AS IT IS WRITTEN

Society of Biblical Literature

Symposium Series

Victor H. Matthews,
Series Editor

Number 50

AS IT IS WRITTEN
STUDYING PAUL'S USE OF SCRIPTURE

AS IT IS WRITTEN

Studying Paul's Use of Scripture

Edited by

Stanley E. Porter

and

Christopher D. Stanley

Society of Biblical Literature
Atlanta

AS IT IS WRITTEN
Studying Paul's Use of Scripture

Copyright © 2008 by the Society of Biblical Literature

All rights reserved. No part of this work may be reproduced or transmitted in any form or by any means, electronic or mechanical, including photocopying and recording, or by means of any information storage or retrieval system, except as may be expressly permitted by the 1976 Copyright Act or in writing from the publisher. Requests for permission should be addressed in writing to the Rights and Permissions Office, Society of Biblical Literature, 825 Houston Mill Road, Atlanta, GA 30329 USA.

Library of Congress Cataloging-in-Publication Data

As it is written : studying Paul's use of Scripture / edited by Stanley E. Porter and Christopher D. Stanley.
    p. cm. — (Society of Biblical Literature symposium series ; 50)
  Includes bibliographical references and indexes.
  ISBN: 978-1-58983-359-3 (paper binding : alk. paper)
  1. Bible. N.T. Epistles of Paul—Relation to the Old Testament. 2. Bible. O.T.—Relation to the Epistles of Paul. I. Porter, Stanley E., 1956– II. Stanley, Christopher D.
  BS2655.R32A75 2008b
  227'.06—dc22   2008027157

16 15 14 13 12 11 10 09 08   5 4 3 2 1
Printed in the United States of America on acid-free, recycled paper
conforming to ANSI/NISO Z39.48-1992 (R1997) and ISO 9706:1994
standards for paper permanence.

Contents

Preface vii

Abbreviations ix

Part 1: Introduction

Paul and Scripture: Charting the Course
Christopher D. Stanley 3

Part 2: Paul's Engagement with Scripture

Quotations
Steve Moyise 15

Allusions and Echoes
Stanley E. Porter 29

Scriptural Language and Ideas
Roy E. Ciampa 41

Biblical Narratives
Steven DiMattei 59

Part 3: Paul and His Audiences

Paul and His Bible: His Education and Access to the Scriptures of Israel
Stanley E. Porter 97

Paul's "Use" of Scripture: Why the Audience Matters
Christopher D. Stanley 125

Synagogue Influence and Scriptural Knowledge among the Christians of Rome
Bruce N. Fisk 157

Part 4: Paul's Intertextual Background(s)

The Meaning of δικαιοσύνη Θεοῦ in Romans: An Intertextual Suggestion
Douglas A. Campbell 189

"Blasphemed among the Nations": Pursuing an Anti-Imperial
  "Intertextuality" in Romans
  Neil Elliott 213

Part 5: "Paul and Scripture" through Other Eyes

Paul and Writing
  Mark D. Given 237

Paul and Postcolonial Hermeneutics: Marginality and/in Early
  Biblical Interpretation
  Jeremy Punt 261

Paul and the Authority of Scripture: A Feminist Perception
  Kathy Ehrensperger 291

Bibliography 321

Contributors 351

Index of Ancient Sources 353

Index of Modern Authors 376

Preface

The editors wish to thank all of the contributors to this volume, as well as the colleagues who attended the sessions of the Paul and Scripture Seminar of the Society of Biblical Literature (SBL) where many of these papers were first delivered. We have been greatly encouraged by the responses of the audiences to these seminar sessions as they listened to the seminar members discussing, sometimes intensely and other times more lightheartedly, but always seriously, how Paul uses Scripture. The seminar will continue to meet through 2010.

The papers in part 3 by Porter, Stanley, and Fisk were all delivered at the SBL meeting in Washington, D.C., in 2006. The papers in part 4 by Campbell and Elliott were delivered at the Society's meeting in San Diego, California, in 2007. The papers in part 5 by Given, Punt, and Ehrensperger were also delivered at the SBL meeting in San Diego, California, in 2007. As editors, we wish to thank all of those who participated both as contributors and as listeners in these sessions, including those who offered critical responses to the papers. They have all been revised in the light of further reflection.

The papers in parts 1 and 2 were written specifically for this volume. When we were planning this volume, we realized that our goals were not limited to presenting the results of the seminar's technical discussions. We also wanted to provide readers with a useful overview of current scholarly study of Paul's use of Scripture, so we invited the contributors in part 2 to write essays that offered general introductions to four of the broad categories of Pauline engagement with Scripture.

Finally, we wish to thank SBL Publications for publishing this volume as part of their SBL Symposium Series. Special thanks go to Victor Matthews for his work as editor of the series and to the staff of SBL Publications for their willingness to produce this volume on a relatively tight schedule. We value their ongoing efforts to promote scholarly dialogue within the field.

ABBREVIATIONS

All abbreviations not in this list, including those of ancient texts, can be found in Patrick H. Alexander et al., *The SBL Handbook of Style* (Peabody, Mass.: Hendrickson, 1999).

AB	Anchor Bible
ABD	*The Anchor Bible Dictionary*. Edited by David Noel Freedman. 6 vols. New York: Doubleday, 1992.
AGJU	Arbeiten zur Geschichte des antiken Judentums und des Urchristentums
AJP	*American Journal of Philology*
AnBib	Analecta biblica
APF	*Archiv für Papyrusforschung*
ASP	American Studies in Papyrology
BECNT	Baker Exegetical Commentary on the New Testament
BibInt	*Biblical Interpretation*
BIOSCS	Bulletin of the International Organization for Septuagint and Cognate Studies
BSac	*Bibliotheca sacra*
BHT	Beiträge zur historischen Theologie
CBQ	*Catholic Biblical Quarterly*
CJ	*Classical Journal*
CQ	*Classical Quarterly*
CRINT	Compendia rerum iudaicarum ad Novum Testamentum
DSS	Dead Sea Scrolls
ESEC	Emory Studies in Early Christianity
EvT	*Evangelische Theologie*
ExpTim	*Expository Times*
FRLANT	Forschungen zur Religion und Literatur des Alten und Neuen Testaments
GRBS	*Greek, Roman, and Byzantine Studies*
HBT	*Horizons in Biblical Theology*
HSCP	*Harvard Studies in Classical Philology*

HTR	*Harvard Theological Review*
HTS	Harvard Theological Studies
IBC	Interpretation: A Bible Commentary for Teaching and Preaching
ICC	International Critical Commentary
IDBSup	*Interpreter's Dictionary of the Bible: Supplementary Volume.* Edited by Keith R. Crim. Nashville: Abingdon, 1976.
JBL	*Journal of Biblical Literature*
JCS	*Journal of Cuneiform Studies*
JGRChJ	*Journal of Greco-Roman Christianity and Judaism*
JQR	*Jewish Quarterly Review*
JSJ	*Journal for the Study of Judaism in the Persian, Hellenistic, and Roman Periods*
JSJSup	Journal for the Study of Judaism Supplement Series
JSNT	*Journal for the Study of the New Testament*
JSNTSup	Journal for the Study of the New Testament Supplement Series
JSOTSup	Journal for the Study of the Old Testament Supplement Series
JSPSup	Journal for the Study of the Pseudepigrapha Supplement Series
LCL	Loeb Classical Library
LD	Lectio divina
LEC	Library of Early Christianity
LXX	Septuagint
MT	Masoretic Text
Neot	*Neotestamentica*
NIB	*The New Interpreter's Bible*. 13 vols. Nashville: Abingdon, 1994–2004.
NICNT	New International Commentary on the New Testament
NIGTC	New International Greek Testament Commentary
NovT	*Novum Testamentum*
NovTSup	Novum Testamentum Supplements
NRSV	New Revised Standard Version
NSBT	New Studies in Biblical Theology
NTG	New Testament Guides
NTM	New Testament Monographs
NTS	*New Testament Studies*
NTTS	New Testament Tools and Studies
PG	Patrologia graeca [= Patrologiae cursus completus: Series graeca]. Edited by J.-P. Migne. 162 vols. Paris: Migne, 1857–1886.
PTMS	Pittsburgh Theological Monograph Series
ProEccl	*Pro ecclesia*

RSR	*Recherches de science religieuse*
RSV	Revised Standard Version
RTR	*Reformed Theological Review*
SBL	Society of Biblical Literature
SBLAcBib	Society of Biblical Literature Academia Biblica
SBLDS	Society of Biblical Literature Dissertation Series
SBLSBL	Society of Biblical Literature Studies in Biblical Literature
SBLSBS	Society of Biblical Literature Sources for Biblical Study
SBLSP	Society of Biblical Literature Seminar Papers
SBLSymS	Society of Biblical Literature Symposium Series
SBLTT	Society of Biblical Literature Texts and Translations
SBLWGRW	Society of Biblical Literature Writings from the Greco-Roman World
SBT	Studies in Biblical Theology
SC	Sources chrétiennes. Paris: Cerf, 1943–.
SE	*Studia evangelica I, II, III (=* TU 75 [1959], 87 [1964], 88 [1964], etc.)
SemeiaSt	Semeia Studies
SFSHJ	South Florida Studies in the History of Judaism
SJOT	*Scandinavian Journal of the Old Testament*
SJT	*Scottish Journal of Theology*
SNTSMS	Society for New Testament Studies Monograph Series
SSEJC	Studies in Early Judaism and Christianity
TAPA	*Transactions of the American Philological Association*
TDNT	*Theological Dictionary of the New Testament.* Edited by Gerhard Kittel and Gerhard Friedrich. Translated by Geoffrey W. Bromiley. 10 vols. Grand Rapids: Eerdmans, 1964–1976.
TENTS	Texts and Editions for New Testament Study
THKNT	Theologischer Handkommentar zum Neuen Testament
TSAJ	Texte und Studien zum antiken Judentum
TZ	*Theologische Zeitschrift*
TU	Texte und Untersuchungen
VT	*Vetus Testamentum*
WBC	Word Biblical Commentary
WUNT	Wissenschaftliche Untersuchungen zum Neuen Testament
YCS	Yale Classical Studies
ZNW	*Zeitschrift für die neutestamentliche Wissenschaft und die Kunde der älteren Kirche*

Part 1
Introduction

Paul and Scripture: Charting the Course

Christopher D. Stanley

1. Introduction

Everyone who has studied the apostle Paul's references to the Jewish Scriptures acknowledges that Paul does strange things with texts—"strange," that is, by modern literary standards. Not only does he fail to cite the sources of most of his quotations, but the wording of his quotations and allusions often diverges significantly from that of the texts that he cites. The sense that he derives from the biblical text also deviates fairly often from what modern readers might see as the "original meaning" of the passages to which he refers. Similar problems can be discerned in the writings of other New Testament authors.

These differences between ancient and modern practices aroused scholarly interest as early as the late 1500s, when Protestant scholars such as Franciscus Junius (1590) and Johannes Drusius (1594) published studies comparing the New Testament quotations with their biblical antecedents.[1] The mid-1700s witnessed a flowering of interest in these questions as a result of William Whiston's claim that the New Testament authors had preserved a more accurate version of the Old Testament text than the one traditionally found in Christian Bibles, which Whiston claimed had been corrupted by ancient Jewish scribes.[2] Not until the nineteenth century, however, did scholars begin to give serious attention to the specific problems associated with

---

1. Franciscus Junius, *Sacrorum parallelorum libri tres* (London: Bishop, 1590); Johannes Drusius, *Parallela sacra* (Frankfurt: Aegidium Radacum, 1594).

2. William Whiston, *An Essay toward Restoring the True Text of the Old Testament* (London: Senex, 1722). Whiston's claims were ably answered by, among others, Johann Carpzov in *A Defense of the Hebrew Bible* (trans. Moses Marcus; London: Bernard Lintot, 1729).

the apostle Paul's use of Scripture.³ By the end of the century, they had identified most of the problems and many of the solutions that have continued to occupy scholars to the present day.

2. Sorting out the Field

Until fairly recently, scholars who investigated Paul's use of Scripture focused primarily on theological and historical questions. The field has broadened substantially over the last two decades with the application of literary and socio-rhetorical methods. Many scholars now seek to combine two or more of these methodologies. Still, a rough typology of approaches can be discerned within the field.

(a) Scholars who view Paul's interpretation of the Jewish Scriptures through a *theological* lens can be divided into two groups. One group, whose pedigree goes back as far as the patristic era, is concerned with the significance of Paul's ideas for Christian faith. Some of the people in this group would regard Paul's teachings and practices, including his handling of Scripture, as normative for the Christian tradition, while others adopt a more critical stance.⁴ The second group of theologically minded scholars is moti-

---

3. Several good surveys of scholarship on Paul's use of Scripture and the related question of "the use of the Old Testament in the New" can be found in the literature; see (in order of publication) F. A. G. Tholuck, "The Old Testament in the New," trans. Charles A. Aiken, *BSac* 11 (1854): 569–76; Crawford H. Toy, *Quotations in the New Testament* (New York: Scribner, 1884), xxxvii–xliii; August Clemen, *Der Gebrauch des Alten Testaments in den neutestamentlichen Schriften* (Gütersloh: Bertelsman, 1895), 1–11; Hans Vollmer, *Die alttestamentlichen Citate bei Paulus* (Freiburg: Mohr, 1895), 6–9; Otto Michel, *Paulus und seine Bibel* (Gütersloh: Bertelsman, 1929; repr., Darmstadt: Wissenschaftliche Buchgesellschaft, 1972), 1–7; E. Earle Ellis, *Paul's Use of the Old Testament* (Edinburgh: Oliver & Boyd, 1957; repr., Grand Rapids: Baker, 1981), 2–5; Merrill Miller, "Targum, Midrash, and the Use of the Old Testament in the New Testament," *JSJ* 2 (1971): 64–78; I. Howard Marshall, "An Assessment of Recent Developments," in *It Is Written—Scripture Citing Scripture: Essays in Honour of Barnabas Lindars* (ed. D. A Carson and H. G. M. Williamson; Cambridge: Cambridge University Press, 1988), 1–21; Richard B. Hays, *Echoes of Scripture in the Letters of Paul* (New Haven: Yale University Press, 1989), 5–14; Christopher D. Stanley, *Paul and the Language of Scripture* (SNTSMS 74; Cambridge: Cambridge University Press, 1990), 4–28.

4. Studies that fit within this tradition include Thomas Randolph, *The Prophecies and Other Texts Cited in the New Testament* (Oxford: Fletcher, 1782); F. A. G. Tholuck, *Das Alte Testament im Neuen Testament* (6th ed.; Gotha: Perthes, 1877); David M. Turpie, *The Old Testament in the New* (London: Williams & Norgate, 1868); Roger Nicole, "The New Testament Use of the Old Testament," in *Revelation and the Bible* (ed. Carl F. H. Henry; Grand Rapids: Baker, 1958); Gleason L. Archer and Gregory D. Chirichigno, *Old*

vated by historical concerns. Their principal goal is to understand the role that Scripture played in the development and content of Paul's thought.[5] Scholars in both groups labor to comprehend how Paul read and interpreted the biblical text insofar as this can be discerned from his letters. Most of the attention has been devoted to Paul's use of explicit quotations, but scholars have also studied his allusions to biblical passages, his references to biblical narratives, and his appropriation of biblical language and concepts. Virtually all of the scholars in this category have been convinced that Paul engages seriously and thoughtfully with the original context of his biblical references.

(b) Among those who have investigated the *historical* context of Paul's use of Scripture, the primary concern has been to understand how Paul's handling of the biblical text compares with the methods of other Jewish (and occasionally non-Jewish) authors. Much of the work in this area aims to show that Paul's treatment of Scripture is not as strange as it might seem to modern readers. Until the middle of the twentieth century, most of the comparisons focused on the exegetical and hermeneutical procedures of the rabbinic literature, whose relevance was accepted by most, although questioned by some.[6] With the discovery of the Dead Sea Scrolls, scholars were presented with a set of texts that not only originated fairly close to the New Testament era but also showed many similarities to the apostle Paul's handling of the Jewish Scriptures. Much of the subsequent historical work on Paul's use of Scripture has sought to clarify the nature and significance of these similarities.[7] From

---

Testament Quotations in the New Testament: A Complete Survey (Chicago: Moody Press, 1983); and Walter C. Kaiser, *The Uses of the Old Testament in the New* (Chicago: Moody Press, 1985).

5. Most of the recent studies of Paul's use of Scripture would fit into this category, including Dietrich-Alex Koch, *Die Schrift als Zeuge des Evangeliums: Untersuchungen zur Verwendung und zum Verständnis der Schrift bei Paulus* (BHT 69; Tübingen: Mohr Siebeck, 1986); D. Moody Smith, "The Pauline Literature," in Carson and Williamson, *It Is Written*, 265–91; J. Ross Wagner, *Heralds of the Good News: Isaiah and Paul "in Concert" in the Letter to the Romans* (NovTSup 101; Leiden: Brill, 2002); and Francis Watson, *Paul and the Hermeneutics of Faith* (London: T&T Clark), 2004.

6. See Guilielmus Surenhusius, *Sefer ha-Meshaweh sive biblos katallages in quo secundum veterum theologorum hebraeorum formulas allegandi et modos interpretandi conciliantur loca ex V. in N.T. allegata* (Amsterdam: Boom, 1713); Johann Christian Carl Döpke, *Hermeneutik der neutestamentlichen Schriftsteller* (Leipzig: Vogel, 1829); Eduard Böhl, *Die alttestamentlichen Citate im Neuen Testament* (Vienna: Braumüller, 1878); Joseph Bonsirven, *Exégèse rabbinique et exégèse paulinienne* (Paris: Beauschesne, 1939).

7. E.g., Ellis, *Paul's Use of the Old Testament*; Richard N. Longenecker, *Biblical Exegesis in the Apostolic Period* (Grand Rapids: Eerdmans, 1974); Anthony Tyrrell Hanson, *Studies in Paul's Technique and Theology* (Grand Rapids: Eerdmans, 1974).

time to time scholars have also compared Paul's practices with the writings of Philo, Josephus, and the Jewish Apocrypha and Pseudepigrapha.

(c) Until fairly recently, the *literary* dimension of Paul's engagement with Scripture had been broadly neglected by biblical scholars. This changed in 1989 with the publication of Richard B. Hays's *Echoes of Scripture in the Letters of Paul*,[8] which offered a highly creative literary interpretation of Paul's echoes and allusions. A century earlier, Hans Vollmer had noted the importance of taking Paul's biblical allusions into account when considering the breadth of his engagement with the text of Scripture, and Otto Michel made a similar point a few decades later, but neither scholar did anything with these observations.[9] Hays, by contrast, made Paul's echoes and allusions the focal point of his study. Nearly all subsequent studies of Paul's use of Scripture are indebted to Hays's work. Literary approaches can also be seen in the writings of several scholars who have examined how Paul engaged with the narrative elements of the Jewish Scriptures.[10] To this point, however, almost no one has asked whether other modes of literary study, such as (post)structuralism, reader-response, and deconstruction, might shed any light on the use of Scripture in Paul's letters.[11]

(d) Relatively few attempts have been made to apply *rhetorical* or *social-scientific* methods to the study of Paul's use of Scripture. Many scholars have pointed out that at least some of Paul's quotations can be understood as responses to biblical arguments that had been raised by others, and scholars have frequently noted in passing that a particular quotation seems designed to lend weight to Paul's argumentation. But studies that focus primarily on the rhetorical dimension of Paul's appeals to the Jewish Scriptures are rare.[12] Even less attention has been given to the kinds of questions typically raised

---

8. New Haven: Yale University Press, 1989. Additional examples of Hays's approach can be seen in his more recent book, *The Conversion of the Imagination: Essays on Paul as Interpreter of Israel's Scripture* (Grand Rapids: Eerdmans, 2005).

9. For more on the books by Vollmer and Michel, see n. 3 above.

10. E.g., Sylvia Keesmaat, *Paul and His Story: (Re)Interpreting the Exodus Tradition* (JSNTSup 181; Sheffield: Sheffield Academic Press, 1999).

11. John G. Lodge offers a reader-response analysis of Rom 9–11, including the relevant quotations, in *Romans 9–11: A Reader-Response Analysis* (University of South Florida International Studies in Formative Christianity and Judaism 6; Atlanta: Scholars Press, 1996). Passing references to the role of Scripture can also be found in John Paul Heil, *Paul's Letter to the Romans: A Reader-Response Commentary* (New York: Paulist, 1987).

12. Two recent books that use rhetorical approaches to analyze Paul's use of Scripture are Christopher D. Stanley, *Arguing with Scripture: The Rhetoric of Quotations in the Letters of Paul* (New York: T&T Clark, 2004); and John Paul Heil, *The Rhetorical Role of Scripture in 1 Corinthians* (SBLSBL 15; Atlanta: Society of Biblical Literature; Leiden: Brill, 2005).

by social scientists, such as the effects of power imbalances and the role of class and gender differences in shaping the production and reception of Paul's repeated references to Scripture.[13]

3. The Cost of Progress

The flowering of interest in Paul's use of Scripture over the last two decades has made this a highly fruitful period for scholarly investigation. Most scholars who work regularly in this area would agree that substantial progress has been made in recent years. This sense of progress can be attributed in part to the application of new methods and in part to a general decline in theological tensions over Paul's handling of Scripture. Few scholars today feel a compelling need to attack or defend the validity of Paul's handling of the Jewish Scriptures, although there are certainly some whose sympathies incline in one direction or the other. As a result, scholarly study has been able to proceed with more independence than in previous eras. Developments in other areas of Pauline studies, such as the rise of the "New Perspective" on Paul, have also helped to reframe the debate in this area. The result has been a proliferation of new methods of study and new interpretations of Paul's use of Scripture.

Unfortunately, the growing diversity of the field has also made it harder for scholars to engage in productive dialogue concerning the role of Scripture in Paul's theology and writings. Prior generations of scholars shared many common ideas about which questions mattered and how one might go about resolving them, even when they disagreed in their conclusions. Today, by contrast, scholars not only employ different methods but also ground their studies on different presuppositions. Some of these presuppositions are complementary, but others are mutually exclusive. For example, some scholars are convinced that Paul's explicit quotations provide the best insights into his engagement with the ideas and language of Scripture, while others find it more useful to study his allusions and echoes or his use of biblical narratives. Some claim that Paul's frequent references to Scripture reveal how profoundly his ideas were shaped by the biblical tradition, while others insist that Paul cited Scripture primarily for rhetorical effect. Some assert that Paul expected his audiences to know and to supply the context of his quotations and allusions, while others reject this presumption as unhistorical.

---

13. Ben Witherington's "socio-rhetorical" commentaries on Romans (*Paul's Letter to the Romans: A Socio-Rhetorical Commentary* [Grand Rapids: Eerdmans, 2004]) and the Corinthian correspondence (*Conflict and Community in Corinth: A Socio-Rhetorical Commentary on 1 and 2 Corinthians* [Grand Rapids: Eerdmans, 1995]) include occasional hints in this direction, but the question receives little explicit attention.

As a result of these and other differences in method, scholarly discussions of Paul's use of Scripture have become increasingly fragmented. Instead of examining the relative strengths and weaknesses of various modes of analysis, scholars more often simply talk past one another. Papers are presented and books and articles written with little or no effort to justify the methods and presumptions used. Scholars who approach the subject using different methods are either dismissed or ignored. Progress is made in particular areas, but little is done to integrate the findings into a coherent whole or to examine places where the use of different methods or presuppositions might lead to different conclusions.

Of course, diversity and disagreement are a normal part of scholarly discourse on any subject. But in an area of research as narrow as Paul's use of Scripture, it seems that scholars ought to be able to converse freely about the strengths and weaknesses of various methods of study and the validity of employing different sets of presuppositions. Instead, most of the discussion and debate seems to take place among people who share common methodologies, with little dialogue across methodological lines. Professional meetings do not allow sufficient time for scholars to debate the premises upon which a particular paper is based, nor is there space in a published article to interact with the many issues that might be raised by people who approach the subject from different methodological perspectives. If the current round of studies is to yield any sense of "assured results," a forum is needed to promote and enable such discussions among scholars.

4. Charting the Course

The Paul and Scripture Seminar of the Society of Biblical Literature was established in 2005 to provide a forum for scholars to discuss methodological questions pertaining to the study of Paul's use of Scripture. The seminar functions as a collective research project whose goal is to identify points of agreement and disagreement among scholars and to clarify the strengths and weaknesses of various ways of analyzing the biblical materials in Paul's letters. Seminar members were chosen for their ability to contribute to such an open-ended project. Prior to the first meeting, the steering committee identified six sets of questions to guide the work of the seminar.

(a) *What do we mean by Paul's "use" of Scripture?* For some interpreters, the central scholarly task is to understand how Paul read and interpreted particular passages. Others focus on the broader question of how Paul incorporated the ideas and language of Scripture into his theology. Still others aim to understand how Paul used Scripture to influence his audience and gain acceptance for the arguments of his letters. How do these various modes of analysis relate to one another? Are they complementary, overlapping, or contradictory? What are the strengths and weaknesses of each approach? Is it possible to integrate all three approaches into a coherent model? What might this look like? Are there other approaches that might enhance the value of such a model?

(b) *What kinds of data yield the best understanding of Paul's engagement with the text of Scripture?* Some scholars focus primarily on the quotations, others on the allusions and echoes, and still others on Paul's references to the storyline or ideas of the Jewish Scriptures. What are the reasons for preferring one type of data over another? What kinds of insights can be gleaned from studying each type? Are some types of data more useful than others, or does the choice of data depend largely on one's purpose? Is it feasible (or desirable) to develop an understanding of Paul that would incorporate all of these types of data? How might our answers to these questions affect our interpretation of Paul and his letters?

(c) *How does one recognize references to Scripture in Paul's letters?* The evidence is clear in the case of explicit quotations, but scholars disagree about the presence and purpose of unmarked references to Scripture in Paul's letters. Are there any reliable criteria for identifying allusions and echoes of Scripture? What purpose do these unmarked references serve in Paul's letters? Are they part of his rhetorical agenda, or do they simply reflect his own pattern of thinking and speaking in biblical terms? Is there any way to know whether Paul is engaging directly with the text of Scripture or relying on earlier Jewish or Christian traditions? Should the appropriation of biblical ideas and motifs count as a form of interaction with the Jewish Scriptures?

(d) *How do Paul's references to the Jewish Scriptures relate to their original context?* Many scholars have sought to demonstrate that Paul engages thoughtfully with the literary and theological context of his biblical references. Others have argued that Paul frequently stretches or ignores the original context when it serves his rhetorical ends. Is there any way to adjudicate this dispute? Might it be possible to develop a set of criteria for evaluating the likelihood that a proposed contextual reading reflects the thinking of Paul rather than the ingenuity of a modern reader? Or is this a hopeless enterprise? Scholars have also claimed that in some cases Paul drew his material from a "testimony book" or some other form of Jewish or Christian tradition rather than relying directly on the text of Scripture. How do we evaluate these claims? What difference might it make for our understanding of Paul and his letters?

(e) *What can we presume about the biblical literacy of Paul's audiences?* Most scholars have concluded from the way Paul cites the Jewish Scriptures that he expected his audiences to be able to recognize the sources of most of his quotations and allusions and to reconstruct and approve his interpretations of particular biblical passages. Others have questioned whether such a model is historically valid or required by Paul's use of Scripture. How can we determine what Paul expected in this area? Were his expectations realistic? How might Paul's audiences have obtained the level of biblical knowledge that most scholars seem to think they possessed? Do studies of ancient literacy shed any light on the subject? What difference does it make how we reconstruct the biblical literacy of Paul's audiences?

(f) *What role does Scripture play in Paul's theology and rhetoric?* In recent years many scholars have insisted that Scripture was foundational to Paul's thinking. Some, however, have disputed this point, arguing that Paul cited Scripture primarily as a rhetorical tool to counter the biblical arguments of his opponents. How do we evaluate the importance of Scripture in Paul's life and thought? How does it compare with other sources of authority that may have influenced his thinking (e.g., tradition, experience, reason)? Did Scripture shape all aspects of his thought, or was its influence stronger in some areas than others? How might we use the evidence of the letters to figure this out?

Whether the seminar can produce agreement on any of these issues remains to be seen. At the very least, however, it will enable participants to understand better the nature and reasons for the differences in scholarly opinion about Paul's use of Scripture, including the arguments used to support different positions. This in turn should lead to more thoughtful and creative studies of the role of Scripture in Paul's letters and theology.

5. The Present Volume

The present volume presents the fruit of the first three years of the seminar's labors. Some of the twelve essays are revised versions of papers that were prepared for the seminar, while others were commissioned especially for this volume. All represent efforts to "push the envelope" in the study of Paul's use of Scripture. The book is divided into four sections, with each section addressing a different set of issues.

The first section contains four essays that examine methodological questions associated with the four major categories of Paul's use of Scripture: explicit quotations (Steve Moyise); allusions and echoes (Stanley Porter); use of biblical language and ideas, such as law, covenant, and prophet (Roy Ciampa); and appropriations of biblical narratives (Steve DiMattei). Each of these essays offers a critical introduction to recent scholarship on the topic, paying special attention to the assumptions and methodological differences that have divided scholars who have studied the issue. The purpose of these essays is to analyze the data as dispassionately as possible and to propose "common-ground" approaches that might prove useful to other scholars who are interested in Paul's use of Scripture.

The second section consists of three papers that investigate various historical questions pertaining to Paul's use of Scripture. As in the first section, the essays focus on critical questions that have received insufficient attention in most of the earlier studies of Paul's engagement with Scripture. The first paper, by Stanley Porter, reviews what we can know or presume about Paul's educational background, including his education in the Jewish Scriptures, and examines how this information might affect our understanding of Paul's use of Scripture. The next two papers investigate how different reconstructions of Paul's audiences can affect our perception of what Paul is doing when he refers to the Jewish Scriptures in his letters. First, Christopher Stanley argues that Paul framed his biblical references for an audience consisting largely of illiterate Gentiles who knew only as much Scripture as they might have learned through oral instruction within the Christian community. Then Bruce Fisk examines the effect of envisioning Paul's intended audience as having a strong background in Judaism, whether as former "God-fearers" or through their continuing association with the synagogue (à la Mark Nanos). Taken together, these two essays show how different views of Paul's intended audience can lead to different understandings of Paul's use of Scripture.

The third section contains two papers that demonstrate the effect of positing different intertextual backgrounds for Paul's statements about God's activity in the letter to the Romans. Douglas Campbell focuses on Paul's "righteousness" language, which he interprets as an allusion to biblical traditions about the "right" actions of a king. In his view, Paul deployed these traditions to explain how God had acted "rightly" as a divine king in vindicating Jesus after his oppression and execution by evil opposing powers. Neil Elliott, by contrast, proposes a Roman imperial background for Paul's repeated references to God's "mercy." According to Elliott, Paul's language pertains directly to the situation in Rome, where Nero's recent decision to allow the Jews to return to the capital has created the impression that they are the undeserving beneficiaries of the emperor's "mercy." Together these papers highlight the complexity of determining the textual and ideological backgrounds of Paul's use of "biblical" terminology.

The last section includes three papers that were designed to extend the boundaries of research into Paul's use of Scripture by using nontraditional methods to investigate Paul's engagement with the biblical text. Mark Given looks at Paul's biblical references through a deconstructive lens that opens up theoretical questions about Paul's view of Scripture (and his religion) that have not been addressed in previous studies of the subject. Jeremy Punt draws on postcolonial theory to explain how Paul used Scripture to construct a discourse of power that both replicated and opposed the power claims of the Roman Empire. Kathy Ehrensperger also examines Paul's discourse of power, using feminist criticism to argue that Paul deployed Scripture in a less "authoritative" mode than many have supposed. All three papers promise to open up new methodological avenues for the analysis of Paul's engagement with the Jewish Scriptures.

Taken together, these essays demonstrate what can be done when scholars take the time to explore the reasons for their differences and try out new approaches to old problems. Even the most constructive dialogue does not always produce agreement, as these essays show. But the transgression of boundaries that occurs when scholars come together and investigate the issues that divide them invariably opens up new territories for scholarly exploration. The editors wish to thank the contributors to this volume for their role in extending the discussion.

Part 2
Paul's Engagement with Scripture

Quotations

Steve Moyise

1. Introduction

An explicit quotation occurs when an author clearly indicates that the words that follow are not his or her own but are taken from another source. In Paul's letters, this is generally marked by an introductory formula, using either a verb of writing ("as it is written") or a verb of speaking ("as Isaiah said"). It can also be indicated by more abbreviated expressions such as γάρ ("for") and ὅτι ("that"), although this makes more demands on the reader, since these terms can also be used to introduce the author's own deductions. For example, Rom 1:17 is generally recognized as Paul's first explicit quotation in Romans ("as it is written, 'The one who is righteous will live by faith'"). But immediately before this, there are three γάρ clauses that could potentially be introducing quoted material: (1) "hence my eagerness to proclaim the gospel to you also who are in Rome, *for* 'I am not ashamed of the gospel'"; (2) "I am not ashamed of the gospel, *for* 'it is the power of God for salvation'"; (3) "to the Jew first and also to the Greek, *for* 'in it the righteousness of God is revealed.'" The fact that these three γάρ clauses are not generally thought to be introducing quoted material is partly because the words that follow look like Paul's own formulations and partly because no specific Old Testament texts spring to mind. However, if there were grounds for believing that a text that said "the righteousness of God is revealed" was well known, we might have to revise that opinion.

Indeed, if the text is particularly well known, it is possible to introduce it without any marker at all. For example, Paul brings his exposition in Rom 9–11 to a close with the words, "O the depth of the riches and wisdom and knowledge of God! How unsearchable are his judgments and how inscrutable his ways!" (11:33). He then continues, "For who has known the mind of the Lord? Or who has been his counselor?" There is nothing to indicate that this phrase is in any way different from the previous words, except that the LXX of Isa 40:13 is almost identical.[1] On the grounds that Isa 40 was an important quarry for the early Christians, it could be argued that Paul does not need to spoil the poetic effect of the two verses by inserting a superfluous "as Isaiah said." On the other hand, the words that follow the Isaiah quotation ("Or who has given a gift to him, to receive a gift in return?") appear to be another quotation, but the words are not very close to any known text. Job 35:7 is probably the closest ("what do you give to him; or what does he receive from your hand"), but the words are absent from the LXX as known to Origen and were hardly well known. If Paul could assume that his readers would know Isa 40:13, he certainly could not assume that they would know Job 35:7.

Thus one of the major challenges in studying Paul's quotations is to explain why some quotations are specifically marked ("Isaiah said"), some are generally marked ("it is written"), and some are not marked at all. The example above suggests that the motive was not to facilitate finding the more difficult texts, since Job 35:7 is far more obscure than Isa 40:13, yet neither of them are marked at all. Is it, then, to highlight the more important texts? The five references to "Isaiah" in Romans (9:27, 29; 10:16, 20; 15:12) certainly leave an impression on the reader, but does it follow that these quotations are more important to Paul than Hab 2:4, which only has a general marker ("it is written")? If this is the case, it is strange that Paul makes his readers wait nine chapters before giving them this vital piece of information. In his work on Rom 2, Timothy Berkley argues that the key texts lying behind Paul's exegesis are Jer 7:9–11; 9:23–24; and Ezek 36:16–27 and that the explicit quotation ("it is written") of Isa 52:5 in Rom 2:24 is simply a convenient summary text. However, it would be difficult to argue that all of the sixty or so explicit quotations in Romans are simply summary texts.[2]

The other conundrum occurs when we have a specific marker but the text that follows does not correspond very closely to any form of text known to us. For example, 1 Cor 3:19 says: "For the wisdom of this world is foolishness with God. For it is written, 'He catches the wise in their craftiness....'" The thought is close to Job 5:12–13, where God "frustrates the devices of the crafty" and "takes the wise in their own craftiness," but the LXX that has come down to us is very different from Paul's words (ὁ δρασσόμενος τοὺς σοφοὺς ἐν τῇ πανουργίᾳ αὐτῶν in Paul, ὁ καταλαμβάνων σοφοὺς ἐν τῇ φρονήσει in the LXX). It is possible that Paul is offering his own translation of the Hebrew, although this is a minority position today. This leaves us with two major

---

1. The LXX connects the two clauses with "and" rather than "or."
2. Timothy W. Berkley, *From a Broken Covenant to Circumcision of the Heart: Pauline Intertextual Exegesis in Romans 2:17–29* (SBLDS 175; Atlanta: Society of Biblical Literature, 2000), 139–40.

options for understanding quotations that differ from any Greek text known to us: (1) Paul has changed the wording, whether for theological or rhetorical reasons or simply for the sake of style; or (2) Paul is using a text that is no longer extant. A generation ago, the latter was often seen as a desperate attempt to save Paul from the accusation of text manipulation, but many scholars today consider this to be a realistic option.[3] As we shall see later, the Dead Sea Scrolls have shown that the text was still somewhat fluid in the first century, although this is not to be exaggerated. They have also shown that texts were copied with a remarkable degree of accuracy.

2. How Do Quotations Work?

Paul is not the only author explicitly to cite other works, so our first question is whether Paul's citations can be understood as part of a general theory of quotation. Unfortunately, the classical rhetorical handbooks have little to say on the subject. Aristotle briefly discusses the citing of ancient witnesses such as Homer and certain well-known proverbs and maxims, but the brevity of his treatment suggests that he was not convinced of its value. He does offer some examples, but they are not very profound: "If you are urging somebody not to make a friend of an old man, you will appeal to the proverb, 'Never show an old man kindness'" (*Rhet.* 1.15). He does, however, make some interesting points. First, he stipulates that the use of maxims should be confined to the older man who is experienced in such subjects. On the lips of the inexperienced, such maxims sound foolish. Second, he suggests that the orator should try to guess the opinions of his listeners and then offer a general truth in support. Thus "if a man happens to have bad neighbors or bad children, he will agree with any one who tells him, 'Nothing is more annoying than having neighbors'" (*Rhet.* 2.21). Third, in order to make a proverb or maxim more persuasive, he suggests adding a judicious comment. Thus the maxim, "We ought not to follow the saying that bids us treat our friends as future enemies: much better to treat our enemies as future friends," is made more convincing by the addition, "for the other behavior is that of a traitor" (*Rhet.* 2.21).

Quintilian notes the practice of the "greatest orators of drawing upon the early poets to support their arguments or adorn their eloquence ... for the charms of poetry provide a pleasant relief from the severity of forensic eloquence" (*Inst.* 1.8.12). This "charm" is not simply adornment, however, for it "makes use of the sentiments expressed by the poet as evidence in support of

---

3. E.g., Florian Wilk, *Die Bedeutung des Jesajabuches für Paulus* (FRLANT 179; Göttingen: Vandenhoeck & Ruprecht, 1998).

his own statements." In *Inst.* 2.7, Quintilian argues that it is more useful for boys to memorize the great works than their own compositions, for this will give them "a plentiful and choice vocabulary and a command of artistic structure and a supply of figures which will not have to be hunted for, but will offer themselves spontaneously from the treasure-house." Such a treasure-house will be useful in court debate, for "phrases which have not been coined merely to suit the circumstances of the lawsuit of the moment carry greater weight and often win greater praise than if they were our own." In other words, utterances that do not spring from the immediate situation are less open to the accusation of bias, for they were taken as "authoritative" before the exigencies of the current situation were known.

Longinus is less interested in quotations as "proofs" than as a means of attaining "the sublime": "it is well that we ourselves, when elaborating anything which requires lofty expression and elevated conception, should shape some idea in our minds as to how perchance Homer would have said this very thing" ([*Subl.*] 14.1). Indeed, "there would not have been so fine a bloom of perfection on Plato's philosophical doctrines, and that he would not in many cases have found his way to poetical subject-matter and modes of expression, unless he had with all his heart and mind struggled with Homer" ([*Subl.*] 13.4). Longinus is aware of the accusation of plagiarism, but he denies it. One is not seeking to pass off someone else's work as one's own; it is more like "taking an impression from beautiful forms or figures or other works of art" ([*Subl.*] 13.4).

Given the importance of Homer in the ancient world, these statements are rather meager, but they do offer a starting point for our discussion. Some scholars think that Paul's use of scriptural quotations can be largely explained by such rhetorical devices, while others see them as peripheral to Paul's main concern of offering an *exposition* or *interpretation* of Scripture. For example, what is the function or purpose of the Habakkuk quotation in Rom 1:17, which Paul quotes in the form ὁ δὲ δίκαιος ἐκ πίστεως ζήσεται ("the righteous by faith will live")? Aristotle might have said that Paul has deftly mingled his words with the words of Habakkuk in order to give the (false) impression that Habakkuk means what Paul means. By omitting the Septuagint's pronoun (ἐκ πίστεώς μου), Paul ensures that it is human faith that is being spoken about. Furthermore, since Paul is introducing himself to the Roman church, he cites a text that he knows (or thinks he knows) will be common ground. In this way, he hopes to gain their confidence for some of the more controversial claims ("all Israel will be saved") that he intends to make later in the letter (11:26).

Quintilian and Longinus would probably have noted that Paul did not need to add the quotation. His programmatic statement about the gospel could quite happily end with the words, "For in it the righteousness of God is revealed through faith for faith." For Quintilian, the advantage of the quotation is that it shows that Paul's statement has not been formulated just to meet the needs of the Roman church but was written long ago. Indeed, judging by the existence of the Qumran pesharim, it might be that such words were treasured as well as transmitted. As Francis Watson has put it, the words speak of the "divinely ordained way to salvation with a clarity and brevity unparalleled in the rest of scripture."[4] Longinus, by contrast, would be more interested in the aesthetic value of the words than in viewing them as a "proof." As a skilled writer, Paul knew when to break off from his own style and introduce words from another source. In this case, the words from Habakkuk have an almost unparalleled succinctness, as each word (righteous, faith, live) is pregnant with meaning and connotation.

Thus it is clear that no single theory of quotation emerges from the handbooks. Some scholars would maintain that such "rhetoric" has little to do with Paul's deep engagement with Scripture in any case; we must look instead to Jewish parallels. Until the discovery of the Dead Sea Scrolls, scholars were limited mainly to rabbinic works,[5] and their favorite "explanation" was that Paul used *gezerah shawah*, or word-links, to move from one quotation to another. Perhaps the most celebrated example was Paul's exposition of Gen 15:6 in Rom 4 ("Abraham believed God, and it was *reckoned* to him as righteousness") by means of Ps 32:1–2 ("Blessed are those whose iniquities are forgiven ... the one against whom the Lord will not *reckon* sin"). Contrary to the tenets of modern historical criticism, Paul assumes that he can correlate the meaning of these two texts, even though they come from different authors and different periods of history. As we shall see later, one of the major differences among scholars who study the Pauline quotations is that some hold a theological viewpoint that essentially approves of such techniques as examples of "intertextuality," while others regard this idea as gratuitous. Such deeply held convictions inevitably affect one's evaluation and analysis of Paul's quotations.

The discovery of the Dead Sea Scrolls is important for our topic in at least three ways: they show that interpreting texts from the standpoint of eschatological fulfillment was not unique to Paul; they show that the text of Scripture was much more fluid than was previously thought; and they show that many of the texts that were important to Paul were also important to the Qumran

---

4. Francis Watson, *Paul and the Hermeneutics of Faith* (London: T&T Clark, 2004), 124.

5. Joseph Bonsirven, *Exégèse rabbinique et exégèse paulinienne* (Paris: Beauchesne, 1939); W. D. Davies, *Paul and Rabbinic Judaism* (London: SPCK, 1948).

community. From the early work of Earle Ellis to the recent *magnum opus* of Francis Watson, each of these three areas has proved fruitful.[6] The point of contention is not so much whether such parallels exist but whether they get to the heart of Paul's hermeneutics. In a formal sense, Paul's application of specific texts to the church ("whatever was written in former days was written for our instruction" [Rom 15:4]) and its "enemies" ("All day long I have held out my hands to a disobedient and contrary people" [10:21]) has parallels with the Qumran application of Scripture to its community ("this concerns all those who keep the Law in the house of Judah" [1QpHab 8]) and its "enemies" ("the Kittim who trample the earth" [1QpHab 3]). But is there a "christological" or "messianic" dimension to Paul's hermeneutics that cannot be paralleled in the Qumran writings? The question can be illustrated if we look again at Paul's interpretation of Hab 2:4:

> I will stand at my watchpost, and station myself on the rampart; I will keep watch to see what he will say to me, and what he will answer concerning my complaint. Then the LORD answered me and said: Write the vision; make it plain on tablets, so that a runner may read it. For there is still a vision for the appointed time; it speaks of the end, and does not lie. If it seems to tarry, wait for it; it will surely come, it will not delay. Look at the proud! Their spirit is not right in them, but the righteous live by their faith. (Hab 2:1–4 NRSV; lit., "but the righteous *will* live by *his* faith")

> For I am not ashamed of the gospel; it is the power of God for salvation to everyone who has faith, to the Jew first and also to the Greek. For in it the righteousness of God is revealed through faith for faith; as it is written, "The one who is righteous will live by faith." (Rom 1:16–17)

The Hebrew text envisages two groups of people, the proud and the righteous, the latter being characterized by their "faithfulness" (אמונה) to God. The Qumran commentator has a particular individual in mind as "the proud" ("this concerns the Wicked Priest.... his heart became proud"), and as one would expect, "the righteous" are those who "observe the law in the house of Judah." Some scholars have argued that Paul likewise has a particular individual in mind as "the righteous," namely, Jesus Christ. Anthony Hanson argued that ὁ δίκαιος ("The righteous One") is used as a messianic title in 1 En. 38:2 and is applied to Jesus in Acts 3:14; 7:52; and 22:14 (and perhaps 1 Pet 3:18; 1 John 2:1).[7] This idea was subsequently taken up by Richard Hays

---

6. E. Earle Ellis, *Paul's Use of the Old Testament* (Edinburgh: T&T Clark, 1957).

7. Anthony Tyrrell Hanson, *Studies in Paul's Technique and Theology* (London: SPCK, 1974), 39–45.

and others as part of a broader argument that Paul's focus was not on the individual's "faithfulness," nor even on the individual's "faith in Christ," but on Christ's own faithfulness, a faithfulness that led him to the cross (Rom 5:18–19; Phil 2:8).[8] In contrast, Joseph Fitzmyer thinks that Paul's focus *is* on the individual's "faith in Christ" and that this idea differs significantly from the meaning that was intended by Habakkuk. Paul has read the text in the light of his Christian beliefs and taken "*pistis* in his own sense of 'faith,' and 'life' not as deliverance from invasion and death, but as a share in the risen life of Christ.… In this way Paul cites the prophet Habakkuk to support the theme of his letter."[9]

Francis Watson also denies that Paul has imposed a "christological" or "messianic" interpretation on the text. He considers it extremely unlikely that Paul had first formulated his gospel as the revelation of God's righteousness ἐκ πίστεως ("of" or "from" faith) and only later discovered that Hab 2:4 is the only text in the whole of Scripture to make such a connection. Much more likely is that Paul began with the Habakkuk text and formulated his doctrine accordingly. Indeed, Watson regards Rom 1:16–17 as virtually a paraphrase of Hab 2:4: "*The one who is righteous* (that is, with a *righteousness* of God, revealed in the gospel) *by faith* (since this righteousness is received *by faith* and is intended for faith) *will live.*"[10] This is not to say that Paul is unwilling to go beyond what the prophet understood. When he gets to Rom 3:21–22, he will specify that this ἐκ πίστεως is uniquely connected with Jesus Christ, something that Habakkuk did not and could not know. However, even here Watson is reluctant to speak about any christological "imposition" on the text, for Habakkuk is told that there is a vision to be made plain now and a vision for the future. In other words, Habakkuk envisages a fuller revelation in the end time, and Paul sees himself as providing it. Paul goes beyond what Habakkuk wrote, but it falls within Habakkuk's "speech-act," which envisages an interpreter such as Paul speaking from the standpoint of its fulfillment.[11]

---

8. Richard B. Hays, "'The Righteous One' as Eschatological Deliverer: A Case Study in Paul's Apocalyptic Hermeneutics," in *Apocalyptic and the New Testament: Essays in Honor of J. Louis Martyn* (ed. Joel Marcus and Marion L. Soards; JSNTSup 24; Sheffield: JSOT Press, 1988), 191–215.

9. Joseph A. Fitzmyer, *Romans: A New Translation with Introduction and Commentary* (AB 33; New York: Doubleday, 1992), 265.

10. Watson, *Paul and the Hermeneutics of Faith*, 48.

11. If this sounds like an *apologia* for Christianity, it should be noted that Watson thinks the Qumran commentator also fits the role; both occupy the same "intertextual field" as latter-day interpreters responding to Habakkuk's "speech-act" in the way that he intended.

3. Does Paul Respect the Context of His Quotations?

The question of whether Paul respects the context of his quotations continues to evoke widely different answers. In the previous example, all three scholars acknowledge that Paul's interpretation differs from the historical meaning that Habakkuk or his hearers/readers could have understood. For some scholars, this is sufficient to conclude that Paul does not respect the context of his quotations. Unlike those of us trained in the historical-critical method, Paul does not appear to show any interest in how the historical Isaiah, Hosea, or Habakkuk would have been understood in their own day (or days, according to modern theories of composition). For example, Paul supports a series of (dubious) accusations against the Jews (Rom 2:17–23) by quoting Isa 52:5 in the form: "The name of God is blasphemed among the Gentiles because of you." A look at the context of Isa 52:5 reveals a significant discrepancy:

> You were sold for nothing, and you shall be redeemed without money. For thus says the Lord GOD: Long ago, my people went down into Egypt to reside there as aliens; the Assyrian, too, has oppressed them without cause. Now therefore what am I doing here, says the LORD, seeing that my people are taken away without cause? Their rulers howl, says the LORD, *and continually, all day long, my name is despised.* Therefore my people shall know my name; therefore in that day they shall know that it is I who speak; here am I. (Isa 52:3–6)

The despising (Hebrew) or blaspheming (Greek) of God's name is occurring not because of the sinfulness of Israel but because of their piteous state ("reside there as aliens"/"oppressed them without cause"/"taken away without cause"). As Brendan Byrne says, "According to both the Hebrew original and the LXX it was Israel's *misfortune* that led to the reviling of God's name by the nations. Paul, however, interprets the LXX phrase 'on account of you' as 'because of your fault,' thereby converting what was originally an oracle of compassion towards Israel into one of judgment."[12] On the other hand, some scholars think such a historical-critical understanding of "context" is too narrow. Hays, for example, notes that Paul quotes Isa 52:7 ("How beautiful are the feet of those who bring good news!") in Rom 10:15, thereby demonstrating that Paul is fully aware of the salvation context of Isa 52:5. That being so, Hays suggests that we should look for a more sophisticated explanation of Paul's use of Isa 52:5: "If Paul reads Isa. 52:5 as a reproach, it is a

---

12. Brendan Byrne, *Romans* (Sacra Pagina; Collegeville, Minn.: Liturgical Press, 1996), 101.

reproach only in the same way that the historical event to which it refers was a reproach."[13] As the argument of Romans unfolds, it becomes clear that Paul does not think that this reproach is final. By the time we get to Rom 11, we discover that the hardening of Israel is temporary and that in the end "all Israel will be saved" (11:26). At this point, the reader will understand that Paul's "misreading" of Isa 52:5 was temporary and that its message of hope is ultimately Paul's message also. In short, the meaning of Isa 52:5 in Rom 2:24 can be understood only from multiple readings of the text. As Hays puts it, "The letter's rhetorical structure lures the reader into expecting Israel's final condemnation, but the later chapters undercut such an expectation, requiring the reader in subsequent encounters with the text to understand the Isaiah quotation more deeply in relation to its original prophetic context."[14]

4. The Mind of Paul or the Understanding of His Readers?

Closely related to the question of Paul's respect for context is another polarity in the study of Pauline quotations. Given what we know of literacy in the first century,[15] is it safe to assume that the recipients of the letter in Rome would have known that the text, "How beautiful are the feet of those who bring good news," occurs two verses after the text, "The name of God is blasphemed among the Gentiles because of you"? Paul has not done much to help them, since (1) the two quotations are separated by eight chapters; (2) the latter occurs in a section that contains references to Leviticus, Deuteronomy, Joel, and other parts of Isaiah; and (3) Paul omits the phrases "on the mountains" and "who announces peace," which would have considerably aided its location. If it is doubtful, then, that Paul's recipients would have been able to make this connection, then either Paul was a poor communicator, misjudging the abilities of his recipients, or such sophisticated understandings of Paul's intentions are misguided.

Christopher Stanley opts for the latter, challenging scholars for assuming that Paul (1) expected his readers to have access to what is mistakenly called "the LXX," as if it existed in a single volume; (2) expected them to know the original context of his quotations and indeed made it a condition for understanding his argument; and (3) expected them to discern the thought

---

13. Richard B. Hays, *Echoes of Scripture in the Letters of Paul* (New Haven: Yale University Press, 1989), 45.

14. Ibid., 46.

15. William V. Harris, *Ancient Literacy* (Cambridge: Harvard University Press, 1989); Harry Y. Gamble, *Books and Readers in the Early Church: A History of Early Christian Texts* (New Haven: Yale University Press, 1995).

processes or prior exegesis that lies behind his specific quotations.[16] Instead, Stanley thinks that Paul generally made it clear how he expected his quotations to be understood. Thus the majority of his recipients would have taken the quotation of Isa 52:5 at face value; hypocritical Jews, like those denounced in Rom 2:21–23, give God a bad name. Technically, the quotation does not support Paul's eventual conclusion that "Jews as a class stand alongside Gentiles as the objects of God's threatened judgment," but it does offer strong support for the "more limited indictment in 2:17–23 of Jews who hypocritically neglect their covenantal obligations."[17] There is no need to adopt a sophisticated hermeneutic based on levels of dissonance with the original meaning. This is a modern historical-critical concern, not a problem for first-century interpreters such as Paul (or Philo or the Qumran pesherists).

Social-science theorists draw a distinction between "emic" explanations (how something might have been explained at the time) and "etic" explanations (how we might explain it today). The distinction is not absolute, since it is *we* who are doing the analysis in both cases, but it is a useful distinction nonetheless. For example, one of the first things we notice about this quotation is the significant difference between the Greek and Hebrew traditions. Paul cites a text that includes the phrases "because of you" and "among the Gentiles," which are absent from any Hebrew text known to us. This naturally affects our explanation of the meaning or significance of the quotation. Whether Paul was aware of this difference is a matter of debate. Given his rabbinic background, it is perhaps more likely than not that he would have known it, but it is nevertheless the Greek text that is the reference of the ascription "it is written." Further, given Stanley's concerns about the readers' knowledge of "the LXX," we can be fairly certain that they would not have known that the Greek text differs from the Hebrew. Thus an emic explanation will view references to this additional textual information as "anachronistic" in any attempt to describe "Paul's use of Scripture."

On the other hand, there is no reason why this material should not be of interest to us today. What has come down to us is a text that we call "Romans" (actually a huge number of manuscripts) that contains other texts embedded within it. Why should we not explore the dynamic between text and intertext with whatever methods prove to be illuminating? Thus the link between the quotations of Isa 52:5 and 52:7 is not an invention of Hays; the link is really there, even if his first readers would likely have missed it. Hays might be over-

---

16. Christopher D. Stanley, *Arguing with Scripture: The Rhetoric of Quotations in the Letters of Paul* (New York: T&T Clark, 2004), 38–61. These three points are my summary of Stanley's nine "questionable assumptions."

17. Ibid., 149.

confident that the original readers would "get it" on subsequent readings of the letter, but it would be discovered eventually. It then becomes a matter of definition as to whether the "meaning" of a quotation is to be located in the author's intention, the reader's perception, or the dynamics of the text itself—remembering, of course, that none of these are "givens," since all have to be "constructed" by the modern interpreter.

Some theorists have therefore pursued the dynamics of quotation without regard to author intention or reader competence. For example, Meir Sternberg highlights the inevitable process of *recontextualization* when a text is severed from its original moorings and forced to serve a different purpose: "However accurate the wording of the quotation and however pure the quoter's motives, tearing a piece of discourse from its original habitat and reconstructing it within a new network of relations cannot but interfere with its effect."[18] On this view, quotations inevitably disturb rather than console, for they introduce a tension between previous contextual meanings and the function or role in the new work. As Harriet Davidson says of Eliot's *The Waste Land*, "The work's meaning is in the tension between its previous contextual definition and its present context."[19] It is easy to see how this could be applied to Paul. For example, there is a tension between Habakkuk's call for faithfulness and Paul's attack on the law; there is a tension between God's pity on Israel in Isa 52 and Paul's accusation against Jews in Rom 2:24; and there is a tension between the catena of Rom 3:10–18, which Paul uses to prove that "no one is righteous, not even one," and the psalms that (mostly) make up the catena, which assume a distinction between the wicked, to whom the accusations are directed, and the righteous.[20] For some scholars, analysis of the Pauline quotations means analysis of the "meaning effects" produced by these discrepancies.

However, this is to treat the quotations individually and largely as "obstacles" to discovering Paul's meaning. Other scholars believe that, taken collectively, they reinforce Paul's message by pointing to an overarching scriptural framework. Thus Ross Wagner claims that Paul wrote Romans "in concert" with Isaiah. The term is suggestive, for it implies harmony rather than discord. According to Wagner, Paul read Isaiah as a three-act play of rebellion, punishment, and restoration and "locates himself and his fellow believers (Jew and Gentile) in the final act of the story, where heralds go forth

---

18. Meir Sternberg, "Proteus in Quotation-Land: Mimesis and the Forms of Reported Discourse," *Poetics Today* 3 (1982): 108.

19. Harriet Davidson, *T. S. Eliot and Hermeneutics: Absence and Interpretation in* The Waste Land (Baton Rouge: Louisiana State University Press, 1985), 117.

20. See Steve Moyise, "The Catena of Rom. 3:10–18," *ExpTim* 106 (1995): 367–70.

with the good news that God has redeemed his people."²¹ This involves a twofold strategy: (1) Paul reads prophecies of Israel's deliverance as prophecies of his own gospel and mission; and (2) Paul reads texts that denounce Israel's idolatry and unfaithfulness as referring to Israel's current resistance to the gospel. This does not create a battlefield, as Sternberg's theory would suggest, for in "claiming that God will be faithful to redeem all Israel, Paul does not lean on the isolated testimony of a few verses from Isaiah. Rather, he taps into a broad and deep stream of thought that is characteristic of Isaiah's vision—a stream of thought, moreover, that is shared by numerous other prophetic texts and that is kept vigorously alive in later Jewish literature."²²

Francis Watson makes a similar point by suggesting that Paul does not offer an exegesis of Scripture, which would require comment on every (significant) detail, but a "construal of the whole from a particular perspective."²³ In the corresponding footnote, he quotes from David Kelsey's book, *The Uses of Scripture in Recent Theology*, followed by his own comment:

> "[W]hen a theologian appeals to scripture to help authorize a theological proposal, he appeals, not just to some aspect of scripture, but to a *pattern* characteristically exhibited by that aspect of scripture, and in virtue of that pattern, he construes the scripture to which he appeals as some kind of *whole*" ... Kelsey shows that an implicit "construal of the whole" may be reconstructed from a theologian's actual *use* of scripture, in relation to which it serves as a kind of hermeneutical framework. There is no reason why this should not apply also to Paul.²⁴

According to Watson, this observation can help us to understand the difficult logic of Gal 3:10–14, where Paul cites texts from Deut 27:26; Hab 2:4; Lev 18:5; and Deut 21:23. Watson suggests that, if we widen our field of view, we will notice that Paul's exposition begins with a reference to Gen 15:6 (Gal 3:6) and ends with a reference to Sinai (Gal 3:19–20). The explicit references to Genesis, Exodus, Leviticus, and Deuteronomy (albeit in a different order) show that Paul is offering an "interpretation of the Torah, a construal of the shape and logic of its fivefold form."²⁵ However, the logic of this form is not straightforward, since the promise of life in Lev 18:5 is at odds with the reality

---

21. J. Ross Wagner, *Heralds of the Good News: Isaiah and Paul "in Concert" in the Letter to the Romans* (NovTSup 101; Leiden: Brill, 2002), 354.
22. Ibid., 297.
23. Watson, *Paul and the Hermeneutics of Faith*, 515.
24. Ibid., 515 n. 1, citing David H. Kelsey, *The Uses of Scripture in Recent Theology* (London: SCM, 1975), 102, emphasis original.
25. Watson, *Paul and the Hermeneutics of Faith*, 517.

of sin and curse in the final chapters of Deuteronomy. Contrary to many so-called "New Perspective" scholars, Watson does not think that Paul is trying to harmonize the quotations in Gal 3; indeed, Paul explicitly states: ὁ δὲ νόμος οὐκ ἔστιν ἐκ πίστεως ("but the law is not of faith"). Taken on their own, the quotations from Deuteronomy look as though they have been "severed" from their original context and forced to mean something different. But Watson argues that Paul is merely doing what the canonical form of the Pentateuch does, that is, providing an interpretative framework for understanding each particular verse. Paul not only respects that framework; he has been deeply influenced by it.

5. Conclusion

Although scholars endeavor to put aside personal prejudices when studying Paul's quotations, it is clear that there are some fundamental commitments that significantly affect one's analysis. For example, if one is convinced by Sternberg's "agonistic" theory of quotation, then attempts to show that Paul respected the context of his quotations or is indebted to a scriptural framework look absurd. It is quite clear that Isaiah or Habakkuk could not have meant what Paul says they meant (especially when Paul's LXX text differs from the Hebrew). On the other hand, if one holds a theological position that locates Paul firmly within his Jewish tradition, one will find Sternberg's language of "tearing a piece of discourse from its original habitat" to be melodramatic, to say the least. Advocates of such a theological position are more likely to adopt a literary theory that speaks of "embedded meaning" or "potential meaning" rather than confining meaning to some originating moment. In this regard, it is interesting to note that Hays, Wagner, and Watson can all speak of Paul "misreading" or even "rewriting" a text, without drawing the conclusion that he took texts out of context. Clearly it depends on what one means by "context."[26]

Similarly, there is sometimes a degree of confusion as to whether emic or etic explanations are being offered. For example, some scholars will explain how Paul got from A to B by suggesting dependence on additional texts or interpretative traditions. This is then used to show that Paul's use of Scripture is not "arbitrary" or ad hoc but conforms to the accepted practices of the day. This is then further used to refute the suggestion that Paul's use of Scripture is in any sense "contrived" or "gratuitous." Others, however, think that such

---

26. See further Steve Moyise, *Evoking Scripture: Seeing the Old Testament in the New* (London: T&T Clark, 2008), 125–41.

explanations are beside the point. Paul may have thought that he could discern the meaning of texts by finding common wording in another text, but he was wrong; language does not work like that. Finally, while Wagner is correct to note that Paul's accusatory use of Isa 52:5 has been facilitated by the LXX's addition δι' ὑμᾶς ("because of you"), this should not disguise the fact that it is not what the Hebrew-speaking Isaiah meant.

A third polarity is similar to the diachronic/synchronic debate. Some scholars think that a quotation formula implies that Paul wants what follows to be understood in the light of the quotation. If this were not the case, what would be the point of drawing attention to it? Other scholars suggest that Paul wants the words of the quotation to be understood in the light of their role or function in the new work. After all, one generally tries to understand the meaning of the particular in the light of the whole. Why should this be any different for embedded quotations? As there seems to be some truth in both of these positions, it is probably best to seek the "meaning" or "significance" of a quotation in the interaction between the connotations it (may) bring with it *and* its role or function in the new work.[27] Thus, in reality, disputes are not so much about whether we should adopt diachronic or synchronic analysis but, in cases of dissonance, which should be granted priority.

Lastly, one might say that the most fundamental question is whether one thinks that the various polarities mentioned above are in principle answerable or whether each side of the polarity has its own validity and needs to be incorporated into a "thick" description of Paul's use of Scripture. I would affirm the latter, which is my reason for being part of this project. Paul's use of quotations is both complex and diverse, and his practice is best understood by analyzing them from different points of view. However, this does not necessarily mean that in particular instances some approaches might not prove more illuminating than others. It is nonetheless important that we not rule some approaches "out of court" from the outset.[28]

---

27. Whether this is best described as dialogical, dialectical, or intertextual is itself an illustration of the point. It depends on what connotations these words bring with them for particular scholars.

28. Those who pursue "ideological criticism" will of course relate this to the purpose or purposes of the modern scholar. Whose interests are served by seeking to demonstrate either the superiority of one method or the validity of multiple interpretations? Whose interests are served by showing that Paul's use of quotations is rational and sophisticated rather than contingent and contrived?

Allusions and Echoes

Stanley E. Porter

1. Introduction

Terminology for reference to extratextual material has become common in New Testament studies, growing in apparent proportion as study of extratextual material has become increasingly manifest in the discipline. As I have noted in a previous study, the language that has been used includes an abundance of disparate terms, often without clear correlation or correlatives.[1] This abundance of terms is often and appropriately reduced to a smaller number. These usually include direct and indirect forms of extratextual reference. In another essay, I identified five categories to include all of the forms of direct and indirect reference to extrabiblical material: formulaic quotation; direct quotation; paraphrase; allusion; and echo.[2] Others have differentiated an even smaller number, some simply using the categories of quotation and allusion to encompass all forms of mediation of extratextual material.[3] Others have simply conflated allusion and echo together into a single category, sometimes

---

1. See Stanley E. Porter, "The Use of the Old Testament in the New Testament," in *Early Christian Interpretation of the Scriptures of Israel: Investigations and Proposals* (ed. Craig A. Evans and James A. Sanders; SSEJC 5; JSNTSup 148; Sheffield: Sheffield Academic Press, 1997), 79–96, here 80.

2. See Stanley E. Porter, "Further Comments on the Use of the Old Testament in the New Testament," in *The Intertextuality of the Epistles: Explorations of Theory and Practice* (ed. Thomas L. Brodie, Dennis R. MacDonald, and Stanley E. Porter; NTM 16; Sheffield: Sheffield Phoenix Press, 2007), 98–110, esp. 107–9. I believe that these categories are still correct, and I will revisit some of the issues regarding such terminology below in addressing specifically matters related to allusion and echo.

3. See Mary M. Talbot, *Fictions at Work: Language and Social Practice in Fiction* (London: Longman, 1995), 49.

referred to as allusive echo.[4] However, the term *echo* has taken on a disproportionately large significance in recent scholarly discussion and is treated here as a separate category from that of allusion (see the discussion below). Quotation (whether introduced by an explicit quotation formula or not) and paraphrase involve direct reference to extratextual material cited by another.

This essay is directly concerned with allusion and echo, the two forms of indirect reference to extratextual material found in the New Testament. I will first examine the notion of allusion, then echo, along the way drawing appropriate distinctions about how to differentiate the two categories, before concluding.

2. Definition of Allusion

The term *allusion* is used for a figure of speech that makes indirect extratextual references. The term has been a stock-in-trade of literary studies for countless years and so has been fairly consistently referenced in the critical literature—even if it has been and remains notoriously difficult to define in specific terms. For example, in one of the standard handbooks of literary study, Holman defines allusion as follows:

> A FIGURE OF SPEECH that makes brief, often casual reference to a historical or literary figure, event, or object.... Strictly speaking, *allusion* is always indirect. It attempts to tap the knowledge and memory of the reader and by so doing to secure a resonant emotional effect from the associations already existing in the reader's mind.... The effectiveness of *allusion* depends on there being a common body of knowledge shared by writer and reader. Complex literary *allusion* is characteristic of much modern writing, and discovering the meaning and value of the *allusions* is frequently essential to understanding the work.[5]

Holman's definition includes several significant elements: (1) reference may be to historical or literary entities, including people, events, or objects; (2)

---

4. Richard B. Hays, *Echoes of Scripture in the Letters of Paul* (New Haven: Yale University Press, 1989), 18–19, citing John Hollander, *The Figure of Echo: A Mode of Allusion in Milton and After* (Berkeley and Los Angeles: University of California Press, 1981), ix.

5. C. Hugh Holman, *A Handbook to Literature* (4th ed.; Indianapolis: Bobbs-Merrill, 1980), 12. Cf. Marlies K. Danziger and W. Stacy Johnson, *An Introduction to the Study of Literature* (Lexington, Mass.: Heath, 1965), 127. An illustration of the complexity of definition is found in the definition offered by Murray H. Abrams, who defines allusion as either "explicit or indirect" (*A Glossary of Literary Terms* [4th ed.; New York: Holt, Rinehart, Winston, 1981], 8). According to my definitions, he conflates paraphrase with allusion.

reference is indirect, as opposed to quotation or paraphrase, both of which are direct; (3) the allusion is intentional on the part of the author toward the reader; (4) allusion may occur without the knowledge of the reader; and (5) allusion is most effective when there is a body of shared knowledge between the author and reader.[6] In other words, allusion is a figure used by the author to reference specific types of material for a functional purpose.

In their introduction to text linguistics, de Beaugrande and Dressler give a useful example of allusion that exemplifies the type of definition offered above, including the functional use of allusion. They note that authors can in theory "draw upon *any* available prior text; but in practice, *well-known* texts are more suitable as being more readily accessible to the receiver audience."[7] They use the example of Christopher Marlowe's poem, "The Passionate Shepherd to His Love." The poem begins with the following lines:

> Come live with me and be my love,
> And we will all the pleasures prove
> That valleys, groves, hills, and fields,
> Woods, or steepy mountain yields.

De Beaugrande and Dressler note several allusive responses to Marlowe's poems. The same year as Marlowe wrote this poem, 1600, Sir Walter Raleigh wrote his "The Nymph's Reply to the Shepherd." The poem begins as follows:

> If all the world and love were young,
> And truth in every shepherd's tongue,
> These pretty pleasures might me move
> To live with thee and be thy love.

Raleigh's response follows the same poetic conventions of rhyme, rhythm and structure as Marlowe's but offers a negative response to the optimism of Marlowe's passionate plea. Raleigh's poem takes Marlowe's conventions seriously, even if he responds negatively to them. In 1612, John Donne wrote a poem, "The Bait," that utilized the framework of Marlowe's poem to create an elaborate sarcastic conceit:

> Come live with me and be my love,
> And we will some new pleasures prove,

---

6. See Charles Duffy and Henry J. Pettit, *A Dictionary of Literary Terms* (rev. ed.; [Denver]: Brown Book, 1952), 4; G. B. Caird, *The Language and Imagery of the Bible* (London: Duckworth, 1980), 33.

7. Robert de Beaugrande and Wolfgang U. Dressler, *Introduction to Text Linguistics* (London: Longmans, 1981), 186.

Of golden sands and crystal brooks,
With silken lines and silver hooks.

This poem begins with quotation as a basis of allusive development for what follows.[8] Donne again follows the conventions but transforms them into an account that disputes them. Others have used this same poem by Marlowe, including Cecil Day Lewis in his ironic "Come Live With Me and Be My Love." Lewis does not accept the poetic or social conventions of Marlowe and the others. As de Beaugrande and Dressler note, there are several types of allusive use found in this small grouping of poems. Raleigh and Donne accept Marlowe's poetic conventions, even though they respond to them by refuting or mocking them, while Lewis rejects the social and societal conventions that Marlowe and the others accept.[9] Nevertheless, as de Beaugrande and Dressler also illustrate, the defining conventions of allusion are maintained in every case. A specific literary work (in this case) is indirectly cited by the subsequent authors, writing to audiences that should be able to at least share the poetic if not societal conventions and hence understand the allusion, whether it is used to support or refute the original poetic stance.

Most New Testament studies, at least the ones that I have surveyed, tend to follow—although more implicitly than explicitly—this understanding of allusion. For example, Michael Thompson in his study of Paul's references to Jesus' teaching in Rom 12:1–15:13 identifies eleven criteria by which one may discern the presence of an allusion (or an echo, according to his categories) to a Gospel source in Paul's letters. The criteria that he outlines include the following: verbal agreement (meaning some shared vocabulary); conceptual agreement; formal agreement; place of the Gospel saying in the dominical tradition; common motivation and rationale; dissimilarity to Greco-Roman and Jewish traditions; the presence of dominical indicators; the presence of tradition indicators; the presence of other dominical echoes or word/concept clusters in the immediate context; the likelihood that the author knew the saying; and exegetical value.[10] We do not need here to evaluate in detail the

---

8. De Beaugrande and Dressler misquote the second line of Donne's poem (*Introduction to Text Linguistics*, 187), corrected here.

9. Ibid., 187–88.

10. Michael B. Thompson, *Clothed with Christ: The Example and Teaching of Jesus in Romans 12.1–15.13* (JSNTSup 59; Sheffield: JSOT Press, 1991), 30–37. See also Grant R. Osborne, *The Hermeneutical Spiral: A Comprehensive Introduction to Biblical Interpretation* (2nd ed.; Downers Grove, Ill.: InterVarsity Press, 2006), 167–69, citing Douglas J. Moo, *The Old Testament in the Gospel Passion Narratives* (Sheffield: Almond Press, 1983), 169; Keven J. Vanhoozer, *Is There a Meaning in This Text? The Bible, the Reader, and the Morality of Literary Knowledge* (Grand Rapids: Zondervan, 1998), 256–57.

viability and usefulness of Thompson's scheme, which I have already done elsewhere.[11] Its major limitation is that it verges on a definition of direct reference, that is, quotation and paraphrase, by considering such items as verbal agreement and formal agreement, and it overspecifies and overdetermines the character of the allusion. However, it does include all five aspects of Holman's definition of allusion, including reference to, in this case, a prior literary work; indirect reference (although note the criticism above); intentionality on the part of the author; a focus upon the author making the allusion rather than the readers recognizing it; and shared common knowledge.

In an earlier study of various instances of allusion, I defined allusion (as opposed to quotation, paraphrase, and echo) as involving the indirect invoking of a person, place, or literary work and noted that it was concerned with bringing the external person, place, or literary work into the contemporary material. Instances of allusion in the New Testament include, for example, references in Gal 4:22–23 to Abraham having two sons (an allusion to Gen 16 and 21); in Gal 4:24 to a covenant being related to Sinai (an allusion to Exod 19–20, etc.); in Gal 4:24–25 to Hagar (an allusion to Gen 16 and 21); and in Rom 4:2–3 to the faith of Abraham (narrated in Gen 15) occurring before Abraham's circumcision in Gen 21 (including the quotation of Gen 15:6 in Rom 4:3). All of these examples fulfill the criteria noted in the definition above.

Despite the validity of this definition, there are still at least two major issues that arise with respect to the use of the notion of allusion. The first concerns the nature of indirect quotation itself. One of the major difficulties in treating allusion is the relationship between allusion and plagiarism. Allusion involves the unacknowledged (indirect) quotation of previous sources. As Ruthven notes, if the use of the allusion is ironic or parodic, one can more readily determine the allusive use, because the author has clearly invoked the allusion in order to make an adverse comment upon it. This leaves no doubt concerning the author's intention in creating the allusion. However, if there is no ironic, parodic, or similar explicit use, the one alluding is vulnerable to the criticism that one is not using allusion to create a deeper referential understanding of the text but may simply be plagiarizing other texts for the sake of creating superficial textual brilliance.[12] In other words, when it is not made clear through the textual reference that the source text is being utilized

---

11. Porter, "Use of the Old Testament," 86–87.

12. K. K. Ruthven, *Critical Assumptions* (Cambridge: Cambridge University Press, 1979), 108–9.

in a functional manner, one may well be accused of using other texts simply to enhance one's own writing, hence the potential charge of plagiarism.

Ruthven's analysis inadvertently raises the issue of intentionality in allusion, which leads to the second issue that must be addressed. There has been a recent shift in understanding of the notion of allusion in New Testament studies that raises questions about the intentionality of the author who engages in allusion. Jeannine Brown, in her recent introduction to hermeneutics, speaks of authors meaning "more than they are fully attending to in any particular utterance."[13] She attributes these types of utterances with their excess of meaning to the fact that the authors of the New Testament were "saturated in the Old Testament," so that we might expect that they will "echo or evoke an Old Testament text or idea without being fully aware that they have done so."[14] She apparently realizes that such unconscious or unintentional invocations raise the question of how to determine whether an allusion is in fact present. On the basis of the discussion above, one might well ask whether it is in fact plagiarism (according to Ruthven) that is present in such a usage. One is able, Brown asserts, to determine whether allusion is present on the basis of two factors: whether such an echo or evocation is "part of the author's communicative intention"; and whether this communicative intention is in "continuity with the author's broader purposes."[15] Brown uses as an example John Steinbeck's novel *Of Mice and Men*, where there is language that may allude to the Bible, even though one cannot determine whether Steinbeck himself consciously intended these possible allusions. Thus Brown wishes to move beyond specific authorial intent to a larger communicative intention or broader authorial purpose as a means of grounding allusion, thus avoiding what might be called an excess of allusive meaning, and possibly plagiarism.

Peter D. Juhl, however, rejects such a formulation. He believes that the "relevance of an author's intention to what his text means is perhaps most obvious in the case of allusion."[16] He cites the example of T. S. Eliot possibly alluding to poems by Donne and Marvell in his poem, "Love Song of J. Alfred Prufrock." Without minimizing the effect that language might have on the

---

13. Jeannine K. Brown, *Scripture as Communication: Introducing Biblical Hermeneutics* (Grand Rapids: Baker, 2007), 108. She seems to rely upon N. T. Wright, *The New Testament and the People of God* (London: SPCK, 1992), 62, who speaks of the text containing things "not present to the author's mind." However, Brown (109 n. 32) believes that such things may still be intended by the author.

14. Brown, *Scripture as Communication*, 108.

15. Ibid., 109, 108.

16. Peter D. Juhl, *Interpretation: An Essay in the Philosophy of Literary Criticism* (Princeton: Princeton University Press, 1980), 58.

reader, Juhl asks whether, if it could be shown that Eliot did not know these poems, one could still claim that the words in dispute were allusions. Juhl claims that one can only meaningfully speak of an author making an allusion if the author is capable of making such an allusion. For example, if there is no possibility of the author making the allusion—say, the supposed allusion was written in a work after the time of the alluding work—then it could not be an allusion. Juhl concludes that this indicates that calling a reference an allusion is only sensible if the author could have alluded to it, that is, if the author knew the work in order to allude to it.[17] Otherwise, the author "could not intend to allude" to another work. Juhl contends that it is "a necessary condition of [an author's] intention to allude" that the author know the item to which the allusion is allegedly being made. Further, the "intention to allude" is a "necessary and sufficient condition" for the cited material to constitute an allusion.[18]

This recent discussion among biblical scholars regarding the intentionality of allusion yields a number of conclusions. (1) As Brown herself admits, some form of intentionality is required to establish an allusion. (2) Biblical scholars need a more precise definition of intentionality in their discussion of allusion. Brown uses varied terms, including communicative intention, which seems for her to constitute a larger category that includes authorial intention and is found at the level of an entire discourse, not within a particular locution. She also speaks about an author's broader purposes, a concept that seems to extend beyond a given work to potentially include the author's entire corpus. She does not, at least in her discussion of allusion, utilize any clear notion of authorial intention. (3) Brown seems to want to insist that verbal similarities are evidence of allusion, rather than distinguishing, as does Juhl, between intentional allusion and unconscious uses of language. (4) Brown seems to admit that potentially allusive language was part of a body of common knowledge shared by author and reader, but Brown's argument still leaves one wondering how to assess whether a particular use of language is in fact allusive, unless one invokes a specific authorial knowledge coupled with an intent to allude. Therefore, it appears that authorial intention is necessary for language to constitute an allusion and to avoid the possibility of the language being confused with plagiarism or simply effective language.

The implications of this discussion for the study of allusion in the New Testament are several. (1) Intentionality appears to be a necessary but not sufficient means by which one can distinguish an allusion. Intentionality on

---

17. Ibid., 59.
18. Ibid., 62.

the part of the author saves an allusion from being merely unconscious plagiarism of an earlier source. However, plagiarism can also be intentional, so intentionality is not enough in and of itself to indicate allusion. (2) Allusion draws upon a common pool of shared knowledge. In an ideal context, both author and reader will understand the allusion, because they have this shared knowledge in common. But allusion can take place even if the reader does not grasp the allusion, because it is authorial intent that defines the presence of an allusion. (3) The purpose of allusion, in order to avoid being merely ornamentation (or even possibly plagiarism), is to draw the earlier person, text, or event into the present text as a means of addressing a particular literary problem. As Wolfgang Iser states, allusions are "functional, not merely imitative."[19] By this he means that an author finds the current literary system deficient in solving a particular literary problem and must therefore draw upon previous solutions to the problem—by invoking people, events, or ideas—to aid in solving the problem. The mere act of alluding does not constitute a solution to the problem, but it does offer a potentially new orientation to the problem so that a new solution can be found.[20]

3. Definition of Echo

The term *echo* is of more recent provenance than allusion, but it has come to be understood in most literary-critical circles as at least related to, if not synonymous with, the notion of allusion. John Hollander's study of what he calls "echoes" in the works of Milton treats echo as a "mode of allusion."[21] This notion of echo (which Richard Hays refers to variously as "allusive echo" or "intertextual echo") is taken up by Hays as the best term to use for indirect textual reference.[22] Thus for Hays and others, echo is tantamount to allusion.

---

19. Wolfgang Iser, *The Act of Reading: A Theory of Aesthetic Response* (Baltimore: Johns Hopkins University Press, 1978), 79.

20. As Iser states, the use of allusion is not meant to be "mere reproduction," as the material cited is introduced without its original context, i.e., "depragmatized and set in a new context" (ibid.).

21. Hollander, *Figure of Echo*. See the subtitle of the work.

22. See Hays, *Echoes of Scripture*, 18–21; see also 29, where he seems to differentiate echo from allusion, but only apparently because he wants to distance his label from authorial intention and provide a looser category. Eventually he pulls back from making a clear distinction. Hays has been followed by numerous scholars, e.g., James D. G. Dunn, "Jesus Tradition in Paul," in *Studying the Historical Jesus: Evaluations of the State of Current Research* (ed. Bruce Chilton and Craig A. Evans; NTTS 19; Leiden: Brill, 1994), 155–78, esp. 159; J. Ross Wagner, *Heralds of the Good News: Isaiah and Paul "in Concert" in the Letter to the Romans* (NovTSup 101; Leiden: Brill, 2002), 9–13 (see 9 n. 36, where he

If this synonymity of the two terms is accepted, then much, if not all, of what was said above would apply to echo, and the terms could simply be conflated. Before commenting upon the validity of this equation, I wish to examine in more detail two sets of defining criteria that Hays posits regarding the notion of echo.

In attempting to define the notion of echo more specifically, Hays first identifies five possibilities for the locus of the echo. This discussion is similar to the comments above regarding the distinguishing features of allusion. His five locative possibilities are: (1) Paul's mind; (2) the original readers of Paul's letter; (3) the text itself; (4) a contemporary act of reading; or (5) an interpretive community.[23] Hays notes that options 1 and 2 locate the echo in "a historical act of communication between persons in the past," whereas options 4 and 5 "locate meaning in the act of reading in the present." Option 3 he calls a "heuristic fiction," because it brackets "out the messy complications of the history behind the text and the experience of readers encountering the text."[24] Hays equates each of these loci with a particular literary-theoretical position. Rather than taking sides in this hermeneutical debate, Hays claims that his working method is "to hold them all together in creative tension" as he engages in contemporary readings of Paul's ancient texts.[25]

Unfortunately, it is not at all apparent how one can hold all five of these positions together in tension, unless the rules of contradiction and exclusion are suspended. Hays mitigates the difficulties of option 2 regarding original readers and their knowledge by substituting what he as a reader can demonstrate that the original readers "would likely have perceived." This is not the same, however, as establishing what these readers did know. Moreover, in defining option 3, Hays states that "we have no access to the author or to the original readers; we have only the text. Consequently, assertions about Paul's intention are intelligible only as statements about the implied author." If this is the case, then options 1 and 2 cannot also be held in "creative tension," because option 1 makes a claim about authorial intention and option 2 about actual readers, while option 3 undermines both. Option 4, accord-

---

agrees with Hays in treating echo and allusion as roughly the same thing). Hays continues to maintain this position. See his *The Conversion of the Imagination: Paul as Interpreter of Israel's Scripture* (Grand Rapids: Eerdmans, 2005), 163–89, where he reprints his defense of *Echoes of Scripture* that first appeared in Craig A. Evans and James A. Sanders, eds., *Paul and the Scriptures of Israel* (JSNTSup 83; SSEJC 1; Sheffield: Sheffield Academic Press, 1993), 70–96.

23. Hays, *Echoes of Scripture*, 26.
24. Ibid., 27.
25. Ibid.

ing to Hays's definition, make all of the other options invalid, as this option states that "claims about intertextual meaning effects are valid if I say so." In other words, one is not concerned with real or even implied authors or readers (neither of which really exists anyway, according to Hays), but only with what he as a contemporary individual reader posits (i.e., there is no appeal to evidence apart from his experience of reading). Option 5 further confuses the situation by laying claim to the validating influence of a "community of readers," even though the other four options are concerned with individual authors and readers, ancient and modern.[26] It is no wonder that Hays appears soon to abandon such a hermeneutical position and adopts what he calls "a single key hermeneutical axiom: that there is an authentic analogy—though not a simple identity—between what the text meant and what is means." He thinks that one might call this a "'common sense' hermeneutics."[27] There are many presuppositions here that could be examined, including Hays's use of analogy, his differentiation between what a text meant and what it means, and whether there is any "common sense" in this at all. What is clear is that it is not self-evident that the term *echo* is needed in such a scheme. If any term were needed, the already well-known term *allusion* might well suffice.

Instead of discussing the particulars of the five options above, Hays instead attempts to develop seven tests for hearing echoes as part of his interpretive scheme. These seven tests merit scrutiny.[28] The first, "availability," asks whether the source of an echo was available to the author and/or the original readers. This leads to an immediate question: If one is writing to an uninformed audience who does not know the source text, does that mean that the echoes are no longer present? If they are comprehensible to another audience, does that mean that the text is now different, or only the audience? Apart from audience perception, what means are available to recognize an echo? This criterion is clearly inadequate. Hays's second criterion is "volume." Defining a metaphor with another metaphor is often dangerous, and this is no exception. Among other points, Hays defines volume in terms of explicit repetition, which appears to be a separate issue related to verbal coherence, which is unmentioned by Hays. Hays's third criterion is "recurrence," which applies a statistical test to determine echoes. This may work for identifying more or less frequent echoes, but it does not seem to be able to determine a singular echo. The final four criteria are "thematic coherence," "historical

---

26. Ibid., 26.
27. Ibid., 27.
28. Ibid., 29–32. Scholars who have scrutinized Hays's criteria regarding echoes are few. See J. Christiaan Beker, "Echoes and Intertextuality: On the Role of Scripture in Paul's Theology," in Evans and Sanders, *Paul and the Scriptures of Israel*, 64–69, esp. 64–65.

plausibility," "history of interpretation," and "satisfaction." As Hays admits, these last four are not so much criteria for determining echoes as they are attempts to establish the interpretation of these echoes. In other words, Hays has offered only three criteria for determining echoes, all of which are very problematic. As Hays says of the last one (satisfaction), "This criterion is difficult to articulate precisely without falling into the affective fallacy, but it is finally the most important test: it is in fact another way of asking whether the proposed reading offers a good account of the experience of a contemporary community of competent readers."[29] It is perplexing that the most important criterion is not in fact a criterion for discovering echoes, only for interpreting them, leaving the question of definition and determination unresolved. As a result, it is not clear that the term *echo* provides a way forward as a useful term for indirect references to extrabiblical material.[30]

This does not mean, however, that the notion of echo cannot serve a purpose in describing the indirect introduction of extratextual material into a text. Whereas allusion invokes a specific person, place, or literary work, the notion of echo may be used for the invocation by means of thematically related language of some more general notion or concept.[31] Echoes are found, for example, in Rom 3:8 with reference to blasphemy, echoing the citation in Rom 2:24 of Isa 52:5, where Paul echoes the language of Isaiah regarding God being blasphemed, and in Rom 11:17–24, where the reference to grafted branches echoes the "branch" language of Isaiah and Jeremiah at various places.[32]

4. Conclusion

This essay has attempted to outline some of the major issues surrounding the use of the terms *allusion* and *echo*. In some recent scholarship that attempts a minimalist differentiation between direct and indirect citation, the terms *allusion* and *echo* are often used interchangeably or as synonyms. In one of the major recent treatments of this topic, Richard Hays uses *echo* as an inclusive term for indirect references to extratextual material. Although I reject Hays's definition of echo, I believe that retention of the two terms *allusion*

---

29. Hays, *Echoes of Scripture*, 31–32.
30. The above paragraph quotes with modifications from Porter, "Use of the Old Testament," 84–85.
31. Hays ends up using the concept of echo for a wide range of material, from reference to very subliminal citations to specific citation of a text. However, he rejects the kind of use that I have defined above (Hays, *Echoes of Scripture*, 24).
32. The above quotes directly from Porter, "Further Comments," 109.

and *echo* as names for separate and distinct forms of indirect citation is probably warranted. Allusion is concerned to bring an external person, place, or literary work into the contemporary text, whereas echo does not have the specificity of allusion but is reserved for language that is thematically related to a more general notion or concept.[33] The use of both concepts seems to imply an intentional use by the author for a particular textual purpose, such as exemplifying or supporting a particular concept. The appeal is based in common knowledge thought to be shared with the readers, although an allusion or an echo can still be present if the recipients fail to know or recognize its presence.

---

33. Quoted from ibid.

Scriptural Language and Ideas

Roy E. Ciampa

The study of Paul's scriptural citations has received the lion's share of attention in the analysis of his use of Scripture, with allusions and echoes receiving more attention recently since the publication of Richard Hays's *Echoes of Scripture in the Letters of Paul*.[1] Our task here is to consider Paul's general use of biblical language and ideas, when he is not citing, alluding to, or echoing specific Old Testament text(s).[2] The concept of intertextuality, important for all discussions of Paul's use of Scripture, is both helpful and a significant challenge for our task. It is helpful in that it affirms that *all* discourse is intertextual and that the relationships between any text and its intertexts are at the heart of textual interpretation. The concept of intertextuality suggests that all discourse depends upon, builds upon, modifies, and/or reacts to prior discourse and the prior use of words, concepts, and ideas. In the words of Julia Kristeva, all discourse is intertextual in that "any text is constructed as a mosaic of quotations, any text is the absorption and transformation of another."[3] As Daniel Boyarin puts it, "Every text is ultimately dialogical in

---

1. New Haven: Yale University Press, 1989.

2. To be sure, there may be other scriptural ideas in play besides those evoked by his citations, allusions, or echoes even when he is citing, alluding to, or echoing Scripture.

3. Julia Kristeva, *Desire in Language: A Semiotic Approach to Literature and Art* (New York: Columbia University Press, 1980), 66. Of course, Kristeva does not limit intertextual influence to a single source, as this quotation might suggest; in her view, every text draws explicitly or implicitly on a vast web of predecessors. For a basic introduction to issues of intertextuality and influence, see the introduction to Udo J. Hebel, ed., *Intertextuality, Allusion, and Quotation: An International Bibliography of Critical Studies* (Bibliographies and Indexes in World Literature 18; New York: Greenwood, 1989); Thaïs E. Morgan, "Is There an Intertext in this Text? Literary and Interdisciplinary Approaches to Intertextuality," *American Journal of Semiotics* 3/4 (1985): 1–40; Jay Clayton and Eric Rothstein, "Figures in the Corpus: Theories of Influence and Intertextuality," in *Influence and Intertextuality in Literary History* (ed. Jay Clayton and Eric Rothstein; Madison:

that it cannot but record the traces of its contentions and doubling of earlier discourses."[4] While the focus often still tends to fall on relationships between particular discrete texts,[5] the point is that every text finds its place within the context of an ongoing discourse about whatever issues it discusses or any ideas that it is building on, responding to, or reacting against. That concept points to the serious challenge posed by the concept of intertextuality, since it becomes clear that detecting all of the intertextual relations between any one text and the many antecedent or later texts to which it relates is an unrealistic goal. An easier but similar goal would be to try to determine all of the ways in which all previous automobile designs influenced the people who designed the next car we see. Some influences may be fairly obvious, and others may be recognized by true aficionados, but surely there would be many influences of which not even the designer is fully conscious.

University of Wisconsin Press, 1991), 3–36. The present study has more in common with American approaches to intertextuality, which generally tend to be more sympathetic toward the identification of particular intertextual sources and influences (intertexts or subtexts) and to the recognition of the place of the author in the literary work. European approaches tend to stress the anonymous and infinite nature of intertextual relationships and to eliminate the author from the investigation. See Susan Stanford Friedman, "Weavings: Intertextuality and the (Re)Birth of the Author," in Clayton and Rothstein, *Influence and Intertextuality*, 146–80. On the issue of the theoretically infinite number of intertextual relationships in a passage, it is relevant to point to Chaim Perelman's focus on the importance of "presence" in argumentative rhetoric, as well as to linguistic theories of prominence, and to note that authors have ways of indicating which intertextual relationships are of particular significance for understanding their discourses. This may well be one of the key roles of citation and allusion in a discourse. Thus statements to the effect that all texts consist of "citations from anonymous sources" must be modified to deal with the fact that some texts have ways of making some of their sources give up their anonymity. The use of citations and other types of references to an authoritative source must be reflected within an approach that has room to recognize levels of prominence that are highlighted by the author's techniques for giving presence to such intertexts while backgrounding others. On allusion and intertextuality, see Carmela Perri, "On Alluding," *Poetics* 7 (1978): 289–307.

4. Daniel Boyarin, *Intertextuality and the Reading of Midrash* (Indiana Studies in Biblical Literature; Bloomington: Indiana University Press, 1990), 14.

5. Richard Hays, for example, defines the "phenomenon of intertextuality" as "the imbedding of fragments of an earlier text within a later one" (*Echoes of Scripture*, 14). Boyarin also goes on to suggest that the concept of intertextuality pushes us to recognize "how later texts interpret and rewrite the earlier ones to change the meaning of the entire canon, and how recognizing the presence of the earlier texts in the later changes our understanding of these later texts as well" (*Intertextuality and the Reading of Midrash*, 16).

Related to the broader type of intertextuality with which we are concerned is the concept of "influence" in the thinking of writers such as Harold Bloom. As Benjamin D. Sommer notes,

> Elements which fall under the rubric of "influence" need not confine themselves to particular words or even images or tropes. Thus Harold Bloom insists repeatedly that he is not interested in echoes of earlier poets' wording or imagery in the work of later poets: "Poetic influence, in the sense I give to it has almost nothing to do with verbal resemblances between one poet and another."[6]

Influence may be exerted not only by passages or books but even by a whole tradition.

> The wider implications of influence study reflect a central difference between influence and allusion: influence is a much broader phenomenon. Whereas allusion posits a relationship between two specific texts (in most cases between particular sets of lines in those texts), influence refers to relations between authors, whole works and even traditions. Thus one may speak not only of the influence of one work on another (say, of Spenser's *Faerie Queene* on Milton's *Paradise Lost*) but of a tradition on a work (the aggadic tale on Agnon's story "Aggadat Hassofer") and of a tradition on a tradition (Greek tragedy on French neo-classicism).[7]

Along similar lines, Sylvia Keesmaat has affirmed that

> texts occur not only in relation to other texts but also in dialogue with other aspects of the cultures in which they occur. Hence an intertextual reference may be to a ritual or a work of art, or indeed to a matrix of ideas which is informed by specific texts, but is not a text in itself.... The writings of Paul also, I suggest, take place within certain "cultural codes" which endow his

---

6. Benjamin D. Sommer, *A Prophet Reads Scripture: Allusion in Isaiah 40–66* (Stanford, Calif.: Stanford University Press, 1998), 14, citing Harold Bloom, *A Map of Misreading* (New York: Oxford University Press, 1975), 19. Bloom's more radical approach stands out clearly earlier in *A Map of Misreading*, where he points out that by poetic influence he does not "mean the passing-on of images and ideas from earlier to later poets. Influence, as I conceive it, means that there are no texts, but only relationships between texts. These relationships depend upon a critical act, a misreading or misprision, that one performs upon another, and that does not differ in kind from the necessary critical acts performed by every strong reader upon every text he encounters" (*Map of Misreading*, 3). This is the strong form of intertextuality that is most common to postmodern literary criticism.

7. Sommer, *A Prophet Reads Scripture*, 14–15.

writings with plausibility. Sometimes these can be traced to specific texts, but more commonly he is drawing on a matrix of ideas which cannot be linked to any specific text but which is shaped and formed by a number of texts (and traditions) within his culture.[8]

As suggested by Keesmaat, it is often impossible to distinguish the direct influence of Scripture from the "indirect" influence of Scripture whereby Paul reflects the influence of early Jewish scriptural understandings as they are found, in part, in postbiblical literature that is based upon a tradition of biblical interpretation.[9]

It is unlikely that any poetic tradition has ever had as much influence over the course of poetry in the Western world as Scripture has had over the discourse of early Judaism and early Christianity. In New Testament studies, however, the bulk of the attention has been devoted to passages that include explicit quotations; other forms of scriptural influence have received less attention.[10]

---

8. Sylvia Keesmaat, "Exodus and the Intertextual Transformation of Tradition in Romans 8.14–30," *JSNT* 54 (1994): 33.

9. What Peter Stuhlmacher says about the hermeneutical context of Paul's reference to God in the prescript of his letter to the Romans ("Theologische Probleme der Römerbriefpräskripts," *EvT* 27 [1967]: 379–80) applies as well to our consideration of other issues Paul touches on in his letters: "The Pauline reference to the Old Testament's testimony of God's gracious election since primeval times can be mastered today only if we can bring ourselves not only to a historically reflected assessment of the Old Testament, but also of the Jewish history of tradition to which the Old Testament leads in New Testament times. Indeed, for the authors of the New Testament and the apostle Paul, the decisive categories of understanding for appropriating the Old Testament tradition arose originally from the Jewish tradition itself." See the second chapter of Brian Rosner's *Paul, Scripture and Ethics: A Study of 1 Corinthians 5–7* (AGJU 22; Leiden: Brill, 1994), entitled "Indirect Dependence: Scriptural Influence through Jewish Moral Teaching" (26–58). He points out that the manner in which early Jewish literature mediates scriptural teaching to its readers is a continuation of the manner in which later biblical books mediate earlier Scriptures to their readers: "Later portions of Scripture, and not just post-Biblical Jewish writings, may have mediated earlier portions of Scripture to Paul. In practice, whether the critical influence came directly from the Pentateuch, or the Prophets and Writings, or Jewish moral teaching may be difficult to determine. The stream of a given moral tradition may have flowed a fair way within the Scriptures before passing through Jewish moral teaching on its way to Paul" (49). Although Rosner's focus is on Paul's ethical teaching, his point is equally valid for other types of teaching as well.

10. To be fair, commentaries often do pay attention to this issue, but studies of Paul's use of Scripture do not.

One of the distinctive characteristics of sectarian or closely knit religious groups (and perhaps other affinity groups) is that their discourse typically takes place within the context of a more narrowly defined, clearly recognized, and fully accepted intertextual framework than other communities. The foundational documents and traditions of such a group play a significant role in establishing the particular intertextual framework within which much of the community's discourse takes place and within which it is understood. That is, each group develops its own jargon, argot, or in-group language habits. The Scriptures of Israel and discourse based on the interpretation of those Scriptures serve as a primary intertextual context for virtually all Jewish religious literature and discourse of the first century.[11] Most if not all forms of early Judaism were communities whose discourse was intertextually linked, both explicitly and implicitly, to Jewish scriptural interpretation.[12] Paul's readers were part of the early messianic Jewish movement in which the Scriptures of Israel and the story of Jesus Christ were mutually interpreting intertexts that

---

11. Charles Perrot suggests that through the Sabbath readings in the synagogue "the text of Moses was seen in its brightest colours, being understood partly through the 'prism' of the prophetic texts and then, by means of the homily, through the aid of all the other 'Writings,' the better to express the Word of God. Finally, the whole Bible was called upon, and the synagogue transformed into a sort of immense 'living concordance' of the sacred text" ("The Reading of the Bible in the Ancient Synagogue," in *Mikra: Text, Translation, Reading and Interpretation of the Hebrew Bible in Ancient Judaism and Early Christianity* [ed. Martin Jan Mulder; CRINT 2.1; Assen: Van Gorcum; Minneapolis: Fortress, 1988], 153). Josephus says that it is to careful knowledge of the law that Jews owed their "admirable harmony": "Unity and identity of religious belief, perfect uniformity in habits and customs, produce a very beautiful concord in human character. Among us alone will be heard no contradictory statements about God.... Among us alone will be seen no difference in the conduct of our lives. With us all act alike, all profess the same doctrine about God, one which is in harmony with our Law and affirms that all things are under His eye" (*C. Ap.* 2.179–181).

12. See James H. Charlesworth, "The Pseudepigrapha as Biblical Exegesis," in *Early Jewish and Christian Exegesis: Studies in Memory of William Hugh Brownlee* (ed. Craig A. Evans and William F. Stinespring; Atlanta: Scholars Press, 1987), 152: "The Pseudepigrapha, like all early Jewish religious writings, generally tended to be in some way exegetical." Richard Hays (*Echoes of Scripture*, 14) points out that that this determinative characteristic of early Judaism has been handed down to its heirs: "The phenomenon of intertextuality … has always played a major role in the cultural traditions that are heir to Israel's Scriptures: the voice of Scripture, regarded as authoritative in one way or another, continues to speak in and through later texts that both depend on and transform the earlier." This is not to deny that there may have been (and, in fact, are) other intertexts of significance. It is only to affirm that no Jewish religious text of the first century (including Paul's letters) can be expected to be fully understood apart from its intertextual relationship with Scripture.

formed the primary foundation for the religious discourse of the community.[13] Discourse that takes place in such a context might be expected to reflect its relationship to this intertextual framework whether or not the authors give it an explicit "presence" through the use of citations or allusions.[14]

Here we will focus on deciding which concepts, terms, and ideas would most likely have been regarded as "biblical" by Paul and other ancient Jews, that is, as having their origin or basis in Scripture, even if they had been developed further in traditions that reflected other historical, cultural, and theological influences. We are concerned with the broad issue of the scriptural background behind the words, concepts, idioms, topics, structures, and concerns found in Paul's letters, including the many subtle or intuitive ways in which Scripture may be influencing the argument of the text. Our concern is not primarily with the teaching of the (Old Testament) Scriptures as they might be interpreted according to modern historical-critical (or other) methods but with how they were (or might have been) understood by Jews (and some Gentiles) in Paul's day, as reflected in the literature and interpretive tendencies of the Second Temple period. Jewish teaching as reflected in its earliest literature serves as a helpful guide to the scriptural understanding of that time.[15] To understand what Paul and/or his readers would have regarded as "scriptural" discourse, that is, discourse based on, influenced by, or engaging with what Scripture said and taught, requires familiarity with the variety of interpretive traditions that may have shaped those perceptions.

Any attempt to establish whether particular ideas found in Paul's letters actually originated entirely from the interpretation of Scripture as opposed to some other cultural and intellectual influence would be a fool's errand.[16] We must content ourselves with the attempt to discern which ideas or concepts Paul (and contemporary Jews and/or Christians) would have considered to

---

13. Certainly other early Jewish groups also interpreted Scripture in the light of certain historical, political, communal, and spiritual experiences. The Maccabean experiment and the Teacher of Righteousness were important keys to the Qumran community's self-understanding and its interpretation of Scripture.

14. Of course, authors do not always provide such an explicit or overt manifestation of the intertextual framework but are more likely to do so when such a manifestation will positively affect the rhetorical effectiveness of the discourse.

15. See also Max Wilcox, "On Investigating the Use of the Old Testament in the New Testament," in *Text and Interpretation: Studies in the New Testament Presented to Matthew Black* (ed. Ernest Best and R. McL. Wilson; Cambridge: Cambridge University Press, 1979), 231–43.

16. Most people do not recognize the extent to which their own interpretations of texts or discourse are influenced by previous interpretations to which they have been exposed.

be based on Scripture.[17] Many of the concepts and interpretations involved naturally owe much of their particular shape to historical, cultural, and theological developments relating to influences outside of Scripture itself. Some of the distinctive influences on those developments may be discerned at times, but most will elude us. The relevant question, then, is whether people who referred to Jesus as "Christ" or to gatherings of Christian believers as "the church" or "the church of God" or who talked about the difference between "this age" and "the age to come" perceived themselves to be dealing with scriptural concepts and whether they would have been so understood by some other Jews as well.[18]

It must be admitted that it is frequently debatable whether Paul is basing his ideas on Jewish/biblical foundations or Greco-Roman ones (see, e.g., the debate over the relevant background to Paul's references to adoption).[19] At times it appears that Paul could be evoking elements that are common to

---

17. Of course, some Jews were prepared to attribute whatever similarities there might have been between pagan thought and literature and Judaism to a dependence upon Moses or borrowing from him on the part of pagan authors. See, e.g., Aristobulus's statements as preserved in Eusebius, *Praep. ev.* 8.10.3–4; 13.12.1–4; 13.13.3–4; Artipanus's statement as preserved in Eusebius, *Praep. ev.* 9.27.4–6; Eupolemus's statement as preserved in Eusebius, *Praep. ev.* 9.26.1; Philo, QG 3.5; 4.152; *Spec.* 4.61; *Prob.* 51–53; *Mos.* 1.2–3; Josephus, *C. Ap.* 2.154–156, 165–168, 256–257, 279–281, 293–295. See also Emil Schürer, *The History of the Jewish People in the Time of Jesus Christ (175 B.C.–A.D. 135)* (rev. and ed. Geza Vermes, Fergus Millar, and Martin Goodman; 3 vols.; Edinburgh: T&T Clark, 1973–1987), 3:582; and James H. Charlesworth's introduction to fragments of lost Judeo-Hellenistic works, where he refers to the "apologetic claim that the best Greek ideas are derived from the Jews," which he says is "generally characteristic" of those fragments (*The Old Testament Pseudepigrapha* [2 vols.; New York: Doubleday, 1983–1985], 2:775).

18. Jewish thinkers and writers of the first Christian century (like Paul) frequently had their understanding of Scripture mediated by the interpretive traditions reflected in the Apocrypha and Pseudepigrapha. On the Pseudepigrapha as exegetical literature, see James H. Charlesworth, "Biblical Interpretation: The Crucible of the Pseudepigrapha," in *Text and Testimony: Essays on New Testament and Apocryphal Literature in Honour of A. F. J. Klijn* (ed. Tjitze Baarda et al.; Kampen: Kok, 1988), 66–78; idem, "The Pseudepigrapha as Biblical Exegesis," in Evans and Stinespring, *Early Jewish and Christian Exegesis*, 139–52; and Devorah Dimant, "Use and Interpretation of Mikra in the Apocrypha and Pseudepigrapha," in Mulder, *Mikra*, 2:379–419.

19. For an argument in favor of the view that Paul's language of adoption reflects a scriptural and Jewish background, see James M. Scott, *Adoption as Sons of God: An Exegetical Investigation into the Background of ΥΙΟΘΕΣΙΑ in the Pauline Corpus* (WUNT 2/48; Tübingen: Mohr Siebeck, 1992). For the contrary argument, see John L. White, *The Apostle of God: Paul and the Promise of Abraham* (Peabody, Mass.: Hendrickson, 1999), 176–91.

both[20] (e.g., his language about the proclamation of good news, or references to a universal reign of God that may be based on Old Testament ideas while also engaging Roman imperial pretensions).

The challenge in identifying and analyzing Paul's broader usages of Scripture is that it is commonly treated as a matter of intuition or individual insight. Although scholars sometimes suggest that those who do not recognize the scriptural influence that they see do not "have ears to hear" or have insufficiently developed intuition, the question of who might be (to change the metaphor radically) wearing the emperor's new clothes is a real one. What criteria might we use to judge whether or not Paul is using scriptural vocabulary or concepts rather than ones that have some other primary background?

The following criteria are suggested with the hope that others might help to improve upon them as discussion continues. Concepts and ideas are more likely to be "scriptural" if: (1) Paul and/or other early Jewish or Christian authors associate them with scriptural quotations, allusions, and/or echoes elsewhere in their writings; (2) they have a distinctive background in the Jewish Scriptures and are typically introduced in Jewish (and early Christian) discourse as Jewish or scriptural concepts; (3) they reflect dissimilarity (in some significant aspect) to Greco-Roman ideas or concepts while also demonstrating similarity to a distinctive (generally known) Jewish concept that has roots in Scripture; or (4) they reflect dissimilarity (in some significant aspect) to Greco-Roman and Jewish ideas or concepts but are explicable in terms of new or alternative interpretations of Scripture inspired by Jesus or by the context and needs of the early church (especially if explicit scriptural support is given for the idea within early Christianity).

We know of some concepts that Paul considered scriptural concepts because of the way they are associated with quotations, allusions, and/or echoes elsewhere in Paul's writings. Paul's more explicit uses of Scripture address a broad range of issues, including justification by faith, the sinfulness of Jews and Gentiles, God's promises to Abraham and David, the salvation of the Gentiles, the Ten Commandments, the goodness of creation, the significance and dangers of idolatry, the reign of Christ, the law's promise of life, and so on. It will normally be safe to conclude that, where Paul addresses these subjects in other contexts without citing or alluding to particular verses of Scripture, he also understands himself to be dealing with biblical concepts

---

20. For an analysis of the background to Paul's cultic atonement metaphors that is sensitive to scriptural, Jewish, and Greco-Roman backgrounds, see Stephen Finlan, *The Background and Content of Paul's Cultic Atonement Metaphors* (SBLAcBib 19; Atlanta: Society of Biblical Literature, 2004).

that are informed by at least those verses that he quotes in his letters.[21] For example, Abraham, David, and the concept of justification are mentioned in a variety of scriptural texts that provide us with part of the scriptural matrix through which Paul understood these themes even when he does not quote or allude to specific texts. We should be cautious, however, about assuming that Paul's readers would have associated references to other biblical themes with particular scriptural backgrounds unless he clearly cites or alludes to that background elsewhere in the same letter. Yet even here it remains possible that the audience would have recognized the concepts or background as being based on Scripture, even if they did not have as clear or full an understanding of the specific scriptural background as did the apostle.

Other concepts that seem obviously "scriptural" in nature include those that have a distinctive background in the Jewish Scriptures and are typically introduced in Jewish (and early Christian) discourse as Jewish or scriptural concepts. For example, in Rom 9:4–5 Paul refers to the Israelites, to whom belong "*the* adoption, *the* glory, *the* covenants, *the* giving of the law, *the* worship, and *the* promises, … *the* patriarchs…, and from them … comes *the* Messiah." Here Paul does not expect there to be any doubt about which adoption, glory, covenants, giving of the law, worship, promises, patriarchs, or Messiah he has in mind. They would be those mentioned in the Scriptures and cherished in Jewish tradition. Similarly, when Paul refers to *the* law and/or *the* prophets, we are confident he means the ones found in or referred to in the Scriptures. In all of these cases, however, there are elements that may well reflect postbiblical developments. In Rom 9:4–5, for example, many questions remain. *Which* promises does Paul have in mind, and how are they understood? What kind of Messiah, exactly? It is not at all clear what Paul has in mind by "the glory," either. Paul's language implies it is a scripturally "known" idea, even if none of his readers could have known exactly what he had in mind or what scriptural basis the idea might have. Even in cases where we have plenty of scriptural background to work from, as in the case of "covenants," Paul does not imply that his readers would have had an encyclopedic knowledge of what they are or how they work; he merely presumes that they should recognize the concept as part of the Jewish scriptural heritage. It is often a challenge for the modern reader to discern the shape and extent of Paul's own understanding of the concepts that he invokes, much less the shape and extent of his readers' understanding.

---

21. Of course, it is not unlikely that Paul may have discussed a topic in Galatians on which he cites a text in Romans without having had that text in mind when he wrote Galatians.

Many times, of course, Paul refers to scriptural ideas in ways that are not clearly marked linguistically as such. These can be recognized due to the fact that they are specifically Jewish ideas (especially ideas that Jews were likely to think had some clear scriptural background) that are left unexplained and seem to suppose that Paul and his readers had some general understanding of what they entail. Students of biblical theology are constantly on the lookout for such concepts. We already see the development of scriptural themes that are no longer identified with a particular text or texts within the Old Testament itself. To give just one example, in discussing Amos's understanding of the Day of the Lord, von Rad suggested that "the prophetic concept of the *eschaton* was also to some extent systematized, that is to say, predictions connected with the expectation of the Day of Jahweh which began from different traditions were to some extent blended."[22]

James Dunn notes "how much Paul seems to have taken for granted that his readers would know what he meant by such key terms as 'righteousness' and 'works of the law.' "[23] Hans Hübner has argued similarly:

> The language of the New Testament, or more precisely the language of the various New Testament authors, is, in the main, shaped through and through by the Old Testament.... It is the old concept of God, it is the old concept of human beings, which time and again shapes the theological thinking of the New Testament authors to a considerable extent. It was not necessary for them to refer to important Old Testament statements and concepts because ... the intellectual and religious world of the Old Testament was self-evident to them as well as, as they probably thought, for their readers.[24]

Peter Stuhlmacher likewise insists that

> alongside the quotations and allusions, the New Testament is related to the Old through the use of a common tradition of language and life experience. This is manifested in a common mode of expression and in common concepts. Some of the many examples are: the creation doctrine which is common to both the Old and the New Testaments, the common idea of the "kingdom of God" (ἡ βασιλεία τοῦ θεοῦ), which is soon to come, the concept of God "dwelling" upon the earth, the belief that there exists a direct

---

22. Gerhard von Rad, *The Message of the Prophets* (New York: Harper & Row, 1965), 99.

23. James D. G. Dunn, *The Theology of Paul the Apostle* (Grand Rapids: Eerdmans, 1998), 16.

24. Hans Hübner, *Die Theologie des Paulus* (vol. 2 of *Biblische Theologie des Neuen Testaments*; Göttingen: Vandenhoeck & Ruprecht, 1993), 18.

relation between the deeds of a person and his or her condition, and the expectation of a resurrection of the dead at the end of time.[25]

We have already mentioned Paul's reference to "the Messiah" in Rom 9:5, but the variety of ways in which Paul uses the word Χριστός raises some interesting issues for our topic. Romans 9:5 is one of the rare instances where the word seems to have a clear titular meaning and thus is frequently translated "the Christ" or "the Messiah." It is commonly thought, however, that for Paul Χριστός typically "functions simply as a way of speaking of Jesus, as a *proper name* for Jesus."[26] Magnus Zetterholm goes so far as to assert that "there is almost complete unanimity among scholars that this expression has become a proper name and that it has lost its messianic overtones almost completely."[27]

Different people draw different conclusions from the same evidence. Dunn points out that, "in fact, there are quite a number of passages in Paul where *Christos* seems to retain something at least of its more titular sense and where we should more properly translate 'the Christ.'"[28] He has in mind passages such as Rom 9:3, 5; 15:3, 7, among others.[29] Besides these places where a titular sense seems more apparent, he also suggests that the use of "Christ" as the equivalent of a proper name "is an astonishing fact" because "it means that at the time of Paul's writing, the Christian claim that Jesus was Messiah was no longer controversial. No longer was it necessary for Paul to argue the case that Jesus was indeed Israel's long-awaited Davidic Messiah."[30] Moo also suggests that "it must be questioned whether a Jew like Paul, who had been converted to a new movement whose distinguishing claim was that God's promised Messiah was none other than Jesus of Nazareth, crucified by the Romans, could ever have fully discarded the rich Jewish associations of the word." He proposes a "middle ground" that accepts that Paul "rarely uses 'Christ' to communicate a theological point to his mainly Gentile audiences" and that "he appears to use the word usually without giving much thought to its significance," while also arguing that "there still clings to the word in Paul's

---

25. Peter Stuhlmacher, *How to Do Biblical Theology* (PTMS 38; Allison Park, Pa.: Pickwick, 1995), 8–9.

26. Ben Witherington III, *Paul's Narrative Thought World: The Tapestry of Tragedy and Triumph* (Louisville: Westminster John Knox, 1994), 133.

27. Magnus Zetterholm, "Paul and the Missing Messiah," in *The Messiah in Early Judaism and Christianity* (ed. Magnus Zetterholm; Minneapolis: Fortress, 2007), 37.

28. Dunn, *Theology of Paul*, 198.

29. Douglas J. Moo also includes 1 Cor 1:3; 10:4; and 12:12 ("The Christology of the Early Pauline Letters," in *Contours of Christology in the New Testament* [ed. Richard N. Longenecker; McMaster New Testament Studies; Grand Rapids: Eerdmans, 2005], 186.

30. Dunn, *Theology of Paul*, 197.

letters, more clearly in some texts than others, an allusion to the Old Testament and Jewish background against which Jesus must be understood."[31]

Interesting intertextual issues are raised by Witherington's observation that "careful scrutiny of the way and places in which Paul uses the term 'Christ' suggests that in the main what Paul means by 'Christ' he has *not* derived from early Jewish ideas about God's anointed, but rather from traditions about the conclusion of Jesus' life and its sequel, coupled with Paul's own Damascus road experience. These events have forced Paul to rethink what it meant for someone to be the Davidic Messiah."[32] This view assumes some understanding (from Scripture and Jewish interpretation) of "the Davidic Messiah," but it also suggests that, rather than being a static concept, it was capable of receiving (and, in fact, had received) new content based on the church's (and Paul's) actual experience of Jesus (Christ). The result is that Jesus' identity is informed by some prior understanding of the Davidic Messiah, while the scriptural concept of the Davidic Messiah is also filled out and informed by what is known about Jesus. Of course, even in Rom 9:5 the fact that the Messiah "is God over all" arguably goes beyond most previous messianic expectations and reflects a filling-out of the concept in light of the church's knowledge of Jesus Christ.[33]

This brings us back to Hübner's statement that in the New Testament we find "the old concept of God." While Paul clearly understands himself and his communities to be worshipers of the God of Israel who is revealed in the

---

31. Moo, "Christology of the Early Pauline Letters," 186-87.
32. Witherington, *Paul's Narrative Thought World*, 133.
33. Many scholars would translate the verse as in the NAB and RSV: "is the Messiah/Christ. God who is over all be blessed forever." In favor of this reading, see James D. G. Dunn, *Romans 9-16* (WBC 38B; Dallas: Word, 1988), 464-69, or the commentaries of Wilckens, Käsemann, and Stuhlmacher. The translation adopted here is persuasively supported by the commentaries of C. E. B. Cranfield (*A Critical and Exegetical Commentary on the Epistle to the Romans* [ICC; 2 vols.; London: T&T Clark, 1975-1979], 2:464-70), Douglas J. Moo (*The Epistle to the Romans* [NICNT; Grand Rapids: Eerdmans, 1996], 565-68), and Robert Jewett (*Romans: A Commentary* [Hermeneia; Minneapolis: Fortress, 2006], 566-69). It also reflects the view of the great majority of the Greek fathers (see Moo, *Romans*, 566 n. 64) and most modern translations (e.g., NRSV, TNIV, NIV, NET). Among other arguments, Cranfield points out that "Pauline doxologies are generally either an integral part of the preceding sentence or else closely connected with it (the doxology referring to a person named in the preceding sentence), and do not stand in complete asyndeton" (*Romans*, 2:467). He also notes that "[w]herever *bārûk* or its Greek equivalent εὐλογητός is used in the Bible in an independent doxology, it is always (apart from one known exception) ... the first word of the sentence, and the same rule is regularly applied also in extra-biblical Jewish usage" (ibid).

Scriptures, his (and his readers') understanding of that God has been radically shaped by his experience of Jesus Christ. This is so much the case that we can speak of Paul's "christological monotheism"; that is, Paul can hardly think of God without thinking of him in relation to Jesus Christ.[34]

Neil Elliott points to another type of dual intertextuality in Paul's use of an important scriptural theme when he reminds us that Paul's declaration "that he was charged by God with securing 'faithful obedience among the nations'" must be understood in light of the fact that "'the obedience of nations' was also the prerogative claimed by the Roman emperor."[35] It seems clear that New Testament authors understood Christ to be the fulfillment of biblical promises about the anticipated reign of God and/or his messianic king over all the earth, based on numerous passages from the Psalms and prophets, including Pss 2; 65; 68; 72; 89; 98; 102; 110; 138; 148; Mic 7; Zech 9; and Dan 7. No doubt the scriptural idea was shaped by Israel's knowledge and experience of world-dominating pagan suzerains.[36] The pretensions of pagan rulers were seen to parody the kind of sovereign rule that God himself is expected to exercise on behalf of his people one day, even as those same pagan reigns may well have informed Jewish understanding (by both comparison and contrast) of what such a reign might look like. Paul's evocation of such a theme would seem to reflect a similar type of mutually informing intertextuality between scriptural background and pagan imperial ideology.

Some scriptural backgrounds, concepts, or images may be identified by the distinctive nature of the parallels between aspects of Paul's thought (or another author's thought) and scriptural teaching on the same subject found

---

34. Cf. N. T. Wright, *The Climax of the Covenant: Christ and the Law in Pauline Theology* (Minneapolis: Fortress, 1992), 99, 114, 116, 119, 129, 132, 136; Richard Bauckham, *God Crucified: Monotheism and Christology in the New Testament* (Grand Rapids: Eerdmans, 1999), 38–40. The dynamic relationship between continuity and discontinuity between previous scriptural understanding and that which takes place in Christ's shadow is reflected in three of the chapter titles from N. T. Wright's *Paul: In Fresh Perspective* (Minneapolis: Fortress, 2005): "Rethinking God" (ch. 5), "Reworking God's People" (ch. 6), and "Reimagining God's Future" (ch. 7). The discontinuities are most apparent in the fact that Paul rejects certain ideas that he evidently took to be "scriptural" before his experience with Christ, i.e., those that oppose either his own interpretations of Scripture or other early Christian interpretations that he accepts.

35. Neil Elliott, "'Blasphemed among the Nations': Pursuing an Anti-imperial 'Intertextuality' in Romans," 214, in this volume.

36. Note how the language of the submission of "peoples, languages, and nations" that is used in relation to the "one like a son of man" in Dan 7:14 relates to the use of the same language with respect to Nebuchadnezzar in 3:4, 7, 29; 4:1; with respect to Belshazzar in 5:19; and with respect to Darius in 6:25.

in the Old Testament or in Jewish teaching that is dependent on the Old Testament. In his study of Paul's dependence on Scripture for his ethical statements in 1 Cor 5–7, Brian Rosner suggested a methodology that could serve as a tool for the discernment of some of the kinds of scriptural influences we are concerned with here.

> The first step in evaluating the use of Scripture … in any New Testament passage is to study the subject of that passage in the Scriptures and related early Jewish literature.… Once this background material has been assembled it should be held up as a mirror against the relevant New Testament passage to see to what extent the influence of Scripture may be reflected. Having listened to the Bible's teaching on a subject one is ready to hear echoes [or recognize the influence of biblical ideas and teachings] in the New Testament.[37]

As suggested above, the parallels discovered through such an investigation are more likely to be considered "scriptural" if they (1) reflect dissimilarity in some significant aspect from Greco-Roman ideas or concepts while also demonstrating similarity to a distinctive (generally known) Jewish concept that has its roots in Scripture, or (2) if they reflect dissimilarity (in some significant aspect) from Greco-Roman *and* Jewish ideas or concepts but are clearly explicable in terms of new or alternative interpretations of Scripture inspired by Jesus or the context and needs of the early church (especially if explicit scriptural support is given for the idea within early Christianity).

We may attempt to reconstruct Paul's own understanding of certain biblical concepts and ideas through the kind of synthesis that is usually performed in theological dictionaries, studying what he says about God, Christ, the Holy Spirit, the church, redemption, new creation, or other topics that we might presume he would understand as "biblical" concepts.[38] Such reconstructions would give us an author-centered perspective[39] that would include both the

---

37. Rosner, *Paul, Scripture and Ethics*, 18.

38. Many of the references in Hans Hübner, *Corpus Paulinum* (vol. 2 of *Vetus Testamentum in Novo*; Göttingen: Vandenhoeck & Ruprecht, 1997), are not so much texts that are being alluded to or echoed in Paul's letters as a listing of the sorts of texts on which the theological ideas communicated by Paul might be based (e.g., his list of parallels to Rom 1:4 on pages 4–8). Romans 1:1–5 is an example of a text that is full of theological statements that do not clearly allude to or echo particular Old Testament texts but are rather built out of biblical traditions about the hope for a Davidic king, resurrection from the dead, the role of the Holy Spirit, and the place of Gentiles in eschatology.

39. In favor of an author-centered approach, see Stanley E. Porter, "The Use of the Old Testament in the New Testament: A Brief Comment on Method and Terminology," in

prior scriptural content that would have been familiar to Paul before his conversion and the new understanding that he acquired in the light of Christ. The differences and relationship between those two sources of understanding could be further explored.

It seems clear that various aspects of the Jewish understanding of God (e.g., sovereignty, jealousy, power, role in creation, faithfulness, wrath against sin, intention to restore/redeem Israel and save Gentiles) are reflected in Paul's thought. Scriptural influence from a variety of passages may also be detected in his references to various biblical characters,[40] the promises made to the patriarchs, God's prophets, the significance and function of angels, the law of Moses (or the law and the prophets), the election and mission of Israel, the tribe of Benjamin, the importance of being children of Abraham (and children of God), the use of cultic language, the ideas of sin against God and idolatry, the Day of the Lord or a final day of judgment (now also the day of Christ), the related themes of divine blessings and curses, and the concept of the gospel. Additional examples can be seen in his views of apostasy, the church, the covenant(s), the Holy Spirit (including the role of the Holy Spirit in prophecy, inspiration, etc.), the Messiah as the Son of God and king over all peoples, the resurrection of/from the dead, the view of God as the Father of his people and of the Messiah, the significance of Jerusalem, and the concepts of righteousness and justice, not to mention his ethical expectations and his use of priestly language to describe his life and ministry. Also included under this heading are Paul's references to the practice and meaning of circumcision and his idea that Jews were expected to keep the law, along with the associated belief that keeping the law might lead people to life or justification or bring them under divine judgment.

The terms "Scripture" or "the Scriptures" are frequently used in relation to particular texts (Rom 4:3; 9:17; 10:11; 11:2; 15:4; Gal 3:8; 4:30; 1 Tim 5:18), but they can also be used without such specific references (Rom 1:2; 1 Cor 15:3–4; Gal 3:22). In a broader sense, Scripture is being "used" whenever it is invoked, regardless of whether the author or readers could have provided a specific justification for the invocation. In Rom 1:2, for example, we are told that the gospel of God about his Son was "promised beforehand through his prophets in the Holy Scriptures." In 1 Cor 15:3–4 we are told that Christ's

---

Early Christian Interpretation of the Scriptures of Israel (ed. Craig A. Evans and James A. Sanders; SSEJC 5; JSNTSup 148; Sheffield: Sheffield Academic Press, 1997), 93, 95–96.

40. Many of Paul's references to people of the Old Testament are text-specific (e.g., Eve in 2 Cor 11:3), while others seem to be more general. While Paul explores some specific texts in Rom 4, his opening reference to Abraham (4:1) entails a general reference to his role as forefather.

death for our sins and his resurrection on the third day were both "according to the Scriptures." In both cases we might be able to guess at a number of the texts that Paul had in mind, but it seems better to think that he is alluding here not to specific texts but to constellations of scriptural interpretations. Similarly, in Gal 3:22 Paul informs us that "the Scripture" has imprisoned all things under sin. The use of the singular ("Scripture") probably suggests that he has a particular text in mind, but it is hardly apparent which text that might be. The parallels in Rom 3:9 and 11:22 and the discussion in 3:9-19 might suggest the kinds of texts that Paul had in mind.

The explicit invocation of Scripture as an authority without referencing any particular text or passage, as in the examples just cited, entails an unusual and remarkable kind of rhetorical employment of Scripture. The analysis of specific rhetorical aspects of the use of biblical language and ideas in Paul's letters would require the adoption of a reader-focused approach, since rhetorical usage depends in significant part on how an author or speaker uses or engages the reader/hearer's prior knowledge and values. To evaluate the rhetorical significance of Paul's use of such general biblical references, we would need to pay attention to the significance of the particular places and ways in which scriptural concepts, ideas, and idioms are evoked in Paul's letters and compare that information with what he says in similar passages where he does not seem to be dependent upon Scripture at all. We would also need to ask how the recognition of the presence of such scriptural influence clarifies our understanding of both the meaning and the effect of the text. In some cases one might expect that there could have been a slight sense of alienation on the part of readers either because they recognized Paul's references to Jewish prerogatives as delineated in Scripture (e.g., in Rom 9:4-5) or because the scriptural material (whether recognized as such by them or not) seemed foreign to them or was brought to bear against them. In other cases the readers' shared knowledge of and appreciation of such background might have helped Paul to build or reinforce a sense of solidarity between himself and his readers.[41] Given the impossibility of certain knowledge of Paul's readers and their sensibilities, it is extremely difficult to explore such rhetorical issues with any great confidence.

It is clear that we have barely scratched the surface in our consideration of Paul's use of general biblical concepts and ideas. There remain many questions that merit further research. Among these we might highlight just a

---

41. For suggestions of how these dynamics might be at work, see the sections in Roy E. Ciampa, *The Presence and Function of Scripture in Galatians 1 and 2* (WUNT 2/102; Tübingen: Mohr Siebeck, 1998), dealing with Paul's status and ethos (69-70, 96-98, 104-5, 126-28, 178, 218).

few. (1) How might we clarify and strengthen the criteria that can be used to discern which of Paul's ideas are partly or mainly based on Scripture or influenced by scriptural traditions?[42] (2) Can and should the list of general biblical concepts and ideas that Paul uses be organized around certain key issues (e.g., creation, patriarchs, exodus traditions, second exodus traditions, moral teaching, eschatology)? (3) What criteria may be used to discern the extent to which later Jewish or Greco-Roman philosophy, ethics, traditions, culture, and so forth have influenced ideas that have biblical background? (4) Might a careful analysis of Paul's use of general scriptural background provide any insight into his understanding of what counted and what did not count as Scripture?[43]

It may well be that the question of the subtle influence of general biblical concepts and ideas on Paul's thinking and his implicit use of them in his writing will pose the greatest challenge as we seek to gain an ever more complete understanding of the use of Scripture in his letters.

---

42. Is there any way in which H. P. Grice's approach (and that of others) to evaluating implicature by the principle of cancelability (see Jay David Atlas, "Presupposition," in *The Handbook of Pragmatics* [ed. Laurence R. Horn and Gregory L. Ward; Blackwell Handbooks in Linguistics 16; Malden, Mass.: Blackwell, 2004], 38–39) might be informally applied to this issue? For instance, does the fact that it would sound strange (although not impossible) to hear someone say, "Paul mentions Israel's election but he does not have in mind what Scripture says about that," or "Paul refers to the resurrection of the dead but he does not have in mind the expectation based on Scripture that God's righteous people would be raised from the dead," help in deciding which ideas are "scriptural" and which are not, or are reactions to such statements equally subjective?

43. Exactly which books Paul would have included in his references to "Scripture" may never be definitively settled, but it seems clear that he expects his readers to know what counts as Scripture and what does not.

BIBLICAL NARRATIVES

Steven DiMattei

1. Introduction

The notion that Paul interprets Scripture typologically has undeniably dominated Pauline scholarship since its inception and easily passes as an unquestionable given. At least since Leonhard Goppelt's pioneering work on τύπος,[1] New Testament scholars have approached the epistles of Paul with the hermeneutical conviction that Paul employs the term τύπος in two distinct ways, indeed with two distinct meanings in mind: (1) as a personal "model" or "example" to imitate and follow;[2] and (2) as a historical "type" conceived hermeneutically in terms of a historical "prefiguration."[3] It has furthermore been asserted that this latter sense, traditionally attributed to Paul's use of τύπος in 1 Cor 10:6 (cf. its adverbial form τυπικῶς at 10:11) and Rom 5:14, is demanded by the exegetical context within which the term is found.[4] Yet it remains unclear whether this sense is actually demanded by its context or whether it is extrapolated from or imposed upon its context on the basis of an a priori hermeneutical conviction on the part of the reader that τύπος means "type" and that Paul's approach to Scripture is typological. For

---

1. See both his 1939 monograph, *Typos: Die typologische Deutung des Alten Testaments im Neuen* (Gütersloh: Bertelsmann, 1939), translated as *Typos: The Typological Interpretation of the Old Testament in the New* [trans. Donald Madvig; Grand Rapids: Eerdmans, 1982]), and his 1969 article "τύπος," *TDNT* 8:246–59.

2. E.g., 1 Thess 1:7; 2 Thess 3:9; and Phil 3:17. Cf. 1 Tim 4:11 and Titus 2:7.

3. In Goppelt's words, a *Vorausdarstellung*.

4. Goppelt, "τύπος," *TDNT* 8:253: "This sense [i.e., the hermeneutical] is demanded in Rom 5:14: Ἀδὰμ ὅς ἐστιν τύπος τοῦ μέλλοντος." For contrasting views, see Otfried Hofius, "The Adam-Christ Antithesis and the Law: Reflections on Romans 5:12–21," in *Paul and the Mosaic Law* (ed. James D. G. Dunn; Grand Rapids: Eerdmans, 2002), 165–206; Karl-Heinrich Ostmeyer, "Typologie und Typos: Analyse eines schwierigen Verhältnisses," *NTS* 46 (2000): 112–31.

example, although a growing number of scholars now concede that Paul's use of the term τύποι in 1 Cor 10:6 is best understood as referring to literary and/or historical *exemplae*[5] and that τυπικῶς at 10:11 means "as examples," many of these same scholars would nonetheless classify Paul's use of Scripture in 10:1–4 as typological. This, evidently, is not a hermeneutical conviction that depends on the meaning and use of the term τύποι in 10:6 but one that has its origins elsewhere, such as patristic readings of Paul's scriptural hermeneutic in the interpretive and apologetic debates of the early church, a topic about which I will have more to say later.

In a similar vein, at least since John Chrysostom's claim that Paul meant to employ the term τύπος in Gal 4:24 rather than the participle ἀλληγορούμενα,[6] Gal 4:21–31 has also been invoked by commentators as an example of Pauline typology. Again, I am not so convinced[7] and rather see this interpretive maneuver as merely another example of reading Paul's use of Scripture through a post-Pauline interpretive lens that was initially formulated by Antiochene exegetes as a response to Origen's portrayal of a Pauline scriptural hermeneutic

---

5. Richard Hays, *Echoes of Scripture in the Letters of Paul* (New Haven: Yale University Press, 1989), nevertheless advocates for a comprehension of τύποι in 10:6 as "types" or "historical prefigurations," yielding the view that Paul read Israel typologically as a prefiguration of the Church (95–102; see also Hays, *The Conversion of the Imagination: Paul as Interpreter of Israel's Scripture* [Grand Rapids: Eerdmans, 2005], 8–12). Yet a sense such as "prefigurations" goes against what Paul has written and makes no sense at all of the context or syntax of 10:6–10, which is one continuous sentence: "These things have become our 'prefigurations' [τύποι] *so that* [εἰς τό] we do not lust after evils, ... are not idolaters, ... do not commit sexual immorality," etc. Within the syntax of this sentence and the larger context of this passage, pedagogical *exemplae* is the only appropriate meaning for τύποι here, and we can be sure that this was both Paul's intended meaning and how his Hellenophone audience would have understood the term. Likewise, in 10:11, "These things happened to them [i.e., the Israelites] 'as prefigurations' [τυπικῶς]" is hardly intelligible, unless one understands τυπικῶς through an anti-Jewish Origenian hermeneutic whereby these events occurred to the Israelites as "shadows" and "copies" of spiritual and celestial realities that the Jews themselves were incapable of deciphering—a sense that Origen pulls from Heb 10:1 and 8:5, a non-Pauline text. As will become clear below, the conviction of Hays and others that 1 Cor 10:1–11 represents Paul's typological interpretation of narratives found in Exodus and Numbers is not born from the term τύποι but is a post-Pauline Christian hermeneutic projected onto the text.

6. *Comm. Epist. ad Gal.* 4:710 (PG 61:662): Καταχρηστικῶς τὸν τύπον ἀλληγορίαν ἐκάλεσεν.

7. For a detailed discussion, see Steven DiMattei, "Paul's Allegory of the Two Covenants (Gal 4:21–31) in Light of First Century Hellenistic Rhetoric and Jewish Hermeneutics," *NTS* 52 (2006): 102–22.

that denied the *historia* of the biblical narrative.⁸ Such claims tell us less about what Paul meant than they do about the apologetic and hermeneutical agenda of early Christian exegetes as they vied to defend Paul's scriptural hermeneutic from contending "heretical" positions. Furthermore, such claims also continue to construe Paul's use of Scripture through an anachronistic a posteriori Christian hermeneutical and theological grid that ends up divorcing Paul from his Jewish context and from other Jewish hermeneutical practices of the first century. Efforts have been made to avoid this charge by arguing that typology has its roots in Jewish reading practices,⁹ a line of reasoning that has even been extended to include Qumran pesharim.¹⁰ Contrary to this common practice, this paper argues that the roots of typological exegesis lie in the early church's use of the term τύπος in relation to a series of interpretive debates that took place in the early church with its diverse socioreligious and apologetic contexts. In this respect, typology is unequivocally a Christian hermeneutic. What Paul and other Jewish exegetes are doing must be redefined and categorized with more appropriate terminology. Thus this paper also attempts to recontextualize Paul's scriptural hermeneutic in general and his use of biblical narrative in particular, by moving away from a methodology that looks for parallels in later Christian exegetical practices and toward one that compares Paul's methods with Jewish hermeneutical practices of the first century and Hellenistic modes of reading historical narratives for purposes of edification.

2. Reassessing the Notion of Pauline Typology

One of the lasting legacies of Goppelt's 1939 monograph has been the conviction that, to put it in E. Earle Ellis's words, "a typological understanding

---

8. See particularly the responses of John Chrysostom and Theodore of Mopsuestia in their commentaries on Gal 4:24. See also Frances Young, *Biblical Exegesis and the Formation of Christian Culture* (Cambridge: Cambridge University Press, 1997), 180–85.

9. See, e.g., Jean Daniélou, *Sacramentum futuri: Études sur les origines de la typologie biblique* (Paris: Beauchesne, 1950); E. Earle Ellis, *Paul's Use of the Old Testament* (Edinburgh: Oliver & Boyd, 1957; repr., Grand Rapids: Baker, 1981), 131, with reference to an alleged "Exodus typology" in the Prophets; Daniel Patte, *Early Jewish Hermeneutic in Palestine* (SBLDS 22; Missoula, Mont.: Scholars Press, 1975); David Instone-Brewer, *Techniques and Assumptions in Jewish Exegesis before 70 CE* (Tübingen: Mohr Siebeck, 1992). The same line of reasoning can be seen in Michael Fishbane, *Biblical Interpretation in Ancient Israel* (Oxford: Clarendon, 1985), who voices reluctance about using this "anachronistic and methodologically problematic" label as a means of talking about Jewish exegetical practices (350–51).

10. E.g., Otto Betz, "Past Events and Last Events in the Qumran Interpretation of History," *Proceedings of the World Congress of Jewish Studies* 6 (1977): 27–34.

of Scripture governed the interpretation of NT writers and continued to be followed, more or less closely, by Irenaeus of Lyons and by the patristic school of Antioch."[11] I would be more inclined to argue, however, that a typological understanding of Scripture did not govern the interpretation of New Testament writers and that this conviction is the result of looking at New Testament uses of the Old, including those of Paul, through a later Christian hermeneutical lens.[12] This may be compared to construing Paul's theology through a post-Pauline Lutheran lens, much of which has now been dismantled by the "New Perspective." Furthermore, such an overreaching conviction does not take into consideration the changing socioreligious dynamics of the early church that inevitably prompted certain exegetical practices to arise as responses to contending views or to potentially "heretical" views of Scripture. Our modern understanding of typological exegesis, for example, which has not changed significantly since Goppelt's initial work, is actually rooted in the hermeneutical and theological concerns of Antiochene exegetes as they attempted to redefine, and even correct, Paul's scriptural hermeneutic in the wake of Origen's invocation of Paul to support his "ahistorical" allegorical method. Thus

---

11. Foreword in Goppelt, *Typos*, ix.

12. The larger issue of the supposedly typological use of the Old Testament in the New is a topic well beyond the scope of this paper. It might briefly be stated, nonetheless, that what has traditionally been labeled as examples of New Testament typology by the pioneers in the field needs to be critically reevaluated. I would be hesitant to claim, for example, that, through the formula ἵνα πληρωθῇ τὸ ῥηθὲν ὑπὸ κυρίου διὰ τοῦ προφήτου, Matthew is using Scripture typologically; that in Luke 4:17–21 Jesus reads Scripture typologically; that Luke's Jesus is using typology when he invokes fire from the heavens, as did Elijah (9:54; 1 Kgs 1:10, 12); that the sign of Jonah (Matt 12:41) is a typological reference; that 1 Peter's use of ἀντίτυπος in 3:21 represents a typological reading of Noah and the flood; or that John's use of the manna tradition (6:47–49) should be understood as typology. In fact, John's highly anti-Judaic interpretation (*contra* Richard Hays's claim that John interprets the manna "Christocentrically and typologically" [*Echoes of Scripture*, 90]) sets up a contrast between the manna that leads to death and the eucharistic bread, Christ himself, which is life. In a similar way, 1 Peter uses ἀντίτυπος to speak about Christian baptism of the Spirit as a "reversed model" of the salvation of the flesh that was brought through Noah's ark. The examples of Elijah and Jonah do not conform to the definition of typological exegesis that springs from the early church; they share more affinities with Jewish practices of constructing narratives on the model of former narratives. Luke's image of Jesus reading Scripture and Matthew's own scriptural interjections are best understood as compositional techniques used to buttress claims that Jesus fulfilled Old Testament prophecies. In fact, the kind of typological exegesis that is associated with the use of the term τύπος in the works of Barnabas, Justin Martyr, Irenaeus, Origen, and, to a lesser degree, the Antiochenes is in fact quite different from what modern scholars label as New Testament typology. For more on this, see below.

our modern tendency to define typology over against allegory, emphasizing that typology deals with historical persons, institutions, and events, while allegory deals merely with words, is a byproduct of this Antiochene-Alexandrian debate,[13] which crystallized around the question of how Paul's expression in Gal 4:24, ἅτινά ἐστιν ἀλληγορούμενα, should be understood.

Before we look at this issue in more detail, two other claims that appear frequently in the scholarly literature need to be addressed. Again, these are already formulated by Goppelt.

> Typology and the typological method have been part of the church's exegesis and hermeneutics from the very beginning.... So far as we can tell, Paul was the first to use the Greek word τύπος (adj. τυπικός) as a term for the prefiguring of the future in prior history. God dealt in a typical way (τυπικῶς) with Israel in the wilderness, in a manner that is a pattern for his dealing with the church in the last days. The fortunes of Israel are types (τύποι) of the experiences of the church (1 Cor 10:11, 6; cf. Rom 5:14). It cannot be demonstrated that the word had this meaning prior to Paul, and in Barnabas, Hermas, and Justin this usage has become firmly established.[14]

The sentiments expressed here are obviously not exclusive to Goppelt's work; one finds these same convictions throughout the secondary literature. For convenience, we should note that three essential claims are being made here: (1) typological exegesis was part of the church's hermeneutic from its beginning, influenced by New Testament typological exegesis;[15] (2) Paul himself

---

13. Whether an actual debate took place between these "schools" is disputed. Nevertheless, we are justified in speaking of an Antiochene response that was elicited, more or less, by the Alexandrian's formulation of Paul's scriptural hermeneutic. See Jean Guillet, "Les exégèses d'Alexandrie et d'Antioche: Conflit ou malentendu?" *RSR* 34 (1947): 257–302; Jean-Noël Guinot, "L'école exégétique d'Antioche et ses relations avec Origène," *Origeniana octava: Origen and the Alexandrian Tradition* (ed. Lorenzo Perrone, in collaboration with P. Bernardino and D. Marchini; 2 vols.; Leuven: Leuven University Press, 2003), 2:1149–66; and Frances Young, "Alexandrian and Antiochene Exegesis," in *The Ancient Period* (vol. 1 of *A History of Biblical Interpretation*; ed. Alan Hauser and Duane Watson; Grand Rapids: Eerdmans, 2003), 334–54.

14. *Typos*, 4–5.

15. Some critics, relying on Luke 4:17–21, have even attempted to claim that Jesus himself interpreted Scripture typologically (Goppelt, *Typos*, 121; Robert M. Grant, *A Short History of the Interpretation of the Bible in the Church* [New York: Macmillan, 1948], 7). One cannot help but notice the theological apologetic in such claims. Furthermore, as with other claims that label New Testament passages as examples of typology (see n. 12 above), Luke's portrait of Jesus reading from Isaiah, whether factual or fictional, is not typology; it is prophecy. See the distinction in Justin, *Dial.* 114.1.

forged the hermeneutical sense of "type" or *Vorausdarstellung* from the term τύπος and was thus the first to use it as such; and (3) the early church, as represented by Barnabas, Hermes, Justin, and Irenaeus, followed Paul in their use of the term τύπος. Such claims need to be critically reevaluated against the literary and historical evidence, especially those that concern pre-Antiochene uses of τύπος. A thorough reevaluation of this literature is beyond the scope of this paper; nevertheless, there is room to enumerate some of the methodological problems associated with these claims and to indicate how τύπος was actually used in the early church, giving rise to typological interpretation independently of Pauline influence.

I start with the second assertion noted above. The line of reasoning behind this argument is usually articulated by asserting that Paul forged a hermeneutical sense of the term τύπος from an inverted understanding of the term's etymological sense.[16] The problem inherent in such assessments is that the link between the term's etymological meaning ("imprint," "mark") and its alleged hermeneutical meaning ("type," "antitype," "hollow form," "*Vorausdarstellung*," "prefiguration") is never demonstrated, only asserted. One gets the impression that this rationale is merely an attempt to make sense of our a priori understanding of τύπος as "type" and to explain how Paul must have derived this meaning from its etymological sense. Second,

---

16. See, e.g., Goppelt, "τύπος," 8:252: "Thus τύπος can be the 'hollow form' which makes an opposite impression on some other material. Paul can adopt the term, which was familiar to him already in the sense of a moulding original, for a technical use consonant with this basic meaning"; C. K. Barrett, *A Commentary on the Epistle to the Romans* (London: Black, 1957), 105: "The word means a visible mark left by some object (e.g., John 20:25). Hence, in metaphor, a type is the mark, a reversed, laterally inverted, mark, which corresponds to the fact that Adam and Christ are reversed images of each other"; Ellis, *Paul's Use of the Old Testament*, 126: "Τύπος occurs fifteen times in the NT. Primarily it signifies the imprint made by a blow, and from this the several NT meanings arise—imprint (Jn 20:25), image (Acts 7:43), form (Rom 6:17), pattern or example (1 Cor 10:6; Heb 8:5). Τύπος may be either the primary concept or the secondary image (e.g., Acts 7:43; Heb 8:5; 9:24), but in typological exegesis the 'type' is usually applied to the OT 'shadow' and the 'antitype' to the NT fulfillment" (note the Origenian hermeneutic of shadow-antitype imposed here on Paul's use of the term); and C. E. B. Cranfield, *A Critical and Exegetical Commentary on the Epistle to the Romans* (ICC; 2 vols.; Edinburgh: T&T Clark, 1975–1979), 1:283: "The word τύπος denotes a mark made by striking (it is cognate with τύπτειν), an impression made by something, such an impression used in turn as a mould to shape something else (e.g. in 6:17), hence a form, figure, pattern, example, and—a specialized use in biblical interpretation—a type in the sense of a person or thing prefiguring (according to God's design) a person or thing pertaining to the time of eschatological fulfillment."

as many commentators have noted,[17] this hermeneutical sense is not attested prior to Paul, nor is it a philologically sound assessment.[18] Moreover, as we shall see, this understanding of τύπος, allegedly forged by Paul and handed down to the church, is not attested in our earliest Christian sources, including those sources mentioned above: Barnabas, Justin, and Irenaeus. Third, commentators often ignore other possible and even probable meanings of τύπος in connection to its usage in 1 Cor 10:6 and Rom 5:14, such as a sense with which Paul was surely familiar, that of "model,"[19] or the sense of the synonymous term παράδειγμα.[20] Finally, rather than demonstrating how Paul forged a hermeneutical sense or how a contextualized analysis of the passages in question supports this meaning, it seems that such evaluations are simply assertions established on the authority and tradition of the secondary literature,[21] which ultimately derives its meaning of "Pauline typology" from

---

17. E.g., Goppelt, "τύπος," 8:252 n. 32; Hofius, "Adam-Christ Antithesis," 181; Simon Légasse, *L'épître de Paul aux Romains* (Paris: Cerf, 2002), 383 n. 59.

18. See particularly Ostmeyer, "Typologie und Typos," 128. Nevertheless, I am not persuaded by this author's proposed etymological sense of "Stammvaterfunktion" for Rom 5:14.

19. Even when "model" is understood as an appropriate—and, I would say, correct—understanding of Paul's use of τύπος in Rom 5:14, commentators are nevertheless compelled to add to this some notion of typology. E.g., James D. G. Dunn, *Romans 1–8* (WBC 38A; Dallas: Word, 1988), 276–77.

20. This sense best suits an understanding of Paul's use of τύποι in 1 Cor 10:6, and it can be confidently concluded that he employed the term with this sense in mind, as he consistently does elsewhere (e.g., 1 Thess 1:7; 2 Thess 3:9; Phil 3:17; and, I would argue, Rom 5:14). See also Margaret M. Mitchell, *Paul and the Rhetoric of Reconciliation: An Exegetical Investigation of the Language and Composition of 1 Corinthians* (Louisville: Westminster John Knox, 1992), who, after meticulously examining the extensive use of rhetorical *exemplae* (παραδείγματα) in the orations of Hellenistic authors (39–60), concludes the same (47 n. 127): Paul's use of τύπος in 1 Cor 10:6 conforms to his uses in Philippians and Thessalonians in addition to Hellenistic uses of παράδειγμα and in some cases τύπος (e.g., Dio Chrysostom, *Or.* 31.56). See the discussion of 1 Cor 10:1–11 below.

21. The secondary literature typically pulls its definition of typology from earlier studies on the subject, from modern literary critics, from the Renaissance, from the Latin Middle Ages, etc., not from a contextualized analysis of the uses of τύπος in the early church nor, for that matter, in Paul. It is through the hermeneutical lens of the former that the latter are then often understood. See, e.g., Kenneth J. Woollcombe, "The Biblical Origins and Patristic Development of Typology," in *Essays on Typology* (ed. G. W. H. Lampe and Kenneth J. Woollcombe; Naperville, Ill.: Allenson, 1957), 39–75; James Barr, *Old and New in Interpretation: A Study of the Two Testaments* (London: Harper & Row, 1966); Elizabeth Achtemeier, "Typology," *IDBSup*, 926–27; Manlio Simonetti, *Profilo Storico dell'Esegesi Patristica* (Rome: Instituto Patristico Augustinianum, 1981); Karl Froehlich, *Biblical Interpretation in the Early Church* (Philadelphia: Fortress, 1984); Walter C. Kaiser,

Antiochene formulations of Paul's hermeneutic in response to Origen's formulation of the same. Thus it is not only Paul's use of τύπος (and indeed his approach to Scripture in general) that is reinterpreted through this Antiochene hermeneutic filter but also those of Barnabas, Justin, and, to a lesser degree, Irenaeus.

Momentarily setting Paul aside, the earliest attested uses of τύπος in exegetical contexts come from the Epistle of Barnabas and the works of Justin Martyr. It is significant to note that these two authors display no knowledge of the epistles of Paul in general and in particular no knowledge of any Pauline hermeneutical sense of the term τύπος. In fact, both authors use the word in conjunction with one of its basic meanings: "image" or "form." Moreover, their exegetical agendas arise from a specific socioreligious dynamic, which might best be explained as a desire to respond to possible Jewish objections to Jesus, a crucified criminal, as God's choice for salvation. Thus their "typological" exegesis—as derived from their use of τύπος—draws attention to the images or forms (τύποι) of the cross that are pre*figured* in the Old Testament. It is at base a visual hermeneutic,[22] not a historical hermeneutic.[23] Thus, Moses with his arms extended in the narrative of Exod 17:8–14 is an "image" of the cross (τύπος τοῦ σταυροῦ).[24] Similarly, the brazen serpent that Moses molds in Num 21:8–9 is an "image" (τύπος) of Jesus (Barn. 12.6–7) or the

---

The Uses of the Old Testament in the New (Chicago: Moody Press, 1985); Hays, *Echoes of Scripture*, 98–101; and Rowan A. Greer, "The Christian Bible and Its Interpretation," in James L. Kugel and Rowan A. Greer, *Early Biblical Interpretation* (LEC 3; Philadelphia: Westminster, 1986), 126–42.

22. Expressed through Barnabas's repeated use of the verb προφαίνω, and Justin's hermeneutical reflection in *Dial.* 114.1, where he articulates that a τύπος is something that is visibly produced (ἐναργῶς πράττεσθαί τι) by the prophetic spirit and that "was a figure of what was to come" (τύπος τοῦ μέλλοντος γίνεσθαι ἦν)—i.e., "images" or "forms" that the prophetic spirit makes (ἐποίει). See the distinction outlined in *Dial.* 90.2 between what the prophets said (εἶπον) and what the prophets did (ἐποίησαν), respectively, revelations through parables and forms (παραβολαῖς καὶ τύποις).

23. That is not to say that it is ahistorical. Again, such distinctions as historical/ahistorical and the emphasis on the historicity of Old Testament τύποι are later formulations. See also Young, *Biblical Exegesis*, 152.

24. Barn. 12.2–3; *Dial.* 91.3; 111.1; 111.2; 131.4. Justin's use of vocabulary is revealing. In *Dial.* 91.3, Justin correlates "the image of Moses with his arms extended," expressed in the Greek as τύπος τῆς ἐκτάσεως τῶν χειρῶν τοῦ Μωϋσέως (note that τύπος cannot be understood as "prefiguration" here) with the "image of the cross" (τύπος τοῦ σταυροῦ), which is also spoken of in *Dial.* 112.2 as "the image of Jesus who was crucified" (εἰκὼν τοῦ σταυρωθέντος Ἰησοῦ)—demonstrating that τύπος and εἰκών were conceived as synonymous terms by Justin and also by Irenaeus. *Contra* Goppelt, "τύπος," 8:252–53.

cross.²⁵ The emphasis is placed not only on the visual form of the cross as revealed in Scripture but also on the expiatory function of the image, which pertains to both the narrative context of the Torah passage and Christ on the cross. In other words, both of these scriptural passages (which are already re-presented in a christological manner) speak of "salvation" through the form of the cross: the Israelites defeat Amalek's men with the aid of Moses holding his arms outspread,²⁶ and Moses forms the brazen "cross" to "save" the people, that is, to expiate their sins. The exegetical apologetic is clear: God chose to expiate the sins of his people through the form (τύπος) of the cross.²⁷

Justin's celebrated typological/iconic²⁸ exegesis of the paschal lamb (*Dial.* 40.1–3), which in his view "was a figure of Christ" (τύπος ἦν τοῦ Χριστοῦ), displays this same theological and exegetical conviction: "For the lamb, while being roasted, gives forth an exterior form [σχηματιζόμενον] resembling the form of the cross [τῷ σχήματι τοῦ σταυροῦ], for one spit transfixes it horizontally from the lower parts up to the head, and another pierces it across the back, and holds up its forelegs." Justin's exegetical point is clear: the roasted lamb, the means through which the sins of the people are expiated, portrays through its exterior shape (σχῆμα) the form (τύπος) of the cross.²⁹ This is quite different from Paul's use of τύπος as well as later uses of the term and their exegetical aims and apologetics. What Justin and Barnabas are searching for in the Old Testament is not historical persons and events but visual forms of the cross inherent in the historical narrative.³⁰ In this sense, typol-

---

25. *Dial.* 91.4; *1 Apol.* 60.3–5. Justin's exegesis seems to suggest that Moses formed the brazen serpent in the form of a cross—a form (τύπος), according to Justin's apologetic, that Plato mistook as a *chi* (X)!

26. This form explains why the author of the Epistle of Barnabas follows this exegesis up with a similar, yet quite different, typological exegesis. Isaiah 65:2 is yet another passage that prophetically announces the salvific "form" of the cross: "All day long I have stretched out my hands to an obstinate people" (12.3).

27. This theology of the cross extends well beyond the parameters of Scripture for Justin. In *1 Apol.* 55, for example, Justin notes the forms of the cross, the means through which God saves, existing in the physical world, as in the sail of a ship or workmen's tools shaped in the form of a cross. Justin comments: "Ponder and see if anything in the world could exist and survive without this sign."

28. Term borrowed from Young, *Biblical Exegesis*, 191.

29. See also *Dial.* 91.2, where the form (σχῆμα) of the brazen serpent was an image (τύπος) of the cross.

30. This basic meaning of τύπος as "form," together with its specific application to the "form" of the cross, seems to have been present already in early Christendom beyond the context of scriptural exegesis, as witnessed, for instance, in a passage from the Acts of Paul

ogy is a Christian, indeed christological, interpretation of Scripture, the apologetic goal of which is to demonstrate visually, in conjunction with prophetic words, that God chose to save his people, to expiate the sins of his people, through the form of the cross. Thus the form of the cross, Jesus on the cross, or Old Testament rites of expiation play a central role in these early typological exegeses.[31]

Similarly, both Irenaeus's use of τύπος and his "typology" develop independently of any Pauline hermeneutical sense of the term τύπος or any alleged Pauline notion of typology. Rather, they are dependent on and influenced by (1) gnostic uses of τύπος to express cosmological and exegetical relationships between earthly happenings and events in the Pleroma, and (2) Irenaeus's particular exegetical project, namely, to demonstrate against the gnostic "economy" that there is but one unified history of salvation, linking events of the Old Testament with those of the New. This is the exegetical trajectory that is usually identified as New Testament typology; however, it is unique to Irenaeus and developed in reaction to gnostic uses of τύπος. For instance, a good part of book 1 of Irenaeus's *Adversus haereses* treats Valentinian cosmology, which uses the term τύπος to express relationships between what happens in the Pleroma and what occurs on earth or in the cosmos. Thus the Valentinians claim that the twelve signs of the zodiac are τύποι of the Dodecade, while the moon, in making its revolution around the heavens in thirty days, is a τύπος of the number of Eons (7.1), and, in general, things below are declared to be τύποι of those above (7.2). In these and similar examples, τύπος simply means "image" or "figure." This conception even extends to their scriptural exegesis.

> Concerning events happening outside the Pleroma, here is what they attempt to extrapolate from Scripture. They claim that the Lord came to suffer his Passion in the end times of the cosmos in order to display the passion which occurred to the last of the Aeons, and to make known through

---

and Thecla, where upon her martyrdom Thecla extends her arms in the form of a cross as she mounts the pyre: ἡ δὲ τὸν τύπον τοῦ σταυροῦ ποιησαμένη ἐπέβη τῶν ξύλων (22.4).

31. Thus, in Barnabas, the following are marked as "forms" or "images" of the cross, or of Jesus' crucifixion: the bull of Lev 16, understood as a sin offering (7.7, 10); the red heifer of Num 19, together with the scarlet wool (7.11; 8.1; Barnabas is working from midrashic traditions here; see the comments by Pierre Prigent in *Épître de Barnabé* [SC 172; Paris: Cerf, 1971], 130–31 nn. 3–4; 166 n. 2; 168 n. 1); and the unaccomplished rite of expiation of the Aqedah (7.3). In Justin's *Dialogue* we have the following: the paschal lamb of Exod 12:6–9 (40.1); the grain offering of Lev 14:10, understood as a purification/expiation (41.1); the prescription to circumcise, again understood figuratively as an expiation (41.4); and, finally, the image of the unicorn in Joseph's benediction in Deut 33:13–17 (134.3).

his own end, the end of the production of the Aeons. They maintain further that the girl of twelve years, the daughter of the ruler of the synagogue, to whom the Lord approached and raised from the dead (Luke 8:41–42), was a τύπος of Achamoth, which their Christ, by extending himself [beyond the bounds of the Pleroma], shaped and led to the perception of that light which had forsaken her. (8.2)

As exemplified above, the term τύπος is used in gnostic exegesis to construct relationships between events of Christ's life and events in the Pleroma.[32] That is to say, the exegetical use of τύπος among these "heretics" has no place for the Old Testament nor for its God, for that matter. The iconic resemblance is built upon happenings in the life of Christ and those in the Pleroma. Irenaeus, by contrast, takes up the same term to construct an exegetical system that highlights, in opposition to his adversaries, the "economy" between happenings in the Old and New Testaments. Irenaeus's typological hermeneutic, in other words, grows out of his particular socioreligious context, wherein he must demonstrate against his gnostic rivals that there is but one God who instructed Jews and Christians alike about Christ and Christian realities through Old Testament τύποι. His invocation of Paul is part of his exegetical apologetic.

> Thus he [God] set upon the people the construction of the tabernacle, the building of the temple, the election of the Levites, sacrifices and oblations also, and all the other services of the law.... However, he instructed a people easily inclined to return to idols, stipulating through repeated appeals to persevere and to serve God, calling them to first principles through secondary, that is, to truths through τύποι, to eternal realities through temporal, to spiritual realities through carnal, and to celestial realities through terrestrial things, as it was also said to Moses: "You shall make all things according to the image [κατὰ τὸν τύπον] of the things you saw on the mountain" (Heb 8:5). For forty days he learned to keep the words of God, the heavenly forms, the spiritual images, and the figures of the things to come [προτυπώσεις τῶν μελλόντων], as also Paul says: "For they drank from the rock that followed them, and the rock was Christ" (1 Cor 10:4). And again, after mentioning the events related in the law, he goes on to say: "Now all these things happened to them in τύποι and were written down for our instruction, upon whom the end of ages has come" (10:11). Therefore, by means of τύποι they learned to fear God and persevere in his service. Thus they had law, instruction, and prophecy of future things.[33]

---

32. See their exegesis of Matt 9:20–21 (*Haer.* 2.23.1) and Luke 2:29 (*Haer.* 1.8.4).

33. *Haer.* 4.14.3. Where possible I have followed the few Greek fragments of this passage and the Greek retrojection from the Latin made by Adelin Rousseau (SC 100; Paris: Cerf, 1965). In the latter, the Latin manuscript's *typum*, *typica*, etc., are translated back

We should first notice how Irenaeus understands the term τύπος in relation to his pedagogical thesis: the Jews were instructed about truths through τύποι, about eternal realities through temporal realities, about spiritual realities through carnal realities, about celestial realities through earthly things. It becomes apparent from this list of dichotomies that Irenaeus is working with the same meaning of the term as the gnostics used, that of "image" or "figure," and is conceptualizing it in the same manner, understanding earthly, corporeal, and terrestrial events as images or figures of celestial and spiritual realities.[34] However, contrary to his rivals, Irenaeus argues (invoking Paul as his authority) that Old Testament τύποι bear witness to Christian celestial and spiritual realities, not those of the Pleroma. This, Irenaeus affirms, was even taught to the Jews, for they themselves were instructed through τύποι, that is, through carnal and earthly things, to comprehend what was to come. Hebrews 8:5 is Irenaeus's prooftext, and we would do well to pay particular attention to how Irenaeus reads and understands the term τύπος in this verse and how he then transfers this meaning to 1 Cor 10:4, 6, and 11. Following from the Hellenistic meaning of τύπος that is exemplified in the above list of earthly-celestial dichotomies, Irenaeus asserts that Moses was instructed about the celestial temple through its terrestrial τύπος. This hermeneutic is then extended to 1 Cor 10:1–11: the Israelites in the desert were likewise instructed about Christ through the spiritual rock, which was an earthly "figure" (τύπος is what Irenaeus understands here) of Christ. In other words, Irenaeus understands Paul's statement that "this rock was Christ" (10:4) through the hermeneutical lens provided to him by his already-Hellenized reading of τύπος in Heb 8:5. This is quite removed from Paul's own meaning and use of τύπος. In fact, Paul does not use the term τύπος in reference to the rock of 10:4, or if he does, it is certainly not in the sense proposed by Irenaeus, which, it must be borne in mind, is Irenaeus's own exegetical creation designed to substantiate his refutation of the gnostics by demonstrating (on the authority of Paul) that the Jews were instructed about Christ and Christian realities in their own sacred Scripture through earthly and cor-

---

to Irenaeus's Greek, so that *per typica ad vera* becomes διὰ τῶν τυπικῶν εἰς τὰ ἀληθῆ; *secundum typum* yields κατὰ τὸν τύπον; and *praefigurationes futurorum* is rendered as προτυπώσεις τῶν μελλόντων. Additionally, it would seem that Irenaeus has the "Antiochene" reading of 1 Cor 10:11 (τύποι συνέβαινον) that is attested in some manuscripts (A D F G sy[b]).

34. Cf. Ptolemy, *Flor.* 5.2 and 5.8, where the adjective τυπικός is used to describe the relationship between corporeal Jewish rituals and their spiritual meanings; also Origen, *Comm. Jo.* 10.110.55, where it is said that corporeal events are τύποι of incorporeal realities.

poreal figures: the rock and the temple. This is then further extended to all the historical events enumerated in this passage: "All these things happened to them in τύποι" (i.e., earthly and corporeal figures). Irenaeus's reading of Paul, therefore, reveals more about Irenaeus's exegetical and theological project than about Paul's hermeneutical intention.[35] In short, Irenaeus's typology is derived from his own unique understanding and application of τύπος, not from some alleged notion of New Testament typology or any Pauline hermeneutical sense of τύπος.[36]

Although confronted with many of the same adversaries as Irenaeus, Origen also had other opponents to contend with. On one side stood the Jews and Jewish literal readings of the law; on the other stood Hellenistic authors such as Celsus who regarded such literal interpretations as folly. Thus, in his attempt to defend Scripture, Origen is pressed to accentuate an allegorical scriptural hermeneutic, for which he invokes Paul as an authoritative representative.[37] Unfortunately, the "Paul" whom Origen predominantly

---

35. Cf. Clement of Alexandria's reading of the same verse (*Paed.* 2.101.1–3), where he clearly articulates that these τύποι are pedagogical *exemplae*—more in line with Paul's own meaning. See also Heb 2:7–4:11

36. The same conclusion must ultimately be drawn from an analysis of Irenaeus's use of τύπος from Rom 5:14, which he also understands as "image," synonymous with εἰκών. In a rather long refutation against those who claim that Jesus was not born of flesh and that Adam will not be saved, Irenaeus, as part of his counterargument, invokes Paul, who "calls Adam himself a τύπος τοῦ μέλλοντος" (*Haer.* 3.22.3). This verse is cited and understood by Irenaeus within the context of a christological interpretation of Gen 1:26, wherein Christ as Logos fashions Adam in his "form and likeness." Thus Irenaeus's theological and exegetical argument is that Christ formed Adam in his image (Gen 1:26), who then carries with him an "image" of Christ's future incarnation (Rom 5:14). Thus, for Irenaeus, this future economy, namely, the salvation of all flesh, including Adam, by the one who would become incarnate in this same flesh, is already stamped onto Adam at his creation. In other words, the linking of Adam and Christ in a unified history of salvation—typically referred to as a "typology"—is not born out of Paul's use of the expression Ἀδὰμ ὅς ἐστιν τύπος τοῦ μέλλοντος but rather from Irenaeus's theological application of it in the context of his christological interpretation of Gen 1:26—best translated in Irenaeus as "an image of the future economy."

37. There are roughly twelve passages that Origen frequently cites to justify his Pauline scriptural hermeneutic, which can be divided as follows: Rom 7:4; 1 Cor 2:10, 12–13; and 2 Cor 3:6, 15–17 bear witness to the spiritual nature of the law, spiritual realities that are only discernable by spiritual means, or the spirit of the Lord manifested through the law; 1 Cor 9:9–10 and Gal 4:24 support the idea that the law must be interpreted allegorically; and 1 Cor 10:4, 11; Col 2:16–17; and Heb 8:5; 10:1 furnish Origen with the idea that the law and its historical narrative are shadows and copies of incorporeal and spiritual realities.

invokes to justify his approach is no Paul at all but the anonymous author of the Epistle to the Hebrews. One cannot overemphasize the role of Heb 8:5 ("they [i.e., the Jews] worship celestial realities in copies and shadows [ὑποδείγματι καὶ σκιᾷ] ... according to the pattern received [κατὰ τὸν τύπον τὸν δειχθέντα]") and 10:1 ("the law is a shadow [σκιάν] of the good things to come") in Origen's conception and formulation of Paul's scriptural hermeneutic.[38] These verses allow Origen to nimbly forge together terms and concepts such as ὑπόδειγμα, σκιά, τύπος, τυπικῶς, and even σῶμα and τὰ σωματικά into a fused hermeneutical system that then identifies all biblical narratives as carnal "shadows" and "copies" of concepts usually expressed through an opposite group of terms: ἐπουράνιος, ἀληθής, πνεῦμα, τὰ πνευματικά, τὰ νοητά, and even τὰ μέλλοντα ἀγαθά (Heb 10:1). This scriptural hermeneutic is further reinforced by combining the expressions ταῦτα τυπικῶς συνέβαινεν from 1 Cor 10:11 (understanding τυπικῶς as synonymous with ὑπόδειγμα, σκιά, and τὰ σωματικά) and ἅτινά ἐστιν ἀλληγορούμενα of Gal 4:24.[39] Both serve as Pauline hermeneutical maxims justifying, for Origen, the allegorical interpretation of all of Scripture's historical narrative, which becomes a mere repository, in shadows and copies, of incorporeal realities.[40]

The Antiochene response to Origen's conception of Paul's allegorical hermeneutic, allegedly supported by Gal 4:24, stresses the historical element in Paul's allegory: "she [i.e., Hagar] corresponds to present-day Jerusalem" (Gal 4:25), retorts Theodore,[41] while Chrysostom claims that Paul improperly

---

38. Heb 8:5a (οἵτινες ὑποδείγματι καὶ σκιᾷ λατρεύουσιν τῶν ἐπουρανίων) is the most important and most often cited text in Origen's construal of his "Pauline" scriptural hermeneutic. See, e.g., *Cels.* 2.2.14, 5.44.13; *Princ.* 4.2.6; *Hom. Jer.* 1.34.2, 6.266.3, 10.91.3; *Philoc.* 1.13; *Comm. Matt.* 16.3.57; *Hom. Lev.* 5.1.48, 10.2.45, 13.1.2; *Hom. Jos.* 12.1, 17.1. See also *Hom. Lev.* 9.2, where Origen praises the scriptural hermeneutic evidenced by Hebrews in general.

39. See particularly *Cels.* 4.43–44; *Princ.* 4.2.6; and *Philoc.* 1.13. It is significant that in the celebrated passage in *Princ.* 4.2.6, Heb 10:1 opens and closes Origen's hermeneutical exposition, so that 1 Cor 10:11 and Gal 4:24 are cited and understood through the hermeneutical lens provided by Heb 10:1—a non-Pauline text. This Origenian hermeneutical lens still influences modern commentaries on Paul's scriptural hermeneutic, as when they draw on language such as "shadow"–"antitype" to describe Paul's scriptural hermeneutic.

40. See *Comm. Jo.* 20.67, 74: "One must interpret allegorically all the Abrahamic history in order to accomplish each of these things spiritually.... All the history of Abraham and the ensemble of what is written relating to him 'were spoken of allegorically' (Gal 4:24)." See also *Cels.* 2.3.8, 4.44.28; *Princ.* 4.2.6; *Philoc.* 1.13; *Comm. Matt.* 10.14.43, 17.34.78; and *Hom. Gen.* 6.1.25, 7.2.19, 10.2.42, 10.5.22.

41. *Commentary on Galatians* 4:22–31 (trans. in Froehlich, *Biblical Interpretation in the Early Church*, 101).

labeled the τύπος as an allegory.[42] The responses of Theodore and Chrysostom accentuated the correspondences to historical events that Paul makes in the allegory of Gal 4:21–31. Their approach, moreover, stands against Origen's assertion that historical events (τὰ ἱστορικά) are not τύποι of historical realities (οὐ ... ἱστορικῶν εἶναι τύπους) but of incorporeal realities (ἀλλά ... νοητῶν; *Comm. Jo.* 10.110.55). The difference, then, between Origen's reading of Paul's scriptural intent inherent in his use of τύπος (and ἀλληγορούμενα) and the Antiochene exegetes' reading of Paul's scriptural intent in his use of τύπος (incorrectly labeled as allegory) is often expressed as the difference between, respectively, "copies and shadows of images" and "images of *pragmata*," where the latter are conceived of as historical realities.[43] Thus, the emphasis on the historicity of the "image" is introduced into the exegetical discourse of the early church. This formulation, however, must be seen in the context of this specific interpretive debate. Thus, as Theodore notes, Paul's allegory refers to realities in his historical present, something that Origen's Paul rarely does. Yet Paul's allegory, in support of Origen, also refers to spiritual realities, such as the Jerusalem above (Gal 4:26). Thus, we must bear in mind that the Antiochene evaluation of Paul's scriptural hermeneutic, like that of Origen, was guided by theological and apologetic concerns that arose as a result of interpretive conflicts within early Christendom. It is not, nor should it be perceived as, a just representation of Paul's scriptural hermeneutic. In other words, Antiochene typology also developed independently of Paul's use of τύπος or of any alleged Pauline typology, even though Paul is apologetically invoked as the authoritative representative of the Antiochene approach to Scripture.

This brief survey of the uses of τύπος in the early church indicates that Paul did not equip the early church with either a hermeneutical sense of the term τύπος or a form of typological exegesis. Instead, both the meaning and the use of τύπος in the scriptural exegesis of the early church developed

---

42. PG 61:662: "He [Paul] improperly called the τύπος allegory. For here is what he wished to say: 'This narrative not only speaks about what has appeared, but it also declares other things [ἄλλα τινά].' Thus why it had been labeled 'allegory.' Now what has it declared? None other than the historical realities present."

43. See *Hom. Ps.* 38.7, where this difference is largely visible in Origen's use of Heb 10:1, which affirms: "The law is a shadow of the good things to come, not the image itself of the things [οὐκ αὐτὴν τὴν εἰκόνα τῶν πραγμάτων]." Origen comments: "Therefore, the law possesses the shadow of the good things to come, not 'the images themselves of realities [*pragmata*],' displaying without a doubt that the image of realities is something other than what Paul calls 'the shadow of the law.'" See also Jean-Noël Guinot, "La typologie comme technique herméneutique," in *Figures de l'Ancien Testament chez les Pères* (Cahiers de Biblia Patristica 2; Strasbourg: Palais Universitaire), 1–34.

within, and as a result of, unique socioreligious contexts wherein potentially harmful or "heretical" scriptural hermeneutics prompted an "orthodox" response.[44] It is thus unlikely that Paul had already coined a hermeneutical sense of the term τύπος or that he interpreted Scripture typologically, even though, it must be granted, Paul is apologetically invoked as the founder of this approach. In short, both Barnabas and Justin developed their typology (i.e., the use of τύπος in their christological exegesis) independently of Pauline influence and in response to specific arguments that were being raised against the Christian claim of a prophesied crucified messiah. Irenaeus's use of τύπος, predominantly influenced by a Hellenistic understanding of the term as exemplified in his reading of Heb 8:5, developed in reaction to gnostic forms of interpretation that, while using the same vocabulary, bypassed the Old Testament and its God. Origen likewise formulated his Paul-inspired scriptural hermeneutic on the basis of Heb 8:5 and 10:1, which formed the hermeneutical lens through which he understood τύποι in 1 Cor 10:6 and τυπικῶς in 10:11. Finally, the Antiochenes' typological exegesis, which initially rests on Paul's use of the term ἀλληγορούμενα, was developed in reaction to Origen's understanding and application of the same term to support his own hermeneutical agenda, which, from the perspective of the Antiochenes, brought into question the historicity of the biblical narrative. We cannot, therefore, speak of a direct Pauline influence on the formation of typological exegesis in the early church other than to acknowledge that the apostle was apologetically invoked as the founder of an "orthodox" Christian hermeneutic by early Christian exegetes.

It will nonetheless be argued that Paul's approach to biblical narrative is typological, even if the early church understood and used τύπος in a different sense than Paul did and even if typological exegesis emerged independently of Pauline influence. But is "typology" really the best term to describes Paul's scriptural hermeneutic? Often typology is (mis)understood as an exegetical procedure that pays particular attention to historical correspondences between a text and its exegetical application. But the typological exegesis that arose in the early church is not necessarily concerned with identifying correspondences between historical realities, as many of the exegeses cited above indicate. An exegesis that attempts to apply, understand, or interpret a biblical narrative in light of the historical circumstances of the exegete is

---

44. Alain Le Boulluec, *La notion d'hérésie dans la littérature grecque, IIe-IIIe siècles* (2 vols.; Paris: Études Augustiniennes, 1985), has treated at length the subject of how "orthodoxy" ultimately was forced to define its ecclesiology, i.e., its practice, doctrines, history, canon—and, I would add, scriptural hermeneutic—in opposition to contending "heretical" doctrines, practices, canon, and scriptural hermeneutics (see particularly 2:554).

not necessarily typological, nor is the effort to understand a contemporary historical event with reference to a past historical event typology. In short, to label Paul's scriptural hermeneutic as "typology" is to read Paul through a later Christian apologetic lens and a modern historicizing hermeneutical grid. But if Paul's approach to biblical narratives is not typological, how better might we label it?

3. Paul's Approach to Biblical Narrative in the Context of First-Century Jewish Hermeneutics

"As a Jew, Paul is a reader of scripture alongside other [Jewish] readers."[45] Francis Watson's words are an apt place to start recontextualizing Paul's scriptural hermeneutic. Although my particular interests and the direction of my inquiry are quite different from those of Watson, I nonetheless agree with his basic premise. Indeed, it hardly seems necessary these days to argue that Paul was a Jew and must therefore be understood within a Jewish context. The problem, however, is that, having construed Paul's hermeneutic as typology, New Testament scholars have actually placed Paul alongside subsequent Christian readers of Scripture and not alongside his Jewish contemporaries. This is certainly odd, considering that for the past thirty years the New Perspective has sought to advocate a view of Paul that is more attuned to his Jewish context. But when it comes to understanding Paul's use of Scripture, this has not always been the case. The tendency among many scholars has been to view Paul through the lens of post-Pauline hermeneutical practices and apologetics, so that, in effect, Paul's approach to Scripture is made to accord with Christian approaches to Scripture.[46] I hope that the preceding survey of how Paul was apologetically invoked as the authoritative representative of an "orthodox" Christian hermeneutic has, to some extent, made this clear. Nonetheless, I suspect that scholars will continue to argue that typology has its roots in pre-Christian Jewish exegesis and that Paul, therefore, is situated among other Jewish exegetes. Certainly there is no denying that Paul applies, reads, and understands Scripture in his historical context as containing instruction for those living in the end times, that is, Paul's own time. But can this rightly be labeled as typology? Is it not more appropriately a hermeneutic that we find in the Judaism of Paul's day, one that exemplifies Jewish hermeneutical assumptions prevalent in Paul's own milieu? Must

---

45. Francis Watson, *Paul and the Hermeneutics of Faith* (London: T&T Clark, 2004), 1.

46. E.g., Hays, *Echoes of Scripture*, 183; to a lesser degree, Sylvia Keesmaat, *Paul and His Story: (Re)interpreting the Exodus Tradition* (JSNTSup 181; Sheffield: Sheffield Academic Press, 1999), 235–37.

not an understanding of Paul's approach to biblical narrative be sought in the context of first-century Jewish hermeneutics?

Since the discovery of the Dead Sea Scrolls, New Testament scholars have, in fact, been doing just this. We know more about Jewish hermeneutical practices today than could possibly have been known in the early twentieth century, when speculation about typological exegesis was in its formative stages, often governed by misinformed ideas about Jewish hermeneutics and by Christian apologetic and theological agendas.[47] The discovery of exegetical practices at Qumran has to a large extent changed this, and we have greatly benefited from the wealth of studies that have sought to compare Paul's use of Scripture with Qumran pesharim, for example. Nonetheless, early studies in the field tended to overstate the similarities by either labeling Qumran pesher as a form of typological exegesis[48] or else identifying Paul's approach to biblical narrative as a form of midrash pesher.[49] Other scholars, in an attempt

---

47. For example, Joseph Bonsirven, *Exégèse rabbinique et exégèse paulinienne* (Paris: Beauchesne, 1939), argues that rabbinic exegesis, in comparison to Paul's, is nothing but a pedantic means of extrapolating from Scripture minute curiosities pertaining to history, grammar, and legal matters and that without typology Scripture is but a simple repository of historical and archeological information devoid of spiritual substance (353; see also 355). Likewise, Goppelt: "The typological use of the OT in the NT has always provided an example of a more profound interpretation of the OT and has motivated the search for a meaning that goes beyond the literal grammatical-historical explanation" (*Typos*, 7). "For us, Christ makes the Jewish interpretation of Scripture seem to be nothing more than a remarkable confusion of truth and error ... a falsification of the core of Scripture" (58). Surprisingly, such apologetics still find their way into discussions about Paul's allegedly Christian typological hermeneutic—a byproduct of these early studies that emphasized stark differences between Jewish and Christian hermeneutical approaches to Scripture where Paul was invoked, obviously, as subscribing to the latter.

48. E.g., Betz, "Past Events and Last Events," 33. Cf. Joseph Fitzmyer's more cautious approach in "The Use of Explicit Old Testament Quotations in Qumran Literature and in the New Testament," in *Essays on the Semitic Background of the New Testament* (London: Chapman, 1971), 3–58, 55. See also F. F. Bruce, *Biblical Exegesis in the Qumran Texts* (London: Tyndale, 1960), 75–88.

49. For example, Ellis (*Paul's Use of the Old Testament*, 139–47), drawing particularly on Krister Stendahl (*The School of Matthew and Its Use of the Old Testament* [Lund: Gleerup, 1954], 182–94), discusses similarities between pesher and Paul by having recourse to the notion of "midrash pesher." However, Timothy Lim ("Midrash Pesher in the Pauline Letters," in *The Scrolls and Scriptures: Qumran Fifty Years After* [ed. Stanley E. Porter and Craig A. Evans; JSPSup 26; Sheffield: Sheffield Academic Press, 1997], 280–91; *Holy Scripture in the Qumran Commentaries and the Pauline Letters* [Oxford: Clarendon, 1997], 123–39) argues that the category of midrash pesher was erroneously construed on a misunderstanding of 4QFlor by William Brownlee, "Bible Interpretation among the Sectarians

to distinguish Paul from the Qumran pesherites, have argued that Qumran pesharim viewed the biblical past as paradigmatic for the future, whereas Pauline and Christian typology saw the past as having been supplanted by the present, the old by the new.[50] This distinction is often reformulated to assert that Paul's hermeneutical assumptions were guided by his unique belief in Jesus as the Christ, an event that had already happened, so that Paul's interpretation of Scripture expressed a promise-fulfillment scenario that was absent from the Qumran sectarians who were still awaiting their Messiah.[51]

Without denying the influence that Paul's faith in Christ had on his hermeneutic, I would nevertheless distinguish between Paul's hermeneutical assumptions—those underlying principles that governed his *approach* to the biblical text—and Paul's Christology, the specific religious conviction that shaped his interpretation. In other words, although Paul's belief in Christ influences and shapes the content of his hermeneutic, it is not to be confused with the underlying hermeneutical assumption that guides his interpretation. The distinction, then, is between content and method: the former is variable and shaped by the specific historical circumstances and theological beliefs of the exegete and/or the community; the latter is the hermeneutical constant that assumes that the text under interpretation speaks to and about the exegete's and/or community's current historical, and often eschatological, situation. What I am proposing, then, is that Paul's approach to biblical narrative was guided by the same hermeneutical assumptions that governed Qumran pesharim[52] and, furthermore, that it is this hermeneutic that best explains Paul's approach to biblical narrative. For instance, one of the central characteristics of pesher exegesis, that which best defines its hermeneutical presupposition, is its contemporizing eschatological interpretation of prophetic texts, sometimes referred to as an "actualization"[53] of the text or as "fulfillment" interpretation.[54] The hermeneutical principles or assumptions

---

of the Dead Sea Scrolls," *BA* 19 (1951): 54–76, and has now largely been abandoned, or at least questioned, by Qumran scholars.

50. Betz, "Past Events and Last Events," 33–35.

51. E.g., Fitzmyer, "The Use of Explicit Old Testament Quotations," 51–54; Lim, *Holy Scripture*, 175.

52. Cf. Bruce, *Biblical Exegesis*, 75–88; J. Ross Wagner, *Heralds of the Good News: Isaiah and Paul "in Concert" in the Letter to the Romans* (NovTSup 101; Leiden: Brill, 2002), 348; and George J. Brooke, *The Dead Sea Scrolls and the New Testament* (Minneapolis: Fortress, 2005), 93–94.

53. Cecil Roth, "The Subject Matter of Qumran Exegesis," *VT* 10 (1960): 51–68.

54. See, e.g., James Charlesworth, *The Pesharim and Qumran History: Chaos or Consensus?* (Grand Rapids: Eerdmans, 2002), 6; Brooke, *The Dead Sea Scrolls*, 60; Geza Vermes, *Scrolls, Scriptures, and Early Christianity* (London: T&T Clark, 2005), 51.

at work in Qumran pesharim are thus often recognized as a conviction that (1) biblical prophecies refer to end times, and (2) the end time is now.[55] In other words, Israel's historical past is to be interpreted in light of the contemporary circumstances or history of the sect, with the added belief that the community is currently living in the end times. As has often been noted, this hermeneutical principle is best exemplified in the pesher on Hab 2:2, where the commentator affirms: "[The interpretation is that] God told Habakkuk to write down that which would happen to the final generation" (1QpHab 7). The prophetic text's core meaning is understood as its contemporized or eschatological meaning, a reading that more than often saw their particular community as having a unique and special place in the history of salvation.[56] Are these not the same hermeneutical principles that govern Paul's approach to biblical narrative, as when he says, "These things [i.e., the events pertaining to the wilderness narrative] ... were written for our instruction, upon whom the end of ages has come"?

One notable difference, however, between Paul's use of Scripture and Qumran pesharim is to be found in the form through which the latter expresses itself. Pesher commentary derives its name from its form: the prophetic verse is cited, followed by the pesher formula, "this is interpreted," and then the interpretation or commentary is given. Even though we have occasions of formulaic citations in Paul ("for it is written"), these are significantly different. When Paul cites Scripture, he rarely if ever provides his reader with such transparent interpretive signals as "the interpretation of this text is this."[57] Usually the scriptural passage is cited in its interpretive context; that is, the interpretative meaning of the base text is already assumed, and the text is simply presented in its contemporized context. For example, in Rom 9:25 Paul cites Hos 2:23: "I will call them my people who were not my people, and her beloved who was not beloved." Unlike pesher, Paul does not provide his readers with a hermeneutical key that bridges text and interpretation, translating Hosea's "my people" as "the Gentiles." He simply assumes the interpretive connection by means of its application: Hosea's "my people" are "the Gentiles." It has often been asserted that Paul cites this passage with no regard for its original context; through its application, the text assumes a new meaning and thus a new context. The hermeneutical assumption at

---

55. Shani Berrin, "Qumran Pesharim," in *Biblical Interpretation at Qumran* (ed. Matthias Henze; Grand Rapids: Eerdmans), 116.

56. Charlesworth, *The Pesharim and Qumran History*, 2.

57. Except perhaps in Gal 4:24, where Paul translates the allegorical sense of the covenant born of the bondwoman back to its literal sense, specifying "this one is Hagar." See also Gal 3:16.

work here, however, mirrors the principles of Qumran pesharim: for Paul, the prophetic text speaks of contemporary events and/or personages, here specifically the Gentiles.[58] The prophetic verse is thus understood not only in the contemporary context to which it is applied but also in its eschatological context. It is precisely this underlying hermeneutical assumption, which is at base a Jewish hermeneutical principle, that allows Paul to cite and use Scripture in the course of arguments that bear on the current, and often specific, historical situations of his churches. In other words, the text bears witness to what is currently happening in Paul's historical present. Thus for Paul, the appropriate and perhaps the only context within which to read and understand the prophetic text is the contemporized eschatological context. It is in this sense that the question of context remains pertinent to understanding Paul's approach to biblical narrative.

Any attempt to understand Paul's use of the biblical narratives excerpted from Exodus and Numbers in 1 Cor 10:1–11 must start by recognizing the pedagogical and eschatological elements inherent in Paul's reading and application of these narratives. These elements are explicitly articulated in 10:11: "These events … were written for our instruction, upon whom the end of ages has come." Thus, Paul's approach to biblical narratives mirrors the Qumran pesherists' approach to prophecy: the base text concerning Israel's past is applied to contemporaneous historical circumstances for the purpose of edification. George Brooke has referred to this as the exhortatory use of Scripture: events in the past are used to warn about or promise the fulfillment of future events.[59] Scripture told the story of Israel's past, a past that taught lessons for the present.[60] Paul's hermeneutic also shares many affinities with Hellenistic modes of reading the historical past as pedagogical *exemplae*, a practice that is especially common in deliberative rhetoric.[61] Aristotle writes, "Examples [παραδείγματα] are most suitable for deliberative

---

58. Cf. Wagner, *Heralds of the Good News*, 85.

59. George J. Brooke, "Biblical Interpretation at Qumran," in *Scripture and the Scrolls* (vol. 1 of *The Bible and the Dead Sea Scrolls*; ed. James Charlesworth; Waco, Tex.: Baylor University Press, 2006), 305–6. As an example, Brooke cites CD 2.14–3.3, where narratives specific to Noah and Abraham serve to warn readers of the life-threatening dangers that come upon those who stray and the benefits that come to those who follow the examples of Noah or Abraham (306).

60. Philip Davies, "Biblical Interpretation in the Dead Sea Scrolls," in Hauser and Watson, *A History of Biblical Interpretation*, 156.

61. Exhortation and deliberative speech obviously share much in common. See Mitchell, *Paul and the Rhetoric of Reconciliation*, 20–64, for an indispensable treatment of the affinities of 1 Corinthians with deliberative rhetoric, one of which is Paul's use of historical examples.

speech, for it is by examination of the past that we divine and judge the future [τὰ μέλλοντα]" (*Rhet.* 1.9.40; see also 2.20). In a similar vein, the orator Andocides asserts, "One must use the past as a guide for the future [περὶ τῶν μελλόντων],"[62] and "the examples [παραδείγματα] furnished by our past mistakes are enough to prevent men of sense from repeating them" (*De pace* 32). The same conviction is expressed in the Greco-Roman period by Aristides: "It is advantageous to draw from past events, the application of well-known examples [παραδείγματα] to the present."[63] As Margaret Mitchell concludes, through the use of examples, "the author brings to mind a past person or situation and either says that the course of action proposed, like the example, will be advantageous, or, in the negative, that the proposed action will, like the example, bring ruin and despair."[64] It should additionally be noted that the historical example is usually drawn from the cultural heritage of the author and his audience, thereby setting forth a past event or well-known individual as an example to be imitated or avoided.[65]

This practice of using one's cultural past as *exemplae* to guide or warn against present or future circumstances recalls what Paul has done in 1 Cor 10, where he refers to a narrative about "our fathers" to provide examples (τύποι) for the present edification of the Corinthian community who risk finding themselves in the same situation as their forefathers, if they continue in their present course of action. Paul's opening rhetorical formula—"I do not want you to be ignorant, brethren, that all our fathers" (10:1)—also mimics Hellenistic conventions for opening a deliberative speech by employing historical *exemplae* for pedagogical aims.[66] Thus there can be little doubt that Paul understands τύποι in 10:6 as synonymous with Hellenistic uses of the term παραδείγματα. Both the context of the passage in general and the syntax of this sentence in particular bear this out: "For these things/events

---

62. *De pace* 2. It is likewise in this respect that Paul's use of Adam as a τύπος τοῦ μέλλοντος (Rom 5:14) must be understood. Adam, through whose transgression death comes to all, Jew and Greek alike, serves as a model of what will happen in the future through Jesus Christ: life will come to all, Jew and Greek alike. As with his use of the historical narratives of the Israelites in the wilderness as τύποι in 1 Cor 10:6, Paul is employing the Hellenistic notion of using the past to divine the future when he presents Adam as "a model of the future."

63. *Or.* 24.23. See Mitchell, *Paul and the Rhetoric of Reconciliation*, 40 n. 97.

64. Mitchell, *Paul and the Rhetoric of Reconciliation*, 40.

65. See the examples cited in Benjamin Fiore, *The Function of Personal Example in the Socratic and Pastoral Epistles* (Rome: Biblical Institute Press, 1986), 26–56. On Paul as example, see 1 Cor 9:24–27; 11:1, etc.

66. See Mitchell, *Paul and the Rhetoric of Reconciliation*, 46–47; Fiore, *The Function of Personal Example*, 50.

have become our examples so that we do not covet evil, ... are not idolaters, ... do not commit sexual immorality...."[67] In this case, Paul's historical *exemplae* serve as warnings for the Corinthian congregation.[68] There is nothing typological about Paul's approach to these biblical narratives. Rather, his methodological approach must be understood in the context of the way historical narratives were understood and used to invest the present with meaning, as seen in Jewish hermeneutical conventions of the first century and the Hellenistic practice of reading past narratives as applicable to and instructional for the present.

There remains, however, the added eschatological emphasis to consider in Paul's use of these narratives. In recounting these narratives, Paul does not simply narrate the past; he also reshapes it, retelling the story and often interjecting elements and themes drawn from the context of the contemporary situation to which the narrative is being applied. On the one hand, it seems certain that Paul understood the events recounted in 1 Cor 10 as past history; this is evident both from his repeated use of the past tense and his reference to "our fathers." On the other hand, the passage includes many narrative details that do not belong to this past history and that are in fact part of the Corinthian community's present history: baptism, a communion of spiritual food and drink, and Christ.[69] How are we to understand this? Is Paul actually narrating a story of the past (i.e., a biblical story) in contemporaneous terms, or is he narrating a Corinthian story dressed up as past history? Or is he doing both?

According to Philip Davies: "It was the story itself, rather then a 'canonical' account of it, that mattered" for the Qumran exegetes.[70] Could this likewise have been the case for Paul? His renarration of the "salvation" of

---

67. Mitchell (*Paul and the Rhetoric of Reconciliation*, 126–65) goes on to show convincingly that all the *paradeigmata* that Paul uses in 10:6–10 are examples of the kind of factionalist behavior that Paul attempts to combat at Corinth.

68. Concerning Paul's rather cryptic expression in verse 11—"these things happened to them [i.e., Israelites] as examples [τυπικῶς]"—one may wish to refer to Ps 78, where many of these same events drawn from the wilderness experience do in fact serve as *exemplae* for the audience of the psalmist. See also Heb 2:7–4:11. Cf. Wayne A. Meeks, "'And They Rose up to Play': Midrash and Paraenesis in 1 Corinthians 10:1–22," *JSNT* 16 (1982): 64–78.

69. However one wishes to understand Paul's assertion that the rock was Christ (10:4), it must be acknowledged that Paul did not mean that the rock was a τύπος of Christ, either in an Irenean or Origenian sense. Nor does Paul understand the rock as a prefiguration of Christ; it *was* Christ. See also Heb 4:2, where the author, while invoking the same wilderness narrative, suggests that the gospel was preached "to them as well."

70. Davies, "Biblical Interpretation in the Dead Sea Scrolls," 156.

the Israelites in the desert via their baptism into Moses and their eating and drinking of a spiritual nourishment that has its source in Christ is shaped by his eschatological interpretation of events at Corinth, that is, the salvation of the Corinthian congregation via their baptism in Christ and their eating and drinking of the eucharistic meal. In this sense, these things have literally become the Corinthians' examples. Past and present, the text and its re-presentation (not to mention its interpretation) seem to coalesce into a single narrative fabric. Not surprisingly, Qumran pesharim display this same tendency toward reshaping the historical story or narrative to suit the contemporized application. Davies notes that, in retelling Israel's past for the purpose of edification, Qumran exegetes did not always strictly adhere to the text and often reshaped its details to suit the contemporary application.[71] Furthermore, like the Qumran exegetes, it seems that Paul also saw a consistent pattern in Israel's history of salvation, such that the historical narratives of Israel's past reveal the manner in which God will act in the eschatological age.[72] This is particularly the case with the narrative elements Paul emphasizes in 1 Cor 10:1–4, which strongly suggests that Paul understood the wilderness narrative as speaking of the events that were to (re)occur in the final generation. In fact, an eschatological understanding of this very narrative appears to have been current in the Judaism of Paul's day, where some believed that in the coming messianic age God would not only send a savior figure like Moses (Deut 18:15) but also rescue his people by the same means used by Moses to save the Israelites in the desert, that is, through baptism,[73] spiritual bread, and the spiritual rock, which would reappear in the messianic age.[74] Thus even if the content of Paul's interpretation is influenced by his belief in Christ, Paul nonetheless understands and applies this narrative in accord with Jewish hermeneutical assumptions—the belief that the prophecies, promises, blessings, and even historical narratives of Scripture

---

71. Davies, "Biblical Interpretation in the Dead Sea Scrolls," 156. See also Brooke, "Biblical Interpretation at Qumran," 303.

72. See Betz, "Past Events and Last Events," 31.

73. It seems that the narrative of the crossing of the Red Sea was also invoked in some early Jewish sources as a reference to proselyte baptism (e.g., b. Ker. 9a). See Richard N. Longenecker, *Biblical Exegesis in the Apostolic Period* (Grand Rapids: Eerdmans, 1999), 102.

74. See especially Targum Onqelos and Targum Pseudo-Jonathan on Num 20:2. See also the detailed discussion in Hermann L. Strack and Paul Billerbeck, *Kommentar zum Neuen Testament aus Talmud und Midrasch* (5 vols.; Munich: Beck, 1926), 3:406–8; Édouard Cothenet, "Prédication et typologie sacramentaire dans la première épître aux Corinthiens (10:1–13)," in idem, *Exégèse et Liturgie II* (LD 175; Paris: Cerf, 1999), 112. Cf. CD 6.3–4, where the "well" is interpreted eschatologically as the Torah.

were being fulfilled in the history and/or historical events of the contemporary community.[75]

Another Jewish reading practice contemporaneous with Paul that sheds considerable light on his understanding and use of biblical narrative is the *haftarah*, by which Torah passages were read through the interpretive lens of prophetic passages.[76] To speak of a *haftarah* reading in Paul seems unwarranted, since scholars do not normally accredit the first century with a *haftarah* liturgical reading practice.[77] However, it is far from coincidental that in Gal 4:21–31 Paul cites first from the Torah (giving a paraphrase of Gen 16–17) and then from Isa 54:1, which in the Palestinian triennial cycle is the *haftarah* reading. Thus already inherent in the passage's liturgical reading that immediately followed Gen 16:1—"Now Sarah, Abraham's wife, had not borne him any children"—is the implicit connection between the barren Sarah and the barren Jerusalem of Isa 54:1.[78] The exegetical link is constructed on thematic and verbal analogies, not on "types." The technique employed, or, as the case may be, handed down to Paul from an already-existing tradition, is decidedly Jewish and is established upon the rabbinic principle of *gezerah shawah*, where the verbal analogy is between οὐκ ἔτικτεν of Gen 16:1 and ἡ οὐ τίκτουσα of Isa 54:1, a link that is more evident in

---

75. Cf. Brooke, "Biblical Interpretation at Qumran," 312.

76. This aspect of *haftarah* is treated by Charles Perrot, *La lecture de la Bible dans la synagogue: Les anciennes lectures palestiniennes du Shabbat et des fêtes* (Hildesheim: Gerstenberg, 1973), 178–85.

77. This consensus, however, is slowly being brought into question. For example, Lawrence Schiffman, "The Early History of Public Reading of the Torah," in *Jews, Christians, and Polytheists in the Ancient Synagogue* (ed. Steven Fine; New York: Routledge, 1999), 44–56, suggests that even post-70 texts, notably Acts 13:13–15 and Luke 4:16–21, lend themselves to the conclusion that a Torah–Prophets reading was practiced prior to the destruction of the temple in 70 C.E. (47–48). More specific to Paul, Mark Nanos, "What Does 'Present Jerusalem' (Gal 4:25) in Paul's Allegory Have to Do with the Jerusalem of Paul's Time, or the Concerns of the Galatians?" (paper presented at the Central States SBL, St. Louis, March 2004), also suggests that Paul's use of Isa 54:1 together with Gen 16:1 may be evidence for the existence of a *haftarah* reading practice in the first century. See also DiMattei, "Paul's Allegory of the Two Covenants," 114–18; Michael Fishbane, "Introduction," in *The JPS Bible Commentary: Haftarot* (Philadelphia: Jewish Publication Society, 2002), xxiii; and Renée Bloch, who notes that such midrashic interpretational techniques as *gezerah shawah*, such as we find here in Paul (see above), largely originate from liturgical reading practices (cited by Geza Vermes, *Scripture and Tradition in Judaism* [StPB 4; Leiden: Brill, 1961], 7).

78. DiMattei, "Paul's Allegory of the Two Covenants," 115.

the Hebrew original, which has לא ילדה in both passages.⁷⁹ On a thematic level, the analogy is construed on the relationship between Sarah's current barrenness and future promised child, on the one hand, and Isaiah's prophetic pronouncement promising sons for Jerusalem after the devastating destruction by the Babylonians that left Jerusalem barren, on the other. Thus preliminarily, it would seem that Paul sees a similar, if not identical, narrative in these two texts.

This idea is reinforced by the recognition that in both texts, Genesis and Deutero-Isaiah, the future—perhaps even the eschatological—fulfillment of sons for the barren ones, Sarah and Jerusalem, is understood in terms of the promises made to Abraham. This is self-evident in the Genesis narrative, while in the Isaian narrative it becomes explicit in 51:1-3, where the prophet calls on his audience, "those who pursue righteousness," to remember the promises of land and descendants that were made to Abraham, the fulfillment of which is understood in terms of the (eschatological) restoration of Zion.⁸⁰ Thus, Paul's allegorical use of the Genesis narrative might plausibly have been shaped by the way he saw Isaiah reading and using the promises that were made to Abraham and his seed—promises that were intimately connected with the heavenly or eschatological Jerusalem and would ultimately be fulfilled in the eschaton. Again, we are working with a contemporizing eschatological Jewish hermeneutic that read prophetic texts as speaking of events that would occur in the last days. Accordingly, the Jerusalem spoken of by the prophet is not read as the historical Jerusalem but as the Jerusalem above. Interestingly, there is a fragment from Qumran that attests this same reading.⁸¹ We can go a step further in inferring that the Qumran sectarians would have seen Isaiah's "righteous ones" (53:1) as a reference to themselves, while Paul's hermeneutic, guided by the same contemporizing eschatological

---

79. C. K. Barrett, "The Allegory of Abraham, Sarah, and Hagar in the Argument of Galatians," in *Rechtfertigung: Festschrift für Ernst Käsemann zum 70. Geburtstag* (Tübingen: Mohr Siebeck, 1976), 1–16, construes the *gezerah shawah* on the term στεῖρα from Isa 54:1 and Gen 11:30, which is the annual Babylonian liturgical reading (12). Yet this is incorrect: Gen 11:30 is absent from the context of Paul's argument, and the *gezerah shawah* is best explained on the verbal linkage articulated above, reflecting the Palestinian cycle.

80. Isa 53:1-3 (LXX): "Hearken to me, those who pursue righteousness and seek the Lord: Look to the solid rock that you have hewn and to the hollow of the pit that you have dug. Look to Abraham your father and to Sarah, who was in labor with you: that he was one, and I called him, and blessed him, and loved him, and multiplied him. And now I will comfort thee, O Zion, and I have comforted all her wilderness, and I shall make her wilderness as the Lord's paradise."

81. 4Q164 frag. 1 interprets Isaiah's desolate Jerusalem as the eschatological new Jerusalem.

premise, would have dictated that they be interpreted as the Gentiles, "those who believe" (Gal 3:9), the sons of Abraham. The Gentiles are thus seen as the heirs of the new Jerusalem because, according to Paul's contemporized eschatological reading of Isaiah, this is exactly what the prophet speaks of at every turn of the page: "the nations" shall be/are being justified and assembled in the end of days.[82]

What Paul's hermeneutic seems to be doing, then, is retrospectively reading the heavenly Jerusalem of Isaiah onto the Sarah of Genesis, so that the latter narrative is conceived, like the prophetic text, as speaking about the eschatological present, albeit allegorically.[83] In other words, Paul allows his eschatological reading of Isaiah to influence his reading of the Abrahamic narrative. Reading through the hermeneutical lens provided by Isaiah, he interprets Sarah's barren-promise-of-heir narrative in a contemporized eschatological manner, so that she is, allegorically speaking, the Jerusalem above. Thus for Paul, both narratives, Isaiah and Genesis, reveal what is currently taking place: the promises are being fulfilled; the sons are being called; Sarah/Jerusalem has produced heirs.[84]

What is interesting is the term Paul uses to label this hermeneutical procedure, "allegory." It is important that we attempt to understand why Paul chose this term rather than having recourse to a Christian apologetic that claims that this is not allegory but typology. It may be stated that in some regards Theodore is correct in asserting that Paul relates his exegesis to "pres-

---

82. Isa 2:2–3; 14:2; 25:5–7; 51:5; 52:15; 54:3; 55:4–5, etc. See DiMattei, "Paul's Allegory of the Two Covenants," 116–17.

83. DiMattei, "Paul's Allegory of the Two Covenants," 118. It might also be said that, if one were to adopt Ross Wagner's idea (*Heralds of the Good News*, 354) that Paul reads Isaiah as a three-part story wherein he locates himself in the last act (i.e., the restoration where heralds go forth with the good news), then it might also be suggested, on the basis of what has been proposed above, that Paul, through the hermeneutical lens provided by Isaiah, reads the Abraham-Sarah narrative as expressing this same eschatological final act, albeit allegorically. This line of interpretation also corroborates Wagner's view that Paul read certain texts, particularly prophetic texts and Torah passages, as narrating the same story (354–55). See also Carol Stockhausen, "2 Corinthians and the Principles of Pauline Exegesis," in *Paul and the Scriptures of Israel* (ed. Craig A. Evans and James A. Sanders; SSEJC 1; JSNTSup 83; Sheffield: Sheffield Academic Press, 1993), 143–64, particularly her second Pauline exegetical procedure (144); and N. T. Wright, *The Climax of the Covenant: Christ and the Law in Pauline Theology* (Edinburgh: T&T Clark, 1991), 265.

84. See Charles Cosgrove, "The Law Has Given Sarah No Children (Gal 4:21–30)," *NovT* 29 (1987): 219–35, who suggests that Paul's reading of Isaiah allows him to see (allegorically) a Sarah who has remained barren until Christ.

ent-day Jerusalem,"[85] but this is the result of the Jewish hermeneutic at play here. For instance, Paul also relates this text to the eschatological Jerusalem from above, a hermeneutical maneuver accomplished through the *haftarah*—again, a Jewish hermeneutic. In short, there is nothing "typological" about Paul's reading of the Genesis narrative. Hagar and Sarah cannot be construed as τύποι of two covenants in any sense of the term.[86] Here, as in his renarration of the wilderness narrative, Paul reshapes the Genesis story to fit the details of the current eschatological context to which he applies the text. This is evident in his re-presentation of Sarah as the "freewoman" (Gal 4:22), a narrative detail found only in the text's applied context. Likewise, Paul's subtle rephrasing of Gen 21:10 from τοῦ υἱοῦ μου Ισαακ (LXX) to τοῦ υἱοῦ τῆς ἐλευθέρας (Gal 4:29) suggests that he not only applied this text to his own interpretive context but also understood the text—the story—in relation to a contemporary context. Yet the existence of this contextual layer does not negate the existence of the biblical context, Israel's historical past. This is where many commentators misinterpret the nature of allegorical narrative. That is to say, allegory has usually been understood and defined in relation to its apologetic function or use, rather than in relation to its Hellenistic rhetorical definition.[87] Regardless how we view allegory, Paul apparently saw in this Hellenistic term an apt expression for the Jewish hermeneutic employed here: biblical narratives speak of what will happen in the final generation. Moreover, Paul might have chosen the term *allegory* to describe this hermeneutical process because it simultaneously allows both narratives, both contexts, to be heard—the biblical and the eschatological.

Thus, there seems to be a latent problem in our use of the adjective *biblical* in our query into Paul's approach to biblical narrative, as it presupposes that Paul read the narratives of his religious tradition as part of a closed, canonical narrative.[88] In other words, the adjective *biblical* assumes that Paul is dealing with a canonical narrative that has a beginning and an ending (i.e.,

---

85. This would be the other half of Paul's allegory: the word "Hagar," which is an allegory of the covenant from Sinai, "corresponds to present-day Jerusalem" (Gal 4:25). See DiMattei, "Paul's Allegory of the Two Covenants," 109–14.

86. See, e.g., the senses surveyed in the patristic literature above: image, form, shadow, copy.

87. See Tryphon, *De tropis* 1.1: "*Allegoria* is an enunciation that while signifying one thing literally, brings forth the thought of something else"; Pseudo-Heraclitus, *Homeric Allegories* 5.2: "The trope that says one thing but signifies something other than what is said is called by the name *allegoria*." See DiMattei, "Paul's Allegory of the Two Covenants," 104–9.

88. The same query is made by Davies, "Biblical Interpretation in the Dead Sea Scrolls," 144, with respect to Qumran uses of Scripture. I largely follow Davies here.

the biblical story or history). However, this may not have been the case for Paul nor, if Philip Davies is correct, for the Qumran exegetes. This has some interesting ramifications for the way we conceptualize Paul's relationship to "biblical" narrative. Of course, we use the adjective only as a convenient label, yet it should be emphasized that what we identify as "biblical narrative," and the many questions that arise from this category, might have been a foreign concept to Paul. The narrative that Paul read in Scripture appears to have been an ongoing narrative, contemporized and historically extended beyond the "biblical" story—a narrative that is not only "written for our sake" but one that is also ultimately about "us." Furthermore, the term *biblical narrative*, by contrast, presupposes not only a canonical narrative with a beginning and an ending but also a contextualized narrative, one that is encompassed by the biblical story and whose meaning is found in this story's context. Thus, it has often been claimed that Paul's use of biblical narrative indicates that Paul has the narrative context in mind. But if "biblical" is a nebulous or flexible category for Paul, then how should we understand the context of Paul's use of historical narrative? Can we speak of Paul as using biblical citations in a contextualized manner if indeed the context within which Paul recasts his story extends beyond what we might identify as "biblical" context? Can we confidently claim that Paul's hermeneutic starts with Scripture or the biblical narrative when the narrative that Paul invokes time and again extends beyond the confines of what we would label as "biblical"?

It would seem, then, that as part of our query into how Paul might have envisioned the narratives of his religious tradition, we are drawn into the larger question of how Paul envisioned the context of those narratives—a question that has received a wealth of attention in recent scholarship.[89] Much of this literature attempts to defend Paul's use of Scripture by arguing, in opposition to the image of Paul taking scriptural verses out of context, that Paul cites scriptural texts with the broader narrative context in mind. Thus, the question of context is constructed around "biblical" context. For example,

---

89. E.g., Hays, *Echoes of Scripture*; Carol Stockhausen, *Moses' Veil and the Glory of the New Covenant: The Exegetical Substructure of II Cor. 3:1–4:6* (Rome: Biblical Institute Press, 1989); Linda Belleville, *Reflections of Glory: Paul's Polemical Use of the Moses-Doxa Tradition in 2 Corinthians 3:1–18* (JSNTSup 52; Sheffield: Sheffield Academic Press, 1991); Keesmaat, *Paul and His Story*; Wagner, *Heralds of the Good News*; Christopher D. Stanley, *Arguing with Scripture: The Rhetoric of Quotations in the Letters of Paul* (New York: T&T Clark, 2004); Scott J. Hafemann, *Paul, Moses, and the History of Israel: The Letter/Spirit Contrast and the Argument from Scripture in 2 Corinthians 3* (Paternoster Biblical Monographs; Waynesboro, Ga.: Paternoster, 2005); and Watson, *Paul and the Hermeneutics of Faith*.

many scholars have argued that, when Paul uses a scriptural verse or narrative, he is alluding to a much larger biblical context. Is this context, then, necessary for the comprehension of Paul's use of Scripture in the course of his argument?[90] This question implies that meaning, for both Paul and his audience, is dependent upon the historical and/or literary context in which the narrative or verse under question was originally written. Yet the question of context might be more complex than is generally acknowledged. Rather than pursuing the issue of context from a modern historical-critical and literary (i.e., "biblical") perspective, it might be more appropriate to construe context from Paul's perspective, from the larger basin of first-century Jewish hermeneutical norms.[91] How would a Jewish exegete such as Paul or a Qumran pesherist have understood "context"? When a prophetic text or historical narrative is cited and used in a contemporizing manner, as is often the case, what is the meaning of "context" from the perspective of the exegete? Is it not the contemporary, and often eschatological, situation to which the text is applied?

Thus far I have suggested that Paul understood biblical narrative in the context of a realized or contemporized eschatology, that is, in relation to his own historical moment. Thus, to a certain degree, the historical events unfolding before Paul's own eyes have happened, as Paul himself declares on occasion, "just as it is written."[92] In other words, Scripture bears witness to Paul's contemporary, even eschatological, present. Thus it would seem that the context within which we should understand Paul's use of Scripture is the one of which, according to the exegete, the citation speaks: the present

---

90. To take just one example, Hafemann concludes his study with an apologetic argument against a scholarly consensus that claims that, "based on his new-found Christian presuppositions ... Paul often creatively reinterpreted the Old Testament with little regard for its original context and contrary to its canonical meaning" (*Paul, Moses, and the History of Israel*, 452). Through a detailed reading of 2 Cor 3, Hafemann demonstrates how this is inaccurate. Yet both of these positions do not quite represent Paul's approach to Scripture. On the one hand, it would seem that Paul does in fact interpret Scripture with no regard to "biblical" context, a practice in accord with Jewish hermeneutical principles of his day that understood Scripture as speaking about events and/or personages of the final generation. On the other hand, it is difficult to know what "original/biblical context" or "canonical meaning" might have meant for Paul and other Jews, since such concepts did not exist. Can we confidently speak of such things in regard to Paul's perspective or understanding of the narratives of his religious traditions?

91. Donald H. Juel ("Interpreting Israel's Scriptures in the New Testament," in Hauser and Watson, *A History of Biblical Interpretation*, 283–303), like me, questions whether or not we have the "right" context in view.

92. Cf. Watson, *Paul and the Hermeneutics of Faith*, 45.

eschatological generation. We thus circle back to our earlier inquiry: What is the appropriate context to understand Paul's use of the wilderness narrative in 1 Cor 10:1–11? We have seen how Paul not only reshapes, applies, and contemporizes the experiences of the Israelites in the wilderness to meet his pedagogical purpose but also recontextualizes the narrative, using language and concepts foreign to the narrative's biblical and historical context. Baptism, spiritual food and drink, and Christ are narrative components that make sense in only one particular context, the Corinthian context. In retelling the narrative, Paul has shifted its context; it is now the Corinthians' story. Would it therefore have been necessary for the Corinthians to know the biblical context of the story that Paul narrates, since that story and its lesson are directed to, and speak about, the Corinthians' current circumstances? In other words, would not the meaning—this is what is at stake when we speak of context—of Paul's use of this story be supplied by the story's applied context, the current eschatological circumstances in the Corinthian congregation, not by the biblical context?

We can pursue this question further by engaging Paul's citation of Exod 32:6: "The people sat down to eat and drink, and rose up to play" (1 Cor 10:7). Surely Paul is alluding to the biblical context of the golden calf narrative, and just as surely his audience needs to know this context in order to grasp Paul's meaning.[93] Yet is the biblical context necessary for the Corinthians to comprehend Paul's use of Scripture here? It is often argued that the golden calf episode, the biblical or narrative context behind Exod 32:6, must have been on Paul's mind and must also be a required piece of information for the Corinthians to understand Paul's use of this verse and his intended meaning in citing it. If, however, the proper context for understanding Israel's past is the present eschatological context—the context about which the text speaks, according to Jewish hermeneutical principles—then the citation can be understood contextually as speaking about the Corinthians' current plight. That is, Exod 32:6 aptly speaks to, and about, the contemporary context. The Corinthians are in fact drinking, playing, and (apparently) eating idol meat at the Lord's Supper, and this behavior has put them in danger of being exterminated, as some of the Israelites were.[94] Thus, the connection between idolatry and eating, drinking, and playing—a connection, it has often been argued,

---

93. See Stanley, *Arguing with Scripture*, 83–90.

94. See particularly 10:14–17, where the simultaneous practice of idolatry and communion in Christ is denounced; 10:18–22, where Paul again denounces communion with Greek gods (*daimones*) via, it would seem, the consciousness of eating idol meat in conjunction with the communion with the Lord (see 10:31). Furthermore, Paul articulates in 11:27, 29, and 31 that the one who eats or drinks frivolously, in an unworthy manner, or

that requires knowledge of the biblical context—is actually made in Paul's correspondence and speaks of the current situation at Corinth (perhaps more so than we can perceive in the letter). Therefore, the relationship between idolatry, on the one hand, and eating, drinking, and playing on the other, need not be sought in the context of the biblical narrative; it can be seen in the Corinthian congregation, especially in the context of the Lord's Supper, where the eating of idol meat has become an issue. Is, therefore, Paul's use of Exod 32:6 meant to invoke the context of the golden calf narrative and those who were slaughtered? Or is it meant to invoke the Corinthian behavior at the Lord's Supper and insinuate their destruction if they do not shape up? If the latter context and lesson is implied, then would the Corinthians have had need of the biblical context of Exod 32:6 to understand the lesson at hand? Is not this renarration of Israel's past for the purpose of edification a self-contained lesson, which, since it speaks to and about current situations, requires no "background information"? Clearly the narrative that Paul recounts is descriptive of the current situation in Corinth.

It has often been claimed that Paul pays meticulous attention to both narrative detail and context in his use of biblical narratives. Although there is a growing body of literature that supports this line of interpretation, I am inclined to make a case for the opposite view, especially when considering the story of Abraham, another narrative that seems to extend beyond the category of "biblical narrative." As in the previous cases, the way we understand context, or the way we imagine Paul to have understood context, is central to our discussion. Does Paul pay particular attention to the narrative detail and biblical context of the Abraham story, or does he pay attention to details and context as they relate to another story, an extrabiblical story? Carol Stockhausen has convincingly shown how, through the attention allotted to narrative details, plot-line, character, and even individual words and concepts, Paul invokes the whole Abrahamic narrative in Gal 3–4. Stockhausen argues that Paul's references to Abraham's belief (Gen 15:6), his blessing that extends to the nations (e.g., 12:3), his singular seed (12:7), the birth of his two sons (Gen 16), and the role of Isaac as his promised heir (21:10) strongly indicate that Paul has the entire story of Abraham in mind and that these individual citations function as "a connected series of statements" through which Paul sets forth the correct interpretation of the story of Abraham.[95] Without contesting Stockhausen's assessment of Paul's use of the Abrahamic narrative, I would

---

with the consciousness that one is eating idol meat at the Lord's Supper/communion will be judged and, Paul implies, end up like "some of them did," i.e., destroyed (see 11:19–22).

95. Stockhausen, "2 Corinthians," 149.

nonetheless like to suggest an alternative understanding. It might be claimed, for example, that the "biblical" details that Paul emphasizes are actually the exegetical linchpins in a new story that he is telling and that they function as narrative details in the context of this new story. In other words, the very terms and themes that are often cited as evidence that Paul is paying close attention to the biblical narrative and its context are exactly the same terms and themes that we find in the narrative and context of the extrabiblical story that Paul is telling. The emphasis that is placed on Abraham's faith, the promises, the seed, and so forth all serve as narrative details in the recontextualized story that Paul is telling, the story about Abraham's promise, the coming of Christ, and the Gentiles as Abraham's promised heirs. We might label this extrabiblical story the "Abraham-Christ narrative."

As we have already seen in Paul's renarration of the wilderness narrative, the "biblical" details that Paul puts forth are often reshaped to suit the story's new context and might not be biblical details at all. In Rom 4, for example, where Paul seemingly invokes the narrative details of Sarah's miraculous pregnancy after having been sterile for so long, while simultaneously noting that Abraham was well beyond his youthful prime, we find that the narrative details and the context within which this story is re-presented are laden with extrabiblical themes and details—themes and details that we actually find in the recontextualized story that Paul is narrating. This is especially visible in Paul's choice of vocabulary: Sarah's "dead" womb and Abraham's "dead" body (4:19); and the God who "brings to life the dead" (4:17).[96] Certainly there is an intensified interest in the narrative details here, but these narrative details do not belong to the biblical story per se nor to its context, but to the Abraham-Christ story. The Genesis narrative about Abraham is no longer *just* about Abraham; "it was also written for our sake."[97] In other words, the storyline is extended beyond the biblical narrative to incorporate elements of the "story" that is presently unfolding before Paul, the Abraham-Christ story.[98] How legitimate is it, then, to speak of Paul using biblical narrative in its context?

To a large degree, then, Paul approaches biblical narrative as if the narrative being told is the historical/eschatological narrative that is currently

---

96. See also Paul's extrabiblical detail of Sarah as the freewoman (Gal 4:22) and his reshaping of Gen 21:10 in Gal 4:30.

97. Cf. James W. Aageson, *Written Also for Our Sake: Paul and the Art of Biblical Interpretation* (Louisville: Westminster John Knox, 1993), 87.

98. See the similar conclusion drawn by Wright, *The Climax of the Covenant*, 264. However, I would be hesitant in using the term "prefigurements" to describe Paul's contemporized reading of Israel's past.

unfolding before his eyes. There is no longer an Abrahamic narrative in Genesis that can be separated from the historical narrative of Paul's own time.[99] We must now speak of an Abraham-Christ narrative. One does not exist apart from the other; it is one narrative history. It starts with Abraham and has its ending (*telos*) in Christ. In short, it is an extrabiblical narrative. Moreover, the context within which we should understand this historical narrative is expanded beyond the biblical context to include Paul's own story. Paul, his Gentile converts, his Jewish brethren, and Christ are all characters in this new drama. Therefore, Paul's use of the Genesis narrative only becomes comprehensible within the context of this larger extrabiblical story. This is especially evident if we draw a parallel between the way Paul uses Scripture and the way, according to scholarly opinion, his opponents in Galatia used Scripture. When his opponents cite the Abrahamic narrative to persuade the Galatians to circumcise, Paul counters by presenting his community not with a different interpretation of the Abrahamic narrative but with a different story, the Abraham-Christ story. So, although Paul does pay attention to the details and context of the narrative, we must recognize that, for Paul, the narrative and its (con)text have changed. In Paul's view, the proper and perhaps the only context within which to read the Abrahamic story is no longer to be found exclusively in Genesis; the proper context is the one provided by Christ. Paul might have called this "lifting the veil" of Scripture.

4. Conclusion

By way of conclusion, we can summarize the convergent ways in which Paul approaches and understands biblical narratives.

(1) Paul interprets biblical narratives from the perspective that Israel's past has pedagogical significance for the present and/or the future. This pedagogical conviction finds parallels in both Jewish and Hellenistic patterns of reading historical narratives for the purposes of edification.

(2) In Paul's case, however, this pedagogical application is usually linked with an eschatological understanding of the narrative. This can be traced to Paul's underlying Jewish hermeneutical assumption, that Israel's historical narratives convey a message for those living in the eschaton. Furthermore, Paul often read this eschatological meaning into the narratives recounted in the Torah through the aid of an a priori eschatological hermeneutic applied to prophetic texts. In this sense, Paul's approach to Torah narratives through the

---

99. Cf. Deutero-Isaiah's use of the Abrahamic narrative (51:1–3) and how Paul might have envisioned Isaiah using the Abrahamic narrative. See also above.

hermeneutical lens of prophetic passages finds affinities with *haftarah* reading practices.

(3) In renarrating Israel's past, Paul often reshapes the story to suit contemporary themes, details, and concerns. Thus, context is shifted and the appropriate context for understanding Paul's renarration of Israel's story becomes the current historical context. This contemporizing or eschatologizing element in Paul's use of biblical narrative is, furthermore, grounded in the conviction that the narrative being recounted in Scripture is now "our" narrative. Thus, for Paul, Scripture justifies and demonstrates how the events of the present, including his calling, Jesus as Christ, the Gentiles' admission into Israel, and so on, are happening just "as it is written."

(4) This approach to Scripture has the ancillary benefit of lending justification and authority to Paul's gospel, since, according to Paul's reading of Scripture, the scriptural narrative bears witness to the events that are currently unfolding in Paul's historical and eschatological present, including the preaching of his gospel.[100] Thus the story that Paul narrates is actually an extrabiblical story, one that extends beyond the boundaries and context of what we might identify as "biblical" or "canonical."

(5) In this shifting of focus from a "biblical" to a "contemporized eschatological" context, we see a Paul whose approach to biblical narrative is firmly founded in Jewish hermeneutical principles. In conclusion, Paul's scriptural hermeneutic shares more affinities with first-century Jewish hermeneutical principles than with later Christian typological exegesis.

---

100. Here I might distance myself from Wagner's conclusion that Paul reads in Isaiah's heralding of the good news "a prefiguration of his own mission" (*Heralds of the Good News*, 356); rather, Paul's eschatological reading of Isaiah dictated that he would understand Isaiah's heralding of the good news as speaking about his own mission, i.e., as speaking about those things that would happen in the final generation.

Part 3
Paul and His Audiences

PAUL AND HIS BIBLE: HIS EDUCATION AND ACCESS TO THE SCRIPTURES OF ISRAEL*

Stanley E. Porter

1. INTRODUCTION

There have been many introductions to Paul's use of Scripture over the last twenty years or so.[1] Most would agree that we have increased in our knowledge of how Paul uses scriptural texts in a variety of ways. Some of these studies have concentrated upon the various forms of the text that Paul used, such as Christopher Stanley's detailed study.[2] As a result, we have a clearer idea of the variety of textual traditions that may have been available to Paul and the ones that he may have drawn upon in his writings. Others have focused upon the various ways in which these texts have been incorporated into Paul's writings. Some of these treatments have been broad in scope, such as Richard Hays's attempt to distinguish various types of intertextuality.[3]

---

* A revised version of this paper is to appear as Stanley E. Porter and Andrew W. Pitts, "Paul's Bible, His Education and His Access to the Scriptures of Israel," *JGRChJ* 5 (2008): 9-41.

1. Some of the issues surrounding this are surveyed in Stanley E. Porter, "The Use of the Old Testament in the New Testament: A Brief Comment on Method and Terminology," in *Early Christian Interpretation of the Scriptures of Israel: Investigations and Proposals* (ed. Craig A. Evans and James A. Sanders; SSEJC 5; JSNTSup 148; Sheffield: Sheffield Academic Press, 1997), 79-96; idem, "Further Comments on the Use of the Old Testament in the New Testament," in *The Intertextuality of the Epistles: Explorations of Theory and Practice* (ed. Thomas L. Brodie, Dennis R. MacDonald, and Stanley E. Porter; NTM 16; Sheffield: Sheffield Phoenix Press, 2006), 98-110.

2. Christopher D. Stanley, *Paul and the Language of Scripture: Citation Technique in the Pauline Epistles and Contemporary Literature* (SNTSMS 74; Cambridge: Cambridge University Press, 1992).

3. Richard B. Hays, *Echoes of Scripture in the Letters of Paul* (New Haven: Yale University Press, 1989).

Others have been more specific, such as Ross Wagner's treatment of the use of Isaiah in Romans.[4] Still others have been concerned not with the way that the texts have been incorporated but with what function the texts played in Paul's writings. Again, Stanley has aided us in deciphering this, as he has analyzed the various rhetorical purposes and effects that resulted from Paul's use of Scripture.[5] Most of these treatments—with the noteworthy exception of Hays and his followers—have concentrated on explicit quotations, especially those that have been marked or indicated with a quotation formula. This has been the case to such an extent that many studies have been limited to treating those passages that are introduced by quotation formulas.

A number of other assumptions also seem to have driven and regulated the study of Paul's use of Scripture. One is that Paul had a relatively low level of education, especially in Greco-Roman circles, even if he was better educated in the rabbinic (or equivalent) traditions of Jerusalem. Another is that there was widespread illiteracy in the ancient world, including the world of Judaism, perpetuated by the fact that writing was difficult, that those competent in writing were difficult to find, that writing materials and people were costly, and that, as a result, books were in limited supply and hard to find. Following on from that is the assumption that, when texts were read in the ancient world, they were read aloud. These are just some of the fairly common assumptions that have been made by Pauline scholars.

In this paper, I intend to address some of these technical issues that accompany the study of Paul's use of Scripture. If we acknowledge that Paul used the texts of the Old Testament (not necessarily the Hebrew Bible), then he must have had access to them in some form. The questions that I wish to raise here are related to how he had access to the texts that he drew upon. Therefore, I wish to address several issues, including: (1) the structure of the educational system in the ancient world and, along with it, the educational level that Paul could reasonably have achieved; (2) the nature of the book culture in the ancient world, including the availability of books and what books were available; (3) the question of reading as a general phenomenon and, in particular, with reference to Paul; and (4) the process by which Old Testament texts became Pauline citations and what we can determine from that process. I will only be able to make suggestive remarks under each heading, but I believe that these observations will open up new insights into how we view Paul as an interpreter of Scripture.

---

4. J. Ross Wagner, *Heralds of the Good News: Isaiah and Paul "in Concert" in the Letter to the Romans* (NovTSup 101; Leiden: Brill, 2002).

5. Christopher D. Stanley, *Arguing with Scripture: The Rhetoric of Quotations in the Letters of Paul* (London: T&T Clark, 2004).

2. Paul and the Greco-Roman Educational System

Paul was born and reared, at least to a certain age, in the city of Tarsus, in Cilicia. One of the most extensive treatments of Tarsus in ancient literary sources is from Strabo (64/63 B.C.E.–21 C.E. at least, according to the *OCD*), the first-century author who would have been writing about Tarsus at the time Paul was born and lived there. Strabo makes a number of important comments about the city. Regarding their philosophical and educational aspirations, he states, "the people at Tarsus have devoted themselves so eagerly, not only to philosophy, but also to the whole round of education in general, that they have surpassed Athens, Alexandria [the two leading centers other than Tarsus], or any other place that can be named where there have been schools and lectures of philosophers" (Strabo, *Geogr.* 14.5.13 LCL). Some of the city's distinguished citizens included Stoic and other types of philosophers and rhetoricians, among them one rhetorician who had been the teacher of Julius Caesar (14.5.14). According to Strabo, there are some things that distinguished the educational system in Tarsus from others, and some of these are of special interest in our consideration of Paul and his education. Strabo says, "But [Tarsus] is so different from other cities that there the men who are fond of learning are all natives, and foreigners are not inclined to sojourn there" (14.5.13 LCL). Whereas it appears that the custom was for young men of other cities to go to another city to study and become educated, it was the custom for Tarsians to stay at home, at least for the initial stages of their education. See further Strabo's subsequent statement: "Neither do these natives [of Tarsus] stay there, but they complete their education abroad; and when they have completed it they are pleased to live abroad, and but few go back home" (14.5.13 LCL).[6] By contrast, other cities, such as Alexandria, had a mix of native students and students from other cities. This description by Strabo of Tarsus is uncannily close to the description of Paul's development that we find in the New Testament. Paul was born and reared in Tarsus (Acts 9:11, 30; 11:25; 21:39; 22:3; cf. Gal 1:21) and so had the possibility of gaining some education there as other Tarsians did, before leaving to complete his education abroad (for Paul, in Jerusalem under Gamaliel [Acts 22:3]) and never returning there to resettle.

In the light of these considerations, there are two pertinent questions to answer. The first revolves around what the educational system would have

---

6. As Daly points out, although Strabo is probably describing primarily Greek-speaking people, he also notes elsewhere (*Geogr.* 4.5.181) that the Romans frequently did likewise. See Lloyd W. Daly, "Roman Study Abroad," *AJP* 71 (1950): 40–58, esp. 40, 55–56.

been like that Paul might have participated in, and what evidence we have that he had been educated within such a system. The nature of his education has direct bearing on the access he would have had to the Bible. The number of educational centers in the ancient world was relatively small. For a Roman intending to "study abroad," the two primary choices were Athens and Rhodes. Further down the list were some of the universities in what is now France, such as Marseilles or Autun, or some of the cities in the East, such as in Asia Minor, and including Mytilene, Ephesus, and Berytus (and later Constantinople).[7] Few went to Alexandria (neither did Paul, it appears!), perhaps, as Daly suggests, because of the political tensions there.[8] Paul, however, being a Tarsian, did not have to worry about going abroad, as the custom was to stay at home, at least to the point where one left for the final educational stages.

We do not know at what age Paul left home. There is much dispute over the interpretation of Acts 22:3 and whether, when Paul refers to being raised in "this city," he is indicating Tarsus, to which he has just referred, or Jerusalem, where he says he studied with Gamaliel, whom he mentions next. Most scholars, on the basis of three factors—their understanding of the educational system, their perception of Paul's Greco-Roman knowledge and education, and his being Jewish—have concluded that Paul was not educated to a very high level in the Tarsian Greco-Roman educational system. There are a number of considerations, however, that make resolution of the specific meaning of Acts 22:3 less important than getting a grasp of the organization of ancient educational systems. The nature of the educational system points to the fact that Paul could have been educated in both Tarsus and Jerusalem.

The traditional and still standard viewpoint is that the Greco-Roman educational system had three successive tiers. This position has been argued by a number of scholars in the past, such as H. I. Marrou, Stanley Bonner, and Donald Clark,[9] and repeated more recently by such scholars as Teresa Morgan and Ronald Hock.[10] The three tiers were the primary school or *ludus litter-*

---

7. On these cities, see Clarence A. Forbes, "Ancient Universities and Student Life," *CJ* 28 (1933): 413–26, esp. 414 on Paul and Tarsus.

8. Daly, "Roman Study Abroad," 55.

9. H. I. Marrou, *A History of Education in Antiquity* (trans. George Lamb; London: Sheed & Ward, 1956), 186–205, 242–54; Stanley F. Bonner, *Education in Ancient Rome: From the Elder Cato to the Younger Pliny* (London: Methuen, 1977), 34–75, 165–276; Donald L. Clark, *Rhetoric in Greco-Roman Education* (Morningside Heights, N.Y.: Columbia University Press, 1957), 9–66.

10. Teresa Morgan, *Literate Education in the Hellenistic and Roman Worlds* (Cambridge: Cambridge University Press, 1998), 21–25; Ronald Hock, "The Educational Curriculum in Chariton's *Callirhoe*," in *Ancient Fiction: The Matrix of Early Christian and Jewish Narrative* (ed. Jo-Ann A. Brant, Charles W. Hedrick and Chris Shea; SBLSymS 32;

arius, the grammar school or *schola grammatici*, and the rhetorical school or *schola rhetoris*. These three were sequentially arranged, so that one attended the primary school first, where one learned the basics of reading and writing, and perhaps some mathematics, before proceeding to the grammar school. At the grammar school, one learned grammar and some composition, including letters, and was introduced to literature, especially the writings of Homer. At the third level, the rhetorical school, one learned rhetoric or oratory and concentrated on various prose authors. This tripartite organization, however, has been revised in the light of recent research. A. D. Booth noticed that, in the ancient evidence, there were many instances where the first teacher of a student served the functions of both the primary teacher and the grammatical teacher. As a result, he suggested that the Greco-Roman educational system, rather than being sequential, was concurrent and socially organized. In his interpretation of the evidence, there were essentially two tracks. The first track, or elementary school, was for those of the lower social orders, including slaves. The second track was for those of status, or the upper class. The latter received elementary education either at home or in the initial stages of their grammatical education. As a result, the system for them consisted of essentially two levels: grammatical and rhetorical education.[11] Even this scheme, however, as Robert Kaster has shown, is overly rigid, as there is abundant evidence that the educational system of the time was much more flexible and less rigid, as well as more subject to regional variation, than previous scholarship has realized. Nevertheless, the evidence that Kaster marshals does seem to support the notion that the distinction between the primary and grammatical teachers was blurred and that their functions overlapped (e.g., there is little evidence that a student going through the grammatical system normally attended primary school), both in Rome and in other places throughout the Greco-Roman world.[12]

Atlanta: Society of Biblical Literature, 2005), 15–36, esp. 17–25, even though he recognizes the evidence against such a scenario.

11. A. D. Booth, "The Schooling of Slaves in First-Century Rome," *TAPA* 109 (1979): 11–19; so also Robert A. Kaster, "Notes on 'Primary' and 'Secondary' Schools in Late Antiquity," *TAPA* 113 (1983): 323–46, here 324, who notes that in the sequential account there was a recognition that many in the elementary school did not go on to the grammar school, and many grammar school students received their elementary tuition privately (although Kaster does not mention any of those who held to this modified view). See also Raffaella Cribiore, *Gymnastics of the Mind: Greek Education in Hellenistic and Roman Egypt* (Princeton: Princeton University Press, 2001), 37, 45.

12. Kaster, "Notes," 328–29, 336–38, 346.

If this is the case—and it seems that the evidence points in this direction—there are important implications for Paul's education. In this revised organization, students began their schooling somewhere around six to eight years old,[13] and they would have finished the grammar school at around twelve or thirteen years. As a Roman citizen and the son of a person with a productive trade (which probably resulted in the citizenship of his father or an earlier relative), Paul would apparently have had sufficient status and economic support to finance and facilitate his attending the grammar school. This chronology is consistent with the ages of man as discussed by the rabbis, according to W. D. Davies. In what is probably a later addition to m. Pirqe 'Abot 5:24 (ca. 150 C.E.), we read, "At five years the Scriptures; at ten years the Mishnah; at thirteen the commandments; at fifteen the Talmud." It was thought that generally at the age of thirteen a boy was made a "son of commandment" and welcomed into the Jewish community.[14] Even though the tradition may be later, this pattern of development is consistent with Paul being reared in a Jewish home in Tarsus and learning the Scriptures while being educated in a Greek grammar school, then, after his Bar Mitzvah (or the equivalent at the time), going to Jerusalem to complete his education in Jewish law and related matters. The word that is translated "reared" in Acts 22:3 does not necessarily mean being reared from birth but may indicate being educated, without reference to when the process began. This means that the verse could be compatible with either Tarsus or Jerusalem, without necessarily restricting his education to one city or the other.[15]

This educational structure is also consistent with the educational framework that Birger Gerhardsson outlines. He notes a number of similarities between the Torah schools and the Greco-Roman schools, parallels that are complementary to the portrait of Paul that I am creating here. Rather than the poets, students in the Torah school would study the Old Testament, and rather than advancing from poets to rhetoric, they proceeded from the written Torah to the oral Torah, or, as they were later codified, from Mishnah to Talmud.[16] Although the evidence for advanced Jewish education is later, from

---

13. Ibid., 336.

14. W. D. Davies, *Paul and Rabbinic Judaism: Some Rabbinic Elements in Pauline Theology* (4th ed.; Philadelphia: Fortress, 1980), 24–25.

15. This has direct implications for interpreting Luke 4:16, which may refer to Nazareth as the place where Jesus was "educated" rather than simply "reared."

16. Birger Gerhardsson, *Memory and Manuscript: Oral Tradition and Written Transmission in Rabbinic Judaism and Early Christianity, with Tradition and Transmission in Early Christianity* (Grand Rapids: Eerdmans, 1998 [1961, 1964]), 56–66, 89–92; cf. Catherine Hezser, *Jewish Literacy in Roman Palestine* (TSAJ 81; Tübingen: Mohr Siebeck, 2001),

the Tannaitic but especially the Amoraic periods, the general pattern was that the few fortunate students who could do so would study with a rabbi and attend a "study house," where they would engage not so much in reading the Torah (basic Torah knowledge would have been assumed) but in disputing over interpretation of the Torah, that is, talmudic discussion.[17] According to this model, then, Paul would have had plenty of time to have been instructed in the written Torah in Tarsus, even as a student of the grammar school and possibly beyond, before leaving for Jerusalem to continue his education with Gamaliel the rabbi on the oral Torah.

As important as the organization of the educational system—and perhaps the most important element for this paper—is the content of the educational system. What exactly would Paul have learned as a student in a grammar school? As noted above, if he did not learn the basics of writing, reading, and arithmetic from a private tutor or at home before entering the school, he must have acquired these skills at the outset. However, there was much more to the grammar-school education than this. Students started with simple exercises in which they learned syllable or word separation and gained increased facility in reading. Students increasingly learned about words and sentences, then about the basic literary features of a text, including punctuation and how to recognize a change of speakers. At this stage the major authors being read were poets, with an eye toward identifying the features of poetic texts and how to evaluate them. The major poet whom students read was "The Poet" Homer (especially his *Iliad*), along with Hesiod, Pindar, and other lyric poets, including contemporary ones such as Callimachus, Euripides the tragedian, Menander, and the like. It appears that there were certain authors who were at the core of the curriculum, while others were more at the periphery.

The students learned to read, recite, and explain these authors; in other words, there was a huge emphasis on the oral and mnemonic character of education. However, there was also a written component. It was during the first century that grammatical study became a more or less fixed part of the grammar-school curriculum. Included here was practice in composition, which centered on the so-called preparatory exercises, or *progymnasmata*.[18] Students learned to compose such forms as fable, narrative, chreia,[19] and

---

39–109; A. R. Millard, *Reading and Writing in the Time of Jesus* (Biblical Seminar 69; Sheffield: Sheffield Academic Press, 2000), 188–92.

17. Hezser, *Jewish Literacy in Roman Palestine*, 94–109, esp. 94–96.

18. See George A. Kennedy, *Progymnasmata: Greek Textbooks of Prose Composition and Rhetoric* (SBLWGRW 10; Atlanta: Society of Biblical Literature, 2003).

19. Ronald F. Hock and Edward N. O'Neil, *The Chreia in Ancient Rhetoric: The Progymnasmata* (SBLTT 27; Atlanta: Scholars Press, 1986); idem, *The Chreia and Ancient*

aphorism and became familiar with such basic rhetorical concepts as confirmation, refutation, commonplaces, eulogy, censure, comparison, ethopeia, prosopopoiia, the thesis, and discussions of law. All were considered necessary preparation for moving to the next stage in education, rhetoric proper. Although not so central to the curriculum as the *progymnasmata*, students at the grammar school also learned how to write letters. Learning to write letters has long been recognized as one of the skills required by those who were training to become professional scribes, but it is increasingly recognized that learning to write letters was a part of grammar-school education as well. Students probably did not learn by copying letters out of books but by constructing them themselves, perhaps under the direct guidance of the teacher.[20]

In regard to the curriculum, there are at least three observations to be made in the light of recent Pauline scholarship. The first concerns the *progymnasmata*. Recent rhetorical studies of Paul's letters attribute to him the ability to use a number of the stylistic characteristics that were commonly taught in the grammar school curriculum.[21] The natural place for Paul to have learned these techniques was in the local grammar school. The second observation concerns the literature read at this stage. It is worth noting the secular authors whom Paul cites or alludes to in his letters[22] or is depicted as citing

---

Rhetoric: Classroom Exercises (SBLWGRW 2; Atlanta: Society of Biblical Literature, 2002). Both of these books, despite recognizing the recent shift regarding education (*Classroom Exercises*, 1–4), still use the three sequential stages in their analysis.

20. See Marrou, *History of Education*, 169–75; Cribiore, *Gymnastics of the Mind*, 185–218 (see also Raffaella Cribiore, *Writing, Teachers, and Students in Graeco-Roman Egypt* [ASP 36; Atlanta: Scholars Press, 1996], esp. the appendixes); Morgan, *Literate Education*, 24; Hock, "Educational Curriculum," 21–23. The epistolary theorists may have relevance here, as they present types or models of letters. However, the only one early enough to be relevant does not present samples of whole letters but characteristic excerpts (see Pseudo-Demetrius). We do not know whether these letter types were copied directly. See Abraham J. Malherbe, *Ancient Epistolary Theorists* (SBLSBS 19; Atlanta: Scholars Press, 1988).

21. See, e.g., Stanley E. Porter, "Paul of Tarsus and His Letters," in *Handbook of Classical Rhetoric in the Hellenistic Period 330 B.C.–A.D. 400* (ed. Stanley E. Porter; Leiden: Brill, 1997), 532–85, esp. 578–83.

22. I take all of the thirteen letters of Paul as authentic and so include them in the discussion below. For issues related to Pauline authorship of the letters, see Lee M. McDonald and Stanley E. Porter, *Early Christianity and Its Sacred Literature* (Peabody, Mass.: Hendrickson, 2000), 388–93, 410–98. Paul no doubt used scribes, but evaluating the influence of the scribes on his writing is difficult, as the evidence can cut both ways. The consistency of the Pauline voice argues for a strong Pauline authorial presence.

or alluding to in Acts.[23] Most of them come from the list of canonical authors mentioned above, including a variety of poets (Menander, *Thais* frag. 218 in 1 Cor 15:33; Aristotle, *Pol.* 3.8.2 in Gal 5:22; Aeschylus, *Eum.* 1014–1015 in Phil 4:4; Pindar frag. from Strabo, *Geogr.* 6.2.8 in 2 Tim 2:7; Epimenides in Titus 1:12; Aratus, *Phaen.* 5 or Epimenides in Acts 17:28; Euripides, *Ion* 8 in Acts 21:39; Euripides, *Bacch.* 794–795 in Acts 26:14).[24] Some speculate that Paul did not know these authors' works but simply cited quotations from major writers that were commonly found in testimonia. If this is so, he was probably exposed to these materials during his grammar-school training (see discussion below). The third observation pertains to Paul as a letter writer. Despite the debate over whether his compositions should be considered letters or epistles, scholarship has continued to recognize that Paul was one of the major letter writers of the ancient world, as the size and character of his letter collection attests.[25] Paul's use of the letter form seems to indicate an author who knew the conventions of letter writing but who also innovated in his use of this form by the development of various subsections of the letter (e.g., expansion of the sender or receiver in the salutation) or of the major sections of the letter (e.g., the thanksgiving or paraenesis).

The chronology of Paul's life and the evidence from his letters and Acts make it plausible that Paul was a product of the Greco-Roman educational system in Tarsus. The structure of the system, including the ages of study and the curriculum, point to Paul having completed grammar school before leaving Tarsus to continue his education in Jerusalem in the rabbinic school. During his grammar-school studies, besides basic literacy and numeracy, Paul would have been exposed to the major poets and authors and learned composition through the *progymnasmata* and letter writing. Whereas he would already have studied the written Torah during his studies in Tarsus, he would have learned the oral Torah in Jerusalem. The evidence indicates that there is nothing in the educational system in Greco-Roman times that prevents Paul from having finished the grammar-school level, and with it gaining the various skills that this system taught.

---

23. On the relationship of the Paul of Acts to the Paul of the letters, see Stanley E. Porter, *The Paul of Acts: Essays in Literary Criticism, Rhetoric, and Theology* (WUNT 115; Tübingen: Mohr Siebeck, 1999).

24. Other references in Paul have an aphoristic quality and may have been learned in a school setting, such as 1 Cor 9:10; 2 Cor 4:6; and Eph 5:14. For other possible knowledge of ancient sources, see Evelyn B. Howell, "St Paul and the Greek World," *Greece & Rome* 2/11 (1964): 7–29, esp. 22–23, cited above.

25. See Ulrich von Wilamowitz-Moellendorff, *Die griechische Literatur des Altertums* (Stuttgart: Teubner, 1912), 232–33.

3. Oral and Book Culture

Paul's ability to read and write is also important for understanding how he utilized Scripture. However, it is not enough to explain how it was that he gained access to and then utilized the texts that he did. In order to understand that, we must understand the interplay of oral and book cultures. There is a tendency in the current climate of biblical interpretation to emphasize the elements of oral culture at the expense of the book culture of the time. I wish to say something about each of them here. The first statement to make, however, is that the situation is much more complex than simply differentiating between oral and written sources and cultures. As Robbins has stated, the situation of terminology needs to be clarified. He differentiates between the following when talking about culture: oral culture, scribal culture, rhetorical culture, reading culture, literary culture, print culture and hypertext culture.[26] I am not sure that we need all of these categories, but the situation is admittedly more complex than simply oral versus written.

I probably do not need to say as much about orality, as this is a subject that has been widely studied lately. The emphasis in recent studies has been upon the oral nature of Judaism and early Christianity, reflecting the fact that they were positioned within the predominantly oral cultures of the ancient Mediterranean Greco-Roman world. Building on the work of scholars such as Walter Ong, Werner Kelber emphasizes the oral dimension of the ancient world and especially of Paul's work. Kelber draws a contrast in Paul's thought between the stultifying effect of the written word, which is equated with the law, and the liberating and spirit-filled oral word. According to Kelber, Paul emphasizes the oral word, which is related to the gospel and its strength and power.[27] Kelber's ideas have been picked up and developed further by a number of scholars,[28] to the point that the oral is sometimes emphasized to the point of dismissing the written.

There is no doubt that oral culture played a significant role in the ancient world. However, there is other evidence from Greco-Roman culture as a whole, and Judaism in particular, that puts this fact into perspective. To

---

26. Vernon K. Robbins, "Oral, Rhetorical and Literary Cultures: A Response," *Semeia* 65 (1994): 75–90, esp. 77. See also Hezser, *Jewish Literacy in Roman Palestine*, 16.

27. Werner Kelber, *The Oral and the Written Gospel: The Hermeneutics of Speaking and Writing in the Synoptic Tradition, Mark, Paul and Q* (Philadelphia: Fortress, 1983), 140–83.

28. Joanna Dewey, "Textuality in an Oral Culture: A Survey of the Pauline Traditions," *Semeia* 65 (1994): 37–64; see also Arthur J. Dewey, "A Re-hearing of Romans 10:1–15," *Semeia* 65 (1994): 109–27.

adapt the terminology of Robbins, there is no need to create a false disjunction between oral and written culture, but there is a need to recognize that there are various levels of written culture within a society, including a less-visible scribal culture that operates alongside the more obvious literary culture. In fact, this is what we find. In the ancient Greek and then Roman worlds, even though there was an emphasis upon orality, such that the major poets wrote for oral performance, the growth of empire brought a need for record-keeping that led to a scribal culture that developed over time into a literary culture. Thus Rosalind Thomas distinguishes between documents and records. There are potentially all sorts of documents written for different purposes. However, a transition takes place when one recognizes that written documents may become records of persons, possessions, or other things. With this recognition comes a certain power in literacy, to the point of developing systematized record-keeping and the like. This is one of the hallmarks of the Roman Empire, especially as evidenced in the papyri remains from Egypt (see section 5, below). The confluence of record-keeping and power can clearly be seen in the tax records that were kept every seven and then every fourteen years.[29] The power to record became the power to tax and the power to maintain control over the people.[30]

In the Jewish culture of the time, there was a somewhat similar developmental phenomenon, as Gerhardsson has pointed out. Gerhardsson offers a more sophisticated (and, as the history of research tells us, more prescient) view of the interplay of orality and literacy than many others. He notes the creative and dynamic role that oral tradition played in the rise of Judaism. He also points out that, a number of centuries before the Christian era, written tradition began to play an important part in Judaism. Gerhardsson's analysis ends up claiming that the written Torah, which Christians would equate with the Old Testament, was complemented by the oral Torah, which constitutes the oral tradition that goes hand in hand with it.

Another factor that is not as fully recognized as it might be is the type of book culture that was present in the first century C.E. The standard position is to dismiss such a notion on the basis of a purported widespread

---

29. See Stanley E. Porter, "The Reasons for the Lukan Census," in *Paul, Luke, and the Graeco-Roman World: Essays in Honour of Alexander J. M. Wedderburn* (ed. Alf Christophersen, Carsten Claussen, Jörg Frey, and Bruce W. Longenecker; JSNTSup 217; Sheffield: Sheffield Academic Press, 2002), 165–88.

30. Rosalind Thomas, *Literacy and Orality in Ancient Greece* (Cambridge: Cambridge University Press, 1992), 132–44; see idem, *Oral Tradition and Written Record in Classical Athens* (Cambridge: Cambridge University Press, 1989); Dewey, "Textuality in an Oral Culture."

illiteracy, the supposed high cost of materials, and the lack of printing technology. Nevertheless, there is ample evidence for a widespread book culture at that time. In some ways, the disparagement of writing and the book culture is an unfounded consequence of a paradigm that draws a sharp disjunction between orality and literacy and then, because the culture is regarded as oral, posits that there must not have been significant written sources. But how under this paradigm do we account for such factors as Galen wandering through a market and seeing books for sale, including some that were attributed to him when he knew that he had not written them?[31] In other words, there was enough of a market for books to make forgery a desirable option for some (although clearly not for Galen, who was incensed). Similarly, the literary tradition associated with Lysias indicates that a significant number of the works attributed to him were known even in ancient times to be forgeries, a problem that has kept scholars busy for years.[32] Likewise, the Qumran community, although a relatively small community living in isolation, was responsible for creating a significantly large number of books.[33] There were also a number of well-known large libraries, such as the ones at Alexandria and Ephesus,[34] together with a number of small private libraries that may have been more important to the book culture than the larger libraries.[35] In fact, books were so plentiful by the first century C.E. that Seneca can denounce what he sees as the ostentatious accumulation of books.[36]

There are two major features of the book culture to note. Without minimizing the importance of orality—or the fact that the major means of "publication" was in terms of oral performance, such as orations, the reading of poetry, lectures delivered in public, and the theater—we must recognize that there was a parallel book culture that was large and significant. There was no publishing industry as we would know it today, but there were never-

---

31. Bruce M. Metzger, "Literary Forgeries and Canonical Pseudepigrapha," *JBL* 91 (1972): 3–24, esp. 4.

32. Kenneth J. Dover, *Lysias and the Corpus Lysiacum* (Berkeley and Los Angeles: University of California Press, 1968), 23–27.

33. Loveday Alexander, "Ancient Book Production and the Circulation of the Gospels," in *The Gospel for All Christians: Rethinking the Gospel Audiences* (ed. Richard Bauckham; Grand Rapids: Eerdmans, 1998), 71–111, esp. 78. See also Hezser, *Jewish Literacy in Roman Palestine*, 498, who thinks that Qumran was "exceptional" but who also notes several other archives, such as that of Babatha and Salome Komaise.

34. See Lionel Casson, *Libraries in the Ancient World* (New Haven: Yale University Press, 2001).

35. Frederic G. Kenyon, *Books and Readers in Ancient Greece and Rome* (Oxford: Clarendon, 1932), 65.

36. Ibid., 80.

theless means of getting books produced.[37] Papyrus, the paper of the ancient world, was widely available and was not expensive. As Thomas Skeat has argued, both on the basis of statements by the ancients and the bountiful evidence of discarded papyri discovered throughout Egypt, the cost of papyrus was reasonable in the ancient world—and very few papyri were ever reused, even if they were blank on one side.[38] The cost of getting a book copied was not exorbitant, ranging from two to four drachmas, which is the equivalent of one to six days' pay.[39]

The second notable feature of the book culture is the nature of that culture itself. Kenyon notes that as early as the fourth century B.C.E. there was a "considerable quantity" of "cheap and easily accessible" books to be found in Athens, which shows that a reading culture was growing even during that time.[40] In Hellenistic Egypt, as indicated by the documentary and especially the literary finds, there were numerous books available, to the point that "Greek literature was widely current among the ordinary Graeco-Roman population," and this was a likely pattern throughout the Hellenistic world.[41] That these books were accessible to a wide range of people is indicated by the fact that the most common literary author found in the papyri is Homer, the major author read in the grammar school.[42]

Access to these books was gained through a variety of means. There was what Loveday Alexander has called a commercial book trade. Alexander notes that the main motivation of authors to publish in ancient times—perhaps not too unlike modern times—was fame, not money. Hence there were not the same kinds of restrictions on access as we have today.[43] Authors themselves would probably have been involved in the "publication" of their books. Raymond Starr notes that the author would have written a rough draft and then had it reviewed by others, such as slaves or friends. Once a final version of the text was formulated, it was circulated to a wider group of friends before being

---

37. Pat E. Easterling and Bernard M. W. Knox, "Books and Readers in the Greek World," in *Greek Literature* (vol. 1 of *The Cambridge History of Classical Literature*; ed. Pat E. Easterling and Bernard M. W. Knox; Cambridge: Cambridge University Press, 1989), 1–41, here 19.

38. T. C. Skeat, "Was Papyrus Regarded as 'Cheap' or 'Expensive' in the Ancient World?" *Aeg* 75 (1995): 75–93.

39. Easterling and Knox, "Books and Readers," 22. See also Kenyon, *Books and Readers*, 24; Millard, *Reading and Writing*, 164–66.

40. Kenyon, *Books and Readers*, 24.

41. Ibid., 34, 36.

42. Cribiore, *Gymnastics of the Mind*, 140.

43. Alexander, "Ancient Book Production," 87–89.

more widely disseminated.⁴⁴ As a result, perhaps the easiest way to secure a book was to borrow a copy from a friend and either have a slave or scribe copy it or make one's own copy. As Alexander notes, Aristotle, Cicero, Galen, and Marcus Cicero the Younger all seem to have employed this process.

There were other means by which books were circulated as well. Alexander notes four. The first is the copying and exchanging of books by professional scribes. Another is the transcribing of orations into written speeches. A third was to copy down oral lectures given by teachers and to circulate them among students. A fourth and final method was to dedicate a book to a patron who may have been involved in the publishing process.⁴⁵ Harry Gamble has noted that there were associations of people connected with book production, so that those who were interested in a particular type of literature would produce and share these books. This could include those who were interested in the Greek text of the Bible (i.e., the Old Greek or Septuagint).⁴⁶ Josephus records that a rebel in Galilee confronted him with "a copy of the law of Moses in his hands" as he tried to work the crowd (Josephus, *Life* 134).⁴⁷

As a result of the book culture, there were a number of types of collections of books that we know about from the ancient world. When, at the end of the fourth century B.C.E., Ptolemy I Soter founded the Museum in Alexandria, he initiated a movement toward standardizing the most substantial Greek texts of antiquity. The mass scale of book production at the Alexandrian library played a crucial role in standardizing both the selection of literary works and the form that they took (book size, material, etc.).⁴⁸ As Pat Easterling and Bernard Knox note, "the corpus of 'best authors' was given official recognition in the classifications made by the scholars of Alexandria and perhaps of Pergamum, and came to exercise a very powerful effect on Greek culture."⁴⁹ Specifying the "canons" of Greek literature (the ten orators, the nine lyric poets, the three tragedians, etc.) is usually accredited to Aristophanes of Byz-

---

44. Raymond J. Starr, "The Circulation of Literary Texts in the Roman World," *CQ* 37 (1989): 313–23, here 313–16.

45. Alexander, "Ancient Book Production," 88–99. See also Loveday Alexander, "The Living Voice: Scepticism towards the Written Word in Early Christian and Graeco-Roman Texts," in *The Bible in Three Dimensions* (ed. David J. A. Clines, Stephen E. Fowl and Stanley E. Porter; JSOTSup 87; Sheffield: JSOT Press, 1990), 221–47.

46. Harry Y. Gamble, *Books and Readers in the Early Church: A History of Early Christian Texts* (New Haven: Yale University Press, 1995), 85.

47. Millard, *Reading and Writing*, 161. Millard notes that Herod had a library of at least forty-four Greek authors and that Philo must have had his own collection of Scriptures, which he used (in Greek!).

48. Easterling and Knox, "Books and Readers," 34.

49. Ibid., 35.

antium. The first formal standardization of a collection of authors seems to have been the formation of the canon of the Attic orators around the time of the Roman Empire. Several writers of antiquity mention this canon, including Caecilius, who wrote the now lost *On the Character of the Ten Orators*, Quintilian (*Inst.* 10.1.76), Lucian (*Scyth.* 10), and Pseudo-Plutarch's *Lives of the Ten Orators*.[50]

Canonization was a common Greek educational practice that allowed the selection of a list of authors from a particular genre to be standardized as the objects of instruction in the schools. Literary collections of poets and canons of various philosophers followed soon after.[51] These collections of authors provided the basis for the educational curriculum, although which authors were emphasized or selected remained much more fluid. In this way, the writings of various canonized authors became the basis for instruction, imitation, and criticism in the Hellenistic schools. The works of Homer were perhaps most affected by this process under the influence of Aristarchus, who successfully standardized Homeric compositions to conform to a common "vulgate" text that is reflected in nearly all Homeric papyri found after the middle of the second century B.C.E.[52] The works of Homer, in particular, were imputed a normative status in Greco-Roman culture that was comparable to, if not on par with, that of the Jewish Scriptures in early Christianity.[53]

Hellenistic authors or speakers who desired to quote from any or all of these canons of literature would have faced some of the same material difficulties that early Christians and Jews would have dealt with in their attempts to cite authoritative texts. The cumbersome nature of scrolls, the lack of ease in navigation, the cost of ownership, and the sheer size of many ancient books all made employing citations from written material impractical. This explains the emphasis upon imitation and memorization in Hellenistic education.[54]

---

50. See Stephen Usher, *Greek Oratory: Tradition and Originality* (Oxford: Oxford University Press, 1999).

51. Hermogenes (*On Ideas*) provides the most extensive survey of classical canons and genres from an ancient source. For analysis of *On Ideas* 2.10–12 as well as the contribution of the Hermogenean analysis of literature more broadly, see Ian Rutherford, "Inverting the Canon: Hermogenes on Literature," *HSCP* 94 (1992): 355–78.

52. See Stephanie West, *Ptolemaic Papyri of Homer* (Papyrologica Coloniensia 3; Cologne: Westdeutscher Verlag, 1967).

53. See Christopher D. Stanley, "Paul and Homer: Greco-Roman Citation Practice in the First Century CE," *NovT* 32 (1990): 48–78, here 51–52; Morgan, *Literate Education*, 144–51.

54. According to Quintilian (*Inst.* 1.1.5; 1.3.1), memorization is the most important element of education. See also Morgan, *Literate Education*, 352; on the function of imitation in advanced levels of education, see Cribiore, *Gymnastics of the Mind*, 220–44.

As Stanley notes with regard to the citation of Homeric literature, "When one takes into account the difficulties associated with unrolling a large scroll to check and find references (hence the frequent reliance on memory in the ancient world), it is ... the faithfulness of the authors of this period to their sources that appears remarkable."[55] However, Stanley may give the Greek memory more credit than it is due. While the majority of Homeric papyri consist of the two major epic poems—the *Odyssey* and the *Iliad*[56]—there is nevertheless an ample papyrological supply of Homerica, various lexica, scholia, anthologies, glossaries, summaries, and paraphrases of Homer's work. P.Mich. inv. 4832 (late second century to first century B.C.E.) provides an example of a Ptolemaic papyrus of an anthology from *Iliad* Σ–T.[57] Other significant Homeric anthologies on papyri include P.Hamb. II 136 (early third century B.C.E.), P.Stras. inv. 2374 (third century B.C.E.), and P.Vindob. G 26740 (second century C.E.). As Renner observes, together "these fragmentary anthologies bear abundant witness to continued popularity through five centuries in Greco-Roman Egypt to a type of study which had probably been in use in the schoolroom since at least Plato."[58] They would have also provided authors with a more manageable form of material than a book-length scroll for citing Homer and other classical authors without having to rely solely on the facility of memory.

Perhaps the most common collection of quoted material that circulated in the Hellenistic world was the Greco-Roman anthology. Greco-Roman anthologies were diverse and abundant, taking a variety of forms (e.g., gnomologia, chreiae, poetry, biography, history, rhetoric, philosophy) and being employed regularly as schooltexts within the educational system.[59] Gnomologies were especially significant in Greco-Roman education. As Morgan insists, "Gnomic schooltexts form part of a long and complex tradition in Greek literature, and one in which Greek literature was part of an even older and more extensive tradition in the literatures of the Near East."[60] These

---

55. Stanley, "Paul and Homer," 54.
56. For a listing of Homeric papyri, see F. Uebel, *APF* 24/25 (1976): 191.
57. For analysis of the form and content of the papyri, see Timothy Renner, "Three New Homerica on Papyrus," *HSCP* 83 (1979): 311–37, here 331–37.
58. Ibid., 333.
59. See Morgan, *Literate Education*, 120–51: non-schooltext anthologies include Pseudo-Phocylides, *Menandri Sententiae*, *Sentences of Sextus*, *Distichs of Cato*, and Stobaeus. The Pythagorean *Golden Verses* is one of the few anthologies that was focused around a single doctrinal system (Morgan, *Literate Education*, 121).
60. Ibid., 120.

anthologies emerged in the Hellenistic period[61] and typically consisted of a collection of sayings on divergent subjects by the same or various authors relevant to individuals at all layers of social strata. Manuscripts of collections of gnomic sayings and various anthologies are in greater number than any other form of schooltexts and were apparently used at every level of education. Quotations from Menander or in Menandrean style were most popular, but sayings from other prose poets are represented as well.[62] While not all of the topical categories for gnomic sayings mentioned in literary sources are found among the schooltext papyri, several emerge with a great deal of consistency, evidencing their important role in early education. Some of these reflect themes[63] that Paul takes up in his letters, such as wealth, "word" and speech, family, women, friends and associates, and old age. The authority of these texts undoubtedly derives "from their being part of classical Greek culture, as well as from the authority which is awarded conventionally to poets of all sorts."[64] Thus it seems clear that literary and papyrological sources confirm the use of literary compilations as a significant aid to authors wishing to cite earlier writings in the production of original compositions. This explains the accuracy and consistency with which Greek authors quoted Homer and other ancient literature.

Philosophers, rhetoricians, and historians were anthologized as well.[65] These collections served as essential compositional tools used by ancient authors for accessing classical literature. As Jonathon Barns has convincingly shown, the famous bee simile was likely employed as a suggestion for students to create compilations of significant poets as a tool for later composition.[66] The simile seems to have been used first by Isocrates (*Demon.* 51) to encourage students to compile collections of poetic writings for study. It takes on a similar connotation in Plutarch (*Rect. rat. aud.* 8.41E), where it refers to philosophers instead of poets. In Lucian (*Pisc.* 6) we find evidence that rhetoricians used philosophical anthologies as a tool to aid in their compositions.

---

61. Plato, *Leg.* 810e–812a contains a reference to an ethical anthology within the classical period that would indicate the selection of ethical texts for educational purposes (Morgan, *Literate Education*, 121).

62. See Morgan, *Literate Education*, 123.

63. Ibid., 125.

64. Ibid., 144.

65. For surveys and lists of Greek anthologies, see Jonathon Barns, "A New Gnomologium: With Some Remarks on Gnomic Anthologies," *CQ* 44 (1950): 126–37, esp. 133–37; idem, "A New Gnomologium: With Some Remarks on Gnomic Anthologies, II," *CQ* NS 1 (1951): 1–19.

66. Barns, "New Gnomologium," 132–34.

Similarly, Seneca (*Ep.* 83) suggests employing a written compilation when composing a literary work. The simile is even employed in early Christianity to refer to the selection of the best pagan authors (Clement, *Strom.* 1.11; 33.6; 6.89.2; PG 31:564). Barns concludes that the form of literary compilation in these examples has relevance to four areas: the selection of literary excerpts; their compilation in writing; their application to education; and their use as an aid to original composition.[67] These selections were made both for pleasure and for intellectual and educational purposes.[68]

Collections of authoritative material took a variety of forms in Hellenistic Jewish sources as well. As far as collections of literature go, there was in New Testament times the notion of the Old Testament as a body of Jewish literature, but, as the discoveries at Qumran indicate, the understanding of the canonical status of many books was still rather fluid. Canons of rabbinical material, whose boundaries became fixed much more quickly, also emerged, including the Mishnah and various compilations of tannaitic tradition such as the Tosefta and the halakic midrashim.[69] As with other writings of the first century, we have testimony to compilations within the Mishnah itself in such texts as Pirqe 'Abot and 'Eduyyot. Similar anthologies are represented in Hellenistic Jewish authors such as Pseudo-Phocylides. Perhaps the most significant Jewish parallels to the Greco-Roman anthologies of classical authors are the collections of excerpts from the Hebrew Bible found in Qumran Cave 4: 4QPatriarchal Blessings, 4QTanhumim (4Q176), 4QOrdinances (4Q159), and especially 4QTestimonia and 4QFlorilegium.[70] The two most significant compilations, 4QTestimonia and 4QFlorilegium, are collections of excerpts revolving around the eschatological hopes of the community. They seem (at least in the case of 4QFlorilegium) to have served liturgical purposes as well.[71] 4QTestimonia contains five passages: Deut 5:28–29; 18:18–19; Num 24:15–17; Deut 33:8–11; and a selection from a book accredited to Joshua. Unlike 4QTestimonia, 4QFlorilegium includes midrashic commentary upon

---

67. Ibid., 134.

68. Compilations for pleasurable reading include P.Petr. II 49; P.Tebt. 3; P.Freib. I 4; P.Oxy. III 622; P.Oxy. IV 671. Barns, "New Gnomologium," 134–35. See the above discussion on gnomologies for various compilations and schooltexts used in education. The literary sources quoted above also evidence the use of anthologies in composition.

69. On the formation of the rabbinic canon, see David Kraemer, "The Formation of Rabbinic Canon: Authority and Boundaries," *JBL* 110 (1991): 613–30.

70. See Robert Hodgson Jr., "The Testimony Hypothesis," *JBL* 98 (1979): 361–78, here 362–65.

71. See George J. Brooke, *Exegesis at Qumran: 4QFlorilegium in Its Jewish Context* (JSOTSup 29; Sheffield: JSOT Press, 1985; repr., Atlanta: Society of Biblical Literature, 2006), 169–78.

its three central selections: 2 Sam 7:10–12; Pss 1:1; 2:1–2 (cf. also 4QTanhumim [4Q176]). What is worth noting is that this evidence seems to support collections of specific excerpted texts that were gathered together in a single document.[72]

In summary, the evidence suggests that there was a book culture that cut across all of the various cultural and ethnic groups of the first century. The result was that there was an abundance of written material available to be read. Some of this was in the form of whole works, while other documents attest to a process of selection and anthologizing. The anthologized texts made access to extended works more manageable as well as providing ease of transportation.

4. Literacy and Reading

The last topic that I wish to address—literacy and reading—does not need to be treated as extensively as the others. Although important, these subjects are not as germane to the topic of how Paul handled Scripture, as it is clear from what has been said that Paul was literate. Nevertheless, I wish to make some statements about literacy in general and then about reading, as a way of rounding out the picture I am creating.

The issue of literacy in the ancient world, and especially among Jews, has become a subject of renewed interest and debate. William Harris's well-known monograph was the first to undertake a historical rather than a social-anthropological study of literacy in the Greco-Roman world.[73] He was not the first to address the issue, but he was the first to study systematically the historical, documentary, and literary evidence and then attempt to quantify the literacy of the ancient world. His work distanced him from those who had emphasized the oral culture of the ancient Greeks[74] and established a target for others to shoot at. Some rejected his findings by claiming that he

---

72. This is in conformity with what has been found in the Gospels as well. For a recent treatment of the issue of collections of biblical texts (testimonia), especially evaluating hypotheses concerning collections of blocks or extended portions of material versus collections of specific texts, see Mark J. Boda and Stanley E. Porter, "Literature to the Third Degree: Prophecy in Zechariah 9–14 and the Passion of Christ," in *Traduire la Bible Hébraïque/Translating the Hebrew Bible: De la Septante à la Nouvelle Bible Segond/From the Septuagint to the Nouvelle Bible Segond* (ed. Robert David and Manuel Jinbachian; Montreal: Médiaspaul, 2005), 215–54, esp. 239–45 on the Gospels.

73. So Hezser, *Jewish Literacy in Roman Palestine*, 21.

74. Such as Eric Havelock, *The Literate Revolution in Greece and Its Cultural Consequences* (Princeton: Princeton University Press, 1982); idem, *The Muse Learns to Write: Reflection on Orality and Literacy* (New Haven: Yale University Press, 1986).

had overestimated the influence and capability of writing, but the majority of critics argued that he had underestimated the impact of literary culture, at least in terms of the Greco-Roman context.[75] Even if his statistics are accurate and not underestimated—that 20–30 percent of men and 10–15 percent of women in the Roman Empire were literate, yielding an overall ratio of no more than 15 percent[76]—he seems to have neglected the fact that even those who were illiterate came into contact with literate culture. For example, a person illiterate in Greek might need to have a contract written out and so would be a part of literate culture by virtue of needing to have this document prepared. This person might also have to deal with the consequences of this act, such as having a document sent in return. Bowman goes so far as to state that a "large proportion" of the 80 percent who may have been formally illiterate were to some degree participants in literate culture. Further, there are many more documents that remain to be deciphered, as well as a number that were destroyed. All of this evidence of literacy needs to be taken into account.[77] Hopkins notes that by Harris's figures there were over two million adult men in the Roman Empire who could read and that this large number would have exerted a significant influence upon the society as a whole.[78] Paul, as a Tarsian of some means and status and the composer of many letters (of which he wrote a part, if not all), would have been one of these two million literate men who exerted cultural (and, in this case, religious) influence on his surroundings.[79]

---

75. See, e.g., Mary Beard, ed., *Literacy in the Roman World* (Journal of Roman Archaeology Supplement Series 3; Ann Arbor: University of Michigan Press, 1991), with essays by Beard, Bowman, and Hopkins; Millard, *Reading and Writing*. The major exception is Hezser, who argues for a significantly lower literacy rate among Jews in Palestine, perhaps as low as 2–3 percent (Hezser, *Jewish Literacy in Roman Palestine*, 496–504). However, Paul was not a Palestinian Jew but a citizen of the Roman world, so he is considered in that light here.

76. William V. Harris, *Ancient Literacy* (Cambridge: Harvard University Press, 1989), 266–67 for summary.

77. The example is from Alan K. Bowman, "Literacy in the Roman Empire: Mass and Mode," in Beard, *Literacy in the Roman World*, 119–31, here 122; see also 121. Harris does take this into account (*Ancient Literacy*, 124).

78. Keith Hopkins, "Conquest by Book," in Beard, *Literacy in the Roman World*, 133–58, here 135.

79. Another factor to consider but that is not directly germane here is that the term "illiterate" was used in Greek to refer to those who did not know how to read or write Greek. They may have been literate in other languages, but those knowing such languages were considered "barbarians." See Herbert C. Youtie, "*Agrammatos*: An Aspect of Greek Society in Egypt," *HSCP* 75 (1971): 161–76.

More germane to the issue of Paul's use of Scripture would be the style of reading in the culture of the time. We have seen that Greco-Roman culture included a complex interplay of oral and literary elements, of which written texts were clearly a part.[80] If we assume that there were books in the ancient world and that Paul had access to some of them (a point that I will explore further below), then the process by which he read them for the sake of using them is worth considering. I am not addressing the issue here of how his letters were read in his churches, although the findings about reading in general do have application in that area.[81]

The standard view is that there was very little silent reading in the ancient world. Within the field of biblical studies, an important article by Paul Achtemeier argues that papyrus was widely available in the ancient world and that books were widely available through libraries and booksellers. Achtemeier points to the large number of extant manuscripts as evidence for the book culture of the ancients, even in the lower classes of the Greco-Roman world. Where Achtemeier has been particularly influential is in his view that all reading was vocalized and hence performed out loud. From this he concludes that all writing came about through vocalization and hence dictation. That is, one either dictated (read aloud) to oneself or to another; in either case, one was writing down what was heard.[82] Achtemeier's view has been influential in subsequent interpretation of Paul's letters, as scholars have attempted to locate and identify the oral features that are to be found in his letters as a result of this dictation process.

This position was called into question almost immediately by Frank Gilliard,[83] but the fact that his statement was buried in the critical notes of *JBL* probably minimized its effect. Gilliard pointed out numerous earlier examples of silent reading. These include Theseus as depicted in Euripides, *Hipp.* 856–874 (fifth century B.C.E.); Demosthenes in Aristophanes, *Eq.* 116–127 (fifth century B.C.E.); the riddle in Antiphanes' *Sappho* (fourth century B.C.E.);

---

80. See Harris, *Ancient Literacy*, 125; cf. Thomas, *Literacy and Orality*.

81. On issues regarding oral delivery, see Thomas H. Olbricht, "Delivery and Memory," in Porter, *Handbook of Classical Rhetoric*, 159–67.

82. Paul J. Achtemeier, "*Omne Verbum Sonat*: The New Testament and the Oral Environment of Late Western Antiquity," *JBL* 109 (1990): 3–27, esp. 15–19. The example of Bishop Ambrose reading silently in the fourth century is often cited. This point is addressed by Michael Slusser, "Reading Silently in Antiquity," *JBL* 111 (1992): 499, who cites another example from the fourth century.

83. E.g., see Frank D. Gilliard, "More Silent Reading in Antiquity: *Non Omne Verbum Sonabat*," *JBL* 112 (1993): 689–94, who notes previous discussion among biblical and classical scholars, where similar confusion reigned.

Alexander the Great (according to Plutarch, *Alex. fort.* 340A; fourth century B.C.E.); Julius Caesar (according to Plutarch, *Brut.* 5; first century B.C.E.); Cicero, *Tusc.* 5.116 and *De or.* 57 (first century C.E.); Augustus (according to Suetonius, *Aug.* 39; second century C.E.; see Gavrilov below); Aristotle (according to the Peripatetic work *Problems* 18.1, 7; final form from fifth century C.E.); and Augustine (*Conf.* 8.12, a text that mitigates the significance of Augustine's amazement at Ambrose being able to read silently; fourth century C.E.).[84] The inevitable conclusion is that there is ample evidence for silent reading in the records of antiquity. In a discussion of the psychology of reading, A. K. Gavrilov analyzes the reading process, commenting upon several of the examples cited above and providing more examples of his own. His additions include a number of passages where "silent reading is more or less certainly implied." Gavrilov also includes lists of passages where the advantages of reading aloud or silently are listed, such as instances of lecturing where ancient writers would silently read their notes while delivering their fully developed lecture.[85]

In short, the evidence seems clear that Greco-Roman culture was increasingly literate, directly and indirectly, and that there were many in this literate culture who could read, both aloud and silently.

5. Paul and the Use of the Old Testament

At this point I wish to bring together some of the strands that I have been discussing above in order to see if they can help us to understand the context in which Paul cites Scripture.

The first step is to gather together the various strands to create a social scenario in which to place Paul. Though orality was significant in the Greco-

---

84. Gilliard, "More Silent Reading," 690–92. Gilliard also cites Bernard Knox ("Silent Reading in Antiquity," *GRBS* 9 [1968]: 421–35, esp. 421–22), who speculates on the absurdity of thinking that every ancient author read everything aloud, such as Didymus's three thousand volumes (Gilliard, "More Silent Reading," 692)!

85. A. K. Gavrilov, "Techniques of Reading in Classical Antiquity," *CQ* NS 47 (1997): 56–73, esp. 70–71. Among the many examples that he cites are Herodotus, *Hist.* 1.123–125; Euripides, *Iph. aul.* 34ff.; *Iph. taur.* 763; Aristophanes, *Nub.* 23; *Av.* 960ff.; *Ran.* 51–52; Xenophon, *Symp.* 4.27; Plato Comicus = Athenagoras 1.8.5b; Menander, *Epitr.* 211ff.; Herodas 4.21–25; Plautus, *Bacch.* 729–995; Cicero, *Fam.* 9.20; Horace, *Sat.* 2.5.51ff.; *Ep.* 1.19.34; Ovid, *Metam.* 9.569; Petronius, *Sat.* 129; Quintilian, *Inst.* 1.1.33–34, 10.3.25; Josephus, *Life* 219–223; Plutarch, *Cat. Min.* 19, 34; *Brut.* 36.1–3; *Ant.* 10; Pliny, *Ep.* 5.3.2; Lucian, *Jupp. trag.* 1; Achilles Tatius, *Leuc. Clit.* 1.6; 5.24; Philostratus, *Vit. Apoll.* 8.1, 31; 4.17; Aristaenetus 1.10.36ff.; Cyril of Jerusalem, *Procatechesis* 14; Ambrose, *Ep.* 47; and Possidius, *Vita S. August.* 31.

Roman world, including the world of Diaspora Judaism, it maintained a complex interplay with literacy and a growing and developing book culture. Paul was born in a city that was one of the leading cities in providing education, especially for its native youths. The nature of the educational system, with its parallel streams, provided opportunities for those like Paul. If we can assume that the portrait of Paul that emerges from the evidence in Acts and the letters is accurate (as I think that it is), then Paul could quite possibly have taken advantage of at least the first part of the liberal arts education that began with the grammar school and finished with the rhetorical school. The fact that he was a Roman citizen from a family of Romans[86] and practiced a trade that was valued in the ancient world indicates that he could have availed himself of the grammar school, if not the rhetorical school, and it seems likely that he did so. Rather than progressing to a rhetorical education, however,[87] he went to Jerusalem for rabbinic training.

Even if Paul were not able to be educated in the Tarsian grammar school, the primary school probably would have been available to him, where he would have gained literacy and numeracy and even some basic compositional skills. However, the sequence of events within the educational system, including his move from Tarsus to Jerusalem to study with Gamaliel, fits very well with what we know about the educational system in Tarsus. If this is the case, then Paul would have been literate and capable of not only reading and writing but also of composing, before he left Tarsus. In addition to his exposure to a range of writers, especially poets, he would have been able to perform the various requirements of the *progymnasmata*, been introduced to letter writing and style, and even had some basic rhetorical training. He would have been able to read and write, probably aloud and silently. His continued education in Jerusalem would have been in some ways the Jewish equivalent of the rhetorical training of the Greco-Roman school, although it is unlikely that he received any formal rhetorical training there. Instead, as a student

---

86. There is no good reason to doubt Paul's Roman citizenship, even if reference is only found in Acts 16:37; 22:25; 25:11–12; 26:32.

87. See Porter, "Paul of Tarsus and His Letters," 533–38, 562–67, and the literature cited there, esp. Stanley E. Porter, "The Theoretical Justification for Application of Rhetorical Categories to Pauline Epistolary Literature," in *Rhetoric and the New Testament: Essays from the 1992 Heidelberg Conference* (ed. Stanley E. Porter and Thomas H. Olbricht; JSNTSup 90; Sheffield: JSOT Press, 1993), 100–122; and Dennis L. Stamps, "Rhetorical Criticism of the New Testament: Ancient and Modern Evaluations of Argumentation," in *Approaches to New Testament Study* (ed. Stanley E. Porter and David Tombs; JSNTSup 120; Sheffield: Sheffield Academic Press, 1995), 129–69, esp. 141–47.

of Gamaliel, he would have studied both the written and the oral Torah and learned enough about disputing points of law to become a Pharisee.

As a literate person in the company of other literate persons (such as those who served as scribes for his letters), Paul would have had access to the necessary materials for the securing, copying, and writing of books, including his letters.[88] Like other letter writers, he probably wrote (or had others write) multiple copies of his compositions for use in making later copies, thereby forming his own letter collection.[89]

This raises the question of what might be meant in 2 Tim 4:23 by the reference to "the parchments." Of course, many will want to dismiss this as a late, non-Pauline text, but that does not answer the question of what the term means. Whether Paul wrote these words or not, these "parchments" could have included any number of "books" from the ancient world, whether the writings of individual authors or anthologies culled from the writings of others, such as Old Testament authors. Given Paul's educational background, we certainly would expect him to be familiar with Greek anthologies as a fundamental part of his early training in literacy and composition. As a Pharisee, Paul would have also likely been exposed to Jewish methods of compiling important verses of Scripture into testimony volumes for easy reference in the propagation of theological agendas or for liturgical purposes.

Moreover, Paul undoubtedly employs the Greek version of the Jewish Scriptures in most of his citations of the Old Testament.[90] Paul's Greek Bible

---

88. I believe that it is impossible for Paul not to have known that he was a major letter writer on the basis of simply seeing how his letters compared to other, more typical letters of the ancient world.

89. See Millard, *Reading and Writing*, 76–77; Stanley E. Porter, "Paul and the Process of Canonization," in *Exploring the Origins of the Bible* (ed. Craig A. Evans and Emanuel Tov; Grand Rapids: Baker, 2008).

90. As an initial point on terminology, "LXX" has taken on a variety of different meanings and is often used in ambiguous and unqualified ways in New Testament studies. As R. Timothy McLay observes (*The Use of the Septuagint in New Testament Research* [Grand Rapids: Eerdmans, 2003], 5), "Sometimes 'LXX' refers to the reading in the Greek Jewish Scriptures that has been judged by the editor of a critical text to be most likely the original reading, that is, what is believed to be the closest approximation that we can make to what was probably written originally by the translator. In other cases 'LXX' may refer to any reading that is found in any Greek manuscript of the Jewish Scriptures, which is not necessarily the original or even a very early reading. It could be any reading or word that appears in any Greek manuscript of a book in the LXX. In the same way, it is often stated that the NT writer quotes the 'LXX' version of a biblical text, as opposed to the Hebrew version or the MT, without any qualification." This ambiguity has led several recent scholars to speak of the Greek Bible in use during the time of the New Testament authors as the

was not a volume that he (or anyone else, for that matter) could have pulled down from the shelf and used to look up a passage but rather a series of scrolls. There is, in fact, no evidence that there was anywhere a collection of Greek manuscripts spanning the entire Old Testament in Paul's day. More than likely, people thought of the Greek text in terms of individual books and their respective scroll(s)—"the LXX" did not exist as a single volume until the propagation of the codex in the second century C.E.[91] These scrolls were the result of two hundred years of scholarship by diverse translators in diverse times and circumstances.[92] As a result, they reflect different translation philosophies and should not be understood monolithically as a coherent, textually stable tradition of Scripture readily available to most first-century Jews and Christians. Thus, as Stanley notes, it is highly unlikely that any one individual or establishment would have had access to the entire collection of Jewish Scriptures in Greek.[93] Poor relations between Paul and many of his fellow Jews may have further limited Paul's and his colleagues' access to the Greek Scriptures.[94] In any case, carrying around a large bag of scrolls for reference in letter composition would have been rather cumbersome (and thus impossible) in Paul's travels.

A likely hypothesis, therefore, is that Paul or one of his early Christian colleagues compiled an anthology of significant biblical texts to be used as liturgical, doctrinal, or compositional tools. This would not have been a foreign compositional aid to Paul, given his Greek and Jewish backgrounds. It is not hard to imagine Paul as a person who was involved in the book culture in a number of ways. He himself might have made use of copybooks or the tablet equivalent. We know that Paul could write, even if he chose to use a scribe in most instances when it came to writing his letters.[95] As part of a

---

"Old Greek" text. See also Leonard Greenspoon, "The Use and Abuse of the Term 'LXX' and Related Terminology in Recent Scholarship," *BIOSCS* 20 (1987): 21–29; Christopher D. Stanley, "'Pearls before Swine': Did Paul's Audience Understand His Biblical Quotations?" *NovT* 41 (1999): 124–44, here 126–28.

91. See Stanley, "Pearls before Swine," 127.

92. For a recent survey of the history and transmission of the Greek Jewish Scriptures, see Natalio Fernández Marcos, *The Septuagint in Context* (Leiden: Brill, 2001). A less technical treatment is found in Karen H. Jobes and Moisés Silva, *Invitation to the Septuagint* (Grand Rapids: Baker, 2000); see also McKay, *Use of the Septuagint*, 100–136.

93. Stanley, "Pearls before Swine," 127.

94. Ibid.

95. There are some who have taken Paul's "signature" in Phlm 19 as if it were an acknowledgment of his illiteracy. This reflects a failure to understand the illiteracy formula, which instead indicates that Paul is legally affirming what he has just said. See Thomas J. Kraus, "Eine vertragsrechtliche Verpflichtung in Phlm19. Duktus und juristischer Hinter-

group that was concerned with Scripture, he might also have had periodic access to Greek and possibly Hebrew scriptural texts for copying. We know that he had scribes and others accompanying him who may have had similar interests and abilities. This same group may have been involved in the copying and dissemination of his own letters.

When we turn to Paul's letters, we find little direct evidence of his compositional techniques. Most likely he cited Scripture both from memory and from written texts, with the latter including both anthologies and manuscripts of entire books. His citations from Greek authors probably came from either memory or such anthologies. Some scholars have suggested that in those places where Paul mentions an author or book by name or cites a series of passages from the same book, he is using a written source, but where he cites an author or book without attribution or brings together passages from different sources to form a combined citation, he is quoting from memory.[96]

For the sake of discussion, let me cite several examples that perhaps illustrate what I am suggesting. In the first half of Rom 9, Paul cites a number of passages from the Pentateuch, with the exception of one passage from Malachi (Gen 21:12 in Rom 9:7; Gen 18:10, 14 in Rom 9:9; Gen 25:23 in Rom 9:12; Mal 1:2–3 in Rom 9:13; Exod 33:19 in Rom 9:14; Exod 9:16 in Rom 9:17). Since these quotations follow the scriptural book order, it appears that Paul may well have used a written source of some type for his quotations from the Pentateuch and then cited Mal 1:2–3 from memory as an example of what is found in Gen 25:23. The pentateuchal passages seem to follow the Greek version, which offers a generally accurate reflection of the Hebrew apart from the combination of Gen 18:10 and 18:14 LXX in Rom 9:9. The exception to this is Exod 9:16, which may have an independent origin (memory?). The quotation from Mal 1:2–3 in Rom 9:13 follows a text where the LXX agrees with the MT.[97]

---

grund," in *Steht nicht geschrieben? Studien zur Bibel und ihrer Wirkungsgeschichte: Festschrift für Georg Schmuttermayr* (ed. Johannes Frühwald-König et al.; Regensburg: Pustet, 2001), 187–200; now in English as "An Obligation from Contract Law in Philemon 19: Characteristic Style and Juridical Background," in Thomas J. Kraus, *Ad Fontes: Original Manuscripts and Their Significance for Studying Early Christianity—Selected Essays* (TENTS 3; Leiden: Brill, 2007), 207–30. The same can be said for Gal 6:11–18. Contra Dewey, "Textuality in an Oral Culture," 52–54.

96. A similar view is suggested, but rejected, by McLay, *Use of the Septuagint*, 26–30.

97. I use the information on the quotations provided by Gleason L. Archer and Gregory Chirichigno, *Old Testament Quotations in the New Testament* (Chicago: Moody Press, 1983), ad loc.

In the second half of Rom 9, Paul includes a series of quotations from the Prophets: Hos 2:25 in Rom 9:25; Hos 2:3 in Rom 9:26; Hos 2:3 and Isa 10:22–23 in Rom 9:27–28; Isa 1:9 in Rom 9:29; and Isa 28:16 in Rom 9:33. Paul again appears to have had a written source for these passages from the Prophets, perhaps a collection of prophetic texts, as several of them (e.g., Hos 2:25; 2:3b; Isa 10:22–23) reflect an independent textual tradition. However, Isa 1:9 is a close rendering into the LXX from the Hebrew, and Isa 28:16 follows the Hebrew. Is it possible that he had two prophetic scrolls, or at least excerpts from them, in front of him? It is also worth considering whether Paul had a scroll of Psalms, or at least an anthology that included significant Psalms excerpts, in front of him when he wrote Rom 3:10–18. This passage contains citations from Ps 14:1–3 in Rom 3:10–12; Ps 5:9 in Rom 3:13; Ps 10:7 in Rom 3:14; and Ps 36:1 in Rom 3:18, all reflecting various features of the Greek version that differ from the Hebrew. Apart from the first citation, the order is biblically sequential, suggesting that Paul may have had an extended collection that followed our scriptural order, if not an actual copy of the book of Psalms. Apart from the odd exception, most of the explicit scriptural citations in Rom 9–10 are taken either from the Pentateuch or from the Prophets. Romans 11 also contains predominantly a mix of citations from the Pentateuch, the Prophets (both Former and Latter), and the Psalms.[98] Paul also cites Isa 59:7–8 in Rom 3:15–17. This may have come to his memory in the moment of dictation, or it may have come from a book of citations that he had in front of him.

6. Conclusion

In this essay I have examined the historical and cultural background of Paul's engagement with the text of the Jewish Scriptures, as a means of providing access into the process behind his actual citation of Scripture. Along the way, I have explored briefly the nature of the Greco-Roman educational system and how Paul may have been involved in it. The nature of his involvement has potential implications for how he cited Scripture and other authors, since it establishes the nature and types of reading that he would have done in the course of his education and beyond. As a result, I believe that it is plausible that Paul's education combined elements of both the Greco-Roman grammar school and Jewish Torah training. His exposure to a range of texts, including both continuous texts and various types of anthologies and collections, helps to account for some of the features of his use of both Scripture and other

---

98. Note Luke 24:44, where the same three are mentioned.

ancient authors. Actual studies of such usage are of necessity preliminary and may well always remain so, because the type of evidence that we have, while suggestive, is indirect and circumstantial. Nevertheless, I am convinced that Paul's involvement in the Greco-Roman and Torah-based educational systems can help to account for both the material that he cites and the way in which he cites it.

Paul's "Use" of Scripture: Why the Audience Matters

Christopher D. Stanley

1. Introduction

Virtually all modern studies of Paul's use of Scripture have focused on the literary, hermeneutical, or theological dimensions of his engagement with the biblical text. Their chief concern has been to develop a fuller and richer understanding of the way Paul read and interpreted his ancestral Scriptures and the role(s) that Scripture played in his theology. In some cases, the quest has been broadened to include an examination of the ways in which Paul's interpretive techniques and conclusions resembled and differed from those of his Jewish contemporaries. Even here, however, the scholarly gaze has remained firmly fixed on the question of how Paul understood the Jewish Scriptures in the light of his Christian faith.

One of the unfortunate side-effects of this emphasis on Paul's hermeneutical activity has been a tendency to neglect the social and rhetorical setting within which Paul's biblical references were framed. For most interpreters, the task is not to explain how Paul's references to the Jewish Scriptures serve to advance a developing argument that was addressed to a particular audience but rather to reconstruct how Paul read and interpreted the biblical text prior to his composition of the letter. The usual method is to read a passage from Paul's letters in tandem with a passage from the Jewish Scriptures that the interpreter regards as the source of Paul's language and then to draw inferences about Paul's understanding of Scripture from the similarities and differences between the two texts. Some scholars limit their attention to a single passage, while others examine a broad range of texts in an effort to develop a thorough understanding of Paul's practices. The goal is the same in either case: to explain how Paul himself interacted with the text of Scripture. Occasionally a scholar will talk about how a particular quotation, allusion, or echo might relate to the concerns or interests of Paul's epistolary audiences, but these observations are mostly limited to passages where Paul is believed to be using Scripture in a polemical sense, as in his repeated references to the Abraham story in Gal 3 and 4 or his "wisdom" quotations in the first three chapters of 1 Corinthians.

In principle, there is nothing wrong with this approach. Paul's letters are saturated with biblical language, and it makes sense to look for patterns that might indicate how his thinking was shaped by the Jewish Scriptures both before and after he became a follower of Jesus. But there are many obstacles that stand in the way of such a task. Some of these obstacles are well known, while others are less obvious.

(1) While many of Paul's biblical references are clearly marked, others are not. Scholars frequently disagree about whether a particular passage in Paul's letters should be taken as an echo or allusion to a specific verse of Scripture or whether it reflects the influence of the Jewish Scriptures on Paul's ordinary patterns of thinking and speaking. Recent efforts to develop a set of criteria for resolving this problem have been helpful, but their application remains highly subjective.[1]

(2) In cases where a reference is evident, scholars sometimes have trouble deciding what biblical text Paul had in mind. Even with marked quotations, there are places where scholars disagree about the identity of the text to which Paul was referring,[2] and there are several passages for which the precise nature of Paul's biblical *Vorlage* is unclear.[3] The fact that Paul frequently modifies the wording of the biblical text to accord with his own interpretive agenda further complicates the picture.[4]

(3) The brevity and ambiguity of Paul's references to the Jewish Scriptures also pose problems for interpreters. Only rarely does Paul engage in an extended exposition of a particular passage of Scripture in which he exposes

---

1. Virtually all scholars who have worked in this area in recent years have relied on the criteria set forth by Richard B. Hays in *Echoes of Scripture in the Letters of Paul* (New Haven: Yale University Press, 1989), 29–33. For a more recent discussion and refinement of these criteria, see Richard B. Hays, "Who Has Believed Our Message? Paul's Reading of Isaiah," in *The Conversion of the Imagination: Paul as Interpreter of Israel's Scripture* (Grand Rapids: Eerdmans, 2005), 25–49.

2. For example, does the quotation in Gal 3:6 refer to Gen 12:3; 18:18; 22:18; or 28:14? Does the unmarked citation in 1 Cor 5:13 refer to Deut 17:1; 19:19; 22:21, 22, 24; or 24:7?

3. See Rom 9:33; 11:3-4; 11:26-27. For a discussion of the textual problems associated with these and other explicit quotations in Paul's letters, see Christopher D. Stanley, *Paul and the Language of Scripture: Citation Technique in the Pauline Epistles and Contemporary Literature* (SNTSMS 74; Cambridge: Cambridge University Press, 1992).

4. For an extended discussion of this phenomenon, see the study cited in the previous note.

his interpretive methods to public view.[5] His usual practice is to embed biblical quotations and allusions into his developing argument and then leave it to his audience to figure out the implied link between his own statements and the biblical texts to which he refers. In many cases, the reasoning behind these references is opaque, as evidenced by the divergent interpretations that scholars have offered for many of Paul's biblical citations.

This last point deserves more attention than it has received. Even scholars who are aware of the methodological problems associated with trying to reconstruct the "original authorial intent" behind a piece of literature speak routinely about how Paul "read" or "interpreted" a particular passage of Scripture, as though Paul's mental activity could be recovered by engaging in a judicious comparison of Paul's letters with the biblical texts to which they refer. In reality, such studies reflect the analytical insights of highly trained contemporary interpreters who have ready access to the texts of Paul's letters and the Jewish Scriptures in easy-to-use print and electronic versions, together with a vast array of published studies in which other scholars have spelled out their ideas concerning how Paul might have understood a particular biblical text. Even with these tools at their disposal, interpreters remain divided over what Paul was doing in many of his references to the Jewish Scriptures. This recognition ought to lead scholars to question the common presumption that Paul expected his ancient audiences to be able to retrace and approve the interpretive activity that lay behind his many references to the text of Scripture. Until recently, however, this presumption has received little attention from scholars. This essay seeks to remedy that oversight.

2. Defining the Audience

One of the principal reasons for the success of Richard Hays's acclaimed book, *Echoes of Scripture in the Letters of Paul*, lies in his thoughtful attention to questions of methodology. Hays harbors no illusions that his readings of Paul's letters can be equated with "what Paul intended" at the moment when he penned his letters. His aim is rather to produce "late twentieth-century readings of Paul informed by intelligent historical understanding."[6] Quoting frequently from the work of literary critic John Hollander,[7] Hays states that

---

5. The most obvious examples are, of course, Rom 4:9–23 and Gal 4:21–31.
6. *Echoes of Scripture*, 27.
7. John Hollander, *The Figure of Echo: A Mode of Allusion in Milton and After* (Berkeley and Los Angeles: University of California Press, 1981). In a later article ("On the Rebound: A Response to Critiques of *Echoes of Scripture in the Letters of Paul*," in *Paul and the Scriptures of Israel* [ed. Craig A. Evans and James A. Sanders; JSNTSup 83; Shef-

his concern is not to investigate what Paul might have intended or what the original audience might have understood but rather to call attention to "the poetic effects produced for those who have ears to hear."[8] In particular, he is interested in the possible presence in Paul's letters of the diachronic trope that Hollander calls "transumption" or "metalepsis." According to Hays (following Hollander), "When a literary echo links the text in which it occurs to an earlier text, the figurative effect of the echo can lie in the unstated or suppressed (transumed) points of resonance between the two texts."[9] The task of the interpreter in this case is to uncover and highlight the suppressed material so that readers who are less familiar with the source text can participate in the "field of whispered or unstated correspondences" that is implicitly set up between the two texts.[10] The bulk of Hays's book is devoted to showing how this might work in particular instances.

The influence of Hays's "metaleptic" approach to analyzing Paul's engagement with the Jewish Scriptures is hard to overstate. The most visible evidence of his influence is the frequency with which one hears scholars using the phrase "those who have ears to hear" when calling attention to what they regard as unstated points of resonance between Paul's letters and a particular biblical text. The presence of so many implicit references to Scripture has led many scholars to conclude that Paul reflected more thoughtfully on the broader literary context of his quotations, allusions, and echoes than has commonly been supposed. The effect has been to insulate Paul from the accusation that he frequently took verses out of context.

In the nearly two decades since Hays's book was published, relatively few questions have been raised about the methodological validity of his approach.[11] In particular, little attention has been paid to the manner in

---

field: Sheffield Academic Press, 1993], 80), Hays also gives substantial credit to Thomas M. Greene, *The Light in Troy: Imitation and Discovery in Renaissance Poetry* (New Haven: Yale University Press, 1982), and Michael Fishbane, *Biblical Interpretation in Ancient Israel* (Oxford: Clarendon, 1985) for shaping his thought.

8. Hays, *Echoes of Scripture*, 19.

9. Ibid., 20.

10. Ibid.

11. Of the five critical essays on Hays's book that appeared (along with a response from Hays) in the 1993 book *Paul and the Scriptures of Israel* (see n. 7), only two (the articles by Evans and Green) explicitly question elements of Hays's methodology. Additional criticisms of Hays's approach can be found in Christopher D. Stanley, *Arguing with Scripture: The Rhetoric of Quotations in the Letters of Paul* (New York: T&T Clark, 2004), 38 n. 2, 47 n. 29. See also Stanley E. Porter, "The Use of the Old Testament in the New Testament: A Brief Comment on Method and Terminology," in *Early Christian Interpretation of the Scriptures of Israel: Investigations and Proposals* (ed. Craig A. Evans and James A.

which Hays applies the insights of John Hollander, Thomas Greene, and the other literary critics whom he cites in his book. A careful review of the works of these critics suggests that Hays has turned their methodological insights in directions that they might not have endorsed.

Unlike his literary-critical mentors, Hays is not content to speak only about "poetic resonances" between Paul's biblical references and the text of Scripture. For Hays, it is important to be able to attribute a significant proportion of these resonances to the hermeneutical activity of Paul himself. As Hays puts it, "If I, having learned something about Paul's historical circumstances and having read the same Scripture that Paul lived in so deeply, discern in his language echoes of that Scripture, it is not improbable that I am overhearing the same echoes that he and his earliest readers might have been able to hear."[12] By the end of the book, Hays is using the fruits of his analyses of various Pauline texts to draw broad conclusions about the manner in which the historical Paul viewed and interpreted his ancestral Scriptures.[13] Much of the material upon which Hays bases his conclusions is derived from his study of Paul's explicit quotations, where it is obvious that Paul intended to refer to particular verses of Scripture. But his findings are also influenced by the results of his investigations of various "echoes" of Scripture in Paul's letters, materials that Hays had earlier indicated cannot be so readily attributed to the intentions of the author.[14] Hays is such an artful reader of texts and such a persuasive writer that few scholars have noticed how he relies on incommensurable materials to support his conclusions about Paul's approach to Scripture.

As it turns out, this questionable mixing of materials does not have a major impact on Hays's understanding of Paul's interpretive activity. Virtually everything that he says in his concluding chapter could have been derived from a study of Paul's quotations without reference to the texts that Hays identifies as "echoes" of the Jewish Scriptures. For example, the quotations by themselves provide sufficient justification for Hays's assertion that,

---

Sanders; SSEJC 5; JSNTSup 148; Sheffield: Sheffield Academic Press, 1997), 79–96; idem, "Further Comments on the Use of the Old Testament in the New Testament," in *The Intertextuality of the Epistles: Explorations of Theory and Practice* (ed. Thomas L. Brodie, Dennis R. MacDonald, and Stanley E. Porter; NTM 16; Sheffield: Sheffield Phoenix Press, 2006), 98–110.

12. Hays, *Echoes of Scripture*, 28.

13. Ibid., 154–92. Virtually every page of this chapter includes references to "Paul as reader of Scripture" (154), "Paul's readings of Scripture" (155), "Paul's construal of Torah" (157), "Paul's hermeneutical procedures" (158), etc.

14. Ibid., 19, 32; see also 156.

for Paul, "The biblical text must be read as a vast texture of latent promise, and the promise must be recovered through interpretive strategies that allow the hidden word to become manifest."[15] The same is true for his conclusion that, "for Paul, original intention is not a primary hermeneutical concern,"[16] along with many similar statements. In fact, a critical examination of Hays's work reveals that the majority of his conclusions concerning Paul's engagement with Scripture are the product of a judicious application of traditional methods of interpretation, not the fruit of a new theoretical approach to Paul's letters.

Nonetheless, there are two aspects of Hays's work that remain open to challenge on methodological grounds. The first is his insistence that Paul's theological outlook was heavily influenced by his reflection on the broader literary contexts of many of the biblical texts to which he refers in his letters. Hays's argument slips into circularity at this point, since his analysis of Paul's letters presupposes his thesis that metalepsis is the key to understanding many of the passing references to Scripture in Paul's letters. This thesis compels Hays to search for evidence of a contextual orientation behind Paul's biblical references and to ignore readings that would suggest a greater disjunction between Paul's letters and the context of his references. Hays is aware of the potential circularity of his argument at this point, and he takes pains to indicate why he thinks that this mode of reading does more justice to Paul's thought than the atomistic or noncontextual readings that have been proposed by other scholars.[17] In the end, however, Hays acknowledges that his reconstruction of Paul's interpretive activity reflects his own aesthetic judgment that such contextualized readings yield the most satisfying readings of Paul's letters.[18] It is unclear how Hays would respond to an interpreter who claimed to find more aesthetic satisfaction in an atomistic or noncontextual reading of Paul's engagement with the Jewish Scriptures.

This leads us to the second and more serious difficulty with the methods used by Hays and his followers. To justify his shift from literary analysis (uncovering poetic resonances) to historical study (elucidating how Paul read and interpreted the biblical text), Hays proposes a "common sense hermeneutics" that is based on the assumption "that readers ancient and modern

---

15. Ibid., 155.

16. Ibid., 156.

17. This is the underlying purpose of Hays's seven criteria for identifying the presence of a biblical echo in a Pauline text (ibid., 29–32).

18. The last of Hays's seven tests for the presence of a biblical echo is "satisfaction," which involves a subjective decision about the cumulative weight of the evidence (ibid., 31–32).

can share a common sense of the text's meaning."[19] In other words, Hays presumes that there is at least a rough analogy between the reading experiences of ancient and modern audiences when they encounter Paul's letters. No such presumption is required for a purely literary reading of the letters, but the conventions of historical analysis require some kind of criteria for testing the validity of claims concerning the past. According to Hays,

> Prominent among these conventions are the convictions that a proposed interpretation must be justified with reference to evidence provided both by the text's rhetorical structure and by what can be known through critical investigation about the author *and the original readers*. Any interpretation must respect these constraints in order to be persuasive within my reading community. Claims about intertextual meaning are strongest where it can credibly be demonstrated that they occur within the literary structure of the text and that they can plausibly be ascribed to the intention of the author *and the competence of the original readers.*[20]

The dual reference to "the original readers" in this formulation is clearly intentional, since Hays could easily have omitted this phrase and limited his attention to Paul's personal engagement with the biblical text. A similar concern for ancient readers can be observed in Hays's first and fifth criteria for testing claims about the presence of biblical echoes in Paul's letters.[21] But the reason for its inclusion is unclear. Why should it matter to Hays whether the "original readers" of Paul's letters could have recognized and understood his references to the Jewish Scriptures? Why does Hays not simply say, "Here are some interesting connections that I have observed between Paul's letters and the biblical texts that he cites, and here is why I think that Paul might have seen them also"? Hays never answers this question.

Surprisingly, Hays pays little attention to whether a particular biblical "echo" might have been intelligible to "the original readers" of Paul's letters in the course of his analysis. Here and there he asks whether an especially obscure reference might have been recognizable to Paul's first-century audiences, but most of the time he simply presumes that Paul's readers will be able

---

19. Ibid., 27–28.
20. Ibid., 28, emphasis added.
21. Under the heading of "Availability," Hays states that the interpreter should ask, "Was the proposed source of the echo available to the author and/or his original readers?" (ibid., 29). Under "Historical Plausibility," he asks, "Could Paul have intended the alleged meaning effect? Could his readers have understood it?" Later in the same section he states that this test "necessarily requires hypothetical constructs of what might have been intended and grasped by particular first-century figures" (30).

to identify the source of his biblical references and recall their broader literary context. Questions about the literary competence of the "original readers" serve primarily as a check against excessively speculative readings of Paul's literary intentions; elsewhere they recede into the background.

The reason why Hays devotes so little practical attention to the "original readers" of Paul's letters is not hard to uncover. According to Hays, "The implied readers of these letters appear to be primarily Gentile Christians with an extensive knowledge of the LXX and an urgent interest in its interpretation."[22] Hays is aware that this description of the implied readers of Paul's letters might not be valid for the "actual original readers" of the letters,[23] yet he fails to follow up on this observation, noting rather meekly that "some such characterization of Paul's actual readers … is not implausible."[24] This virtual equation of the implied audience with the actual audience of Paul's letters allows Hays to sidestep the thorny question of whether Paul's first-century audiences would have been capable of recognizing and following his many allusive references to the Jewish Scriptures, together with the related question of whether this was in fact what Paul expected. The question makes little difference to Hays's analysis of Paul's own engagement with the biblical text, but it plays a vital role in his reconstruction of Paul's rhetoric, since Hays believes that Paul included echoes and allusions in his letters as part of a conscious attempt to lead his first-century audiences into a deeper understanding of the meaning of the texts to which he refers. For Hays, Paul's echoes and allusions serve to invite his audiences to recall the broader literary context from which the reference was selected and to rethink the meaning of the passage under the tutelage of Paul's own Christian reading of the text.

Hays clearly underestimates the demands that this view of Paul's rhetoric places on a first-century audience. For the model to work, Paul's audience must first be able to recognize the presence of an unmarked echo or allusion in one of Paul's letters. This would require not only a deft ear but also a fairly substantial knowledge of the Jewish Scriptures, since the texts to which Paul alludes include verses that are rarely if ever cited by other Jewish or Christian authors. Next, the audience must be able to recall in a fair amount of detail the broader literary context of the referenced text. This is a crucial step, since Hays's approach is predicated on the belief that Paul expected his audiences

---

22. Ibid., 29. Whether this is in fact an accurate description of the "implied readers" of Paul's letters will be addressed at a later point.

23. According to Hays, "Whether the actual original readers of the letters fit this description is a question that must be distinguished carefully from the literary question about the implied reader as an intertextual phenomenon" (ibid., 201 n. 92).

24. Ibid.

to draw links between the texts to which he refers and the scriptural contexts from which those texts were extracted. From here, the audience must be able to discern accurately how Paul is interpreting the passage in question, since he rarely spells out the reasoning behind his references to the biblical text. Some scholars would raise the bar still higher by asserting that Paul expected his audiences to be capable of making informed judgments about how his interpretation of the biblical text resembled and differed from other teachers whom they might have heard in the past. Finally, the audience must be willing to accept these hypothetical reconstructions of Paul's meaning as valid, since the rhetorical weight of his biblical references would be undermined if the audience were to judge Paul's readings of Scripture to be unacceptable or unconvincing. Presumably their receptiveness would have been unaffected by the tensions and suspicions that frequently existed between Paul and his audiences or by the fact (acknowledged by Hays) that "Paul repeatedly interprets Scripture in ways that must have startled his first audience."[25]

While it is not impossible that this is what Paul expected, it seems unlikely that Paul would have placed such heavy interpretive demands upon his audiences. In fact, a closer examination of Hays's model suggests that his concern to uncover "metaleptic" references to Scripture in Paul's letters has led him to misinterpret the purpose and effects of Paul's biblical rhetoric.

In the first place, the idea that Paul's first-century audiences would have possessed the degree of biblical literacy presupposed by Hays's approach is historically implausible. Unless Paul's congregations were highly anomalous, the great majority of their members would have been illiterate and thus unable to read the Jewish Bible for themselves. His letters also suggest that most of his addressees came from non-Jewish (i.e., "Gentile") backgrounds where many of them would have been ignorant of the content of the Jewish Scriptures. Even if Paul had been aware of the existence of some kind of "Bible training program" in the churches to which he wrote, he had no way of knowing precisely which passages his audiences would recognize, apart from texts that he had taught them or verses that were commonly employed in Christian teaching and preaching.[26] If Paul expected his first-century audiences to be

---

25. See ibid., 1. Hays frequently refers to Paul "transforming" the meaning of texts (e.g., 1, 45) and offering "revisionary" readings of Scripture (66, 81). Elsewhere he refers to Paul's "innovative interpretive strategy" (114) and remarks on the "audacity" of a particular interpretive move (112). Occasionally he uses stronger language, describing one Pauline reference as a "stunning misreading" of the text of Scripture and another as "historically outrageous" (45, 82). Despite these problems, however, Hays's hypothetical readers always seem to go along with Paul's readings.

26. All of these points will be developed further in the latter part of this essay.

able to recognize, recall to memory, and engage in thoughtful reflection upon the broader literary context of all of his unmarked references to the Jewish Scripture, he was a thoroughly incompetent rhetor. No ancient author would have so radically misjudged his audience.

The same objection applies to Hays's presumption that Paul meant for his audiences to figure out and embrace the reasoning behind his many references to the Jewish Scriptures. If contemporary scholars with all of their resources have been unable to come to agreement about how Paul was interpreting the biblical text in many cases, it is hard to see how Paul could have thought that his original audiences would have been capable of reconstructing his reasoning. It is even more difficult to believe that Paul overlooked the possibility that the biblically literate members of his audience might have objected to his often tendentious readings of the Jewish Scriptures. In fact, one can point to several places in Paul's letters where an ancient reader who was capable of consulting the original context of Paul's biblical references might have concluded that the text of Scripture offered more support for the views of Paul's opponents than for Paul.[27] When we add to this mix the tensions that often existed between Paul and the elite members of his congregations, it becomes virtually incomprehensible that Paul would have trusted these people not only to accept his revisionist readings of Scripture without complaint but also to assist their fellow believers in grasping his meaning.[28] Some may even have relished the opportunity to point out the flaws in Paul's arguments and thus undermine his authority. Once again, Hays's model implies that Paul was an incompetent rhetor who failed to anticipate potential problems with his audience.

In summary, Hays's contention that Paul inserted biblical references into his letters as a means of guiding his first-century audiences toward a new way of reading the Jewish Scriptures rests on shaky historical ground. This is not to say that Paul never engaged in such a practice—passages such as Rom 4:1–25 and Gal 4:21–31 show clearly that Paul was capable of employing such a rhetorical strategy when he wished to do so—but the number of passages in which Paul explains to his audience how he is interpreting the text of Scripture is quite small. Most of the time he simply weaves biblical references

---

27. For example, see the discussion of Gal 3:6–14 in Stanley, *Arguing with Scripture*, 121–30, which is summarized later in this essay.

28. This is clearly the case in 1 Corinthians, where Paul repeatedly sides with the poorer members against the (presumably literate) elite members of the congregation (see Gerd Theissen, *The Social Setting of Pauline Christianity: Essays on Corinth* [Philadelphia: Fortress, 1982]), and arguably so in the case of Galatians, where the opponents appear to be offering their own text-based interpretation of the Jewish Scriptures.

into his argument and then relies on the surface structure of the argument to call attention to the points that he wants his audience to draw from the biblical text.[29] In many cases he also revises the wording of the text so that it comports more closely with his argument.[30] Taken together, these techniques suggest to the audience that there is no need for them to consult the original context of the passage to which Paul refers; if they want to know what the text means, all they have to do is listen to Paul.

A clear exception to this pattern can be seen in several passages where Paul alludes to a particular biblical passage or story in the expectation that the audience will be able to supply the portions that he omits. In these cases the meaning of the reference is lost unless the audience is familiar with the missing material. Examples include 1 Cor 10:1–12 and 2 Cor 3:7–18, where he assumes that the Christians in Corinth are aware of certain key episodes from the exodus narrative; Gal 3:6–8, 16, 28 and 4:21–31, where he refers allusively to various aspects of the Abraham narrative (cf. Rom 4:1–25; 9:6–13); and Rom 5:12–21, where his argument presupposes at least a minimal acquaintance with the story of Adam's fall in Gen 3. Yet the amount of biblical material that the audience is expected to supply in these passages is fairly limited. The pattern varies from letter to letter, but virtually all of the references concern materials that were well-known in early Christianity: the creation stories, the ancestral narratives (primarily the story of Abraham), the exodus saga, and a few of the more important laws of Torah.[31] These are precisely the kinds of materials that one would expect to be passed on by word of mouth in a community of illiterates. How much Paul expected his audiences to know about these passages is unclear, since his references are highly selective. But the type and amount of biblical knowledge that would have been required to follow Paul's biblical argumentation is consistent with what we might expect from a functionally illiterate Gentile audience who had received a modest amount of biblical instruction in a Christian setting.

Taken as a whole, these observations suggest that Paul was aware of the limited biblical knowledge of his intended audiences and crafted his arguments to suit their capabilities. Instead of expecting his audiences to remember and reflect on the original context of his biblical references, Paul

---

29. This point is developed at great length in Stanley, *Arguing with Scripture* (see n. 11 above), especially chapters 5–8.

30. For a summary of the ways in which Paul commonly adapts the wording of his explicit quotations, see Stanley, *Paul and the Language of Scripture*, 338–50.

31. For more on this point, see the discussions in Stanley, *Arguing with Scripture*, 75–78, 114–18, 136–42, concerning what Paul assumes about the biblical literacy of the Christians in Corinth, Galatia, and Rome.

seems to have made a serious effort to communicate to his audiences how he wished for his references to be understood. The success of this effort did not hinge on anyone being able to reconstruct Paul's biblical hermeneutic or approve his handling of the biblical text. All that was needed was for an audience to be able to follow Paul's developing argument (no easy feat!) and to accept his interpretations of Scripture as valid.

3. From Implied to Real Audiences

If this view of Paul's biblical rhetoric is correct, it still tells us only what kind of audience Paul had in mind when he dictated his letters, that is, the "implied audience" of the letters.[32] It says nothing about the actual literary capabilities of the people to whom Paul addressed his letters. We must always allow for the possibility that Paul underestimated or overestimated the amount of biblical knowledge that his audiences possessed, thereby limiting the effectiveness of his biblical rhetoric. From what we know of Paul, he was not always a good judge of how people would understand his letters.

So where might we turn for information about the biblical literacy and reading abilities of the people to whom Paul's letters were addressed? The first step is to admit that we can never really know the answers to these questions, since our only information comes from the letters themselves, and they are open to multiple interpretations. But we can determine what counts as a historically responsible presumption concerning the abilities of Paul's audiences by examining what can be known about literacy levels in general and biblical literacy in particular in the ancient world. Studies of the social makeup of Paul's churches have consistently shown that the great majority of people in Paul's churches came from nonelite and non-Jewish backgrounds, although some may have attended a Jewish synagogue prior to joining the Christian community. Unless we see evidence to the contrary, we should assume that Paul was at least broadly aware of the abilities and limitations of his audiences and that he took these factors into account when composing his letters, since this is one of the primary tasks of an effective rhetor.

On the general subject of literacy in the ancient world, the evidence is fairly clear. In his acclaimed study of ancient literacy, William Harris concluded that no more than 10–20 percent of the populace would have been

---

32. Hays's contention that "the implied readers of these letters appear to be primarily Gentile Christians with an extensive knowledge of the LXX and an urgent interest in its interpretation" (Hays, *Echoes of Scripture*, 29) is rooted in his presumption that Paul expected his readers to engage in "metaleptic" readings of his biblical references, a position that the present essay is designed to refute.

able to read or write at any level during the classical, Hellenistic, and Roman imperial periods.[33] Virtually all elite males would have been literate, but their numbers were too small in relation to the broader society to have much influence on the overall literacy figures.[34] Harris points to a number of factors that inhibited the growth of literacy in both Greek and Roman societies: the absence of any widespread network of schools (and the high cost of attending the ones that existed); the costliness of books (and the lack of public libraries from which they might be borrowed); the ready availability of intermediaries (scribes, literate slaves, etc.) to carry out chores that required literacy; the strength of ancient memories, which made writing less vital to ordinary people; and the general absence of any significant social, economic, or religious motivation for societal leaders to commit resources to the promotion of popular literacy.[35]

In a subsequent investigation of books and literacy in early Christianity, Harry Gamble concluded that, even if the early church had a disproportionate number of craftspeople and small business workers among its numbers, the number of Christians who could read and write during the first few centuries

---

33. William V. Harris, *Ancient Literacy* (Cambridge: Harvard University Press, 1989), 272, 284, 328–30. Of course, literacy levels were lower for women than for men throughout the ancient world; see Susan Guettel Cole, "Could Greek Women Read and Write?" in *Reflections of Women in Antiquity* (ed. Helene P. Foley; New York: Gordon & Breach, 1981), 219–45; Raffaella Cribiore, *Gymnastics of the Mind: Greek Education in Hellenistic and Roman Egypt* (Princeton: Princeton University Press, 2001), 74–101. The general validity of Harris's findings is affirmed (with some reservations) by the scholars who examined his work in the series of essays in Mary Beard, ed., *Literacy in the Roman World* (Journal of Roman Archaeology Supplement Series 3; Ann Arbor: University of Michigan Press, 1991). Allan Millard (*Reading and Writing in the Time of Jesus* [Sheffield: Sheffield Academic Press, 2000], 154–84) offers a more optimistic assessment of the data, but nearly all of his examples pertain to the practices of upper-class and "professional" writers (i.e., scribes), not ordinary working people. The same is true for the recent study by John F. A. Sawyer, *Sacred Languages and Sacred Texts* (London: Routledge, 1999), 44–58, who compounds the problem by commingling materials from different periods.

34. Harris, *Ancient Literacy*, 29–30, 103, 157.

35. Ibid., 11–35. Recently Cribiore has suggested that Harris may have oversimplified the social context of education in the ancient world and overlooked some of the less formal modes of education that occurred. In particular, she argues that a significant minority of the population might have been able to gain at least a rudimentary understanding of letters and numbers, although even this was "not much more than the ability to copy a brief text and read a list of words or a short passage from an author previously rehearsed" (*Gymnastics of the Mind*, 131). In the end, she agrees with Harris that "mass education and majority literacy did not exist in the ancient world" (17; see also 50, 60, 76, 86, 163, 184, 187, 249).

C.E. would not have exceeded the upper end of the range specified by Harris.[36] As Gamble puts it,

> It cannot be supposed that the extent of literacy in the ancient church was any greater than that in the Greco-Roman society of which Christianity was a part.... Not only the writing of Christian literature, but also the ability to read, criticize and interpret it belonged to a small number of Christians in the first several centuries, ordinarily not more than about 10 percent in any given setting, and perhaps fewer in the many small and provincial congregations that were characteristic of early Christianity.[37]

For this reason, says Gamble, "We must assume ... that the large majority of Christians in the early centuries of the church were illiterate, not because they were unique but because they were in this respect typical."[38]

What about the Jewish members of Paul's congregations? Biblical scholars have long assumed that literacy rates were relatively high among the Jews of antiquity, since written texts played a key role in Jewish worship and Jews relied heavily on written texts to guide their daily conduct. The Dead Sea Scrolls contain verses that speak of the community studying the laws of Torah together (1QS VI, 6–8; VIII, 11–12), and Josephus claims that Jews were trained to read and discuss their sacred texts throughout the Mediterranean world (*C. Ap.* 2.18; 2.25; 2.178). The Mishnah and Talmud also refer to schools in which apparently literate young boys were trained to study the Torah.[39]

In recent years, however, a number of studies have suggested that literacy levels might not have been as high among the Jews of antiquity as scholars have supposed.[40] Closer inspection of the literary evidence indicates that the

---

36. Harry Y. Gamble, *Books and Readers in the Early Church: A History of Early Christian Texts* (New Haven: Yale University Press, 1995), 2–11.

37. Ibid., 5.

38. Ibid., 6. Pieter J. J Botha ("Greco-Roman Literacy as Setting for New Testament Writings," *Neot* 26 [1992]: 195–215) offers a similar view: "If early Christianity reflects a fair cross section of society, it would follow that a rather small percentage within those groups were literate. What is probably true in any case is that we have a completely disproportionate impression of an extremely small group of Christians" (211).

39. See the extensive discussion of the evidence in Catherine Hezser, *Jewish Literacy in Roman Palestine* (TSAJ 81; Tübingen: Mohr Siebeck, 2001), 39–110.

40. In addition to the book by Hezser cited in the previous note, see Meir Bar-Ilan, "Writing in Ancient Israel and Early Judaism, Part Two: Scribes and Books in the Late Second Commonwealth and Rabbinic Period," in *Mikra: Text, Translation, Reading and Interpretation of the Hebrew Bible in Ancient Judaism and Early Christianity* (ed. Martin Jan Mulder; CRINT 2.1; Assen: Van Gorcum; Philadelphia: Fortress, 1988), 21–38; idem,

texts that have been used to argue for widespread Jewish literacy are in fact speaking about special subgroups within the broader Jewish community (the elite peers of Josephus, the priest-centered Dead Sea Scrolls community) or developments that arose later than the first century (the Torah-centered rabbinic schools). Additionally, comparative studies of literate cultures suggest that ancient Palestine lacked virtually all of the social factors necessary for the growth of widespread literacy.[41]

In her recent exhaustive review of the literary and inscriptional evidence for literacy in Roman Palestine, Catherine Hezser concluded that less than 10 percent of the Jewish population would have been able to read simple texts and sign their names throughout the imperial era.[42] Hezser describes Jewish literacy using the image of concentric circles.

> At the center one has to imagine a very small number of highly literate people who could read literary texts in both Hebrew/Aramaic and Greek. Then there was another, slightly broader circle of those who could read literary texts in either Hebrew/Aramaic or Greek only. They were surrounded by people who could not read literary texts but only short letters, lists, and accounts. A broader proportion of the population may have been able merely to identify individual letters, names, and labels. They as well as the vast majority of their entirely illiterate contemporaries had access to texts through intermediaries only.[43]

Perhaps the best that can be said at this point is that the evidence that has often been cited for widespread Jewish literacy in antiquity is questionable. Thus while it is quite reasonable to suppose that the Jewish members of Paul's churches would have been familiar with common biblical stories and key texts from their experience in Jewish synagogues, it would be hazardous to assume that they were capable of reading the text of Scripture (or any other text) on their own. As Hezser puts it, "Most Jews will have been aware of the symbolic value of the Torah, ... but [they] did not study its contents or participate in the intellectual discourse which developed among its experts. They may have occasionally listened to scholarly disputes, attended Torah-readings in synagogues, and memorized some central texts and stories, but they did

---

"Illiteracy in the Land of Israel in the First Centuries C.E.," in *Essays in the Social Scientific Study of Judaism and Jewish Society* (ed. Simcha Fishbane et al.; Hoboken, N.J.: Ktav, 1992), 2:46–61.

41. Heszer, *Jewish Literacy in Roman Palestine*, 37–38 (summary), 39–250 (full development).

42. Ibid., 496.

43. Ibid., 473.

not actually study the text of Torah for themselves."[44] In short, the presence of Jews in the early Christian churches tells us little or nothing about the overall literacy levels of the people to whom the New Testament documents were addressed, including the letters of Paul.

Occasionally scholars have suggested that Paul knew that the literate members of his churches made a practice of teaching their illiterate brothers and sisters the content of the Jewish Scriptures, so that he could reasonably expect his audiences to recognize and recall the broader literary context of the biblical texts that he mentions in his letters.[45] Unfortunately, this proposal overlooks the many social barriers that would have hindered such a system. At the most basic level, it is anachronistic to think that the illiterate masses who labored from sunup to sundown simply to survive would have had either the time or the intellectual proclivity to sit around with their social superiors and listen to biblical texts being read and discussed or to ask thoughtful questions about their content. It is even less likely that the early Christian house-churches, which as far as we know met only once a week, developed a system for training their illiterate members to memorize vast sections of the Jewish Scriptures, particularly when there is no mention of such a practice anywhere in the New Testament.[46]

As for the small number of literate elites in Paul's churches, it seems unlikely that many of them would have studied the Jewish Scriptures for themselves on a regular basis. Only the local synagogue would have owned a significant number of biblical scrolls, and the tensions that often existed between synagogue authorities and the followers of Jesus would have made it difficult for many Christians (especially non-Jews) to gain access to them.[47]

---

44. Ibid., 200 (see also 456).

45. Discussed most recently by J. Ross Wagner, *Heralds of the Good News: Isaiah and Paul "in Concert" in the Letter to the Romans* (NovTSup 101; Leiden: Brill, 2002), 33–39.

46. This is not to say that such feats of memory were impossible for illiterate people, only that there is no evidence for the existence of any sort of program or mechanism in the early churches for promoting this kind of activity. The Jewish synagogue is not an analogous situation, since even illiterate Jews were trained to know the content of their Scriptures from childhood. To gain a rough idea of how much an audience might be able to absorb and memorize as a result of weekly exposure to oral readings from Scripture, one only need think about the massive biblical illiteracy that characterizes many contemporary Christian churches despite the ready availability of written texts and nearly universal literacy.

47. While it seems reasonable to suppose that a wealthy Diaspora synagogue might have owned copies of all of the scrolls that we call "the LXX," we have no clear evidence to that effect. This expectation also presupposes that there was a standard collection of texts that a synagogue would want to own, a notion that many scholars would reject for

The sheer cost of purchasing some of the longer biblical scrolls would also have limited their availability, although it is possible that some of the wealthier Christians may have purchased a scroll or two for personal or congregational use.[48] Ordinarily, literate Christians who were interested in the Jewish Scriptures would have copied excerpts onto wax tablets, papyrus scrolls, or parchment notebooks during times when they had access to biblical scrolls, in addition to relying on their memories.[49] Some of these people may have

---

this period. As Harry Gamble notes, "The Scriptures of Judaism comprised not a single book but a collection of scrolls, five of the Torah and more of the prophetic books. These books were relatively costly, and their availability even to all synagogues cannot be taken for granted" (*Books and Readers*, 214).

48. Scholars who have highlighted the costliness and relative scarcity of books in antiquity include Harris, *Ancient Literacy*, 193–96, 224–25, and Millard, *Reading and Writing*, 164–65. Gamble is more ambivalent: on the one hand, he claims that "because the matter of their cost almost never comes up [among Christian authors], expense does not appear to have been an obstacle" (*Books and Readers*, 237; see also 231), yet he also speaks of "the small minority who were both literate and had the money to buy books" (88; see also 214). T. C. Skeat has argued that papyrus and written scrolls were in fact cheaper than other scholars have thought (discussed by Brian Abasciano in "Diamonds in the Rough: A Reply to Christopher Stanley Concerning the Reader Competency of Paul's Original Audiences," *NovT* 49 [2007]: 160 n. 32), while Cribiore has noted that the cost factor was less significant as one moved up the social scale: "Expensive for a farmer or villager, papyrus was nevertheless quite affordable in more elevated social milieus" (*Gymnastics of the Mind*, 147–48). The key question, however, is not whether people could afford to buy individual sheets of papyrus as writing materials but how many people in Paul's churches (which seem to have attracted few people of means) had sufficient funds to purchase a scroll of the Torah or the book of Isaiah.

49. For evidence concerning the common practice of note-taking in antiquity and its significance for the apostle Paul, see Stanley, *Paul and the Language of Scripture*, 73–78. Individuals for whom we have evidence of note-taking while reading include Socrates (according to Xenophon), Aristotle, Cicero, Pliny the Elder, Seneca, Plutarch, and Aulus Gellius. Several techniques were available: to copy the texts directly onto a papyrus scroll, to use one of the sturdier parchment notebooks that were already becoming available by this time, or to take notes onto a wax tablet (using a stylus) and then transfer them later to a more permanent repository. According to Harris (*Ancient Literacy*, 194), codices of up to ten wax tablets were common, with each tablet able to hold fifty or more words per side. Jocelyn Penny Small (*Wax Tablets of the Mind* [London: Routledge, 1997], 149) calls attention to a third-century C.E. relief of a boy holding a writing case containing his writing equipment (pens, ink, and knife) and remarks that "anyone doing research in a library, public or private, would carry such a writing case as well as tablets or papyri for taking notes." For more on the technology of note-taking, see Gamble, *Books and Readers*, 50–53; Millard, *Reading and Writing*, 63–69; Small, *Wax Tablets of the Mind*, 149–50, 169–74, 177–81; Cribiore, *Gymnastics of the Mind*, 153–57; C. H. Roberts and T. C. Skeat, *The Birth of the Codex* (Oxford: Oxford University Press for the British Academy, 1983), 18–29; Pat

read their notes aloud or quoted from memory in the Christian gatherings, but there is little reason to think that the physical scrolls would have been available for reading and exposition in most of the Christian house-churches. For ordinary first-century Christians, a first-hand encounter with a scroll of a biblical text was probably an unusual event.[50]

Even when the literate members of Paul's churches had access to the Jewish Scriptures, other factors would have hindered their ability to engage intelligently with the biblical text. Ancient scrolls had no chapter or verse divisions or other textual markers to aid the reader in locating specific passages, and ancient readers had no concordances or other tools to assist them.[51] As a result, only people who possessed a thorough knowledge of the Jewish Scriptures (invariably Jews) would have been capable of chasing down a particular passage in a biblical scroll. Others would have had to rely on these people for guidance. Second, Christians from non-Jewish backgrounds—the great majority by the time the New Testament texts were written—frequently entered the church with no idea of where to look for the biblical verses that were cited by Paul and other early Christian writers.[52] Those who were literate

---

E. Easterling and Bernard M. W. Knox, "Books and Readers in the Greek World," in *Greek Literature* (vol. 1 of *The Cambridge History of Classical Literature*; ed. Pat E. Easterling and Bernard M. W. Knox; Cambridge: Cambridge University Press, 1989), 18; Frederic Kenyon, *Books and Readers in Ancient Greece and Rome* (Oxford: Clarendon, 1932), 91–92.

50. Even if the words of Scripture were read aloud when Paul's churches gathered for worship (see 1 Tim 4:13), this need not imply that the actual biblical scrolls were present. Notebooks filled with biblical excerpts could have served the same purpose (see Gamble, *Books and Readers*, 214). Interestingly, there is no mention of public Scripture-reading in the few passages where Paul himself speaks about corporate worship (1 Cor 11:17–34; 14:1–40; see also Eph 5:19–20). Harry Gamble issues a similar warning against the uncritical assumption "that scripture reading belonged from the outset to specifically Christian worship or, if it did, that it played the same role that it did in the synagogue" (*Books and Readers*, 212). Like others, however, he eventually concludes that Paul's expectations concerning his readers' familiarity with Scripture imply that the Jewish Scriptures were regularly read and taught in the Pauline congregations (212–13). Joanna Dewey, after a careful survey of the evidence, concludes that "there is no evidence that Scripture readings were important in the worship of Paul's communities and it seems unlikely that they occurred at all" ("Textuality in an Oral Culture: A Survey of the Pauline Traditions," *Semeia* 39 [1994]: 52).

51. For a discussion of the problems associated with locating and retrieving specific passages in ancient books, see Small, *Wax Tablets of the Mind*, 14–25.

52. Of course, non-Jews were familiar with Jewish beliefs and practices, including their reverence for a collection of holy texts, but they did not (so far as we know) read the Jewish Scriptures for themselves. Even the literati of Greco-Roman society had wild ideas about the content of the Jewish Scriptures; see the citations in Menahem Stern, ed., *Greek*

and had attended Jewish synagogues (i.e., "God-fearers") might have had at least a general idea of the location of certain well-known passages, but most of their biblical knowledge would have come from oral sermons by synagogue leaders. Literate Gentiles who had studied biblical scrolls for themselves while attending the synagogue would have been quite rare.

In summary, the evidence suggests that not more than a few individuals in any given church, that is, those recruited from the educated (Jewish or non-Jewish) elites, would have been capable of reading and studying either the early Christian writings or the Jewish Scriptures for themselves, and many of them would have found it difficult to engage regularly with the biblical text.[53] Jewish Christians and non-Jews who had attended Jewish synagogues as "God-fearers" might have recognized biblical references that escaped Christians from non-Jewish backgrounds, but there is no reason to think that more than a handful (if any) would have been capable of recalling the literary context of less common passages or looking up biblical verses for themselves.

If this is correct, it makes little sense to suppose (as Hays does) that Paul inserted biblical references into his letters as a means of inviting his audiences to reflect in a new way on the broader context of his references. The same is true for Hays's contention that Paul was attempting to train his audiences to imitate his "revisionary" readings of Scripture.[54] Both of these theories are grounded in a view of Paul's audiences that pays little attention to current scholarly understandings of the literary capacities of a typical first-century audience. The only time when we can be confident that Paul expected his audiences to know and recall the context of a biblical reference is when he

---

and Latin Authors on Jews and Judaism (3 vols.; Jerusalem: Israel Academy of Sciences and Humanities, 1974–1984), and the discussion in Louis H. Feldman, *Jew and Gentile in the Ancient World* (Princeton: Princeton University Press, 1993). The earliest non-Jewish source that reveals a familiarity with the content of the Jewish Scriptures is an admiring quotation from Gen 1 in Pseudo-Longinus's *On the Sublime* toward the end of the first century.

53. Dewey reaches the same conclusion in "Textuality in an Oral Culture," 47–54. For more on the subject, see Pieter J. J. Botha, "Greco-Roman Literacy"; idem, "The Verbal Art of the Pauline Letters: Rhetoric, Performance and Practice," in *Rhetoric and the New Testament: Essays from the 1992 Heidelberg Conference* (ed. Stanley E. Porter and Thomas H. Olbricht; JSNTSup 90; Sheffield: Sheffield Academic Press, 1993), 409–28.

54. It is interesting to note that these claims about Paul attempting to influence his audiences to read the text of Scripture in a new way are largely absent from Hays's earlier essays that were recently republished in Hays, *Conversion of the Imagination* (see n. 1). The sole exception is the first essay in the volume, "The Conversion of the Imagination: Scripture and Eschatology in 1 Corinthians" (1–24), which not surprisingly was the last to be written.

cites only the relevant points of a story or other passage and leaves it to his audience to fill in the gaps, as in his allusive references to the Abraham narrative in Rom 4:1–24 and Gal 3:6–9 or the exodus story in 1 Cor 10:1–11 or 2 Cor 3:7–18. Even here we cannot be sure that Paul's initial audiences would have perceived his interpretations as "revisionary," since this assumes that the audiences were familiar with other readings of the text before they encountered Paul's version. For many of them, Paul's interpretation might not have differed substantially from what they had already learned in Christian circles.

These observations about Paul's audiences in no way detract from the many valuable insights that Richard Hays and his followers have put forward concerning the manner in which Paul himself read and interpreted the Jewish Scriptures. In fact, Hays's careful attention to the broader literary context of Paul's biblical references has convinced many scholars that they had underestimated the thoughtfulness with which Paul reflected on the Jewish Scriptures. Even scholars who disagree with Hays's readings of specific texts remain indebted to him for the questions that he raises and the thoughtful and elegant manner in which he frames his answers. Clearly, the figure of metalepsis has proved to be a useful tool in the hands of scholars who know how to wield it.

Like all tools, however, this one can be misused. It is interesting to note that neither of the two literary critics whom Richard Hays cites as his primary theoretical influences makes the same mistake that Hays does in conflating historical and literary audiences.[55] In *The Figure of Echo*, John Hollander focuses on the activity of the literate reader who is familiar with a range of texts and thus capable of recognizing them when they are referenced in a later text. No poetic trope is involved unless a reference can be recognized. As Hollander puts it,

> The reader of texts, in order to overhear echoes, must have some kind of access to an earlier voice, and to its cave of resonant signification, analogous to that of the author of the later text. When such access is lost in a community of reading, what may have been an allusion may fade in prominence; and yet a scholarly recovery of the context would restore the allusion, by revealing the intent as well as by showing means.[56]

---

55. On the influence of John Hollander and Thomas Greene on Hays's thought, see Hays, *Echoes of Scripture*, 14–21, 27, 173–78; idem, "On the Rebound," 43, 46, 59, 72, 80, 82, 95–96.

56. Hollander, *Figure of Echo*, 65–66. The subtitle of the book ("A Mode of Allusion in Milton and After") indicates clearly that Hollander is concerned with the activities of a

In other words, the contemporary scholarly reader can bring the trope to life even if it would have been overlooked by the original audience. This is precisely what Hays is doing with Paul's letters: presenting a scholarly retrieval of an earlier voice that Paul might arguably have heard in Scripture. The results are of course speculative, but no more so than for any other author.

Problems arise, however, when Hays tries to bring Paul's historical audience into the analytical picture. Hays overlooks the vast gulf that separates the cultured readers of Milton's poetry (the subject of Hollander's study) from the ancient audiences to whom Paul addressed his letters. The materials that Hollander analyzes in his book were written for a literate audience that was familiar with many classic works of literature and attuned to the presence of poetic echoes and allusions. Paul's letters, by contrast, were written for a very different type of audience, one that was largely illiterate and possessed only a limited acquaintance with the text of Scripture. By ignoring this difference, Hays has constructed a model of Paul's rhetoric of Scripture that is historically invalid. What Paul offers to his audiences is not a direct encounter with the voice of Scripture but a highly selective interpretation of that voice. Not surprisingly, that voice consistently upholds Paul's arguments. Few of Paul's original hearers would have been in a position to argue with his readings.

In a similar way, Thomas Greene, another of Hays's stated influences, seeks to uncover how literate authors of the Renaissance period engaged with earlier texts and incorporated them into their writings.[57] Greene's study is heavily author-centered; he has almost nothing to say about Renaissance authors using references to earlier works to influence their readers to adopt revisionist interpretations of the works that they cite. Greene does talk about authors struggling with the meaning and influence of earlier texts and rewriting them for later times, but the struggles that he describes take place in the creative psyche of the author.[58] The revisionist effects of the new literary product are apparent only to other literate people (whether ancient or modern) who are familiar with the author's literary predecessors.[59]

---

literate age; Hollander's discussion of the literary figure that he calls "metalepsis" must be understood against the backdrop of these ideas.

57. Greene, *Light in Troy* (see n. 7).

58. Ibid., 37–48. In his overview of ancient modes of literary imitation (54–80), Greene never asks how literate readers might have responded to an author's deviations from a known literary forebear.

59. Unlike Hays, Greene distinguishes between allusions, i.e., "usages of earlier texts that the reader must recognize in order to read competently," and repetitions, "whose provenance my be obscure or irrelevant and matters little for the reading of the poem" (*Light in Troy*, 49). Hollander makes a similar distinction between allusion, which requires

In summary, interpreters of Paul's letters can learn much from Hays's thoughtful attempts to make sense of Paul's engagement with the text of Scripture, but they should be wary about imitating Hays's use of "metalepsis" as a tool for describing how ancient audiences might have interpreted Paul's biblical references. Historical studies suggest that most of the people in Paul's audiences would have been incapable of drawing the kinds of interpretive inferences that Hays and his followers believe that Paul wanted them to derive from his references. Either Paul was rhetorically inept in failing to take account of the literary capabilities of his audiences or Hays and his followers have misjudged what Paul was doing with his biblical references. We cannot have it both ways.

4. Taking the Audience Seriously

Two brief examples will illustrate how different constructions of Paul's audiences can affect the way we understand the use of Scripture in Paul's letters. One comes from a passage that is tangential to Paul's arguments (2 Cor 4:13), the other from a passage that plays a central role in his theological reflection (Gal 3:6–14). The first reading of each passage will highlight some of the problems that might arise if the audience were to make a serious effort to recall the broader context of Paul's biblical reference, retrace his interpretation of the passage, and approve his handling of the biblical text. This is what Hays suggests that Paul expected his audiences to do. The second reading will look at the same passage through the eyes of an audience that knows only as much of the Scriptures as Paul presupposes in the letter in which the passage appears. The discussion of both passages is intentionally narrow, highlighting only those points that relate to the question at hand.[60] The purpose of these examples is to demonstrate some of the difficulties that arise from a more critical application of Hays's model.

4.1. 2 Corinthians 4:13

The citation of Ps 115:1 (LXX) in 2 Cor 4:13 is one of the more obscure biblical references in the Pauline corpus. The quotation (together with the application

---

intentionality on the part of the author and a common library of texts linking author and audience, and echo, which can be present regardless of whether it is intended by the author or recognized by the original audience (*Figure of Echo*, 64–65). Both authors seem to regard allusion as a conscious rhetorical strategy and repetition/echo as a poetic trope that has no obvious rhetorical value.

60. Both examples are adapted from Stanley, *Arguing with Scripture*, 98–101, 121–30.

that follows in 4:13–15) occupies a fairly minor position in a lengthy chain of arguments that Paul brings forward to defend his ministry against questions that had been raised by some of the Corinthians (2:14–6:10). The function of the quotation is difficult to characterize. It does not serve as a "proof" for a specific argument; in fact, its link to the preceding verses is so loose that the audience would likely have been puzzled by its appearance.

The interpretive comments that frame the verse seem to suggest that Paul viewed the quotation (or wanted the Corinthians to view it) as a biblical warrant for his own ministry of preaching Christ despite all manner of troubles and opposition (see 4:1, 8–11). The quotation consists of only three words in the Greek (ἐπίστευσα, διὸ ἐλάλησα), but Paul makes the most of every syllable. Just as the psalmist "believed" and therefore "spoke," says Paul, "So also we [i.e., Paul, using the editorial "we"] believe and therefore keep on speaking" the message about Jesus' resurrection and the future resurrection of those who follow him (4:14).[61] The shift from the aorist tense in the quotation to the present tense in Paul's interpretation is significant: he continues to have faith and to preach about Christ despite the troubles enumerated in 4:8–11. When read in this way, the quotation does function somewhat like a "proof," since it serves to justify Paul's ministry, as do the other arguments in this portion of his letter.

So what might the Corinthians have made of this quotation? An audience that knew the source of the reference would have been taken aback by Paul's handling of the passage. While he follows the wording of the biblical text precisely, the sense in which he uses the verse diverges so far from the original context as to raise questions about Paul's reliability as an interpreter. In the standard edition of the LXX, the verse that Paul quotes is the first verse of a new psalm (Ps 115:1) rather than the midpoint, as in the Hebrew (Ps 116:10), but the issue is the same in either case: what the psalmist "spoke" was not "good news" as in Paul's case but rather a word for which he was "humbled" by God.[62] The tone of complaint continues into the next verse, so Paul could

---

61. As many commentators have noted, Paul's introductory comment, "having the same spirit of faith," constitutes an implicit claim that his experience of faith parallels that of the psalmist.

62. In the Hebrew text, the second line reports what the author said in his time of trouble ("I am greatly afflicted"); in the Greek text, on the other hand, the quotation is replaced by a statement describing what transpired after the "speaking" ("and I was greatly humbled"). Abasciano insists that the psalmist's words here carry no negative connotation, since they are rooted in an attitude of "faith" ("I believed") and appear in a psalm of thanksgiving ("Diamonds in the Rough," 173–75). But there are other psalms of thanksgiving in which the psalmist speaks of being humbled after engaging in negative patterns

not possibly have misunderstood the context. The problem remains even if we assume that the audience would have recognized a link between the sufferings of Paul described in 2 Cor 4:8–12 and those of the psalmist.[63] Apart from this broad point of contact, the context of the psalm would have offered little help in clarifying the link that Paul had in mind, so the Corinthians would have had to figure out for themselves the significance of the reference.[64] An audience that was familiar with the psalm might well have been disturbed by the discrepancy between the original sense of the words that Paul cites and the way in which he uses them in his argument. This in turn could have led them to question whether they could trust Paul's skills as an interpreter.

An audience that knew nothing about the source of the reference, by contrast, would have had to infer the meaning of the quotation from the letter itself. The clearest piece of evidence appears in the introductory phrase, where Paul declares that he has "the same spirit of faith" as the psalmist, which in turn leads him to "speak" as did the psalmist. From the verses that precede the quotation, the audience could have inferred that Paul's use of the words "faith" and "believing" in 4:13 was simply another way of speaking about how he perseveres in his ministry despite obstacles.[65] From the ensuing verses they could have discerned that the "speaking" mentioned in 4:13 referred to Paul's

---

of speech (e.g., Pss 29:7–8 LXX, 72:13–15 LXX), and this is probably what Ps 116:10 meant in the Hebrew. Moreover, Abasciano's interpretation of ἐπίστευσα in v. 1 as an expression of faith disconnects the word from v. 2, where the psalmist summarizes his speech in the words, "Every man is a liar." The psalm is awkward however it is to be interpreted, but the assumption that Paul's language in 2 Cor 4:13 serves as a reliable guide to its meaning is dubious at best.

63. Several commentators have noted the references to sufferings in both passages and suggested that Paul may have had the parallel in mind, though the meaning implied by the link remains unclear; see Philip E. Hughes, *Paul's Second Epistle to the Corinthians* (Grand Rapids: Eerdmans, 1962), 146–47; Margaret E. Thrall, *A Critical and Exegetical Commentary on the Second Epistle to the Corinthians* (2 vols.; ICC; Edinburgh: T&T Clark, 1994), 1:340–41.

64. Most commentators seem to think that Paul simply ran across a set of words that sounded like a good "motto" for his ministry and then copied them down (or memorized them) for later use without regard for their original context. Jan Lambrecht typifies this view: "Since in the psalm the 'speaking out' addresses God it is rather unlikely that Paul, who changes that speaking into preaching to people, intends to refer to the broader context of that psalm" (*Second Corinthians* [Collegeville, Minn.: Liturgical Press, 1999], 74). For an argument to the contrary, see Frances Young and David F. Ford, *Meaning and Truth in 2 Corinthians* (Grand Rapids: Eerdmans, 1987), 63–69.

65. This would be true even if the audience failed to understand the somewhat tortured imagery of 4:11–12 that immediately preceded the quotation, since the idea runs throughout the passage.

ministry of preaching about Jesus and the future resurrection. With the help of these interpretive cues, they could have figured out that Paul was implicitly claiming that the example of the psalmist served as a model for his own behavior. Exactly why Paul should have chosen to quote this particular verse of Scripture would have remained unclear, but a sympathetic audience could have concluded that Paul's ability to apply a biblical text such as this to himself reinforced the validity of his ministry.

4.2. GALATIANS 3:6–14

The overall argument of Gal 3:6–14 is well-known and need not detain us here. Most of the scholarly disagreements over the meaning of this passage pertain directly or indirectly to the manner in which Paul uses Scripture to support his arguments. But few scholars have asked how these arguments might have appeared to the Galatians. The answer depends on how well they knew the context of the verses to which Paul refers in this difficult passage.

An audience that knew the original context of all of Paul's quotations in Gal 3:6–14 would have found Paul's arguments from Scripture both helpful and confusing. On the one hand, Paul's references to Abraham in 3:6–9 would have appeared both clear and convincing to an audience that knew the Abraham narrative and shared Paul's Christian presuppositions. Both of the quotations that Paul adduces (from Gen 15:6 in 3:6 and Gen 12:3 in 3:8) are central to the stories in which they appear, and both would have evoked memories of God's promises to Abraham (and thus to Israel) and Abraham's faithful response. In both cases the sense that Paul derives from the verse is consistent with the original context, though a careful reader would have noticed that Paul has adapted the wording of the second quotation slightly to highlight the connection.[66] The fact that Paul repeats key words from the quotation in his interpretive comments ("believe" in 3:7, "justify" in 3:8, "blessed" in 3:9) would have strengthened the impression that Paul's interpretation of the Abraham story was true to the text. From these verses a sympathetic audience could have drawn the conclusion that the Scriptures of Judaism upheld Paul's claim that faith alone is the basis for God's acceptance of Gentiles (i.e., the Galatians).

---

66. The replacement of πᾶσαι αἱ φυλαί with πάντα τὰ ἔθνη and the related omission of τῆς γῆς has no basis in the textual tradition of Gen 12:3. While it is possible that Paul has accidentally conflated the wording with the very similar language of Gen 18:18, it seems more likely that Paul has substituted a close synonym to make the application of the verse to "Gentiles" (τὰ ἔθνη) more apparent. See the discussion in Stanley, *Paul and the Language of Scripture*, 237.

The same cannot be said for the quotations in 3:10–14, where a literate audience could have found ample reason to question the validity of Paul's biblical argumentation.

(1) In the case of 3:10 (quoting Deut 27:26), the primary problem is the apparent conflict between the wording of the quotation and Paul's assertion in the first part of the verse. Where the quotation pronounces a curse on the person who does not continually follow the requirements of Torah, Paul appears to apply the curse to those who seek to *comply* with the laws of Torah.[67] This blatantly contradicts the original sense of Deut 27, which contains a long series of curses on individuals who violate specific provisions of Torah.[68] The fact that the verse fails to support Paul's assertion (and could, in fact, be read as upholding the views of his opponents) could have raised serious questions about the legitimacy of Paul's handling of Scripture and perhaps of his entire argument.[69]

(2) A similar situation arises in the case of the quotation in 3:11. When comparing Paul's interpretation with the original context of Hab 2:4, the audience would have discovered significant discrepancies. By dropping the word

---

67. Martin Luther saw the problem clearly: "Now these two sentences of Paul and Moses seem clean contrary. Paul saith: Whoever shall do the works of the law, is accursed. Moses saith: Whoever shall not do the works of the law is accursed. How shall the two sayings be reconciled together? Or else (which is more) how shall the one be proved by the other?" (*A Commentary on St. Paul's Epistle to the Galatians* [ed. Philip S. Watson; London: Clarke, 1953], 244). For an extended discussion of the problem and recent attempts to resolve it, see Christopher D. Stanley, "'Under a Curse': A Fresh Reading of Gal 3.10–14," *NTS* 36 (1990): 481–511.

68. The contradiction could be avoided if the informed audience understood the "curse" in 3:10a as a threat rather than a present reality (see Stanley, "Under a Curse," 497–501). But since most modern interpreters have overlooked this solution to the problem, we should not assume that it would have been evident to the Galatians.

69. Additional questions might have arisen from the fact that Paul quotes Deut 27:26 in a form that differs greatly from the standard LXX text. While some of the deviations can probably be traced to the use of a different *Vorlage*, others are clearly Pauline adaptations, such as the insertion of the words, "everything that is written in the book of the law" (cf. Deut 28:58) in place of "all the words of this law" in the middle of the verse. The cumulative effect of the variations and adaptations is to dehistoricize the text by eliminating all references to the covenant ceremony in Deuteronomy. But the language of the resultant quotation is not inconsistent with the original context of Deut 27, so the audience might not have found serious reason to be concerned. For a fuller discussion of how the wording of the quotation relates to Deut 27:26, see Stanley, *Paul and the Language of Scripture*, 238–43.

μου from the quotation and ignoring the first clause of the verse,[70] Paul has converted a statement about God's faithfulness into a proleptic reference to Christian faith in God. A critical reader might have noticed that neither the verse that Paul quotes nor the broader context actually supports Paul's assertion in 3:11a, since there is nothing in Hab 2:4 that speaks against the biblical requirement that the people of God should follow the laws of Torah. All that Paul's opponents had to do to undermine his argument was to point out (as they had no doubt done already) that obedience to Torah was the best and only way to express one's (Christian) faith toward God.

(3) As with the previous two verses, an audience that was aware of the context of Paul's quotation might well have concluded that the verse that Paul quotes in Gal 3:12 actually lends more support to the views of his opponents than to Paul's position, since Lev 18:5 says clearly that obedience to God's laws is the pathway to "life." As in 3:11, the counterargument to Paul's position is obvious: there is nothing in Lev 18 that pits faith against obedience to Torah, so the followers of Jesus should obey the laws of Torah as an expression of their faith in God. Contrary to his intentions, Paul's clumsy handling of Scripture in 3:10–12 might actually have persuaded an audience that knew the context of his quotations to embrace the views of his opponents.

(4) The final quotation in this passage, the excerpt from Deut 21:23 in 3:13, would have added more fuel to the audience's growing distrust of Paul's handling of Scripture. A glance at the original passage would have shown them that the verse that Paul quotes here actually refers to the ancient practice of hanging the dead body of a convicted criminal on a tree for public display,

---

70. The LXX of Hab 2:4 diverges sharply from the MT: "If he (?) should draw back, my soul will not be pleased with him (?); the righteous person will live by my faith(fulness)." The subject of the initial verb is unclear; a masculine antecedent is required by the αὐτῷ at the end of the clause, but there is no obvious referent in the broader context. The sense of the verse will not allow a continuation of the reference to καιρός in v. 3a (despite the marginal note to this effect in *A New English Translation of the Septuagint and the Other Greek Translations Traditionally Included under That Title* [ed. Albert Pietersma and Benjamin G. Wright; New York: Oxford University Press, 2007], and taking ἐρχόμενος as the antecedent (i.e., reading the word as an indefinite nominal participle rather than an adverbial participle modifying ἥξει) is awkward as well. The only other alternative, to supply an indefinite human subject (he/she), as in the translation above, leaves the verse disconnected from the broader context. Perhaps it was this very disconnection from the context that led Paul to disregard the context when he adopted this verse as a motto for his gospel (see Rom 1:17). For more on the text of Hab 2:4, see Stanley, *Paul and the Language of Scripture*, 83–84. For the argument that Paul grounded his use of Hab 2:4 on a serious engagement with the broader context of Habakkuk, see Hays, *Echoes of Scripture*, 39–41; Francis Watson, *Paul and the Hermeneutics of Faith* (London: T&T Clark, 2004), 78–126.

not the redeeming death of a crucified Messiah. Only by extracting the verse from its original context and revising its wording can Paul claim that it refers to the death of Jesus.[71] For an audience that was aware of the original context, the tendentiousness of such a reading would have been utterly glaring.

Thus we see that an audience that was familiar with the original context of Paul's quotations in Gal 3:10–13 would have been led inexorably toward a point of view that was the opposite of what Paul intended. When they compared Paul's interpretive comments with the original context, such an audience would have discovered that the passages not only failed to support Paul's arguments but could in fact be understood as upholding the views of his opponents. The fact that Paul had changed the wording of the text in several instances to create a closer fit with his argument might have reinforced their suspicions. Taken together, the evidence suggests that Paul did not expect his actual addressees in Galatia to be capable of checking his references in this manner.

The experience of an audience that was unfamiliar with the context of Paul's quotations would have been quite different. The only text of Scripture that Paul clearly requires his hearers to know in Gal 3:6–14 is the story of Abraham, to which he refers several times in 3:6–9. As we noted earlier, Paul's handling of this passage is broadly consistent with the original storyline, although he obviously reads it through a Christian lens. As a result, the audience would likely have concluded that the text of Scripture supported Paul's position.[72]

When they came to the dense biblical argumentation of Gal 3:10–13, on the other hand, an audience that was ignorant of the original context of Paul's quotations would have had to rely on Paul's interpretive comments for their understanding of the verses that he cites, since he makes no explicit reference to their original contexts. As a result, they would have been unaware of most of the problems that arise from a comparison of Paul's quotations with their original context.

---

71. Two revisions can definitely be attributed to Paul: the omission of ὑπὸ θεοῦ (clearly an embarrassment when applied to Jesus' death) and the replacement of κεκατηραμένος with ἐπικατάρατος from 3:10 (to eliminate the verbal implication that the "curse" was pronounced before the victim was "hung on a tree"). For more on the way Paul handles the wording of the quotation, see Stanley, *Paul and the Language of Scripture*, 245-48.

72. Such an audience might not have recognized 3:6 as a quotation, since the marking is ambiguous (καθώς is always followed by γέγραπται when used with quotations in Paul's letters), but this would not have seriously interfered with their understanding of the passage.

(1) The conflict between Paul's statement and the verse that he cites in 3:10 is evident even without consulting the original context. An audience that knew the verse only from Paul's letter would doubtless have found Paul's argument obscure at this point. But since they could not consult the original context for clarification, they would have had no choice but to leave the tension unresolved as they continued through the letter.

(2) The quotation from Hab 2:4 in Gal 3:11b would probably have passed by the audience unnoticed unless they had encountered the same verse elsewhere, since the statement is not marked as a quotation. The second part of the verse is clearly meant to ground the assertion in the first part, but Paul gives no sign that he is quoting a verse of Scripture here as opposed to issuing his own pronouncement on the subject. The relation of 3:11 to 3:10 is unclear, but a sympathetic audience would have found nothing here to hinder them from following Paul's argument.[73]

(3) The quotation from Lev 18:5 in Gal 3:12b is also unmarked, but the fact that the second clause stands in syntactical tension with the first part of the verse (i.e., the pronouns have no antecedents) would have signified that a quotation was present. The meaning of the quotation might have seemed a bit obscure at first due to the dangling pronouns, but in the wake of 3:10 the audience could probably have figured out that the word "them" referred to the precepts of Torah and that 3:12a aimed to contrast the "doing" of Torah with the way of (Christian) faith. Since they would have been unaware of Paul's questionable application of the verse from Leviticus, their questions would have centered on the validity of Paul's assertion in the first part of the verse, not on the quotation. The fact that Paul could quote a verse of Scripture to reinforce his point may have helped to commend his argument to such an audience, although even they might have wondered if the quotation actually upheld Paul's assertion in the first part of the verse.[74]

---

73. The first part of 3:11 ("that no one is justified before God by Torah") appears on the surface to be a blatant contradiction of the quotation in 3:10. But since audiences normally assume that an author's argument is coherent until proven otherwise, a possible solution would be to take 3:11a as a restriction of 3:10b, implying that no one actually lives up to the requirement of Deut 27:26. Of course, Paul does not actually say this, and many scholars have argued that the thought is foreign to Paul (see the discussion in Stanley, "Under a Curse," 482–83). But it is easy to see how the language of the passage might lead one to that (possibly incorrect) conclusion. The problem arises from the terseness of Paul's language in 3:10–12, which requires the audience to figure out the inner links of the argument for themselves. This includes both the transitions between the verses and the relation between Paul's assertions and the verses that he cites to support them.

74. Anyone who had been exposed to Judaism might have found reason to question Paul's assumption that a concern for "doing" the Torah necessarily implies a lack of "faith."

(4) As with the other verses in this section, an audience that was ignorant of the context of Paul's quotations would have had no reason to question his treatment of Deut 21:23. Their only cue to the meaning of the verse would have come from Paul's framing comments, where the verse is applied to the death of Jesus on the cross. The logic of the primary argument would still have been obscure, since Paul simply assumes that the audience can figure out how Jesus being "cursed" on the cross could have redeemed others from the "curse of the law" (see 3:10).[75] But the meaning of the quotation (and its application to Jesus) would have been clear as long as the audience accepted the implied equivalence between crucifixion and being "hanged on a tree." Here again the fact that Paul could appeal to the authoritative text of Scripture in support of his argument would have commended his position to the audience.

On the whole, then, an audience that was unaware of the context of Paul's quotations would have found little cause for concern and ample reason to be persuaded by Paul's arguments from Scripture in Gal 3:6–14. Of course, the argument that the quotations were meant to support is by no means clear, and the audience might not have been willing to grant the validity of all of Paul's assertions. But with the possible exception of 3:10, nothing in the quotations would have detracted from the argument. The fact that Paul could quote Scripture in his favor might even have inclined the audience to give him the benefit of the doubt in questionable cases.

In summary, it seems clear that the response of the Galatians to Paul's arguments in Gal 3:6–14 would have been heavily conditioned by their prior familiarity with the biblical text. Those with an extensive knowledge of Scripture would have found Paul's quotations troubling, to say the least, and some might even have concluded that a contextual reading of Paul's quotations offered more support for the views of Paul's opponents than for Paul. By contrast, those who knew less about the context of Paul's quotations would have been insulated from these problems.

The inconsistency between "faith" and "doing" is simply taken for granted in these verses, not argued. In fact, Paul's opponents could have used the quotations in 3:11–12 to argue for the opposite position (i.e., the priority of Torah over faith) by reversing the quotations and changing a few of the words in the framing verses. Doing this yields the following (non-Pauline) argument: "It is obvious that no one is justified by God through faith (alone), because (Scripture says,) 'The one who does these things will live by them.' But the righteousness that comes through Torah (nonetheless) requires faith, since (it says,) 'The righteous person will live by faith.'"

75. Perhaps he had used similar language when he was with them (see 3:1), so that he had reason to believe that they would be able to grasp his point.

While we must be careful about generalizing from such limited data, the reactions that we have posited for each of these audiences lends prima facie support to the thesis that Paul constructed his biblical arguments for an "implied audience" that was incapable of consulting the original context of most of his biblical references. As it turns out, this internal evidence coheres well with the external evidence provided by recent studies of literacy and illiteracy in the ancient world. It also agrees with what we know about the difficulties that even literate Christians would have faced in accessing and using biblical scrolls. Taken together, these diverse lines of evidence suggest that Paul recognized and took seriously the limited biblical literacy of his audiences and framed his arguments in such a way that the illiterate members of his audience could have grasped his essential point without having to rely on others to explain to them how he was interpreting the Jewish Scriptures.[76]

---

76. This point is developed more fully in Stanley, *Arguing with Scripture* (see n. 11).

Synagogue Influence and Scriptural Knowledge among the Christians of Rome

Bruce N. Fisk

1. Paul's Use of Scripture in Romans

In an important monograph on the rhetoric of biblical quotations in Paul's epistles, Christopher Stanley gives particular attention to Paul's first-century audiences and to the problem of assessing their competence as readers. The problem, as Stanley sees it, is that scholars too easily equate Paul's "intended" or "implied" audience with his letters' actual recipients:

> Paul routinely assumes that his audience not only accepts the authority of the Jewish Scriptures but also knows the biblical text well enough to supply the background and context for many of his quotations. In some cases he requires the audience to infer how a quotation fits into his broader argument as well. This evidence had led most scholars to conclude that Paul's first-century addressees must have been reasonably familiar with the text of the Jewish Scriptures, whether from Paul's earlier teaching or their own study, since Paul would not have made impossible demands upon his audience.[1]

For a number of reasons, Stanley is not at all sure that the assumptions Paul made about his audiences were always correct.[2] Scholars may err, then, if they too readily equate Paul's ideal audience with the facts on the ground in Paul's churches (including Rome) and if they assume uncritically the success of Paul's speech acts. According to Stanley, literacy rates in the Christian community would not have been substantially higher than in the general

---

1. Christopher D. Stanley, *Arguing with Scripture: The Rhetoric of Quotations in the Letters of Paul* (New York: T&T Clark, 2004), 38; see also 48, 56 n. 48.
2. Ibid., 65.

population, where the upper limit was likely between 10 and 20 percent,[3] and Paul's audiences would not have had "relatively free access" to Jewish Scriptures in Greek, in any case.[4] Accordingly, Paul would not have expected his Gentile audiences "to recognize and appreciate his many allusions and other unmarked references to the Jewish Scriptures."[5] Paul does sometimes assume (e.g., Rom 4:9–22; 9:10–13; 11:1–4; Gal 3:6–9; 4:21–31) that his audience will be familiar with "the background and context of specific verses" of Scripture,[6] but a number of his Scripture citations (e.g., Rom 2:24; 9:25–26; 10:5–8, 18; 1 Cor 14:21; 2 Cor 4:13; Gal 3:10) "diverge ... far from any obvious contextual reading," so that we should not assume that he was engaging his audience on the level of biblical exegesis.[7]

Stanley's approach to the study of Paul's readers posits "three idealized groups"—the *informed audience*, the *competent audience*, and the *minimal audience*—each of whom would have heard Paul's letter differently.[8] According to Stanley, few in Paul's actual first-century audiences would have belonged to the first group, those most able to recognize his scriptural citations and allusions, recall their source, and feel the full impact of his exegesis. Stanley grounds this contention on the belief that "except for the few people who had attended the synagogue as Jewish sympathizers, no one in Paul's churches had any significant knowledge of the Jewish Scriptures before entering the Christian Church."[9]

There are several implicit claims in this statement, each of which merits attention: (1) synagogue attendance would normally have led to a knowledge of the Scriptures; (2) Paul's churches were predominantly Gentile; (3) only a few of those Gentiles came from the ranks of the synagogue-attending "God-fearers"; and (4) in order to enter the Christian church, those few God-fearing Gentiles severed their ties with the synagogue.

---

3. Ibid., 41, 44–45.

4. Ibid., 41.

5. Ibid., 48. On this point Stanley (ibid., 47 n. 29, 38 n.2) takes to task both Richard B. Hays, *Echoes of Scripture in the Letters of Paul* (New Haven: Yale University Press, 1989), 27–28, and J. Ross Wagner, *Heralds of the Good News: Isaiah and Paul "in Concert" in the Letter to the Romans* (NovTSup 101; Leiden: Brill, 2002), 33–39.

6. Stanley, *Arguing with Scripture*, 43; see also 2, 172.

7. Ibid., 55–56 and n. 46.

8. See ibid., 68–69 for a delineation of these three constructs. Briefly, the *informed* audience "knows the original context of every one of Paul's quotations"; the *competent* audience "knows just enough of the Jewish Scriptures to grasp the point of Paul's quotations in their current rhetorical context"; and the *minimal* audience has "little specific knowledge about the content of the Jewish Scriptures."

9. Ibid., 45; see also 64–65, 68.

In order to evaluate these claims, we must pose several questions. Most important among these are: What do we know about the way Scripture was read and studied in the early synagogues? And what role, if any, did the synagogue play in the ongoing theological and biblical formation of the earliest Christian communities?

The limited goal of this essay is to explore these questions in the context of Paul's epistle to the Romans, a letter well known for its extensive and sophisticated appeals to Scripture. Judging by the frequency and range of both marked and unmarked citations in the letter, Paul appears to assume not only that his Roman readers affirmed biblical authority but also that they enjoyed substantial biblical knowledge. As we have seen, however, Paul's assumptions may be incorrect. Was there, then, a positive correlation between Paul's assumptions about his "ideal" readers and the social-historical reality of early Roman Christianity?[10] Stanley may be right that "the letter gives us little more than [Paul's] best guess as to what they might have known," since he had not even visited the city,[11] but it is not hard to imagine Paul knowing things about his readers that we latecomers do not. Perhaps he knew, for example, whether or not many of his (predominantly Gentile) readers had longstanding associations with (predominantly Jewish) communities where Israel's sacred texts were kept, read, and proclaimed. If the contingent situation of Paul's readers is *an* (even if not *the*) interpretive key to the argument of Romans, including its appeals to Scripture, as many scholars contend,[12]

---

10. A contingent purpose for Romans has been increasingly axiomatic since F. C. Baur's seminal essay, "Über Zweck und Veranlassung des Römerbriefs und die damit zusammenhängenden Verhältnisse der römischen Gemeinde," *Tübinger Zeitschrift für Theologie* 3 (1836): 59–178. See Wolfgang Wiefel, "The Jewish Community in Ancient Rome and the Origins of Roman Christianity," in *The Romans Debate* (ed. Karl P. Donfried; rev. ed.; Peabody, Mass.: Hendrickson, 1991), 85; A. J. M. Wedderburn, *The Reasons for Romans* (Minneapolis: Fortress, 1991), 4; Chrys Caragounis, "From Obscurity to Prominence: The Development of the Roman Church between Romans and 1 Clement," in *Judaism and Christianity in First Century Rome* (ed. Karl P. Donfried and Peter Richardson; Grand Rapids: Eerdmans, 1998), 246–47, 263.

11. Stanley, *Arguing with Scripture*, 141; see also 65.

12. See n. 10. Doubtful on this point is Hays: "To read Romans in light of conjectures about its historical purpose within Paul's ministry is … a surprisingly unsatisfying speculative exercise" (*Echoes of Scripture*, 35). Similarly dubious is Wagner: "A reader-focused approach to Paul's use of scripture in Romans that depends heavily on a reconstructed *historical* audience is clearly inadequate by itself for interpreting the letter on historical, let alone literary or theological, grounds" (*Heralds of the Good News*, 34). Even less inclined to put stock in reconstructions of the situation in Rome is Luke T. Johnson, *Reading Romans: A Literary and Theological Commentary* (New York: Crossroad, 1997), 196 (see also

we would do well to learn all we can about Paul's Roman readers, including their channels of communication, lines of influence, meeting structures, and relationships with their non-Christian Jewish contemporaries. Accordingly, two historical questions animate this study: What can we know about the historical relationship between church and synagogue in mid-first century Rome? And how much has the synagogue shaped, schooled, and influenced Paul's earliest Roman readers?

2. Historical Contingencies in First-Century Rome

2.1. The Edict of Claudius

At some point during the rule of Emperor Claudius (41–54 C.E.), some, perhaps many, Jews were expelled from Rome.[13] Orosius (385–420 C.E.) dates the expulsion to Claudius's ninth year, or 49 C.E., during the period Claudius was campaigning to restore Rome's ancient rites and constrain foreign cults (47–52 C.E.):

> Josephus reports, "In his ninth year the Jews were expelled by Claudius from the city." But Suetonius, who speaks as follows, influences me more: "Claudius expelled from Rome the Jews constantly rioting at the instigation of Christ [*Christo*]." As far as whether he had commanded that the Jews rioting against Christ [*Christum*] be restrained and checked or also had wanted the Christians, as persons of a cognate religion, to be expelled, it is not at all to be discerned.[14]

196–99), who sees Paul's comments as "hypothetical/typical," addressing "chronic issues facing the first urban Christians," and not as "a specific response to a crisis in the Roman church or churches." Johnson's findings rest in part on the contrast he detects between the "thicker" discussion of the actual situation in Galatians and in 1 Corinthians and Paul's more "muted" and "vague" remarks in Romans.

13. For a rigorous treatment of the sources and circumstances related to the edict, see Rainer Riesner, *Paul's Early Period: Chronology, Mission Strategy, Theology* (Grand Rapids: Eerdmans, 1998), 157–201.

14. *Historiae adversum paganos* 7.6.15–16: Anno eiusdem nono expulsos per Claudium urbe Iudaeos Iosephus refert. sed me magis Suetonius mouet, qui ait hoc modo: Claudius Iudaeos inpulsore Christo adsidue tumultuantes Roma expulit; quod, utrum contra Christum tumultuantes Iudaeos coherceri et conprimi iusserit, an etiam Christianos simul uelut cognatae religionis homines uoluerit expelli, nequaquam discernitur. The English translation is from Dixon Slingerland, "Suetonius Claudius 25.4, Acts 18, and Paulus Orosius' *Historiarum Adversum Paganos Libri VII*: Dating the Claudian Expulsion(s) of Roman Jews," *JQR* 83 (1992): 137.

Dio Cassius (ca. 160–ca. 229 C.E.), possibly referring to the same episode, describes a ban on public meetings early in Claudius's reign:

> As for the Jews, who had again increased so greatly that by reason of their multitude it would have been hard without raising a tumult to bar them from the city, he [Claudius] did not drive them out, but ordered them, while continuing their traditional mode of life, not to hold meetings.[15]

Since several aspects of this expulsion may bear on early Roman Christianity and, in particular, on early relations between church and synagogue, a closer look at the evidence is called for.

2.2. Chrestus and Christus

Presumably the imperial expulsion punished those who were fomenting chaos in the capital. For many scholars, Suetonius's use of *Chrestus* suggests that the tumult raged between *Christian* and *non-Christian* Jews. Suetonius (or his source) adopted the alternative spelling for *Christus*—*Chrestus* being a common Roman name—and mistakenly thought Jesus was actively aggravating the status quo in Rome during the reign of Claudius.

Although widely held,[16] this view is not without problems. On the face of it, Suetonius does not link the conflict to teachings or debates *about* Chrestus but rather to Chrestus's *personal presence*.[17] That Suetonius knows enough

---

15. Dio Cassius, *Historia Romana* 60.6.6-7 (Cary, LCL): τούς τε Ἰουδαίους πλεονάσαντας αὖθις, ὥστε χαλεπῶς ἂν ἄνευ ταραχῆς ὑπὸ τοῦ ὄχλου σφῶν τῆς πόλεως εἰρχθῆναι, οὐκ ἐξήλασε μέν, τῷ δὲ δὴ πατρίῳ βίῳ χρωμένους ἐκέλευσε μὴ συναθροίζεσθαι. Gerd Lüdemann (*Paul, Apostle to the Gentiles: Studies in Chronology* [Philadelphia: Fortress, 1984], 164-71) claims Dio's support to date the expulsion to 41 C.E. The majority of scholars, however, distinguish the ban from the expulsion as two separate historical events. Representing the majority view are F. F. Bruce, *The Acts of the Apostles: The Greek Text with Introduction and Commentary* (Grand Rapids: Eerdmans, 1951), 342-43; John M. G. Barclay, *Jews in the Mediterranean Diaspora: From Alexander to Trajan (323 BCE–117 CE)* (Berkeley and Los Angeles: University of California Press, 1999), 303-6; Ben Witherington, *Acts of the Apostles: A Socio-Rhetorical Commentary* (Grand Rapids: Eerdmans, 1998), 541.

16. For defense of the now-common equation of *Chrestus* and *Christ*, see Wiefel, "Jewish Community," 92-93; Wedderburn, *Reasons for Romans*, 54-59; Thomas R. Schreiner, *Romans* (BECNT; Grand Rapids: Baker, 1998), 12-15; Witherington, *Acts of the Apostles*, 540-41; Rudolf Brändle and Ekkehard Stegemann, "The Formation of the First 'Christian Congregations' in Rome in the Context of the Jewish Congregations," in Donfried and Richardson, *Judaism and Christianity*, 118.

17. Mark D. Nanos, *The Mystery of Romans* (Minneapolis: Fortress, 1996), 378-79; Slingerland, "Dating the Claudian Expulsion," 136-37; Stephen Benko, "The Edict of Claudius of A.D. 49 and the Instigator Chrestus," *TZ* 25 (1969): 406-18.

to refer to *Christiani* (note the *i*) is clear from *Nero* 16.2. Nor does Luke at Acts 18:2 hint that Aquila and Prisca were Christians at the time they were forced to leave Rome.[18] Luke may take the couple's prior Christian allegiance for granted, since he says nothing about their conversion after meeting Paul, but it is also possible that the pair offered Paul lodging simply because they shared a trade and sought strength in numbers, and that sustained contact with Paul led to their conversion.[19]

Furthermore, we are hard pressed to show that Luke was aware of any Jewish-Christian tensions in Rome. None of the Roman authorities who interrogate Paul—Gallio (Acts 18), Felix (Acts 24), Festus (Acts 25), and Agrippa (Acts 26)—seem aware of a recent imperial edict against Christian Jews, nor are the Roman officials inclined to see a Jew such as Paul as a threat to public order.[20] Acts depicts Paul arriving in Rome and meeting with Jewish leaders who turn out to be only vaguely aware of the Christian sect and its reputation and genuinely, even positively, curious about Paul's gospel (Acts 28:21–22).[21] If the expulsion was official state retaliation for intra-Jewish debates about Jesus, it is hard to understand why Luke would not exploit the point, given how often Acts chronicles other episodes of Jewish rejection of Jesus.[22]

Even if the term *Chrestus* does refer to Jewish disputes *over Jesus*, as many contend, it remains to be decided what exactly the intra-Jewish dispute was about. At least two possibilities merit consideration: (1) whether or not to acknowledge Jesus as Israel's Messiah; and (2) whether or not to include Gentiles among God's people, in Jesus' name, without their observing the law.

It is easy to imagine the first question provoking hostilities *in Jerusalem*, where religious leaders might feel directly indicted, but it is unlikely that debates about Jesus' messianic status would provoke a major disturbance *in*

---

18. Aquila is called "a certain Jew" (τινα Ἰουδαῖον; Acts 18:2), not, say, a "certain disciple," the expression Luke uses for Paul's presumed brothers in Christ (τινας μαθητάς) in Acts 19:1.

19. For the claim that Prisca and Aquila were already Christians before meeting Paul, see Wiefel, "Jewish Community," 93; Wedderburn, *Reasons for Romans*, 54; and, tentatively, Philip F. Esler, *Conflict and Identity in Romans: The Social Setting of Paul's Letter* (Minneapolis: Fortress, 2003), 100–101. Questioning this assumption is Nanos, *Mystery of Romans*, 377, following Benko, "Edict of Claudius," 413.

20. Similarly Nanos, *Mystery of Romans*, 377–78.

21. Ibid., 375–78.

22. Ibid., 376. This point is weakened if, with Ernst Haenchen, we see Luke willfully understating the Christian presence in Rome in order to give Paul credit for introducing Christianity to the capital ("The Book of Acts as Source Material for the History of Early Christianity," in *Studies in Luke-Acts* [ed. Leander Keck and J. Louis Martyn; Philadelphia: Fortress, 1980], 258–78).

Rome, since, as Reidar Hvalvik remarks, "Jewish doctrine concerning the Messiah was not fixed, and theological orthodoxy was not a central issue in the first century."[23] Alternatively, one might expect the second question—about the validity of a law-free gospel—to rile law-observant Jews in Rome, whether or not they identified with Jesus. In other words, if the edict of Claudius constitutes evidence of a "Pauline" form of Christianity in the capital by or before 49 C.E.,[24] the battle lines might separate not pro- and anti-*Jesus* forces but pro-*law* Jews (Christian or not) and law-free Jews and Gentiles.

These objections may not be decisive, but they are weighty enough to caution us against declaring the *Chrestus/Christos* connection firmly established.[25] It is at least possible that an otherwise unknown Chrestus stirred up enough nationalistic, even messianic, fervor among Roman Jews to incur imperial wrath and provoke expulsion. In other words, there may have been tensions in the Roman Jewish community of the 40s and 50s that had nothing to do with Jesus of Nazareth,[26] in which case it would be unwise to use the expulsion of *Jews* as the cornerstone of one's historical reconstruction of Jewish-*Christian* relations in Rome.

2.3. THE SCOPE OF THE EXPULSION

Another relevant consideration is the scope of the expulsion. How many Jews were affected? Estimates of the Jewish population in Rome during the first

---

23. Reidar Hvalvik, "Jewish Believers and Jewish Influence in the Roman Church until the Early Second Century," in *Jewish Believers in Jesus: The Early Centuries* (ed. Oskar Skarsaune and Reidar Hvalvik; Peabody, Mass.: Hendrickson, 2007), 181.

24. See Wedderburn, *Reasons for Romans*, 57–58. This development might even be dated earlier if, with Francis Watson, we imagine that the ban on public meetings in 41 C.E. chronicled by Dio Cassius was an earlier attempt by Claudius to address the same problem. See Francis Watson, *Paul, Judaism and the Gentiles: A Sociological Approach* (SNTSMS 56; Cambridge: Cambridge University Press, 1986), 93. Watson contends elsewhere ("The Two Roman Congregations: Romans 14:1–15:13," in Donfried, *Romans Debate*, 209) that "Gentile Christianity at Rome is … Pauline Christianity" in the sense that Paul's own converts and associates (especially those mentioned in Rom 16) were responsible for establishing a law-free form of Christianity in Rome. See also Hvalvik, "Jewish Believers," 182.

25. Similarly Dixon Slingerland, "Chrestus: Christus?" in *New Perspectives on Ancient Judaism 4* (ed. A. J. Avery-Peck; Lanham, Md.: University Press of America, 1989), 43.

26. So Marcus Borg, "A New Context for Romans XIII," *NTS* 19 (1972–1973): 211–12; E. A. Judge and G. S. R. Thomas, "The Origin of the Church at Rome: A New Solution?" *RTR* 25 (1966): 81–94; Nanos, *Mystery of Romans*, 379–80; Benko, "Edict of Claudius," 412–14. In response, Wedderburn (*Reasons for Romans*, 55) asks whether a growing, potentially destabilizing political movement would not have drawn a much harsher reaction from Rome than mere expulsion.

century range from 15,000 to 50,000, making Jews one of the largest groups of foreigners in the capital.[27] These figures are cobbled together from clues and hints in the sources, and the margin of error is no doubt wide,[28] but it is difficult to imagine so large a population being forcibly removed from the city. It is one thing to pass an edict, quite another to enforce it.[29]

Of course, Jews, like other imperial subjects, were not all treated equally under the law. Some could be expelled easily, while others required due process. Four broad classes can be identified:[30] (1) *slaves* were punishable by their master or the state; (2) *peregrini* (free-born foreign subjects) and (3) *latini Iuniani* (manumitted slaves without full citizenship) occupied intermediate classes that could be expelled by magistrates without trial; while (4) *citizens* could be expelled only after conviction in criminal court.

Most Roman Jews probably came from the lower classes and thus were more susceptible to deportation orders but also more difficult to monitor. Some, however, would have acquired citizenship and enjoyed a measure of legal protection.[31] The conclusion of John Barclay regarding the social and economic location of Rome's Jews is commendably cautious: "Such evidence as we possess indicates that the Jewish community in Rome ranged across the social strata, from Greek-speaking illiterates to Romanized court favourites."[32] Philo's sweeping account of the situation in Rome is relevant here:

> He was aware that the great section of Rome on the other side of the Tiber is occupied and inhabited by Jews, most of whom were Roman citizens emancipated ['Ρωμαῖοι δὲ ἦσαν οἱ πλείους ἀπελευθερωθέντες]. For having been

---

27. James S. Jeffers, "Jewish and Christian Families in First-Century Rome," in Donfried and Richardson, *Judaism and Christianity*, 129–30; Barclay, *Jews in the Mediterranean Diaspora*, 295 and n. 32.

28. See Brändle and Stegemann, "Formation," 120. For Rome under Augustus, see Josephus, *Ant.* 17.299–303; *War* 2.280; under Tiberius, see Suetonius, *Tib.* 36; Josephus, *Ant.* 18.81–84; Tacitus, *Ann.* 2.85.

29. James C. Walters ("Romans, Jews and Christians: The Impact of the Romans on Jewish/Christian Relations in First Century Rome," in Donfried and Richardson, *Judaism and Christianity*, 177, n. 11) cites Tacitus's reference to an ineffectual Senatorial edict expelling astrologers from Italy (*Ann.* 12.52).

30. Leonard Rutgers, "Roman Policy toward the Jews: Expulsions from the City of Rome During the First Century C.E.," in Donfried and Richardson, *Judaism and Christianity*, 97–98.

31. On the socioeconomic status of Roman Jews, see Jeffers, "Jewish and Christian Families," 129–31; Robert Jewett, *Romans: A Commentary* (Hermeneia; Minneapolis: Fortress, 2007), 55.

32. Barclay, *Jews in the Mediterranean Diaspora*, 318.

brought as captives to Italy they were liberated by their owners and were not forced to violate any of the native institutions.³³

If we can trust Philo's assessment that during the rule of Claudius many Jews in Rome, although formerly prisoners of war, had gained freedom and even citizenship,³⁴ a wholesale expulsion of all Roman Jews would have been legally complicated and extremely problematic.

Further uncertainty about the scope of the expulsion of the Jews is tied to the fact that Suetonius's statement about the expulsion—*Iudaeos impulsore Chresto assidue tumultantes Roma expulit*—may be translated two ways: (1) "Since the Jews constantly made disturbances at the instigation of Chrestus, he expelled them from Rome"; or (2) "He expelled from Rome the Jews [who were] constantly making disturbances at the instigation of Chrestus."³⁵ The first reading implies that most, or even all, Jews were embroiled in the tumult, as one might also infer from the language of Acts 18:2: προσφάτως ἐληλυθότα ἀπὸ τῆς Ἰταλίας ... διὰ τὸ διατεταχέναι Κλαύδιον χωρίζεσθαι πάντας τοὺς Ἰουδαίους ἀπὸ τῆς Ῥώμης. The second, more restrictive reading limits the expulsion to those causing the disturbance, in which case Luke's claim that *all* Jews had to leave Rome would be one more instance of Lukan hyperbole.³⁶ Perhaps, then, the expulsion only targeted a minority of the city's Jewish population, say, a handful of ringleaders or the members of only a few synagogues.³⁷ A small-scale expulsion would explain why other historians of the period (Luke excepted) fail to mention it.³⁸

---

33. Philo, *Legat.* 155 (Colson, LCL).

34. So Barclay, *Jews in the Mediterranean Diaspora*, 289; see also Jewett, *Romans*, 55.

35. See William L. Lane, "Social Perspectives on Roman Christianity during the Formative Years from Nero to Nerva: Romans, Hebrews, 1 Clement," in Donfried and Richardson, *Judaism and Christianity*, 196–244; Nanos, *Mystery of Romans*, 374. The first translation above follows J. C. Rolfe's LCL translation of Suetonius, *The Lives of the Caesars*.

36. For hyperbolic uses of πᾶς in Luke-Acts, see Luke 1:3; Acts 1:1; 2:5; 3:18; 8:1, etc. See also Witherington, *Acts of the Apostles*, 106, 539; Riesner, *Paul's Early Period*, 192.

37. For "ringleaders," see, tentatively, Hvalvik, "Jewish Believers," 183–84; James D. G. Dunn, *Romans 1–8* (WBC 38A; Dallas: Word, 1988), xlix. Brändle and Stegemann ("Formation," 126) suggest that the edict only affected *Christian* Jews. With regard to the "synagogues" reading, William Lane ("Social Perspectives") suggests that perhaps Jews from only one or two synagogues of some eleven to fifteen in the city were forced out. Similarly Peter Lampe, *From Paul to Valentinus: Christians at Rome in the First Two Centuries* (trans. Michael Steinhauser; Minneapolis: Fortress, 2003), 12–14; Nanos, *Mystery of Romans*, 376, who cites Slingerland, "Dating the Claudian Expulsion," 127–44, in support of a limited expulsion of a subset of troublesome Jews. Conversely, Riesner (*Paul's Early Period*, 200; see also 192–93) cautions against *under*estimating the scope of the expulsion.

38. Tacitus first mentions the Roman Christians in his account of the great fire of 64

2.4. Jews and Christians in Rome after the Expulsion

Scholars agree that in its earliest stages Christianity across the empire spread outward from the synagogue.[39] Thus, the first Jesus-followers in Rome would almost certainly have been Jews, proselytes, and God-fearers with strong Jewish ties.[40] By the mid-50s, however, Paul seems to assume that most Christians in Rome are Gentiles.[41] The following excerpts from Paul's letter are notable in this regard.

> through whom we have received grace and apostleship to bring about the obedience of faith *among all the Gentiles* for the sake of his name, *including yourselves* who are called to belong to Jesus Christ.... I want you to know, brothers and sisters, that I have often intended to come to you ... in order that I may reap some harvest *among you as I have among the rest of the Gentiles*.[42] (Rom 1:5, 13; all translations NRSV)

C.E. and shows no awareness of their role in any earlier controversies. Josephus mentions the expulsion under Tiberius in 19 C.E. (*Ant.* 18.81–84) but knows, or notes, nothing about one under Claudius. It hardly seems necessary, however, to conclude on this basis, as does, e.g., Harry J. Leon (*The Jews of Ancient Rome* [Philadelphia: Jewish Publication Society, 1960], 27), that the expulsion did not happen. See further Judge and Thomas, "Origin of the Church at Rome," 86; Nanos, *Mystery of Romans*, 379–80.

39. See Wiefel, "Jewish Community," 89: "The mission of early Christianity was usually started in synagogues." Likewise, Douglas Moo, *The Epistle to the Romans* (NICNT; Grand Rapids: Eerdmans, 1996), 4, 9, 11–12. For evidence of this pattern, see Acts 13:42–47; 14:1–6; 17:1–5; 18:4; 19:8–9. Wiefel ("Jewish Community," 89 n. 37) suggests that "Luke's somewhat schematic sequence [in Acts] may still, in principle, be an accurate portrayal of early Christian missionary practice."

40. Note the mention in Acts 2:10 of "visitors from Rome, both Jews and proselytes." See also Wedderburn, *Reasons for Romans*, 50; Walters, "Romans, Jews and Christians," 176. For secondary literature supporting the Jewishness of early Roman Christianity, see Lane, "Social Perspectives," 203 nn. 16 and 18.

41. See Johnson, *Reading Romans*, 5; Brändle and Stegemann, "Formation," 124. Defending a Gentile majority among the intended readers of Romans are Wiefel, "Jewish Community," 93 (*contra* Ropes and Lietzmann); Dunn, *Romans 1–8*, xliv–l; Moo, *Romans*, 9–13. See also Ambrosiaster (375 C.E.) *Ad Romanos*. On whether to distinguish Paul's historical audience from the audience that he encodes in the letter (his "ideal reader"), see Wagner, *Heralds of the Good News*, 34–35 (who sees "no strong reason" to assume a sizeable Gentile majority in the Roman churches); Hays, *Echoes of Scripture*, 29 and n. 92; Mark D. Nanos, "A Rejoinder to Robert A. J. Gagnon's 'Why the "Weak" at Rome Cannot Be Non-Christian Jews'" (http://www.marknanos.com/Gagnon-rejoinder-6-20-03.pdf): 11; and Esler, *Conflict and Identity*, 110–11.

42. Esler (*Conflict and Identity*, 111–15) ably represents the minority view that these

For I could wish that I myself were accursed and cut off from Christ for the sake of my own people, my kindred according to the flesh. *They are Israelites*, and to *them* belong the adoption, the glory, the covenants, the giving of the law, the worship, and the promises; to *them* belong the patriarchs, and from them, according to the flesh, comes the Messiah. (Rom 9:3–5)

Now *I am speaking to you Gentiles*. Inasmuch then as *I am an apostle to the Gentiles*, I glorify my ministry in order to make my own people jealous, and thus save some of *them*. For if *their* rejection is the reconciliation of the world, what will *their* acceptance be but life from the dead! ... But if some of the branches were broken off, and *you*, a wild olive shoot, were grafted in *their* place to share the rich root of the olive tree, do not boast over the branches. If *you* do boast, remember that it is not *you* that support the root, but the root that supports *you*. *You* will say, "Branches were broken off so that I might be grafted in." That is true. *They* were broken off because of *their* unbelief, but *you* stand only through faith. So do not become proud, but stand in awe. For if God did not spare the natural branches, perhaps he will not spare *you*. ... For if *you* have been cut from what is by nature a wild olive tree and grafted, contrary to nature, into a cultivated olive tree, how much more will these natural branches be grafted back into their own olive tree. ... As regards the gospel *they* are enemies of God for *your* sake; but as regards election *they* are beloved, for the sake of their ancestors. ... Just as *you* were once disobedient to God but have now received mercy because of *their* disobedience, so *they* have now been disobedient in order that, by the mercy shown to *you*, *they* too may now receive mercy. (Rom 11:13–15, 17–21, 24, 28, 30–31)

Nevertheless on some points I have written to *you* rather boldly by way of reminder, because of the grace given me by God to be *a minister of Christ Jesus to the Gentiles* in the priestly service of the gospel of God, so that *the offering of the Gentiles* may be acceptable, sanctified by the Holy Spirit.[43] (Rom 15:15–16)

Now to God who is able to strengthen you according to my gospel and the proclamation of Jesus Christ, according to the revelation of the mystery that was kept secret for long ages but is now disclosed, and through the prophetic writings *is made known to all the Gentiles* ... to bring about the obedience of faith. (Rom 16:25–26)

---

verses reflect a Judean perspective and do not imply that Paul's principal audience was Gentile.

43. See also 15:8–13.

A parenthetical remark in Rom 7:1—γινώσκουσιν γὰρ νόμον λαλῶ—is sometimes taken as evidence to the contrary, on the assumption that those who "know the law" must be Jewish. Even here, however, a predominantly Gentile readership cannot be ruled out. Not only are there clues in the immediate context (e.g., 6:19-20) that Paul has former pagans in his sights, but the explanatory aside itself would add little to his argument if he were addressing law-observant Jews. If even here Paul's implied readers are Gentiles, then the likelihood of a synagogue connection is further increased, as James Dunn observes: "The fact that Paul could assume a reasonable knowledge of the Torah strengthens the likelihood that the bulk of gentile converts had previously been adherents to the Jewish synagogues in Rome or elsewhere."[44] Of course, whether Paul's assumption was justified and what constitutes a "reasonable" knowledge of Torah are questions difficult to answer.

Complementing this evidence from the body of the letter is the list of names in Rom 16.[45] Of the twenty-six people mentioned by name in 16:3-15, Paul identifies only three of them as his συγγενεῖς (see 16:7, 11). Since it is difficult to explain why Paul would call only some Jews his kins(wo)men, and since Paul had clear theological interest in emphasizing the ethnic status of any Jewish believers in the Roman church—they would lend support to Paul's remnant argument (11:1-5)—it is reasonable to conclude that a substantial majority of Paul's named acquaintances in Rome were Gentile.[46] Whether

---

44. Dunn, *Romans 1-8*, 359; see also A. Andrew Das, *Solving the Romans Debate* (Minneapolis: Fortress, 2007), 83-87.

45. This assumes that Rom 16 was originally part of the letter, *contra* T. W. Manson, "St. Paul's Letter to the Romans—And Others," in *Studies in the Gospels and Epistles* (ed. Matthew Black; Manchester: Manchester University Press, 1962), 225-41, now in Donfried, *Romans Debate*, 3-15; E. J. Goodspeed, "Phoebe's Letter of Introduction," *HTR* 44 (1951): 55-57. For arguments defending the integrity of the letter, see Das, *Solving the Romans Debate*, 16-23; Wedderburn, *Reasons for Romans*, 12-18; Peter Lampe, "The Roman Christians of Romans 16," in Donfried, *Romans Debate*, 217-21; Dunn, *Romans 9-16* (WBC 38B; Dallas: Word, 1988), 884; Schreiner, *Romans*, 6-10.

46. See Lampe, "Roman Christians of Romans 16," 224-25 (and n. 38), who concludes that "most people in the Roman church were of Gentile origin but had lived as sympathizers on the margins of the synagogues before they became Christian." See idem, *From Paul to Valentinus*, 74-75. Similarly, Jewett, *Romans*, 61. Paul's theological interests are not considered by Karl P. Donfried, "A Short Note on Romans 16," in Donfried, *Romans Debate*, 44-52, who argues (with H. Leon, against W. Marxsen) that the names in Rom 16 "could easily belong to Roman Jews" (48). Donfried's inscriptional evidence does show that Roman Jews often took non-Jewish names, but this insight can hardly be inverted to claim that people with non-Jewish names in Rom 16 are probably Jewish! In a category of their own are Aquila and Prisca, whose Jewishness (his, at least) is attested in Acts 18:2. These two head Paul's list of contacts in Rome and are called not συγγενεῖς but συνεργοί,

all of these individuals, Gentile or otherwise, belonged to Paul's target audience in Rome is less clear, given the nature of Paul's second-person formula in 16:3–16—[*you*] *please greet so-and-so* [*for me*]—which might possibly imply that the named individuals were related only *indirectly* to the letter's recipients.[47] It is doubtful, however, that we should distinguish too sharply between these individuals and the letter's recipients, given the inclusive note sounded in Paul's opening address: πᾶσιν τοῖς οὖσιν ἐν Ῥώμῃ ἀγαπητοῖς θεοῦ κλητοῖς ἁγίοις (1:7).

In light of these observations about the letter's implied readers, most scholars have concluded that Gentiles made up a sizeable majority of Paul's intended audience. How did this Gentile majority come about? Was it caused by a steady infusion of converts, or does it owe much to a sudden, mass deportation of Jews? I have suggested that the evidence that Claudius ordered this expulsion to punish Jewish disputes *over Jesus* is inferential and relatively weak and that we know neither the scope of the expulsion nor precisely who was affected. It follows that it is precarious to attempt to explain how, if at all, this expulsion altered Jew-Gentile relations in the church(es) at Rome. Regrettably, we really do not know what impact the edict had on the composition, structure, leadership, and governance of the Christian community in Rome. Nor can we say with confidence what it was like for Christian Jews such as Prisca and Aquila[48] to return from exile and (re)connect with fellow believers in the capital.[49]

Enthusiasts of the *Chrestus* = *Christ* hypothesis would, of course, beg to differ. They contend that the shift from predominantly *Jewish* origins to predominantly *Gentile* membership was likely a direct consequence of (or greatly accelerated by) the expulsion: once Jewish Christians were forced out of the capital, the city's church(es) came under the leadership of Gentiles. This, in turn, explains the Jew-Gentile tensions in the church at the time Paul wrote Romans several years after the expulsion: the non-law-observant Gentile

---

Paul's associates in mission. Their special, cherished status may be why Paul does not call them kins(wo)men, or it may be that, since Prisca is Gentile, the term cannot rightly be applied to them both. That a Jew is host to one of Rome's largely Gentile house churches (Rom 16:5) should caution us against overstating racial tensions.

47. Das, *Solving the Romans Debate*, 101–103, helpfully summarizes the investigations of T. Y. Mullins, J. L. White, S. Stowers, and R. M. Thorsteinsson into ancient Greek letters. On three typical closing greetings in ancient letters, including this second-person type (using ἀσπάζομαι), see Hans-Josef Klauck, *Ancient Letters and the New Testament: A Guide to Content and Exegesis* (Waco, Tex.: Baylor University Press, 2006), 24–25.

48. Prisca and Aquila, whose expulsion from Rome is noted in Acts 18:2, are back in the capital in the mid-50s when Paul writes Rom 16:3.

49. See Wiefel, "Jewish Community," 94; Leon, *Jews of Ancient Rome*, 27–28.

leadership resented the sudden influx of returning, law-observant Jews. Wolfgang Wiefel explains it this way:

> Expulsion of Jews from Rome also meant *the end of the first Christian congregation* in Rome, which up until then had consisted of Jewish Christians. In Paul's letter to the Romans, written a few years after these events, we meet *a new congregation*.... [Jewish-Christians returning to Rome] found a *"new"* Christian congregation *completely different* in organizational structure and spiritual outlook from the *old* one which had existed in the synagogue.[50]

James Walters makes a similar point:

> When Jewish Christians and Gentile Christians (who lived like Jews) returned to Rome after the edict had lapsed, they encountered Christians whose socialization had changed markedly. Not only were Christians assembling in house churches that were independent of Jewish gatherings, these house churches were populated by persons who—for the most part—no longer observed Sabbath and dietary laws and who were not eager to resume such behaviors, as Romans 14:1–15:13 indicates.[51]

These claims are certainly bold in their suggestion that in the space of five or six years, due largely to an imperial edict and the resultant physical separation, the roles of Jews and Gentiles within the Roman church have been reversed. Undoubtedly, the broad appeal of this proposal can be traced to its putative ability to explain Paul's argument in Romans, especially Rom 9–15. The question is whether the tensions that Paul addresses in these chapters requires so great a rift or whether evidence for a "monolithic hostility" (Mark Nanos's phrase) toward Roman *Jewish* believers is lacking. A reasonable case can be made that the situation Paul presupposes in his letter is shaped less by a recent upheaval or sudden crisis than by what Mark Nanos calls "the strain of different opinions developing within communities concerned with proper belief and behavior for the people of God."[52] Later we shall examine Nanos's thesis that the predominantly Gentile Roman church was still under the aegis of the (non-Christian) Jewish synagogue when Paul wrote Romans. Here we simply register doubts about whether appeals to the Claudian expulsion and its aftermath are necessary, let alone sufficient, to explain the tensions and conflicts that were dividing the community that

---

50. Wiefel, "Jewish Community," 93 and 96, emphasis added.
51. Walters, "Romans, Jews and Christians," 178; see also Hvalvik, "Jewish Believers," 192, 198–99.
52. Nanos, *Mystery of Romans*, 381.

Paul addresses in Romans. Perhaps the question is whether a persuasive account of the letter's historical context must include this crisis or whether a less dramatic, more quotidian explanation might prove equally satisfactory. Such is the contention of Mark Nanos: "The tensions addressed in Romans ... are precisely the kinds of tensions that would have been unfolding in synagogues as the Christian adherents grew in number and developed a subgroup identity (with additional meetings in their homes for worship and instruction)."[53]

3. The Synagogue: Matrix of Early Roman Christianity?

The evidence considered thus far fails to show that Jews and Jewish Christians were engaged in hostile, public debates in the Rome of the late 40s C.E., let alone that there had been a full-scale "parting of the ways" between synagogue and church. The little we do know about Claudius's edict and its aftermath should caution us against presuming that a Roman Christian community once dominated by Jews came suddenly, due to intra-Jewish hostilities and an imperial edict, to be dominated by Gentiles who, before long, resented Jewish repatriation after the death of Claudius. To adopt this perspective is to link one's interpretation of Romans to a catena of unproven inferences:[54] (1) the *inferred* impact (Gentile dominance in the Christian community, triumphalism, elitism) (2) of the *presumed* return (after Claudius's death) (3) of *large numbers of* Christian Jews (4) who were *likely* expelled in 49 C.E.

With so much focus on the Claudian expulsion, it is easy to exaggerate evidence of ethnic resentment, schism, and social distance and, perhaps, to miss signs of overlap, Jew-Gentile interaction, and positive Jewish influence on early Roman Christianity. By contrast, without Claudius's edict dominating the skyline, we are in a better position to see possible signs of the influence that Rome's Jewish community—its synagogues, leadership, and practices—had on the Jesus movement.

---

53. Nanos, *Mystery of Romans*, 384. Similarly, Esler, *Conflict and Identity*, 106, who finds the expulsion hypothesis "unnecessary" and "speculative" (102).

54. Scholars similarly reluctant to weight heavily the edict of Claudius in their historical reconstructions of the setting of Romans include Nanos, *Mystery of Romans*, 372–87; Wagner, *Heralds of the Good News*, 34; Jerome Murphy-O'Connor, *Paul: A Critical Life* (New York: Oxford University Press, 1996), 333; Rutgers, "Roman Policy," 105–6; Steve Mason, "'For I Am Not Ashamed of the Gospel' (Rom 1.16): The Gospel and the First Readers of Romans," in *Gospel in Paul* (ed. L. Ann Jervis and Peter Richardson; JSNTSup 108; Sheffield: JSOT Press, 1994), 254–87.

3.1. Roman Synagogues

No synagogue structures survive from ancient Rome. A few miles away, however, on the outskirts of Ostia, Rome's ancient port, the remains of a hall, 25 x 13 meters in size, mark the site of a fourth-century synagogue. The earliest layers of this site appear to date from the reign of Claudius and suggest an earlier public building suitable for synagogue services.[55] If so, this would not merely be the oldest known synagogue building in the Diaspora; it would encourage us to expect similar dedicated structures in nearby Rome.[56] This need not mean that every "synagogue" or "prayer (house)" in Rome was, in our period, a dedicated building with distinctive architecture; limited resources and legal constraints would mean that some Jewish congregations would gather in multipurpose buildings that would offer archaeologists few clues as to the range of their utilization. But given several centuries of Jewish presence in the Roman capital and the common practice of benefaction, the likelihood of dedicated structures in Rome is substantial. As Philip Esler observes, "We would expect that at a fairly early stage wealthy Judeans or well-disposed outsiders … would dedicate an existing building, or part of one…, or have a new edifice erected for use as a meeting place."[57]

The existence in Rome of dedicated synagogue structures, sometimes called προσευχαί, is further confirmed by Philo, who writes of Augustus's accommodating stance toward the Jews:

> He was aware that the great section of Rome on the other side of the Tiber is occupied and inhabited by Jews ['Ιουδαίων].... He knew therefore that they have houses of prayer [προσευχὰς] and meet together in them, particu-

---

55. On the date and function of the structure, see Anders Runesson, "The Oldest Original Synagogue Building in the Diaspora: A Response to L. Michael White," *HTR* 92 (1999): 409–33. Runesson is responding to L. Michael White, "Synagogue and Society in Imperial Ostia: Archaeological and Epigraphic Evidence," *HTR* 90 (1997): 23–58, reprinted in Donfried and Richardson, *Judaism and Christianity*, 30–68, who contends that the building was erected in the early second century as a two-story private insula and not adapted for synagogue use until the late second century. Agreeing with Runesson's first-century date are A. Thomas Kraabel, "Unity and Diversity among Diaspora Synagogues," in *The Synagogue in Late Antiquity* (ed. Lee I. Levine; Philadelphia: ASOR, 1987), 51; and Esler, *Conflict and Identity*, 95.

56. See Donald D. Binder, *Into the Temple Courts: The Place of Synagogues in the Second Temple Period* (SBLDS 169; Atlanta: Scholars Press, 1999), 336.

57. Esler, *Conflict and Identity*, 89 (see also 94–95), following Wayne Meeks, *The First Urban Christians: The Social World of the Apostle Paul* (New Haven: Yale University Press, 1983), 80.

larly on the sacred Sabbaths when they receive as a body a training in their ancestral philosophy [ὅτε δημοσίᾳ τὴν πάτριον παιδεύονται φιλοσοφίαν].... Yet nevertheless he neither ejected them from Rome... nor took any violent measures against the houses of prayer [τὰς προσευχάς], nor prevented them from meeting to receive instructions in the laws [οὔτε ἐκώλυσε συνάγεσθαι πρὸς τὰς τῶν νόμων ὑφηγήσεις]. (Philo, *Legat.* 155–157 [Colson, LCL])

To these arguments from archaeology, historical probability, and written testimony we can add evidence from Roman catacomb and *hypogea* inscriptions. A survey of about forty inscriptions identifies some ten different synagogues, at least four of which probably existed in the first century: three are named after individuals (Augustus, Agrippa, Volumnius); a fourth, called the "Synagogue of the Hebrews," may have been the first synagogue in the city.[58] If we are right about the first-century dating of these four synagogues, we should probably assume there were others, perhaps many others, given the size of the Jewish population in Rome. Philo's reference to the destruction during the rule of Caligula of synagogues (τὰς προσευχάς) in Alexandria, "of which there are many in each section of the city" (πολλαὶ δέ εἰσι καθ' ἕκαστον τμῆμα τῆς πόλεως), lends further credence to this assumption (Philo, *Legat.* 132 [Colson, LCL]).

Several of these synagogues would have been located in the Trans-Tiber region of Monteverde, a densely populated and relatively poor part of the city.[59] We should not, however, conclude that Roman Judaism was uniformly destitute or devoid of honor. There would have been significant economic disparities from one synagogue to the next. We should also imagine different organizing principles at work: some groups would gather for convenience, others due to a shared profession, still others because of a shared country of origin.[60] To name synagogues after figures such as Augustus and (probably Marcus) Agrippa (d. 12 B.C.E.) likely signals collective gratitude for measures that made Jewish life in the Diaspora more tolerable. It may also suggest political savvy, communal vigor, and self-confidence.[61]

---

58. Lee I. Levine, *The Ancient Synagogue: The First Thousand Years* (New Haven: Yale University Press, 1999), 97; see also Wiefel, "Jewish Community," 90.

59. Levine, *Ancient Synagogue*, 265. See also Philo, *Legat.* 155, cited above. On the distribution of synagogues in other districts, see Jewett, *Romans*, 57; Barclay, *Jews in the Mediterranean Diaspora*, 316; and the sources cited in n. 80 below.

60. Lee I. Levine, "The Second Temple Synagogue: The Formative Years," in Levine, *Synagogue in Late Antiquity*, 15.

61. Peter Richardson, "Augustan-Era Synagogues in Rome," in Donfried and Richardson, *Judaism and Christianity*, 29.

Almost certainly this predominantly blue collar, high-density region of the city, this vibrantly Jewish enclave, was also home to many of the earliest Christian gatherings—hybrid assemblies of Jews, proselytes, and sympathetic God-fearers eager to advance beyond the rank of outsider.[62] To the extent that the first generation of Roman Christians emerged from within this context, we should expect them to follow many of the same patterns, gathering in diverse household groups here and there across the district. That Paul nowhere refers to "*the* church at Rome" should come as no surprise if, as Dunn suggests, "the Christian house congregations shared the same sort of fragmented existence as did the wider Jewish community."[63]

3.2. Synagogue Leadership and Organization

There is no evidence that Rome's Jews were governed by a single arch-council, Sanhedrin, or *gerousia*. Inscriptions mention many synagogue officials—there are some fifty references to the *archon* alone—but nothing suggests that these rulers had more than local authority. Evidently each synagogue was autonomous and could adopt its own distinct practices with varying degrees of accommodation to Roman culture.[64] According to Wolfgang Wiefel, the inscriptional evidence points to:

> a diverse community of individually structured congregations whose esteemed officials are responsible for their religious and social functions. But we have also noticed the absence of a single, controlling organization supervising the individual synagogues. There is no organizational head such as the ethnarch in Alexandria who, together with a council of Jews, represented all other Jews before the authorities.[65]

---

62. On locating the earliest Christian communities in *Trastevere* and other regions of the city, see Lampe, *From Paul to Valentinus*, ch. 3, esp. 38–44.

63. Dunn, *Romans 1–8*, lii.

64. See Levine, *Ancient Synagogue*, 265–66.

65. Wiefel, "Jewish Community," 91; followed by Hvalvik, "Jewish Believers," 185. See also Barclay, *Jews in the Mediterranean Diaspora*, 316 and n. 85. Shaye J. D. Cohen describes the synagogue as "predominantly a democratic lay organization" with no central office (Pharisaic or otherwise) empowered to set and enforce standards ("Were Pharisees and Rabbis the Leaders of Communal Prayer and Torah Study in Antiquity? The Evidence of the New Testament, Josephus, and the Early Church Fathers," in *Evolution of the Synagogue: Problems and Progress* [ed. Howard Clark Kee and Lynn H. Cohick; Harrisburg, Pa.: Trinity Press International, 1999], 89–105, here 103). Even the attempted extradition of Jews from synagogues in Damascus (Acts 9:1–2) requires only the moral authority of the high priest in Jerusalem, not a Diaspora-wide system of synagogue governance. The

How did the earliest Roman Christians relate to this decentralized system of governance? Christian evangelists and missionaries could have gained access to individual synagogues without broad, official sanction. Whether they were welcomed or shunned, embraced or punished, would depend on dynamics and relations within each synagogue rather than on city-wide policies. Whatever influence Roman synagogues could exert on the emerging Christian movement would have been local and ad hoc rather than systematic or coordinated.

Did some of Rome's Christ-following Jews and Gentiles continue to gather under the aegis and authority of local synagogues? Was Roman "Christianity" during the 40s and 50s largely a set of subgroups within Judaism? A positive answer to these questions might go a long way to explaining why Paul could assume a measure of biblical literacy among his predominantly Gentile readers. Mark Nanos contends, largely against the scholarly grain, that the Christians Paul addressed in Romans had continuing ties to Rome's synagogues. As Nanos puts it, Paul's Roman readers "lived out their identities in Jewish social space."[66] That is, the (predominantly) Gentile recipients of Romans were "to be found within subgroups of believers in Jesus, still entirely located within the synagogues of Rome and functioning in lively, sometimes distressing contact, in view of the expectations of the Jewish community (or communities) regarding conduct appropriate for them."[67]

According to this proposal, Paul's Gentile readers were in direct, regular, meaningful contact with real (not merely theoretical) non-Christian Jews. Indeed, on Nanos's reading of Rom 13:1-7, Paul calls the Roman Christians to acknowledge and submit to *synagogue* (not *state*) authorities. Nanos contends that his proposal explains a number of otherwise problematic dimensions of Paul's epistle:[68] (1) Paul's positive statements about the law (Rom 3:1-2; 7:12-16; 9:4); (2) Paul's hope of provoking jealousy among his Jewish kinsmen (11:13-14);[69] (3) Paul's concern for "the one who is weak in faith" (ὁ ἀσθενῶν τῇ πίστει; 14:1);[70] (4) the absence of instructions to church leaders;[71]

---

punishment inflicted "by Jews" described in 2 Cor 11:24 reflects synagogue authority at the local level.

66. Nanos, "A Rejoinder," 12.

67. Mark D. Nanos, "The Jewish Context of the Gentile Audience Addressed in Paul's Letter to the Romans," *CBQ* 61 (1999): 284; see also 295, 297, 304.

68. See ibid., 297-303.

69. Nanos, *Mystery of Romans*, 247-51.

70. Ibid., 85-165.

71. Contrast 1 Clement's considerable interest in church officials, on which see Caragounis, "From Obscurity to Prominence," 274-77.

and (5) Paul's assumptions about his readers' substantial knowledge of Scripture (7:1; 15:4; etc.).[72]

Although ingenious and insightful, Nanos's proposal is not without problems at the level of exegesis, as Andrew Das and Robert Gagnon, among others, have pointed out.[73] Nanos's reading of Rom 13:1–7, for example, requires us to attach unlikely meanings to some of Paul's words (e.g., μάχαιρα in 13:4) and cannot explain why Paul's call for submission makes no obvious reference to behaviors or contexts that are specifically Jewish. Not only is there no clear evidence (unless we find it in this passage) that Paul saw the Christian community in Rome or elsewhere as standing under the religious authority of synagogue leadership, but the absence of a centralized governing council that spanned Rome's many synagogues would have made a call for Christians to submit to governing *religious* authorities odd and, perhaps, even inscrutable to his readers.[74]

After the critics have had their say, however, several elements of Nanos's bold thesis may remain. Jewish and Gentile Christians in Rome may be less isolated from the synagogue than is often assumed. Followers of Christ may have gathered regularly not only in exclusively Christian house-churches but also in predominantly non-Christian synagogues, as Peter Lampe suggests:

> Before Christianity and Judaism separated, law-abiding Jewish Christians and uncircumcised Gentile Christians might very well have coexisted in the synagogues. Let us consider this: *Sebomenoi* worshiped on the fringes of a synagogue without being circumcised. The first Gentile Christians, i.e., the first *sebomenoi* won over by the Christian gospel of Jewish Christians, would have simply *continued* worshiping at the periphery of their synagogue. Thus, inasmuch as Jews and uncircumcised *sebomenoi* coexisted in a synagogue, also Law-abiding Jewish Christians and uncircumcised Gentile Christian *sebomenoi* coexisted in the synagogue.[75]

---

72. Nanos, "Jewish Context," 289.

73. Das, *Solving the Romans Debate*, 115–48; Robert A. J. Gagnon, "Why the 'Weak' at Rome Cannot Be Non-Christian Jews," *CBQ* 62 (2000): 64–82. See also Jewett, *Romans*, 71–72; Schreiner, *Romans*, passim.

74. Nanos, *Mystery of Romans*, 289–336. Counter-evidence might be found in Acts 28:17, 21–25, where Luke says Paul called together those preeminent (οἱ πρῶτοι) among the Jews. Were these official (elected, appointed, authorized) leaders from various synagogues?

75. Lampe, *From Paul to Valentinus*, 69. Lampe, however, is among those who infer a separation of urban Roman Christianity from "the federation of synagogues" by the time Paul wrote Romans (16).

Proponents of the *Chrestus* = *Christ* hypothesis, after all, see little reason to doubt that ties existed between Roman Christians and Jewish synagogues at least through 49 C.E., the most likely year of the expulsion.[76] If, however, Claudius's expulsion was not tied explicitly to emerging Christianity, or if its scope was narrow and its impact limited, a few more years of substantive overlap are not at all implausible. During this period Gentile Christians would have continued to experience sustained and substantial exposure to Israel's Scriptures.

3.3. PUBLIC READING OF TORAH

Historical studies suggest that the synagogue service of the pre-70 period included three more or less standard elements—precisely the same three activities that are known to have been central to synagogue services in the Talmudic period (ca. 200–600 C.E.): communal prayer, sermon, and public reading of Torah.[77]

For the first of these (communal prayer), evidence for standard patterns in pre-70 synagogue gatherings is sparse, though the name προσευχή ("[house of] prayer"), used widely for synagogues in the Diaspora, strongly suggests that prayers were among the ritual elements of the gathering.[78] Perhaps it was because Diaspora participants did not often visit the temple, where prayer was a daily occurrence, that organized prayers found their way into the liturgical life of local communities.[79] The absence of evidence for established patterns of public prayer might explain why the few surviving pre-70 syna-

---

76. Das, *Solving the Romans Debate*, 170.

77. Levine, "Second Temple Synagogue," 7–31; James Strange, "Ancient Texts, Archaeology as Text, and the Problem of the First-Century Synagogue," in Kee and Cohick, *Evolution of the Synagogue*, 27–45. For the talmudic period, see Avigdor Shinan, "Sermons, Targums, and the Reading from Scriptures in the Ancient Synagogue," in Levine, *Synagogue in Late Antiquity*, 98–110.

78. Communal prayer, however, need not mean set recitations with fixed texts and unison performance. See E. P. Sanders, *Judaism: Practice and Belief 63 BCE–66 CE* (Philadelphia: Trinity Press International, 1992), 202–8. For evidence of Jewish influence upon early Christian prayer, see Stephen G. Wilson, *Related Strangers: Jews and Christians, 70–170 C.E.* (Minneapolis: Fortress, 1995), 224–29.

79. Levine, "Second Temple Synagogue," 19–23; Martin Hengel, "Proseuche und Synagoge," in *The Synagogue: Studies in Origins, Archaeology and Architecture* (ed. Joseph Gutmann; New York: Ktav, 1975), 27–54. Levine ("Second Temple Synagogue," 22) conjectures that, in the Gentile context of the Diaspora, the term *proseuche* was more overtly religious and descriptive than *synagogue*. Strange ("Ancient Texts," 29–30) posits some form of set prayer in first-century synagogue liturgy.

gogue structures do not all face Jerusalem, since Torah-reading alone did not call for a Jerusalem orientation. It is similarly difficult to discern any clear patterns in the early development of synagogue homilies, both in terms of form and content.[80]

Unlike prayer and preaching, however, the evidence for regular public reading of Torah in pre-70 synagogues is solid. Not only is the Jews' centuries-old regard for Torah well documented,[81] but Josephus, Philo, the New Testament, rabbinic literature, and archaeological evidence concur that "scriptural readings constituted the core of contemporary Jewish worship in the synagogue" during the late Second Temple period.[82] The first-century C.E. *Theodotus* inscription, our best archaeological evidence on the subject, identifies a threefold purpose for one particular Jerusalem synagogue: "for reading the Law and studying the commandments, and as a hostel ... for the needs of itinerants from abroad."[83] As the need arose, Torah reading would have been accompanied by Greek and/or Aramaic translation,[84] as well as Haftarah readings (see Luke 4; Acts 13) and expository homilies. Philo describes a typical synagogue service in his *Hypothetica*:

> What then did he [Moses] do? He required them to assemble in the same place [αὐτοὺς εἰς ταὐτὸν ἠξίου συνάγεσθαι] on these seventh days, and sitting together in a respectful and orderly manner [καὶ καθεζομένους μετ' ἀλλήλων σὺν αἰδοῖ καὶ κόσμῳ] hear the laws read so that none should be ignorant of them [τῶν νόμων ἀκροᾶσθαι τοῦ μηδένα ἀγνοῆσαι χάριν]. And indeed they do always assemble and sit together, most of them in silence except when it is the practice to add something to signify approval of what is read. But some priest who is present or one of the elders reads the holy

---

80. Levine, *Ancient Synagogue*, 134; idem, "Second Temple Synagogue," 17–18. For evidence of reading and supplementary teaching in the synagogue, see Mark 1:21; 6:1–6; Matt 13:54–58; Luke 4:15–17, 20–22, 28; Acts 13:15–16, 42; 15:21; Josephus, *War* 2.291; Philo, *Hypoth.* 7.12–13; *Spec.* 2.62; and other sources cited in Bruce N. Fisk, *Do You Not Remember? Scripture, Story and Exegesis in the Rewritten Bible of Pseudo-Philo* (JSPSup 37; Sheffield: Sheffield Academic Press, 2001), 42 n. 88.

81. E.g., *Let. Aris.* 176–177, 1 Macc 3:48; 12:9 (cf. 2 Macc 8:23); Josephus, *War* 2.229–231 (par. *Ant.* 20.115–117), 292.

82. Levine, *Ancient Synagogue*, 134, 138; Sanders, *Judaism*, 197–202. See Josephus, *C. Ap.* 2.175; *Ant.* 16.43; Philo, *Legat.* 155–156; *Somn.* 2.127; *Hypoth.* 7.12; *Prob.* 81–82 [on Essene practice]; *Opif.* 128; Luke 4:16–22; Acts 13:14–15; 15:21. See also Levine, "Second Temple Synagogue," 7–31.

83. Cited in Levine, "Second Temple Synagogue," 17. See also Alan Millard, *Reading and Writing in the Time of Jesus* (Sheffield: Sheffield Academic Press, 2000), 110–11.

84. Levine, *Ancient Synagogue*, 139, takes the production of the Septuagint as evidence for Torah-reading practices in third-century B.C.E. Alexandria.

laws to them and expounds them point by point [ἀναγινώσκει τοὺς ἱεροὺς νόμους αὐτοῖς καὶ καθ' ἕκαστον ἐξηγεῖται] till about the late afternoon, when they depart having gained both expert knowledge of the holy laws [τῶν τε νόμων τῶν ἱερῶν ἐμπείρως ἔχοντες] and considerable advance in piety. (Philo, *Hypoth.* 7.12–13 [Colson, LCL])

However much Luke has embellished his account of Jesus' homecoming, it nevertheless constitutes further evidence that Scripture reading and exposition were thought to be elements of a typical synagogue service during the mid-first century C.E.:

He went to the synagogue on the sabbath day, as was his custom. He stood up to read, and the scroll of the prophet Isaiah was given to him. He unrolled the scroll and found the place where it was written: "The Spirit of the Lord is upon me, because he has anointed me to bring good news to the poor...." And he rolled up the scroll, gave it back to the attendant, and sat down. The eyes of all in the synagogue were fixed on him. Then he began to say to them, "Today this scripture has been fulfilled in your hearing." All spoke well of him and were amazed at the gracious words that came from his mouth. (Luke 4:16–22, NRSV)

Specificity concerning the form and frequency of Torah reading in the late Second Temple period has proven elusive. We are hard pressed to know, for example, at what point the reading of Torah became a weekly affair. Nevertheless, the practice of reading holy texts, repeatedly and liturgically, would have set Judaism apart from Greco-Roman paganism, where no such practice was to be found,[85] and would have ensured that Jews, proselytes, and regularly attending God-fearers would be exposed over time to substantial portions of the Torah and quite possibly to the Prophets and Psalter as well.

In addition to the public reading of Scripture, we have reason to suspect that levels of literacy (however defined) would have been higher among Jews and synagogue-influenced Christian Gentiles (i.e., God-fearers) than in Greco-Roman society at large. Josephus assumes that the law enjoins parents to teach children to read and to know both the laws and the deeds of their forefathers: καὶ γράμματα παιδεύειν ἐκέλευσεν καὶ τὰ περὶ τοὺς νόμους καὶ τῶν προγόνων τὰς πράξεις ἐπίστασθαι.[86] The Testament of Levi is equally adamant about the need for biblical literacy: διδάξατε ... ὑμεῖς τὰ τέκνα

---

85. See ibid., 139 nn. 81–82; Harry Gamble, *Books and Readers in the Early Church* (New Haven: Yale University Press, 1995), 18–19.

86. *C. Ap.* 2.204. See also *Ant.* 4.211, and see Martin Hengel, *Judaism and Hellenism: Studies in Their Encounter in Palestine during the Early Hellenistic Period* (trans. John

ὑμῶν γράμματα ἵνα ἔχωσι σύνεσιν ἐν πάσῃ τῇ ζωῇ αὐτῶν ἀναγινώσκοντες ἀδιαλείπτως τὸν νόμον τοῦ θεοῦ (13:2). Beyond the cultural value that Jews attached to literacy, public reading, and formal study, the earliest Christians, eager to defend the legitimacy of their novel claims, may have felt additional pressure to understand Israel's Scriptures.[87]

Whether Paul's extensive and intensive use of Scripture in Romans should be counted as further evidence for a Roman Christian community with strong ties to the synagogue and its reading practices is difficult to judge. But surely Paul's frequent and sophisticated appeals to Scripture count for something. Did Paul cite Scripture in part to remind Gentiles of the fundamentally *Jewish* nature of his gospel? Could Paul expect that his letter, as it circulated, would be read in dozens of diverse house-churches, each with its own distinct pattern of interaction with the local synagogue, its practices and resources? Did Paul have reason to assume that many, even most, churches had adopted synagogue reading practices? As we have seen, there are good reasons to think the answer to all these questions may be, "Yes."

3.4. SYNAGOGUE AS CONTEXT AND MODEL FOR EMERGING CHRISTIANITY

To what extent did the early Roman Christians inherit and perpetuate Jewish practices of Scripture reading and study? Wayne Meeks was perhaps the first to compare systematically Paul's communities with a range of contemporary groups and organizations: the Roman household; the voluntary association; the synagogue; and the philosophic or rhetorical school.[88] Various scholars have defended one or another of these groups as the best model for understanding the formation and identity of the earliest Christian churches.

As early as 1975, however, John Gager had looked to the structure of the Diaspora synagogue for help in explaining the early Christians' use of Scripture, as well as their leadership, liturgy, and social order. More recently, both James Burtchaell and Judith Lieu have flagged the importance of the Jewish synagogue in the formation of Paul's churches. For Burtchaell, the relevant continuity concerns the officers presiding over the liturgy; for Lieu, the syna-

---

Bowden; 2 vols.; Philadelphia: Fortress, 1974), 1:78–83, and the additional sources cited there.

87. See Gamble, *Books and Readers*, 7–20.

88. Meeks, *First Urban Christians*, 74–110. To Meeks's list we might add the secret societies that guarded the ancient mysteries. See Richard S. Ascough, *What Are They Saying about the Formation of Pauline Churches?* (New York: Paulist, 1998); Bruce N. Fisk, "Paul: Life and Letters," in *The Face of New Testament Studies* (ed. Scot McKnight and Grant R. Osborne; Grand Rapids: Baker, 2004), 314–15 and the sources in nn. 120–21.

gogal matrix of the early church was what encouraged the conversion of many Gentile "God-fearers" to Christianity.[89] In this context, the provocative thesis of Mark Nanos—that Romans addresses (predominantly Gentile) Christians who continued to move in (predominantly non-Christian) Jewish synagogue circles—has encouraged us to consider ways in which the synagogue and its leadership may have continued to influence the Roman church for some time after the Christian gospel had made inroads.[90]

Almost certainly, Jew-Gentile-Christian relations in Rome were complicated. Not only would Gentile "God-fearers" in the Diaspora have displayed a "broad range of degrees of attachment" to Judaism,[91] but a similar diversity would have marked Jewish-Christian relations in the period before the proverbial "parting of the ways," however that parting is understood.[92] Indeed, we should be open to the possibility that synagogue influence on Roman Christianity extended into the waning decades of the first century, a possibility that might explain the extensive use of both Scripture and postcanonical Jewish traditions in 1 Clement, a subapostolic epistle likely authored by a Roman Gentile in the 90s. In this regard, Peter Lampe's comments bear repeating: "*Christians from the sphere of influence of the synagogues*, Jewish Christian as well as Gentile Christians, exercised an astonishing influence on the formation of theology in urban Roman Christianity in the first century. These Christians

---

89. John G. Gager, *Kingdom and Community: The Social World of Early Christianity* (Englewood Cliffs, N.J.: Prentice Hall, 1975); James T. Burtchaell, *From Synagogue to Church: Public Services and Offices in the Earliest Christian Communities* (New York: Cambridge University Press, 1992); Judith M. Lieu, "Do God-Fearers Make Good Christians?" in *Crossing the Boundaries: Essays in Biblical Interpretation in Honour of Michael D. Goulder* (ed. Stanley E. Porter, Paul Joyce, and David E. Orton; Biblical Interpretation Series 8; Leiden: Brill, 1994), 329–45. On the disputed category of "God-fearers" (cf. Acts 10, 13, 16–18) within first-century Judaism, see especially J. Andrew Overman and Robert S. MacLennan, eds., *Diaspora Jews and Judaism: Essays in Honor of, and in Dialogue with, A. Thomas Kraabel* (SFSHJ 41; Atlanta: Scholars Press, 1992); John J. Collins, *Between Athens and Jerusalem: Jewish Identity in the Hellenistic Diaspora* (2nd ed.; Grand Rapids: Eerdmans, 2000), 264–70. For a concise summary of the debate and references in both Jewish and Roman sources to the phenomenon, see Dunn, *Romans 1–8*, xlvii–xlviii.

90. Nanos, "Jewish Context," 283–304; idem, *Mystery of Romans*, 75, 84, 85–165. Nanos's proposal thus moves beyond the consensus view, illustrated by Dunn (*Romans 1–8*, liii), that the Roman Christians "were not yet clearly distinguished from the wider Jewish community."

91. Collins, *Between Athens and Jerusalem*, 270; Dunn, *Romans 1–8*, xlvii.

92. This is a notoriously problematic concept. The challenge of determining how and when "Christianity" emerged as a movement distinct from "Judaism" is taken up in James D. G. Dunn, *Jews and Christians: The Parting of the Ways, A.D. 70 to 135* (Grand Rapids: Eerdmans, 1992); and Wilson, *Related Strangers*.

from the sphere of influence of the synagogues presumably formed the majority."[93]

One might imagine that Jewish attitudes towards Christians would fall along a continuum ranging from exclusion to embrace, as summarized below.

Hostile opposition and exclusion	— for theological reasons related to offensive dining practices, nonenforcement of food laws, and Gentile inclusion without circumcision (Acts 15:1-2; 22-23) — for hermeneutical reasons related to the battle over the right to interpret Israel's Scripture — for christological reasons related to belief in a crucified and risen Messiah — for political reasons related to the potential for conflict, political instability, and Roman reaction — for cultural or linguistic reasons that have little to do with specifically Christian convictions
Ignorance	— because they were largely unaware of Jesus and the early Christian movement, having only a vague acquaintance with the views of certain opponents (Acts 28:21-22)[94] (a few hundred Roman Christians among 50,000 Jews represents about 0.5%)
Benign indifference	— because they were physically/geographically/culturally distinct from the house synagogues/churches where Jesus' followers met — because they were unable to meet together due to physical constraints imposed by the meeting place — because they were unaware of significant differences between Jesus' followers and other sects in Rome, insofar as many Christians adhered faithfully to all essential aspects of Judaism[95]

---

93. Lampe, *From Paul to Valentinus*, 76 (emphasis original).
94. On the challenge of gleaning from Acts 28:21-22 information on church-synagogue relations in Rome, see Das, *Solving the Romans Debate*, 144-46.
95. On a "Judaizing Christianity" in Rome, see Wedderburn, *Reasons for Romans*, 51, citing Ambrosiaster (fourth century). Wedderburn counts Hebrews, if addressed to

	— because they were inclined to co-exist with other diverse and even conflicting expressions of Judaism
	— because they were disinterested insofar as the Jesus movement represented such a small percentage of the synagogue population in Rome and lacked the political clout of the older branches and sects
Sympathy, affirmation, and embrace	— because of geographical links to Palestine or approval of Jesus' teaching
	— because Jesus' followers were turning Gentiles toward Israel's God
	— because they supported an inclusive, less nationalistic brand of Judaism
	— because they acknowledged Jesus as a prophet or even as Israel's Messiah

As for Roman Christian attitudes toward non-Christian Jews, we should probably imagine that the followers of Jesus would have displayed a similarly diverse set of perspectives, only some of which would be reflected in Paul's letter to the Romans (e.g., 11:17–21). Given Rome's cultural and religious diversity and the lack of coordinated governance in the Jewish community, Jews and God-fearers drawn to the Jesus movement would have gathered in diverse house churches and synagogues across the city to test and confirm their new commitments. These meetings, as James Dunn suggests, "would probably not, in the first instance, be thought of as opposed to the life and worship of the wider Jewish community."[96] To the extent that Paul could presume a vibrant Jewish matrix for early Roman Christianity, he would have had reason to expect that his many appeals to Israel's Scripture, whether largely rhetorical or soberly exegetical, would resonate with an audience that was both sympathetic and knowledgeable.

---

the church at Rome (Heb 13:24), as evidence that Christians in Rome were feeling drawn to abandon their loyalty to Jesus and fellow-Christians (10:25) by turning or returning to non-Christian synagogue attendance.

96. Dunn, *Romans 1–8*, xlviii. For a summary of research on house-churches in Rome, emphasizing the impact of architecture and space on group identity, see Esler, *Conflict and Identity*, 102–7, 120–25.

4. Conclusions

I began this study by posing two questions: (1) What can we know about the historical relationship between church and synagogue in mid-first century Rome? (2) How much has the synagogue shaped, schooled, and influenced Paul's earliest Roman readers?

I conclude by summarizing our modest findings. It remains to be seen whether these remarks will withstand scrutiny and, if so, how much exegetical payoff we should expect from them.

(1) Although most of Rome's many synagogues were located in the Trans-Tiber quarters, they differed widely in configuration (neighborhood, profession, origin), practices, rituals, and degree of openness to non-Jews and Christians.

(2) There was no central governing body for Jews across Rome; each synagogue or prayer house had independent status and local leadership.

(3) An impressive number of Gentiles were attracted in varying degrees to the beliefs and rhythms of Judaism, with interests ranging from curiosity to conversion. These adherents likely frequented synagogue buildings and attended religious services; perhaps some even provided financial subsidies.

(4) A central pillar of synagogue ritual in our period was the reading, study, and (likely) teaching of Torah. It is reasonable to assume the stability and regularity of additional liturgical elements including Haftarah readings, prayers, and homilies.

(5) There is good reason to think that many scholars have overstated the ideological gaps and social tensions between non-Christian Jews and Christian Gentiles in Rome during our period. For the years prior to Paul's Roman epistle, the burden of proof should rest with those who wish to argue for a wide chasm between (largely non-Christian) Jewish and (largely Gentile) Christian communities with little opportunity for exchange and mutual influence.

(6) There is also reason to suspect that the prevailing patterns of synagogue worship, including the public reading and study of Torah, influenced and shaped the culture of early Christianity in Rome. Gentile followers of Jesus would have varied widely in their familiarity with Torah, depending on the resources, leadership, and practice of the synagogues that they attended and the extent, intensity, and duration of their contact with a particular Jewish community.

(7) It is precarious to make claims based solely on evidence within Romans about the competence of Paul's actual first readers. In light of what other sources tell us about synagogue practice, however, and given the lack of evidence that Rome's Christian community had uniformly severed its ties

with the synagogue, it does not appear unreasonable to think that many of those who first read or heard Paul's letter would have enjoyed considerable prior, and ongoing, exposure to a number of the scriptural passages Paul cites. Paul's best guess about his readers' competence may not be far off.

Part 4
Paul's Intertextual Background(s)

The Meaning of δικαιοσύνη Θεοῦ in Romans: An Intertextual Suggestion*

Douglas A. Campbell

Richard Hays suggested some time ago that Rom 1:17 is informed by Ps 98:2-3 (97:2-3 LXX).[1] On first considering this claim, I rejected it as unlikely.[2] I have since, however, reversed that judgment and now hold the suggestion to be both probable and highly significant. To note the issue of significance briefly: if this intertext lies behind 1:17, then it enfolds—or at least directly informs—Paul's first use of δικαιοσύνη Θεοῦ in Romans. This Old Testament text might then provide us with critical insight into the meaning of that important but much-contested phrase in Paul, perhaps rather as Hab 2:4 arguably informs the apostle's use elsewhere in Romans

---

* This essay appears as "An Echo of Scripture in Paul, and Its Implications," in *The Word Leaps the Gap: Essays in Honor of Richard B. Hays* (ed. Katherine Grieb, Kavin Rowe, and Ross Wagner; Grand Rapids: Eerdmans, 2008); and Douglas A. Campbell, *The Deliverance of God* (Grand Rapids: Eerdmans, 2008), ch. 17, §2.3. Reprinted by permission of the publisher; all rights reserved.

1. Richard B. Hays, *Echoes of Scripture in the Letters of Paul* (New Haven: Yale University Press, 1989), 36-37. Others have since noted some sort of connection, apparently independently of Hays: see C. E. B. Cranfield, *A Critical and Exegetical Commentary on the Epistle to the Romans* (2 vols.; ICC; London: T&T Clark, 2004), 1:96 (parenthetically and without further comment); Robert Jewett, *Romans: A Commentary* (Hermeneia; Minneapolis: Fortress, 2007), 143, citing Klaus Haacker, *Der Brief des Paulus an die Römer* (THKNT 6; Leipzig: Evangelische Verlagsantsalt, 1999), 41; also Robert Morgan, *Romans* (NTG; Sheffield: Sheffield Academic Press, 1995), 20-21, cited by A. Katherine Grieb, *The Story of Romans: A Narrative Defense of God's Righteousness* (Louisville: Westminster John Knox, 2002), 11 n. 21. Mark Seifrid cites this text as central to the broader debate but never connects it with Rom 1:16-17; see *Christ, Our Righteousness: Paul's Theology of Justification* (NSBT 9; Downers Grove, Ill.: InterVarsity Press, 2000), 38-40.

2. One of the mistakes in my *The Rhetoric of Righteousness in Romans 3:21-26* (JSNTSup 65; Sheffield: JSOT Press, 1992).

of πίστις.³ But in order to generate this significance, the suggestion must of course first prove true, and our subsequent discussion will address this challenge in two stages.

First we must revisit the specific question of the echo itself that was posed initially by Hays: Does Rom 1:17 demonstrably echo Ps 98? Many have not detected this connection in the past. But if we conclude that it is likely, then we will have to explore the further semantic consequences of this realization—the broader echo chamber of the initial sounding, so to speak—since these have been largely overlooked. And I will suggest, in a move beyond Hays's initial work, that this echo generates a broad and rich resonance through Romans in terms of the ancient discourse of kingship. It is *this* particular chord that Paul is sounding with the strategic phrase δικαιοσύνη Θεοῦ, mediated by the text of Ps 98, which is a psalm of divine kingship. Δικαιοσύνη Θεοῦ denotes for Paul nothing less than the decisive saving act of deliverance by the divine King of his royal appointed representative, that is, the resurrection and enthronement of Jesus (the) Christ.

The first stage in this demonstration—the detection of the initial echo—can be dealt with relatively quickly. However, the second—its orchestration in terms of the discourse of kingship—is more complex and controversial and will take us a little longer.

1. An Echo of Scripture in Romans 1:17

The detection of scriptural echoes is a delicate matter,⁴ but an accumulation of various indicators suggests to me that Hays was absolutely right to assert that Paul is echoing the opening verses of Ps 98 in Rom 1:16-17—an echo

---

3. See Rom 1:17; 3:5, 21, 22, 25, 26; 10:3 (2x); 1 Cor 1:30; 2 Cor 5:21; Phil 3:9. Literature on this debate is voluminous; an excellent introductory survey and bibliography is supplied by John Reumann in his series of entries "Righteousness (Early Judaism)," "Righteousness (Greco-Roman World)," and "Righteousness (NT)," *ABD* 5:736-73. The suggestion concerning πίστις was made by Richard Hays as well, in *The Faith of Jesus Christ: The Narrative Substructure of Galatians 3:1-4:11* (2nd ed.; Grand Rapids: Eerdmans, 2002).

4. Hays's own initial treatment of the methodological issues in *Echoes of Scripture* (esp. 29-32) is difficult to better; his criteria for detecting an echo are presented again and revised in his "'Who Has Believed Our Message?': Paul's Reading of Isaiah," in idem, *The Conversion of the Imagination: Paul as Interpreter of Israel's Scripture* (Grand Rapids: Eerdmans, 2005), 25-49. Some helpful recent refinements are undertaken by Leroy Huizenga, in dialogue in particular with the semiotic theories of Umberto Eco and Stefan Alkier; see especially "Dictionaries, Encyclopedias, and the Model Reader," ch. 1 in "The Akedah in Matthew" (unpublished Ph.D. diss., Duke University, 2006), 43-101.

that encloses the critical phrase in which we are currently interested. The psalm reads (Ps 97:2-3 in the LXX, the version of the Old Testament that Paul generally uses[5]):

² ἐγνώρισεν κύριος τὸ σωτήριον αὐτοῦ,
ἐναντίον τῶν ἐθνῶν ἀπεκάλυψεν τὴν δικαιοσύνην αὐτοῦ.
³ ἐμνήσθη τοῦ ἐλέους αὐτοῦ τῷ Ἰακὼβ
καὶ τῆς ἀληθείας αὐτοῦ τῷ οἴκῳ Ἰσραήλ·
εἴδοσαν πάντα τὰ πέρατα τῆς γῆς τὸ σωτήριον τοῦ θεοῦ ἡμῶν.

Paul then writes in Rom 1:16-17:

¹⁶ δύναμις γὰρ Θεοῦ ἐστιν εἰς σωτηρίαν παντὶ τῷ πιστεύοντι,
Ἰουδαίῳ τε πρῶτον καὶ Ἕλληνι.
¹⁷ δικαιοσύνη γὰρ Θεοῦ ἐν αὐτῷ ἀποκαλύπτεται
ἐκ πίστεως εἰς πίστιν καθὼς γέγραπται κ.τ.λ.

There are three distinguishable indicators that underpin the judgment that Paul is echoing this psalm passage: phraseological, lexicographical, and thematic. There is, first, an echo of a clause (i.e., of a potentially self-sufficient phrase) and not merely of isolated words here; compare δικαιοσύνη γὰρ Θεοῦ ... ἀποκαλύπτεται in the target text with ἀπεκάλυψεν τὴν δικαιοσύνην αὐτοῦ from the source text. Although these syntagms are not precisely the same, they are essentially so: the same substantive, δικαιοσύνη, with a genitive denoting the same subject, God (Θεοῦ/αὐτοῦ), being developed by the same verb, ἀποκαλύπτω, although in different tenses and voices. It is worth noting, moreover, that this basic clause and association in the two texts is unequalled in its proximity, whether elsewhere in Paul or in the LXX.[6] Second, this essentially phraseological echo is accompanied in both texts by a parallel to δικαιοσύνη constructed with "salvation," the word σωτηρία occurring once in Rom 1:16 and its cognate twice in Ps 98.[7] So a close lexical associ-

---

5. Dietrich-Alex Koch's conclusion in 1986, which still seems plausible; see *Die Schrift als Zeuge des Evangeliums: Untersuchungen zur Verwendung und zum Verständnis der Schrift bei Paulus* (BHT 69; Tübingen: Mohr Siebeck, 1986).

6. Intriguingly, the Hebrew texts Isa 56:1 and CD 20.20 are close to this clause, as Haacker notes (*Der Brief des Paulus an die Römer*, 41). But the LXX blunts the echo of Isaiah in the Greek, translating צדקה with ἔλεος, and Paul's reproduction of a clause from Qumran directly is, of course, unlikely. Romans 3:21-22 is also a partial exception to this claim, although there the verb has changed to a synonym, φανερόω.

7. Strictly speaking, the LXX uses the neuter adjective τὸ σωτήριον at this point.

ation seems to confirm the initial syntagmatic echo.[8] But, third, a series of broader thematic similarities is apparent as well. Both texts discuss an antithesis between Jews and pagans (Ἰουδαῖος versus Ἕλληνος in Romans; τὰ ἔθνη versus Ἰακώβ/οἶκος Ἰσραήλ in the psalm), in relation to which God is acting.[9] Moreover, in both texts God is acting to make something known, this point being made in Ps 98 by further verbs of knowledge and of sight.[10] Finally, the aorist tenses in the psalm corroborate Paul's later temporal emphases in Rom 3:21–26 that the divine saving event has taken place "now," in the sense of the immediate past and the present, as against the future. God *has* acted. So the unusual temporality of the two texts—which is a crucial argumentative point in Romans for Paul—is identical as well.

In my view, this is an impressive accumulation of evidence, the force of which is difficult to deny. Phraseological, lexical, and three thematic echoes all reinforce one another in suggesting a connection, and more general considerations seem only to enhance these implications.[11] In view of all this evidence, some relationship between Ps 98:2–3 and Rom 1:16–17 looks almost certain. Hays's initial perception was, in my opinion, profoundly right. We will need to consider in due course why Paul does not mark this quotation explicitly, as

---

8. This correlation is very significant, because it limits the relevant background texts to those that speak of *iustitia salutifera*. Moreover, this particular action occurs (as Morgan points out in *Romans*, 20–21) primarily in the Psalter, though there is a significant cluster of such instances in Isaiah.

9. This emphasis is apparent in the context preceding Rom 1:16–17 as well, where Paul has been speaking of his apostolic commission (to) Ἕλλησίν τε καὶ βαρβάροις, σοφοῖς τε καὶ ἀνοήτοις.

10. There is even a hint of priority of action toward Judaism in Ps 98, as God is said to have remembered his mercy and fidelity to Israel, something the pagan nations there "see." This arguably echoes the overt statement of Jewish priority in Rom 1:16b—Ἰουδαίῳ τε πρῶτον καὶ Ἕλληνι—although I would not want to press this point. I supply an additional explanation for this phrase in my extensive study of justification questions in Paul, *The Deliverance of God: An Apocalyptic Rereading of Justification in Paul* (Grand Rapids: Eerdmans, forthcoming), ch. 19.

11. It is widely conceded that Paul quotes and alludes to Scripture repeatedly through Romans. Within this practice, it is also evident that he makes extensive use of texts from the Psalms (see esp. 3:10–18 and 20a in the immediate setting). Romans 3:21–22, which is so closely constructed to 1:17, is little more than a pastiche of scriptural texts—except, that is, at *this* point, where the disclosure of the δικαιοσύνη Θεοῦ is stated, so the lacuna has now been addressed. Admittedly, this last argument may be a little opaque in the present setting, but it is, I would suggest, ultimately quite significant. If 3:21–22 is demonstrably a pastiche of intertexts, then we might expect some intertext to emerge here as well, as indeed Ps 98:2–3 does. For detailed development of this argument, see my *Deliverance of God*, ch. 15.

he does his other key intertexts in Romans;[12] this particular scriptural usage is allusive rather than overt. But I will suggest an explanation for this reticence shortly. It is important for now to investigate the semantic implications of this intertextual linkage further—the moment at which previous exploration of this connection has tended to falter. And here we enter the second, more complex phase in our intertextual exploration.

2. Paul and the Ancient Discourse of Kingship

Psalm 98 is a psalm of divine kingship[13] and contains (as we will see in more detail shortly) terminology and themes characteristic of that ancient Jewish discourse: a discourse that interwove in turn with broader conceptions of kingship, both divine and human, throughout the ancient Near East. The discourse of kingship had profoundly ancient roots but was also very much alive—sometimes in new variations—in Paul's day. This raises the possibility that the phrase δικαιοσύνη Θεοῦ is operating within that broader discourse and is colored by its distinctive concerns. Our investigation of this possibility will unfold in an analysis of five subordinate questions: (1) the general contours of the ancient discourse of kingship; (2) the meaning(s) of "right" actions by a king; (3) the presence (or absence) of this discourse in Romans; (4) the probable meaning of δικαιοσύνη Θεοῦ in Rom 1:17; and (5) the implications for the construal of δικαιοσύνη Θεοῦ in relation to the covenant. In navigating these questions, we will be drawing upon certain recent scholarly advances in relation to Jesus' messiahship, resurrection, and lordship, some of which have recently been pressed through Romans, although in a rather preliminary way.

2.1. The Ancient Discourse of Kingship

Psalm 98 is part of a widespread ancient discourse concerning kingship and its particular ascription by pious Jews to their God.[14] It is one of the classic

---

12. That is, with a quotation formula, usually γέγραπται.
13. Hays does not develop this point, referring rather to lament and exile, which are not to be excluded from the interpretation either of Paul or of Romans but do not seem so directly relevant here (see *Echoes of Scripture*, 38). Seifrid is sensitive to this connotation but, as noted above, does not connect it directly to the key texts and phrases in Romans; see *Christ, Our Righteousness*, 39.
14. Keith W. Whitelam provides an excellent summary and bibliography in "King and Kingship," *ABD* 4:40–48; see also J. H. Eaton, *Kingship and the Psalms* (SBT 2/32; London: SCM, 1976); James Luther Mays, *The Lord Reigns: A Theological Handbook to the Psalms*

expositions of this discourse as identified by Gunkel and Begrich in 1933. They pointed in particular to Pss 47, 93, and 96–99,[15] all of which name God explicitly at a certain point as "king" (see here 98:6). Psalm 98 is typically theocentric throughout, speaking primarily of acts by God on his people's behalf in terms thought appropriate for the divine ruler: acts of salvation, deliverance, order, and judgment. These acts are accomplished by God's "right hand" or "holy arm." The people then respond with rejoicing and thanksgiving, and this response is typically hyperbolic; it is literally orchestrated, and other facets of creation join in as well (presumably because they are also ruled by God the King): the sea and its contents, the world and all who dwell in it, the rivers, and the mountains. Significantly, because the scope of the divine King's rule is cosmic, these acts are visible to and indeed affect the pagan nations in addition to Israel.

Numerous other texts, both within and outside the Jewish scriptural tradition, freight this discourse in various ways.[16] But the complex data can be simplified (as is necessary here) by the recognition that much of it is characterized by a root metaphor concerning God—the metaphor precisely of God as a king.[17] The content of that image was generated largely by historical, human kingship, although presumably in the form of ideal types. God the

---

(Louisville: Westminster John Knox, 1994); J. Richard Middleton, *The Liberating Image: The Imago Dei in Genesis 1* (Grand Rapids: Brazos, 2005). A brief account more directly relevant to our concerns here is Richard J. Bauckham, *God Crucified: Monotheism and Christology in the New Testament* (Carlisle, U.K.: Paternoster, 1998), 9–13.

15. Gunkel and Begrich denoted these texts as "enthronement psalms" (as noted by Whitelam, "King and Kingship," 43). Significantly, Sigmund Mowinckel had earlier worked with a much more extensive range of texts, so the enthronement psalms provide a very minimalist data pool. Mowinckel includes Pss 8; 15; 24; 29; 33; 46; 48; 50; 66a; 75; 76; 81; 82; 84; 87; 114; 118; 132; 149; and Exod 15:1–18; the data can arguably be broadened still further.

16. The Hellenistic and Roman data should not be ignored; see esp. Aristotle, *Pol.* 3.14–18; 5.10–11; Seneca, *De clementia*; Dio Chrysostom, *Disc.* 1–4 (see also *Disc.* 62). See Erwin R. Goodenough, "The Political Philosophy of Hellenistic Kingship," *YCS* 1 (1928): 55–102; Bruno Blumenfeld, *The Political Paul: Justice, Democracy, and Kingship in a Hellenistic Framework* (JSNTSup 210; Sheffield: Sheffield Academic Press, 2001).

17. I draw here on the terms and method of George Lakoff; see especially his *Moral Politics: How Liberals and Conservatives Think* (2nd ed.; Chicago: University of Chicago Press, 2001); see also his earlier classic study (with Mark Johnson), *Metaphors We Live By* (2nd ed.; Chicago: University of Chicago Press, 2003). His work is discussed in more detail in my *Deliverance of God*, esp. chs. 1 and 7. Root metaphors have been applied to Paul's thought previously by John L. White, although in a rather different way from here; see *The Apostle of God: Paul and the Promise of Abraham* (Peabody, Mass.: Hendrickson, 1999), 3–59.

King and the ideal human king were images that mutually interpreted one another, a fact that draws other illuminating texts into the elaboration of the discourse (especially Pss 2; 45; 72; 89; 110).[18]

We learn from these texts (supported by studies of ancient iconography, etc.) that ancient kings, and ancient gods conceived of as kings, had a fundamental duty of care in relation to their people.[19] This could unfold in two basic ways.

First, if a king's people were in some sort of difficulty, it was the monarch's duty to resolve that difficulty. If they were oppressed or invaded, the king was obliged to deliver or defend them. But this function was often narrated in the ancient Near East in cosmic terms (partly, no doubt, to underwrite the need for a king in the first place). Indeed, it was frequently in the first instance the divine king's duty to establish cosmic order, slaying or controlling the monsters of chaos that threatened the cosmos with instability or dissolution.[20] Alternatively, it was the chaotic waters bordering the world that needed to be controlled (and so on). Cosmic and more recognizably political activities thus intertwine throughout this discourse—and entirely deliberately. However, all of these actions, whether concretely political or more mythical and ritual, revolve around the basic notion of a ruler acting to save his people from disorder and oppression and to establish them in (relative) freedom and safety, whether that ruler is divine, human, or an alliance of the two.

Complementing this principal type of saving and ordering activity is the second broad duty incumbent on the divine and human monarchs, namely, sustaining a condition of peace and prosperity. Once order has been established, or reestablished, it is the duty of the divine monarch and/or the divinely appointed monarch to preserve it. It is worth noting that the "being" of kings, whether divine or human, is consequently inseparable from their activity. Kings are what they do; character and activity are correlative notions

---

18. Strong boundaries in the evidence should not be drawn between Jewish, ancient Near Eastern, and more recent Hellenistic and Roman discourses.

19. See the later medieval and aristocratic notions of *royaume* and *noblesse oblige*; see also, most importantly, Ps 72, where this duty is often spelled out explicitly. Whitelam ("King and Kingship," 42) states more discursively (in relation specifically to human kingship) that "the justification of kingship with its centralized social structure was based upon a guarantee of order, security, prosperity, fertility, etc., in return for loyalty and subservience."

20. The desire to control the forces of chaos was widespread in the ancient Near East, although in different local forms: cf. the Egyptian ideology of the pharaoh as the Lord of *ma'at*, as against the Babylonian epic *Enuma Elish*, where Marduk establishes a right to rule by defeating the sea monster Tiamat. Ugaritic material evidences similar notions as well. For references, see Whitelam, "King and Kingship," 45.

in this relation. We can now note some further common elements in this discourse that are relevant to our unfolding concerns.

As has already been intimated, an important alliance generally holds between the divine king and an appointed earthly representative, who is also a king, although in a derivative sense. Numerous variations on this basic dynamic are observable, including the strand in the Old Testament that rejects this relationship altogether ("no king for Israel but God"). Yet even in this radical variant, divine kingship is effected through appointed earthly agents or representatives who act with authority that they receive by way of delegation from the divine ruler, often as they are inspired by the divine Spirit. Usually, however, such figures are royal and part of a divinely ratified dynasty, "the Lord" establishing "the lord." (This alliance cries out for an ideological analysis, but this is not our present concern.) The earthly king, then, is usually involved in the fulfillment of his duties in both sacral and overtly political and military activities, although these interpenetrate in ancient societies. The establishment and preservation of cosmic and political order are his responsibility, so cultic and political capacities are developed to carry out his duties in those respective spheres. Accordingly, there is an important observable relationship between the palace and the temple (not to mention the military), one that influences much of the Old Testament.[21] David and Solomon dominate the kingly ideals as they are presented by the Old Testament, David acting overtly more as a deliverer of his people, the one who creates order, and Solomon as the establisher of a suitably impressive cultus over which he presides (see esp. 1 Kgs 3:1–2, 5–6; 7:13–51; 8–9), thereby sustaining that order and prosperity. But he is also, of course, the archetypally wise ruler (see 1 Kgs 2:6, 9; 3:9, 12, 16–28; 4:29–34; 5:7, 12; 10:23–24). The key symbols of scepter, crown, and throne (especially this last) are plainly evident in much of this material.[22]

2.2. "Right" Actions by a King

We must now ask the critical question in the present relation: What is a "right" action by a divine king or his appointed human representative? It can be seen almost immediately that the answer depends very much on the par-

---

21. The celebration of the human king as the "son of God" at an annual enthronement festival in ancient Israel has been much debated. Fortunately, this question does not have to be decided here.

22. See Whitelam, "King and Kingship," 42, although arguably he overlooks the emphatically gender-coded symbolism of multiple beautiful wives and concubines; see esp. 2 Sam 16:20–22 and 1 Kgs 2:13–25.

ticular setting of a given action within the broader discourse. A right action may be a dramatic act of intervention that saves or reorders—a fundamentally liberating action that presumably will have a correspondingly oppressive effect on any opposing, hostile forces that are defeated. Alternatively, it may be an ongoing act that sustains peace and/or prosperity or an act that judges a given situation accurately in terms of the ethical rectitude of parties contending at law, thereby maintaining social order.[23]

Furthermore, because the ancient king combines in his person executive and judiciary functions, right actions can be described using terms drawn from either of these fields, although here the most important semantic crossover is probably the deployment of more strictly forensic terminology in relation to executive activity, the language of the law court being used to describe what a modern person would view as an executive political action. Hence, if a right action by a king is described using forensic terminology and imagery such as "verdict" or "judgment," we might nevertheless be speaking of an essentially performative, oppressive or liberating event (these two acts often go together), as against a more strictly retributive procedure (i.e., also performative but with an indicative dimension predicated on appropriate retribution). A military victory, a proclamation of the Jubilee, and an arbitration of a difficult civil case can all be described as "judgments" by the king, and certainly all of these ideally ought to be "right" as well, but they are "right" in very different senses.[24] Such language is still detectable in modern political discourse, although not as frequently; for example, an election result might be described as a "judgment," without meaning by this a retributive action. The immediate context must therefore tell us what kind of activity is in view at any given moment. The language of "rightness" is often deployed in the Old Testament in the specific setting of kingship, using all of these specific senses.[25]

Most important for our discussion here, δικαιοσύνη not infrequently denotes a liberating or delivering act, an action whereby it is "right" for either

---

23. All of these actions are widely attested, in relation to both God and human kings, in the Old Testament.

24. I distinguish these in a more detailed discussion elsewhere in terms of forensic-nonretributive and forensic-retributive actions. In the former, the rectitude of the parties being judged is irrelevant; the action is usually grounded in the right action, and hence character, of the primary actor, i.e., God or the king. In the latter, the rectitude of those being judged is relevant and needs to be assessed accurately by God or the king, so that the resulting judgment rightly reflects that prior ethical calculus. For more discussion, see my *Deliverance of God*, ch. 16.

25. See the excursus at the end of this essay.

God the King or his appointed king to set someone free. Previously some interpreters have referred to this particular subset of the data of δικαιοσύνη in the Old Testament as *iustitia salutifera* because of the frequent occurrence of notions of salvation in the immediate context, and these references have assisted our recognition of this usage as fundamentally liberatory.[26] But we might now have a better explanation of just why the term functions in this way on occasion. It is right in certain circumstances for the king to act to deliver, especially if his clients or his people are in some sort of difficulty. It is his duty to set them free, to save them. Similarly, God the King can act in such terms to deliver his appointed human king, provided that this king has done nothing heinously wrong (or, alternatively, that he has repented sufficiently of any such sins). Again, in these circumstances, it is right for God to act to save.[27]

It might be objected here that this ancient discourse is not especially significant for the New Testament; after all, by the first century C.E. Israel had not been ruled by a Davidic king for a very long time. However, vigorous New Testament debates unfolding along various axes suggest that, although the specifics of the discourse are far from clear, its presence is both significant and undeniable. The current discussions of the relevance of the Roman imperial cult and Augustan ideology to the New Testament (especially to Paul) and the widespread data—especially in the Synoptic Gospels—concerning the "kingdom of God" (or its close equivalent) suggest this conclusion almost immediately.[28] This discourse was still very much in play, in all its subtle local variations, in the New Testament era.

---

26. This material was emphasized in a classic study by Hermann Cremer, *Die paulinische Rechtfertigungslehre im Zusammenhange ihrer geschichtlichen Voraussetzungen* (Gütersloh: Bertelsmann, 1899). A useful brief overview is supplied by J. J. Scullion, "God's ṣedeq-ṣĕdāqâ: Saving Action" in "Righteousness (OT)," *ABD* 5:731-34.

27. The conviction seems to be widespread in the Old Testament that God "cares" and hence can be appealed to directly for help in all sorts of difficult circumstances, irrespective of any claim on that help that might be generated by the appellant's ethical state. Sometimes that putative basis for a claim is introduced, but often it is not, and at times it is even directly disavowed in a repentant mode.

28. Many other debates could be added to these two, such as the stilling of the storm pericopes, which arguably present Jesus as the Divine Warrior, or the triumphal entry. Wright gives an especially vigorous account of the presence of royal themes in Jesus' life in *Jesus and the Victory of God* (Minneapolis: Fortress, 1996), esp. chs. 6-13 (198-653); the relevant data is listed in an appendix, "'Kingdom of God' in Early Christian Literature," 663-70. An interesting application to a Pauline text of themes especially associated with the Divine Warrior is Timothy G. Gombis, "Ephesians 2 as a Narrative of Divine Warfare," *JSNT* 26 (2004): 403-18.

2.3. Divine Kingship in Romans and the Early Church

With these broader observations in place, we can turn to consider an important contextual question in relation to Paul. Is a discourse of divine kingship operative in Romans? This specific query touches on several important debates that are currently unfolding within New Testament studies.

Since the seminal work of Wilhelm Bousset, theological development in the early church has been viewed by many interpreters panoramically as a slow progression from limited, theologically primitive, Jewish, particular notions to a liberated, theologically mature, Hellenistic, universal gospel that is perhaps best exemplified by John.[29] This famous paradigm has greatly influenced the reconstruction of almost every New Testament question, figure, and text, whether Jesus, the pre-Pauline church, Paul himself, or the figures who wrote after him, such as the authors of the Gospels. There have consequently been strong methodological tendencies to detach Paul's understanding of Jesus from "early," "low," and Jewish christological categories such as Messiah and to interpret it instead in terms of "later," "higher" (although not necessarily "high/the highest"!), and Hellenistic categories, within which stratum the apostle's use of the title "Lord" is generally included. This is often combined with emphases on a spiritual rather than a bodily resurrection and a supposed disinterest in the teaching and life of the historical Jesus.[30] All these concerns have, of course, influenced the interpretation of Paul's most discursive letter, Romans, leading to a certain myopia at key points that we must try briefly in what follows to redress.[31]

Various scholars have for some time been attempting to roll back the broad agenda of Bousset, and with some success.[32] N. T. Wright, for exam-

---

29. Wilhelm Bousset, *Kyrios Christos: A History of the Belief in Christ from the Beginnings of Christianity to Irenaeus* (trans. J. E. Steely; Nashville: Abingdon, 1970).

30. I would add that this agenda also integrates in certain useful ways with the predominant Protestant way of construing Paul's soteriology, which emphasizes individualism, liberation from the crabbed constraints of the law, and the atoning death of Christ—i.e., justification. For a more detailed description of this soteriology and its various theological and social legitimations, see my *Deliverance of God*, esp. chs. 1, 6, and 9.

31. An accessible overview of this and related trends can be found in Larry W. Hurtado, *Lord Jesus Christ: Devotion to Jesus in Earliest Christianity* (Grand Rapids: Eerdmans, 2003), 1–29. For more detailed engagements, see the following note.

32. Among others, see especially Bauckham, *God Crucified*; Joseph A. Fitzmyer, "The Semitic Background of the New Testament *Kyrios*-Title," in *The Semitic Background of the New Testament* (Grand Rapids: Eerdmans, 1997), 115–42; idem, "New Testament *Kyrios* and *Maranatha* and Their Aramaic Background," in *To Advance the Gospel: New Testament Studies* (2nd ed.; Grand Rapids: Eerdmans, 1998), 218–35; Martin Hengel, "Christological

ple, has vigorously reemphasized the Jewishness and messiahship of Jesus, his bodily resurrection, and his exalted lordship (which ought to be understood, furthermore, in a thoroughly Jewish sense). He is in the process of pressing these emphases through the thought of Paul, the argument of Romans, and the general theological development of the early church.[33] It is not necessary to endorse all of the details of Wright's various claims and arguments—which are numerous—in order to find these basic corrections to Bousset's paradigm plausible.[34] Indeed, they appear to participate in a new paradigm that is gathering momentum within New Testament studies, at least in certain quarters. But Wright's principal corrections are of great moment for our present discussion.

If interpreters approach Paul and Romans with ears freshly attuned to the importance and integration of Jesus' messiahship, resurrection, and exaltation to lordship, the textual surface of the letter begins to shift in some interesting new directions. Initially, it becomes apparent that these themes have simply been underemphasized by much previous interpretation. So, for example, resurrection is a much more prominent theme in Romans than most commentators seem to have realized, as is Jesus' Davidic descent. But following these realizations it rapidly begins to emerge that the various recovered motifs are not just isolated points of emphasis for Paul, that is, spots where his authentic Jewishness and/or his continuity with the thinking of the early church is gratifyingly apparent. Rather, they are tightly integrated concerns that fulfill important argumentative and theological roles.[35] I would suggest,

---

Titles in Early Christianity," in *The Messiah: Developments in Earliest Judaism and Christianity* (ed. James H. Charlesworth; Minneapolis: Fortress, 1992), 425–48; idem, "'Sit at My Right Hand!' The Enthronement of Christ at the Right Hand of God and Psalm 110:1," in *Studies in Early Christology* (Edinburgh: T&T Clark, 1995), 119–225; Larry W. Hurtado, *One God, One Lord: Early Christian Devotion and Ancient Jewish Monotheism* (2nd ed.; London: T&T Clark, 1998); idem, *Lord Jesus Christ*, passim; C. Kavin Rowe, "Romans 10:13: What Is the Name of the Lord?" *HBT* 22 (2000): 135–73. See also the works by N. T. Wright in the following note.

33. Wright's principal treatments are *The Climax of the Covenant: Christ and the Law in Pauline Theology* (Edinburgh: T&T Clark, 1991); idem, *The New Testament and the People of God* (London: SPCK, 1992); idem, *Jesus and the Victory of God*; idem, "Romans," *NIB* 10:393–770; and idem, *The Resurrection of the Son of God* (Minneapolis: Fortress, 2003). He refers to numerous shorter studies, many on Romans, in these major works.

34. Arguably, there are insensitivities in certain aspects of his work, not to mention occasional gaps; for a slightly different account of the resurrection, e.g., see Dale C. Allison Jr., *Resurrecting Jesus: The Earliest Christian Tradition and Its Interpreters* (London: T&T Clark, 2005). I am assuming here, however, that his basic claims are plausible.

35. Sensitivity to narrative and intertextuality are vital here—thus the importance of the work of Richard Hays (see n. 1).

however, that while Wright and others have begun the resulting process of reinterpretation,[36] the addition of one or two more insights can bring still greater clarity and cogency to our reappropriation of the letter's argument.

I recommend that these recovered emphases be correlated in a significant interplay with the ancient discourse of kingship, which in Romans is now focused on—and in a real sense *realized by*—Jesus Christ. Indeed, an entire theological complex constructed in these terms is discernible within Romans, although it is clearly subtle. This integrated program is signaled *in nuce* by Paul's famous opening statements in Rom 1:1b-4, a passage that we begin to recognize as programmatic for much of the rest of Romans:[37]

> Paul, a servant of Jesus Christ, called to be an apostle, set apart for the gospel of God, which he promised beforehand through his prophets in the holy scriptures, the gospel concerning his Son, who was descended from David according to the flesh and was declared to be Son of God with power according to the Spirit of holiness by resurrection from the dead, Jesus Christ our Lord. (NRSV)

Christ's messiahship and lordship are here affirmed by his resurrection from the dead, which functions, furthermore, as a *heavenly enthronement*. This enthronement is effected by the Spirit of sanctification, who in the Old Testament sanctifies the cult and the people of God and anoints the king. Equally importantly, this event is widely attested by the Jewish Scriptures—both Torah and Prophets. Moreover, it is an explanation of Jesus' sonship. He is the Son of God because, as for any divinely appointed king, God has now become his Father. So he is the King of Israel not only by descent, as a "son of David," but also by royal enthronement; his "coronation" has already taken place. As a sanctifying act, this must somehow implicitly effect the broader reconciliation of God with creation and his people, presumably overcoming the oppressive and even chaotic forces that seek to disrupt that relationship. Order should be established and prosperity realized and preserved. So, entirely predict-

---

36. The work of Daniel Kirk is also of significance in this relation; see his *Unlocking Romans: Resurrection and the Justification of God* (Grand Rapids: Eerdmans, 2008).

37. Wright makes this point clearly: "The Christology of 1:3-4 is by no means an isolated statement attached loosely to the front of the letter but not relevant to its contents. It is the careful, weighted, programmatic statement of what will turn out to be Paul's subtext throughout the whole epistle (see also 9:5; and 15:12, the final scriptural quotation of the main body of the letter)"; later he also points to 5:12-21 and "all the elements of chaps. 6-8 that follow from it" (*Romans*, 413, 415-19, quoting 417 and 418). Robert Jewett (*Romans*, 96-98, 103-8) provides a nuanced analysis in full dialogue with the extensive secondary discussion.

ably, the appointed ambassadors of that reconciliation, like Paul, are sent out to establish the appropriate submission and fidelity to this ruler in the rest of the world by way of their delegation ("apostleship") and proclamation ("gospel")—so 1:1b and 5-6.

This is an essentially narrative account—a story rich with theological import—that links Jesus' messiahship, resurrection, and lordship. Clearly, many Old Testament texts that speak of divine and human kingship will resonate with it. Scholars debate many further issues within these broad assertions, but most of those debates do not concern us at this point.[38] What matters here is more limited: the implicit evidence that this basic narrative is mobilized by Paul throughout much of the rest of Romans. We can note five points where this narrative emerges in a conspicuous way, followed by two further, supplementary pieces of evidence.

(1) In Rom 5:1–11 God *reconciles* a hostile world to himself through the Christ-event (see esp. 5:10–11). Here Paul describes the divine act in quite distinctive language that resonates with the language of diplomatic, political, and royal circles (and invariably so whenever a delegate is involved, as indicated by the presence of πρεσβευ- language).[39] There is, moreover, a complementary use of royal "access" language in 5:2, in relation to which this reconciliation takes place. Then, in 5:14, an emphatic use of the terminology of government begins, with Paul speaking repeatedly of what are in effect two kingdoms, with two "rules," respective services, and even enslavements, and a military relationship of hostility and/or victory. These emphases continue through subsequent chapters in the letter.[40]

---

38. It is not, for example, immediately apparent how "high" this Christology is. Paul's use of "lord" here could be divine, entirely human, or roaming somewhere in between. But this question is best addressed in relation to Rom 10:9–13; see especially Rowe, "What Is the Name of the Lord?" It should be asked in due course whether this material represents Paul's thought exhaustively or is presupposed by him in relation to his auditors. It must suffice here to indicate that I view it as a shared basis for discussion, Paul's own position pushing rather radically beyond it, although in continuity with it; for further justification of this claim, see my *Deliverance of God*, esp. ch. 19.

39. Jewett surveys the "reconciliation debate" in Paul in *Romans*, 364–66, noting that detailed studies by F. Hahn, M. Hengel, and C. Breytenbach support the reading being suggested here. Jewett also discusses "access" in 347–50, although without linking the two debates.

40. So, for example, Paul uses the verb [συμ]βασιλεύω a total of only ten times, but six of those are in this section of Romans: see 5:14, 17 [2x], 21 [2x]; 6:12 (also 1 Cor 4:8 [3x] and 15:25, where the royal connotations of this term are explicit). In 8:15 and 21 he uses δουλεία, elsewhere only in (the closely similar) Gal 4:24 and 5:1. In 8:37 he speaks of ὑπερνικάω, a hapax legomenon.

(2) In Rom 8 the theme of heavenly enthronement and glorification of Christ that was signaled in 1:2–4 reemerges. In 8:15–17 those who cry "Abba Father" receive "sonship" or "adoption" (υἱοθεσία), becoming "children of God," "and if children, also heirs—heirs of God and fellow heirs with Christ." Paul affirms here (and in Gal 4:6) this cry's appropriateness for Christians, who participate in the "firstborn," namely, Jesus (see also Rom 8:29–30). His resurrection, understood also as a heavenly enthronement (see esp. 8:34: ἐν δεξιᾷ τοῦ Θεοῦ), explains the access that Christians now have "in him" to the inheritance that he has received, their status as children of God like him, and the consequent appropriateness of their cry to a God now characterized as "Father." Such father-son language and affirmations, in the context of adoption, inheritance, and glorification, seem best explained by texts such as Ps 89 and the broader discourse of divine kingship.[41] The preserved Aramaism in Rom 8:15 is meanwhile a marker of this christological tradition's antiquity within the early church. We seem to be in touch here, then, with an early explanation of the resurrection—as the heavenly enthronement and glorification of Jesus and as his consequent affirmation as Messiah and Lord, who will rule the cosmos on behalf of his divine Father.

(3) Kavin Rowe has pointed out that Paul's repeated affirmations of lordship in Rom 10:9–13 draw on important Old Testament intertexts and are rooted in the entirely Jewish monotheistic veneration of Yahweh as the only true God. Moreover, the affirmation of Jesus' lordship, which is included unavoidably by Paul in this central Jewish confession, is confirmed by his resurrection—a connection illuminated best by the interpretation of the resurrection as the enthronement of the Messiah, Jesus, *as* Lord.[42] Paul's unusual reference to "the Christ" in 9:5 is comprehensible in part as an anticipation of his later use of this narrative.[43]

---

41. αὐτὸς ἐπικαλέσεταί με Πατήρ μου εἶ σύ, θεός μου καὶ ἀντιλήμπτωρ τῆς σωτηρίας μου· κἀγὼ πρωτότοκον θήσομαι αὐτόν, ὑψηλὸν παρὰ τοῖς βασιλεῦσιν τῆς γῆς (Ps 89:26–27 [88:27–28 LXX]). Note also the use of δικαιοσύνη to describe benevolent and salvific acts of God in 89:14 and 16 (15 and 17 LXX), in parallel with κρίμα, ἔλεος, εὐδοκία, καύχημα, and ἀλήθεια. It may also be legitimate to detect an influence from Ps 110 at this point in the reference to God's right hand—another royal enthronement psalm, of course, and one much used by the early church. See Donald H. Juel, *Messianic Exegesis: Christological Interpretation of the Old Testament in Early Christianity* (new ed.; Minneapolis: Augsburg Fortress, 1998), 135–50.

42. Rowe, "What Is the Name of the Lord?"

43. Indeed, this subsection of Romans is arguably replete with various messianic and royal connotations, most notably perhaps of wisdom. For more details, see my *Deliverance of God*, ch. 19.

(4) Although it is often overlooked, Rom 15:12 effects the closure of the main letter body by affirming Jesus' Davidic lineage through a citation of Isa 11:10 (see also 42:4 LXX, which is closely accompanied by the divine King's δικαιοσύνη in 42:6). With this reference to "the root of Jesse," which resumes the Davidic claims of 1:3, Paul not only concludes his substantive discussion but also fashions a messianic inclusio around most of the letter's discursive material.[44]

(5) Although almost entirely unnoticed, Rom 16:20—Θεὸς τῆς εἰρήνης συντρίψει τὸν Σατανᾶν ὑπὸ τοὺς πόδας ὑμῶν ἐν τάχει—echoes 1 Cor 15:25-27 and reflects underlying messianic readings of Pss 8 and 110 (specifically, 8:6 and 110:1). Both Ps 8 and Ps 110, when applied to Christ, speak of his messianic enthronement (implicitly linked to the resurrection) followed by a further process of subjugating all of Christ's enemies, which will be consummated at his second coming, "so that God might be all in all" (1 Cor 15:28b).[45] Hence, not only does 16:20 echo the royal discourse, but it even seems to deploy that discourse—via Ps 8—opposite the Adamic theme that is so important to Paul in much of Romans.[46]

---

44. The discourse's connotations are arguably detectable to an even more significant degree if the contexts of the three other texts quoted are explored—so Ps 18:49 (certainly) and Deut 32:43 (a book that generally assumes the kingship of God); Ps 117:1 seems too brief to set up any such resonances. For some elaboration of these claims, see Hays, *Echoes of Scripture*, 70–73; idem, "Christ Prays the Psalms: Paul's Use of an Early Christian Exegetical Convention," in *The Future of Christology: Essays in Honor of Leander E. Keck* (ed. Abraham J. Malherbe and Wayne A. Meeks; Minneapolis: Fortress, 1993), 122–36, esp. 134–35; Wright, *Romans*, 733, 744–49, esp. 748.

45. This royal reading resumes the language of Gen 3:15, along with the surrounding narrative. There are no direct linguistic signals of a connection between Rom 16:20 and Gen 3:15, so that the echo, if it exists, must be fundamentally narrative. Nevertheless, Dunn suggests that Gen 3:15 was a staple of Jewish hope, citing Ps 91:13; T. Sim. 6:6; T. Levi 18:12 (to which we should add T. Zeb. 9:8); Luke 10:18–19 (a text that includes a note of joy, like Rom 16:19–20). This view is supported by *TDNT* 5:81, Michel, Käsemann, Stuhlmacher (*Der Brief an die Römer* [Göttingen: Vandenhoeck & Ruprecht, 1989], 223), and Cranfield (*Romans*, 2:905).

46. Wright, like Dunn, points rather to Ps 91:13, which is actually a markedly less apposite intertext. (In particular, there is no connection with 1 Cor 15:25–27.) Somewhat curiously, he nevertheless detects the Adamic allusion, routing that through Luke 10:17–19 (cf. Rev 12:10–11). The strongest intertextual echo in this subsection for Wright is the evocation of the Jesus saying recorded in Matt 10:16 by 16:19b, which does not disturb the set of resonances being suggested in 16:20 (*Romans*, 764–65). These connections are all clearer in 1 Cor 15:25–27 and are further affirmed and explained by Eph 1:20–22 and Heb 1–2 (see esp. 1:13; 2:6–8a). See Anthony C. Thiselton, *The First Epistle to the Corinthians: A Commentary on the Greek Text* (NIGTC; Grand Rapids: Eerdmans, 2000), 1230–36. Hays

These five texts all develop the clues that are supplied by Paul in Rom 1:2-4. We can see in each of these other places a narrative of Jesus' heavenly enthronement informing Paul's argument, a narrative that describes Jesus as Son, Christ, "firstborn," and Lord, because of his enthronement by the resurrection. At this point he has entered his inheritance, an act that in Paul's view opens up that inheritance for all who indwell him, whether Jew or pagan. This description of the Christ-event rotates around the resurrection and interprets it in terms of the discourse of divine and human kingship.

If it is granted that these five texts are points where a robust narrative Christology developed in terms of ancient kingship emerges conspicuously into Paul's argument, it seems plausible to detect other points where such a discourse is operative in Romans, if not so overtly. At least two further texts are worth noting.

(6) Paul cites Ps 143:2 (142:2 LXX), suitably modified, rather pregnantly in 3:20a: διότι ἐξ ἔργων νόμου οὐ δικαιωθήσεται πᾶσα σὰρξ ἐνώπιον αὐτοῦ. This quotation is, of course, interesting in and of itself, but, as several scholars have noted, Ps 143 speaks repeatedly of God's δικαιοσύνη (cf. esp. 143:1, 11), and this contextual material can hardly be coincidental when Paul is about to resume that motif emphatically in Rom 3:21, 22, 25, and 26.[47] It seems, then, that the rest of the psalm is implicit within Paul's allusion, at least in some sense. Perhaps less obvious is the way the psalm echoes many of the key themes in the discourse of divine kingship. It does not itself function within that discourse, but it does articulate an element that functions within it, and this seems entirely deliberate. Psalm 143 is a prayer for help grounded overtly in the goodness of God and his works that also specifically disavows help from God in response to the supplicant's piety. That is, this psalm *specifically repudiates retributive activity by God*, acknowledging that this would result in condemnation rather than assistance. So the psalmist observes (quite rightly in the view of much of the Christian tradition) that no one is entitled to help from God couched in such terms, because "no one living is righteous before you." The ground for any divine assistance must therefore be the divine character, which must in turn be compassionate and should result in liberat-

---

also puts these points succinctly, introducing Mark 12:35-37 into the mix for good measure! See Richard B. Hays, *First Corinthians* (IBC; Louisville: John Knox, 1997), 265-66. The future tense of the verb inclines me to suspect that Ps 110 is to the fore in the echo in 16:20, but probably only marginally. Moreover, Satan is presumably one of the enemies who will eventually be placed under the feet of God.

47. Classic studies are Richard B. Hays, "Psalm 143 and the Logic of Romans 3," *JBL* 99 (1980): 107-15; William S. Campbell, "Romans iii as a Key to the Structure and Thought of the Letter," *NovT* 23 (1981): 22-40.

ing—and correspondingly oppressive! (see 143:3, 12)—actions. Such behavior is directly compatible with either the divine or the human king rescuing one of his charges, as he ought to, merely by virtue of his own duty of care. This dyad of intertextual echoes in Rom 1–3 thereby reproduces the much broader pattern of such echoes in the Psalter itself. Both are informed by a basic perception concerning the goodness of God.

(7) Finally, we should note that in 1:17b a messianic reading of Hab 2:4[48] foregrounds Christ's resurrection and eternal life in relation to the gospel as it is disclosed by the δικαιοσύνη of God: "the righteous one, through fidelity, will live." The letter's auditors are thereby prompted to find some connection between the gospel (i.e., the announcement of the divine King's good news through his appointed representative), Jesus' resurrection, and God's δικαιοσύνη.

2.4. The Meaning of δικαιοσύνη Θεοῦ in Romans 1:17 in Relation to Psalm 98:2

We should recall now the insight that catalyzed this investigation: Richard Hays's observation that the phrase δικαιοσύνη Θεοῦ and its immediate development in Rom 1:17 echoes Ps 98. If we supplement that insight by the additional observations that Ps 98 is a psalm of divine kingship and that Romans itself develops the ancient discourse of kingship in relation to Christ explicitly from its outset, and repeatedly throughout its body (*contra* Bousset et al.), then the conclusion seems to follow ineluctably that the phrase δικαιοσύνη Θεοῦ is best interpreted in the light of that discourse as well. Such a reading fits Paul's local argument perfectly, resumes the opening concerns of 1:2–4 neatly, and integrates with the contextual hints we receive from specific lexical data elsewhere in Paul.[49] In the light of this broader frame, we can now invest this phrase with the meaning appropriate to its particular function within that broader discourse: it speaks of a decisive saving and delivering act of power by God, the divine King,[50] on behalf of his royal representative, Jesus. Note that Christ is not being judged (or oppressed) by God here; he is being resurrected! So, δικαιοσύνη Θεοῦ must mean in 1:17 "the deliver-

---

48. This reading is now most frequently associated with the advocacy of Hays in *The Faith of Jesus Christ* (132–41; see also the introduction to the second edition, xxxvii). A few interpreters from an earlier generation of scholars had made this connection, but Hays is the most prominent current advocate of the reading. I find Hays's interpretation entirely plausible.

49. See especially my *Deliverance of God*, ch. 17.

50. This sets up another resonance with 1:4, which also speaks of δύναμις.

ance of God," or something closely equivalent.[51] This is the specific content of the righteous act that God has undertaken on behalf of his messianic agent, Christ: the act of resurrection, empowerment, and heavenly enthronement after his oppression and execution by evil opposing powers. It is "right" for God to act in this way on behalf of his chosen Son, who has been unfairly executed. It remains, then, only to ask why the psalm is present allusively rather than overtly.

I suggest that it is precisely the allusive activation of this broader discourse, and the critical enthronement narrative within it, that lies behind Paul's subtle use of the text of Ps 98 in Rom 1:17. The words of Ps 98:2–3 serve to *mediate* this construct—a discourse composed of scriptural texts that now operates at one remove from those texts—as a distinguishable theological entity. Hence, the detection of this particular scriptural text plays no overt rhetorical role in the broader argument; the Roman Christian auditors are not supposed to be impressed by Paul's citation here of an authoritative Jewish text (as they are by his citation of Hab 2:4 in 1:17b). They are merely meant to understand what he is talking about in more general terms, and they should be able to do so insofar as they inhabit this Jewish Christian discourse concerning Jesus' resurrection and kingship. Paul is merely using the words of Ps 98:2–3 to say here what he wants to say (and presumably in a way that other Christians have already formulated and so can recognize), that God the King has acted to save his messianic Son.[52]

An explanation of the similar reticence of Paul with respect to this discourse in the rest of Romans is hinted at here as well, although it cannot be developed fully in this essay. As the detailed argument of Romans continues to unfold, it becomes apparent that the ancient discourse of kingship is not so much elaborated as presupposed. Paul does not seem intent to describe or to justify it as much as to interact with and exploit it in support of various contingent goals in relation to the Christians at Rome. It seems to be traditional theology that the Roman Christians share with both Paul and the Jerusalem church—an integrated, Jewish, and perhaps surprisingly "high" christological narrative that smoothly links Jesus' messiahship, sonship, resurrection, and exalted heavenly lordship. Paul then builds from this shared theology toward his more specific rhetorical points in Romans.

---

51. That is, "the salvation of God" or "the redemption of God." At this point my recommendations overlap with an insightful study by Peter Leithart, "Justification as Verdict and Deliverance: A Biblical Perspective," *ProEccl* 16 (2007): 56–72.

52. This rhetorical qualification should serve to meet some of the concerns about Hays's methodology as expressed in Christopher D. Stanley, *Arguing with Scripture: The Rhetoric of Quotations in the Letters of Paul* (London: T&T Clark, 2004).

2.5. The Relationship to the Covenant

With these realizations offering an explanation of the discourse's subtle quality, it remains only to note the possible covenantal resonances of the phrase, since these have recently been proposed by other scholars as the invariable central content of δικαιοσύνη Θεοῦ (not least by N. T. Wright). In the eyes of many, this phrase means nothing more nor less than "the covenant faithfulness of God."[53]

If the phrase δικαιοσύνη Θεοῦ is located within the broader discourse of divine kingship, then covenantal associations are clearly not far away, and any such reading is not far from the truth. The earthly king was ratified at times by a particular covenant, and the divine King could structure his relationships with Israel directly in terms of a covenant, as the book of Deuteronomy perhaps most overtly attests.[54] It is certainly fair, then, to detect a covenantal strand within this discourse (and possibly also in relation to this phrase, which operates within it). Indeed, there is something profoundly right about any such assertion, because it grasps and emphasizes that *God's fidelity is intrinsic to any act of salvation.* For God to save implies necessarily and immediately that God has, in that act, acted faithfully.[55] Yet broader cov-

---

53. Wright, esp. *Romans*, 397–406, 413, 464–78. Hays himself endorses this reading at times as well; see, e.g., "Justification," *ABD* 3:1129-33, although he tends to speak of Christ's death and resurrection in the same breath, which links up with my recommendations here. Somewhat curiously, James D. G. Dunn, although on the opposite side of many questions from Wright and Hays, concurs on this issue; see his *Romans 1-8* (WBC 38A; Dallas: Word, 1988), 40–42.

54. Moshe Weinfeld suggests that it is modeled on an Assyrian suzerainty treaty and hence fundamentally covenantal; see his *Deuteronomy 1-11: A New Translation with Introduction and Commentary* (AB 5: New York: Doubleday, 1991). So construed, it is also arguably generous, although it remains conditional. (The royal covenant evident elsewhere in the Old Testament looks unconditional.) This potential concession to contractual theology in certain covenantal forms is further cause for caution with the interpretation of δικαιοσύνη Θεοῦ in this sense; cf. the elegant analysis and warnings of J. B. Torrance, "Covenant and Contract: A Study of the Theological Background of Worship in Seventeenth-Century Scotland," *SJT* 23 (1970): 51–76; idem, "The Contribution of McLeod Campbell to Scottish Theology," *SJT* 26 (1973): 295–311; idem, "Preface to the New Edition of John McLeod Campbell," in John McLeod Campbell, *The Nature of the Atonement* (Edinburgh: Handsel, 1996), 1–16.

55. The order of this set of predications must be noted carefully. *We know that God is faithful because he has acted to save.* Hence, we do not *ground* that act of salvation *on* his faithfulness, as if these two dispositions could be prioritized, humanly speaking, and the latter made the basis of the former. Rather, we grasp two complementary aspects of God's personhood, which is now disclosed definitively in Christ. Some of the important salva-

enantal associations—that is, in terms of a more elaborate arrangement—are not always central and hence not determinative or invariable. They may or may not be mentioned in connection with an act by a divine or human king in the Old Testament. Such acts can take more specific senses depending on their context, as we have seen, and are not always directly linked to a *covenant* (as in fact Ps 98 demonstrated earlier). Covenantal connotations are consequently *possible* but not *necessary* semantic resonances of the phrase δικαιοσύνη Θεοῦ, so we would need contextual information to activate them in Paul.

In short, δικαιοσύνη Θεοῦ *might* denote a righteous act by the divine King in fidelity to his covenant with Israel, that is, an act of covenant faithfulness (and so perhaps an act that is πίστις or described in terms of ἀλήθεια). Or it could denote a dramatically liberating act on behalf of Israel (σωτηρία/ σωτήριον) that might (or might not) be syntactically elaborated as, among other things, an act of covenant faithfulness. Or it might denote a saving act undertaken without reference to the covenant, or even in defiance of Israel's repeated violations of the covenant, and so be rooted merely in God's benevolence (ἔλεος). It might even denote an oppressive act against God's enemies—a righteous action—that has nothing to do with a covenant with those targeted by the action (i.e., a κρίμα). Finally, it might denote a retributive act that has nothing to do with a covenant but is oriented around the perception of an innocent person or group being accused or the guilty being acquitted (again a κρίμα, although of a different sort).[56]

It is not surprising, then, that the phrase δικαιοσύνη Θεοῦ or its close equivalent is sometimes found in the same textual locations as covenantal notions in the Old Testament (just as similar considerations apply to links with creation). Both are elements within the discourse of divine kingship,[57] so that the phrase may possess legitimate covenantal resonances. In later usage, however, these have to be established explicitly, not merely assumed. The covenant was not a central, standard, or invariable element in the discourse of divine kingship and hence in the phrase δικαιοσύνη Θεοῦ. We must let Romans itself tell us how this complex discourse is being activated.

In the immediate location of 1:16–17, including its particular allusion to Ps 98, I see nothing that explicitly activates these specific resonances. The

---

tion-historical implications implicit here are sketched in my *The Quest for Paul's Gospel: A Suggested Strategy* (London: T&T Clark, 2005), 63–68.

56. Many further semantic variations are conceivable. The phrase might denote a right but wrathful action by God against Israel, or it might denote a judgment or a posture within a trial between God and Israel—a more retributive scenario.

57. Similar observations apply to any resonances with Roman imperial ideology.

phrase seems rather to be oriented in a fundamentally *christocentric* direction. It speaks not of the covenant with Israel—although it certainly has implications for that!—but rather of the inauguration of the age to come by way of Christ's enthroning resurrection. It speaks therefore of a liberating act that has implications for all of humanity, including but not limited to Israel. Romans 3:21-22 and 23-26 confirm these suspicions rather strongly, as the claims of these later, related texts point ahead to the universal arguments of Rom 4–8.[58] The "right" act of God in relation to Christ, resurrecting him from the dead and enthroning him on high, has implications for all of creation. Israel is implicitly included here, but this does not exhaust its implications. Ernst Käsemann's classic study was correct in emphasizing precisely the *eschatological* nature of this "right" act;[59] a new creation has been inaugurated.

Somewhat ironically, the psalm that Paul echoes in Rom 1:17 makes this point nicely. While Ps 98:2 speaks of the saving deliverance that is being effected by God in plain view of the pagan nations, 98:3 goes on to articulate in a syntactical development that this action is an act of fidelity to the house of Israel. The same considerations seem to apply to the phrase δικαιοσύνη Θεοῦ when Paul deploys it later in Romans with specific reference to Christ. Christians suggest that the resurrection of Christ is ultimately an act of fidelity toward Israel and therefore the supreme expression of covenant loyalty and fulfillment by God. But these claims are not implicit in the semantic content of the phrase itself; they are related theological claims that must be argued for, since in certain respects they are by no means obvious. Thus Paul himself goes on to make an extensive case in Rom 9–11 that his christological claims *should* be so understood (see also 15:8). As his argumentative maneuvers unfold there, it becomes increasingly obvious that these implications are far from uncontested. Hence, to claim that he is merely semantically unpacking δικαιοσύνη Θεοῦ is to overstrain his language, as well as to ignore what he does syntactically and argumentatively.

It needs to be emphasized in closing, then, that this reading does not exclude Israel from the Christ-event for Paul—far from it. We have merely reached a semantic judgment that, when Paul deploys the phrase δικαιοσύνη Θεοῦ, especially in the early argumentative stages of Romans, he is not speaking of something that is overtly and fundamentally covenantal and hence rooted in the past and in a certain conception of history. He is discussing a liberating and eschatological act of God in Christ, a fundamentally present

---

58. For further elaborations of these hints, see my *Deliverance of God*, esp. chs. 15–17.

59. Ernst Käsemann, "The Righteousness of God in Paul," in *New Testament Questions of Today* (London: SCM, 1969), 168–82. I hope that this essay can be viewed as an attempt to build on Käsemann's central insights, not to overthrow or deny them.

and future event performed by the resurrecting God, which therefore arguably introduces a reconceptualization of history.

In sum, I would suggest that, on internal grounds, δικαιοσύνη Θεοῦ in Paul denotes a singular, saving, liberating, life-giving, eschatological act of God in Christ.[60] The intertextual echo of Ps 98:2 (LXX 97:2) detected in Rom 1:16–17—in combination with other clues—nuances this act in terms of the rich and powerful ancient Near Eastern discourse of divine kingship. In this particular instance, it denotes Christ's heavenly enthronement by God after his faithful death at the hands of his enemies—one of which was death—as God's appointed messianic agent and the cosmos's κύριος. Clearly, this is a singular, saving, liberating, life-giving, eschatological act of God. In undertaking this act in Christ, God is operating as a divine king should, delivering his captive creation from its bondage through his appointed royal representative. He is therefore doing the "right" thing, acting as his character and role demand. In this way δικαιοσύνη Θεοῦ in Romans is, in essence, an intertextually mediated reference to the deliverance of God.

EXCURSUS: THE RELATIONSHIP BETWEEN
RIGHT ACTION AND KINGSHIP IN THE PSALTER

The densest concentration of δικαιοσύνη terminology in the setting of kingship—where it most frequently denotes a liberating act—is in the Psalter: see especially (LXX) Pss 44:5, 8; 47:11; 49:6; 71:1, 2, 3, 7; 88:15, 17; 95:13; 96:2, 6; 97:2 (the text to which Paul alludes in Rom 1:17), 9; 98:4; 117:19. The liberating notion of δικαιοσύνη occurs in many other psalms as well, so this semantic field overlaps with the discourse of kingship but is not coterminous with it. For God's liberating righteousness, see also (LXX) Pss 5:10; 7:18; 9:9; 21:32; 30:2; 34:24, 28; 35:7, 11; 39:10, 11; 50:16; 68:28; 70:2, 15, 16, 18, 24; 84:11, 12, 14; 87:13; 102:17; 110:3; 111:3, 9; 118:7, 40, 62, 75 [?], 106, 123, 138 [?], 142 [2x], 160, 164; 142:1 (a reference that is especially significant for Paul), 11; 144:7. But this is hardly a problem for my case here. It simply suggests that this perception of the character of God was widespread and perhaps also that the discourse of divine kingship was more widely known than is often recognized, perhaps either tacitly or as a hidden transcript.

In sum, about 80 of the 336 instances of δικαιοσύνη in the LXX occur in the Psalter—around 25 percent. Approximately 50 of those 80 instances describe God, and then almost invariably in a liberating, salvific sense. Half a dozen of those instances, and several more important instances describing the

---

60. See my *Deliverance of God*, ch. 17, §2.2.

human king in the same terms, occur in texts that are indisputably enthronement psalms or texts denoting some other aspect of ancient kingship. This is where the lexical and thematic fields overlap especially clearly. Psalm 98 (97 LXX) operates within that intersection.

The correlation with various salvific terms is also worth noting because it reinforces these claims. Δικαιοσύνη occurs in close relation to salvific terms in the LXX almost entirely in the Psalter and Isaiah. See the strong connections between liberation, salvation, and δικαιοσύνη in Pss (LXX) 16:1, 15; 39:10, 11, 17 (see also 39:14, 18); 50:16 (a psalm traditionally linked to David and his repentance for his adultery with Bathsheba); 70:2, 15, 16, 18, 24; 71:1–4 (a psalm about ideal human kingship); 84:8, 11–14 (a psalm oriented more toward the land); 97:1b–2, 9 (the psalm that launched this entire investigation; see also 97:3); 117:14, 19, 21; 118:40–41, 121–123, 169–176.

The links with salvation and kingship are, however, perhaps even more overt in Isaiah: see (LXX) 39:8 (where King Hezekiah is grateful for δικαιοσύνη [prosperity] in his day); 51:5–11; 59 (esp. 59:14, 17; overt royal instances of God triumphing through a rehearsal of the ancient combat myth); 62 (see esp. 62:1, 2); 63:1–6, 8–9 (note the liberative sense of δικαιοσύνη; the related theme of God as "father" is also prominent in 63:7–64:11). The *maintenance* of prosperity, in part through "due process," is apparent in 60:17, 18 and intermingles with the liberating sense in 61:8, 11 (see the closely related language in Amos 5:7, 24; also 5:12, 15; 6:12).

"Blasphemed among the Nations": Pursuing an Anti-imperial "Intertextuality" in Romans

Neil Elliott

The larger project from which this essay is drawn is a book-length reading of Romans as a sustained interaction with themes and tropes of Roman imperial ideology, rather than (as conventionally understood) an interaction with Judaism, the "Jewish doctrine of redemption," or Jewish "exclusivism" or "ethnocentrism."[1] First I sketch an approach to Romans that adapts the notion of "intertextuality" to the larger rhetorical environment of Roman imperial ideology contemporary with Paul; then I offer a single "sample" reading using this approach.

1. Empire and the Obedience of Nations

One premise of what follows is that empires require ideological legitimation.[2] The impossibility of achieving through force the willing consent of peoples whose labor and resources empires would claim for their own generates tremendous tension within an empire's ideological system, a contradiction so threatening that it must be suppressed through ideological mechanisms that

---

1. This essay relies on parts of chs. 1, 3, and 5 of *The Arrogance of Nations: Reading Romans in the Shadow of Empire* (Minneapolis: Fortress, 2008), where the arguments here are fleshed out in greater detail, and is published with the permission of Fortress Press.

2. Essential works include Peter A. Brunt, *Roman Imperial Themes* (Oxford: Clarendon, 1990); Paul Zanker, *The Power of Images in the Age of Augustus* (Ann Arbor: University of Michigan Press, 1988); and S. R. F. Price, *Rituals and Power: The Roman Imperial Cult in Asia Minor* (Cambridge: Cambridge University Press, 1984); all of these are excerpted in Richard A. Horsley, ed., *Paul and Empire: Religion and Power in Roman Imperial Society* (Harrisburg, Pa.: Trinity Press International, 1997).

Fredric Jameson has termed "strategies of containment."[3] The ideology of the Roman Empire, no less than contemporary imperial ideology, was preoccupied with the challenge of "winning the hearts and minds" of conquered peoples.

Examining the constellation of rhetorical topoi enlisted by Roman imperial ideology offers a necessary lens for reading Romans. Paul declared that he was charged by God with securing "faithful obedience among the nations" (Rom 1:5, my trans.). That statement is a guide to the purpose of the letter and an indication of the political dimension of Paul's rhetoric. Because "the obedience of nations" was also the prerogative claimed by the Roman emperor, interpreting Romans requires that we situate Paul's rhetoric in a wider field of discourses, across different social locations, in which coercion and consent, obedience and subjection, were aligned or opposed to each other.

Admittedly, the coercive aspect of the empire that Rome built is a delicate subject for some contemporary observers,[4] but it is clear enough that the topoi of imperial propaganda were (and are) the ideologically necessary instruments for representing actual power relationships in the public transcript. An agrarian tributary empire, particularly one as "parasitic" as Rome's, had specific ideological requirements.[5]

---

3. Fredric Jameson, "On Interpretation," in idem, *The Political Unconscious: Narrative as a Socially Symbolic Act* (Ithaca, N.Y.: Cornell University Press, 1981), 17–102 (esp. 52–53).

4. Classicist Clifford Ando objects that reading literature produced by the Roman elite with suspicion is a modern "anachronistic cynicism" (*Imperial Ideology and Provincial Loyalty in the Roman Empire* [Berkeley and Los Angeles: University of California Press, 2000], 67).

5. See Gerhard E. Lenski's extended discussion of agrarian empires in *Power and Privilege: A Theory of Social Stratification* (New York: McGraw-Hill, 1966), chs. 8 and 9. Roland Boer argues for shifting analysis away from Marx's category of "mode of production" to the more flexible concept of "regimes of allocation," distinguishing between tribute, "war machine," corvée labor, slavery, and patron-client regimes of allocation, and identifying the last two especially with the Roman world (*Marxist Criticism of the Bible* [Sheffield: Sheffield Academic Press, 2003], 244–45). G. E. M. de Ste. Croix observes that, while slavery was an indispensable component of the Roman economy, it was only one form of unfree labor. The Roman economy depended on both the ownership of land and the control of unfree labor: "It was these assets above all which enabled the propertied class to exploit the rest of the population" (*Class Struggle in the Ancient Greek World: From the Archaic Age to the Arab Conquests* [Ithaca, N.Y.: Cornell University Press, 1980], 33, 133–34). Peter Garnsey and Richard Saller offer a very similar assessment in *The Roman Empire: Economy, Society, and Culture* (Berkeley and Los Angeles: University of California Press, 1987), chs. 3–5.

We should read Romans alert to the pervasive role of imperial ideology in its rhetorical environment. But because themes of justice, mercy, faith, and the destiny of peoples were perceived and treated differently in different social locations, we require a method that allows us to measure "the impact of domination on public discourse" in a specific society.[6] Toward that end, James C. Scott has distinguished between what he calls the "public transcript," that is, the zone of direct interaction between dominant and subordinate classes, and the "hidden transcripts of the subordinate," on one hand, and the "hidden transcript of the dominant," on the other (see the table below).

"Hidden" and "Public Transcripts" as Described by James C. Scott

Hidden transcript of the dominant	Public transcript (with roles and expectations for subordinate and dominant classes)	Hidden transcript of the subordinate
Distinct from the role of the powerful in the public transcript; "hidden" because constrained by prevalent ideology.	Expressed in the "public" sphere as this is defined by the dominant classes, the public transcript includes roles assigned to the weak and the dominant, the powerless and the powerful alike; yet these are under constant negotiation in "the most vital arena for ordinary conflict, for everyday forms of class struggle."	Distinct from the role of the subordinate in the public transcript; "hidden" because constrained by coercive force.

Scott's work focuses on contemporary societies (especially modern Malaysia), but biblical scholars have seen the worth of applying his categories to the early Roman Empire as well. It is precisely the difference between the solemn assurances the elite gave their subjects regarding their altruism and benevolence and the candor with which they admitted their rapacity to one another in private that allows us to distinguish the hidden transcript of the powerful from the public transcript.[7]

---

6. James C. Scott, *Domination and the Arts of Resistance: Hidden Transcripts* (New Haven: Yale University Press, 1990), 5.

7. See Richard A. Horsley, ed., *Hidden Transcripts and the Arts of Resistance* (SemeiaSt 48; Atlanta: Society of Biblical Literature, 2004). Brunt makes the same point when he observes that Cicero's "own personal opinions can only be properly elicited from his inti-

The hidden transcript of the dominant is "an artifact of the exercise of power. It contains that discourse—gestures, speech, practices—which is excluded from the public transcript by the ideological limits within which domination is cast." The powerful can speak with candor when they know they are alone among their peers "and can let their hair down." Such hidden transcripts are of particular value because the full *public* transcript offers only occasional, accidental glimpses into the actual motives of the powerful; as Scott observes, "Dominant groups often have much to conceal, and typically also have the wherewithal to conceal what they wish."[8]

As to the "hidden transcript" of the subordinate in the first century C.E., we recognize that expressions of outright defiance to Roman rule were rare, desperate, and doomed. The paucity of direct first-hand evidence is precisely what we should expect on Scott's analysis of the effects of domination upon discourse. Unable to express their resistance openly, subordinate groups must ordinarily rely on strategies of indirection and disguise or else seek the safety of anonymity. There is abundant indirect evidence for "a permanent current of hostility" on the part of the masses in Rome to "senatorial misrule and exploitation" from the time of the Republic onward.[9] But the occasional surprise expressed by the elite when a gesture of courage sparked an explosion of popular unrest suggests that the common people more usually were constrained to suppress their dissatisfaction.[10] Defiance surfaced in strategies of anonymity that Scott calls the "everyday forms of class struggle."[11] Strategies of "political disguise" included graffiti, effigies anonymously erected in public,[12] and spontaneous street demonstrations (termed "riots" by the elite).[13] The alternatives available to subordinate groups are more complex,

---

mate letters," when he had no particular reason to "veil or distort his real views" ("*Laus Imperii*," in *Roman Imperial Themes*, 288–89).

8. Scott, *Domination and the Arts of Resistance*, 5.

9. De Ste. Croix, *Class Struggle*, 352–53. See Michael Parenti, *The Assassination of Julius Caesar: A People's History of Ancient Rome* (New York: New Press, 2003), 38, 42, 59–83.

10. Parenti, *Assassination of Julius Caesar*, 117–18, quoting Plutarch, *Caes.* 6.1-4.

11. Scott, *Domination and the Arts of Resistance*, 36–37, 136, 150–51, 14. On the Roman "mob," see de Ste. Croix, *Class Struggle*, 357, 361.

12. On graffiti as an important source for nonelite perceptions, see Justin J. Meggitt, *Paul, Poverty, and Survival* (Studies of the New Testament and Its World; Edinburgh: T&T Clark, 1998); Parenti, *Assassination of Julius Caesar*. Edward Champlin (*Nero* [Cambridge: Harvard University Press, 2003], 91) discusses anonymous expressions of disdain for the emperor.

13. Scott, *Domination and the Arts of Resistance*, 136–52, 20–22; Meggitt, *Paul, Poverty, and Survival*, 34–35. The movement surrounding the populist land reformer Tiberius

then, than a naked choice between silence and defiance. What Scott calls the "strategic uses of anonymity," including collective action and the anonymity of the crowd, reflects "a popular tactical wisdom developed in conscious response to the political constraints realistically faced," that is, the constant threat of violent suppression.[14] In the era when Romans was written, forms of anonymous protest directed at Nero in particular—anonymous jokes circulating through the capital, graffiti appearing on public walls overnight—mocked the key claims of imperial propaganda, ridiculing Nero's extravagant building projects, mocking his claim to be descended from the ancient Trojan hero Aeneas, and, after 59, taunting him as his mother's murderer as well,[15] despite his calculated efforts in the theater (ably discussed by Edward Champlin) to identify that act as the embodiment of mythic themes of justified matricide.[16]

Scott's insights into the dialectic of defiance and caution are hardly a modern discovery. No less erudite an observer than Philo of Alexandria provided an analysis very similar to Scott's when he contrasted the "untimely frankness" (παρρησία ἄκαιρον) of those who resisted Rome openly but at an inopportune time, with the caution (εὐλαβεία) that is more usually appropriate to the public square. "When the times are right," Philo explains, "it is good to set ourselves against the violence of our enemies and subdue it; but when the circumstances do not present themselves"—as is usually the case in history, Scott suggests—"the safe course is to stay quiet."[17] "Staying quiet" clearly implies the self-restraint that keeps an oppositional transcript hidden. Typically, expressions of protest or resistance in the Judean literature are

---

Gracchus relied on mass action and graffiti alike; see Plutarch, *Ti. C. Gracch.* 21.2–3; Parenti, *Assassination of Julius Caesar*, 217.

14. Scott, *Domination and the Arts of Resistance*, ch. 6.

15. In graffiti, Romans scorned the pretension that the emperor bore Apollo's image, comparing him instead to an official enemy (Suetonius, *Nero* 39); see Champlin, *Nero*, 91–92.

16. See Champlin, *Nero*, ch. 4.

17. Philo, *Somn.* 2.92 (emphasis added). On the significance of this passage for an appropriate understanding of Philo's politics, see Erwin R. Goodenough, *An Introduction to Philo Judaeus* (2nd ed.; Oxford: Blackwell, 1962), 55–62; on its relevance for an adequate understanding of rhetoric in the Roman period, see my "Romans 13:1–7 in the Context of Imperial Propaganda," in Horsley, *Paul and Empire*, 196–204; on these texts as examples of "hidden transcripts," see my essays "The 'Patience of the Jews': Strategies of Resistance and Accommodation to Imperial Cultures," in *Pauline Conversations in Context: Essays in Honor of Calvin J. Roetzel* (ed. Janice Capel Anderson, Philip Sellew, and Claudia Setzer; JSNTSup 221; Sheffield: Sheffield Academic Press, 2002), 32–42, and "Strategies of Resistance and Hidden Transcripts in the Pauline Communities," in Horsley, *Hidden Transcripts*, 97–122. Scott's term for what Philo calls "caution" (εὐλαβεία) is "tactical prudence" (*Domination and the Arts of Resistance*, 15).

couched in veiled or muted terms, but we may presume they offer glimpses into a deeper, richer hidden transcript of resentment that ultimately erupted in rebellion.

2. The "Public Transcript" in Nero's Rome

It is vitally important to distinguish "public" and "hidden transcripts" in ancient literature. The phenomena that Scott discusses are not aspects inhering in texts as such, so that if we only spent sufficient time staring at a text (like Romans) through the right methodological lens we could confirm its character as one or the other. *No ancient text spontaneously reveals itself as a "hidden transcript,"* and sheer assertion that one text or another is such a hidden transcript will not convince reasonable contemporary readers. As Cynthia Briggs Kittredge rightly warns, in applying Scott's work to biblical studies, we necessarily depend on a *historical reconstruction* of a particular historical context and of the way in which power constrained the discourse of social groups in that context.[18] We must also rely on *comparisons* with actual contemporary texts that show telltale fissures between the public contestation of power and statements that vary from the normative expectations of the public transcript.

Along with important works by S. R. F. Price on symbol and ritual of the imperial cult and by Paul Zanker on the ideological purpose of mass-manufactured and distributed imagery, Edward Champlin's recent study of Nero's age allows us to say a great deal about the cultural environment in the city to which Paul wrote. Champlin emphasizes the rich repertoire of statuary, monument, inscription, and (of special relevance with regard to this emperor) theater, all of which conveyed "a single, powerful message regarding the inevitability and rightness of the imperial regime."[19] Champlin's observations about the constricted sphere of public discourse in ancient Rome bear out Scott's argument regarding the constraints of power in the public transcript, which remains a zone of contestation. After the accelerated consolidation of power in the single figure of the emperor, the marginalization of the first two "public" zones, public meetings and elections, meant that, by the mid-first century C.E., "the outlet provided by the games became even more important."[20] The constraints imposed on the public transcript meant that direct dissent was suppressed. For that reason, Champlin shows, "Roman theatrical

---

18. Cynthia Briggs Kittredge, "Reconstructing 'Resistance' or Reading to Resist: James C. Scott and the Politics of Interpretation," in Horsley, *Hidden Transcripts*, 145–55.
19. Champlin, *Nero*, 94.
20. Ibid., 63.

audiences were extraordinarily quick to hear the words spoken and to see the actions presented on stage as offering pointed commentary on contemporary life."[21] Champlin speaks of a "remarkable sensitivity on the part of the audience": "audiences *expected* to find contemporary relevance" in stage productions.[22]

3. The Question of Criteria

If we apply Champlin's observations to the immediate environment in which Paul's letter was read, or rather, performed,[23] we should ask what *oblique* commentary might have been detected by the "remarkable sensitivity" of a Roman audience. On what basis might we identify anything that Paul says as having a bearing, however indirectly, on contemporary events in Rome?

In his landmark discussion of "intertextual echo" in Paul's letters, Richard B. Hays identified seven "tests" for identifying likely allusions in one text (e.g., Romans) to another (e.g., Isaiah or the Psalms).[24] These tests are just as applicable to the themes of myth and ideology that so charged the air of the imperial capital. Under the rubric of *availability*, Hays asks, "Was the proposed source of the echo available to the author and/or original readers?" Here we can have no doubt that through mass dissemination by means of imagery, ceremonial, and panegyric, themes of imperial propaganda saturated the cities of the Roman Empire. (Indeed, recognizing the overwhelming "availability" of imperial themes in Paul's environment, we may wonder whether the energy devoted to determining how conversant Paul's non-Judean hearers were with the Septuagint might better be directed to another symbolic repertoire with which they were *undoubtedly* more familiar.)[25] Under *historical plausibility*, Hays asks whether Paul could have intended the alleged meaning effect and whether his readers could have understood it. Precisely here Champlin's observations about the "remarkable sensitivity" of Roman audiences to irony, double entendre, and other forms of indirect commen-

---

21. Ibid., 95.
22. Ibid., 96, 103.
23. On the oral performance of ancient letters, see Joanna Dewey, "Textuality in an Oral Culture: A Survey of the Pauline Traditions," *Semeia* 65 (1994): 37–65; Antoinette Clark Wire, "Performance, Politics, and Power: A Response," *Semeia* 65 (1994): 129.
24. Richard B. Hays, *Echoes of Scripture in the Letters of Paul* (New Haven: Yale University Press, 1989), 29–33.
25. Hays himself regards this question as "intriguing" and worthy of further investigation; see *The Faith of Jesus Christ: The Narrative Substructure of Galatians 3:1–4:11* (2nd ed.; Grand Rapids: Eerdmans, 2002), xl–xlii.

tary must be taken seriously into account. Under *volume,* Hays is concerned with "the degree of explicit repetition of words or syntactical patterns, but other factors may also be relevant: how distinctive or prominent is the precursor text?" Here the case with regard to themes from imperial ideology is necessarily much murkier, because Paul neither quotes nor alludes to any imperial declarations (although the contemporary recognition of an allusion to official propaganda in 1 Thess 5:3 bears note), nor does he quote from recognizable Roman works such as the *Aeneid.* But this only makes Hays's reference to "other factors" all the more important. Themes that loom large in Romans—justice, mercy, piety, and virtue—were *overwhelmingly* "distinctive and prominent" in Roman imperial ideology as well.

Hays considers another criterion, the *history of interpretation,* as "one of the least reliable guides for interpretation" precisely because the interpretation of Paul's letters has been so long dominated by theological agendas. We are nevertheless at a turning point in the history of interpretation in which political themes and allusions in Paul's writings are increasingly recognized.[26]

On the basis of Hays's criteria, I contend that there is at least a prima facie case for reading Romans with the same "remarkable sensitivity" to political connotations that was evident in the Roman theater. Indeed, given that Paul's letter would have been read in a much less surveilled social site, we may suppose that the sort of expectations that Champlin describes for the theater might have been heightened there.

4. A Test Case: The Topos "Mercy" (Clementia)

"We are blasphemed among the nations," Paul protested (Rom 2:24, citing Isa 52:5). The Christian interpretive tradition has long read the broader context of this quotation, in which Paul engages an interlocutor in a diatribal conversation, as an effort to accuse or "indict" a Jew (and, thus, Judaism) for arrogance, hypocrisy, moral presumption, and/or a smug ethnocentrism. Under that assumption, however, it becomes difficult to identify who "we" are here: Paul and his Jewish interlocutor? Paul and his Christ-believing audience? Paul and his apostolic colleagues who advocate a law-free mission?

In his recent magisterial commentary, Robert Jewett manages to conflate all of these possibilities in what he calls "a wonderful piece of rhetorical jujitsu" on the part of the apostle. Though Paul is (in Jewett's view) still

---

26. N. T. Wright notes that imperial themes were "almost entirely screened out" in the work of the Pauline Theology Section of the SBL through the 1980s and early 1990s: "Paul's Gospel and Caesar's Empire," in *Paul and Politics: Ekklesia, Israel, Imperium, Interpretation* (ed. Richard A. Horsley; Philadelphia: Trinity Press International, 2000), 162.

engaged in an antagonistic diatribal address to a Jew (since 2:17), here he "shrewdly brings his audience into the dialogue": "we" means "we believers," who are being slandered by people *like the Jewish antagonist* ("the insidious interlocutor").[27] But this alleged "jujitsu" resembles more the tangle of a rhetorical game of Twister. The Roman non-Judean audience is expected to understand (on this view) that Paul is addressing an antagonistic Jew, who is addressed in the first-person plural at 3:1 and 3:9 but who is *not* included in the first-person plural of 3:8, where they (the non-Judean audience) *are* included in an antagonistic accusation *against* the "insidious" Jew. Just this tangle is the inevitable result when we make the a priori assumption that the purpose of Romans is to *defend* the law-free mission against Jewish antagonism.

I contend, instead, that the "slander" to which Paul refers is one that he shares *with his Jewish interlocutor,* who is *not* his antagonist. This interchange is of a piece with the larger rhetorical address since 2:17, which is directed (I argue) *not* against a Jewish *antagonist* but to a Jewish conversation *partner* in an effort to convince a non-Judean audience that accountability to God is universal—and thus includes them as well. (That is the explicit argument in 6:1–15.) The rhetorical burden in the earlier chapters, Rom 2–3, is to address the (mistaken) perception that mercy, especially on God's part, constitutes an exemption from accountability (addressed explicitly in 2:3–5).

4.1. "Mercy" in Imperial View

Upon Nero's accession, one of the ways in which he exercised his personal prerogative as emperor was to extend "clemency" to those who had suffered punishment or exile at the hands of his stepfather. These included Judeans whom Claudius had expelled from Rome, under circumstances that tell us more about Roman policy than about the character or conduct of the city's Judean population. Almost all commentators on Romans today cite this expulsion as part of the background for Paul's letter. Normally this has meant explaining why the "Gentiles" in the Roman churches would have had reason to look down on their Judean neighbors. Some interpreters go further, however, attributing failure or malfeasance to these neighbors and implying that the Judeans had deserved Claudius's severe response. Such characterizations of the Judean population perpetuate the perceptions of hostile Romans in

---

27. Robert Jewett, *Romans: A Commentary* (Hermeneia; Minneapolis: Fortress, 2007), 250–51.

Paul's own day, implying that Judeans were undeserving of the mercy that Nero had deigned to show them.

It is just this perception that Paul opposes in Romans. Relying on familiar techniques appropriate to the diatribe, he elicits from a fictitious Judean character the strident denial of any presumption on *divine* mercy (2:17–24). But if Judeans, who have been given tremendous privileges by God, cannot presume on these to exempt them from accountability before God, how much less can others! To presume that divine punishment long withheld is evidence of God's indulgence would be a disastrous mistake, one that Paul seeks to prevent the Roman assemblies from making. But that very presumption was ready at hand *in the ideology of Roman imperialism*.

4.2. The Mercy of the Augusti

From the perspective of imperial ideology, mercy is the prerogative of the powerful, appropriate only when the object of mercy is truly powerless and submissive. Within the logic of empire, "mercy" is not something that is due to others under any obligation that might present a restraint on the exertion of power. In Paul's day, Roman imperial ideology construed "mercy" as the sole prerogative of those who enjoyed absolute power.[28] There was no contradiction here, since mercy was by definition the right of the conqueror over those who submitted, just as the insolent who dared to resist earned their chosen fate. Given the options of destruction and subjection, the vanquished would naturally be grateful to be spared.[29]

Clementia was "the operative principle after ongoing conquests and submission of other peoples," Karl Galinsky observes.[30] It was one of the virtues celebrated on the golden shield that the Senate donated to Augustus after his victories and one of the chief virtues of which the emperor boasted in the *Res Gestae*. After Augustus, *clementia* became a standard claim on the part of his successors as well.[31] Upon Claudius's death (likely at the hands of Nero's mother), Nero promised the Senate that he would reign with a mercy surpassing any of his predecessors except Augustus.[32] The speech that Seneca wrote for the young Nero one or two years before Romans was written, "On Mercy" (*De clementia*), is widely credited with having had a moderating effect on the

---

28. Cicero, *Resp.* 3.15; Virgil, *Aen.* 6.851–853.
29. Karl Galinsky, *Augustan Culture* (Princeton: Princeton University Press, 1998), 82–85.
30. Ibid.
31. Tacitus, *Ann.* 12.12–13.
32. Suetonius, *Nero* 10; Tacitus, *Ann.* 13.4.

young emperor, although it might also have been the case that Nero's excesses grew to be far more obvious after he required his advisor to commit suicide, causing his early years to appear milder in comparison. *De clementia* combines lofty rhetoric with abject flattery and cold political calculation. It warns that mercy must be dispensed in moderation, since according to the common wisdom, "mercy upholds the worst class of men, since it is superfluous unless there has been some crime," it being self-evident that Roman justice sufficed to preserve the innocent. "An indiscriminate and general mercy" would undermine public morality. The people must be kept under the rein.[33]

Clementia was, then, the indulgence shown by a sovereign to his unworthy subjects, an undeserved favor that highlighted his moral superiority over them. Two particular occasions on which imperial clemency was proclaimed bear directly on the occasion of Romans. One is Claudius's order suppressing civil unrest in Alexandria in 41 C.E. The other is Nero's order, probably in 54 C.E., rescinding his stepfather's expulsion of Judeans from the city of Rome.

The first episode and its dénouement are instructive in regard to the malleability of "ethnicity" during this period. If, in the provinces, participation in the imperial cult held out for the ambitious the prospect of "becoming Roman, staying Greek,"[34] some at least of Philo's contemporaries sought to "become Alexandrian, staying Judean."[35] They thought it reasonable to seek recognition as both Alexandrian citizens and members of the Judean *politeia*. Their neighbors opposed this plea by protesting the Judeans' unsuitability to participate in the Roman order. Their supposed origins as lower-class Egyptians and their contempt for the rites of others showed that the Judeans could never take their place among enlightened peoples who accepted the Roman gods alongside their own. The catastrophe in Alexandria was not just an episode of "ethnic" tension: it was a case of rivalry among colonized peoples jockeying against each other for the favor of the colonial power. We must note also the imperial construal of the situation. Claudius knew that far from a squabble between ethnic groups, the anti-Judaic bloc had stirred up trouble in clear defiance of Roman policy, attempting to triangulate with Flaccus against the Judeans. Claudius rejected the strategy and condemned its architects.[36] But

---

33. Seneca, *De clem*. 1.2.1–2; 1.4.2; 1.12.4; 2.2.2; see Miriam T. Griffin, *Nero: The End of a Dynasty* (London: Routledge, 1994), 104.

34. Greg Woolf, "Becoming Roman, Staying Greek: Culture, Identity, and the Civilizing Process in the Roman East," *Proceedings of the Cambridge Philological Society* 40 (1994): 116–43; idem, "Beyond Romans and Natives," *World Archaeology* 28 (1995): 339–50.

35. Shaye J. D. Cohen, *The Beginnings of Jewishness: Boundaries, Varieties, Uncertainties* (Berkeley and Los Angeles: University of California Press, 1999), 67.

36. Peter Schäfer emphasizes that the conflict was "first and foremost a political

he also warned the Judeans not to import troublemaking compatriots from Syria, indicating that, from the Roman point of view, the Judeans were, like the Alexandrians, potentially troublesome residents of the Eastern provinces who must learn their place in the Roman order. Note, finally, the emperor's claim of unparalleled benevolence. Regardless of the effects of Roman policy; regardless of whatever miseries and injustices were left without redress, it was to be understood that he had Alexandria's best interests at heart.

As to the expulsion of Judeans from Rome in 49 C.E., H. Dixon Slingerland has offered a compelling explanation that is based not in conjecture about specific Jewish actions or putative Jewish characteristics but in Roman policy. Claudius was simply continuing his predecessors' policy of seeking to control Judeans and adherents to other foreign "superstitions" in the city. As Leonard Rutgers has shown, the impulse behind this imperial policy was not a religious concern but a political one. "It was quite common for the Roman authorities to expel easily identifiable groups from Rome in times of political turmoil. Such expulsions were ordered not for religious reasons, but rather to maintain law and order." The Judeans were "just a convenient group whose expulsion could serve as an example to reestablish peace and quiet among the city populace at large."[37]

When the Judeans who had been expelled from the city by Claudius were allowed to return by Nero soon after his accession, they returned to a city in which much of the community life that they had previously known was in disarray.[38] In an influential 1970 article, Wolfgang Wiefel catalogued the expressions of contempt leveled against Judeans by their Roman neighbors in the latter half of the first century C.E. They were scorned as beggars and fortune-tellers infesting the public parks; they scraped by on a miserable diet, apparently without adequate access to decent kosher food.[39] They were

---

drama in the triangle of Flaccus, Gaius Caligula, and the Alexandrians. The Jews are the innocent victims of a political conflict of interests" (*Judeophobia: Attitudes toward the Jews in the Ancient World* [Cambridge: Harvard University Press, 1997], 143).

37. H. Dixon Slingerland, *Claudian Policymaking and the Early Imperial Repression of Jews at Rome* (Atlanta: Scholars Press, 1997); Leonard Rutgers, "Roman Policy toward the Jews: Expulsions from the City of Rome during the First Century C.E.," in *Judaism and Christianity in First-Century Rome* (ed. Karl P. Donfried and Peter Richardson; Grand Rapids: Eerdmans, 1994), 104–8. On this point, Rutgers offers an important corrective to Slingerland's study, which emphasizes antipathy toward non-Roman religion as the primary motive of Roman policy toward the Jews. See, at greater length, Elliott, *Arrogance of Nations*, 91–100.

38. Jewett speaks of a consensus that Romans is an occasional letter and relies on the date of the edict of Claudius for establishing the date of the letter (*Romans*, 3, 18–20).

39. Wolfgang Wiefel, "The Jewish Community in Ancient Rome and the Origins of

derided as "the weak" in the city.⁴⁰ Although there is no reason to attribute these characterizations to the effect of the expulsion under Claudius alone, we may reasonably assume that this event, together with the subsequent return of the former exiles, made a lasting impression. While officially Judeans still enjoyed the emperor's favor, Nero's own advisor, Seneca, complained that noxious Judean practices had spread among the non-Judean populace, a development that he found doubly offensive, since "the conquered [*victi*] have given their laws to the conquerors [*victores*]."⁴¹ Given that the assemblies to which Paul wrote were "surrounded by a society marked by its aversion and rejection of everything Jewish," Wiefel found it understandable that in Romans Paul should strive to instill a different attitude toward Israel among his audience.

But we can say more about the attitudes against which Paul struggled in this letter. As we have seen, in 41 C.E. Claudius portrayed his severe posture toward the Judeans of Alexandria as being milder than they deserved due to his benevolence. Upon Claudius's death in 54 C.E., Nero set himself to conspicuously reversing his stepfather's policies as a way of demonstrating his superior clemency. One of these gestures, we may safely presume, was to allow the exiled Judeans to return to Rome.⁴²

Given all that we have seen regarding the representation of imperial clemency in official imagery and propaganda, we may hazard an informed guess regarding how this action was perceived among the Judeans' neighbors. First, Nero allowed them to return not to improve their lot but to enhance his own prestige as a benevolent and merciful ruler. But Seneca himself had reminded Nero that, in the common view, "mercy upholds the worst class of men" and that "an indiscriminate and general mercy" would undermine Nero's credibility.⁴³ We can imagine that non-Judeans in Rome would have looked upon these returning exiles not only as the wretched and broken people that they appeared but *as the undeserving beneficiaries of imperial largesse,* troublemakers who had escaped being held accountable for their misdeeds. They were, in Seneca's phrase, "the worst class of men," being upheld by misdirected mercy.

Roman Christianity," in *The Romans Debate* (rev. ed.; ed. Karl P. Donfried; Peabody, Mass.: Hendrickson, 1991), 85–101, esp. 96–101; see also Hans-Werner Bartsch, "Die antisemitischen Gegner des Paulus im Römerbrief," in *Antijudaismus im Neuen Testament?* (ed. Willehad Paul Eckert, Nathan Peter Levinson, and Martin Stöhr; Munich: Kaiser, 1967); idem, "Die historische Situation des Römerbriefes," *SE* 4/TU 102 (1968): 282–91.

40. Horace, *Sermones* 1.9.
41. Seneca, in a lost treatise, *De superstitione,* as quoted by Augustine, *Civ.* 6.10.
42. Suetonius, *Nero* 10.
43. Seneca, *De clem.* 1.2.1–2; 1.4.2; 1.12.4; 2.2.2; see Griffin, *Nero,* 104.

4.3. A Warning against Presuming on Mercy (Romans 2–3)

Paul's stylized conversation with a Judean in Rom 2–3 is a rhetorical device aimed precisely at combating this prejudicial conclusion on the part of his *non-Judean* audience. "We are blasphemed among the nations," Paul protests (Rom 2:24). One effect of Paul's rhetoric in the beginning of Romans is to drive a wedge between his hearers and the sort of arrogant presumption that characterized the imperial house (1:18–32). In a stylized second-person address to a fictitious interlocutor, Paul then warns against a self-deluding hypocrisy that presumes upon God's mercy as an escape from accountability to God. *All* are accountable to God and will be judged according to their works (2:1–16). It becomes clear as the letter progresses that this fictitious address has a very real hortatory burden: Paul warns his Roman audience against misconstruing their status "in Christ" as a presumption on God's mercy.[44] The consequences that he draws out in 6:1–23 are specifically relevant to those who have been baptized into Christ: they are not to misconstrue the grace that they have received as an opportunity to presume on divine mercy, to "continue in sin that grace may abound."

Here we may compare Paul's rhetoric with the way Roman imperial propaganda presented the "clemency" of the Augusti as the exercise of a sovereign's prerogative toward the *undeserving*. Where Seneca advised the emperor to be judicious in his granting of amnesty, out of concern that too-great leniency would undermine the public perception of the emperor's power, Paul insists that God's "kindness and forbearance" are the expression of God's power. God's mercy produces repentance, faithfulness, and obedience. It cannot, therefore, compromise God's justice; to the contrary, God's mercy is the public manifestation of God's justice—*insofar as those who have received mercy are thereby moved to respond in obedience*.

Another comparison is even more central to the larger purpose of the letter. When Romans has been read as a treatise on salvation, the apostrophe in 2:17–3:9 has been read as an indictment of "the Jew," intended to show both that the Jew needs Paul's gospel as much as the "Gentile" and that the Jew is in greater danger of resisting the gospel because of a false presumption. This "characteristic Jewish boast" must be "demolished" by proving that the Jew is just as guilty of disobedience as the sinners described in 1:18–32. But this reading, based in part on a mistranslation of 3:19, misses the point of Paul's

---

44. On the hortatory thrust of this section, see Neil Elliott, *The Rhetoric of Romans: Argumentative Constraint and Strategy and Paul's Dialogue with Judaism* (JSNTSup 45; Sheffield: JSOT Press, 1990), 146–52.

argument. It is hard to imagine a Jew who would have been surprised by Paul citing the Jewish Scriptures to argue for Jewish accountability to Israel's God. Paul's point—addressed to a non-Judean audience—is that the Jewish Scriptures establish God's claim on the whole world, *not* just upon Judeans. All the world—not just Judeans—is accountable to God.[45] Paul's stylized address to a Judean in 2:17–3:9 is thus meant not to indict "the Jews" or to criticize Judaism but to enlist a fellow Judean as a witness in order to make an important point to his non-Judean audience.

Here it is crucially important that we understand how Paul's use of diatribal techniques functions.[46] No one has done more to help us understand Paul's use of diatribal techniques in Rom 2–3 than Stanley K. Stowers. In *The Diatribe and Paul's Letter to the Romans* (1981) and *A Rereading of Romans* (1994), he demonstrated that the sudden rhetorical turn to second-person-singular address at 2:1 was not a rhetorical "trap" for the Jew but fit a broad pattern of moral exhortation in which speech-in-character was used as "a personal indictment of any of the audience to whom it might apply." It is "anachronistic and completely unwarranted to think that Paul has only the Jew in mind in 2:1–5 or that he characterizes the typical Jew."[47]

By contrast, in 2:17–24 Paul clearly has "the Jew" in mind. Here again, however, Stowers's insights into the function of diatribal techniques sufficed to establish that Paul was not addressing the attitudes of actual Judean opponents in his Roman audience. Stowers's case rested in part on the careful distinction of different diatribal techniques, including the use of (1) *objections,* clearly signaled as such; (2) rhetorical questions, imperatives, or accusations intended to convict the fictitious interlocutor of wrong thinking or hypocrisy (*elenchos*-rhetoric), sometimes indicated by a negative term of address; and (3) rhetorical questions leading to *false conclusions,* often indicated by an invitation to consider consequences. All of these forms are clearly evident in Romans. Just here, however, some categorical confusion distorts Stowers's reading of diatribal elements in the letter. Unfortunately, Stowers does not carefully maintain the distinctions between diatribal techniques that he has identified. The result is a confused reading of the diatribal address in

---

45. On the difference that a comma makes in the translation of 3:19, see ibid., 142–46; on the diatribe in Rom 2–3, see Elliott, *Arrogance of Nations,* 100–107.

46. I discuss this passage in greater detail in Elliott, *The Rhetoric of Romans,* 127–57; idem, *Arrogance of Nations,* 100–107.

47. Stanley K. Stowers, *The Diatribe and Paul's Letter to the Romans* (SBLDS 57; Chico, Calif.: Scholars Press, 1981), 110–12; so again in *A Rereading of Romans: Gentiles, Jews, Justice* (New Haven: Yale University Press, 1994), 153.

Rom 2–3 that fundamentally misunderstands Paul's purpose in this section and in the letter as a whole.

Stowers reads Rom 2:17–24 as a series of "indicting rhetorical questions." The picture that the apostle paints, according to Stowers, is

> not just of the pretentious person but of the pretentious moral and religious leader and teacher. The "Jew" here pretends to have a special relationship with God. He boasts ... of his relation to God.... Bragging about what one does not truly possess is the chief mark of the pretentious person. He also boasts in the law while breaking it. This person pretends to have great ethical knowledge, knowledge of the law and of God's will. Finally, he pretends to be a teacher and moral guide to others, although he does not embody what he teaches.[48]

But (against Stowers) the person whom Paul addresses is *not* "bragging about what [he] does not truly possess." To the contrary, Paul is clear that the Judean *does* possess these things (see Rom 9:4–5).[49] Neither do we hear Paul's Judean interlocutor admit that he has broken the law; indeed, Paul has so structured the dialogue at this point that he has no opportunity to respond. Stowers insists (and I agree) that the apostrophe is not meant as Paul's characterization of Jews as such. But the question remains: Just what is Paul's purpose here? Stowers has given different answers: either Paul is simply showing off, providing the Roman church with a sample of his rhetorical skill by showing the sort of diatribal technique of which he is capable,[50] or he is hurling a long-distance invective at perceived Judean opponents in Jerusalem.[51]

These judgments fail to follow through on Stowers's own insights into the function of diatribe. According to Stowers, the use of speech-in-character and of rhetorical questions addressed to a fictitious interlocutor was normally "didactic" in purpose. All of the apostrophes in Romans, he wrote, "indict pretentious and arrogant persons. Rather than indicating a polemic against the Jew, the apostrophes in Romans censure Jews, Gentiles, and Gentile Christians alike. None are excluded from the censure of the pretentious."[52] These conclusions follow naturally from Stowers's discussion of the normal didactic or hortatory effect of diatribal techniques. But Stowers does not follow through to the logical conclusion of these observations with regard

---

48. Stowers, *Diatribe and Paul's Letter*, 96, 112–13.
49. Elliott, *The Rhetoric of Romans*, 130–31.
50. Stowers, *Diatribe and Paul's Letter*, 179–80, 182 (emphasis added); idem, *A Rereading of Romans*, 168.
51. Stowers, *A Rereading of Romans*, 150–51.
52. Ibid., 152, 176–77.

to the apostrophe to "the Jew" in 2:17–24. This apostrophe is a device aimed at criticizing attitudes among *Paul's non-Judean audience* in a fundamentally hortatory letter.

We may compare the apostrophe in 2:17–24 with the one in 2:1–6. In the earlier passage, Paul levels an accusation against a hypothetical interlocutor, using indicative statements: "Therefore you are without excuse, O mortal, everyone who judges, for in that by which you judge another you condemn yourself, *for you who judge do the same things.*" In 2:17–24, by contrast, Paul asks his hypothetical *Judean* interlocutor a series of questions: "Do you not teach yourself? ... Do you steal? ... Do you commit adultery? ... Do you rob temples? ... By transgressing the law, do you dishonor God?" Here, however, he does not wait for an answer, so he cannot deliver a guilty verdict comparable to 2:1.[53] The apostrophe here remains *conditional*: *if* you steal, commit adultery, and rob temples, *then* you dishonor God; *then,* the verdict of Scripture would apply (2:24). *Then* your circumcision would avail you nothing (2:25). The apostrophe imaginatively embodies the assertion that Paul has already made in 2:12–13: "As many as have sinned in the law will be judged by the law."

It would be hard to imagine a self-respecting Judean arguing *against* Paul here: Which of his contemporaries would have protested that being a Judean in fact gave one a license to sin? But Paul's Judean contemporaries are not his target. The non-Judeans in Rome are. It is *they* who need to hear that Judeans do not, in fact, presume on God's grace and mercy to indulge their sins.

That is just what the audience hears when Paul's Judean interlocutor at last gets a chance to talk back in 3:1–9. Here again, Stowers's insights into diatribe style provide keys to interpretation; here again, however, Stowers fails to follow through with these insights. Stowers has shown that, in general, teachers employing diatribal style would use leading questions and false conclusions to move their fictitious hearer to the right conclusion. Puzzlingly, however, in his 1981 study Stowers read the rhetorical questions in 3:1, 3, 5, 7, 8, and 9 not as Paul's leading questions but as *objections* from the Jewish interlocutor. (In 1994, he modified this outline, but he continued to read 3:1 and 9 as objections.) This way of construing the dialogue puts "the Jew" on the defensive, recoiling from Paul's earlier questions in 2:17–24. His supposed protest, "Then what advantage does the Jew have?" implies that he had previ-

---

53. The point is obscured, unfortunately, in the Nestle-Aland (27th ed.) Greek text, which ends all these phrases with a question mark except the last, which it ends with a semicolon. (The RSV and NRSV insert a question mark.) The earliest surviving manuscript of Romans to include punctuation marks, Codex Sinaiticus, has a question mark at the end of 2:23; see my *The Rhetoric of Romans*, 128–29.

ously assumed that his "advantage" was precisely the license to get away with theft, adultery, and the robbing of temples. But this is scarcely credible *even as a fictitious dialogue*. To the contrary, as I argued in *The Rhetoric of Romans* (1990), on the basis of Stowers's own discussion of diatribal technique, we should read the questions in 3:1–9 not as objections from the interlocutor but as *Paul's* leading questions and the answers as his dialogue partner's appropriate drawing of right conclusions and rejection of wrong conclusions.[54]

The conversation thus runs as follows:

3:1	Paul's leading question	Then what advantage has the Jew? Or what is the value of circumcision?
3:2	Interlocutor's response	Much in every way. For, in the first place, the Jews were entrusted with the oracles of God.
3:3	Paul	What if some were unfaithful? Will their faithlessness nullify the faithfulness of God?
3:4	Interlocutor	By no means! Although everyone is a liar, let God be proved true …
3:5	Paul	But if our injustice serves to confirm the justice of God, what should we say? That God is unjust to inflict wrath on us? (I speak in a human way.)
3:6	Interlocutor	By no means! For then how could God judge the world?
3:7, 8	Paul	But if through my falsehood God's truthfulness abounds to his glory, why am I still being condemned as a sinner? And why not say (as some people slander us by saying that we say), "Let us do evil so that good may come"?
3:8c	Interlocutor	Their condemnation is deserved!
3:9a	Paul	What then? Do we have any defense (against God's judgment)?
3:9b	Interlocutor	No, not at all; for we have already charged that all, both Jews and Greeks, are under the power of sin …

---

54. See the table contrasting Stowers's reading of the diatribe and mine in *Arrogance of Nations*, 105–6, 205–6 n. 74.

This way of reading the diatribe more naturally conforms to Stowers's insights about the way teachers could use leading questions in fictitious dialogues to shape the perceptions and attitudes of their audiences. But it fundamentally changes our perception of Paul's purpose. He is not *indicting* a Judean who recoils in self-protection and protest; rather, he is *enlisting* a Judean colleague who heartily endorses his conclusion. Yes, says his witness, *if* I have committed the sins you describe, I most assuredly deserve judgment! To expect otherwise would be to dishonor God—and to justify the reprehensible allegations raised against my people by the nations—if we should imagine that we may "do evil that good may come." Far better for me to be judged than for God's honor to be impugned! The Judean interlocutor is not concerned to protect his privilege over against God's claim; to the contrary, he enthusiastically agrees with Paul that Judeans enjoy no defense against God's judgment.[55]

The non-Judean audience overhearing this conversation is meant to learn an important lesson *about Judeans*. Regardless of the emperor's claims to magnanimity, and regardless of the more scurrilous generalizations to be heard in the Roman street about the returning exiles as unworthy beneficiaries of Nero's clemency, present circumstances in Rome had little to do with genuine mercy or with the justice of God.

Here we are in touch with the character of Paul's argumentation as the dissociation of concepts.[56] Paul's rhetoric drives toward the distinction of the present from the future, or more precisely, the dissociation of the present, *as the failed realization of God's purposes in history*, from the future, *as the complete realization of those purposes*. The full revelation of God's justice is yet to come. That will be a day of judgment: of glory and honor for those who have endured in doing right, but wrath and punishment for all who have done evil (2:6–11). In place of the present regime of arrogance and pretension, corruption and contempt for the truth, *that* day will bring a universal and inescapable judgment according to works. Until now, the world has seen

---

55. The question in 3:9 has often been read as a repetition of 3:1, the unusual Greek form προεχόμεθα taken either as an active middle ("are we any better off?" NRSV) or a passive ("are we at a disadvantage?" NRSV note), but the verb is a genuine middle, meaning "raise a defense for oneself" or "put up a defense." When the Judean is asked whether he shares the presumption of being exempt from God's judgment (2:1–6), he immediately gives an exemplary response: "Not at all!" See Nils Dahl, "Romans 3:9: Text and Meaning," in *Paul and Paulinism: Essays in Honour of C. K. Barrett* (ed. Morna D. Hooker and Stephen G. Wilson; London: SPCK, 1982), 184–204, here at 194; J. C. O'Neill, *Romans* (London: Penguin, 1975), 68; and Elliott, *The Rhetoric of Romans*, 132–33, 141.

56. Chaim Perelman and Lucie Olbrechts-Tyteca, *The New Rhetoric: A Treatise on Argumentation* (trans. John Wilkinson and Purcell Weaver; Notre Dame, Ind.: University of Notre Dame Press, 1969), 411–50.

spectacular examples of God's wrath being revealed (1:18–32), but until now, history has more usually been the arena of God's forbearance of sins (3:25). God's kindness and mercy have provided a temporary reprieve, allowing time to repent, but that time is drawing quickly to an end. To read the present disposition of power and privilege as the climax of history would be a grave mistake. To join in the delusion that the exercise of imperial prerogative constitutes genuine mercy and that justice means no more than brokering favor regardless of desert, would be morally disastrous.

4.4. The Manifestation of Mercy in History

Paul's stylized conversation with "a Judean" in Rom 2–3 thus anticipates the argument of Rom 9–11. There, too, the relation of God's mercy to the present moment in history is at the theological heart of the issue. Understanding divine mercy aright is necessary to discerning the will of God, "the good and acceptable and perfect," but given imperial realities, it also sets one inevitably at odds with the mentality of the present age (12:1–2).

But Paul's chief concern in Rom 9–11 is not to diagnose the inadequacy in Israel's thinking. His more urgent objective is to guide his non-Judean audience to a correct perception of Israel's present circumstances. God has been found by those who did not seek God, that is, the nations (10:20, quoting Isa 65:1), but God has also stretched out his hands to an untrusting people, Israel (10:21, quoting Isa 65:2). This is, again, not a final determination of "who is in and who is out" but a description of God's persistent efforts to bring *both* Israel and the nations to salvation (the δὲ in 10:21 is conjunctive, not adversative). God has not abandoned his people (11:1).

The dissociative logic in these chapters is coherent and powerful. Present circumstances are only a guide to the future if one knows the deep logic, the "mystery," which Paul reveals. Without it, the non-Judeans in Rome are able only to draw the conclusions to which the cold logic of imperial ideology leads them: those who appear in the streets as the *victi* of imperial power, the losers of history's proud march, are in fact God-forsaken. That conclusion, Paul warns, is a fatal mistake, for it attributes to the empire the power to determine the future, and that power is God's alone.

Nero's court claimed that the humble circumstances of Judeans in the streets of Rome were as much as the wretched of the earth could hope to receive from imperial mercy and far more than they deserved. Against that claim, Paul contemplates a dramatic reversal that constitutes a repudiation of imperial logic. History's course has *not* reached its climax in the mercy of the emperor. Rather, those who now *appear* to be "enemies," *persona non grata* in the imperial dispensation, in fact suffer their present ignominy "for your sake." In reality, they are the elect, beloved "for the sake of the ances-

tors" (11:28). This is the "mystery" Paul reveals to the Roman ἐκκλησία. History has not yet run its course. Rather, he tells his audience, we stand on the very brink of the fulfillment of God's purposes. It is *God* who has brought upon Israel a temporary "hardening," in order to achieve a broader redemption than anyone could anticipate when God will have mercy on all. Until that moment, it is *God* who has "imprisoned all in disobedience" (11:31–32), just as it is God who has subjected the world to futility and corruption (8:20–21). It is an imperial boast—not a Judean one—that provokes the apostle's rebuttal.

Part 5
"Paul and Scripture" through Other Eyes

Paul and Writing

Mark D. Given

1. Introduction

The hardest task confronting any New Testament scholar is to come up with an idea or an argument that is at the same time fresh, interesting, and not too far-fetched.[1]

The idea for this essay occurred to me at the first meeting of the SBL's new Paul and Scripture Seminar in 2005. For that meeting, each of us was asked to make a ten-minute statement about our ideas for the seminar, the tasks that we considered most important for a group that would be meeting annually over the next seven years to address this topic. Most of the members suggested methodological matters, especially literary-critical questions brought to the forefront by the seminal work of Richard Hays and rhetorical-critical issues popularized especially by the recent work of Chris Stanley.[2] A few members were also interested in ideological questions of the sociohistorical and political variety. Only a couple of us emphasized the importance of spending some time on the issue of what Scripture *is* for Paul—Paul's "theory of Scripture," one might say—and examining our own theories of Scripture. This essay is an initial attempt to state my theory of what Scripture is for Paul.[3]

---

1. John Ashton, *The Religion of Paul the Apostle* (New Haven: Yale University Press, 2000), 244.

2. Richard B. Hays, *Echoes of Scripture in the Letters of Paul* (New York: Yale University Press, 1989); Christopher D. Stanley, *Arguing with Scripture: The Rhetoric of Quotations in the Letters of Paul* (New York: T&T Clark, 2004).

3. Note well how I have constructed this sentence. While some aspects of Dale Martin's reflections on how "texts don't mean; people mean with texts" remain problematic to me, I fully agree that interpreters must take responsibility for the meanings they *construct*

Of course, it is not as if this question has never been addressed in the history of interpretation. The issue is present in Protestant biblical scholarship as early as Luther and becomes prominent among the neo-orthodox, Bultmann being a prime example. In this tradition, the possibility opened up of seeing the issue not only as a matter of Paul and Scripture but of Paul and script, Paul and writing. The title of this paper, "Paul and Writing," signals that this topic will not be narrowly pursued in the way that the topic of "Paul and Scripture" is often treated. Indeed, my discussion of Paul and writing will be woven into a very broad context, a theory of Paul's religion.

2. A Theory of Paul's Religion: Apocalyptic Logocentrism

> Many responsibilities begin in dreams, and many transfigurations of the tradition begin in private fantasies. Think, for example, of Plato's or St Paul's private fantasies—fantasies so original and utopian that they became the common sense of later times.[4]

Let me say immediately that I am not offering *the* theory of Paul's religion. Scholars today who specialize in "theory of religion" are leery of "grand theories" that claim to have all the answers. Instead, we must rely on a variety of theories (anthropological, psychological, sociological, rhetorical, philosophical, etc.) that illuminate various aspects of whatever phenomena we choose to classify as religion.[5] Therefore, I am only offering one possible philosophical theory of Paul's religion, one that trades upon one of the most basic insights of deconstruction's critique of the Western philosophical tradition. I think the time for this approach is ripe, especially given the recent positive interest taken in Paul by a variety of philosophers.[6] Surprisingly, however, little has

---

while reading Scripture. See Dale B. Martin, *Sex and the Single Savior* (Louisville: Westminster John Knox, 2006), esp. 1–35.

4. Richard Rorty, "Is Derrida a Transcendental Philosopher?" in *Derrida: A Critical Reader* (ed. David Wood; Oxford: Blackwell, 1992), 237–38. Against Culler, Norris, and Gasché, Rorty argues that Derrida fits in the company of Plato and Paul, not that of "rigorous" philosophers.

5. See, e.g., Ivan Strenski, *Thinking about Religion: An Historical Introduction to Theories of Religion* (Malden: Blackwell, 2006), esp. 337–45; Willi Braun and Russell T. McCutcheon, eds., *Guide to the Study of Religion* (London: Cassell, 2000).

6. E.g., Giorgio Agamben, *The Time That Remains: A Commentary on the Letter to the Romans* (Stanford, Calif.: Stanford University Press, 2005); Alain Badiou, *Saint Paul: The Foundation of Universalism* (Stanford, Calif.: Stanford University Press, 2006); Slavoj Žižek, *The Fragile Absolute, or Why Is the Christian Legacy Worth Fighting For?* (New York: Verso, 2000); idem, *The Puppet and the Dwarf: The Perverse Core of Christianity* (Cambridge:

been written about Paul's particular form of logocentrism aside from Daniel Boyarin's excellent contribution.[7] Even less has been written about its possible implications for his attitude toward Scripture.[8]

A brief definition of logocentrism will serve as the guiding thread for this entire essay.[9] Logocentrism is Derrida's shorthand term for the Western

---

MIT Press, 2003). A major problem with some of these philosophical forays into Paul is that they are often completely out of touch with current scholarship on the subject. While it is clear from my own work that I believe there are still valid insights in the ways thinkers such as Augustine, F. C. Baur, Luther, and Bultmann read Paul, much recent philosophical interpretation of Paul shows no awareness of how radically such classic readings have been problematized in the wake of the "New Perspective" on Paul.

7. Daniel Boyarin, *A Radical Jew: Paul and the Politics of Identity* (Berkeley and Los Angeles: University of California Press, 1994). Brian Ingraffia attempts "to demonstrate ... that Derrida's deconstruction of the logocentrism of Western thought undermines only the human *logos* of Greek and modern rationalism, not the divine *logos* of biblical, Christian theology" (Brian D. Ingraffia, *Postmodern Theory and Biblical Theology: Vanquishing God's Shadow* [Cambridge: Cambridge University Press, 1995], 213). However, Ingraffia's reference to "the human *logos* of Greek ... rationalism" reveals how little he understands the concept of "logocentrism." The Greek *logos* was every bit as much a theological concept as the Christian one. What did *logos*, actually *Logos*, mean to the Stoics?

8. While I agree with Kathy Ehrensperger that Derridean deconstruction can and should be applied to expose the logocentrism of Paulinism, she argues that Paul himself is not logocentric. Although she agrees that Paul is a Hellenistic Jew, she tries to minimize the amount of Hellenism in Paul. See Kathy Ehrensperger, "'Let Everyone be Convinced in His/Her Own Mind': Derrida and the Deconstruction of Paulinism," in *Society of Biblical Literature 2002 Seminar Papers* (SBLSP 41; Atlanta: Scholars Press, 2002), 53–73; idem, *That We May Be Mutually Encouraged: Feminism and the New Perspective in Pauline Studies* (London: T&T Clark, 2004), 47–53, 125–54. There are varieties of logocentrism, and that is why I speak here of explicating Paul's particular form of it. It is a Hellenistic-Jewish apocalyptic logocentrism, not a purely Hellenistic one—as if such a thing existed. But, as the texts examined in this paper will show, it is a logocentrism nonetheless. See also references in n. 28 below.

9. There are many full discussions available on all facets of deconstruction, so I will not be offering a crash course on such matters here. A classic highly readable introduction is Jonathan Culler, *On Deconstruction* (Ithaca, N.Y.: Cornell University Press, 1982), esp. 85–225. A delightful *entrée* is John D. Caputo, ed., *Deconstruction in a Nutshell: A Conversation with Jacques Derrida* (New York: Fordham University Press, 1997). As is often lamented, the interaction between deconstruction and biblical studies continues to occur at the margins of the historical-critical enterprise. For a recent assessment, see Yvonne Sherwood, ed., *Derrida's Bible (Reading a Page of Scripture with a Little Help from Derrida)* (New York: Palgrave Macmillan, 2004), 7–11. Some philosophers of religion and theologians have engaged with deconstruction in fascinating ways, e.g., John D. Caputo, *The Prayer and Tears of Jacques Derrida: Religion without Religion* (Bloomington: Indiana University Press, 1997); and Graham Ward, *Barth, Derrida, and the Language of Theology*

privileging of "speech over writing, immediacy over distance, identity over difference, and (self-) presence over all forms of absence, ambiguity, simulation, substitution, or negativity."[10] Therefore, among other things, deconstruction is a strategy for uncovering this privileging. In the history of Western philosophy that stretches back at least to Plato, existentialism would appear to mark the final outworking of this tradition, with its intense preoccupation with Being and beings and its supreme valorization of Present-ness, an experience, however, that is always frustrated by the differing and deferring of time and space (i.e., *différance*). Derrida, especially through his deconstructive readings of Heidegger, critiques this tradition, so that a second step in my own reading of Paul could involve a similar deconstruction, noting the self-contradictions that emerge from his logocentrism.[11] That, however, is not my focus here. My more modest goals are (1) to explicate how thoroughly logocentric Paul is by analyzing the logocentric symptoms displayed by a number of his texts; (2) to reveal the distinctive characteristics of his particular manifestation of logocentrism, namely, apocalyptic logocentrism, and argue that it can serve as a theory of his religion; and (3) to highlight how this theory can explain his complex attitude toward Scripture and writing.

2.1. 1 Thessalonians

From the beginning to the end of Paul's fragmented corpus, his logocentrism is readily apparent. Beginning with 1 Thessalonians, probably his earliest extant letter, Paul says, "Our Gospel came to you not in word only, but also in power and in the Holy Spirit and with full conviction, just as you know what kind of persons we proved to be among you for your sake" (1 Thess 1:5). The effectiveness of Paul's *logos* depends on the real presence of God within it. He gives thanks that, "when you received the Word of God that you heard from us, you accepted it not as a human word but as what it really is, God's Word, which is also at work in you believers" (2:13). Moreover, as we will see more fully in the case of 2 Cor 3, Paul's own legitimacy ("what kind of persons we proved to be") is somehow bound up with this presence. While "dead letter" is usually associated with written texts, even spoken words can be empty for

---

(Cambridge: Cambridge University Press, 1995). A recent work of particular interest for Paul scholars is Theodore W. Jennings Jr., *Reading Derrida/Thinking Paul: On Justice* (Cultural Memory in the Present; Stanford, Calif.: Stanford University Press, 2006).

10. Jacques Derrida, *Dissemination* (trans. Barbara Johnson; Chicago: University of Chicago Press, 1981), 4.

11. See esp. Jacques Derrida, *Of Spirit: Heidegger and the Question* (trans. Geoffrey Bennington and Rachel Bowlby; Chicago: University of Chicago Press, 1989).

Paul if they do not proceed from the mouth of a person filled with the Spirit of Christ so that they become vehicles of the presence of God.[12] As epistemologically doubtful as this may sound to moderns and postmoderns, Paul *literally* believed that the presence of Christ was in him and speaking through him and that this spiritual presence was what made his *logos* effective.[13]

Given his apocalyptic logocentric presuppositions about the power of the Gospel, the frequent rejection of it must have been very mysterious to him. His frustration led him in the direction of the ancient equivalent of modern conspiracy theory.[14] The "god of this world" must be responsible (2 Cor 4:4)! While I think that some New Testament scholars underestimate the degree to which Paul believed a real war was going on in which Satan was actually winning many battles, I also think that Paul was ultimately unsatisfied with this explanation alone. This is why we see him revealing the secret in Rom 11 that the hardening of part of Israel to the Gospel is actually God's doing and only temporary, a surreptitious plan designed to save everyone.

Paul longs for the presence of the Thessalonians: "But we, brothers and sisters, being taken away from you for a short time in presence, not in heart, endeavored the more eagerly to experience your presence with great desire, because we wanted to come to you—I, Paul, again and again—but Satan hindered us" (1 Thess 2:17-18; see also 3:6 and 10). What is obviously presumed by this sentence, although it bears emphasis, is that resorting to a letter instead of a visit is, as so often stated, a substitute for Paul's presence.[15] Indeed, it is made necessary by a demonic aspect of the form of this world, the activity of Satan, the great divider, separator, and interrupter of divine spiritual presence.[16]

Later we get a glimpse of Paul's eschatological utopia. From the moment of the *parousia*, the being-there, the *presence* of the Lord (1 Thess 4:15; see also 5:23), believers "will always be with the Lord" (4:17; see also 3:13; 5:10). It is interesting to observe how Paul formulates the consummation of his

---

12. Cf. the concept in Acts 9:15-17. See the discussion of Paul's Spirit in Mark D. Given, *Paul's True Rhetoric: Ambiguity, Cunning and Deception in Greece and Rome* (ESEC 7; Harrisburg, Pa.: Trinity Press International, 2001), 46-60.

13. However, this did not lead to Paul forsaking rhetoric. No doubt, he believed that the Spirit inspires rhetoric.

14. See Mark D. Given, "On His Majesty's Secret Service: The Undercover Ethos of Paul," in *Rhetoric, Ethic, and Moral Persuasion in Biblical Discourse* (ed. Thomas H. Olbricht and Anders Eriksson; ESEC 11; New York: T&T Clark, 2005), 196-213.

15. See the excellent discussion of this aspect of ancient epistolary literature in Hans-Josef Klauck, *Ancient Letters and the New Testament: A Guide to Context and Exegesis* (Waco, Tex.: Baylor University Press, 2006), 189-93.

16. See the article cited in note 14.

relationship with the Thessalonians in 2:19: "For what is our hope or joy or crown of boasting—is it not precisely you in the presence of our Lord Jesus at his *parousia*?" In the *parousia*, the desire for presence will be fully satisfied, as believers will be fully present not only to the Lord but also to one another in perfect *koinonia*. This is what gives Paul's logocentrism its distinctive apocalyptic form. It is not simply a state of mind or a mode of being that values "immediacy over distance, identity over difference, and (self-) presence over all forms of absence." It includes the fervent and expectant hope that immediacy, identity, and (self-)presence will be fully attained in the future.[17]

And what of writing? "Now concerning love of the brothers and sisters, you do not need to have anyone write to you, for you yourselves have been God-taught to love one another" (1 Thess 4:9).[18] Already in the letter that provides our first glimpse of Paul, a letter that quotes no Scripture at all, it would appear that empowerment to love, and thus to fulfill the whole law (Gal 5:14), does not come through writing. It comes through knowing God and being taught by him. There are several ways to interpret what Paul means by *theodidaktos*, and I would not want to exclude any of them precipitously, including the possibility that Paul is referring to Lev 19:18.[19] However, as the shorter and probably more original form of 1 Cor 8:12–13 says, "If anyone thinks to have arrived at knowledge, that one does not yet know as one ought to know. But if anyone loves, that one is known."[20] It is one thing to know

---

17. Therefore I do not agree with Boyarin that it is "a serious hermeneutic error to make one's interpretation of Paul depend on the apocalyptic expectation, which is after all not even mentioned once in Galatians, rather than the apocalyptic fulfillment which has already been realized in the vision of the crucified Christ according to the spirit, Christ's spirit, Paul's, and that of the Galatians" (*Radical Jew*, 36). Paul's own perspective is that "if for this life only we have hoped in Christ, we are of all people most to be pitied" (1 Cor 15:19; see also Rom 8:18–25). The vision already attained is but a foretaste for Paul, as he does not expect his hope for a new humanity, "a new creation" (Gal 6:15), to be fulfilled in "this present evil age" (1:4). Maintaining this perspective is important for addressing the cultural problems of similarity and difference explored by Boyarin. Paul *may* have desired a spiritual universe of the Same in the age to come, but one can make a strong case that he recognized—or came to recognize—the harmfulness of trying to realize that goal in this age.

18. See 1 John 1:26–27.

19. See the alternatives in Abraham J. Malherbe, *The Letters to the Thessalonians* (AB 32B; New York: Doubleday, 2000), 244–45. Several involve the concept of being taught through the Spirit. Actually, Malherbe omits Lev 19:18, but see Wayne A. Meeks, *The Origins of Christian Morality: The First Two Centuries* (New Haven: Yale University Press, 1993), 154.

20. See Gordon D. Fee, *The First Epistle to the Corinthians* (NICNT; Grand Rapids: Eerdmans, 1987), 367–68, for a thoroughly persuasive defense of the shorter P^{46} reading. My translation differs from Fee's only in the use of inclusive language.

through precept or Scripture that God commands love, but from Paul's point of view one must also be known by God, intimately, one might say, in order to be able to fulfill this commandment that fulfills all commandments. His neologism *theodidaktos* is probably an attempt to capture that thought.

2.2. 1 Corinthians

The pervasive discourse of Spirit in this letter is, of course, highly symptomatic of logocentrism. To give only a few examples, as early as 2:1–5 Paul is using the same legitimating rhetoric we saw in 1 Thessalonians: "My speech and my proclamation were not with plausible words of wisdom but with a demonstration of the Spirit and of power, so that your faith might rest not on human wisdom but on the power of God" (2:4–5). It is not the logical content of the proclamation—moronic by worldly standards!—that makes the Gospel persuasive (1:23) but the actual presence and power of God conveyed by it, namely, the Spirit.

Chapter 13 is a passage too often marginalized in the Pauline corpus, but I think that it takes us close to the heart of Paul's religion. In that chapter, Paul contrasts the provisional and partial nature of prophecy, tongues, and knowledge, things that were *dividing* the Corinthians, with what will happen when "the complete" comes (13:10). Over against these sources of division and separation, Paul sets love with its images of full intimacy and full presence, such as being "face to face" and "knowing fully as I have been fully known."[21] "Knowing fully as I have been fully known" is as powerful an expression of logocentrism as one can imagine. In it, presence and self-presence are united.[22] Therefore, there is an intimate relationship between 1 Cor 13 and 12. Rather than spiritual gifts creating division in the church, they should be a penultimate manifestation of the eschatological unity of love described in 1 Cor 13, since they all come from "one and the same Spirit" (12:4, 9, 11, 13).

In 1 Cor 15, the anthropological aspects of Paul's apocalyptic logocentrism come more fully into view. Paul explains at some length what a resurrection body is. *Pace* traditionalist interpreters who continue to create convoluted interpretations of the passage in order to reconcile it with the quite

---

21. Although Paul would certainly argue that by ἀγάπη he means something far more "spiritual" than physical intimacy, surely sexual imagery is influencing his expression here, as is so often the case in mystical religious language. Marriage, of course, is spoken of as *two becoming one* in Paul's Jewish culture.

22. In addition, in 1 Cor 15 the ultimate outcome, after all opposition to God and his Messiah is destroyed, is that "God may be all in all" (15:28).

different conceptions in the Gospels and later orthodox Christian doctrine, Paul insists that a resurrection body is constructed entirely of one substance, *pneuma*.[23] Why so? One reason is to facilitate participation or incorporation. As Dale Martin puts it,

> Christians currently partake of two natures: because they possess pneuma, they share something with the heavenly natures; because they are also made up of sarx and psyche, they share something with the earth, Adam, animals, birds, fish, and even dirt (15:39–40, 47–48). The transformation expected at the eschaton will cause the Christian body to shed the lower parts of its current nature and be left with the purer, transformed part of the pneuma. Christians will have bodies without flesh, blood, or soul—composed solely of pneumatic substance—light, airy, luminous bodies. The presupposition underwriting Paul's argument here is that the nature of any body is due to its participation in some particular sphere of existence. It gets its identity only through participation.[24]

As Martin explains earlier, many ancient philosophers held that "the reason why the normal human body cannot experience immortality is that it occupies a relatively low place on the spectrum of stuff, which ranges from fine, thin, rarefied stuff down to gross, thick, heavy stuff."[25] Therefore, it makes sense that in order to enjoy immortality with God a person must be transformed into the same stuff as God, *pneuma*. Identity is valued over difference. Furthermore, the only way one could be fully self-present would be to be composed entirely of one substance. A being composed of multiple substances, flesh and spirit, is by nature divided against itself, creating that inner conflict of flesh and spirit that Paul and other ancient moral philosophers often spoke of.[26] Instead, in the apocalyptic logocentric "end," God must "be all in all" (1 Cor 15:28).

---

23. For an excellent discussion of the concept of the resurrected body in 1 Cor 15, see Dale B. Martin, *The Corinthian Body* (New Haven: Yale University Press, 1995), 104–36, esp. 123–29. Also, see David E. Aune, "Anthropological Duality in the Eschatology of 2 Cor 4:15–5:10," in *Paul beyond the Hellenism/Judaism Divide* (ed. Troels Engberg-Pederson; Louisville: Westminster John Knox, 2001), 215–40; Alan F. Segal, *Life after Death: A History of the Afterlife in Western Religion* (New York: Doubleday, 2004), 399–440.

24. Martin, *The Corinthian Body*, 132.

25. Martin discusses the views of Plutarch, Marcus Aurelius, Cicero, Philo, Apollonius of Tyana, and Epictetus (ibid., 113–17).

26. See Boyarin, *A Radical Jew*, 57–85, passim.

2.3. 2 Corinthians

The classic passage pertaining to writing in Paul is 2 Cor 3:1–4:15, so I will give it a more extended treatment here and return to it later.[27] I find the argument that he is under considerable Hellenistic influence here to be quite convincing, and this influence is certainly relevant to comprehending his form of logocentrism.[28] Interpreters have already suspected that a Hellenistic devaluation of writing is influencing Paul's letter/Spirit dichotomy in 3:6ff. For example, while commenting on 1 Cor 3:6, Furnish refers to the "oft-cited passage from Plato's *Phaedrus*": 275D–276E.[29] Furnish explains:

> The metaphor of commendatory letters is further extended when Paul describes by what agency and on what material they have been inscribed: *not with ink but with the Spirit of the living God; not on stone tablets but on tablets that are human hearts*. An oft-cited passage from Plato's *Phaedrus* provides a detailed exposition of the thesis that "written words" (*logous gegrammenous*, 275D) are but the faint "image" (*eidōlon*) of "the living, breathing word" (*ton logon zōnta kai empsychon*, 276A). Socrates argued (276C–E) that truth is not effectively sown "in ink … through a pen" (*melani … dia kalamou*), in "gardens of letters" (*in grammasi kērous*), but only by "the dialectic method," whereby truth is planted "in a fitting soul" (*psychēn prosēkousan*). In this connection, one may recall that Paul himself regards his own letters as but a poor substitute for his actual presence with those whom he addresses (see, e.g., 10:9–11; 1 Cor 4:14, 18–21; 5:3–5). This point of view corresponds to one frequently expressed by ancient letter writers (see Thraede 1970) and may also reflect, as Rivken suggests (1978:275), Paul's background in Pharisaism, with its concern for the *un*written Torah and for traditions orally conveyed (cf. ibid., 241–43).[30]

This all makes sense to me, and I have quoted it at length as a reminder that interpreters have found it quite plausible that Paul was influenced by the very type of logocentrism Derrida theorized. However, I want to offer some fur-

---

27. For something closer to an exegesis of this passage, see my *Paul's True Rhetoric*, 118–26.

28. Paul is clearly multicultural, a cultural hybrid. As Boyarin puts it, echoing Joyce, "Jewgreek is Greekjew" (*A Radical Jew*, 79). See the essays in Troels Engberg-Pedersen, ed., *Paul in His Hellenistic Context* (Minneapolis: Fortress, 1995); idem, *Paul beyond the Judaism/Hellenism Divide*.

29. Victor Paul Furnish, *II Corinthians* (AB 32A; New York: Doubleday, 1984), 195.

30. Furnish, *II Corinthians*, 195. On ancient letters more generally, see Klauck, *Ancient Letters and the New Testament*.

ther observations, with an eye toward Paul's particular form of apocalyptic logocentrism.

I begin by noting that this entire passage is part of an apology. This is apparent from what I take to be the thesis of 2 Corinthians, expressed in 2:15–17:

> For we are the aroma of Christ to God among those who are being saved and among those who are being destroyed; to the one a fragrance from death to death, to the other a fragrance from life to life. Who is fit for these things? For *we* are not—*like so many*—peddlers of God's Word, but in Christ we speak as persons of sincerity, as persons sent from God and standing in his presence.

Recognition that this is the thesis of the letter, and that the passage with which we are concerned is part of the ensuing first argument in favor of it, clarifies much about the passage when combined with an awareness of the basic characteristics of apocalyptic logocentrism. Paul begins by comparing himself and his colleagues to aromas or fragrances. They are rather airy sorts, and I do not say that just to be funny but rather to call attention to how this characterization already hints that their activity is *pneumatic* in nature. We hear also, of course, that these are spiritual matters of life and death. Then Paul states the fundamental question, one that goes by so fast that we may miss its crucial significance in the thesis: "Who is fit for these things?" The NAB captures the sense of the question even better when it says, "Who is qualified for this?" The next sentence forcefully answers that question. It is not peddlers of the Word of God who are qualified but "persons of sincerity … persons sent from God and *standing in his presence*." This motif of standing in his presence is going to be taken up in the ensuing argument in a very creative way, and this is where our theory of religion is most helpful. In apocalyptic logocentrism, the ideal state is unmediated presence. Therefore, the measure of one's success as an apostle, standing in God's presence, is not the ability to mediate but rather to reflect. In apocalyptic logocentrism, to mediate is to fail, if by mediation one means the performance of some indispensable function that places the mediator permanently between two persons. Such forms of mediation involve re-presenting, but reflection is a matter of presenting or présenting. Therefore, what Paul will go on to find wrong with the peddlers of God's Word, Moses the man, *and Moses the text*, is that in one way or another they all function as mediators, not reflectors, as re-presenters, not présenters.

Comparison (*synkrisis*) is a typical strategy in apologetic discourse, and the comparisons here encompass contrasts between Paul and the peddlers of God's Word, Paul and Moses, and Paul and Moses' respective ministries, which also happen to involve different types of texts. What is wrong with the peddlers of God's Word is exemplified by the "super-apostles," who are not forms of presence but forms of "simulation" and "substitution," as expressed quite clearly by Paul's other title for them, the pseudo-apostles. In 2 Cor 11:4 he speaks of those who "preach another Jesus than the one we preached ... a different spirit from the one you received ... [and] a different Gospel from the one you accepted." These are purveyors of forms of simulation and substitution. Indeed, these peddlers of God's Word rely on actual letters of commendation written with ink rather than living letters written with the Spirit. In addition, as Paul says repeatedly, they represent something different, not the same.

Moving on to Moses the man, Paul quite shockingly puts him in the same camp as the peddlers of God's Word by homologizing their activities, though in a somewhat veiled fashion. I do not limit 3:12–18 to only one interpretation, but I am going to state the one that makes the most sense to me in light of the dynamics of apocalyptic logocentrism. Paul asserts repeatedly in 3:7–11 that the ministry of death once had *doxa*. *Doxa* can mean many things. Most naturally, in this context one might think of "divine presence." Paul would be saying that the glory of God was only temporarily present with Moses and his covenant, but both have been surpassed by a ministry that has permanent spiritual presence. However, *doxa* can also mean "reflection," as in a reflected radiance. So Paul's figurative interpretation of what Moses was trying to do by putting a veil over his face is that he was trying to hide the fact that his ministry was only temporary (3:13).[31] This makes Moses a (dis)simulator who was trying to substitute his own temporary ministry for the permanent one, much like the peddlers of God's Word who preach a different Jesus, a different spirit, and a different Gospel.

So, as Paul continues his contrast at the beginning of 2 Cor 4, we must ask with whom is he contrasting himself when he says, "We have renounced the shameful things that one hides; we refuse to practice cunning or to falsify God's Word; but by the open statement of the truth we commend ourselves to the conscience of everyone in the sight of God"? Is the contrast with the peddlers or Moses? Or is it that Moses is the paradigm of their simulation and substitution? Whatever one decides, Paul goes on to state clearly what an ideal apostle does in 4:5–6 when he says, "For what we preach is not ourselves, but Jesus Christ as Lord, with ourselves as your servants for Jesus' sake. For it is the God who said, 'Let light shine out of darkness,' who has shone in our hearts to give the light of the knowledge of the glory of God in the face

---

31. This and the following verses, of course, invite comparison with Rom 10:4, where Christ is "the end of the law."

of Christ." True apostles are reflectors, not mediators, and when the perfect comes, everyone will reflect the same image, the image of the Same, God.

In a paper so indebted to Derrida, I would be remiss not to include what he had to say about this passage in "A Silkworm of One's Own (Points of View Stitched on the Other Veil)."[32] This is a fascinating essay that, in the words of Gil Anidjar, "constitutes a high point" in "Derrida's momentous reflections and reinscriptions of the notion of revelation."[33] It is one of the most intensely personal and intricately complex of Derrida's weavings or embroideries, so having to single out the Pauline thread in it is unfortunate, though necessary.

The major sections of the essay are structured around a travel itinerary. Section 1 is "On the Way to Buenos Aires, 24–28 November 1995" (311–28); section 2 is "Santiago de Chile–Valparaiso, 29 November–4 December 1995" (328–44); and section 3 is "São Paulo, 4 December–8 December 1995" (344–55). Throughout the essay, Derrida expresses an intense exhaustion with all aspects of the "veil." For example,

> You must understand me, you see, and know what it is to be weary, in this case, to be weary of a figure and its truth, of a strophe, a trope and the folds of the said truth when it plays itself out with so many veils. Infinite weariness, what do you expect, I want to end it all. Protest, attestation, testament, last will, manifesto against the shroud: I no longer want to write on the veil, do you hear, right on the veil or on the subject of veil, around it or in its folds, under its authority or under its law, in a word neither on it nor under it. With other *Schleiermachers* of all sorts I have used and abused truth—as untruth of course, come come, *et passim*, and of revelation and unveiling as veiling, of course, in so many languages. Go and see if I'm lying.[34]

In opposition to the logic or topic of the veil, Derrida sets that of the shawl, that is, the Jewish prayer shawl, the tallith: "The uniqueness of the reference, the untranslatable carry of the ferrence prevents a tallith, which one cannot and must not get rid of, from being or becoming, like every veil, merely a figure, a symbol, a trope. Does this mean that the literality *of* 'tallith,' my tallith, is irreducible?" The unspoken answer is clearly yes, and at this point São Paulo becomes the destination of Derrida's weary journey in more ways than one, for the last section of the essay is a rather impassioned "epistle against Saint Paul."[35] First, he comments on "*the Epistle to the Romans*":

---

32. Jacques Derrida, *Acts of Religion* (ed. Gil Anidjar; New York: Routledge, 2002), 311–55.
33. Anidjar in ibid., 309.
34. Derrida, *Acts of Religion*, 323.
35. Ibid., 346.

Its author thought he knew the literality of the letter. He prided himself on being able to distinguish, for the first time, he no doubt thought, wrong, the circumcision of the heart, according to the breath and the spirit, from the circumcision of the body or flesh, circumcision "according to the letter."[36]

He next quotes the classic passage on the veiling of women in 1 Cor 11:3–10, and says,

> And this very mild, this terrible Paul dares, for he dares with all the daring whose monstrous progeniture are our history and culture (see the erections of São Paulo the proud), this Paul who preferred a good Greek to a bad Jew, this Paul who claimed to know literally what is the breath of spirit and teach it to the Jew so that he would become a good Jew, better than the good Greek, this Paul dares to leave us to judge, he dares to say, to say to us (Jews or Greeks?) that he leaves us to judge.[37]

This leads into a brief discussion of the veiling controversy in the French school system. Derrida explains that he is against both those who prescribe and those who forbid the veil. Then he gets back to Paul, moving on to 2 Corinthians:

> And we hadn't finished, I haven't finished with Saint Paul. The one who wanted to veil the heads of women and unveil those of men, that very one denounced Moses and the children of Israël. He accused them of having given in to the veil, of not having known how to lift the veil, the veil over the face of God, the veil over the covenant, the veil on the heart. The Messiah, the Man-God and the two Resurrections, *voilà* the great Unveiler. Perhaps it's because of this that, at his death, the veil of the temple tore. After having recalled that the "service of death, engraved in letters on stones," was "in such glory that the Benéi Israël were unable to fix their eyes on the face of Moshè because of the glory of his face, ephemeral however," Saint Paul wonders how the service of the breath or the spirit (therefore of life and not death) would not be still more glorious, more luminous. And this light is *unveiling*.[38]

At this point, Derrida immediately quotes 2 Cor 3:12–16 and 4:3–4.

---

36. Ibid., 344. In a footnote, Derrida directs the reader to Rom 2:25–29 and Gal 6:11–17.
37. Ibid., 346.
38. Ibid., 346–47.

Of course, "spirit" forms one of the connecting threads in the three preceding excerpts. It belongs to the logic of the veil. It is the real behind the veil, which is the mere symbol. The veil is the material that blocks and re-presents, barring ultimate access to the really real, the Spirit. Instead of this tired logic and topic, Derrida longs for something new in this essay:

> *the thought of the event without truth unveiled or revealed*, without phallogocentrism of the greco-judeo-paulino-islamo-freudo-heideggeriano-lacanian veil, without phallophoria, i.e., without procession or theory of the phallus, without veiling-unveiling of the phallus, or even of the mere place, strictly hemmed in, of the phallus, living or dead. This culpable edging of the phallus, the edges of this cut which support the veil and hold it out like a tent or an awning, a roof, a canvas, this theoretical toilet of the phallus is not other than the concept, yes, the concept in itself, the possibility of the concept, of the concept in itself.[39]

Certainly it would be somewhat of an understatement to say that Derrida found Paul to be logocentric. He presents him as a key thread in the multicultural veil of Western logocentrism. Paul is indeed one of the great Unveilers for whom presence lies beyond all forms of absence, ambiguity, simulation, substitution, or negativity.[40]

2.4. Romans

At the end of Rom 8, Paul waxes eloquent as he asserts, "I am convinced that neither death, nor life, nor angels, nor rulers, nor things present, nor things to come, nor powers, nor height, nor depth, nor anything else in all creation, will be able to separate us from the love of God in Christ Jesus our Lord" (8:38–39). Not only the obvious obstacles, but literally every created thing and the very dimensions of the universe will give way to the consummation

---

39. Ibid., 350, emphasis added.
40. In the final pages of "A Silkworm of One's Own," Derrida, in a variety of ways, gives voice to a form of the messianic that has become associated with him in such terms as "faith without religion," "religion without religion," and "apocalypse without apocalypse." In this case, a meditation on his tallith becomes the vehicle for its expression: "I love it and bless it with a strange indifference, my tallith, in a familiarity without name or age. As if faith and knowledge, another faith and knowledge, a knowledge without truth and without revelation, were woven together in the memory of an event to come, the absolute delay of the verdict, of a verdict to be rendered and which is, was, or will make itself arrive without the glory of a luminous vision. My white tallith belongs to the night, the absolute night. You will never know anything about it, and no doubt neither will I" (ibid.).

of immediate and eternal love. Since unmediated, total presence is the utopia of Paul's religion, then *all* aspects of the "form of this world" (1 Cor 7:31) are, to quote again from our definition of logocentrism, "forms of absence, ambiguity, simulation, substitution, or negativity." However, they are all "passing away." Paul, consciously or not, was creating a hierarchy of value based on the degree to which any of the forms of this world, seen or unseen, encourage or impede realization of presence. We have already begun to see that these forms include those of apostles. We will soon see more clearly that they include forms of writing.

Turning our attention to Rom 10, the logocentric symptoms we have observed so far resonate with a reading of Paul associated with Luther and most fully developed in neo-orthodoxy, especially by Bultmann. Appropriately enough, at the heart of Bultmann's *Theology of the New Testament*, that is, at almost the exact center of the two-volume work, we read the following statement: *"the salvation-occurrence is nowhere present except in the proclaiming, accosting, demanding, and promising word of preaching."* Immediately Bultmann adds that "a merely 'reminiscent' historical account referring to what happened in the past cannot make the salvation-occurrence visible." Then a few sentences later we read, "Consequently, in the proclamation[,] Christ himself, indeed God Himself, encounters the hearer, and the 'Now' in which the preachèd word sounds forth is the 'Now' of the eschatological occurrence itself (II Cor. 6:2)."[41] "Word" and "presence" along with many equivalent expressions return repeatedly in tandem in the following thirty pages. References to Rom 10 are frequent,[42] and 10:6–10 may be characterized as the catalyst of two passages that are crucial for understanding Bultmann's entire theology, his discussions of faith as "confession" and "hope."[43]

These sections presuppose a reading of Rom 10:6–8 that takes us to the heart of Bultmann's word-presence Christology, that is, his own Pauline-aided, and Heideggerian-abetted, logocentrism and phonocentrism.[44] One

---

41. Rudolf Bultmann, *Theology of the New Testament* (one-volume edition; New York: Charles Scribner's Sons, 1955), 301–2, emphasis original.

42. Ibid., 301, 306, 307, 312, 314 (twice), 316 (twice), 317 (twice), 318 (twice), 319, 320.

43. Ibid., 317–20.

44. Derrida assumed a close relationship between Paul and Heidegger, one that sometimes amounts to intellectual plagiarism. E.g., after exposing Heidegger's "foreclosure" of the Hebrew *ruah* behind his linguistico-historical triad of *pneuma-spiritus-Geist*, Derrida says, "Without being able to invoke here the vast corpus of prophetic texts and their translations, without doing any more than recalling what makes it permissible to read a whole tradition of Jewish thought as an inexhaustible thinking about fire; without citing the evidence from the Gospels of a pneumatology which has an ineradicable relationship of

does not require a mediator to ascend into heaven or to descend into the abyss to make Christ present (10:6–7). For Bultmann, this would no doubt be trying to establish faith by searching for the Christ "according to the flesh" (2 Cor 5:16), the historical Jesus. Therefore, the "word of proclamation" can be "no mere report about historical incidents." Instead, grace itself is "*actively present in the word*," since "*the word is near*" (Rom 10:8). Or, as he had already said, "In the proclamation, Christ himself, indeed God Himself, encounters the hearer," a thought encountered repeatedly throughout the central sections of this work. Certainly, as Bultmann himself concedes, he goes beyond Paul in his insistence on the degree to which the "salvation-occurrence" in the "Now" of the "word of proclamation" eclipses the importance of "the mere report of historical incidents."[45] This preoccupation with "present-ness," the "Now," "self-understanding," "authenticity," and so forth reflects Bultmann's well-known debt to existentialism.[46] Nevertheless, it seems to me that Bultmann is reflecting a comparable logocentric and phonocentric desire for immediate presence as we have been observing in Paul's own logocentrism, a desire strongly rooted in his apocalypticism. However, Bultmann's desire is hardly for a presence through the word in the literal sense Paul that would have approved.[47] Between Paul and Bultmann stands Heidegger's "destruction" of the metaphysics that would allow for a *real* presence like Paul's Spirit. Heidegger's influence motivates Bultmann to argue erroneously that Paul is already beginning to reject the notion of Spirit "as a material."[48] Nevertheless,

---

translation with *ruah*, I will refer only to one distinction, made by Paul in the First Epistle to the Corinthians (2:14), between *pneuma* and *psyche*. Corresponding to the distinction between *ruah* and *néphéch*, it belongs—if it is not its opening—to the theologico-philosophical tradition in which Heidegger continues to interpret the relationship between *Geist* and *Seele*" (*Of Spirit*, 101). This leads to a footnote that links Paul to Luther (137–38). Derrida is exposing the fact that concepts of *Geist* that the Nazi Socialist Heidegger claimed to be only fully realized by German philosophy in the German language were already present in ancient Jewish texts and that Paul may be the "opening" of the theological-philosophical tradition in which Heidegger stands.

45. E.g., Bultmann, *Theology of the New Testament*, 319.

46. For an introduction to his hermeneutic, see Rudolf Bultmann, *New Testament and Mythology and Other Basic Writings* (ed. and trans. Schubert M. Ogden; Philadephia: Fortress, 1984).

47. Although his statement that grace is "*actively present in the word*" makes one wonder.

48. *Theology of the New Testament*, 334. Like Beker, I cannot agree with Bultmann that Paul's apocalyptic worldview can be demythologized while staying true to his thought. See J. Christiaan Beker's critique in *Paul the Apostle: The Triumph of God in Life and Thought* (Philadelphia: Fortress, 1984), 140–43, 146–49.

what I take to be the real, although not fully realized, insight of Bultmann's (mis)reading is the implication that the essence of Paul's apocalypticism is a desire for im-mediate presence. What remains true to Paul is the notion that mouth and ear are the proper media for this message.[49] The "word that is near" in Rom 10:8 is defined not as Scripture but as "the word of faith that we preach." It is "on the lips" and "in the heart." So while Scripture can play a corroborating role in presenting the "word that is near," Paul presupposed that this Word is available only through proclamation (Rom 10:14–17): "So faith comes from hearing, and hearing by the preaching of Christ" (10:17). Here we begin to sense Paul's own phonologism and phonocentrism. Scripture on its own cannot bear "the Word." The voice, "preaching," is privileged over writing. Therefore, both consequently and necessarily, faith comes through *hearing*.

In 2 Cor 3, life under the new covenant is pictured as a process of being metamorphosized into the image of the Lord from one degree of glory to another (3:18), a process that will be completed when he appears (see Phil 3:21). Therefore, what might we expect Paul's attitude to be toward a covenant "engraved in letters on stone" (2 Cor 3:7)? The answer is implicit when he reinscribes Deut 30:12–14 as a text about the Word of faith, not the law (Rom 10:6–8). In context, Deut 30:12–14 is precisely about the nearness, the present-ness, and the *life*-giving or *death*-dealing *pharmakon*-like effects of the law. No one needs to ascend into heaven or cross the sea to obtain it, for it is "in your mouth and in your heart." For Paul, what is in the mouth and heart is the spiritual presence of Christ. Paul has transferred the life-giving or death-dealing present-ness of the law to the "Word of faith" (Rom 10:8; see also 2 Cor 2:16). The Word supplements by filling up what is lacking in the law—it is the "goal" prepared for but unreachable through the law. In addition, by taking the law's place, it is the law's "end."

3. Apocalyptic Logocentrism and Writing

Does all this apply to the law only? What about Scripture? Paul is, overall, more positive toward Scripture than law, and some interpreters have emphasized the difference between letter (*gramma*) and script (*graphē*). To be sure, they are not exactly the same thing, but the contrast between the two has been exaggerated. The possibility of a metonymical overlap between "script," "Scripture," "law," "old covenant," and "Moses" tends to be ignored.

---

49. Even though, as noted above, the logocentric superiority of speech over writing is no guarantee that the Word will not be empty.

For example, since Richard Hays, using texts such as Gal 3:8, wants to claim that "Paul thinks of *Graphē* (Scripture) as alive and active," he must radically separate it from *gramma*.[50] Nevertheless, Paul says that a veil lies over the Israelites' minds when the old covenant is read in 2 Cor 3:14 and when *Moses* is read in the next verse.[51] Are we really to suppose that the *gramma*, the old covenant, and "the read Moses" are easily separable from one another or all three from *Graphē*? One wonders where the law (*nomos*) would fit into this neat dichotomy of *gramma/graphē*, especially when confronted with a text such as Gal 3:22–23, where the very same constraining function is attributed to both *graphē* and *nomos*.[52] Or what about Rom 3:19–20? Here Paul clearly refers to the immediately preceding list of denunciations quoted mainly from the Psalms (also Ecclesiastes, Proverbs, Isaiah, and Leviticus). Yet in doing so, he says, "Now we know that whatever *the law* says it speaks to those who are under the law, so that every mouth may be stopped and the whole world may be accountable to God. For no flesh will be justified in his sight by works of the law, since through the law comes knowledge of sin." "The law," in this case, is a metonym for Scripture.

The errors attendant upon turning the *gramma/graphē* distinction into a firm exegetical principle are exemplified by Schrenk, when he says, "The word which is near (R. 10:8) is not the *gramma* but Scripture, which is self-attesting through the Spirit of Christ."[53] In point of fact, the very verse cited, Rom 10:8, explicitly defines "the Word that is near" not as Scripture but as "the Word of faith that we preach." It is "on the lips" and "in the heart."

Speaking for the moment with a Johannine accent, Paul no longer searches the scriptures thinking that "in them you have life" (John 5:39). This is because he has discovered that the source of life is not a text but an apocalypse (Gal 1:12), an encounter with a living being, a Spirit.[54] Paul knew, however, that not everyone was privileged to have such a direct experience.

---

50. Hays, *Echoes of Scripture*, 106.

51. Indeed, Hays himself, in a brilliantly suggestive passage, declares that "a coherent reading of 2 Cor 3:12–18 is possible only if we recognize that in these verses a metaphorical fusion occurs in which Moses *becomes* the Torah"; shortly thereafter he speaks of "the dreamlike transfiguration of Moses from man into text" (ibid., 144–45, emphasis original).

52. See Bernardin Schneider, "The Meaning of St. Paul's Thesis 'The Letter and the Spirit,'" *CBQ* 15 (1953): 163–207, which shows, on the basis of a survey of the use of *gramma* before and during Paul's time, that it was used for particular written laws and for written law taken as a whole (188–91).

53. Gerhard Schrenk, "γράμμα/γραφή," *TDNT* 1:768.

54. On Paul's apocalyptic mysticism, see Alan F. Segal, *Paul the Convert* (New Haven: Yale University Press, 1990), 34–71.

How, then, could they experience something salvific? Through "the light of the Gospel of the glory of Christ who is the likeness of God" (2 Cor 4:4). I have been capitalizing *Gospel* throughout this essay because for Paul it has divine power, divine presence, quite unlike writing. Although one may read the old covenant or Moses for centuries, Christ will never be found there (2 Cor 3:14–15). The problem is not that *the text* is veiled, hiding Christ the spiritual signified within a living Text, but rather that the mind of *the reader* is hardened. Only by the reader being equipped with something outside the cosmic (textual) apparatus, *only by first turning away from the text* toward the Lord, can the promise of Scripture be recognized (e.g., 1 Cor 15:3–4; Rom 1:2; 3:21; 15:4). Is it any surprise that the Lord to whom the reader turns *is* the Spirit (2 Cor 3:17–18)? For Paul, in a certain way, spiritual exegesis must be spiritual eisegesis. The "first installment" of the Spirit (ἀρραβῶνα, 2 Cor 1:22; 5:5) is the source of the believing reader's competency. Paul's is a spiritual hermeneutic (1 Cor 2:9–16).[55]

Spirit in Paul is an active material power that can invade and transform people, giving them abilities they never had before.[56] It is nothing less than the active presence and power of God.[57] That is why Paul asks those who want to be under the law, "Does he who supplies the Spirit to you and works miracles among you do so by works of the law or by *hearing* with faith?" (Gal 3:5). "Works of the law," which in the context of Galatians is primarily a fleshly writing on the flesh, is opposed to "hearing with faith," a spiritual writing on the heart.[58] *For Paul, no Life, no Power, no Presence is ever to be expected from writing, the letter, the law.* If it were, the law would be against the promises of God, which is also to say, in conflict with Paul's doctrine of justification by faith alone: "For if a law had been given *that could make alive*, then righteousness would indeed be by the law" (Gal 3:21). What makes righteousness possible? What is able to "make alive"? The Spirit. Why can the law not make alive? Because the law is devoid of Spirit. For Paul, *there is nothing in the text.*

---

55. See the discussion in Given, *Paul's True Rhetoric*, 95–101.
56. "For I will not venture to speak of anything except what Christ has accomplished through me to win obedience from the Gentiles, by word and deed, by the power of signs and wonders, by the power of the Holy Spirit" (Rom 15:19); "My speech and my proclamation were not with plausible words of wisdom, but with a demonstration of the Spirit and of power" (1 Cor 2:4).
57. "And we have received *not the spirit of the world but the Spirit that is from God*, that we might understand the gifts bestowed on us by God" (1 Cor 2:12).
58. "He is a Jew who is one inwardly, and real circumcision is a matter of the heart, spiritual and not literal. His praise is not from men but from God" (Rom 2:29). See the discussion in Boyarin, *A Radical Jew*, 78–81, 86–95.

Recognition of this point is crucial. If we miss this, we will be tempted to turn him into Philo or an Alexandrian church father, neither of whom fully shared his apocalyptic pessimism toward the things—even the good things—of this world. Paul does not search for the Spirit in the Letter.[59] The reason he does not emerges from the preceding discussion: *the text has no agency, no power, and no life of its own.* Paul is no less logocentric and phonocentric in this matter than Luther, Heidegger, and Bultmann.

It is crucial to see that, in Paul's allegory in 2 Cor 3, the veil lies over the mind, not the text. First, the mind must be penetrated by the Spirit conveyed by the Gospel through the mouth and ear. There is a quite simple apocalyptic logocentric "common sense" going on here. Since a text is a material testimony to the absence of the author, and in this case the absence of the Author of Life, one is deceived if one thinks that Life is present in the text or is mediated through the text. It is as if one's mind is hardened or a veil lies over one's heart and mind (3:14–15). In short, once the veil is removed and one stands in the presence of Christ through the Spirit, one sees that the text had nothing salvific to offer. One can see that, when "Moses writes that the one who practices the righteousness that is based on the law shall live by it" (Rom 10:5; see also Gal 3:12; Lev 18:5), it is a deception.[60]

Therefore, I still believe J. Louis Martyn is on the right track concerning Lev 18:5.[61] Martyn suggests that what Paul is trying to say to the Galatians through the example of the scriptural contradiction set forth in 3:11–12 can be expressed in an emended form of 1 John 4:1: "Beloved [Galatians, in light of the Teachers' work in your midst], do not believe every spirit [or every text], but test the spirits [and the texts] to see whether they are from God."[62] In the same vein, he also suggests that "the wording of 1 Cor 7:19 itself suggests that Paul uses the expression 'the commandments *of God*' because he presupposes something he does not explicitly state: Not all the commandments come from God!"[63]

---

59. See Wai-Shing Chau, *The Letter and the Spirit: A History of Interpretation from Origen to Luther* (American University Studies 7/167; New York: Lang, 1995).

60. See discussion in Given, *Paul's True Rhetoric*, 122–26. See also Francis B. Watson, *Paul and the Hermeneutics of Faith* (London: T&T Clark, 2004), 291–96.

61. J. Louis Martyn, "The Textual Contradiction between Habakkuk 2:4 and Leviticus 18:5," in *Theological Issues in the Letters of Paul* (Nashville: Abingdon, 1997), 183–208.

62. J. Louis Martyn, *Galatians* (AB 33A; New York: Doubleday, 1997), 334. On the fascinating possibility of explaining the divided voice of the law presupposed by Paul on the basis of a plurality of angelic authors, see Watson, *Paul and the Hermeneutics of Faith*, 280–81. I am, however, offering a simpler explanation.

63. Martyn, *Galatians*, 519.

Would such an idea be unthinkable for Paul? Recently while reading Philo's *Questions and Answers on Exodus*, I was struck by his answer to a question concerning Exod 24:13: "Why does Moses, who has been summoned alone, go up not alone but with Joshua?" (*QE* 1.43). One of his answers is that "rightly, therefore, does he go up as an assurance [εἰς πίστιν] of two most necessary things: one, of the election of the contemplative race, and the other, that the law should be considered not as an invention of the human mind but as a divine command and divine words" (*QE* 1.43).

Philo's second reason answers a thought that could occur to any thinking person possessing a healthy skepticism: perhaps Moses did not receive the law from God while on the mountain but wrote it himself. Philo counters the idea by suggesting that Joshua was taken along "as a proof" that this was not the case. Certainly Paul does not suggest that the law was the invention of Moses. However, perhaps he does suggest something else that also could have occurred to any thinking person possessing a healthy skepticism in an age quite familiar with the tendency of scribes to alter texts. Paul could be suggesting that Moses sometimes mixed his own words in with God's words. Perhaps we should speak not only of "the textual contradiction" in the law but of "the textual corruption" in it.

Notice that, after Paul has made his subtle shift from stone tablets to the "Moses" read in his own day, he also restates the candor versus concealment theme of 2 Cor 3:12–13 in a new way: "Therefore, having this ministry as ones who have received mercy, we do not act badly.[64] On the contrary, we have given up disgraceful concealments, not practicing cunning nor *corrupting* the Word of God, but rather by a manifestation of the truth we commend ourselves to everyone's conscience before God" (2 Cor 4:1–2). Perhaps this is the *coup de grâce* of Paul's comparison of himself and his ministry with Moses and a low blow to deliver against the scribe par excellence. Moses the scribe corrupted the text, the words of God. What would be Paul's prime example of such a textual corruption? As he puts it, "*Moses writes* concerning the righteousness that comes from the law that 'the person who does these things will live by them.' But the righteousness that comes from faith *says*..." (Rom 10:5–6a). This happens to be the only place in Paul's letters where we read "Moses

---

64. On the translation of *egkakeō* as "act badly," see Given, *Paul's True Rhetoric*, 118. Murray J. Harris rightly notes that "found only in Koine Greek, the verb *egkakeō* basically means 'behave badly,' especially in a cowardly (*kakos*) fashion or in reference to a culpable omission" (*The Second Epistle to the Corinthians* [NIGTC; Grand Rapids: Eerdmans, 2005], 323). Nevertheless, like every other commentator known to me, he then goes on to distinguish this meaning from the "NT meanings" without considering the possibility that the basic Koine meaning might be quite appropriate to the context in 4:1.

writes." I would not have been surprised to find him use the expression elsewhere,[65] but even if he had, we would still have to read this occurrence contextually. What Moses *writes* is contrasted with "what the righteousness that comes from faith *says*." Further, what Moses writes in Lev 18:5 is to his advantage, since it lends a salvific purpose and permanency to his ministry that, according to Paul, God never intended it to have. Yet Paul's charge here seems rather ironic, given that he himself is notorious for rewriting the Writing in ways that magnify the importance of his ministry![66]

None of this is to say that Paul did not consider most of the script to be Scripture, "the oracles of God" (Rom 3:2). He certainly believed that God said most of what God is reported to have said there. Nevertheless, these archived words of God are not the "Word of God" for Paul.[67] The Word of God is something Paul hears and proclaims in the present. Once one grasps the logic of Paul's apocalyptic logocentrism, debating whether Paul had a negative attitude toward the law (*nomos*) but a positive one toward Scripture (*graphē*) is beside the point. From the standpoint of apocalyptic logocentrism, even if the first stone tablets written by the finger of God himself had not been destroyed, they would still have been powerless because what brings Life is the Spirit, the presence of God; they would instead mark the absence of that Life-giving Presence. What is "alive and active" for Paul is not Scripture but the Spirit of God.

As I stated at the beginning, this essay is an initial attempt at stating Paul's theory of Scripture. It is a work in progress, so at this point I cannot write a proper conclusion. But to sum it up as it is, I have presented apocalyptic logocentrism as a theory of Paul's religion. What Paul looks forward to is an unmediated and uninterrupted experience of the presence of Christ: *parousia*. To be in this presence is to be in the presence of God and to be fully self-present. Longing for pure presence is the underlying cause of logocentrism and one that Paul fully exhibits through a variety of symptoms. Paul's eschatology, far from insulating him from logocentrism, actually explains why his case of

---

65. However, is it not fascinating that the name Moses occurs only nine times in Paul and that these are limited to Romans and the Corinthian letters?

66. It is well known, of course, that Paul and other New Testament writers regularly misquote the scriptures in such a way as to make them fit their arguments better. One can reply, "Well, that's what everyone did back then," but the point still stands. On the liberties that Paul takes with key details of the story of Moses and the veil, in addition to the standard commentaries and monographs, see now the concise treatment by Peter Balla in *Commentary on the New Testament Use of the Old Testament* (ed. G. K. Beale and D. A. Carson; Grand Rapids: Baker, 2007), 753–62.

67. See further the discussion in Given, *Paul's True Rhetoric*, 133.

it is especially acute. Once one grasps the logic of Paul's religion, his Hellenistic-Jewish apocalyptic logocentrism, it comes as no surprise that he exhibits an ambivalent attitude toward writing in general, including Scripture, and that he favors the living "breath" (*pneuma*) of divinely inspired Speech, Word, Gospel.

From 2 Cor 3–4 it is easy to see where Paul locates himself and his covenant in relation to each of the logocentric binary oppositions: "speech over writing, immediacy over distance, and identity over difference." Paul is one of the "ministers of a new covenant, not of letter but of Spirit, for the letter kills, but the Spirit gives life" (3:6). These words apply no less to Scripture than to letter. Does this mean that Paul was a Harnack where Scripture is concerned? No, it simply means that he knows that Scripture is one of the forms of this world that can be used either to forward or to impede the goal of Presence. Scripture for Paul is what you make of it. If you try to make it a source of life, a way of salvation, or a means of righteousness, then it becomes one of the "forms of absence, ambiguity, simulation, substitution, or negativity." If you remove the veil and see that it is not a means of righteousness, a way of salvation, or a source of life, then it becomes "the oracles of God," "holy and just and good," and even "spiritual."

Paul and Postcolonial Hermeneutics: Marginality and/in Early Biblical Interpretation*

Jeremy Punt

1. Introduction: The Appeal of Postcolonial Biblical Criticism

The application of postcolonial criticism to the New Testament (and the letters of Paul) is a relatively recent phenomenon that carries with it a number of subtle presuppositions. This is not the venue to discuss such issues at length, but it is worth noting that at least one important point is presupposed in all such investigations: the imperial context of the New Testament documents. The Pauline literature originated within the sociopolitical context of the Roman Empire,[1] which found expression not only in public manifestations of power and control (i.e., through its rulers, armies, and conventions) but also in more subtle ways.[2] As Richard Horsley has observed, "Imperial power relations operated in complex ways through cultural-religious forms integrally related

---

* The financial assistance of the South African National Research Foundation (travel grant) and Stellenbosch University is gratefully acknowledged. The title of the paper is deliberately ambiguous, since the paper not only investigates Paul's use of the Scriptures of Israel from a postcolonial perspective but also examines the applicability and potential usefulness of labelling Paul's own hermeneutics as "postcolonial."

1. Fernando Segovia refers to "the massive presence and might of the Roman Empire, master and lord of the entire Circum-Mediterranean, with its thoroughly accurate if enormously arrogant classification of the Mediterranean Sea as *mare nostrum*" ("Biblical Criticism and Postcolonial Studies: Towards a Postcolonial Optic," in *The Postcolonial Bible* [ed. R. S. Sugirtharajah; Bible and Postcolonialism 1; Sheffield: Sheffield Academic Press, 1998], 57).

2. Richard Horsley provides a brief but useful catalogue of the strategies used by the Roman Empire to maintain its authority and control: disruption and displacement of subject peoples; slavery; patronage; the imperial cult; and public rhetoric. See Richard A. Horsley, "Introduction," in *Paul and the Roman Imperial Order* (ed. Richard A. Horsley; Harrisburg, Pa.: Trinity Press International, 2004), 1–23.

to social-economic forms of domination, and not simply by the sword."³ Just as Paul's Jewish upbringing and identity and the sociocultural context of a pervasive Hellenism are important for the interpretation of the apostle's letters, so also the imperial setting largely informed and even determined the daily lives and minds of people across the first-century Mediterranean world.

Postcolonial biblical criticism is eminently suitable to address the complexities emerging from both historical and discursive colonialism. Employing notions such as "mimicry" and "hybridity," for example, it is capable of providing frameworks for understanding the formation and cultivation of identities influenced by the broad-ranging exercise of hegemony and control.⁴ The validity of postcolonial criticism for studying biblical texts has been established over the last two decades⁵ and has now moved beyond the stage where it needs elaborate arguments in favor of either its value or its significance. Postcolonial criticism is not a monolithic enterprise, nor is it beyond criticism,⁶ but its usefulness for the study of the New Testament appears to be settled.

One subject to which postcolonial criticism has yet to be applied is the apostle Paul's engagement with the Scriptures of Israel. Accordingly, this essay will explore the relationship between Paul's hermeneutics and his (sense of) marginality, a perspective that invites a postcolonial reflection on his hermeneutics. The focus here is on understanding Paul's scriptural hermeneutics in a first-century *imperial* context, with special attention to discursive colonialism⁷ and its effects—or, to be slightly more precise, discursive hegemony.

---

3. Ibid., 3.

4. Hegemony in postcolonial thought is "domination by consent" (Gramsci), "the active participation of a dominated group in its own subjugation," regardless of the fact that the subjugated might outnumber those exercising power over them or the oppressor or army of occupation might have the advantage in terms of instruments of subjugation. "In such cases … the indigene's desire for self-determination will have been replaced by a discursively inculcated notion of the greater good, couched in such terms as social stability … and economic and cultural advancement" (cf. Stephen D. Moore, *Empire and Apocalypse: Postcolonialism and the New Testament* [The Bible in the Modern World 12; Sheffield: Sheffield Phoenix, 2006], 101).

5. Scholars who have contributed significantly to the development of postcolonial biblical studies in recent years include Boer, Brett, Moore, Segovia, Sugirtharajah, and others. For a recent overview of some of these studies, see the annotated bibliography in Moore, *Empire and Apocalypse*, 124–51.

6. See Stephen D. Moore and Fernando F. Segovia, eds., *Postcolonial Biblical Criticism: Interdisciplinary Intersections* (Bible and Postcolonialism; London: T&T Clark, 2005).

7. Although historical and discursive colonialism cannot be totally divorced from each other, it is important to note the distinction between the two, particularly in the first-century context, where the focus has long been limited to the historical aspects of

Scholars are in agreement that scriptural quotations, allusions, and echoes formed an integral part of Paul's reasoning and arguments,[8] but little attention has been given to the question of how the Scriptures were implicated in Paul's multifaceted engagement with discourses of power—in other words, how the Scriptures were involved in (i.e., used in various ways), implicated in (i.e., enlisting Scripture as authoritative agent), and influenced (i.e., Scripture was rewritten) the discourses of power in the Pauline letters. Given that Paul's letters, like other ancient texts, were produced "in the shadow of empire,"[9] this contribution is a preliminary investigation of the conceptual resources offered by postcolonial theory in an area where such notions have not generally been actively employed. In short, my aim is to examine the significance of a postcolonial approach for investigating Paul's use of Scripture within the first-century imperial setting.

2. How Is a Postcolonial Approach *Hermeneutically* Helpful?

2.1. The Roman Empire, Paul, and Discourses of Power[10]

As I observed in an earlier publication, postcolonial biblical criticism can

---

the Roman Empire. This has led to a reluctance to take seriously the complexity of the imperial context, which included more than Roman dominance through military power and politico-administrative hegemonic institutions and mechanisms, although these certainly played a role. Similarly, this essay is not primarily addressing the question about the audience(s) of Paul's letters and their relationship to the historical-institutional face of the empire, whether in its central or local constructions; in contrast, it investigates Paul's powerful rhetoric and its significance for the establishment of alternative communities since "[a]t no point that we can now recapture was there a 'first Christianity' distinct from its verbal expression" (Averil Cameron, *Christianity and the Rhetoric of Empire: The Development of Christian Discourse* [Sather Classical Lectures 57; Berkeley and Los Angeles: University of California Press, 1991], 32).

8. Although differences remain regarding Paul's purpose in and style of using the Jewish Scriptures, few scholars today would deny the pervasive role of the Scriptures and the influence of a broader scriptural framework in Paul's thought as found in his letters. See James W. Aageson, *Written Also for Our Sake: Paul and the Art of Biblical Interpretation* (Louisville: Westminster John Knox, 1993); Richard B. Hays, *Echoes of Scripture in the Letters of Paul* (New Haven: Yale University Press, 1989), esp. 1–5; J. Ross Wagner, *Heralds of the Good News: Isaiah and Paul "in Concert" in the Letter to the Romans* (NovTSup 101; Leiden: Brill, 2002), esp. 356–57.

9. Segovia, "Biblical Criticism and Postcolonial Studies," 57.

10. "Power" is used here in the sense of claiming and exercising authority over others through deploying material and other means of control, and not simply as the ability to achieve goals within a social system.

best be described as a variety of hermeneutical approaches characterized by their political nature and their ideological agenda.[11] Postcolonial criticism is not simply ideological criticism reinscribed; its textual politics ultimately involve both a hermeneutic of suspicion and a hermeneutic of retrieval or restoration. It studies not only colonial history, where it sees imperialism and hegemony operating in different forms and at different levels, but also the complex aftermath of colonialism, which is shaped by a history of both repression and repudiation. In short, it involves exposé as well as restoration and transformation.[12] Postcolonial criticism is intrinsically tied to hermeneutics, but it represents a shift in emphasis, a strategy of reading that attempts to point out what was missing in previous analyses, as well as to rewrite and correct.

One insight of postcolonial studies important to the argument here is that the postcolonial condition is about more than subscribing to either of two extremes, of choosing either submission or subversion. Instead, it comprises "unequal measures of loathing and admiration, resentment and envy, rejection and imitation, resistance and cooption, separation and surrender."[13] As a result, individuals whose experiences have placed them in a state of postcoloniality have an intricate task of reflecting on these complexities in a clear yet nuanced way.[14]

Much has been written about the different ways in which Paul encountered the Roman Empire and its politics, but for our purpose two broad conclusions stand out. First, Paul did not frame his reaction to Rome as an attack on the imperial center itself, since he interacted primarily with local structures of power that were instilled, maintained, and linked to the Roman

---

11. Jeremy Punt, "Postcolonial Biblical Criticism in South Africa: Some Mind and Road Mapping," *Neot* 37 (2003): 59–85, here 59.

12. A postcolonial perspective acknowledges the complexity of cultural and political configurations and structures that form boundaries between the opposing sides of the powerful and the marginalized within a hegemonic context (see Homi K. Bhabha, *The Location of Culture* [London: Routledge, 1994], 173). This was certainly the case in the power imbalance that existed between the Romans and any of their subjected peoples, including the Jews in Palestine and in Diaspora.

13. Moore, *Empire and Apocalypse*, x.

14. In the words of Fernando Segovia ("Biblical Criticism and Postcolonial Studies," 57), "How do the margins look at the 'world'—a world dominated by the reality of empire—and fashion life in such a world? How does the center regard and treat the margins in the light of its own view of the 'world' and life in that world? What images and representations of the other-world arise from either side? How is history conceived and constructed by both sides? How is 'the other' regarded and represented? What conceptions of oppression and justice are to be found?"

Empire (understood here as a regime complete with its materiality, institutions, customs, and conventions). Second, Paul's opposition to the Roman Empire was not primarily at the level of narrow political rhetoric, in the sense of matching claims regarding the emperor with counterclaims about Jesus Christ. Instead, Paul addressed the empire as a broader, regime-like sociopolitical and sociocultural complex,[15] crafting an anti-imperial rhetoric that combined political, social, and religious insights.[16]

Positioning Paul sociopolitically requires more than presenting an appropriate portrayal of the Roman Empire in the various institutionalized, material guises that it took throughout the territories over which it exercised control. Paul was also involved in a broad discourse of power,[17]

---

15. The image of the emperor as consistently distant, aloof, and physically secluded in the imperial court is corrected by Fergus Millar's dictum that "the emperor was what the emperor did." The emperors' personal involvement in the distribution of justice while on military campaigns often included extensive communications by means of letters and decrees. It is from these communications between the emperors and various individuals and groups of people that "the immensely complex network of relationships which bound the emperor to the educated bourgeoisie of the cities" emerged (Fergus Millar, *The Emperor in the Roman World (31 BC—AD 337)* [London: Duckworth, 1977], 6–9). For our discussion, two important implications should be noted: (1) this network of relationships underwrote the wide-ranging interaction between the imperial court and the citizens (with few exceptions, predominantly the locally powerful people or elite, according to Millar, ibid., 11), and (2) the local citizenry's negotiations with the emperor give credence to the understanding of hegemony as "domination by consent" as a fair description of the first-century imperial situation.

16. See Simon R. F. Price, "Response," in *Paul and the Roman Imperial Order* (ed. Richard A. Horsley; Harrisburg, Pa.: Trinity Press International, 2004), 175–83. Although it cannot be dealt with here, the messiness of scholarly constructions of empire has often been the object of criticism; see the critique of Stanley K. Stowers ("Paul and Slavery: A Response," *Semeia* 83/84 [1998]: 297–302) against what he sees as Horsley's totalizing schemes.

17. In the sense meant by Foucault: "Not the majestically unfolding manifestation of a thinking, knowing, speaking subject, but, on the contrary, a totality, in which the dispersion of the subject and his continuity with himself [sic] may be determined" (*The Archaeology of Knowledge* [trans. A. M. Sheridan Smith; London: Tavistock, 1972], 55). Simon R. F. Price argues for an analytical understanding of power. Rather than being a possession of the emperor, power "is a term for analyzing complex strategic situations." Rather than being primarily politically qualified, power is manifest in many different ways or relationships, all of which pervade and constitute society ("Rituals and Power," in *Paul and Empire: Religion and Power in Roman Imperial Society* [ed. Richard A. Horsley; Harrisburg, Pa.: Trinity Press International, 1997], 65–71). However, to refer to Paul's discourse of power as an "ideological *intifada*" (Neil Elliott, *Liberating Paul: The Justice of God and the Politics of the Apostle* [Bible and Liberation 6; Maryknoll, N.Y.: Orbis, 1994],

ably assisted by a sophisticated rhetorical skill but also informed by a variety of other influences besides the ever-widening and usurping creep of the Roman Empire. These influences included (without claiming to be exhaustive) his own ethnic identity and Jewish traditions; the tensions that existed among the followers of Christ and various other contenders and claims to the emerging Christian tradition in his time; socioeconomic conditions that included the practices of patronage and slavery; social status concerns, including citizenship-status; the broader Greco-Roman philosophical, religious, and related traditions; and, not least, his personal convictions, ideals, and aspirations.[18] Paul's own discourse of power was rooted largely in his claims to apostleship[19] and the authority that he derived from his experience of God's revelation to him (e.g., Gal 1:1, 16).[20] But there was another important factor that both contributed to and was constituted by Paul's discourse of power: his use of biblical traditions.

2.2. Paul's Discourse of Power and the Role of Scripture

Over the last few decades renewed interest has led to considerable growth in the study of the reception of the Old Testament in the New Testament.[21]

---

184), particularly in the letter to Romans (esp. 12:2), may be too strong. Such a description tends to obscure elements of Paul's participation in a rhetoric of power, especially when one recognizes how ideological posturing cannot be conceived apart from its influence and effects on its adversaries.

18. The point here is not to describe the nature of Paul's rhetoric but to note that, when compared with other contemporary discourses, it was characterized by the same tendencies toward inclusivity and multiplicity or elasticity that could be found in both the prevailing and later Christian discourses (see Cameron, *Christianity and the Rhetoric of Empire*, 7–9).

19. Christopher D. Stanley (*Arguing with Scripture: The Rhetoric of Quotations in the Letters of Paul* [New York: T&T Clark, 2004], 36) notes that Paul's explicit quotations of the Jewish Scriptures occur only in letters where the defense of his apostolic ministry and apostleship was at issue. While the apologetic objective can be discerned in 1 and 2 Corinthians and Galatians, his explanation of the quotations in Romans as "attempts to establish a favorable balance of power with the Roman Christians prior to his impending visit" (36 n. 61) is not compelling.

20. Cf. Sandra Hack Polaski, *Paul and the Discourse of Power* (Gender, Culture, Theory 8; Sheffield: Sheffield Academic Press, 1999), 24–28, 43.

21. Both terms, "Old Testament" and "New Testament," are contested, in biblical studies generally and in "Old Testament in the New Testament" studies in particular. I prefer to use the terms "Scriptures of Israel" (or simply "the Scriptures") and "biblical traditions." To use "Hebrew Bible" in this context does not do justice either to its few Aramaic chapters or to the indications that Paul used a Greek version (LXX). The term "Jewish Scriptures" tends

This recent round of activity has invited forays into areas of research that go well beyond the methods of earlier studies that focused on source-critical and historical questions and the relation between biblical quotations and their source texts.[22] An important area for further research is the extent to which scriptural hermeneutics became involved and implicated in the powerful and totalizing discourse that developed within early Christianity.[23] Throughout the ancient world, people attributed great power to language[24] in general and to spoken, written, and other (e.g., visual) forms of rhetoric[25] in particular as mechanisms of social control. The early Christians were simply following in the footsteps of the Roman Empire before them when they developed an all-encompassing rhetorical (or propaganda) strategy that echoed the rhetoric of empire.[26]

---

to bestow an ethnic or at least national identity on these documents, which they might have acquired in Paul's day but did not always have during the earlier periods of their development and transmission.

22. Continued in more recent studies such as Mogens Müller, "Hebraica Sive Graeca Veritas: The Jewish Bible at the Time of the New Testament and the Christian Bible," *SJOT* 2 (1989): 55–71; idem, "The Septuagint as the Bible of the New Testament Church," *SJOT* 7 (1993): 194–207; and Christopher D. Stanley, *Paul and the Language of Scripture: Citation Technique in the Pauline Epistles and Contemporary Literature* (SNTSMS 74; Cambridge: Cambridge University Press, 1992). While such interests are not the focus of this study, my essay admits to the hermeneutical variety and diversity in Paul's use of the Scriptures. I am certainly not arguing that Paul always employed the same techniques for appropriating the Scriptures (e.g., midrash *and* allegory in Galatians) or that he used them (whether by citation, allusion, or echo) for the same purpose every time (e.g., Paul reinterpreted Abraham's story in Gal 4:21–5:1 *and* used it to bolster his argument in Gal 3).

23. This claim extends recent appeals for research into the rhetorical impact of Paul's quotations, including investigating the influence and effectiveness of such quotations for the lives of the original audiences (as in Stanley, *Arguing with Scripture*). This involves both teasing out the involvement of quotations in Pauline discourse and considering the effect of Paul's quotations on his rhetoric and his rhetorical identity.

24. Underlined by the notion that "the Christian God is modelled on language" (Cameron, *Christianity and the Rhetoric of Empire*, 6).

25. The investigation of Christian discourse in the first-century imperial context requires attention to both sides of this "two-way process," since Christian discourse also made an impact on the society that influenced it (ibid., 4). While this inherent reciprocity is acknowledged, the focus here is on the relation between the imperial setting and Paul's hermeneutics, in particular, and his discourse of power, more generally. The possible reciprocal feedback of Paul's discourse on his audiences is not specifically addressed, although it is certainly implied, even if only for the implicit readers or audience.

26. See ibid., esp. 20.

As I noted earlier, postcolonial theory has not been widely used as a heuristic device for explaining early biblical hermeneutics, or Pauline hermeneutics in particular, and the attempt here is only a first step. It is a particularly pertinent need, however, since it is Paul who established the pattern that Christianity would be a matter of articulation and interpretation.[27] Paul helped to form early Christianity into a religion that was characterized not primarily by ritual or even ethical behavior but centrally and crucially by teaching, interpretation, and definition: "As Christ 'was' the Word, so Christianity *was* its discourse or discourses."[28] In Paul's discourse of power—without discounting his essentially oral-based context—a new reality was constructed through the use of texts. Paul and his fellow followers of Christ were engaged in formulating an alternate world, a world that was built upon the framework of Judaism in interaction with the material context of the Roman Empire in which they lived and wherein they experienced various forms of Greek philosophy, pagan practice, and contemporary social ideas at first-hand level.[29]

Already in his use of writing as "long-distance communication," Paul's actions engaged the imperial context, since writing—apart from its other uses—was essential for the establishment and maintenance of the Roman Empire. In the predominantly illiterate first-century world, "writing was both an instrument of power and a symbol of power."[30] The privilege and power attached to writing was based on the importance of literacy in a context where the ability to use language, particularly written language, went along

---

27. "Its subsequent history was as much about words and their interpretation as it was about belief or practice," although the two can never be thoroughly separated, as is illustrated by the way the outcome of the ecumenical Council of Nicea (325 c.e.) eventually turned on a single letter of a word (ibid., 12, 21). In the view of Guy G. Stroumsa, this focus on interpretation and translation, coupled with the use of a codex beyond the cultic setting, was a "revolutionary" development that played a vital role in the missionary success of Christianity in the later Roman Empire. See "Early Christianity—A Religion of the Book?" in *Homer, the Bible, and Beyond: Literary and Religious Canons in the Ancient World* (ed. Margalit Finkelberg and Guy G. Stroumsa; Jerusalem Studies in Religion and Culture 2; Leiden: Brill, 2003), 153–73.

28. Cameron, *Christianity and the Rhetoric of Empire*, 32.

29. Ibid., 11–12, 21. The textual construction of a new world was accomplished by social practice or lifestyle and through control and discipline (ibid., 21), both of which can already be discerned in Paul and his hermeneutics. See Stroumsa, "Early Christianity," 153–73, esp. 156 on the early Christians' use of the Septuagint as a canon of authoritative texts that was central to their (sense of) identity.

30. Joanna Dewey, "Textuality in an Oral Culture: A Survey of the Pauline Traditions," *Semeia* 65 (1994): 37–65 (44); see also Stroumsa, "Early Christianity," 163.

with leadership.³¹ Paul's written or textual strategy reveals his ambivalent position. Paul's writings engaged the powers of the day (at least by measuring up to empire through establishing a counterdiscourse that was also textually inscribed) while also exercising and increasingly formulating his own discourse of power. Moreover, and particularly important here, Paul went a step further and invoked (both directly and indirectly) the Scriptures of Israel as an authoritative source. It can thus correctly be claimed that "Paul's critique of Caesar's empire was firmly grounded in his Jewish heritage."³²

It was through a specific form of oral-literacy,³³ namely, Paul's use of the Jewish Scriptures as sanctioning or authorizing agent in a discourse of power, that he could both challenge and critique imperial discourse. It was by this same means that his position and authority as leader were underwritten.³⁴ Since words were powerful in the first century, sacred words even more so, Paul's use of texts for the purpose of authenticating arguments in a world of orality was not exceptional.³⁵ In his arguments, Scripture often served as both starting point and criterion.³⁶ In polemical contexts, he used Scripture as a final court of appeal, since it was for him sacred—proceeding from God— and thus had ultimate authority.³⁷ Paul's invocation of the Scriptures of Israel

---

31. Harry Y. Gamble, *Books and Readers in the Early Church: A History of Early Christian Texts* (New Haven: Yale University Press, 1995), 9–10.

32. N. T. Wright. "Paul's Gospel and Caesar's Empire," in *Paul and Politics: Ekklesia, Israel, Imperium, Interpretation: Essays in Honor of Krister Stendahl* (ed. Richard A. Horsley; Harrisburg, Pa.: Trinity Press International, 2000), 160–83, here 181.

33. Given the oral character of first-century religious propaganda and the revolutionary nature of literacy developments among early Christians, this literacy (as seen in Paul's letters) was nevertheless oral in form (Stroumsa, "Early Christianity," 162).

34. It is interesting to note that Thiselton (pursuing Moore's ideas) grounds Paul's mode of argument in his appeals to the Scriptures of Israel and reason (Anthony C. Thiselton, *The First Epistle to the Corinthians: A Commentary on the Greek Text* [NIGTC; Grand Rapids: Eerdmans, 2000], 15–16).

35. See Stroumsa, "Early Christianity," 163.

36. The privileged role of the "inspired interpreter" often exceeded the fixed wording of texts in ancient hermeneutics. Speaking of the Dead Sea Scrolls, Geza Vermes argues that "exegetical elasticity matches the textual elasticity of the Qumran Bible. It still requires an explanation. I believe this should be sought in the paramount doctrinal authority of 'the Priests, the sons of Zadok, the guardians of the Covenant'" (*Scrolls, Scriptures and Early Christianity* [Library of Second Temple Studies 56; London: T&T Clark, 2005], 67). Vermes stresses the importance of a fixed canon and final texts in communities that base their existence on texts and their interpretation, although he also notes that "if 'orthodoxy' depends on privileged priestly teaching, the particular wording of the Bible seems to be less important" (67 n. 18).

37. Moisés Silva, "Old Testament in Paul," in *Dictionary of Paul and His Letters* (ed.

as authority against Roman imperialist discourse was rooted in the content of the Scriptures, but also in their role of presenting a legitimate, alternative history that served as ground for authoritative claims. A good example is found in 1 Thess 5:2–3, where Paul's challenge to the much vaunted "peace and security" that the Roman Empire fondly claimed to have established[38] invokes the intertextual echo of Jer 6:14 regarding the falsehood of a pseudo-peace. In short, Paul's literacy established his authority, which he then maintained through the exercise of his literacy capabilities. In this dynamic interrelationship, the Scriptures of Israel played a central role in providing building blocks for an alternative construction of reality and in sanctioning or authorizing the Pauline discourse.

2.3. PAUL, HERMENEUTICS AND MARGINALITY

Investigating Pauline hermeneutics in a context of imperial rhetoric invites a postcolonial perspective, with its particular foci, to raise different questions, highlighting aspects of and tensions in texts that other approaches and methodologies might not focus on. Postcolonial biblical criticism is not a methodology per se but rather an approach that embodies a range of intellectual, theoretical, ideological, and other stances, positions, and approaches. As a result, it offers a variety of vantage points from which to reread the rereadings or interpretations found in the New Testament.

One of the first points that must be acknowledged is that Paul, like other early Christians, found himself in a marginalized position. Christians were members of a *religio illicita* and thus outsiders not only to the broader political scenario, whether for religious or other reasons, but increasingly also to estab-

---

Gerald F. Hawthorne, Ralph P. Martin, and Daniel G. Reid; Leicester: Inter-Varsity Press, 1993), 630–42, here 638–39; see also Carol K. Stockhausen, "Paul the Exegete," *Bible Today* 28 (1990): 196–202, here 196–97. Silva disagrees with von Harnack, who held that Paul merely invoked Scripture as a "tool" in polemic with his Judaizing opponents, noting that Paul also invoked Scripture on issues where he differed from tradition, as in Gal 3, where Paul argues that the law does not give life, as the Old Testament states. For another interpretation, see James M. Scott, "For As Many As Are of the Works of the Law Are Under a Curse (Galatians 3.10)," in *Paul and the Scriptures of Israel* (ed. Craig A. Evans and James A. Sanders; JSNTSup 83; Sheffield: Sheffield Academic Press, 1993), 187–221.

38. See John Dominic Crossan and Jonathan L. Reed, *In Search of Paul: How Jesus's Apostle Opposed Rome's Empire with God's Kingdom: A New Vision of Paul's Words and World* (New York: HarperSanFrancisco, 2004), 164; Luise Schottroff, "The Dual Concept of Peace," in *The Meaning of Peace: Biblical Studies* (ed. Perry B. Yoder and Willard M. Swartley; trans. Walter Sawatsky; Studies in Peace and Scripture 2; Louisville: Westminster John Knox, 1992), 156–63, here 157.

lished forms of religion, both Jewish[39] and otherwise. The second important point is that Paul's rhetoric of power, although dictated in part by his marginal position, at times comes close to the rhetoric of empire that he engaged and deflected in his letters.[40] This basic ambivalence, whereby the apostle along with the majority of others suffered marginalization but also vied for power, is extended through participation in a colonial/imperial context.[41] In the context of an authoritarian, imperialist society, subalterns typically challenge each other for the favor of the powerful as they vie with one another to establish their power and influence. In such a situation, the quest for self-definition means that identity and group-formation must be constructed, disputed, and negotiated,[42] regardless of how little or insignificant these activities might seem in comparison to the might of imperial hegemony.

The relationship between hermeneutics and marginality is complex and cannot be fully explored here. But one point that is relevant to our analysis of Paul's use of Scripture is the twofold nature of marginality. Marginality is a concept of degree, not absolutes,[43] which means that it must be understood in relation to the contexts from which it is taken and the relationships deemed to have given birth to it.[44] In some instances, marginality is enforced

---

39. While not explicitly purporting to pursue a postcolonial approach, some scholars have recently shown themselves alert to the ambiguity of Paul's position as a marginal Jew (e.g., Calvin J. Roetzel, *Paul: A Jew on the Margins* [Louisville: Westminster John Knox, 2003]; Daniel Boyarin, *A Radical Jew: Paul and the Politics of Identity* [Critical Studies in Jewish Literature, Culture, and Society 1; Berkeley and Los Angeles: University of California Press, 1994]). This is not to discount Boyarin's strong claims that Paul allegorized away Jewish distinctiveness and therefore Jewish identity.

40. Cameron makes a similar point, comparing early Christians to the likes of Nero, Pliny, Tacitus, and Suetonius, although she stresses how the Christians' use of language, in writing and otherwise, increasingly approximated the rhetoric of empire. This, in her opinion, was the first step on Christianity's road to becoming a world religion (*Christianity and the Rhetoric of Empire*, 14).

41. Although there are some problematic elements in Roetzel's claims concerning Paul, he realizes the ambivalence that lies behind Paul's hermeneutics: "So while Paul's scriptural interpretation found a simplification when refracted through the lens of his apocalyptic myth, his hermeneutic was complicated by inclusive tendencies set loose by his gospel" (*Paul*, 36).

42. David Frankfurter, "Violence and Religious Formation: An Afterword," in *Violence in the New Testament* (ed. Shelly Matthews and E. Leigh Gibson; New York: T&T Clark, 2005), 140–52, here 140–44.

43. Roetzel, *Paul*, 8.

44. Marginality is invoked for different purposes by the powerful: to further their own interests and suppress the voices and longings of others; to preserve the status quo and fend off political, cultural, religious, or other challenges to the powerful group; or

by oppressive forces from outside the group, as the powerful seek to establish themselves as the center of the society. In the process, they create a sense of alienation, estrangement, and marginalization in others. In other cases, marginality is taken up and claimed by the members of a subaltern group and so becomes a place of "radical openness and possibility."[45] The powerless, who now find themselves at the periphery, marginalized or even in a liminal state,[46] are able to utilize their marginality as an opportunity for radical possibility. What is considered as "given," as "reality," can be reimagined, and a new reality can be envisaged, construed, and lived.[47]

Focusing on the liminality of Paul's social position can help us to reflect on the ambivalence displayed in Paul's engagement with the Scriptures of Israel, as he not only confirmed these traditions but also reinterpreted, challenged, and, at times, subverted them. The Scriptures were the signifying practices for Paul's faith and theological understanding, at once the fount of wisdom and knowledge for the future and yet fulfilled in the present in Christ. At a meta-level, Paul's use of the Scriptures of Israel implied that his whole project was linked to a group that was regarded—by themselves as well as others—as marginal in the first century, that is, the Jews. Yet, at the same time it was through explicit and subtle appeals to the Scriptures of Israel that he sought to establish his own authority, and it was through their reality-constructing possibilities that a new discourse of power was formatted and formulated.

3. Paul and Postcolonial Hermeneutics: 2 Corinthians 10–13

Before we turn to a specific passage where these interrelationships between hermeneutics, power, and marginality are especially evident, there is another important aspect of the recent perception-shifting work on the Roman

---

simply to discredit alternative ideological positions as wrong or evil. In short, marginality can be used to prop up personal beliefs and social interests in the face of criticism or theoretical challenges (see Roetzel, *Paul*, 8).

45. Bell Hooks, *Yearning: Race, Gender and Cultural Politics* (Boston: South End Press, 1990), 153; see also R. S. Sugirtharajah, "Introduction: The Margin as Site of Creative Revisioning," in *Voices from the Margin: Interpreting the Bible in the Third World* (ed. R. S. Sugirtharajah; Maryknoll, N.Y.: Orbis, 1995), 1–8.

46. Liminality is related to a situation (or position) of transition and therefore deals with the in-between-ness of the transitory—being neither here nor there, on the threshold but also destabilized, without power, not belonging.

47. Roetzel, *Paul*, 2.

Empire that needs to be emphasized,[48] since it affects our understanding of Paul's hermeneutical strategy toward the Scriptures of Israel. It can no longer be maintained that the empire was monolithic or that its authority was simply imposed in a top-down way upon its passive and interest-less would-be subjects. To the contrary, that which we call "the empire" was essentially a distillation of sustained interactions between rulers and subjects. This does not mean that military might—and the exercise of it—was inconsequential, nor that "oppression" and "subjection" are unfair words to use with reference to Rome's imperial power. But the existence and operation of empire was made possible through a series of ongoing choices and negotiations between subjects and rulers; amidst the political maneuvering and overtures of the imperial mighty ones, "inferiors negotiate[d] new positions for themselves."[49]

At least two implications flow immediately from this adjusted understanding of the Roman Empire and its discursive imperialism or hegemony. First, Paul and the communities that he addressed found themselves in a hegemonic situation that was largely characterized by consensual (in the Gramscian sense) domination.[50] Second, Paul's role amidst these first-century communities of the followers of Christ was an ambivalent one, with the apostle claiming and negotiating power across a broad front, including political as well as other dimensions. In his engagement with the imperial context, Paul's references and allusions to the Scriptures of Israel contributed—at least within his circle of influence—to the challenge or even the subversion of the powerful and their claims. Paul's letters evidence a profound commitment to the Scriptures of Israel, and his scripturally based arguments show him to be deeply rooted in his Jewish context and its prevailing traditions.[51] It is

---

48. It may be a commonplace to assert that religion never excluded politics in the Roman Empire (e.g., Alan F. Segal, "Response: Some Aspects of Conversion and Identity Formation in the Christian Community of Paul's Time," in Horsley, *Paul and Politics*, 184–90), but it is worrying that little effort is made with the political element or with using tools that are capable of identifying, exposing, and investigating the political dimensions of the Pauline writings.

49. Price, "Response," 176.

50. The evidence of uprisings and revolts in the areas where Paul claimed to have been working as an apostle is scarce and probably represented instances where the exception (insurrection) proved the rule (negotiated domination).

51. E.g., Kathy Ehrensperger, "New Perspectives on Paul but No New Perspectives in Feminist Theology," in *Gender, Tradition and Romans: Shared Ground, Uncertain Borders* (ed. Cristina Grenholm and Daniel Patte; New York: T&T Clark, 2005), 227–55. This does not mean, of course, that first-century Judaism was monolithic or that Paul was necessarily representative of Judaism in some general sense. For a fairly extensive consideration of

therefore no surprise that he would enlist biblical citations and allusions as an essential element of his challenge to the imperial rhetoric of power.

These and other insights associated with postcolonial analysis can be traced in Paul's Corinthian correspondence.[52] In particular, Paul's animated defense of his ministry and apostleship in 2 Cor 10–13 displays both his anti-imperial, marginal hermeneutics and his discourse of power.[53] Whereas the rhetorical pitch of the letters is often described as pastoral, aimed at providing ethical guidance against the background of a reaffirmation of the *parousia* and (future) eschatology in general,[54] scholars are increasingly recognizing

---

how, beyond simply quoting from the Scriptures, Paul "lived" in his Bible, invoking and interacting with the Psalms, the prophets (Jeremiah, Ezekiel, and Isaiah), and the wisdom literature (Proverbs, Sirach, and the Book of Wisdom), see Frances M. Young and David F. Ford, *Meaning and Truth in 2 Corinthians* (Biblical Foundations in Theology; London: SPCK, 1987), 60–84.

52. At the time of Paul's writings, the recent history of the city would have still been fresh in the memories of the recipients of the letters. Corinth was sacked by Roman legions in 146 B.C.E. under the leadership of general Lucius Mummius and was only reestablished in 44 B.C.E. by Julius Caesar as a Roman colony (Colonia Laus Julia Corinthiensis). The city was set up according to a Roman rather than a Greek model, as attested by the large number (almost 1,200) of inscriptions found there, of which the majority were "official" and often connected to dedications to the emperors. Freedmen, veteran Roman soldiers, and tradesmen and laborers settled in the city due to its strategic economic importance, and they were later joined by immigrants from the East. Corinth held strategic value for Paul's ministry, offering many possibilities for expansion given the location of the city and its trade connections (Thiselton, *The First Epistle to the Corinthians*, 2–6, 17–22).

53. Unlike a letter such as Romans, the Corinthian correspondence was at first glance not directed at a community in the heart of the empire and should therefore be a good test case for analyzing the use of Scriptures in Paul's rhetoric of power. As a composite letter, 2 Corinthians may be an even less obvious choice for arguing the case of a postcolonial analysis of Paul's use of Scripture, not least since it contains only six explicit quotations (4:6, 13; 6:2; 8:15; 9:9; 10:17—and the last one might be a repetition of 1 Cor 1:31). Even if the quotations in 2 Cor 6:16–18 (from Lev 26:11; Ezek 37:27; Isa 52:11, 4; Ezek 20:34, 41; 2 Sam 7:14; 2 Sam 7:8) are not taken as a later interpolation as part of 2 Cor 6:14–7:1 (as argued by Stanley, *Arguing with Scripture*, 97–98 n. 1; *contra* Young and Ford, *Meaning and Truth*, 62), 2 Corinthians still has relatively few quotations when compared with Romans, 1 Corinthians, and Galatians.

54. The apocalyptic-eschatological strain that is found in 1 Corinthians is not simply about reining in the overly enthusiastic Corinthian followers of Christ; the apocalyptic tradition is essentially anti-empire; in contemporary parlance, it anticipated "regime-change" (cf. Jörg Rieger, *Christ and Empire: From Paul to Postcolonial Times* [Minneapolis: Fortress, 2007], 48–49). If one follows the suggestions of Wright ("Paul's Gospel," 161–62) that Paul's high ecclesiology saw the establishment of churches as "colonial outposts of the empire that is to be" and that as a missionary in religious garb he acted as "ambassador of

the strongly subversive or anti-imperial language of these letters, whether on the surface or at more subtle levels.

First, a few general remarks on 2 Cor 10–13 are in order.[55] When crafting 2 Cor 10–13, Paul was evidently hard-pressed to defend his apostolic status, and consequently his position as messenger as well as his message, against challenges from others whom he calls "super-apostles" (τῶν ὑπερλίαν ἀποστόλων, 11:5, 12:11) and "false apostles" (ψευδαπόστολοι, 11:13).[56] The four chapters of 2 Cor 10–13 are generally treated as a unit. Whatever one thinks about the letter's integrity, these chapters fit in well with the broader Corinthian correspondence, with its subversive yet authoritative tone.[57]

Second, Paul's reasoning is embedded in Jewish scriptural tradition and therefore requires an attempt to understand Pauline hermeneutics as encompassing more than direct quotations.[58] Interestingly, 2 Cor 10–13 is framed

---

a king-in-waiting" setting up and organizing groups of loyal followers whose lives were based on the reality created by his story, the connection between pastoral and political is particularly emphasized. In a similar way, Richard Horsley ("1 Corinthians: A Case Study of Paul's Assembly as an Alternative Society," in Horsley, *Paul and Empire*, 242–52) claims that in 1 Corinthians Paul formulated strategies for how the Corinthian community was to establish itself as "a community of a new society alternative to the dominant imperial society" (244).

55. The integrity of 2 Corinthians is often disputed, with many seeing it as a composite letter of which the following constituent parts are identified in various combinations with one another and the letter as a whole: 1:1–2:13 and 7:5–16 (Paul's boasting); 2:14–7:4 (the apostolic office; from which 6:14–7:1 is often omitted as a later interpolation); 8–9 (Jerusalem collection); 10–13 (Paul's defense of his apostolic ministry, seen by some as part of the "tearful" letter of 2 Cor 2:3–4; 7:8). Cf. Rudolf Bultmann, *The Second Letter to the Corinthians* (trans. Roy A. Harrisville; Minneapolis: Augsburg, 1985), 16–18. Other scholars argue for the literary integrity of 2 Corinthians, e.g., Murray J. Harris, *The Second Epistle to the Corinthians: A Commentary on the Greek Text* (NIGTC; Grand Rapids: Eerdmans, 2005), 8–51.

56. Some scholars argue that these were two different groups, with the first being a sarcastic and derogatory reference to the Twelve or the original apostles and the second indicating (self-appointed?) envoys from the Jerusalem church (see Harris, *Second Epistle to the Corinthians*, 74).

57. Early in 1 Corinthians Paul was already challenging the conventions of his time, contrasting general perceptions about wisdom and folly with those of God (1 Cor 1:18–31) and claiming that "the rulers of this age" (τῶν ἀρχόντων τοῦ αἰῶνος τούτου; i.e., both conventional wisdom and current rulers) "are passing away" (καταργουμένων, 2:6). In 1 Cor 1:19, Paul underlines this claim with a quotation from Isa 29:14.

58. In 2 Corinthians, the Jewish feel of the letter emerges early, with the typical Jewish liturgical blessing, *berakah* (εὐλογητός, 2 Cor 1:3; see 11:31). Elsewhere in the New Testament, εὐλογητός is found in the epistolary greetings in Eph 1:3 and 1 Pet 1:3; other occurrences are found in Luke 1:68; Rom 1:28; 9:5. It is the Psalms, the prophets (Jeremiah

by two direct quotations, with Jer 9:22–23 (2 Cor 10:17)[59] supporting Paul's claim to be boasting "in the Lord" and Deut 19:15 (2 Cor 13:1) indicating the requisite number of witnesses for sustaining a claim.[60] Various other allusions strengthen the scriptural setting of Paul's argument, including his appeal to the "meekness and gentleness/fairness of Christ" in 10:1 (διὰ τῆς πραΰτης καὶ ἐπιεικείας τοῦ Χριστοῦ), words that were also used with reference to God (e.g., LXX Ps 85:5; Ps 44:5) and King David (LXX Ps 131:1); his references to the serpent's deception of Eve (2 Cor 11:3); and his strong appeal to his own heritage and tradition (being a Hebrew, an Israelite, and a descendant of Abraham, 11:22).

Third, in 2 Cor 10–13 Paul construes his position as being largely informed by practices of hegemony, which he at the same time reappropriates for his own purposes. In 2 Cor 10 the metaphorical focus is on weaponry and making war, and battle-imagery is used in setting the polemics of the scene as much as in subverting the positions of the powerful. In 2 Cor 11, Paul recounts the physical abuse that he had experienced when punished by Jews as well as his close encounter with a Roman governor, not to mention what today would be called "acts of God." In 2 Cor 12, he describes his personal situation using the notion of strength in weakness, which he relates to his concern for the community in Corinth, before returning to considerations of strength and weakness in the final chapter.

3.1. MIMICRY AND AMBIVALENCE: PAUL'S IDEOLOGICAL HERMENEUTICS (2 CORINTHIANS 10)

The ideological concerns in Paul's hermeneutics are wide-ranging and worthy of investigation in themselves. For now, however, our comments will be restricted to tracing how two concepts that are often used in postcolonial analysis, ambivalence and mimicry, function within his discourse of power, and more particularly how these concepts provide important angles for understanding Paul's use of Scripture. Any serious investigation of the

---

in particular), and the wisdom literature that provide the intertext for 2 Corinthians; see Young and Ford, *Meaning and Truth*, 61–62. Various other scriptural episodes are recalled in 2 Corinthians, such as the ministry of Moses in 3:6–18.

59. The quotation is not accompanied by an introductory formula in 2 Cor 10:17, as in 1 Cor 1:31. Stanley surmises that, mindful of its earlier use, the audience would probably have recognized it as a quotation (Stanley, *Arguing with Scripture*, 98 n. 1).

60. The actual influence of this law of evidence (in addition to Deut 19:15; see also 17:6) in first-century Jewish society is difficult to determine, but its echoes surface twice with reference to Jesus in the Gospels (Matt 18:16; John 8:17).

influence of ideological concerns[61] on Paul's hermeneutical enterprise and his rhetoric of power must take into account the ambivalence that is inherent in the imperial or hegemonic situation. Hegemony generally carries with it signs of destabilization and subversion, since the ambivalence residing in hegemony distorts the seemingly simple and straightforward claims of imperial discourse. Disclosing this ambivalence thus poses "an immanent threat to both 'normalized' knowledge and disciplinary powers."[62]

Paul's argument in 2 Cor 10 in defense of his ministry is an interestingly strong discourse with serious ideological undertones. As a carefully structured rhetorical argument, it boils down to a double challenge: to the powers of the day, represented by his opponents; and to the accompanying, operational rhetoric of power. This is evident in Paul's references to an "engagement in a battle that is not fleshly" (οὐ κατὰ σάρκα στρατευόμεθα, 10:3) and to weapons that are "not fleshly": "for the weapons of our battle are not fleshly but divinely powerful to the extent of destroying strongholds" (τὰ γὰρ ὅπλα τῆς στρατείας ἡμῶν οὐ σαρκικὰ ἀλλὰ δυνατὰ τῷ θεῷ πρὸς καθαίρεσιν ὀχυρωμάτων, 10:4).[63] This leads Paul to further challenge "arguments" (λογισμούς, 10:4) and every "proud obstacle" (ὕψωμα ἐπαιρόμενον, 10:5) offered in opposition to the knowledge of God.

This act of taking up the terminology of the powerful and turning it to his own purposes can be understood as an example of catachresis.[64] Catachresis is a concept in postcolonial thought introduced by Gayatri Spivak to refer to the recycling or redeployment of colonial and imperial culture and propaganda by the colonized for their own purposes. Catachresis is thus at once an act of creative appropriation that turns the rhetorical instruments of their colonial owners against them, a strategy of counterappropriation that redirects and reflects the appropriative incursions of imperialist discourse, and a device of subversive adaptation that creates a parody through strategic misrepresentation.[65] In this way mimicry becomes mockery, exposing the falsity of the

---

61. Ideology is, of course, "a source of social power," not merely a supplementary or secondary aspect of it; ideology is "integral to the multiple, varied, and overlapping networks of power that constitute society" (Cameron, *Christianity and the Rhetoric of Empire*, 11, referring to Mann).

62. Bhabha, *Location of Culture*, 86.

63. In the later Pauline tradition, warfare is comprehensively spiritualized so that it came to represent the Christian life; it was picked up, for example, by the claim in Eph 6:12–18 that Christians' warfare is not against "flesh and blood."

64. Originally, a Greek term meaning "misuse" or "misapplication" (see Moore, *Empire and Apocalypse*, 105).

65. Ibid., 106. In 2 Cor 12:2, Paul is again "playing the fool" and thus refrains from referring to himself directly, even downplaying his own accomplishments. Paul is doing

claims made by the powerful, deriding their conventional rhetoric through exaggeration and misapplication, and imitating the claims of empire and its associates in order to make them appear ridiculous.

Paul's mimicry of empire did not stand aloof from the biblical traditions but was instead authorized through the inclusion of references to the Scriptures of Israel in his argumentation. Indeed, the biblical traditions formed the parameters of his position,[66] including but going beyond the quotation of Jer 9:22-23 in 2 Cor 10:17 (ὁ δὲ καυχώμενος ἐν κυρίῳ καυχάσθω, "Let him who boasts, boast in the Lord").[67] In this rhetoric of weakness, which recalls the claims that he made in 1 Cor 1, Paul aimed to expose the pride and arrogance of the opponents. The contrast is not between Paul and the opponents but between God's power and wisdom and the weakness and folly of the opponents. Criticizing the opponents' reliance upon wisdom, riches, and strength,[68] Paul cites Jeremiah's criticism of any pride that is not rooted in the glory given by God.[69]

At a certain level, then, Paul appropriated the imperial sensibilities of his day in dealing with issues of authority and power in 2 Corinthians and mimicked the empire. Mimicry is a product of the imposition of the colonizer's

---

more here than simply using irony to vindicate himself in place of a Stoic line of argumentation (so Ralph P. Martin, *2 Corinthians* [WBC 40; Waco, Tex.: Word, 1986], 389). Jerry W. McCant, *2 Corinthians* (Readings: A New Biblical Commentary; Sheffield: Sheffield Academic Press, 1999), 13-15, discusses 2 Cor 10-13 as "parody" in the more general sense of the word. In view of Paul's claim in 1 Cor 4:3 that to be judged by the Corinthians is "a small thing" (εἰς ἐλάχιστον), the potential for parody in a subsequent defense is great. One can read 2 Cor 11:1-12:18 as Paul's *foolish discourse* where he uses parody to expose, condemn, humiliate, and persuade his readers of the errors of his opponents' ways in a way that is similar to the techniques used by both earlier (e.g., the Platonic Socrates) and contemporary (esp. the Cynic) philosophers.

66. Echoes of texts such as Zech 4:6, "Not by might, nor by power, but by my Spirit, said the Lord of hosts," reverberate in 2 Cor 10-13. When Deut 19:15 is quoted in 2 Cor 13:1 in support of Paul's warning concerning his upcoming visit to Corinth, Paul aimed to show beyond doubt that he derived his power from God through Christ, since he (Christ) "was crucified in weakness, but lives by the power of God" (13:4a).

67. Generally speaking, "boasting" (καυχάομαι, καύχησις, and καύχημα) is used in 2 Cor 1-9 in a positive sense, referring to appropriate boasting, while in 2 Cor 10-13 it refers to inappropriate, i.e., vindictive or apologetic, boasting (see Young and Ford, *Meaning and Truth*, 13-14; the difference is denied by Harris, *Second Epistle to the Corinthians*, 33). Καυχάομαι is used 37 times in the New Testament, with 35 of these uses occurring in Paul and 17 in 2 Cor 10-12 alone (see Harris, *Second Epistle to the Corinthians*, 726 n. 113).

68. The destruction of the wisdom of the wise and the pride of the high and mighty is an important theme also in Isaiah (e.g., 29:14; 2:10-17).

69. Young and Ford, *Meaning and Truth*, 72-74.

culture on the colonized, which results not only in the coercing of the colonized but also in the valorization of the colonizer's culture, with a view to its internalization and replication by the colonized.[70] The replication, however, is never perfect, nor does the colonizer intend it to be so, since perfect replication would erase the all-important boundaries of power between colonizer and colonized. The result is cultural mimicry. The discourse of mimicry is governed by a further ambivalence in that it entails a risk for the colonizer that the colonized will in fact use mimicry to mock and therefore subtly challenge and subvert the control and authority of the colonizer by subverting the colonizer's narcissistic claim to self-identity.[71] Thus mimicry is ambivalent not only in its insistence on and desistence from mimesis but also in the risk that it poses to colonizers of having their culture parodied.[72] In Paul's case, his mimicry of empire may create the impression that he had internalized and replicated the colonizer's culture, but it is the ambivalence of colonial or hegemonic discourse that he employed to his own advantage.[73] In his discourse of power, Paul mimicked empire through a twofold rhetoric of foolishness and weakness.

3.2. Hermeneutics and Othering: Weakness and Paul's Politics of Difference (2 Corinthians 11)

From a postcolonial perspective, the processes of assuming or describing human existence as identity are complex and entail the acknowledgement that "cultural and political identity are constructed through a process of alterity."[74]

---

70. "Colonial mimicry" is a concept coined by Homi Bhabha (see *The Location of Culture*, 85–92). Rieger (*Christ and Empire*, 20 n. 37) disputes Bhabha's insistence that the ambivalence flowing from mimicry is necessarily a surface effect, arguing that it can also be symptomatic of repression (in the Freudian sense)—although these options are not necessarily mutually exclusive.

71. Bhabha, *The Location of Culture*, 85–92.

72. Moore, *Empire and Apocalypse*, 110.

73. As was shown by Elizabeth Castelli (*Imitating Paul: A Discourse of Power* [Literary Currents in Biblical Interpretation; Louisville: Westminster John Knox, 1991]), mimesis was an important mechanism through which Paul stabilized his own discourse of power.

74. Bhabha, *The Location of Culture*, 175. The greatest form of epistemic violence for postcolonial theorists is the project according to which the colonial subject is established as "the Other" (see Gayatri C. Spivak, "Can the Subaltern Speak?" in *The Post-colonial Studies Reader* [ed. Bill Ashcroft, Gareth Griffiths, and Helen Tiffin; London: Routledge, 1995], 24–28). Some scholars have argued that it was Paul's focus on the cross (see 1 Cor 2:2), as the symbol of ultimate violence in the first century c.e., that informed his "penchant for violence" (John G. Gager and E. Leigh Gibson, "Violent Acts and Violent Language in the Apostle Paul," in Matthews and Gibson, *Violence in the New Testament*, 19).

This notion of "alterity" is important in Paul's letters, which were largely based upon a hermeneutical approach informed by an apocalyptic interpretation of the Christ-events,[75] all of which already anticipated radical otherness. The contemporary world ruled by the Roman Empire was seen as the evil age and thus the domain of Satan.[76] Paul accused his opponents in 2 Cor 11:13–15[77] of excelling in subterfuge and trickery, since as "his slaves/servants," they, like their master Satan, who "disguises himself as an angel of the light" (11:14), disguise themselves as "slaves" or "servants of righteousness" (11:15).[78] This is not to say that Paul directly equated his opponents in Corinth or elsewhere with the Roman authorities and their local minions, or to suggest that Paul identified the Roman Empire or the emperor with Satan. Yet we must be alert to Paul's first-century context, where politics were perceived both broadly (as distant, uninfluencible, overweening power) and narrowly (as rules and regulations concerning taxes, movement, etc.) at the same time, and where contrasting, opposing, and negative views were conflated and perceived to reflect various sides of the same coin. These tensions emerge in an interesting way in Paul's construction of his own identity, that is, through "othering."

---

75. See recently Ehrensperger, "New Perspectives," 234; Roetzel, *Paul*; also Young and Ford, *Meaning and Truth*, 122–24. Although there is a tension in Paul's apocalyptically focused approach to Scripture, it did not amount to a "simplification" inasmuch as the "inclusive tendencies" in his hermeneutic cannot be ascribed to his gospel only (so Roetzel, *Paul*, 36). Was it perhaps the universalistic focus of Paul's shared apocalyptic framework that nudged him toward some form of inclusivity in his interpretation of Scripture?

76. Satan (Σατανάς) is mentioned relatively frequently in 2 Corinthians. In 2:11, Paul linked his forgiveness of the Corinthian offenders to his concern to avoid Satan gaining advantage over the followers of Christ. The reference to ὁ ὄφις ("serpent") who deceived Eve in 11:3 is most likely also to Satan, underlining the deceitfulness of the imperial age. In 12:7 it is the "thorn in the flesh" that is described as a "messenger of Satan." Elsewhere in the authentic Pauline letters, references to Satan can be found only in Rom 16:20; 1 Cor 5:5; 7:5; and 1 Thess 2:18. In the deutero-Paulines, references appear in 2 Thess 2:9 and 1 Tim 1:20; 5:15. The word "devil" (διάβολος) does not occur in the authentic letters, only in the deutero-Pauline letters (Eph 4:27; 6:11; 1 Tim 3:6, 7, 11; 2 Tim 2:26; 3:3; Titus 2:3).

77. This text forms the conclusion to 2 Cor 10:1–11:15 with its numerous accusations against Paul's opponents, including not being submissive to Christ, having no authority from God, claiming success without having been appointed to Corinth, professing a different gospel, proving to be a financial burden to the Corinthians, and being deputies of Satan and deceitful operators (see Harris, *Second Epistle to the Corinthians*, 664).

78. In the wisdom literature and the Psalms, the trickery and deceitfulness of the wicked are also important topics. While their challenge is directed at the upright person, their actions are indicative of their ignorance about God and the fact that all wisdom proceeds from God (Sir 1:1, 11). "Boasting" is also an important concept in the wisdom literature, as it is in Psalms and Jeremiah (Young and Ford, *Meaning and Truth*, 78–80).

When Paul constructed his identity in 2 Cor 11, he did so with constant reference to himself as the "Other," construing himself from and with reference to a position of weakness.[79] In 2 Cor 11, Paul recounted the physical punishment that he had experienced at the hands of Jews (ὑπὸ Ἰουδαίων, 11:24), enumerating five lashings and one stoning, as well as his timely escape from the persecution of King Aretas, governor of Damascus (11:32–33)[80] and his experiences with "acts of God," including being shipwrecked and adrift at sea (11:25). Paul's catalogue of sufferings in 11:25–28 includes references to various other dangers that were brought about by his journeys: dangers experienced due to hazardous travel ways ("rivers"), antagonism ("robbers," his "own people" [ἐκ γένους], "Gentiles" [ἐξ ἐθνῶν], "false brethren"), location ("city," "wilderness," "at sea"), and circumstances ("toil and hardship," "sleepless nights," "hunger and thirst," "often without food," "in cold and exposed").

Paul's catalogue of sufferings at the hands of humans, nature, and God also established a link between identity and agency. In contemporary thought, subjectivity is firmly fixed in language, so that an all-important question is, "how can one account for the capacity of the subject in a post-colonial society to resist imperialism and thus to intervene in the conditions which appear to construct subjectivity itself?"[81] Paul's argument in 2 Cor 11 has to be read in tandem with 2 Cor 12, where he states that the confirmation of his human frailty and mortality had shown him clearly whom he should credit as the source of life and power.[82] The same sentiment expressed in the autobiographical reference in 12:9–10 is echoed in Paul's statement of confidence in 4:10–15, where he both trusts in the resurrection of Christ and appropriates the confidence of the psalmist[83] (ἔχοντες δὲ τὸ αὐτὸ πνεῦμα τῆς πίστεως

---

79. "Paul's own life modelled authority and power in stark contrast to the authority and power of the Roman Empire," as he became "a fool, weak, poor, a victim of torture and homeless" (Rieger, *Christ and Empire*, 51, with reference to 2 Cor 11:21–27).

80. According to his own testimony, Paul was often on the wrong side of the (local) law for disturbing the peace or being a public menace, with the result that he appeared before magistrates and spent time in jail (see Phlm 1, 9, 13; Phil 1:7, 12–14, 16; 1 Thess 2:2; 1 Cor 4:9; 2 Cor 1:8–9; 11:23). See Elliott, *Liberating Paul*, 183.

81. Stephen Slemon, "The Scramble for Post-Colonialism," in Ashcroft, Griffiths, and Tiffin, *The Post-colonial Studies Reader*, 45–52.

82. Young and Ford, *Meaning and Truth*, 63.

83. While Paul did not model his argument on the Psalms, his embeddedness in the Scriptures made the Psalms important in his thoughts. In 2 Corinthians, we find references specifically to the *hallel* psalms (Pss 112–117 LXX), which were used in the synagogues at the great festivals (Young and Ford, *Meaning and Truth*, 68–69). The great festivals also had an important political angle related to God's saving acts and the demise of the political enemies of Israel and the Jews (see the brief summary in Pheme Perkins, *Reading the New*

κατὰ τὸ γεγραμμένον, "having the same spirit of faith as that which is written," 4:13).

The strong appeal that Paul made to the events in 2 Cor 11, through which he established his alterity[84] characterized by weakness, implies that this catalogue of events was much more than a distraction. In fact, Paul used these events to his advantage, making them serve as a recommendation for him and probably also for the particular gospel message he preached. Paul's rhetoric of weakness and powerlessness was central to his discourse of power, challenging imperial discourse while establishing his own, which was dependent upon biblical traditions. The conceptualization and portrayal of textual and personal "others" in Paul's hermeneutical enterprise is not restricted to his adversaries but functions here also autobiographically, as Paul's identity-construction is informed by broader sentiments from the biblical traditions. While his references to "acts of God" could probably be explained more easily within a context undergirded by notions of testing in order to be proven worthy, as appears in the biblical and some philosophical traditions, it is his acknowledgement and to some extent his valorization of his conflicts with local authorities that is remarkable, particularly in the way Paul used these conflicts to inform and describe his identity.

3.3. Identity and Hybridity: Foolishness and Paul's Politics of Identity (2 Corinthians 12)

Hybridity is another important concept in postcolonial thought, but here the focus will be limited to the hybrid character of the hermeneutics that are typically operative in postcolonial contexts. Analyzing this process requires coming to terms with the "complex psychic interpenetration of colonizer and colonized."[85] Hybridity is molded by mimicry, which functions as colonial

---

Testament: An Introduction [rev. ed.; Mahwah, N.J.: Paulist, 1988], 46–48). Theologically, Paul more directly modeled his rhetoric of weakness on the example of Jesus as Paul chose to depict him in Phil 2:6–11, in particular.

84. Some scholars have argued that Paul challenged and effectively neutralized the hierarchical categories of his time with their marginalizing effects, without erasing the difference between the categories. According to this view, Paul's insistence on "oneness in Christ" subverted both "repressive sameness" and "imperial oneness" (e.g., Brigitte Kahl, "No Longer Male: Masculinity Struggles behind Galatians 3.28?" *JSNT* 79 [2000]: 37–49). Other scholars see a similar temporal subversion reflected in Paul's notion of the displacement of the "elements of the world" (Gal 4:3, 9) through knowledge of God (see J. Louis Martyn, *Theological Issues in the Letters of Paul* [Nashville: Abingdon, 1997], 100–101, 393–406).

85. Moore, *Empire and Apocalypse*, 109.

domination and coercion, but hybridity goes beyond mimicry, since it redefines and reconstructs the colonizers. Hybridity in identity and hermeneutics goes beyond what can be called a weak sense of hybridity that regards all cultures as essentially syncretistic,[86] however true that may be at a general level. Thus our discussion of Paul and hybridity[87] must not demand too much from a well-known text such as 1 Cor 9:22b, "I have become all things to all men" (τοῖς πᾶσιν γέγονα πάντα). Nor should the discussion of Paul's multicultural (pluricultural) identity be restricted to the question of how far his Jewish background or identity was infused with Hellenism[88] generally or to other more specific Greco-Roman influences such as his education or his possible Roman citizenship status.[89] As in later Christian writings, Paul's discourse is not characterized as much by radical uniqueness as by creative inventiveness, where the familiar is taken over and reworked or (re)appropriated, where the known is used to indicate and formulate the unknown.[90] Appeals to and the use of the Scriptures of Israel function as an important component in this reappropriating discourse.

Hybridity is a helpful concept for articulating the multiple and complex range of activities that take place in negotiating identity in the postcolonial context and attempting to understand the effects of the engagement between colonizer and colonized. In fact, it is in hybridity that liminality is established, in what Homi Bhabha calls a "third space" that neither subsumes the culture of the colonizer or colonized nor merges the two. Hybridity does not imply a separate third culture[91] but rather a process of continuous construction or

---

86. E.g., seeing Paul as a "hybrid synthesis of multiple cultural and colonial identities" (Robert P. Seesengood, "Hybridity and the Rhetoric of Endurance: Reading Paul's Athletic Metaphors in a Context of Postcolonial Self-Construction," *Bible and Critical Theory* 1 [2005]: 1–16, here 3).

87. The postcolonial situation that consists of the relationship between colonizers and colonized is one of ambivalence, entailing the simultaneous attraction to and repulsion by empire (see Bhabha, *The Location of Culture*, 123–38).

88. The impact of the Hellenistic milieu is discernible, for example, in the list of vices in 2 Cor 12:20–21 and elsewhere (Rom 1:29–31; 13:13; 1 Cor 5:9–11; 6:9–10).

89. Paul's comments in Phil 3:4–11 about giving up claims based on his Jewish descent and heritage, which was recognized by the Roman Empire and accompanied by certain privileges, is sometimes interpreted to illustrate Paul's distancing himself from empire (Rieger, *Christ and Empire*, 51), but this argument requires more attention within the framework of Paul's rhetoric of weakness.

90. Cameron, *Christianity and the Rhetoric of Empire*, 25.

91. As Bhabha stresses (*The Location of Culture*, 173), "The incommensurability of cultural values and priorities that the postcolonial critic represents cannot be accommodated within theories of cultural relativism or pluralism."

formation and deconstruction of cultures, reflecting the recognition that cultures are always constructed. Culture is never "pure, prior, original, unified or self-contained; it is always infected by mimicry, self-splitting, and alterity. In a word, it is always already infected by hybridity."[92]

Hybridity informs and marks Paul's argument about wisdom in the Corinthian letters generally[93] and in 2 Cor 12 in particular. In 2 Cor 12:11, Paul claims γέγονα ἄφρων ("I have been a fool"), only five verses after he declared in 2 Cor 12:6 οὐκ ἔσομαι ἄφρων ("I shall not be a fool"). Both of these statements form part of his larger argument about his credentials and therefore his authority as apostle. Paul's argument is built on contesting the conventional considerations about wisdom and the basis for such considerations. His argument forms part of a larger rhetoric of wisdom and foolishness that at least in part constitutes the Corinthian correspondence as a discourse of power. But Paul's discourse of power is not disconnected from the imperial discourse. The link that he sets up between "wisdom" and "rulers" is not incidental, and his claims regarding the overturning of wisdom and folly resonate in a context where the emperors set great stock by learning generally and where, more practically, the emperor was the ultimate bestower of justice.[94] "In short, from the very beginning of empire, there was a demand that the emperor should behave as a *basileus* who heard the petitions of his subjects and answered them with verbal or written pronouncements which were themselves effective and legal acts."[95]

With his appeal to a different understanding of wisdom and his insistence on breaking through that which was conventional, Paul challenged the discourse of empire while simultaneously invoking a new discourse of power through his rhetoric. In the process, he leaned strongly on the Scriptures of Israel for both authentication and authority. Paul's position was contrary to that of the Roman Empire, which he intentionally subverted through his own rhetorical claims. Yet he was also engaged in a negotiation of power with both the discursive colonialism of the Romans and the recipients of his letters, and

---

92. Ibid., 19–39, esp. 37–39; Moore, *Empire and Apocalypse*, 111.

93. Without claiming direct dependence or even an authorial link, the Jer 9:22–23 quotation, which also appeared in 2 Cor 10:17, provides an important intertextual link between the arguments of 1 Cor 1–3 and 2 Cor 10–13. The "boasting" motif is picked up also in 2 Cor 10:8; 11:16; 12:6. For hybridity elsewhere in Paul as a characteristic of his athletic *topos*, see Seesengood, "Hybridity and the Rhetoric of Endurance," 1–16. Seesengood points out that hybridity at once disrupts colonial identities, resists colonial authority, and reconstructs the identities of colonizer and colonized.

94. See Millar, *The Emperor in the Roman World*, 3–14.

95. Ibid., 11.

even in some sense with the Scriptures of Israel, which were granted a new meaning through their induction into Paul's hermeneutics.

3.4. Marginal Hermeneutics: Confluence and Tension (2 Corinthians 13)

The interplay between operational marginality (i.e., marginality in action) and hermeneutics is characteristically marked by a contradictory yet inherent confluence and tension between the two categories. Marginality is inherent to hermeneutics, since the interpretive process simultaneously constructs and subverts, reinforces and destabilizes, confirms and challenges, decenters and recenters. Marginality refers to the condition of living on the outside, or on the periphery. In some cases it can include liminality, or living between center and periphery.[96] Both of these concepts can be constructively developed[97] in biblical interpretation, but neither should be idealized. Constructive uses of marginality and liminality can pose a serious challenge to conventional interpretations, that is, to the official reading, the traditional and proper way of understanding.[98] Yet marginality and liminality should not be idealized, since both are imposed conditions even when they are taken up and reconstructed by the affected, and both are also messily imbued with the interests of those who are on the margins and in liminal positions.

The hermeneutical marginality of Paul's use of the Scriptures of Israel is evidenced both in its production of alternative readings and in the surplus of meaning generated by his readings. As a rule, those who are part of the "establishment" in a particular era are limited and regulated by the status quo, which at once provides for them and limits them to what the system can offer them. Conversely, those who find themselves outside the system are

---

96. Whereas a hermeneutics of marginalization describes the assignment of marginality from the outside, a hermeneutics of marginality refers to places where marginality is taken up and creatively exploited through redrawing the boundaries and shifting the relationship between center and periphery.

97. Paul's claim for his own marginality is best expressed in his list of his sufferings (2 Cor 11:25–28), which makes clear that his marginal status was a claimed position that served an important function in his discourse of power. Included here is his explicit disavowal of his opponents, whom he admits to deliberately subverting (11:12).

98. Moreover, "the affective experience of social marginality transforms our critical strategies" (Homi K. Bhabha, "Postcolonial Criticism," in *Redrawing the Boundaries: The Transformation of English and American Literary Studies* [ed. Stephen Greenblatt and Giles B. Gunn; New York: Modern Language Association of America, 1992], 437–65; see also Bhabha, *The Location of Culture*, 172), in the sense that a dynamic power is released in and through vulnerability.

frequently stumped in their efforts to participate in the system, yet their marginality gives them access to approaches and responses that lie beyond the regulated system. Thus the marginal position carries with it the advantage of an alternative perspective, a view from the underside that is not accessible from the mainstream. Surplus energies and enjoyment can also be gained from a marginal position, since the surplus is at once inaccessible to those of the status quo and, importantly, beyond their control and thus subversive of the system.[99] Paul's hermeneutical activity shows that he benefited from this surplus of the margins, as seen in his reappropriation of the conventional and the imperial.

The ambivalence of Paul's rhetoric of power also influenced his hermeneutics in the way it implicated his (re)appropriation of the Scriptures in his arguments.[100] Paul's argument against wisdom and strength rests on the rhetorical skill with which he employs and redeploys "foolishness" and "weakness" to serve his own purposes. He deplored the conventional categories of intellect and power as markers of foolishness and weakness while at the same time using this distinction to reestablish his position and authority in the Corinthian congregation(s) and to subvert the claims of his challengers. As elsewhere, the Scriptures of Israel served as the anchor points for Paul's arguments, securing and authorizing his rhetoric and embedding it within a larger scriptural framework that implicitly challenges the empire as the primary defender of the conventional wisdom of Paul's day. At the same time, the Scriptures functioned as the authorizing agent for Paul's own efforts to retain his authority and power within the Corinthian church, providing the mainstay for his rhetoric of power.[101]

---

99. Rieger, *Christ and Empire*, 9.

100. The relatively few direct quotations in Paul's letter to the Corinthians should not be taken as a retreat from engagement with the Scriptures in a more comprehensive way, as though he concluded that his scriptural interpretations will not carry sufficient weight to make his arguments credible to the audience in Corinth (so Stanley, *Arguing with Scripture*, 98). In fact, Paul engaged the Scriptures rather comprehensively in these letters, allowing them to inform his views on his apostleship and ministry (e.g., the comparison with the ministry of Moses).

101. Paul's earlier invocation of and allusion to the psalmist's confidence in the Lord (see nn. 51, 58, 78, and 83 above), with which he (Paul) aligned himself, pervades the Corinthian correspondence and has to be remembered here too. Linking up with the Psalms, Paul substantiated his similar prophetic claim to having received divine authority but also subscribed to the wisdom tradition's subversion of convention and power—even if Paul's appropriation of these texts in 2 Corinthians went beyond their use in their originating contexts.

Paul's strong words in 2 Cor 13 take up the prophetic words of Jeremiah, claiming that, for all his insistence upon weakness, Paul acts with final authority, deciding what will remain and what will be destroyed. In 2 Cor 13:1–10 Paul again uses a rhetoric of weakness, but now with the direct warning in 13:10 (and in 10:8 as well; see also 12:19–20) that he will not shrink back from exercising the authority he received from God to build up and to tear down (κατὰ τὴν ἐξουσίαν ἣν ὁ κύριος ἔδωκέν μοι εἰς οἰκοδομὴν καὶ οὐκ εἰς καθαίρεσιν). With the direct quotation of Jer 9:22–23 in 2 Cor 10:17 already indicating Paul's use of the prophetic literature in the Scriptures, the building up and tearing down language further recalls Jer 24:6 and 51:34. Paul aligns himself with the prophet and his authority as spokesperson of God, authorized to act on God's behalf.[102] Margins and center are shifting again, with Paul utilizing the Scriptures to reinforce his authority against the challenge of his opponents. This in turn has implications for his positioning of himself, his opponents, and the other members of the Corinthian community, not to mention the (position of the) Scriptures themselves.

4. Paul's Hermeneutical Challenge: Margins and Center

It is most likely correct to argue that Paul was opposed to Caesar's empire not because it was *empire* but because it was *Caesar's* and because Caesar claimed divine status and honors that Paul believed belong only to God.[103] However, a further step down this road is required: we must be alert to the possibility that Paul is engaging in a construction of empire in his own discourse of power. We must be careful not to try so hard to rehabilitate Paul that we become oblivious to Paul's own tendency to assert a subtle form of hegemony.[104]

Paul's position was always ambiguous. On the one hand, he was the apostle to the "Others" in the eyes of his Jewish tradition, that is, a marginal Jew challenging the hegemonic power of discursive Roman imperialism and engaging some of its agents along the way. On the other hand, he was keen to impose his authority and to ensure that he kept the upper hand in the dis-

---

102. Whether Paul's purpose here is to indicate his sense of the fulfilment of Jeremiah's prophecy (so Young and Ford, *Meaning and Truth*, 70–72) is doubtful; the primary goal of the citation seems to be the sanctioning effect and the authority that Paul claims by using it.
103. Wright, "Paul's Gospel," 164.
104. On Paul's exercise of his power and authority, cf. Cynthia Briggs Kittredge, *Community and Authority: The Rhetoric of Obedience in the Pauline Tradition* (HTS 45; Harrisburg, Pa.: Trinity Press International, 1998); Polaski, *Paul and the Discourse of Power*.

course of power that he established and maintained throughout his letters.[105] As a result, his use of Scripture cannot be limited to either an anticolonialist or a colonizing role and function. This raises an important question, in oversimplified form: Was Paul an agent of empire (Roman or otherwise), or was he a subaltern speaking back to empire? To help us answer questions such as these, we must pay attention to the place of Paul's hermeneutics within his discourse of power.[106]

The hermeneutical challenge that confronted Paul was informed by the tension between center and margins. Paul frequently opted for the margins (see Rom 12:16; 1 Cor 1:28; Gal 2:10) and willingly provided theological rationale for his position of solidarity with the powerless by referring to the example of Christ (e.g., Phil 2:6–11). By showing Christ to be a Lord who is not in solidarity with the powerful, Paul positioned his own discourse as a challenge to the Roman system, since Roman law favored the elite and propertied classes.[107] Although Paul's use of the Scriptures of Israel cannot be limited to this concern, his writings and his biblical hermeneutics reveal an ongoing interest in the question of how to deal constructively with this tension between center and margins without allowing the one to assimilate the other or collapsing the one into the other.

However, as Paul's rhetoric further suggests, his own convictions, ideals, and motivation were not without presuppositions and biases, informed by

---

105. In Second Temple Judaism, the formation and constitution of the canon was never a focal part of the sectarian debate, as would later be the case in Christianity. However, Jewish sectarian self-definition was characterized by conflicting interpretations of the Scriptures during the time of the New Testament (Shaye J. D. Cohen, *From the Maccabees to the Mishnah* [LEC; Philadelphia: Westminster, 1987], 133–34). This is the broader context within which Paul's use of the Scriptures needs to be located. See Frankfurter, "Violence and Religious Formation," 144–50, on the use of legends of violence to provide a hegemonic group or culture with the pretense of persecution or suffering so that they can claim the identity of "victim" and so mobilize and legitimize violence against "the other," usually a minority group.

106. Hermeneutics implicitly acknowledges the "otherness" of others, so that otherness and marginality are inherent in the practice of hermeneutics. Interpreters do not have the last word, "for in hermeneutics one never ceases to listen to 'the other'" in whatever form (see Anthony C. Thiselton, "Can Hermeneutics Ease the Deadlock? Some Biblical Exegesis and Hermeneutical Models," in *The Way Forward? Christian Voices on Homosexuality and the Church* [ed. Timothy Bradshaw; 2nd ed.; Grand Rapids: Eerdmans, 2004], 145–96, here 146). The concern of hermeneutics with otherness, marginality, and liminality is therefore not surprising, but expected. Yet given its intricate and complex relationship with otherness, hermeneutics is also from the outset implicated in issues of power, since it involves the construction of interpretive positions and interests.

107. Elliott, *Liberating Paul*, 186; Rieger, *Christ and Empire*, 52.

what seems to have been his robust conscience (see Stendahl). On the one hand, Paul's mimicry of empire and his hybrid identity, formed and informed by empire and biblical hermeneutics, implied a degree of marginalization for him and ensured his liminality. In short, he occupied a position of transition, of in-between-ness. On the other hand, Paul's discourse of power, informed by a rhetoric of weakness (e.g., Phil 2:5–11; 2 Cor 10–13) and foolishness (e.g., 1 Cor 1–4), served both as a challenge to imperial discourse and as authority and sanction for his own discourse of power.

5. Conclusion

Paul's letters issued a strong if subtle challenge to the Roman Empire, a challenge that was supported and authorized by, and to some extent built upon, the results of his interpretation of the Scriptures of Israel as he sought to enlist the scriptural framework and even specific quotations to prove the veracity of his message and apostleship. At the same time, however, Paul was implicated in his own discourse of power, as quotations from Scripture also served to underwrite *his* claims, authorize *his* position, and justify *his* arguments and position.[108] In Paul's understanding, his own ministry was so thoroughly entangled with and connected to the Scriptures that his adversaries' stance toward Paul reflected their stance toward the Scriptures.[109] In addition, since the Scriptures of Israel carried divine authority, Paul obtained no less than divine sanction for his mission and message through the direct and indirect claims that he made in his interpretation and use of the Scriptures of Israel.

How useful is it, then, to use postcolonial criticism as a tool for understanding Paul's hermeneutics as a particular manifestation of the first-century hermeneutics found in the New Testament? The question is especially pertinent since postcolonial criticism is a properly (post)modern endeavor, bearing "witness to the unequal and uneven forces of cultural representa-

---

108. Space does not allow for a discussion here, but a fuller treatment of "marginalization" in Paul's letters would also include an analysis of the position of the Scriptures of Israel in Paul's thought. Paul's use of texts and themes from the Scriptures invariably displaced these ideas from their scriptural framework and (to some extent at least) upset the biblical framework as a whole. This is what Daniel Boyarin has in mind in *A Radical Jew* when he accuses Paul of allegorizing away the uniqueness of Israelite history and Jewish life. See also Stanley, *Arguing with Scripture*, 28–29, regarding Meir Sternberg's work on the displacement effect of quotations.

109. Stanley, *Arguing with Scripture*, 40, is probably right in arguing that the authority of the Scriptures was widely acknowledged in the early Christian church, so that Paul's appeals to the Scriptures would have greatly contributed to his powerful position in the early church.

tion involved in the contest for political and social authorities within the modern world order."[110] The value of a postcolonial approach lies primarily in its ability to highlight the interactive relationships that invariably form both colonizer and colonized and to provide conceptual and analytical tools for their investigation. In the case of Paul, a postcolonial approach enables us not only to recognize Paul's challenge to the powers-that-be—imperial and otherwise—but also to see how that challenge rubbed off onto Paul himself, influencing his stance and shaping his response toward the powerful while also shaping his overall outlook and rhetoric.

---

110. Bhabha, "Postcolonial Criticism," 487.

PAUL AND THE AUTHORITY OF SCRIPTURE: A FEMINIST PERCEPTION

Kathy Ehrensperger

1. THE AUTHORITY OF SCRIPTURE AND THE EXERCISE OF POWER

The fact that Paul in a significant number of passages in his letters refers explicitly or implicitly to the Scriptures is taken as obvious evidence that he perceived Scriptures as an authority not only for his own life but also for the life of the Christ-followers he addresses.[1] This perception of the Scriptures as the unquestioned authority at least in the life of Paul (and most likely the other apostles as well) constitutes the starting point of such excellent and divergent analyses as Christopher D. Stanley's two monographs, Richard Hays's monograph and volume of essays, and J. Ross Wagner's volume on Isaiah in Romans, to name only a few.[2] Although these analyses differ in their focus, methodology, and conclusions,[3] they in different ways presuppose that the reference to "the authority of Scripture" is self-explanatory, and thus none of these approaches critically discusses the notion of "the authority of Scripture." Hays asserts that Paul's arguing is deeply shaped by and engaged

---

1. E.g., Christopher D. Stanley, who states that "from the way Paul refers to the Jewish Scriptures in his letters, it seems clear that he not only accepted the sacred text as authoritative for his own life but also expected a similar response from his audiences" (*Arguing with Scripture: The Rhetoric of Quotations in the Letters of Paul* [New York: T&T Clark, 2004], 40); see also Richard B. Hays, *Echoes of Scripture in the Letters of Paul* (New Haven: Yale University Press 1989), 165.

2. Cf. Christopher D. Stanley, *Paul and the Language of Scripture: Citation Technique in the Pauline Epistles and Contemporary Literature* (SNTSMS 74; Cambridge: Cambridge University Press, 1992); idem, *Arguing with Scripture*; Hays, *The Conversion of the Imagination: Paul as Interpreter of Israel's Scripture* (Grand Rapids: Eerdmans, 2005); idem, *Echoes of Scripture*; J. Ross Wagner, *Heralds of the Good News: Isaiah and Paul "in Concert" in the Letter to the Romans* (NovTSup 101; Leiden: Brill, 2002).

3. Stanley, *Arguing with Scripture*, 11, 20.

with Scripture and that he is concerned not "to assert his own authority over Scripture" but to maintain in a "dialectical struggle" the integrity of his proclamation of the gospel in relation to Scripture and vice versa.[4] However, this does not clarify why and in what sense the integrity of Scripture needs to be maintained in Paul's view nor how the integrity of Scripture is linked to its authority. Hays also does not elaborate on the meaning of "authoritative text" when he asserts that "Paul is seeking to ground his exposition of the gospel in Israel's sacred texts."[5] Wagner, too, asserts a dynamic interrelationship between Scripture, theology, and mission in the Pauline letters. He views Paul as a hermeneutical theologian who "proclaims and interprets the gospel and Israel's scriptures," for whom Isaiah's words are "a weighty and palpable presence" and for whom a set of writings are "scripture," that is, holy writ.[6] Although Wagner occasionally mentions the purpose of Paul's scriptural references, speaking of them as explanatory, keys to understanding, or as witnesses to the gospel and/or to God's faithfulness,[7] he claims that they primarily add the weight of cumulative authority to a Pauline argument, without discussing further the issue of authority and power.[8] In a similar way, Stanley seems to take it for granted that Paul refers to Scripture "in order to ground an argument or settle a dispute."[9] As long as the authority of Scripture

---

4. Hays, *Echoes of Scripture*, 158–59. Hays also notes that Paul regards the voice of Scripture as authoritative in one way or another (14). Concerning Paul, he states that "his faith ... is one whose articulation is inevitably intertextual in character, and Israel's Scripture is the 'determinate subtext that plays a constitutive role' in shaping his literary production" (16).

5. Ibid., 34.

6. Wagner, *Heralds of the Good News*, 1–2.

7. Ibid., 46, 358, 356.

8. Ibid., 352. At the end of his study Wagner quotes Michael Fishbane's characterization of the Pharisees as "purveyors and creators" of haggadic exegesis and views this as an appropriate description also for Paul (357 n. 43). I am in agreement with Wagner on this, but I also think that the implications of Fishbane's characterization need to be further explored, as they promise to provide a challenge to many aspects of reading Paul. See Wagner's approval of Fishbane's statement: "[They] appear to live with 'texts-in-the-mind'—that is, with texts (or traditions) which provide the imaginative matrix for evaluating the present, for conceiving of the future, for organizing reality (the inchoate, the negative, the possible), and even for providing the shared symbols and language of communication. With aggadic *traditio* the world of Israelite culture is thus one which talks and thinks, which imagines and reflects, and which builds and rejects, *through* the traditions" (357, quoting Michael Fishbane, *Biblical Interpretation in Ancient Israel* [Oxford: Oxford University Press, 1989], 435).

9. Stanley, *Arguing with Scripture*, 40.

is acknowledged, says Stanley, "direct quotations from the holy text would be greeted with respect and (Paul hoped) submission."[10]

It comes as no surprise that studies such as these, which imply that "the authority of Scripture" is self-explanatory, come to the conclusion that biblical references, quotations, and allusions are a tool in Paul's argumentative strategy to exercise power over the addressees and render them obedient, that is, submissive to his views. Of course, such studies recognize that the function of Paul's references to Scripture is not restricted to his exercise of power and authority; they can serve other purposes as well, such as illustrating, explaining, and motivating.[11] But these other functions depend, according to Stanley, on the acceptance of the authority of the Jewish Scriptures, when he maintains that "the quotation achieves its rhetorical effect as long as the audience acknowledges the authority of the Jewish Scriptures and accepts Paul's reputation as a reliable interpreter of the holy text."[12] Stanley is of the view that, since the Scriptures represent the authority of God, a reference to Scripture would resolve any dispute. He therefore sees an element of force in almost all Pauline scriptural references, "since the very act of adducing a quotation is a covert attempt to increase the audience's receptiveness to the passage in which it appears."[13]

Such approaches operate with a paradigm of power and authority that identifies power with "power-over" and power-over with domination. However, as the contemporary debate on the nature of power demonstrates, this is a limited perception of power and authority.[14] From the perception of power as power-over, that is, as a means to dominate others and demand their submission, conclusions are drawn concerning the meaning of "the authority of Scripture" without further analysis.[15] The conclusion that Scripture is referred

---

10. Ibid., 59.

11. Ibid., 38.

12. Ibid., 60.

13. Ibid., 182. Stanley also mentions that there may also be an element of playfulness inherent in Paul's scriptural references, but he does not elaborate further on this aspect in relation to authority and power (183).

14. See the discussions in Steven Lukes, *Power: A Radical View* (2nd ed.; Oxford: Blackwell, 2005); Hannah Arendt, *On Violence* (London: Allen Lane, 1970); Thomas E. Wartenberg, *The Forms of Power: From Domination to Transformation* (Philadelphia: Temple University Press, 1990); Kathy Ehrensperger, *Paul and the Dynamics of Power: Communication and Interaction in the Early Christ-Movement* (London: T&T Clark, 2007), 16–34.

15. Although Stanley does refer to the issues surrounding the perception of "written oracles," his discussion still operates with a paradigm of power as "power-over" in the vein of a command-obedience structure (*Arguing with Scripture*, 58–60).

to with the intention of settling an argument without further debate, or with the expectation that submission to the authors' views is achieved, is coherent with such a perception of power and authority.

Without denying that the references to Scripture in the Pauline letters are of great significance and have something to do with a perceived "authority of Scripture," I would like to question the assumption that this "fact" in and of itself actually clarifies sufficiently the function and purpose of these scriptural references. It remains to be specified what the "authority of Scripture" actually means. Two major questions are involved in such an analysis: (1) What are the Scriptures to which such authority is attributed by Paul and the other leaders of the early Christ-movement, the recognition of which they expected from the Gentile communities they had founded?[16] (2) What is meant by the terms "power" and "authority" when attributed to the Scriptures? Both questions require further interdisciplinary research, but due to constraints of space, I will focus here on the second question, that is, on the nature of power and authority, although I am aware that the first question is linked with it. The specific questions on which I will focus are: What happens if Paul's references to Scripture are analyzed in conversation with paradigms of power that differ from those mentioned above? What difference does this make to our perception of the "authority of Scripture" and subsequently to our evaluation of the function of Paul's scriptural references?

2. Divergent Perceptions of Power

Contemporary discussions of "power" are invariably shaped or at least influenced by the thought and writings of Max Weber. Debates have evolved in agreement, variation, or differentiation from Weber's classical definition of power as "the probability that one actor within a social relationship will be in a position to carry out his own will despite resistance, regardless of the basis on which this probability rests." A similar view appears earlier in the same work when he states, "Power means every chance within a social relationship

---

16. For more on the important discussion concerning the implications of the flexible boundaries and textual fluidity of the Jewish Scriptures (and the implications of these insights), see David L. Dungan, *Constantine's Bible: Politics and the Making of the New Testament* (Minneapolis: Fortress, 2007), 1–19; Emanuel Tov, "The Status of the Masoretic Text in Modern Editions of the Hebrew Bible: The Relevance of the Canon," in *The Canon Debate* (ed. Lee Martin McDonald and James A. Sanders; Peabody, Mass.: Hendrickson, 2002), 234–51; Eugene Ulrich, *The Dead Sea Scrolls and the Origins of the Bible* (Grand Rapids: Eerdmans, 1999), 79–98.

to assert one's will even against opposition."[17] Although Weber acknowledges that domination is a specific application of power, he nevertheless perceives the exercise of power-over in the vein of domination to be one of the most important elements of social interaction.

This perception of power has been differentiated and challenged from numerous perspectives in the last three decades.[18] Other scholars, in clear distinction from Weber, perceive power as a capacity or ability to do something, to have an effect on something, that is, as the "power-to" achieve what an individual or a group set out to do.

2.1. HANNAH ARENDT AND COMMUNICATIVE POWER

An early significant challenge to the perception of power as power-over, and thus as inherently dominating or at least dangerous, was formulated by the German political theorist Hannah Arendt in her analysis *On Violence* (1970). According to Arendt, the logical consequence of a definition of power as power-over, that is, in the vein of a command-obedience model, is a perception that accepts that violence is the ultimate form of power. Violence is merely a particular means by which power can be exercised. This identifies power with domination in its various forms, which in her view has nothing to do with power. She argues that power is "the human ability not just to act but to act in concert." As such, power must be distinguished from other modes of human interaction such as strength, force, authority and violence.[19] Arendt notes that "power is indeed of the essence of all government, but violence is not."[20] She even maintains that "power and violence are opposites; where the one rules absolutely, the other is absent."[21] Violence always invokes a command-obedience structure, whereas power is neither command nor rule but collaboration in action, "the human ability not just to act but to act in concert."[22]

---

17. Max Weber, *The Theory of Social and Economic Organization* (ed. Talcott Parsons; Glencoe, Ill.: Free Press), 152; see also 16.
18. I cannot elaborate on this discussion in detail here, but I will return later to specific aspects of the debate concerning power in the form of power-over. For a more detailed discussion, see Ehrensperger, *Paul and the Dynamics of Power*, 16–22.
19. Arendt, *On Violence*, 44–47.
20. Ibid., 51.
21. Ibid., 56. This is only a conceptual distinction; Arendt is well aware that, "in the real world," power and violence are more often than not inextricably intertwined.
22. Ibid., 44.

In addition to drawing a clear distinction between power and violence, Arendt, in agreement with Foucault and others, is of the view that power is not something that one can possess, not some kind of stuff that some have—enabling them to store it and then exercise it over others—while others do not. She argues that power exists only in its actualization; it "is always ... a power potential and not an unchangeable, measurable, and reliable entity like force or strength"; it "springs up between men when they act together and vanishes the moment when they disperse."[23] Thus power derives from reciprocal collective action; that is, it is inherently intertwined with action that takes place within a web of relationships with other actors. Its main purpose is to establish and maintain this relational web or network.[24]

Arendt's definition has been criticized as too limited a perception, as it excludes any strategic aspects from an analysis of power.[25] Habermas and others have emphasized that the strategic aspect of power (i.e., power-over) cannot be excluded from a definition and critical discussion of power, since otherwise the dimension that is most troublesome, and indeed has attracted the most interest from scholars who study the exercise of power, would not be addressed at all.

2.2. Feminist Theories of Power

Despite this critique, feminist theorists such as Amy Allen have drawn significantly on Hannah Arendt's ideas in their search for a concept of power that moves beyond a command-obedience, domination-subordination model. This search is motivated by the fact that traditional concepts of power tend to lead to a limited perception of women in patriarchal societies as powerless victims of male domination. In contrast to this, Allen views Arendt's concept of power as enabling a perception of power that takes into account that people who are in situations of subordination are not merely powerless victims of oppression. Even when this is the primary factor determining their lives, there are many circumstances in which they are nevertheless able to form communities and to act in concert. Such acts of community formation and solidarity, although they do not change the overarching situation of oppression, are forms of "power in action" through which people are active

---

23. Hannah Arendt, *The Human Condition* (Chicago: University of Chicago Press, 1958), 200.

24. See Amy Allen, "Power, Subjectivity, and Agency: Between Arendt and Foucault," *International Journal of Philosophical Studies* 10 (2002): 131–49.

25. See Jürgen Habermas's distinguished critique of Arendt in "Hannah Arendt's Communications Concept of Power," *Social Research* 44 (1977): 3–24.

agents within limited dimensions of their lives. The mere fact of forming such groups can be an act of mutual empowerment despite and within a situation of domination.²⁶ Arendt's analysis thus provides a basis for a perception of power that moves beyond the dichotomy of domination and subordination.

Arendt's analysis of power contributes significantly to a perception of power as empowerment, but Allen nonetheless perceives her ideas as too limited. Allen calls for a perception of power that takes both the communicative and the strategic aspects of power into account. She proposes a concept of power that integrates aspects of Michel Foucault's work with Arendt's approach. Allen distinguishes three forms of power: power-over, power-to, and power-with. Power-over implies an asymmetrical relationship between agents that is often, although not necessarily, characterized by domination and subordination. Power-to is consistent with both asymmetrical and symmetrical relationships; it represents strategic power exercised to achieve a certain goal. Power-with implies a symmetrical relationship. These dimensions of power hardly ever occur in "pure" form, and they are not clearly separable from each other. In real life, they are more often than not intertwined.²⁷

2.3. What Is Authority?

The differentiation of power into power-over, power-to, and power-with, with its emphasis on relationality, leaves open the question of how authority should be understood in a specific situation, particularly the authority of a set of texts. Although Arendt deals with the question of authority, she addresses contemporary issues relating to the authority of institutions or people rather

---

26. On the power of subordinate groups in the context of domination, see James C. Scott, *Domination and the Arts of Resistance: Hidden Transcripts of Power* (New Haven: Yale University Press, 1990), 108–35. There are similarities between Allen's development of Arendt's approach and Scott's analysis in their focus on the empowering dimension of community for subordinate groups/subcultures, but Scott sees this "hidden transcript of power" more in the vein of a reversal of power structures. In that sense he does not operate with an alternative paradigm of power but with a reversal of the power-over paradigm. See also Neil Elliott, "Strategies of Resistance and Hidden Transcripts in the Pauline Communities," in *Hidden Transcripts and the Arts of Resistance: Applying the Work of James C. Scott to Jesus and Paul* (ed. Richard A. Horsley; SemeiaSt 48; Atlanta: Society of Biblical Literature, 2004), 118.

27. Arendt was well aware of this fact. After her definitions of the various categories of power, she states, "It is perhaps superfluous to add that these distinctions, though by no means arbitrary, hardly ever correspond to watertight compartments in the real world, from which they are drawn" (*On Violence*, 46).

than texts.[28] Nevertheless, her insistence that authority should by no means be confused with domination, force, or violence is worth noting. According to Arendt, "Since authority demands obedience, it is commonly mistaken for some form of power and violence. Yet authority precludes the external means of coercion; where force is used authority itself has failed."[29] Arendt clearly perceives authority as something that includes a hierarchical relationship between those involved. Although her analysis of authority is of limited value for our purposes, her identification of different dimensions within power and authority discourses is worth pursuing further. I will not elaborate on her distinction between authority and power, a distinction that seems to me less conclusive than Arendt supposes. What I consider significant is her insistence that both authority and power need to be distinguished from force and violence. To me, Arendt's view of authority implies the presence of a hierarchical dimension that she would not designate as power because it does not emerge out of a community acting in concert with each other.[30] This exclusion of asymmetry and hierarchy, or power-over, from her discussion of power is anachronistic, as critics of Arendt have demonstrated.[31] Nevertheless, her insight that there is a dimension in human interaction that is hierarchical but not coercive is important.

This aspect has been further developed by theorist Thomas Wartenberg, who has contributed a useful working hypothesis for relationships that involve hierarchies, that is, relationships that are patterned according to a power-over paradigm without being adequately accounted for in a command-obedience paradigm of power. He refers to a model of exercising power-over that takes as its working paradigm an educational setting. The relationship between student and teacher, or parent and child, is clearly asymmetrical, but the exercise of power over the student or child cannot be adequately described according to a domination-subordination pattern. The power that is exercised serves the purpose of supporting or empowering the "weaker" partner in the rela-

---

28. Arendt does not see her analysis as seeking to define "authority in general"; she is concerned rather with "a very specific form which had been valid throughout the Western World over a long period of time" (*Between Past and Future: Six Exercises in Political Thought* [London: Faber & Faber, 1961], 92).

29. Ibid., 92–93.

30. For a critical discussion of Arendt's perception of power as limited to "the human ability to act, that is to act in concert," see Habermas, "Hannah Arendt's Communications Concept of Power," and my discussion in Ehrensperger, *Paul and the Dynamics of Power*, 22–26.

31. See Habermas, "Hannah Arendt's Communications Concept of Power"; Amy Allen, *The Power of Feminist Theory: Domination, Resistance, Solidarity* (Boulder, Colo.: Westview, 1999), 126–30.

tionship. The aim of such a hierarchical relationship is transformative in the sense that the hierarchy is understood to be temporally limited. Inherent in the exercise of power-over in such a relationship is the idea that it will render itself obsolete. In order for the exercise of power to be empowering, the use of coercion, force, or violence must be ruled out. If coercion or domination infiltrate the relationship, the aim and purpose of the latter is compromised. Wartenberg calls such power exercised over others "transformative power."[32] I think that this paradigm of transformative power could well contribute to an understanding of authority, and of the authority of Scripture in particular, by providing a tool for understanding Paul's use of power in an asymmetrical yet nondominating way.[33] What remains to be clarified through a more detailed analysis than can be provided here is in what sense the emphasis on the relationality of power and authority that has been demonstrated (convincingly, in my view) by Arendt, Habermas, Allen, and others impinges on our understanding of the authority of the Scriptures.[34]

3. The Authority of Written Texts

3.1. Writing and Texts in the Greco-Roman World

In the context of the first century, the fact that Paul refers repeatedly to and interacts with a set of texts that he regards as "Scripture" is both unique (from a non-Jewish perspective) and not unique (from a Jewish perspective). When looking from a perspective outside of Judaism, Paul's practice of referring repeatedly to a particular set of texts, thereby indicating that these texts are of extraordinary significance for both the author and the readers or audience, is a phenomenon that, to say the least, must have seemed strange. The perception that a set of texts (even without the later idea of a canon of texts)[35] could express and/or incorporate all that is of decisive value and importance for a particular people is unique within the Mediterranean

---

32. Wartenberg, *Forms of Power*, 191–200; Ehrensperger, *Paul and the Dynamics of Power*, 27–29.

33. Ehrensperger, *Paul and the Dynamics of Power*, 117–36. See also Elisabeth Schüssler Fiorenza, *The Power of the Word: Scripture and the Rhetoric of Empire* (Minneapolis: Fortress, 2007), 56–68.

34. It is inconceivable from this analysis that there can be some inherent essence, or natural quality, in a set of texts that renders them authoritative. The authority of a set of texts can only emerge in the context of a community that attributes a specific value to a particular set of texts and thereby recognizes them as their Scriptures. See 3.2 below.

35. See the references cited in n. 16 above.

region of the time.[36] It is also unclear whether literacy and thus written texts in general held the same significance and garnered the same high esteem as in contemporary (Western) societies.[37] The high esteem given to education by the elites of Greco-Roman and other societies in antiquity should not be taken as evidence per se for a high regard for literacy.[38] James Crenshaw, for example, maintains that "in the ancient Near East education preceded literacy."[39] Even in Greco-Roman societies, "[e]loquent speech remained the most characteristic feature of Graeco-Roman civilization, even in its most learned manifestations."[40] Thus the question might at least be raised as to whether written texts per se held particular value.

In fact, considerable indications point in a different direction. Written texts, and thus the skills of writing and reading, were not in themselves valued as indications of excellent education or of education as such. They were viewed rather as subservient tools and skills that were useful and relevant insofar as they supported educational discourses.[41] The use of a book in itself was not regarded as advisable; to the contrary, Rosalind Thomas notes that "you must not navigate out of a book" was a contemporary proverb, signifying that one needed first-hand experience to learn a craft: "(a book) might be grossly inadequate unless backed up by the help of a teacher himself." Thomas also argues that "a text might be regarded more as an aid to memorization of what had been passed on orally by a teacher, as a reminder of those who know."[42] When it comes to the specific values that were assigned to written

---

36. See Stanley, *Arguing with Scripture*, 40.

37. Birger Gerhardsson, *Memory and Manuscript: Oral Tradition and Written Transmission in Rabbinic Judaism and Early Christianity* (Uppsala: Gleerup, 1961), 123–26; Samuel Byrskog, *Story as History—History as Story: The Gospel Tradition in the Context of Ancient Oral History* (WUNT 123; Tübingen: Mohr Siebeck, 2000), 116–30.

38. *Contra* Joanna Dewey, who maintains that "in a world in which most people were nonliterate, writing was both an instrument of power and a symbol of power.... Nonliterates would honor reading and writing as symbols of culture and status; they would also fear them as instruments of social and political oppression" ("Textuality in an Oral Culture: A Survey of the Pauline Traditions," *Semeia* 65 [1994]: 44, 47).

39. James L. Crenshaw, *Education in Ancient Israel: Across the Deadening Silence* (New York: Doubleday, 1998), 279.

40. Rosalind Thomas, *Literature and Orality in Ancient Greece* (Cambridge: Cambridge University Press, 1992), 159.

41. See David M. Carr, *Writing on the Tablet of the Heart: Origins of Scripture and Literature* (Oxford: Oxford University Press, 2005), 111–73; Richard A. Horsley, *Scribes, Visionaries, and the Politics of Second Temple Judea* (Louisville: Westminster John Knox, 2007), 90–108; Ehrensperger, *Paul and the Dynamics of Power*, 120–26.

42. Thomas, *Literature and Orality*, 161. On the significance of oral performance, see

and spoken words, it is most likely that notions such as Aristotle's permeated Greco-Roman elite society. In his view, "Spoken words are the symbols of mental experience and written words are the symbols of spoken words. Just as all men have not the same writing, so all men have not the same speech sounds, but the mental experiences, which these directly symbolize, are the same for all, as also are those things of which our experiences are images."[43] In other words, although the spoken and the written words are both outer forms of an ideal spiritual reality and meaning, the spoken word is related directly to this transcendent reality, whereas the written is merely the secondary record of these more immediate (spoken) symbols. [44]

This perception of written texts as holding secondary significance, or even as something inferior to speech and oral transmission, may in fact have caused problems for Paul. He apparently shared with his fellow Jews the perception of a particular set of texts as having high significance, and he presupposes the same perception within the newly formed, predominantly Gentile groups of Christ-followers. Given that the members of the *ekklesia* whom Paul addresses are predominantly non-Jews, Paul's expectation that they should respond positively to a reference to something that "stands written" is at least open to question and should not be taken as self-evident.

In a context where the value of writing and literacy were at least ambiguous, the special role that a set of texts played for the Jews was noted also by non-Jews, who held rather bizarre ideas about the content of these texts.[45] This Jewish perception that a single set of texts is highly significant was at odds with the dominant perception of the significance of texts as such. This in turn raises questions about the common assumption that Paul's references to this set of texts as "Scripture" per se would have added power and authority to his argumentation. If such a practice was in fact alien to the audience,

---

also Martin S. Jaffee, "The Oral-Cultural Context of the Talmud Yerushalmi: Greco-Roman Paideia, Discipleship and the Concept of Oral Torah," in *Transmitting Jewish Traditions: Orality, Textuality, and Cultural Diffusion* (ed. Yaakov Elman and Israel Gershoni; New Haven: Yale University Press, 2000), 31–37.

43. Aristotle, *Int.* 16a.3–8, quoted in Naomi Seidman, *Faithful Renderings: Jewish-Christian Difference and the Politics of Translation* (Chicago: University of Chicago Press, 2006), 81. See also Louis H. Feldmann, *Jew and Gentile in the Ancient World* (Princeton: Princeton University Press, 1993), 204.

44. See Seidman's thought-provoking analysis of the literal/spiritual dichotomy in Western linguistics and theories of translation in *Faithful Renderings*, 73–114; see also Daniel Boyarin, *A Radical Jew: Paul and the Politics of Identity* (Berkeley and Los Angeles: University of California Press, 1994), 14–15.

45. Feldman, *Jew and Gentile*, 149–70; Peter Schäfer, *Judeophobia: Attitudes toward Jews in the Ancient World* (Cambridge: Harvard University Press, 1997), 161–73.

Paul's scriptural references would not necessarily be received as appeals to some higher authority, nor would they be heard as something that settles a dispute or closes the conversation.

3.2. Written Tradition: Jewish Perspectives

There can be no doubt that a set of texts, referred to as "the Scripture(s)" by Paul, was of very high significance for all groups within first-century Judaism. Whatever other common denominators they might have had, these varied and divergent groups all related to a particular set of texts as having key importance to them. I am reluctant to use terms such as "authoritative" or "sacred," as I think that we should try to clarify further what such terms actually mean in relation to a set of texts rather than presuming that the application of such labels clarifies the issue. In the first place, it should be noted that, although all known Jewish groups related to a set of texts, this set is not identical to the later canon of the Christian Old Testament or the Jewish Tanak. The emergence of a set of texts that is regarded as especially significant by a group is a process that involves open boundaries. The boundaries are open concerning not only the inclusion of specific writings but also the versions of the texts themselves. Thus Dungan maintains that "the term *scripture* refers to a semidurable, semifluid, *slowly evolving* conglomeration of sacred texts."[46] Some subset of these texts was most likely shared by all Jews, but others were not.

The Qumran findings may serve as an illustration. It is obvious that the question of which writings were regarded as "Scripture" by the Qumranites cannot be answered conclusively. An awareness of the fluidity concerning what was perceived to be included in this "set of texts," including the wording of the texts themselves, renders a straightforward reference to some "authority of Scripture" questionable. The term "Scripture" refers not to a clearly defined set of texts but to a "cloud of sacred texts,"[47] as Dungan calls them. Thus, in addition to inquiring in what sense the Scriptures are significant, we need to ask about the implications for the notion of "the authority of Scriptures" if there is no commonly agreed collection of texts. A reference to "the Scriptures" does not tell us clearly what an author actually had in mind. In reality, "one man's interpreter is another's Scripture," since "the corpus of what constitutes 'Scripture' and is therefore the object of interpretation changed over time and varied from one group of readers to the next."[48]

---

46. Dungan, *Constantine's Bible*, 2.
47. Ibid., 3.
48. James L. Kugel, *The Bible as It Was* (Cambridge: Harvard University Press, 1997), 35.

In addition to the "fuzzy boundaries" of the collections of writings that were perceived to be "Scriptures," the issue of the fluidity of the actual text of these writings also raises questions concerning the perception of the authority of the Scriptures. Textual critics, especially since the emergence of newer findings at Qumran, emphasize that the reconstruction of one single version as "the original version" of any book of what would later be the canonical Hebrew Scriptures seems to be impossible. This leads Emanuel Tov to suggest that "it may be time to abandon the whole idea of 'reconstructing the original text.'"[49] Indeed, the often-blurred boundaries between text and interpretation raise questions about biblical interpretation in antiquity "at almost the most elemental level." Moshe Bernstein asks, "When does the writing of a biblical text cease and when does a biblical interpretation begin? When and where do we stop talking about the Bible and begin talking about the re-written Bible?"[50] This observation raises significant questions about whether word order or the existence of different versions of a particular text were issues that were debated, and if so, in what sense.[51]

Given that both the collection of texts regarded as significant and the wording of the texts themselves were fluid to some extent, in what sense can such a "cloud of sacred texts" be involved in the life and discourses of communities who hold them as significant enough to transmit them across generations? To put it another way, what does a reference to "sacred scriptures" (1 Macc 12:9) invoke in the life of a community? In what sense are such Scriptures significant? What do they contribute to the power and authority discourse of communities relating to such Scriptures?

3.3. THE JEWISH SCRIPTURES, AUTHORITY, AND POWER

Despite the fuzzy boundaries of the collection and the fluidity of the texts within the collections, there can be no doubt that by the time of the Second Temple there was a shared conviction within Judaism that some set of texts encompassed the most important traditions of the Jewish people. Since these traditions were all related to the divine in some way or another, such a col-

---

49. Tov, "The Status of the Masoretic Text," 248. See Stanley, *Arguing with Scripture*, 92.

50. Moshe J. Bernstein, "The Contribution of the Qumran Discoveries to the History of Early Biblical Interpretation," in *The Idea of Biblical Interpretation: Essays in Honor of James L. Kugel* (ed. Hindy Najman and Judith H. Newman; JSJSup 83; Leiden: Brill, 2004), 227.

51. See Stanley, *Paul and the Language of Scripture*, 83–251; Dietrich-Alex Koch, *Die Schrift als Zeuge des Evangeliums: Untersuchungen zur Verwendung und zum Verständnis der Schrift bei Paulus* (BHT 69; Tübingen: Mohr Siebeck, 1986).

lection was referred to as "the Scripture(s)," the Torah of Moses, and so forth, although the attribute "sacred" does not occur as frequently as might be expected. Within the Jewish Scriptures, references occur in 1 Macc 12:9 using the term τὰ βιβλία τὰ ἅγια, whereas Paul refers once to γραφαὶ ἅγίαι (Rom 1:2) and once to ὁ νόμος ἅγιος and ἡ ἐντολὴ ἁγία (Rom 7:12). In addition, 1 Macc 1:56–57 attributes symbolic meaning to the Torah-scroll itself, and there are Second Temple texts that refer to the Scriptures as "sacred," indicating that they were perceived as linked to the divine realm in a way similar to sacred spaces or oracles in Greco-Roman tradition.[52]

Thus while the significance of a collection of texts described as sacred for the different Jewish groups of the first century can be affirmed, it is far from self-evident what this actually meant. The fact that a collection of texts was perceived to carry traditions that were important for the community as a whole (and the "school" or group in particular) does not in itself disclose any information concerning the sense in which these texts were significant. The term "traditions" hints at the content of such a collection. The transmission of traditions that are related to the divine is of course not peculiar to Judaism, but to transmit these traditions in a written form that is light enough to travel is. This peculiarity is noted, for example, in 1 Macc 3:48, where a parallel between the function of the Torah and certain pagan practices is drawn: "They opened the book of the law to inquire into those matters about which the Gentiles consulted the images of their gods."

The traditions that were transmitted in written form in Judaism all represent and are related to the divine realm. That writing acquired a significance that went beyond the technical function of serving as a back-up system for memory is indicated by some of the scriptural narratives themselves. From a historical perspective, it appears that written texts attained a central role in Judaism only after the exile, upon the return of some Jews to Judea. But materials that attribute a special significance to written words of God can be found in earlier traditions.[53] Thus Jeremiah is requested to write and rewrite proph-

---

52. See the references to Philo and Josephus in Pieter W. van der Horst, "Was the Synagogue a Place of Sabbath Worship before 70 CE?" in *Jews, Christians, and Polytheists in the Ancient Synagogue* (ed. Steven Fine; New York: Routledge, 1999), 34–35; Seth Schwartz, "Language, Power, and Identity in Ancient Palestine," *Past and Present* 148 (1995): 24.

53. I find Hindy Najman's position concerning such preexilic traditions quite conclusive. She maintains that, in order for Ezra's introduction of a "written" tradition to be accepted as authoritative, there must have been some dimension of continuity with previous traditions in order for these to be intelligible and effective ("The Symbolic Significance of Writing in Ancient Judaism," in Najman and Newman, *The Idea of Biblical Interpretation*, 140). Najman also refers to Kugel, *The Bible as It Was*, 17.

ecies, and it seems that the preservation of these written texts is the means by which a future effect of the prophecy, the repentance and return of the people to God, is secured (Jer 36).[54] Ezekiel is also reported to have had a special connection with a written text that contained the Word of God. In Ezek 2:8–3:3, the prophet is invited to eat and digest a scroll—and only when he has internalized the "word of God" is he able to proclaim the words of God to the people.[55] In a similar way Moses, the "prophet of the prophets" in Jewish tradition, is given the privilege of rewriting the word of God on tablets after he had shattered the tablets containing the text that God himself had written (Exod 32:16; 34:27). These traditions witness to the significance of written words as testifying to the will and promises of God. However, the written tradition is significant not because it is written but because it transmits the traditions of the ancestors. The fact that it is tradition is more important than the fact that it is written.[56] It is significant to note that the written text that is finally transmitted is not written by the hands of God, nor is the transmitted written text identified anywhere as the direct production of God.[57] The transmitted written text is attributed to Moses, Jeremiah, Ezekiel, and others, and, although at certain points it is identified as a record of the word of God, it is never called directly "the word of God." This careful distinction between the divine word and the written record of the divine word has bearings on the perception of the authority and subsequent interpretive traditions of the Scriptures, including their role in the Pauline letters. I will discuss this further below, but first attention needs to be given to two other issues that have an impact on the role and authority of Scripture—the communal dimension and the interpretive process—both of which are inherently intertwined with the existence of sacred tradition in the form of Scripture in Judaism.

The context in which a clearly identifiable, central role is attributed to a collection of written texts as "Scriptures" emerges with the return of some Jews from exile. The central unifying event for the community that had to

---

54. See Najman, "Symbolic Significance of Writing," 161–65.

55. As Najman observes, "Like the first set of divine testimonial tablets in Exodus, this divinely written text will not be directly accessible to the Israelite readers. Instead, Ezekiel must internalize the text and then present the material which he has now, quite literally, digested" (ibid., 170).

56. See Hindy Najman, *Seconding Sinai: The Development of Mosaic Discourse in Second Temple Judaism* (JSJSup 77; Leiden: Brill, 2003), 4. Najman refers to the work of Francesca Rochberg-Halton, who describes the process of authorization in first millennium B.C.E. Mesopotamian writings ("Canonicity in Cuneiform Texts," *JCS* 36 [1984]: 134–36).

57. The narrative of Exod 32 depicts a scenario in which the text written by the finger of God (32:16) is lost, shattered by Moses in his anger (32:19).

reorganize itself in the context of return was, as attested in Neh 8:1–8, "neither revelation mediated by a prophet, nor the coronation of a Davidic king.... Instead the central event was a public reading of the Mosaic Torah by Ezra who was said to be both priest and scribe and who had interpreters at hand to supply explanations."[58] Two aspects are of crucial significance here. First, the text is read to the members of the community, not to a sole ruler-king figure. Concerning this quite remarkable scenario, Kugel notes that "the incident does provide a useful index for the growing role of Scripture in this community.... The Torah if it is to function as a central text for the community must truly be their common property, and properly understood by everyone."[59] Thus the hearing and responding to the guidance of the Torah, the written tradition that would also be referred to as the Scriptures, is the responsibility not of an elite but of the entire people. As a community, not as subordinates to a ruler, they are responsible for their life as people of God. The incident reported here in Nehemiah and Ezra witnesses to the fact that no text or collection of texts can become "Scripture" without a community that perceives such a collection as more than a mere record of events in the past. The narrative scene upon the return from exile shows how a text is accepted as "Scripture" by a community—the people re-enact the story of their ancestors accepting the Torah at Mount Sinai as the guidance for their way of life.[60]

---

58. Najman, *Seconding Sinai*, 33.

59. Kugel, *The Bible as It Was*, 22.

60. As William A. Graham notes, "A text becomes 'scripture' in active, subjective relationship to persons and as part of a cumulative communal tradition. No text, written or oral or both, is sacred or authoritative in isolation from a community" (*Beyond the Written Word: Oral Aspects of Scripture in the History of Religion* [Cambridge: Cambridge University Press, 1987], 5). There is a democratic dimension in the narrated interaction between Scripture, interpretation, and community here that resonates with aspects of Phyllis Trible's approach as described by Schüssler Fiorenza, who speaks of "the biblical text or scripture as a pilgrim, who has been a conversation partner of believing communities throughout the centuries and still is today. Such a conversation between scripture and believer is ongoing, mutually corrective, and of reciprocal benefit" (*The Power of the Word*, 65). Schüssler Fiorenza maintains that a more critical hermeneutic must be applied in order to unveil "the imperial functions of authoritative scriptural claims that demand obedience and acceptance.... A critical biblical reading ... understands biblical authority not as something that requires subordination and obedience, but as a resource for creativity, courage and solidarity" (67). While Schüssler Fiorenza's focus is on the meaning of the authority of Scripture in contemporary discourse, her emphasis has bearings on our perception of the function of Scripture in the Pauline letters.

The second characteristic that needs to be noted is the fact that the reading of the texts is accompanied by interpretation. This refers to a perception and practice of interpretation that, ever since the attribution of a special role to written tradition as related to the divine realm, is inherently intertwined with this process. Nowhere is there a reference to a set of such texts as "Scriptures" without interpretation of these texts, even where the text is clearly referred to as the record of the words of God. To identify the written words as records of words of God does not render interpretation, the search for meaning in these words, obsolete. Simply reading the texts, or referring to them without interpretation, was apparently perceived to be meaningless. The text of the Scriptures does not speak for itself! The transmission of written texts as "Scriptures" is envisaged from the very beginning as a process that is accompanied by practices of interpretation.[61] These two dimensions, the response-ability of the community and the inherent relation between Scripture and interpretation, point to a perception and practice of "religious"[62] authority that does not fit a paradigm of power-over exercised in the vein of domination or according to a command-obedience paradigm. The Scriptures (of Judaism) fulfilled not just one role but, as Bernstein notes, many roles in all aspects of Jewish life and creativity,[63] and none of these roles fit easily into a one-dimensional perception of power and authority.

It could be argued that this perception of the roles of Scripture is an ideological construct by a (scribal) elite who wanted to claim that Torah/the Scripture was accepted in a quasi-democratic process by the entire people and that the situation on the ground differed significantly in the first century from this idealized picture of Nehemiah. Thus Snyder reconstructs a scenario that attributes to "scribes" a rather exclusive access to the Scriptures and their interpretation. This in turn creates an extreme power hierarchy between those who know and those who are ignorant, thereby maintaining a structure

---

61. Concerning the Torah, Michael E. Stone writes, "The very fact that the divine law was written created the necessity to base in it by a process of exegesis, the whole corpus of unwritten law which it, needs be, engendered" ("Three Transformations in Judaism: Scripture, History and Redemption," *Numen* 32 [1985]: 220); see also Kathy Ehrensperger, *That We May Be Mutually Encouraged: Feminism and the New Perspective in Pauline Studies* (New York: T&T Clark, 2004), 65–91; Kugel, *The Bible as It Was*, 1–49.

62. The term is anachronistic, as there was no such concept as "religion" in antiquity. I cannot elaborate on this here, but see Ehrensperger, *Paul and the Dynamics of Power*, 9–13; Philip F. Esler, *Conflict and Identity in Romans: The Social Setting of Paul's Letter* (Minneapolis: Fortress, 2003), 3–8.

63. Bernstein, "Contribution of the Qumran Discoveries," 237.

of domination.⁶⁴ In a brief section Snyder then depicts Paul in the vein of such supposedly powerful "scribes" who restrict access to the Scriptures to an exclusive group. Implicit in Snyder's model is the belief that Paul created a structure of power-over in his churches according to a command-obedience model, which easily leads to domination.⁶⁵

There are a number of issues that would need to be discussed here, but for our purpose it is sufficient to note that Snyder's reconstruction does not take sufficiently into account what recent research demonstrates concerning the significance of orality and memory in the ancient world⁶⁶ and the presence of synagogues throughout Palestine and the Mediterranean Diaspora in Paul's day.⁶⁷ Both of these strands of research contribute to an informed reconstruction of a scenario involving the diverse roles of Scripture and the familiarity of nonelites with the texts of Scripture that come close to the image depicted in Nehemiah and Ezra, even if this image is an idealized reconstruction. Although it is far from clear how discourses of interpretation should be understood, it seems inconceivable that there could be a scenario in which access to an interpretive community is restricted to a class of scribes and literate people. The assumption that a conversation over the meaning of a text or tradition can only take place among people who have a formal education is an anachronistic, literate-driven perception. Certainly Josephus and Philo depict a different image of the role of Scripture in first-century Judaism.⁶⁸ Moreover, several New Testament passages (e.g., Acts 18:6; Mark 6:2-3; John 6:25-59) refer to controversial discussions over the understanding of texts read during synagogue gatherings, indicating that interpretation was not the privilege of an exclusive elite but of the community.

---

64. Cf. H. Gregory Snyder, *Teachers and Texts in the Ancient World: Philosophers, Jews, and Christians* (London: Routledge, 2000), 181-89.

65. Ibid., 194-205.

66. See Gerhardsson, *Memory and Manuscript*; Byrskog, *Story as History*; Richard Bauckham, *Jesus and the Eyewitnesses: The Gospels as Eyewitenss Testimony* (Grand Rapids: Eerdmans, 2006); Jaffe, "The Oral-Cultural Context"; Stephen C. Barton, Loren T. Stuckenbruck, and Benjamin G. Wold., eds., *Memory in the Bible and Antiquity* (WUNT 212; Tübingen: Mohr Siebeck, 2007).

67. Lee I. Levine, *The Ancient Synagogue: The First Thousand Years* (2nd ed.; New Haven: Yale University Press, 2005); Birger Olsson and Magnus Zetterholm, eds., *The Ancient Synagogue: From Its Origins until 200 C.E.* (Stockholm: Almqvist & Wiksell, 2004). See also Albert L. A. Hogeterp, who notes that "within first century CE Jewish culture of scriptural interpretation, the synagogue was an important place for the reading and interpretation of Scripture" (*Paul and God's Temple: A Historical Interpretation of Cultic Imagery in the Corinthian Correspondence* [Leuven: Peeters, 2006], 244).

68. Ehrensperger, *Paul and the Dynamics of Power*, 119-26.

Even if the act of reading in a synagogue setting was the privilege of men educated for this task, the access to such an education was not as exclusively limited to a tiny elite, as it was in Greco-Roman society in general. In addition, inherent to the narrative of Ezra reading the Scriptures to the community, not to a ruler or an elite, is a "democratic" element that undermines any elitist claims to power and authority.[69] There is no institutional restriction on access to the Scriptures and no institutional control or restriction over its interpretation. The fact that certain groups claimed superiority for their interpretation over the interpretations of others and that such claims involved power struggles shows that there existed neither a concept of "original" meaning nor any kind of institution that could have instigated any interpretive decisions as binding upon all Jews. Except for the commonly accepted duties concerning the temple and its ritual practices, including calendrical issues pertaining to the celebration of Shabbat and the festivals, there is no evidence for any body or authority exercising control over divergent interpretations.[70]

Whether divergent interpretations invariably lead to power struggles or separation among different groups is at least questionable. Concerning the group at Qumran, it has been proposed that interpretive issues concerning the calendar played a partial, although probably not decisive, role in their supposed opposition to the temple hierarchy. A later rabbinic tradition concerning the schools of Hillel and Shammai could be an indication to the contrary. Despite their differences over interpretation of the Torah, the tradition says that they lived in mutual esteem and friendship (b. Yebam. 14a–b).[71] This rabbinic evidence for a degree of debate and interaction among different Jewish groups over the interpretation of Scripture that did not provoke separation or hostility is mirrored in the Gospel narratives that speak of Jesus interacting with the Pharisees (e.g., Luke 5:17–24; 7:36–50; 11:37–54). The

---

69. Stone notes that "the writing down of sacred scripture set in movement processes which combined with political events to undermine high-priestly authority" ("Three Transformations," 220).

70. Günter Stemberger concludes, as far as the Second Temple period is concerned, that "die Frage nach Entscheidungsfindung und—durchsetzung (bleibt) völlig offen. Religiöse Kontrolle und Vereinheitlichung hielten sich in ganz engen Grenzen" ("Mehrheitsbeschlüsse oder Recht auf eigene Meinung? Zur Entscheidungsfindung im Rabbinischen Judentum," in *Literatur im Dialog: Die Faszination von Talmud und Midrasch* [ed. Susanne Plietzsch; Zurich: Theologischer Verlag Zürich, 2007], 20). On perceptions of the role of the temple in different groups during the Second Temple period, see Hogeterp, *Paul and God's Temple*, 27–114.

71. Whether this is an idealized reconstruction or a historical fact, it indicates that at the time of writing this scenario was presented as the ideal for relating to each other in difference and mutual respect.

conversations are not depicted as hostile in every case, nor even as essentially negative. Most important, they witness to a practice of conversation (sometimes including table-fellowship) that is based on a shared interest: life according to the Scriptures. This image of interaction and conversation between Jesus and Pharisees, as depicted by some of the Gospel narratives, may not have been as unique as has previously been thought. It is found again in Acts (5:33–39; 22:3; 23:1–10), and it could well mirror a practice that was shared by other Jews also. As Hogeterp notes, the role of the Pharisees as teachers and interpreters of Torah need not have been a "one-way didactic interaction between Pharisees and common people. Expositions of Scripture in Palestinian synagogues could convey ideas and norms which developed out of debates between the pluriform Jewish movements.... This is more likely to have been the case than a supposed segregation of closed movements with a homogenous system of beliefs and practices."[72]

Despite differences in interpretation and the differing conclusions to which they led, the diverse groups within Judaism did recognize a specific collection of texts as their Scriptures, that is, as most decisive for shaping and providing guidance for their way of life. Most of the texts used by a particular group were probably shared with other groups. In this sense it could be said they regarded this pluriform collection of texts as authoritative. But this shared perception of the existence of a set of Scriptures (whatever their precise contours) by no means settled or closed the at-times controversial conversation over the meaning of the texts in relation to issues of contemporary life. The almost "unimaginable number of forms" of interpretation found in Second Temple Judaism offer an impressive literary witness to this conversation in all its diversity.[73] Thus the acknowledgement of a collection of Scriptures as "Word of God" and in that sense as sacred and authoritative actually includes the search for interpretation and meaning. The fact that this collection contained diverse texts in itself indicates that diversity is at the heart of the Scriptures. They were perceived as living words of God that produce diversity and ongoing vivid debates over meaning rather than closing such debates. To refer to the Scriptures thus constitutes not a claim to divine authority on the part of the conversation partners but rather an indication that they perceive themselves as participating in a discourse that is shaped by a perception of life and the world according to the Scriptures, that is, according to a Jewish social and symbolic universe. At the center is the relationship with the one God who has committed himself in his covenant and promises

---

72. Hogeterp, *Paul and God's Temple*, 250–51.
73. Bernstein, "Contribution of the Qumran Discoveries," 237.

to his people Israel. To refer to the Scriptures as a way of participating in a relationship is something entirely different from a so-called "use" of Scripture as prooftext or a reference to divine authority on the part of the interpreter. It could better be described as a reference to one's foremost loyalty and an acknowledgement of being a response-able participant in a life and discourse rooted in the guidance of the God of Israel.

The hierarchy in the relationship between God and his people is not adequately described when perceived as including dominating power. I have argued elsewhere that "the power of God is perceived as relationality which rules out any form of force, coercion, or domination. God calls Israel not into a new realm of domination, but into a realm of interdependence."[74] Applying feminist terminology in the vein of Hannah Arendt, the power of God could be described as power-over in the sense of transformation, in that God is committing himself in a relationship, the covenant, which is maintained neither by domination nor by force or coercion but by care for the other (i.e., the people). The aim of the relationship is to empower and thus enable people to unfold their potential as empowering communities through the process of exercising power-with so that they can "act in concert." The perception of Scriptures as the record of the Word of God cannot but mirror such an understanding of power and authority. Since they have something to do with this nondominating relationship between God and his people, to perceive them as authoritative in the sense of force or coercion is in contradiction to their actual contents. To live in the realm of this God means to be in a relationship for which the renunciation of power in the sense of domination is constitutive. The actual practice of the way of life that is in accordance with this relationship is neither engraved in stone nor written on parchment but needs to be rediscovered and enacted again and again in an ongoing conversation within a community that perceives itself to be called by God. Viewed in this light, it would be anachronistic to perceive these Scriptures as being inherently authoritative in the vein of domination. The attribute "divine" or "sacred" does not add some kind of essence to these traditions but rather indicates that they refer to a specific relationship of highest value. The character of the relationship and of the dimension of authority and power within it are inseparably intertwined. Inasmuch as power is not something that someone can possess, but only emerges (according to Arendt) when people act together in concert, the power of Scriptures unfolds as a community interacts with and responds to its words and traditions. These provide guidance insofar as people commit themselves to seek guidance through them and entrust themselves to

---

74. Ehrensperger, *Paul and the Dynamics of Power*, 164.

them as the testimony to the living God. Without a community, that is, without partners in conversation, the Scriptures cannot be part of a discourse of power. Power emerges in the interaction of a community in conversation with each other and with the Scriptures. Thus, although the Scriptures are credited with many divergent roles in the Second Temple period, to attribute to them some force of coercion or dominating power seems unwarranted and inappropriate.[75] I am convinced that there is something in Paul's emphasis that comes close to Arendt's perception of "power as the ability to act in concert" when he refers to the Scriptures as part of a discourse of encouragement and empowerment (Rom 15:4).

4. Paul, Power, and the Authority of Scripture

4.1. Paul as a Participant in Jewish Interpretive Discourse

There is no doubt that Paul was part of and participated in the social and symbolic universe of first-century Judaism. He participated in the interpretive conversation over the meaning of Scriptures before and after his call experience. Taking into account what has been argued above, that the perception of the Scriptures as authoritative included interpretation in a diversity of forms, stances, and communities, leads us to see Paul as part of a tradition of interpretation that includes conversation and diversity. Paul's self-designation as a Pharisee (Phil 3:5) indicates more precisely that he had been educated in Jerusalem and was therefore able to participate in an interpretive discourse that was at least bilingual.[76] His identification of himself as a "Hebrew of Hebrews" may be a way of referring to this bilingualism, although other meanings cannot be ruled out.[77] Clearly this supposed bi- or even trilingual-

---

75. Stanley draws attention to the potential force that may be exercised by a scriptural quotation in *Arguing with Scripture*, 181–82.

76. Hogeterp has demonstrated this point convincingly, in my view, since there are no indications of Pharisaic education outside Jerusalem (*Paul and God's Temple*, 202–35). See also the work of Jan Dochhorn, who in a detailed linguistic study argues that Rom 16:20a is evidence that Paul participated in a "polyglotte Schriftgelehrsamkeit." He thus maintains, "Es spricht also einiges dafür, dass Paulus als kundiger Rezipient eines hebräisch-aramäischen Wissens zu gelten hat" ("Paulus und die polyglotte Schriftgelehrsamkeit seiner Zeit: Eine Studie zu den exegetischen Hintergründen von Röm.16.20a," *ZNW* 98 [2007]: 210).

77. Schwartz discusses the use of Hebrew as an identity sign in the context of the striving for Jewish independence during the two revolts ("Language, Power, and Identity," 18–31), while also cautioning against an anachronistic perception of general multilingualism in Judea and Galilee during the Second Temple period.

ism of Paul is interesting on a linguistic and cultural level and raises all sorts of issues concerning translation, but this is not the aspect that is most significant for the purpose of this essay. The significance of finding traces of bi- or trilingualism in Paul's Greek scriptural references lies in the evidence that this provides for understanding Paul's interpretive context. I am convinced by the arguments that locate Paul's schooling in Jerusalem and therefore view him as a participant in Jewish interpretive discourse.[78] Paul's interaction with and reference to the Scriptures in his conversations with the assemblies of Christ-followers that he addresses in his letters should be analyzed with this in mind.

The embeddedness of Paul in first-century Jewish interpretive discourse has implications for our perception of the function of the references to Scripture in Pauline discourse. Issues of source and target,[79] authors and addressees, speakers and audiences, invariably come into play here.[80] I will focus here primarily on the source, that is how we should perceive the function of the scriptural references and the possible "power-play" that is inherent in the factuality of these references by Paul and his apostolic co-workers in Christ.[81]

One of the functions of Paul's references to the Scriptures, and of his letters more generally, is neatly summarized by Origen in his note that Paul "taught the church that he had gathered from among the Gentiles how to understand the Book of the Law" (*Hom. Exod.* 5.1). I concur with this perception that one of the roles of Paul can be accurately described as that of a teacher.[82] To teach the Gentile members of the Christ movement the implications of the way of life in Christ implied that they had to learn the ways of the Lord/God as outlined in the Scriptures. In order to grasp what it means to be/live in Christ, Gentile converts had to be socialized into the Jewish

---

78. Hogeterp, *Paul and God's Temple*, 202–34; Ehrensperger, *That We May Be Mutually Encouraged*, 142–60.

79. See Umberto Eco, *Mouse or Rat? Translation as Negotiation* (London: Phoenix, 2004), 81–103.

80. This is a dimension of Paul's use of Scripture to which Stanley has drawn attention in a significant way (*Arguing with Scripture*, 38–61); see his analyses of the audience's capacity to grasp the meaning of particular scriptural references (75–196).

81. I am aware that a similar evaluation is necessary regarding the addressees' reception of Paul's biblical references, particularly the question of the amount of contextual knowledge that they brought to their hearing of the Pauline letters, and that such an evaluation would most likely result in conclusions that differ from the ones achieved through the present focus on Paul's perception of Scripture.

82. Ehrensperger, *Paul and the Dynamics of Power*, 117–34.

scriptural symbolic and social universe.[83] Such a process, like any successful educational process, is one of transformation, which of course includes an asymmetrical relationship between teacher and student. But the exercise of power-over in such a relationship has as its purpose to render itself obsolete. In order to be transformative, it can be neither dominating nor coercive; it must be based on trust, providing guidance and encouragement.[84] Those who, like Paul, have invited people to join the Christ-movement and thus to begin an educational/socializing process of learning Christ (which implies learning about Christ and the Scriptures and thus gaining a growing sense and understanding of being in a relationship with the one God of Israel) cannot but try to live the relationship that they initiated according to the pattern of the Scriptures and Christ. In the Scriptures, the relationship of God and his people is sometimes depicted in the vein of a parent-child or teacher-student model, a relationship that is based on nothing but trust (faith).[85] The perception of the power discourse in Paul's relationship to his communities as transformative together with the perception of the Scriptures as the record of the Word of God whose exercise of power consists in a renunciation of any form of domination has significant implications for our perception of the function of the scriptural references in the Pauline letters. The location of the scriptural discourse as a part of, and a participation in, the first-century Jewish discourse of interpretation is another decisive factor that influences our perception of Paul's reasoning with Scripture and the power and authority discourse inherent in it. The significance of this is often overlooked, as it implies not only that Paul had at some stage in his life been part of Jewish conversations over the meaning of Scripture but also that he continued to be a participant in these conversations. He was part of an interpretive community that perceived the Scriptures as authoritative, whether the members of this community were Christ-followers or not. Moreover, he did not work as an isolated apostolic interpreter of the Scriptures but as one of a team.[86]

---

83. S. Scott Bartchy, "'When I'm Weak, I'm Strong': A Pauline Paradox in Cultural Context," in *Kultur, Politik, Religion, Sprache-Text* (vol. 2 of *Kontexte der Schrift: Wolfgang Stegemann zum 60. Geburtstag*; ed. Christian Strecker; Stuttgart: Kohlhammer, 2005), 54–60.

84. See 2.2 above and Ehrensperger, *Paul and the Dynamics of Power*, 180–83.

85. Cf. Hanan A. Alexander, "God as Teacher: Jewish Reflections on a Theology of Pedagogy," *Journal of Beliefs and Values* 22 (2001): 5–17; Rolf Rendtorff, *The Canonical Hebrew Bible: A Theology of the Old Testament* (Leiden: Deo, 2005), 618–21.

86. Ehrensperger, *Paul and the Dynamics of Power*, 35–62.

4.2. The Authority of Scripture and the Challenge of Apostleship in 2 Corinthians

For the purpose of this essay I will focus on a number of passages in the Pauline letters where Paul's role and understanding of apostleship is challenged and where he refers to Scriptures in the course of his argumentation, as it seems most likely that a power discourse is involved in such passages. I will focus here on 2 Corinthians, but it would be equally interesting to pursue analyses of other passages in light of the above insights. I will limit this sketchy survey to explicit references, although I think that Paul's scriptural reasoning encompasses far more than direct quotations.

Although it is generally agreed that in this letter(s) Paul sees a need to confront challenges to his role and understanding as an apostle head on, the references to the Scriptures are not as frequent as one would expect if their function was to support his authority claims over against the Corinthian community. Moreover, the passages where Paul addresses the issue most directly, such as 2 Cor 1:5–11; 3:1–3; 4:7–15; 6:1–10; and 10–13, include only occasional references to the Scriptures, whereas elsewhere in the letter the density is higher, matched only by the references in Romans, which does not address challenges to his role and understanding of apostleship.[87] This comes as a surprise if one presupposes that Paul, particularly in a situation where he is involved in a controversy about his role, should have tried to establish his power and authority through an appeal to a higher, divine authority. The scattered references in 2 Corinthians seem to indicate that something different is going on.

In 2 Cor 1:5–11, there are no references to the Scriptures, but Paul here sets the tone for what is to follow. The focus of his understanding of apostleship—not only his own but the role of apostles generally within the movement—has something to do with a factor that is difficult to swallow from the perspective of the Greco-Roman value system: suffering and weakness as characteristics of true leaders, introduced at the beginning of the letter.[88]

In 3:1–3, when the questions concerning his apostolic credentials become explicit in relation to his lack of a letter of recommendation, Paul does refer to the Scriptures. His language in 3:3 ("and you show that you are a letter from Christ delivered by us, written not in ink but with the Spirit of the living

---

87. Stanley argues that the peculiarity of the scriptural references in 2 Corinthians and Galatians is due to the fact that Paul prior to referring to the Scriptures has to reestablish his authority as an apostle of Christ (*Arguing with Scripture*, 177).

88. See the more detailed discussion in Ehrensperger, *Paul and the Dynamics of Power*, 104–6.

God, *not on tablets of stone but on tablets of human hearts*"), although not a direct and identifiable quotation, serves as an explanatory or illustrating formulation rather than as a reference to some higher authority in support of his position. His description of the Corinthian assembly of Christ-followers is framed in terms of the social and symbolic universe to which this group is supposed to relate and from which its identity is formed. The Corinthians are expected to define their identity as Christ-followers according to the Scriptures of Israel, that is, in a Jewish way, though without becoming Jews.[89]

In 2 Cor 4:7–15, Paul describes and acknowledges the great difficulties that formed part of his experience as an apostle. Working within a value system that perceived suffering and weakness as signs of failure, Paul tries to demonstrate that such experiences are inherent to life in Christ under the contextual circumstances of life under Roman rule.[90] The verse of Scripture cited in 4:13 has been regarded as rather obscure.[91] Even without taking the literary context of the psalm referred to into account, I consider this to be an example of Paul demonstrating how deeply his life and language are entrenched in the Scriptures. He describes experiences of harshness that not only raised questions about his role and understanding of apostleship but also, as he mentioned in the opening paragraph of the letter, led him to the fringes of death, leaving him with nothing but trust in God to cling to. To refer to words from the Psalms in relation to such experiences may be to refer to the language of prayer that is most appropriate in situations such as these. The reference to the words of the psalm is in harmony with Paul's references to his hardships as unavoidable implications of his role as an apostle. This is an example of living with "the text in mind," which provides the imaginative and interpretive matrix for evaluating present experiences.[92] Thus, although Paul does address issues concerning the perception of apostleship within the Christ-movement, the scriptural reference here does not serve as a proof imbued with claims to divine authority. Rather than indicating the presence of a discourse of domination, this is an example of Paul sharing the empowerment and consolation that he gets through the words of the Scriptures (διὰ ὑπομονῆς καὶ διὰ τῆς παρακλήσεως, Rom 15:4).

---

89. On identity formation and the role of Scripture, see William S. Campbell, *Paul and the Creation of Christian Identity* (London: T&T Clark, 2006), 54–67.

90. See Neil Elliott, "Paul and the Politics of the Empire," in *Paul and Politics: Ekklesia, Israel, Imperium, Interpretation. Essays in Honour of Krister Stendahl* (ed. Richard A. Horsley; Harrisburg, Pa.: Trinity Press International, 2000), 17–39.

91. Stanley, *Arguing with Scripture*, 98.

92. See the quotation from Fishbane cited in n. 8 above.

In 2 Cor 6:1–10, the biblical reference in 6:2 stands in obvious relation to the admonition that the Corinthians should not miss the chance of hearing and responding to the grace of God. This is explained by way of an interpretation of the quotation from Isa 49:8. The interpretation explains the reference by identifying the present time as the time when God has intervened in support of his people. In the ensuing verses, Paul explains once again that his experiences of trouble and hardship should not be interpreted by the Corinthians as evidence against his and the other apostles' proclamation of the gospel. But the identification of the time in which the assembly of Christ-followers now live is not introduced to add weight to Paul's claim to power and domination; instead, it functions to explain the eschatological significance of the time in which they now live. The references in the following verses (6:16–18) serve to illustrate and explain the identity of these Christ-followers as the temple of God. Thus, rather than being part of a discourse of domination and authority, I would describe them as part of a discourse of education (διδασκαλία).

The only more or less explicit reference to the Scriptures in the chapters where Paul most passionately outlines and advocates his understanding of apostleship is found in 2 Cor 10:17. If references to the Scriptures were a strong weapon in the arsenal[93] of Paul's defense of his understanding of apostleship, it could be expected that we would find a significant number of such references in passages where he deals with precisely what in his view constitutes apostleship. The only quality that he attributes to himself and his colleagues on the basis of the Scriptures is that he "boasts"—but "in the Lord." This reference actually supports what he argues throughout the letter, that a leader in this movement cannot shape his role and self-understanding according to perceptions of leadership, power, and authority that conform to the value system of the dominating Greco-Roman world. The "world" to which Christ-followers ought to look for guidance and orientation is not "this world" (Rom 12:1–21) but the scriptural world of the Jewish people and Christ. Thus if boasting is required—and Paul makes it crystal clear that he enters this ring of boasting competition most reluctantly—it can only be boasting in God.

When we take into account what I have argued above, it becomes clear that Paul's language here includes a perception of leadership or apostleship that orients itself on a God whose "use" of power consists in his renunciation of domination. Thus to "boast in the Lord" implies that, to be a true apostle in this movement, one must not follow the pattern of this world but abstain from

---

93. Cf. Stanley, *Arguing with Scripture*, 186.

using power in a coercive or dominating way. The reference to Scripture does not add authoritative weight to the argument but is an attempt to guide the addressees' understanding of leadership and power toward an understanding that is rooted in the Scriptures.

4.3. Conclusion

Although this is only a sketchy overview of some passages of 2 Corinthians, it emerges that the power discourse of which the scriptural references are a part can hardly be described as a discourse of domination or a means by which a debate would be closed. These references are indeed part of a power discourse, but it cannot be argued from the above analyses that Paul referred to the Scriptures to add to his own voice some divine dimension. There is here no claim to divine authority on the part of Paul, nor is there an indication that the references to the Scriptures serve the purpose of closing the debate, of being the final word that would allow no further discussion. The issue at stake for Paul is that the Jewish scriptural world provides an alternative to the dominating worldview of Paul's Gentile Christ-followers. This must have been challenging for former Gentiles, as it required a very substantial reorientation of their perception of life and the world they lived in.[94] The interpretation of the Christ-event in light of these Scriptures, and of these Scriptures in light of the Christ-event, certainly provoked discussion among Jews, both Christ-followers and non-Christ-followers.[95]

That the social and symbolic universe of the Scriptures constituted the context from within which Christ-followers were supposed to live was a non-negotiable presupposition for Paul as well as for his colleagues in leadership roles. Whether this meant that the Scriptures provided a reference point for some kind of absolute authority is questionable, in my view. On the one hand, Paul was convinced that there could be no other symbolic universe if one had chosen to join the Christ-movement, since this meant placing one's trust in the one God of Israel. But precisely this trust was a trust in a God whose

---

94. See Bartchy, "When I'm Weak."

95. I cannot elaborate on this aspect here, but I think that this mutually interactive aspect of early Christian interpretation needs to be further clarified. The early Christ-followers interpreted the Christ-event in light of the Scriptures, following the Jewish interpretive practice that tried to understand a contemporary event in light of tradition. The sequence cannot be reversed, as the Christ-event has no meaning apart from it being interpreted in light of the tradition of the Scriptures. Thus to postulate that Paul reads Israel's Scriptures in light of the Christ-event does not clarify the issue sufficiently, since the question of the context for interpreting the Christ-event is not clarified.

power consisted not in the exercise of domination but in empowerment for life. To relate to this authority implied that one was called to respond as a response-able member of the movement.[96] This is the vein in which I see Paul referring to the Scriptures: as an encouragement to empower people to life in Christ, as when he maintains that "this was written for our instruction, that by the steadfastness and by the encouragement of the scriptures we might hope" (Rom 15:4).

More research is needed into Paul's reasoning with the Scriptures from the perspective proposed here. But what can be concluded at this stage is that the apostle referred to the Scriptures in a variety of ways, such as illustrating and elaborating what he meant and demonstrating the symbolic and social world into which these Gentiles were to be socialized. References to Scripture also served to teach and guide Paul's communities into the ways of Christ. But Paul did not refer to the Scriptures in order to introduce prooftexts or to issue a final word that cannot be challenged. He lived and argued with the Scriptures in a way that mirrored the creative and diverse practices of interpretation that were practiced in first-century Judaism.[97] For Paul, the word of God is alive, not static, and thus a word of God would never close a debate. It would serve rather to empower the debaters and thus to promote a response-able hearing by the community involved.

---

96. See Ehrensperger, *Paul and the Dynamics of Power*, 155–78.

97. Levinas's comment concerning talmudic reasoning is appropriate here: "While the sages of the Talmud seem to be doing battle with each other by means of biblical verses, and to be splitting hairs, they are far from such scholastic exercises. The reference to a biblical verse does not aim at appealing to authority—as some thinkers drawn to rapid conclusions might imagine. Rather, the aim is to refer to a context which allows the level of the discussion to be raised and to make one notice the true import of the data from which the discussion derives its meaning" (Emmanuel Levinas, *Nine Talmudic Readings* [trans. Annette Aronowicz; Bloomington: Indiana University Press, 1990], 21). An aspect of this is noted by Stanley, *Arguing with Scripture*, 182–83.

Bibliography

Aageson, James W. *Written Also for Our Sake: Paul and the Art of Biblical Interpretation*. Louisville: Westminster John Knox, 1993.
Abasciano, Brian. "Diamonds in the Rough: A Reply to Christopher Stanley Concerning the Reader Competency of Paul's Original Audiences." *NovT* 49 (2007): 153–83.
Abrams, M. H. *A Glossary of Literary Terms*. 4th ed. New York: Holt, Rinehart, Winston, 1981.
Achtemeier, Elizabeth. "Typology." *IDBSup*, 926–27.
Achtemeier, Paul J. "*Omne Verbum Sonat*: The New Testament and the Oral Environment of Late Western Antiquity." *JBL* 109 (1990): 3–27.
Agamben, Giorgio. *The Time That Remains: A Commentary on the Letter to the Romans*. Stanford, Calif.: Stanford University Press, 2005.
Alexander, Hanan A. "God as Teacher: Jewish Reflections on a Theology of Pedagogy." *Journal of Beliefs and Values* 22 (2001): 5–17.
Alexander, Loveday. "Ancient Book Production and the Circulation of the Gospels." Pages 71–111 in *The Gospel for All Christians: Rethinking the Gospel Audiences*. Edited by Richard Bauckham. Grand Rapids: Eerdmans, 1998.
———. "The Living Voice: Scepticism towards the Written Word in Early Christian and Graeco-Roman Texts." Pages 221–47 in *The Bible in Three Dimensions*. Edited by David J. A. Clines, Stephen E. Fowl, and Stanley E. Porter. JSOTSup 87. Sheffield: JSOT Press, 1990.
Allen, Amy. *The Power of Feminist Theory: Domination, Resistance, Solidarity*. Boulder, Colo.: Westview, 1999.
———. "Power, Subjectivity, and Agency: Between Arendt and Foucault." *International Journal of Philosophical Studies* 10 (2002): 131–49.
Allison, Dale C. *Resurrecting Jesus: The Earliest Christian Tradition and Its Interpreters*. London: T&T Clark, 2005.
Ando, Clifford. *Imperial Ideology and Provincial Loyalty in the Roman Empire*. Berkeley and Los Angeles: University of California Press, 2000.
Archer, Gleason L., Jr., and Gregory D. Chirichigno. *Old Testament Quotations in the New Testament: A Complete Survey*. Chicago: Moody Press, 1983.

Arendt, Hannah. *Between Past and Future: Six Exercises in Political Thought.* London: Faber & Faber, 1961.

———. *The Human Condition.* Chicago: University of Chicago Press, 1958.

———. *On Violence.* London: Allen Lane, 1970.

Ascough, Richard S. *What Are They Saying about the Formation of Pauline Churches?* New York: Paulist, 1998.

Ashton, John. *The Religion of Paul the Apostle.* New Haven: Yale University Press, 2000.

Atlas, Jay David. "Presupposition." Pages 29–52 in *The Handbook of Pragmatics.* Edited by Laurence R. Horn and Gregory L. Ward. Blackwell Handbooks in Linguistics 16. Malden, Mass.: Blackwell, 2004.

Aune, David E. "Anthropological Duality in the Eschatology of 2 Cor 4:15–5:10." Pages 215–40 in *Paul beyond the Hellenism/Judaism Divide.* Edited by Troels Engberg-Pedersen. Louisville: Westminster John Knox, 2001.

Badiou, Alain. *Saint Paul: The Foundation of Universalism.* Stanford, Calif.: Stanford University Press, 2006.

Barclay, John M. G. *Jews in the Mediterranean Diaspora: From Alexander to Trajan (323 BCE–117 CE).* Berkeley and Los Angeles: University of California Press, 1999.

Bar-Ilan, Meir. "Illiteracy in the Land of Israel in the First Centuries C.E." Pages 46–61 in vol. 2 of *Essays in the Social Scientific Study of Judaism and Jewish Society.* Edited by Simcha Fishbane, Stuart Schoenfeld, and Alain Goldschläger. 2 vols. Hoboken, N.J.: Ktav, 1992.

———. "Writing in Ancient Israel and Early Judaism, Part Two: Scribes and Books in the Late Second Commonwealth and Rabbinic Period." Pages 21–38 in *Mikra: Text, Translation, Reading and Interpretation of the Hebrew Bible in Ancient Judaism and Early Christianity.* Edited by Martin Jan Mulder. CRINT 2.1. Philadelphia: Fortress, 1988.

Barns, Jonathan. "A New Gnomologium: With Some Remarks on Gnomic Anthologies." *CQ* 44 (1950): 126–37.

———. "A New Gnomologium: With Some Remarks on Gnomic Anthologies, II." *CQ* NS 1 (1951): 1–19.

Barr, James. *Old and New in Interpretation: A Study of the Two Testaments.* London: Harper & Row, 1966.

Barrett, C. K. "The Allegory of Abraham, Sarah, and Hagar in the Argument of Galatians." Pages 1–16 in *Rechtfertigung: Festschrift für Ernst Käsemann zum 70. Geburtstag.* Tübingen: Mohr Siebeck, 1976.

———. *A Commentary to the Epistle to the Romans.* London: Harper, 1957.

Bartchy, S. Scott. "'When I'm Weak, I'm Strong': A Pauline Paradox in Cultural Context." Pages 49–60 in *Kultur, Politik, Religion, Sprache-Text.* Vol. 2 of *Kontexte der Schrift: Wolfgang Stegemann zum 60. Geburtstag.* Edited by Christian Strecker. Stuttgart: Kohlhammer, 2005.

Bartsch, Hans-Werner. "Die antisemitischen Gegner des Paulus im Römerbrief." Pages 27–43 in *Antijudaismus im Neuen Testament? Exegetische und systematische Beiträge*. Edited by Willehad Paul Eckert, Nathan Peter Levinson, and Martin Stöhr. Abhandlungen zum christlich-jüdischen Dialog 2. Munich: Kaiser, 1967.

———. "Die historische Situation des Römerbriefes." *SE* 4/TU 102 (1968): 282–91.

Bauckham, Richard. *God Crucified: Monotheism and Christology in the New Testament*. Grand Rapids: Eerdmans, 1999.

———. *Jesus and the Eyewitnesses: The Gospels as Eyewitness Testimony*. Grand Rapids: Eerdmans, 2006.

Baur, F. C. "Über Zweck und Veranlassung des Römerbriefs und die damit zusammenhängenden Verhältnisse der römischen Gemeinde." *Tübinger Zeitschrift für Theologie* 3 (1836): 59–178.

Beale, Gregory K., and D. A. Carson, eds. *Commentary on the New Testament Use of the Old Testament*. Grand Rapids: Baker, 2007.

Beard, Mary, ed. *Literacy in the Roman World*. Journal of Roman Archaeology Supplement Series 3. Ann Arbor: University of Michigan Press, 1991.

Beaugrande, Robert de, and Wolfgang Dressler. *Introduction to Text Linguistics*. London: Longmans, 1981.

Beker, J. Christiaan. "Echoes and Intertextuality: On the Role of Scripture in Paul's Theology." Pages 64–69 in *Paul and the Scriptures of Israel*. Edited by Craig A. Evans and James A. Sanders. SSEJC 1. JSNTSup 83. Sheffield: JSOT Press, 1992.

———. *Paul the Apostle: The Triumph of God in Life and Thought*. Philadelphia: Fortress, 1984.

Belleville, Linda. *Reflections of Glory: Paul's Polemical Use of the Moses-Doxa Tradition in 2 Corinthians 3:1-18*. JSNTSup 52. Sheffield: Sheffield Academic Press, 1991.

Benko, Stephen. "The Edict of Claudius of A.D. 49 and the Instigator Chrestus." *TZ* 25 (1969): 406–18.

Bernstein, Moshe J. "The Contribution of the Qumran Discoveries to the History of Early Biblical Interpretation." Pages 215–38 in *The Idea of Biblical Interpretation: Essays in Honor of James L. Kugel*. Edited by Hindy Najman and Judith H. Newman. JSJSup 83. Leiden: Brill, 2004.

Berrin, Shani. "Qumran Pesharim." Pages 110–33 in *Biblical Interpretation at Qumran*. Edited by Matthias Henze. Studies in the Dead Sea Scrolls and Related Literature. Grand Rapids: Eerdmans, 2005.

Betz, Otto. "Past Events and Last Events in the Qumran Interpretation of History." *World Congress of Jewish Studies* 6 (1977): 27–34.

Bhabha, Homi K. *The Location of Culture*. London: Routledge, 1994.

———. "Postcolonial Criticism." Pages 437–65 in *Redrawing the Boundaries:*

The Transformation of English and American Literary Studies. Edited by Stephen Greenblatt and Giles B. Gunn. New York: Modern Language Association of America, 1992.

Binder, Donald D. *Into the Temple Courts: The Place of Synagogues in the Second Temple Period.* SBLDS 169. Atlanta: Society of Biblical Literature, 1999.

Bloom, Harold. *A Map of Misreading.* New York: Oxford University Press, 1975.

Blumenfeld, Bruno. *The Political Paul: Justice, Democracy, and Kingship in a Hellenistic Framework.* JSNTSup 210. Sheffield: Sheffield Academic Press, 2001.

Boda, Mark J., and Stanley E. Porter. "Literature to the Third Degree: Prophecy in Zechariah 9–14 and the Passion of Christ." Pages 215–54 in *Traduire la Bible Hébraïque/Translating the Hebrew Bible: De la Septante à la Nouvelle Bible Segond/From the Septuagint to the Nouvelle Bible Segond.* Edited by Robert David and Manuel Jinbachian. Montreal: Médiaspaul, 2005.

Boer, Roland. *Marxist Criticism of the Bible.* Sheffield: Sheffield Academic Press, 2003.

Böhl, Eduard. *Die alttestamentlichen Citate im Neuen Testament.* Vienna: Braumüller, 1878.

Bonner, Stanley F. *Education in Ancient Rome: From the Elder Cato to the Younger Pliny.* London: Methuen, 1977.

Bonsirven, Joseph. *Exégèse rabbinique et exégèse paulinienne.* Paris: Beauschesne, 1939.

Booth, Alan D. "The Schooling of Slaves in First-Century Rome." *TAPA* 109 (1979): 11–19.

Borg, Marcus. "A New Context for Romans XIII." *NTS* 19 (1972–73): 205–18.

Botha, Pieter J. J. "Greco-Roman Literacy as Setting for New Testament Writings." *Neot* 26 (1992): 195–215.

———. "The Verbal Art of the Pauline Letters: Rhetoric, Performance and Practice." Pages 409–28 in *Rhetoric and the New Testament: Essays from the 1992 Heidelberg Conference.* Edited by Stanley E. Porter and Thomas H. Olbricht. JSNTSup 90. Sheffield: Sheffield Academic Press, 1993.

Bousset, Wilhelm. *Kyrios Christos: A History of the Belief in Christ from the Beginnings of Christianity to Irenaeus.* Translated by John E. Steely. Nashville: Abingdon, 1970.

Bowman, Alan K. "Literacy in the Roman Empire: Mass and Mode." Pages 119–31 in *Literacy in the Roman World.* Edited by Mary Beard. Journal of Roman Archaeology Supplement Series 3. Ann Arbor: University of Michigan Press, 1991.

Boyarin, Daniel. *Intertextuality and the Reading of Midrash.* Indiana Studies in Biblical Literature. Bloomington: Indiana University Press, 1990.

———. *A Radical Jew: Paul and the Politics of Identity.* Critical Studies in Jewish Literature, Culture, and Society 1. Berkeley and Los Angeles: University of California Press, 1994.

Brändle, Rudolf, and Ekkehard Stegemann. "The Formation of the First 'Christian Congregations' in Rome in the Context of the Jewish Congregations." Pages 117–27 in *Judaism and Christianity in First Century Rome.* Edited by Karl P. Donfried and Peter Richardson. Grand Rapids: Eerdmans, 1998.

Braun, Willi, and Russell T. McCutcheon, eds. *Guide to the Study of Religion.* London: Cassell, 2000.

Brooke, George J. "Biblical Interpretation at Qumran." Pages 287–319 in *Scripture and the Scrolls.* Vol. 1 of *The Bible and the Dead Sea Scrolls.* Edited by James Charlesworth. Waco, Tex.: Baylor University Press, 2006.

———. *The Dead Sea Scrolls and the New Testament.* Minneapolis: Fortress, 2005.

———. *Exegesis at Qumran: 4QFlorilegium in its Jewish Context.* JSOTSup 29. Sheffield: JSOT Press, 1985. Repr., Atlanta: Society of Biblical Literature, 2006.

Brown, Jeannine. *Scripture as Communication: Introducing Biblical Hermeneutics.* Grand Rapids: Baker, 2007.

Bruce, F. F. *The Acts of the Apostles: The Greek Text with Introduction and Commentary.* Grand Rapids: Eerdmans, 1951.

———. *Biblical Exegesis in the Qumran Texts.* London: Tyndale, 1960.

Brunt, Peter A. *Roman Imperial Themes.* Oxford: Clarendon, 1990.

Bultmann, Rudolf. *The Second Letter to the Corinthians.* Translated by Roy A. Harrisville. Minneapolis: Augsburg, 1985.

———. *Theology of the New Testament.* One-volume edition. Translated by Kendrick Grobel. New York: Charles Scribner's Sons, 1955.

Burtchaell, James T. *From Synagogue to Church: Public Services and Offices in the Earliest Christian Communities.* New York: Cambridge University Press, 1992.

Byrne, Brendan. *Romans.* Collegeville, Minn.: Liturgical Press, 1996.

Caird, G. B. *The Language and Imagery of the Bible.* London: Duckworth, 1980.

Cameron, Averil. *Christianity and the Rhetoric of Empire: The Development of Christian Discourse.* Sather Classical Lectures 57. Berkeley and Los Angeles: University of California Press, 1991.

Campbell, Douglas A. *The Deliverance of God: An Apocalyptic Rereading of Justification in Paul.* Grand Rapids: Eerdmans, forthcoming.

———. *The Rhetoric of Righteousness in Romans 3:21–26.* JSNTSup 65. Sheffield: JSOT Press, 1992.

Campbell, John McLeod. *The Nature of the Atonement.* 6th ed. New York: Macmillan, 1886. Repr., Edinburgh: Handsel, 1996.

Campbell, William S. *Paul and the Creation of Christian Identity.* London: T&T Clark, 2006.

———. "Romans iii as a Key to the Structure and Thought of the Letter." *NovT* 23 (1981): 22–40.

Caputo, John D. *The Prayer and Tears of Jacques Derrida: Religion without Religion.* Bloomington: Indiana University Press, 1997.

———, ed. *Deconstruction in a Nutshell: A Conversation with Jacques Derrida.* New York: Fordham University Press, 1997.

Caragounis, Chrys. "From Obscurity to Prominence: The Development of the Roman Church between Romans and 1 Clement." Pages 245–79 in *Judaism and Christianity in First Century Rome.* Edited by Karl P. Donfried and Peter Richardson. Grand Rapids: Eerdmans, 1998.

Carpzov, Johann. *A Defense of the Hebrew Bible.* Translated by Moses Marcus. London: Bernard Lintot, 1729.

Carr, David M. *Writing on the Tablet of the Heart: Origins of Scripture and Literature.* Oxford: Oxford University Press, 2005.

Casson, Lionel. *Libraries in the Ancient World.* New Haven: Yale University Press, 2001.

Castelli, Elizabeth. *Imitating Paul: A Discourse of Power.* Literary Currents in Biblical Interpretation. Louisville: Westminster John Knox, 1991.

Champlin, Edward. *Nero.* Cambridge: Harvard University Press, 2003.

Charlesworth, James H. "Biblical Interpretation: The Crucible of the Pseudepigrapha." Pages 66–78 in *Text and Testimony: Essays on the New Testament and Apocryphal Literature in Honour of A. F. J. Klijn.* Edited by Tjitze Baarda et al. Kampen: Kok, 1988.

———. *The Pesharim and Qumran History: Chaos or Consensus?* Grand Rapids: Eerdmans, 2002.

———. "The Pseudepigrapha as Biblical Exegesis." Pages 139–52 in *Early Jewish and Christian Exegesis: Studies in Memory of William Hugh Brownlee.* Edited by Craig A. Evans and William F. Stinespring. Atlanta: Scholars Press, 1987.

———, ed. *The Old Testament Pseudepigrapha.* 2 vols. New York: Doubleday, 1983.

Chau, Wai-Shing. *The Letter and the Spirit: A History of Interpretation from Origen to Luther.* American University Studies 7/167. New York: Lang, 1995.

Ciampa, Roy E. *The Presence and Function of Scripture in Galatians 1 and 2.* WUNT 2/102. Tübingen: Mohr Siebeck, 1998.

Clark, Donald L. *Rhetoric in Greco-Roman Education.* Morningside Heights, N.Y.: Columbia University Press, 1957.

Clayton, Jay, and Eric Rothstein. "Figures in the Corpus: Theories of Influence and Intertextuality." Pages 3–36 in *Influence and Intertextuality in Literary*

History. Edited by Jay Clayton and Eric Rothstein. Madison: University of Wisconsin Press, 1991.

Clemen, August. *Der Gebrauch des Alten Testaments in den neutestamentlichen Schriften.* Gütersloh: Bertelsman, 1895.

Cohen, Shaye J. D. *The Beginnings of Jewishness: Boundaries, Varieties, Uncertainties.* Berkeley and Los Angeles: University of California Press, 1999.

———. *From the Maccabees to the Mishnah.* LEC. Philadelphia: Westminster, 1987.

———. "Were Pharisees and Rabbis the Leaders of Communal Prayer and Torah Study in Antiquity? The Evidence of the New Testament, Josephus, and the Early Church Fathers." Pages 89–105 in *Evolution of the Synagogue: Problems and Progress.* Edited by Howard Clark Kee and Lynn H. Cohick. Harrisburg, Pa.: Trinity Press International, 1999.

Cole, Susan Guettel. "Could Greek Women Read and Write?" Pages 219–45 in *Reflections of Women in Antiquity.* Edited by Helene P. Foley. New York: Gordon & Breach, 1981.

Collins, John J. *Between Athens and Jerusalem: Jewish Identity in the Hellenistic Diaspora.* 2nd ed. Grand Rapids: Eerdmans, 2000.

Cosgrove, Charles. "The Law Has Given Sarah No Children (Gal 4:21–30)." *NovT* 29 (1987): 219–35.

Cothenet, Édouard. "Prédication et typologie sacramentaire dans la première épître aux Corinthiens (10:1–13)." Pages 107–22 in idem, *Exégèse et Liturgie II.* LD 175. Paris: Cerf, 1999.

Cranfield, C. E. B. *A Critical and Exegetical Commentary on the Epistle to the Romans.* 2 vols. ICC. London: T&T Clark, 1975–1979.

Cremer, Hermann. *Die paulinische Rechtfertigungslehre im Zusammenhange ihrer geschichtlichen Voraussetzungen.* Gütersloh: Bertelsmann, 1899.

Crenshaw, James L. *Education in Ancient Israel: Across the Deadening Silence.* New York: Doubleday, 1998.

Cribiore, Raffaella. *Gymnastics of the Mind: Greek Education in Hellenistic and Roman Egypt.* Princeton: Princeton University Press, 2001.

———. *Writing, Teachers, and Students in Graeco-Roman Egypt.* ASP 36. Atlanta: Scholars Press, 1996.

Crossan, John Dominic, and Jonathan L. Reed. *In Search of Paul: How Jesus's Apostle Opposed Rome's Empire with God's Kingdom. A New Vision of Paul's Words and World.* New York: HarperSanFrancisco, 2004.

Culler, Jonathan. *On Deconstruction.* Ithaca, N.Y.: Cornell University Press, 1982.

Dahl, Nils. "Romans 3:9: Text and Meaning." Pages 184–204 in *Paul and Paulinism: Essays in Honour of C. K. Barrett.* Edited by Morna D. Hooker and Stephen G. Wilson. London: SPCK, 1982.

Daly, Lloyd W. "Roman Study Abroad." *AJP* 71 (1950): 40–58.

Daniélou, Jean. *Sacramentum futuri: Études sur les origines de la typologie biblique.* Paris: Beauchesne, 1950.
Danziger, Marlies K., and W. Stacy Johnson. *An Introduction to the Study of Literature.* Lexington, Mass.: Heath, 1965.
Das, Andrew. *Solving the Romans Debate.* Minneapolis: Fortress, 2007.
Davidson, Harriet. *T. S. Eliot and Hermeneutics: Absence and Presence in The Waste Land.* Baton Rouge: Louisiana State University Press, 1985.
Davies, Philip. "Biblical Interpretation in the Dead Sea Scrolls." Pages 144–66 in *The Ancient Period.* Vol. 1 of *A History of Biblical Interpretation.* Edited by Alan J. Hauser and Duane F. Watson. Grand Rapids: Eerdmans, 2003.
Davies, W. D. *Paul and Rabbinic Judaism: Some Rabbinic Elements in Pauline Theology.* 4th ed. Philadelphia: Fortress, 1980.
Derrida, Jacques. *Acts of Religion.* Edited with an introduction by Gil Anidjar. New York: Routledge, 2002.
———. *Dissemination.* Translated with an introduction and additional notes by Barbara Johnson. Chicago: University of Chicago Press, 1981.
———. *Of Spirit: Heidegger and the Question.* Chicago: University of Chicago Press, 1989.
Dewey, Arthur J. "A Re-hearing of Romans 10:1–15." *Semeia* 65 (1994): 109–27.
Dewey, Joanna. "Textuality in an Oral Culture: A Survey of the Pauline Traditions." *Semeia* 65 (1994): 37–65.
Dimant, Devorah. "Use and Interpretation of Mikra in the Apocrypha and Pseudepigrapha." Pages 379–419 in *Mikra: Text, Translation, Reading and Interpretation of the Hebrew Bible in Ancient Judaism and Early Christianity.* Edited by Martin Jan Mulder. CRINT 2.1. Assen: Van Gorcum, 1988.
DiMattei, Steven. "Paul's Allegory of the Two Covenants (Gal 4:21–31) in Light of First Century Hellenistic Rhetoric and Jewish Hermeneutics." *NTS* 52 (2006): 102–22.
Dochhorn, Jan. "Paulus und die polyglotte Schriftgelehrsamkeit seiner Zeit: Eine Studie zu den exegetischen Hintergründen von Röm. 16.20a." *ZNW* 98 (2007): 189–212.
Döpke, Johan Christian Carl. *Hermeneutik der neutestamentlichen Schriftsteller.* Leipzig: Vogel, 1829.
Donfried, Karl P. "A Short Note on Romans 16." Pages 50–60 in *The Romans Debate.* Edited by Karl P. Donfried. Peabody, Mass.: Hendrickson, 1991.
Dover, Kenneth J. *Lysias and the Corpus Lysiacum.* Berkeley and Los Angeles: University of California Press, 1968.
Drusius, Johannes. *Parallela sacra.* Frankfurt: Aegidium Radacum, 1594.
Duffy, Charles, and Henry Pettit. *A Dictionary of Literary Terms.* Rev. ed. Denver: University of Denver Press, 1952.

Dungan, David L. *Constantine's Bible: Politics and the Making of the New Testament*. Minneapolis: Fortress, 2007.

Dunn, James D. G. "Jesus Tradition in Paul." Pages 155–78 in *Studying the Historical Jesus: Evaluations of the State of Current Research*. Edited by Bruce Chilton and Craig A. Evans. NTTS 19. Leiden: Brill, 1994.

———. *Jews and Christians: The Parting of the Ways, A.D. 70 to 135*. Grand Rapids: Eerdmans, 1992.

———. *Romans*. WBC 38A–B. Dallas: Word, 1988.

———. *The Theology of Paul the Apostle*. Grand Rapids: Eerdmans, 1998.

Easterling, Pat E., and Bernard M. W. Knox. "Books and Readers in the Greek World." Pages 1–41 in *The Cambridge History of Classical Literature. I. Greek Literature*. Edited by Pat E. Easterling and Bernard M. W. Knox. Cambridge: Cambridge University Press, 1989.

Eaton, J. H. *Kingship and the Psalm*. London: SCM, 1976.

Eco, Umberto. *Mouse or Rat? Translation as Negotiation*. London: Phoenix, 2004.

Ehrensperger, Kathy. "'Let Everyone be Convinced in His/Her Own Mind': Derrida and the Deconstruction of Paulinism." Pages 53–73 in *Society of Biblical Literature 2002 Seminar Papers*. SBLSP 41. Atlanta: Scholars Press, 2002.

———. "New Perspectives on Paul: New Perspectives on Romans in Feminist Theology?" Pages 227–55 in *Gender, Tradition and Romans: Shared Ground, Uncertain Borders*. Edited by Cristina Grenholm and Daniel Patte. Romans through History and Culture Series. New York: T&T Clark, 2005.

———. *Paul and the Dynamics of Power: Communication and Interaction in the Early Christ-Movement*. London: T&T Clark, 2007.

———. *That We May Be Mutually Encouraged: Feminism and the New Perspective in Pauline Studies*. New York: T&T Clark, 2004.

Elliott, Neil. *The Arrogance of Nations: Reading Romans in the Shadow of Empire*. Minneapolis: Fortress, 2008.

———. *Liberating Paul: The Justice of God and the Politics of the Apostle*. Bible & Liberation 6. Maryknoll, N.Y.: Orbis, 1994.

———. "The 'Patience of the Jews': Strategies of Resistance and Accommodation to Imperial Cultures." Pages 32–42 in *Pauline Conversations in Context: Essays in Honor of Calvin J. Roetzel*. Edited by Janice Capel Anderson, Philip Sellew, and Claudia Setzer. JSNTSup 221. Sheffield: Sheffield Academic Press, 2002.

———. "Paul and the Politics of the Empire." Pages 17–39 in *Paul and Politics: Ekklesia, Israel, Imperium, Interpretation: Essays in Honour of Krister Stendahl*. Edited by Richard A. Horsley. Harrisburg, Pa.: Trinity Press International, 2000.

———. *The Rhetoric of Romans: Argumentative Constraint and Strategy and Paul's Dialogue with Judaism.* JSNTSup 145. Sheffield: JSOT Press, 1990.

———. "Romans 13:1–7 in the Context of Imperial Propaganda." Pages 196–204 in *Paul and Empire: Religion and Power in Roman Imperial Society.* Edited by Richard A. Horsley. Harrisburg, Pa.: Trinity Press International, 1997.

———. "Strategies of Resistance and Hidden Transcripts in the Pauline Communities." Pages 97–122 in *Hidden Transcripts and the Arts of Resistance: Applying the Work of James C. Scott to Jesus and Paul.* Edited by Richard A. Horsley. SemeiaSt 48. Atlanta: Society of Biblical Literature, 2004.

Ellis, E. Earle. *Paul's Use of the Old Testament.* Edinburgh: Oliver & Boyd, 1957. Repr., Grand Rapids: Baker, 1981.

Engberg-Pedersen, Troels, ed. *Paul beyond the Judaism/Hellenism Divide.* Louisville: Westminster John Knox, 2001.

———. *Paul in His Hellenistic Context.* Minneapolis: Fortress, 1995.

Esler, Philip F. *Conflict and Identity in Romans: The Social Setting of Paul's Letter.* Minneapolis: Fortress Press, 2003.

Fee, Gordon D. *The First Epistle to the Corinthians.* NICNT. Grand Rapids: Eerdmans, 1987.

Feldman, Louis H. *Jew and Gentile in the Ancient World.* Princeton: Princeton University Press, 1993.

Fernández Marcos, Natalio. *The Septuagint in Context.* Leiden: Brill, 2001.

Finlan, Stephen. *The Background and Content of Paul's Cultic Atonement Metaphors.* SBLAcBib 19. Atlanta: Society of Biblical Literature, 2004.

Fiore, Benjamin. *The Function of Personal Example in the Socratic and Pastoral Epistles.* AnBib 105. Rome: Biblical Institute Press, 1986.

Fishbane, Michael. *Biblical Interpretation in Ancient Israel.* Oxford: Clarendon, 1985.

———. *The JPS Bible Commentary: Haftarot.* Philadelphia: Jewish Publication Society, 2002.

Fisk, Bruce N. *Do You Not Remember? Scripture, Story and Exegesis in the Rewritten Bible of Pseudo-Philo.* JSPSup 37. Sheffield: Sheffield Academic Press, 2001.

———. "Paul: Life and Letters." Pages 283–325 in *The Face of New Testament Studies.* Edited by Scot McKnight and Grant Osborne. Grand Rapids: Baker, 2004.

Fitzmyer, Joseph A. "New Testament *Kyrios* and *Maranatha* and Their Aramaic Background." Pages 218–35 in *To Advance the Gospel: New Testament Studies.* 2nd ed. Grand Rapids: Eerdmans, 1998.

———. *Romans: A New Translation with Introduction and Commentary.* AB 33. New York: Doubleday, 1992.

———. "The Semitic Background of the NT *Kyrios*-Title." Pages 115–42 in *The Semitic Background of the New Testament*. Grand Rapids: Eerdmans, 1997.

———. "The Use of Explicit Old Testament Quotations in Qumran Literature and in the New Testament." *NTS* 7 (1960–61): 297–333. Repr. as pages 3–58 in *Essays on the Semitic Background of the New Testament*. London: Chapman, 1971.

Forbes, Clarence A. "Ancient Universities and Student Life." *CJ* 28 (1933): 413–26.

Foucault, Michel. *The Archaeology of Knowledge*. World of Man: A Library of Theory and Research in the Human Sciences. Translated by A. M. Sheridan Smith. London: Tavistock, 1972.

Frankfurter, David. "Violence and Religious Formation: An Afterword." Pages 140–52 in *Violence in the New Testament*. Edited by Shelly Matthews and E. Leigh Gibson. New York: T&T Clark, 2005.

Friedman, Susan Stanford. "Weavings: Intertextuality and the (Re)Birth of the Author." Pages 146–80 in *Influence and Intertextuality in Literary History*. Edited by Jay Clayton and Eric Rothstein. Madison: University of Wisconsin Press, 1991.

Froehlich, Karl. *Biblical Interpretation in the Early Church*. Sources of Early Christian Thought. Philadelphia: Fortress, 1984.

Furnish, Victor Paul. *II Corinthians*. AB 32A. New York: Doubleday, 1984.

Gager, John G. *Kingdom and Community: The Social World of Early Christianity*. Englewood Cliffs, N.J.: Prentice Hall, 1975.

Gager, John G., and E. Leigh Gibson. "Violent Acts and Violent Language in the Apostle Paul." Pages 13–21 in *Violence in the New Testament*. Edited by Shelly Matthews and E. Leigh Gibson. New York: T&T Clark, 2005.

Gagnon, Robert A. J. "Why the 'Weak' at Rome Cannot Be Non-Christian Jews." *CBQ* 62 (2000): 64–82.

Galinsky, Karl. *Augustan Culture*. Princeton: Princeton University Press, 1998.

Gamble, Harry Y. *Books and Readers in the Early Church: A History of Early Christian Texts*. New Haven: Yale University Press, 1995.

Garnsey, Peter, and Richard Saller. *The Roman Empire: Economy, Society, and Culture*. Berkeley and Los Angeles: University of California Press, 1987.

Gavrilov, A. K. "Techniques of Reading in Classical Antiquity." *CQ* NS 47 (1997): 56–73.

Gerhardsson, Birger. *Memory and Manuscript: Oral Tradition and Written Transmission in Rabbinic Judaism and Early Christianity, with Tradition and Transmission in Early Christianity*. Lund: Gleerup, 1961. Repr., Grand Rapids: Eerdmans, 1998.

Gilliard, Frank D. "More Silent Reading in Antiquity: *Non Omne Verbum Sonabat.*" *JBL* 112 (1993): 689–94.
Given, Mark D. "On His Majesty's Secret Service: The Undercover Ethos of Paul." Pages 196–213 in *Rhetoric, Ethic, and Moral Persuasion in Biblical Discourse*. Edited by Thomas H. Olbricht and Anders Eriksson. ESEC 11. New York: T&T Clark, 2005.

———. *Paul's True Rhetoric: Ambiguity, Cunning and Deception in Greece and Rome*. ESEC 7. Harrisburg, Pa.: Trinity Press International, 2001.
Gombis, Timothy G. "Ephesians 2 as a Narrative of Divine Warfare." *JSNT* 26 (2004): 403–18.
Goodenough, Erwin R. *An Introduction to Philo Judaeus*. 2nd ed. Oxford: Blackwell, 1962.

———. "The Political Philosophy of Hellenistic Kingship." *YCS* 1 (1928): 55–102.
Goodspeed, Edgar J. "Phoebe's Letter of Introduction," *HTR* 44 (1951): 55–57.
Goppelt, Leonhard. *Typos: The Typological Interpretation of the Old Testament in the New*. Translated by Donald Madvig. Grand Rapids: Eerdmans, 1982.
Graham, William A. *Beyond the Written Word: Oral Aspects of Scripture in the History of Religion*. Cambridge: Cambridge University Press, 1987.
Greene, Thomas M. *The Light in Troy: Imitation and Discovery in Renaissance Poetry*. New Haven: Yale University Press, 1982.
Greenspoon, Leonard. "The Use and Abuse of the Term 'LXX' and Related Terminology in Recent Scholarship." *BIOSCS* 20 (1987): 21–29.
Grieb, A. Katherine. *The Story of Romans: A Narrative Defense of God's Righteousness*. Louisville: Westminster John Knox, 2002.
Guillet, Jean. "Les exégèses d'Alexandrie et d'Antioche: Conflit ou malentendu?" *RSR* 34 (1947): 257–302.
Guinot, Jean-Noël. "L'école exégétique d'Antioche et ses relations avec Origène." Pages 1149–66 in *Origeniana octava: Origen and the Alexandrian Tradition*. Edited by Lorenzo Perrone in collaboration with P. Bernardino and D. Marchini. Leuven: Leuven University Press, 2003.

———. "La typologie comme technique herméneutique." Pages 1–34 in *Figures de l'Ancien Testament chez les Pères*. Cahiers de Biblia Patristica 2. Strasbourg: Palais Universitaire, 1989.
Haacker, Klaus. *Der Brief des Paulus an die Römer*. THKNT 6. Leipzig: Evangelische Verlagsantsalt, 1999.
Habermas, Jürgen. "Hannah Arendt's Communications Concept of Power." *Social Research* 44 (1977): 3–24.
Haenchen, Ernst. "The Book of Acts as Source Material for the History of Early Christianity." Pages 258–78 in *Studies in Luke-Acts*. Edited by Leander Keck and J. Louis Martyn. Philadelphia: Fortress, 1980.

Hafemann, Scott. *Paul, Moses, and the History of Israel: The Letter/Spirit Contrast and the Argument from Scripture in 2 Corinthians 3*. Tübingen: Mohr Siebeck, 2005.

Hanson, Anthony Tyrrell. *Studies in Paul's Technique and Theology*. Grand Rapids: Eerdmans, 1974.

Harris, Murray J. *The Second Epistle to the Corinthians: A Commentary on the Greek Text*. NIGTC. Grand Rapids: Eerdmans, 2005.

Harris, William V. *Ancient Literacy*. Cambridge: Harvard University Press, 1989.

Havelock, Eric. *The Literate Revolution in Greece and Its Cultural Consequences*. Princeton: Princeton University Press, 1982.

———. *The Muse Learns to Write: Reflection on Orality and Literacy*. New Haven: Yale University Press, 1986.

Hays, Richard B. "Christ Prays the Psalms: Paul's Use of an Early Christian Exegetical Convention." Pages 122–36 in *The Future of Christology: Essays in Honor of Leander E. Keck*. Edited by Abraham J. Malherbe and Wayne A. Meeks. Minneapolis: Fortress, 1993.

———. *The Conversion of the Imagination: Paul as Interpreter of Israel's Scripture*. Grand Rapids: Eerdmans, 2005.

———. *Echoes of Scripture in the Letters of Paul*. New Haven: Yale University Press, 1989.

———. *The Faith of Jesus Christ: The Narrative Substructure of Galatians 3:1–4:11*. 2nd ed. Grand Rapids: Eerdmans, 2002.

———. *First Corinthians*. IBC. Louisville: John Knox, 1997.

———. "On the Rebound: A Response to Critiques of *Echoes of Scripture in the Letters of Paul*." Pages 70–96 in *Paul and the Scriptures of Israel*. Edited by Craig A. Evans and James A. Sanders. JSNTSup 83. Sheffield: Sheffield Academic Press, 1993.

———. "Psalm 143 and the Logic of Romans 3." *JBL* 99 (1980): 107–15.

———. "'The Righteous One' as Eschatological Deliverer: A Case Study in Paul's Apocalyptic Hermeneutics." Pages 191–215 in *Apocalyptic and the New Testament: Essays in Honor of J. Louis Martyn*. Edited by Joel Marcus and Marion L. Soards. JSNTSup 24. Sheffield: JSOT Press, 1988.

Hebel, Udo J., ed. *Intertextuality, Allusion, and Quotation: An International Bibliography of Critical Studies*. Bibliographies and Indexes in World Literature 18. New York: Greenwood, 1989.

Heil, John Paul. *Paul's Letter to the Romans: A Reader-Response Commentary*. New York: Paulist, 1987.

———. *The Rhetorical Role of Scripture in 1 Corinthians*. SBLSBL 15. Atlanta: Society of Biblical Literature; Leiden: Brill, 2005.

Hengel, Martin. "Christological Titles in Early Christianity." Pages 425–48 in

The Messiah: Developments in Earliest Judaism and Christianity. Edited by James H. Charlesworth. Minneapolis: Fortress, 1992.

———. *Judaism and Hellenism.* 2 vols. Translated by John Bowden. Philadelphia: Fortress, 1974.

———. "Proseuche und Synagoge." Pages 27–54 in *The Synagogue: Studies in Origin, Archaeology and Architecture.* Edited by Joseph Gutmann. New York: Ktav, 1975.

———. *Studies in Early Christology.* Edinburgh: T&T Clark, 1995.

Hezser, Catherine. *Jewish Literacy in Roman Palestine.* TSAJ 81. Tübingen: Mohr Siebeck, 2001.

Hock, Ronald F. "The Educational Curriculum in Chariton's *Callirhoe.*" Pages 15–36 in *Ancient Fiction: The Matrix of Early Christian and Jewish Narrative.* Edited by Jo-Ann A. Brant, Charles W. Hedrick, and Chris Shea. SBLSymS 32. Atlanta: Society of Biblical Literature, 2005.

Hock, Ronald F., and Edward N. O'Neil. *The Chreia and Ancient Rhetoric: Classroom Exercises.* SBLWGRW 2. Atlanta: Society of Biblical Literature, 2002.

———. *The Chreia in Ancient Rhetoric: The Progymnasmata.* SBLTT 27. Atlanta: Scholars Press, 1986.

Hodgson, R. "The Testimony Hypothesis." *JBL* 98 (1979): 361–78.

Hogeterp, Albert L. A. *Paul and God's Temple: A Historical Interpretation of Cultic Imagery in the Corinthian Correspondence.* Leuven: Peeters, 2006.

Hollander, John. *The Figure of Echo: A Mode of Allusion in Milton and After.* Berkeley and Los Angeles: University of California Press, 1981.

Holman, C. Hugh. *A Handbook to Literature.* 4th ed. Indianapolis: Bobbs-Merrill, 1980.

Hooks, Bell. *Yearning: Race, Gender, and Cultural Politics.* Boston: South End Press, 1990.

Hopkins, Keith. "Conquest by Book." Pages 133–58 in *Literacy in the Roman World.* Edited by Mary Beard. Journal of Roman Archaeology Supplement Series 3. Ann Arbor: University of Michigan Press, 1991.

Horsley, Richard A. "1 Corinthians: A Case Study of Paul's Assembly as an Alternative Society." Pages 242–52 in *Paul and Empire: Religion and Power in Roman Imperial Society.* Edited by Richard A. Horsley. Harrisburg, Pa.: Trinity Press International, 1997.

———. "Introduction." Pages 1–23 in *Paul and the Roman Imperial Order.* Edited by Richard A. Horsley. Harrisburg, Pa.: Trinity Press International, 2004.

———. *Scribes, Visionaries, and the Politics of Second Temple Judea.* Louisville: Westminster John Knox, 2007.

———, ed. *Paul and Empire: Religion and Power in Roman Imperial Society.* Harrisburg, Pa.: Trinity Press International, 1997.

Horst, Pieter W. van der. "Was the Synagogue a Place of Sabbath Worship before 70 CE?" Pages 18–43 in *Jews, Christians, and Polytheists in the Ancient Synagogue*. Edited by Steven Fine. New York: Routledge, 1999.

Howell, Evelyn B. "St Paul and the Greek World." *Greece & Rome* 2/11 (1964): 7–29.

Hübner, Hans. *Corpus Paulinum*. Vol. 2 of *Vetus Testamentum in Novo*. Göttingen: Vandenhoeck & Ruprecht, 1997.

———. *Die Theologie des Paulus*. Vol. 2 of *Biblische Theologie des Neuen Testaments*. Göttingen: Vandenhoeck & Ruprecht, 1993.

Hughes, Philip E. *Paul's Second Epistle to the Corinthians*. NICNT. Grand Rapids: Eerdmans, 1962.

Huizenga, Leroy. "The Akedah in Matthew." Ph.D. diss., Duke University, 2006.

Hurtado, Larry W. *Lord Jesus Christ: Devotion to Jesus in Earliest Christianity*. Grand Rapids: Eerdmans, 2003.

———. *One God, One Lord: Early Christian Devotion and Ancient Jewish Monotheism*. 2nd ed. London: T&T Clark, 1998.

Hvalvik, Reidar. "Jewish Believers and Jewish Influence in the Roman Church until the Early Second Century." Pages 179–216 in *Jewish Believers in Jesus: The Early Centuries*. Edited by Oskar Skarsaune and Reidar Hvalvik. Peabody, Mass.: Hendrickson, 2007.

Ingraffia, Brian D. *Postmodern Theory and Biblical Theology: Vanquishing God's Shadow*. Cambridge: Cambridge University Press, 1995.

Instone-Brewer, David. *Techniques and Assumptions in Jewish Exegesis before 70 CE*. Tübingen: Mohr Siebeck, 1992.

Iser, Wolfgang. *The Act of Reading: A Theory of Aesthetic Response*. Baltimore: Johns Hopkins University Press, 1978.

Jaffee, Martin S. "The Oral-Cultural Context of the Talmud Yerushalmi: Greco-Roman Paideia, Discipleship and the Concept of Oral Torah." Pages 27–73 in *Transmitting Jewish Traditions: Orality, Textuality, and Cultural Diffusion*. Edited by Yaakov Elman and Israel Gershoni. New Haven: Yale University Press, 2000.

Jameson, Fredric. *Political Unconscious: Narrative as a Socially Symbolic Act*. Ithaca, N.Y.: Cornell University Press, 1981.

Jeffers, James S. "Jewish and Christian Families in First-Century Rome." Pages 128–50 in *Judaism and Christianity in First Century Rome*. Edited by Karl P. Donfried and Peter Richardson. Grand Rapids: Eerdmans, 1998.

Jennings, Theodore W., Jr. *Reading Derrida/Thinking Paul: On Justice*. Cultural Memory in the Present. Stanford, Calif.: Stanford University Press, 2006.

Jewett, Robert. *Romans: A Commentary*. Hermeneia. Minneapolis: Fortress, 2007.

Jobes, Karen H., and Moisés Silva. *Invitation to the Septuagint*. Grand Rapids: Baker, 2000.
Johnson, Luke T. *Reading Romans: A Literary and Theological Commentary*. New York: Crossroad, 1997.
Johnson, Mark, and George Lakoff. *Metaphors We Live By*. 2nd ed. Chicago: University of Chicago Press, 2003.
Judge E. A., and G. S. R. Thomas. "The Origin of the Church at Rome: A New Solution?" *RTR* 25 (1966): 81–94.
Juel, Donald H. "Interpreting Israel's Scriptures in the New Testament." Pages 283–303 in *The Ancient Period*. Vol. 1 of *A History of Biblical Interpretation*. Edited by Alan J. Hauser and Duane F. Watson. Grand Rapids: Eerdmans, 2003.

———. *Messianic Exegesis: Christological Interpretation of the Old Testament in Early Christianity*. New ed. Minneapolis: Augsburg Fortress, 1998.
Juhl, Peter D. *Interpretation: An Essay in the Philosophy of Literary Criticism*. Princeton: Princeton University Press, 1980.
Junius, Franciscus. *Sacrorum parallelorum libri tres*. London: Bishop, 1590.
Käsemann, Ernst. "The Righteousness of God in Paul." Pages 168–82 in *New Testament Questions of Today*. London: SCM, 1969.
Kahl, Brigitte. "No Longer Male: Masculinity's Struggles behind Galatians 3.28?" *JSNT* 79 (2000): 37–49.
Kaiser, Walter C. *The Uses of the Old Testament in the New*. Chicago: Moody Press, 1985.
Kaster, Robert A. "Notes on 'Primary' and 'Secondary' Schools in Late Antiquity." *TAPA* 113 (1983): 323–46.
Keesmaat, Sylvia. "Exodus and the Intertextual Transformation of Tradition in Romans 8.14–30." *JSNT* 54 (1994): 29–56.

———. *Paul and His Story: (Re)Interpreting the Exodus Tradition*. JSNTSup 181. Sheffield: Sheffield Academic Press, 1999.
Kelber, Werner. *The Oral and the Written Gospel: The Hermeneutics of Speaking and Writing in the Synoptic Tradition, Mark, Paul and Q*. Philadelphia: Fortress, 1983.
Kennedy, George A. *Progymnasmata: Greek Textbooks of Prose Composition and Rhetoric*. SBLWGRW 10. Atlanta: Society of Biblical Literature, 2003.
Kenyon, Frederic G. *Books and Readers in Ancient Greece and Rome*. Oxford: Clarendon, 1932.
Kirk, J. R. Daniel. *Unlocking Romans: Resurrection and the Justification of God*. Grand Rapids: Eerdmans, 2008.
Kittredge, Cynthia Briggs. *Community and Authority: The Rhetoric of Obedience in the Pauline Tradition*. HTS 45. Harrisburg, Pa.: Trinity Press International, 1998.

———. "Reconstructing 'Resistance' or Reading to Resist: James C. Scott and the Politics of Interpretation." Pages 145–55 in *Hidden Transcripts and the Arts of Resistance*. Edited by Richard A. Horsley. SemeiaSt 48. Atlanta: Society of Biblical Literature, 2004.

Klauck, Hans-Josef. *Ancient Letters and the New Testament: A Guide to Context and Exegesis*. Waco, Tex.: Baylor University Press, 2006.

Koch, Dietrich-Alex. *Die Schrift als Zeuge des Evangeliums: Untersuchungen zur Verwendung und zum Verständnis der Schrift bei Paulus*. BHT 69. Tübingen: Mohr Siebeck, 1986.

Kraabel, A. Thomas. "Unity and Diversity among Diaspora Synagogues." Pages 49–60 in *The Synagogue in Late Antiquity*. Edited by Lee I. Levine. Philadelphia: American Schools of Oriental Research, 1987.

Kraemer, David. "The Formation of Rabbinic Canon: Authority and Boundaries." *JBL* 110 (1991): 613–30.

Kraus, Thomas J. *Ad Fontes: Original Manuscripts and Their Significance for Studying Early Christianity—Selected Essays*. TENTS 3. Leiden: Brill, 2007.

———. "Eine vertragsrechtliche Verpflichtung in Phlm 19. Duktus und juristischer Hintergrund." Pp. 187–200 in *Steht nicht geschrieben? Studien zur Bibel und ihrer Wirkungsgeschichte: Festschrift für Georg Schmuttermayr*. Edited by Johannes Frühwald-König et al. Regensburg: Pustet, 2001.

Kristeva, Julia. *Desire in Language: A Semiotic Approach to Literature and Art*. New York: Columbia University Press, 1980.

Kugel, James L. *The Bible as It Was*. Cambridge: Harvard University Press, 1997.

Kugel, James L., and Rowan Greer. *Early Biblical Interpretation*. LEC 3. Philadelphia: Westminster, 1986.

Lakoff, George. *Moral Politics: How Liberals and Conservatives Think*. 2nd ed. Chicago: University of Chicago Press, 2001.

Lambrecht, Jan. *Second Corinthians*. Collegeville, Minn.: Liturgical Press, 1999.

Lampe, G. W. H., and K. J. Woollcombe, eds. *Essays on Typology*. Naperville, Ill.: Allenson, 1957.

Lampe, Peter. *From Paul to Valentinus: Christians at Rome in the First Two Centuries*. Translated by Michael Steinhauser. Minneapolis: Fortress, 2003.

———. "The Roman Christians of Romans 16." Pages 216–30 in *The Romans Debate*. Edited by Karl P. Donfried. Peabody, Mass.: Hendrickson, 1991.

Lane, William L. "Social Perspectives on Roman Christianity during the Formative Years from Nero to Nerva: Romans, Hebrews, 1 Clement." Pages 196–244 in *Judaism and Christianity in First Century Rome*. Edited by Karl P. Donfried and Peter Richardson. Grand Rapids: Eerdmans, 1998.

Le Boulluec, Alain. *La notion d'hérésie dans la littérature grecque, IIe–IIIe siècles*. 2 vols. Paris: Études Augustiniennes, 1985.

Légasse, Simon. *L'épître de Paul aux Romains*. Paris: Cerf, 2002.

Leithart, Peter. "Justification as Verdict and Deliverance: A Biblical Perspective." *ProEccl* 16 (2007): 56–72.

Lenski, Gerhard E. *Power and Privilege: A Theory of Social Stratification*. New York: McGraw-Hill, 1966.

Leon, Harry J. *The Jews of Ancient Rome*. Philadelphia: Jewish Publication Society, 1960.

Levinas, Emmanuel. *Nine Talmudic Readings*. Translated by Annette Aronowicz. Bloomington: Indiana University Press, 1990.

Levine, Lee I. *The Ancient Synagogue: The First Thousand Years*. 2nd ed. New Haven: Yale University Press, 2005.

———. "The Second Temple Synagogue: The Formative Years." Pages 7–31 in *The Synagogue in Late Antiquity*. Edited by Lee I. Levine. Philadelphia: American Schools of Oriental Research, 1987.

Lieu, Judith M. "Do God-Fearers Make Good Christians?" Pages 329–45 in *Crossing the Boundaries: Essays in Biblical Interpretation in Honour of Michael D. Goulder*. Edited by Stanley E. Porter, Paul Joyce, and David E. Orton. Biblical Interpretation Series 8. Leiden: Brill, 1994.

Lim, Timothy. *Holy Scripture in the Qumran Commentaries and the Pauline Letters*. Oxford: Clarendon, 1997.

———. "Midrash Pesher in the Pauline Letters." Pages 280–91 in *The Scrolls and the Scriptures: Qumran Fifty Years After*. Edited by Stanley E. Porter and Craig A. Evans. JSPSup 26. Sheffield: Sheffield Academic Press, 1997.

Lodge, John G. *Romans 9–11: A Reader-Response Analysis*. University of South Florida International Studies in Formative Christianity and Judaism 6. Atlanta: Scholars Press, 1996.

Longenecker, Richard N. *Biblical Exegesis in the Apostolic Period*. Grand Rapids: Eerdmans, 1974.

Lüdemann, Gerd. *Paul, Apostle to the Gentiles: Studies in Chronology*. Philadelphia: Fortress, 1984.

Lukes, Steven. *Power: A Radical View*. 2nd ed. Oxford: Blackwell, 2005.

Luther, Martin. *A Commentary on St. Paul's Epistle to the Galatians*. Edited and translated by Philip S. Watson. London: Clarke, 1953.

Malherbe, Abraham, J. *Ancient Epistolary Theorists*. SBLSBS 19. Atlanta: Scholars Press, 1988.

———. *The Letters to the Thessalonians*. AB 32B. New York: Doubleday, 2000.

Manson, T. W. "St. Paul's Letter to the Romans—And Others." Pages 225–41 in *Studies in the Gospels and Epistles*. Edited by Matthew Black. Manchester: Manchester University Press, 1962.

Marrou, H. I. *A History of Education in Antiquity*. Translated by George Lamb. London: Sheed & Ward, 1956.

Marshall, I. Howard. "An Assessment of Recent Developments." Pages 1–21 in *It Is Written—Scripture Citing Scripture: Essays in Honour of Barnabas Lindars*. Edited by D. A. Carson and H. G. M. Williamson. Cambridge: Cambridge University Press, 1988.

Martin, Dale B. *The Corinthian Body*. New Haven: Yale University Press, 1995.

———. *Sex and the Single Savior*. Louisville: Westminster John Knox, 2006.

Martin, Ralph P. *2 Corinthians*. WBC 40. Waco, Tex.: Word, 1986.

Martyn, J. Louis. "The Textual Contradiction between Habakkuk 2:4 and Leviticus 18:5." Pages 183–208 in *Theological Issues in the Letters of Paul*. Nashville: Abingdon, 1997.

Mason, Steve. "'For I Am Not Ashamed of the Gospel' (Rom 1.16): The Gospel and the First Readers of Romans." Pages 254–87 in *Gospel in Paul: Studies on Corinthians, Galatians and Romans for Richard N. Longenecker*. Edited by L. Ann Jervis and Peter Richardson. JSNTSup 108. Sheffield: JSOT Press, 1994.

Mays, James Luther. *The Lord Reigns: A Theological Handbook to the Psalms*. Louisville: Westminster John Knox, 1994.

McCant, Jerry W. *2 Corinthians*. Readings: A New Biblical Commentary. Sheffield: Sheffield Academic Press, 1999.

McDonald, Lee Martin, and Stanley E. Porter. *Early Christianity and Its Sacred Literature*. Peabody, Mass.: Hendrickson, 2000.

McLay, R. Timothy. *The Use of the Septuagint in New Testament Research*. Grand Rapids: Eerdmans, 2003.

Meeks, Wayne A. "'And They Rose Up to Play': Midrash and Paraenesis in 1 Corinthians 10:1–22." *JSNT* 16 (1982): 64–78.

———. *The First Urban Christians: The Social World of the Apostle Paul*. New Haven: Yale University Press, 1983.

———. *The Origins of Christian Morality: The First Two Centuries*. New Haven: Yale University Press, 1993.

Meggitt, Justin J. *Paul, Poverty, and Survival*. Studies of the New Testament and Its World. Edinburgh: T&T Clark, 1998.

Metzger, Bruce M. "Literary Forgeries and Canonical Pseudepigrapha." *JBL* 91 (1972): 3–24.

Michel, Otto. *Paulus und seine Bibel*. Gütersloh: Bertelsman, 1929. Repr., Darmstadt: Wissenschaftliche Buchgesellschaft, 1972.

Middleton, J. Richard. *The Liberating Image: The* Imago Dei *in Genesis 1*. Grand Rapids: Brazos, 2005.

Millar, Fergus. *The Emperor in the Roman World (31 BC–AD 337)*. London: Duckworth, 1977.

Millard, Alan. *Reading and Writing in the Time of Jesus*. Biblical Seminar 69. Sheffield: Sheffield Academic Press, 2000.

Miller, Merrill. "Targum, Midrash, and the Use of the Old Testament in the New Testament." *JSJ* 2 (1971): 64–78.

Mitchell, Margaret M. *Paul and the Rhetoric of Reconciliation: An Exegetical Investigation of the Language and Composition of 1 Corinthians*. Louisville: Westminster John Knox, 1992.

Moo, Douglas J. "The Christology of the Early Pauline Letters." Pages 169–92 in *Contours of Christology in the New Testament*. Edited by Richard N. Longenecker. McMaster New Testament Studies. Grand Rapids: Eerdmans, 2005.

———. *The Epistle to the Romans*. NICNT. Grand Rapids: Eerdmans, 1996.

Moore, Stephen D. *Empire and Apocalypse: Postcolonialism and the New Testament*. The Bible in the Modern World 12. Sheffield: Sheffield Phoenix, 2006.

Moore, Stephen D., and Fernando F. Segovia, eds. *Postcolonial Biblical Criticism: Interdisciplinary Intersections*. Bible and Postcolonialism. London: T&T Clark, 2005.

Morgan, Robert. *Romans*. NTG. Sheffield: Sheffield Academic Press, 1995.

Morgan, Teresa. *Literate Education in the Hellenistic and Roman Worlds*. Cambridge: Cambridge University Press, 1998.

Morgan, Thaïs E. "Is There an Intertext in This Text? Literary and Interdisciplinary Approaches to Intertextuality." *American Journal of Semiotics* 3/4 (1985): 1–40.

Moyise, Steve. "The Catena of Rom. 3:10–18." *ExpTim* 106 (1995): 367–70.

———. *Evoking Scripture: Seeing the Old Testament in the New*. London: T&T Clark, 2008.

Müller, Mogens. "Hebraica Sive Graeca Veritas: The Jewish Bible at the Time of the New Testament and the Christian Bible." *SJOT* 2 (1989): 55–71.

———. "The Septuagint as the Bible of the New Testament Church." *SJOT* 7 (1993): 194–207.

Murphy-O'Connor, Jerome. *Paul: A Critical Life*. New York: Oxford University Press, 1996.

Najman, Hindy. *Seconding Sinai: The Development of Mosaic Discourse in Second Temple Judaism*. JSJSup 77. Leiden: Brill, 2003.

———. "The Symbolic Significance of Writing in Ancient Judaism." Pages 139–73 in *The Idea of Biblical Interpretation: Essays in Honor of James L. Kugel*. Edited by Hindy Najman and Judith H. Newman. JSJSup 83. Leiden: Brill, 2004.

Nanos, Mark D. "The Jewish Context of the Gentile Audience Addressed in Paul's Letter to the Romans." *CBQ* 61 (1999): 283–304.

———. *The Mystery of Romans*. Minneapolis: Fortress, 1996.

———. "A Rejoinder to Robert A. J. Gagnon's 'Why the "Weak" at Rome Cannot Be Non-Christian Jews.'" Online: http://www.marknanos.com/Gagnon-rejoinder-6-20-03.pdf.

———. "What Does 'Present Jerusalem' (Gal 4:25) in Paul's Allegory Have to Do with the Jerusalem of Paul's Time, or the Concerns of the Galatians?" Paper presented at the annual meeting of the Central States Region of the SBL. St. Louis, March 2004.

Nicole, Roger. "The New Testament Use of the Old Testament." Pages 135–51 in *Revelation and the Bible: Contemporary Evangelical Thought*. Edited by Carl F. H. Henry. Grand Rapids: Baker, 1958.

O'Neill, J. C. *Romans*. London: Penguin, 1975.

Olbricht, Thomas H. "Delivery and Memory." Pages 159–78 in *Handbook of Classical Rhetoric in the Hellenistic Period 330 B.C.–A.D. 400*. Edited by Stanley E. Porter. Leiden: Brill, 1997.

Olsson, Birger, and Magnus Zetterholm, eds. *The Ancient Synagogue: From Its Origins until 200 C.E.* Stockholm: Almqvist & Wiksell, 2003.

Osborne, Grant R. *The Hermeneutical Spiral: A Comprehensive Introduction to Biblical Interpretation*. 2nd ed. Downers Grove, Ill.: InterVarsity Press, 2006.

Ostmeyer, Karl-Heinrich. "Typologie und Typos: Analyse eines schwierigen Verhältnisses." *NTS* 46 (2000): 112–31.

Overman, J. Andrew, and Robert S. MacLennan, eds. *Diaspora Jews and Judaism: Essays in Honor of, and in Dialogue with, A. Thomas Kraabel*. SFSHJ 41. Atlanta: Scholars Press, 1992.

Parenti, Michael. *The Assassination of Julius Caesar: A People's History of Ancient Rome*. New York: New Press, 2003.

Patte, Daniel. *Early Jewish Hermeneutic in Palestine*. SBLDS 22. Missoula, Mont.: Scholars Press, 1975.

Perelman, Chaim, and Lucie Olbrechts-Tyteca. *The New Rhetoric: A Treatise on Argumentation*. Translated by John Wilkinson and Purcell Weaver. Notre Dame, Ind.: University of Notre Dame Press, 1969.

Perkins, Pheme. *Reading the New Testament: An Introduction*. Rev. ed. Mahwah, N.J.: Paulist, 1988.

Perri, Carmela. "On Alluding." *Poetics* 7 (1978): 289–307.

Perrot, Charles. *La lecture de la Bible dans la synagogue: Les anciennes lectures palestiniennes du Shabbat et des fêtes*. Hildesheim: Gerstenberg, 1973.

———. "The Reading of the Bible in the Ancient Synagogue." Pages 137–59 in *Mikra: Text, Translation, Reading and Interpretation of the Hebrew Bible in Ancient Judaism and Early Christianity*. Edited by Martin Jan Mulder. CRINT 2.1. Assen: Van Gorcum, 1988.

Pietersma, Albert, and Benjamin G. Wright, eds. *A New English Translation of the Septuagint and the Other Greek Translations Traditionally Included under That Title.* New York: Oxford University Press, 2007.

Polaski, Sharon H. *Paul and the Discourse of Power.* Gender, Culture, Theory 8. Sheffield: Sheffield Academic Press, 1999.

Porter, Stanley E. "Further Comments on the Use of the Old Testament in the New Testament." Pages 98–110 in *The Intertextuality of the Epistles: Explorations of Theory and Practice.* Edited by Thomas L. Brodie, Dennis R. MacDonald, and Stanley E. Porter. New Testament Monographs 16. Sheffield: Sheffield Phoenix, 2006.

———. "Paul and the Process of Canonization." In *Exploring the Origins of the Bible.* Edited by Craig A. Evans and Emanuel Tov. Grand Rapids: Baker, 2008.

———. *The Paul of Acts: Essays in Literary Criticism, Rhetoric, and Theology.* WUNT 115. Tübingen: Mohr Siebeck, 1999.

———. "Paul of Tarsus and His Letters." Pages 532–85 in *Handbook of Classical Rhetoric in the Hellenistic Period 330 B.C.–A.D. 400.* Edited by Stanley E. Porter. Leiden: Brill, 1997.

———. "The Reasons for the Lukan Census." Pages 165–88 in *Paul, Luke, and the Graeco-Roman World: Essays in Honour of Alexander J. M. Wedderburn.* Edited by Alf Christophersen, Carsten Claussen, Jörg Frey, and Bruce W. Longenecker. JSNTSup 217. Sheffield: Sheffield Academic Press, 2002.

———. "The Theoretical Justification for Application of Rhetorical Categories to Pauline Epistolary Literature." Pages 100–122 in *Rhetoric and the New Testament: Essays from the 1992 Heidelberg Conference.* Edited by Stanley E. Porter and Thomas H. Olbricht. JSNTSup 90. Sheffield: JSOT Press, 1993.

———. "The Use of the Old Testament in the New Testament: A Brief Comment on Method and Terminology." Pages 79–96 in *Early Christian Interpretation of the Scriptures of Israel: Investigations and Proposals.* Edited by Craig A. Evans and James A. Sanders. SSEJC 5. JSNTSup 148. Sheffield: Sheffield Academic Press, 1997.

Price, S. R. F. "Response." Pages 175–83 in *Paul and the Roman Imperial Order.* Edited by Richard A. Horsley. Harrisburg, Pa.: Trinity Press International, 2004.

———. "Rituals and Power." Pages 47–71 in *Paul and Empire: Religion and Power in Roman Imperial Society.* Edited by Richard A. Horsley. Harrisburg, Pa.: Trinity Press International, 1997.

———. *Rituals and Power: The Roman Imperial Cult in Asia Minor.* Cambridge: Cambridge University Press, 1984.

Prigent, Pierre, trans. *Épître de Barnabé.* SC 172. Paris: Cerf, 1971.

Punt, Jeremy. "Postcolonial Biblical Criticism in South Africa: Some Mind and Road Mapping." *Neot* 37 (2003): 59–85.
Rad, Gerhard von. *The Message of the Prophets*. New York: Harper & Row, 1965.
Randolph, Thomas. *The Prophecies and Other Texts Cited in the New Testament*. Oxford: Fletcher, 1782.
Rendtorff, Rolf. *The Canonical Hebrew Bible: A Theology of the Old Testament*. Leiden: Deo, 2005.
Renner, Timothy. "Three New Homerica on Papyrus." *HSCP* 83 (1979): 311–37.
Richardson, Peter. "Augustan-Era Synagogues in Rome." Pages 17–29 in *Judaism and Christianity in First Century Rome*. Edited by Karl P. Donfried and Peter Richardson. Grand Rapids: Eerdmans, 1998.
Rieger, Jörg. *Christ and Empire: From Paul to Postcolonial Times*. Minneapolis: Fortress, 2007.
Riesner, Rainer. *Paul's Early Period: Chronology, Mission Strategy, Theology*. Grand Rapids: Eerdmans, 1998.
Robbins, Vernon K. "Oral, Rhetorical and Literary Cultures: A Response." *Semeia* 65 (1994): 75–90.
Roberts, C. H., and T. C. Skeat. *The Birth of the Codex*. Oxford: Oxford University Press for the British Academy, 1983.
Rochberg-Halton, Francesca. "Canonicity in Cuneiform Texts." *JCS* 36 (1984): 127–44.
Roetzel, Calvin J. *Paul: A Jew on the Margins*. Louisville: Westminster John Knox, 2003.
Rorty, Richard. "Is Derrida a Transcendental Philosopher?" Pages 235–46 in *Derrida: A Critical Reader*. Edited by David Wood. Oxford: Blackwell, 1992.
Rosner, Brian S. *Paul, Scripture and Ethics: A Study of 1 Corinthians 5–7*. AGJU 22. Leiden: Brill, 1994.
Roth, Cecil. "The Subject Matter of Qumran Exegesis." *VT* 10 (1960): 51–68.
Rowe, C. Kavin. "Romans 10:13: What Is the Name of the Lord?" *HBT* 22 (2000): 135–73.
Runesson, Anders. "The Oldest Original Synagogue Building in the Diaspora: A Response to L. Michael White." *HTR* 92 (1999): 409–33.
Rutgers, Leonard. "Roman Policy toward the Jews: Expulsions from the City of Rome during the First Century C.E." Pages 93–116 in *Judaism and Christianity in First Century Rome*. Edited by Karl P. Donfried and Peter Richardson. Grand Rapids: Eerdmans, 1998.
Rutherford, Ian. "Inverting the Canon: Hermogenes on Literature." *HSCP* 94 (1992): 355–78.
Ruthven, K. K. *Critical Assumptions*. Cambridge: Cambridge University Press, 1979.

Sanders, E. P. *Judaism: Practice and Belief 63 BCE–66 CE*. Philadelphia: Trinity Press International, 1992.
Sawyer, John F. A. *Sacred Languages and Sacred Texts*. London: Routledge, 1999.
Schäfer, Peter. *Judeophobia: Attitudes toward the Jews in the Ancient World*. Cambridge: Harvard University Press, 1997.
Schiffman, Lawrence. "The Early History of Public Reading of the Torah." Pages 44–56 in *Jews, Christians, and Polytheists in the Ancient Synagogue*. Edited by Steven Fine. New York: Routledge, 1999.
Schneider, Bernardin. "The Meaning of St. Paul's Thesis 'The Letter and the Spirit.'" *CBQ* 15 (1953): 163–207.
Schottroff, Luise. "The Dual Concept of Peace." Pages 156–63 in *The Meaning of Peace: Biblical Studies*. Edited by Perry B. Yoder and Willard M. Swartley. Translated by Walter Sawatsky. Studies in Peace and Scripture 2. Louisville: Westminster John Knox, 1992.
Schreiner, Thomas R. *Romans*. BECNT. Grand Rapids: Baker, 1998.
Schürer, Emil. *The History of the Jewish People in the Time of Jesus Christ (175 B.C.–A.D. 135)*. Revised and edited by Geza Vermes, Fergus Millar, and Martin Goodman. 3 vols. Edinburgh: T&T Clark, 1973–1987.
Schüssler Fiorenza, Elisabeth. *The Power of the Word: Scripture and the Rhetoric of Empire*. Minneapolis: Fortress, 2007.
Schwartz, Seth. "Language, Power, and Identity in Ancient Palestine." *Past and Present* 148 (1995): 3–47.
Scott, James C. *Domination and the Arts of Resistance: Hidden Transcripts of Power*. New Haven: Yale University Press, 1990.
Scott, James M. *Adoption as Sons of God: An Exegetical Investigation into the Background of ΥΙΟΘΕΣΙΑ in the Pauline Corpus*. WUNT 2/48. Tübingen: Mohr Siebeck, 1992.
———. "For as Many as Are of the Works of the Law Are under a Curse (Galatians 3.10)." Pages 187–221 in *Paul and the Scriptures of Israel*. Edited by Craig A. Evans and James A. Sanders. JSNTSup 83. Sheffield: Sheffield Academic Press, 1993.
Seesengood, Robert P. "Hybridity and the Rhetoric of Endurance: Reading Paul's Athletic Metaphors in a Context of Postcolonial Self-Construction." *Bible and Critical Theory* 1 (2005): 1–16.
Segal, Alan F. *Life after Death: A History of the Afterlife in Western Religion*. New York: Doubleday, 2004.
———. *Paul the Convert*. New Haven: Yale University Press, 1990.
———. "Response: Some Aspects of Conversion and Identity Formation in the Christian Community of Paul's Time." Pages 184–90 in *Paul and Politics: Ekklesia, Israel, Imperium, Interpretation: Essays in Honor of Krister*

Stendahl. Edited by Richard A. Horsley. Harrisburg, Pa.: Trinity Press International, 2000.
Segovia, Fernando F. "Biblical Criticism and Postcolonial Studies: Towards a Postcolonial Optic." Pages 49–65 in *The Postcolonial Bible*. Edited by R. S. Sugirtharajah. Bible and Postcolonialism 1. Sheffield: Sheffield Academic Press, 1998.
Seidman, Naomi. *Faithful Renderings: Jewish-Christian Difference and the Politics of Translation*. Chicago: University of Chicago Press, 2006.
Seifrid, Mark. *Christ, Our Righteousness: Paul's Theology of Justification*. NSBT 9. Downers Grove, Ill.: InterVarsity Press, 2000.
Sherwood, Yvonne, ed. *Derrida's Bible (Reading a Page of Scripture with a Little Help from Derrida)*. New York: Palgrave Macmillan, 2004.
Shinan, Avigdor. "Sermons, Targums, and the Reading from Scriptures in the Ancient Synagogue." Pages 98–110 in *The Synagogue in Late Antiquity*. Edited by Lee I. Levine. Philadelphia: American Schools of Oriental Research, 1987.
Silva, Moisés. "Old Testament in Paul." Pages 630–42 in *Dictionary of Paul and His Letters*. Edited by Gerald F. Hawthorne, Ralph P. Martin, and Daniel G. Reid. Leicester: Inter-Varsity Press, 1993.
Simonetti, Manlio. *Profilo Storico dell'Esegesi Patristica*. Rome: Instituto Patristico Augustinianum, 1981.
Skeat, T. C. "Was Papyrus Regarded as 'Cheap' or 'Expensive' in the Ancient World?" *Aegyptus* 75 (1995): 75–93.
Slemon, Stephen. "The Scramble for Post-Colonialism." Pages 45–52 in *The Post-colonial Studies Reader*. Edited by Bill Ashcroft, Gareth Griffiths, and Helen Tiffin. London: Routledge, 1995.
Slingerland, H. Dixon. "Chrestus: Christus?" Pages 133–44 in *New Perspectives on Ancient Judaism 4*. Edited by Alan J. Avery-Peck. Lanham, Md.: University Press of America, 1989.
———. *Claudian Policymaking and the Early Roman Repression of Jews at Rome*. Atlanta: Scholars Press, 1997.
———. "Suetonius Claudius 25.4, Acts 18, and Paulus Orosius' *Historiarum Adversum Paganos Libri VII*: Dating the Claudian Expulsion(s) of Roman Jews." *JQR* 83 (1992): 127–44.
Slusser, Michael. "Reading Silently in Antiquity." *JBL* 111 (1992): 499.
Small, Jocelyn Penny. *Wax Tablets of the Mind: Cognitive Studies of Memory and Literacy in Classical Antiquity*. London: Routledge, 1997.
Smith, D. Moody. "The Pauline Literature." Pages 265–91 in *It Is Written—Scripture Citing Scripture: Essays in Honour of Barnabas Lindars*. Edited by D. A. Carson and H. G. M. Williamson. Cambridge: Cambridge University Press, 1988.

Snyder, H. Gregory. *Teachers and Texts in the Ancient World: Philosophers, Jews, and Christians*. London: Routledge, 2000.
Sommer, Benjamin D. *A Prophet Reads Scripture: Allusion in Isaiah 40–66*. Stanford, Calif.: Stanford University Press, 1998.
Spivak, Gayatri C. "Can the Subaltern Speak?" Pages 24–28 in *The Post-colonial Studies Reader*. Edited by Bill Ashcroft, Gareth Griffiths, and Helen Tiffin. London: Routledge, 1995.
Stamps, Dennis L. "Rhetorical Criticism of the New Testament: Ancient and Modern Evaluations of Argumentation." Pages 129–69 in *Approaches to New Testament Study*. Edited by Stanley E. Porter and David Tombs. JSNTSup 120. Sheffield: Sheffield Academic Press, 1995.
Stanley, Christopher D. *Arguing with Scripture: The Rhetoric of Quotations in the Letters of Paul*. London: T&T Clark, 2004.
———. "Paul and Homer: Greco-Roman Citation Practice in the First Century CE." *NovT* 32 (1990): 48–78.
———. *Paul and the Language of Scripture: Citation Technique in the Pauline Epistles and Contemporary Literature*. SNTSMS 74. Cambridge: Cambridge University Press, 1992.
———. "'Pearls before Swine': Did Paul's Audience Understand His Biblical Quotations?" *NovT* 41 (1999): 124–44.
———. "'Under a Curse': A Fresh Reading of Gal 3.10–14." *NTS* 36 (1990): 481–511.
Starr, Raymond J. "The Circulation of Literary Texts in the Roman World." *CQ* 37 (1989): 313–23.
Ste. Croix, G. E. M. de. *Class Struggle in the Ancient Greek World: From the Archaic Age to the Arab Conquests*. Ithaca, N.Y.: Cornell University Press, 1980.
Stemberger, Günter. "Mehrheitsbeschlüsse oder Recht auf eigene Meinung? Zur Entscheidungsfindung im Rabbinischen Judentum." Pages 19–40 in *Literatur im Dialog: Die Faszination von Talmud und Midrasch*. Edited by Susanne Plietzsch. Zurich: Theologischer Verlag Zürich, 2007.
Stern, Menahem, ed. *Greek and Latin Authors on Jews and Judaism*. 3 vols. Jerusalem: Israel Academy of Sciences and Humanities, 1974–1984.
Sternberg, Meir. "Proteus in Quotation-Land: Mimesis and the Forms of Reported Discourse." *Poetics Today* 3 (1982): 107–56.
Stockhausen, Carol K. "2 Corinthians and the Principles of Pauline Exegesis." Pages 143–64 in *Paul and the Scripture of Israel*. Edited by Craig A. Evans and James A. Sanders. Sheffield: Sheffield Academic Press, 1993.
———. *Moses' Veil and the Glory of the New Covenant: The Exegetical Substructure of II Cor. 3:1–4:6*. AnBib 116. Rome: Biblical Institute Press, 1989.
———. "Paul the Exegete." *Bible Today* 28 (1990): 196–202.

Stone, Michael. "Three Transformations in Judaism: Scripture, History and Redemption." *Numen* 32 (1985): 218–35.
Stowers, Stanley K. *The Diatribe and Paul's Letter to the Romans*. SBLDS 57. Chico, Calif.: Scholars Press, 1981.
———. "Paul and Slavery: A Response." *Semeia* 83/84 (1998): 291–93.
———. *A Rereading of Romans: Gentiles, Jews, Justice*. New Haven: Yale University Press. 1994.
Strange, James. "Ancient Texts, Archaeology as Text, and the Problem of the First-Century Synagogue." Pages 27–45 in *Evolution of the Synagogue: Problems and Progress*. Edited by Howard Clark Kee and Lynn H. Cohick. Harrisburg, Pa.: Trinity Press International, 1999.
Strenski, Ivan. *Thinking about Religion: An Historical Introduction to Theories of Religion*. Malden: Blackwell, 2006.
Stroumsa, Guy G. "Early Christianity—A Religion of the Book?" Pages 153–73 in *Homer, the Bible, and Beyond: Literary and Religious Canons in the Ancient World*. Edited by Margalit Finkelberg and Guy G. Stroumsa. Jerusalem Studies in Religion and Culture 2. Leiden: Brill, 2003.
Stuckenbruck, Loren T., Stephen C. Barton, and Benjamin Wold, eds. *Memory in the Bible and Antiquity*. WUNT 212. Tübingen: Mohr Siebeck, 2007.
Stuhlmacher, Peter. *Der Brief an die Römer*. Göttingen: Vandenhoeck & Ruprecht, 1989.
———. *How to Do Biblical Theology*. PTMS 38. Allison Park, Pa.: Pickwick, 1995.
———. "Theologische Probleme der Römerbriefpräskripts." *EvT* 27 (1967): 374–89.
Sugirtharajah, R. S. "Introduction: The Margin as Site of Creative Revisioning." Pages 1–8 in *Voices from the Margin: Interpreting the Bible in the Third World*. Edited by R. S. Sugirtharajah. Maryknoll, N.Y.: Orbis, 1995.
Surenhusius, Guilielmus. *Sefer ha-Meshaweh sive biblos katallages in quo secundum veterum theologorum hebraeorum formulas allegandi et modos interpretandi conciliantur loca ex V. in N.T. allegata*. Amsterdam: Boom, 1713.
Talbot, Mary M. *Fictions at Work: Language and Social Practice in Fiction*. London: Longman, 1995.
Theissen, Gerd. *The Social Setting of Pauline Christianity: Essays on Corinth*. Philadelphia: Fortress, 1982.
Thiselton, Anthony C. "Can Hermeneutics Ease the Deadlock? Some Biblical Exegesis and Hermeneutical Models." Pages 145–96 in *The Way Forward? Christian Voices on Homosexuality and the Church*. Edited by Timothy Bradshaw. 2nd ed. Grand Rapids: Eerdmans, 2004.
———. *The First Epistle to the Corinthians: A Commentary on the Greek Text*. NIGTC. Grand Rapids: Eerdmans, 2000.

Tholuck, F. A. G. *Das Alte Testament im Neuen Testament*. 6th ed. Gotha: Perthes, 1877.

———. "The Old Testament in the New." Translated by Charles A. Aiken. *BSac* 11 (1854): 569–76.

Thomas, Rosalind. *Literacy and Orality in Ancient Greece*. Cambridge: Cambridge University Press, 1992.

———. *Oral Tradition and Written Record in Classical Athens*. Cambridge: Cambridge University Press, 1989.

Thompson, Michael. *Clothed with Christ: The Example and Teaching of Jesus in Romans 12.1–15.13*. JSNTSup 59. Sheffield: JSOT Press, 1991.

Thrall, Margaret. *A Critical and Exegetical Commentary on the Second Epistle to the Corinthians*. ICC. Edinburgh: T&T Clark, 1994.

Torrance. J. B. "The Contribution of McLeod Campbell to Scottish Theology." *SJT* 26 (1973): 295–311.

———. "Covenant and Contract: A Study of the Theological Background of Worship in Seventeenth-Century Scotland." *SJT* 23 (1970): 51–76.

Tov, Emanuel. "The Status of the Masoretic Text in Modern Editions of the Hebrew Bible: The Relevance of the Canon." Pages 234–51 in *The Canon Debate*. Edited by Lee Martin McDonald and James A. Sanders. Peabody, Mass.: Hendrickson, 2002.

Toy, Crawford H. *Quotations in the New Testament*. New York: Scribner, 1884.

Turpie, David M. *The Old Testament in the New*. London: Williams & Norgate, 1868.

Ulrich, Eugene. *The Dead Sea Scrolls and the Origins of the Bible*. Grand Rapids: Eerdmans, 1999.

Usher, Stephen. *Greek Oratory: Tradition and Originality*. Oxford: Oxford University Press, 1999.

Vermes, Geza. *Scripture and Tradition in Judaism*. Leiden: Brill, 1961.

———. *Scrolls, Scriptures and Early Christianity*. Library of Second Temple Studies 56. London: T&T Clark, 2005.

Vollmer, Hans. *Die alttestamentlichen Citate bei Paulus*. Freiburg: Mohr, 1895.

Wagner, J. Ross. *Heralds of the Good News: Isaiah and Paul "in Concert" in the Letter to the Romans*. NovTSup 101. Leiden: Brill, 2002.

Walters, James C. "Romans, Jews and Christians: The Impact of the Romans on Jewish/Christian Relations in First Century Rome." Pages 175–95 in *Judaism and Christianity in First Century Rome*. Edited by Karl P. Donfried and Peter Richardson. Grand Rapids: Eerdmans, 1998.

Ward, Graham. *Barth, Derrida, and the Language of Theology*. Cambridge: Cambridge University Press, 1995.

Wartenberg, Thomas E. *The Forms of Power: From Domination to Transformation*. Philadelphia: Temple University Press, 1990.
Watson, Francis B. *Paul and the Hermeneutics of Faith*. London: T&T Clark, 2004.
———. *Paul, Judaism and the Gentiles: A Sociological Approach*. SNTSMS 56. Cambridge: Cambridge University Press, 1986.
———. "The Two Roman Congregations: Romans 14:1–15:13." Pages 203–15 in *The Romans Debate*. Edited by Karl P. Donfried. Peabody, Mass.: Hendrickson, 1991.
Weber, Max. *The Theory of Social and Economic Organization*. Edited by T. Parsons. Glencoe, Ill.: Free Press, 1957.
———. *Wirtschaft und Gesellschaft: Grundriss der verstehenden Soziologie*. Tübingen: Mohr, 1925.
Wedderburn, A. J. M. *The Reasons for Romans*. Minneapolis: Fortress, 1991.
Weinfeld, Moshe. *Deuteronomy 1–11: A New Translation with Introduction and Commentary*. AB 5. New York: Doubleday, 1991.
West, Stephanie. *Ptolemaic Papyri of Homer*. Papyrologica Coloniensia 3. Cologne: Westdeutscher Verlag, 1967.
Whiston, William. *An Essay toward Restoring the True Text of the Old Testament*. London: Senex, 1722.
White, John L. *The Apostle of God: Paul and the Promise of Abraham*. Peabody, Mass.: Hendrickson, 1999.
White, L. Michael. "Synagogue and Society in Imperial Ostia: Archaeological and Epigraphic Evidence." *HTR* 90 (1997): 23–58.
Wiefel, Wolfgang. "The Jewish Community in Ancient Rome and the Origins of Roman Christianity." Pages 85–101 in *The Romans Debate*. Edited by Karl P. Donfried. Rev. ed. Peabody, Mass.: Hendrickson, 1991.
Wilamowitz-Moellendorff, Ulrich von. *Die griechische Literatur des Altertums*. Stuttgart: Teubner, 1912.
Wilcox, Max. "On Investigating the Use of the Old Testament in the New Testament." Pages 231–43 in *Text and Interpretation: Studies in the New Testament Presented to Matthew Black*. Edited by Ernest Best and R. McL. Wilson. Cambridge: Cambridge University Press, 1979.
Wilk, Florian. *Die Bedeutung des Jesajabuches für Paulus*. FRLANT 179. Göttingen: Vandenhoeck & Ruprecht, 1998.
Wilson, Stephen G. *Related Strangers: Jews and Christians 70–170 C.E.* Minneapolis: Fortress, 1995.
Wire, Antoinette Clark. "Performance, Politics, and Power: A Response." *Semeia* 65 (1994): 129.
Witherington, Ben, III. *Acts of the Apostles: A Socio-Rhetorical Commentary*. Grand Rapids: Eerdmans, 1998.

———. *Conflict and Community in Corinth: A Socio-Rhetorical Commentary on 1 and 2 Corinthians*. Grand Rapids: Eerdmans, 1995.

———. *Paul's Letter to the Romans: A Socio-Rhetorical Commentary*. Grand Rapids: Eerdmans, 2004.

———. *Paul's Narrative Thought World: The Tapestry of Tragedy and Triumph*. Louisville: Westminster John Knox, 1994.

Woolf, Greg. "Becoming Roman, Staying Greek: Culture, Identity, and the Civilizing Process in the Roman East." *Proceedings of the Cambridge Philological Society* 40 (1994): 116–43.

———. "Beyond Romans and Natives." *World Archaeology* 28 (1995): 339–50.

Wright, N. T. *The Climax of the Covenant: Christ and the Law in Pauline Theology*. Edinburgh: T&T Clark, 1991.

———. *Jesus and the Victory of God*. Minneapolis: Fortress, 1996.

———. *The New Testament and the People of God*. London: SPCK, 1992.

———. *Paul: In Fresh Perspective*. Minneapolis: Fortress, 2005.

———. "Paul's Gospel and Caesar's Empire." Pages 160–83 in *Paul and Politics: Ekklesia, Israel, Imperium, Interpretation: Essays in Honor of Krister Stendahl*. Edited by Richard A. Horsley. Harrisburg, Pa.: Trinity Press International, 2000.

———. *The Resurrection of the Son of God*. Minneapolis: Fortress, 2003.

———. "Romans." *NIB* 10:393–770.

Young, Frances. "Alexandrian and Antiochene Exegesis." Pages 334–54 in *The Ancient Period*. Vol. 1 of *A History of Biblical Interpretation*. Edited by Alan J. Hauser and Duane F. Watson. Grand Rapids: Eerdmans, 2003.

———. *Biblical Exegesis and the Formation of Christian Culture*. Cambridge: Cambridge University Press, 1997.

Young, Frances, and David F. Ford. *Meaning and Truth in 2 Corinthians*. Biblical Foundations in Theology. Grand Rapids: Eerdmans, 1987.

Youtie, Herbert C. "*Agrammatos*: An Aspect of Greek Society in Egypt." *HSCP* 75 (1971): 161–76.

Zanker, Paul. *The Power of Images in the Age of Augustus*. Ann Arbor: University of Michigan Press, 1988.

Zetterholm, Magnus. "Paul and the Missing Messiah." Pages 31–55 in *The Messiah in Early Judaism and Christianity*. Edited by Magnus Zetterholm. Minneapolis: Fortress, 2007.

Žižek, Slavoj. *The Fragile Absolute, or Why is the Christian Legacy Worth Fighting For?* New York: Verso, 2000.

———. *The Puppet and the Dwarf: The Perverse Core of Christianity*. Cambridge: MIT Press, 2003.

Contributors

Douglas A. Campbell is Assistant Professor of New Testament at the Duke University Divinity School in Durham, North Carolina, U.S.A.

Roy E. Ciampa is Associate Professor of New Testament and chair of the Division of Biblical Studies at Gordon-Conwell Theological Seminary in South Hamilton, Massachusetts, U.S.A.

Steven DiMattei is Visiting Assistant Professor in the Honors College at the University of Houston in Houston, Texas, U.S.A.

Kathy Ehrensperger is Senior Lecturer in New Testament Studies at the University of Wales, Lampeter, U.K.

Neil Elliott is Acquiring Editor in Biblical Studies at Fortress Press and teaches biblical studies at Metropolitan State University and United Theological Seminary in the Twin Cities in Minneapolis, Minnesota, U.S.A.

Bruce N. Fisk is Professor of New Testament at Westmont College in Santa Barbara, California, U.S.A.

Mark D. Given is Associate Professor and director of the graduate program in Religious Studies at Missouri State University in Springfield, Missouri, U.S.A.

Stanley E. Porter is President, Dean, and Professor of New Testament at McMaster Divinity College in Hamilton, Ontario, Canada.

Steve Moyise is Professor of New Testament at the University of Chichester in Chichester, West Sussex, U.K.

Jeremy Punt is Associate Professor of New Testament at Stellenbosch University in Stellenbosch, South Africa.

Christopher D. Stanley is Professor of Theology at St. Bonaventure University in St. Bonaventure, New York, U.S.A.

Index of Ancient Sources

Hebrew Bible/Old Testament

Genesis
- 1:26 — 71
- 3 — 135
- 3:15 — 204
- 11:30 — 84
- 12:3 — 90, 126, 149
- 12:7 — 90
- 15 — 33
- 15:6 — 19, 26, 33, 90, 149
- 16 — 33, 90
- 16–17 — 83
- 16:1 — 83
- 18:10 — 122
- 18:14 — 122
- 18:18 — 126
- 21 — 33
- 21:10 — 85, 90, 91
- 21:12 — 122
- 22:18 — 126
- 25:23 — 122
- 28:14 — 126

Exodus
- 9:16 — 122
- 12:6–9 — 68
- 15:1–18 — 194
- 17:8–14 — 68
- 19–20 — 33
- 24:13 — 257
- 32 — 305
- 32:6 — 89, 90
- 32:16 — 305
- 33:19 — 122, 305
- 34:27 — 305

Leviticus
- 14:10 — 68
- 16 — 68
- 18 — 151
- 18:5 — 26, 151, 153, 256, 258
- 19:18 — 242
- 26:11 — 274

Numbers
- 19 — 68
- 20:2 — 82
- 21:8–9 — 66
- 24:15–17 — 114

Deuteronomy
- 5:28–29 — 114
- 17:1 — 126
- 17:6 — 276
- 18:15 — 82
- 18:18–19 — 114
- 19:15 — 276, 278
- 19:19 — 126
- 21:23 — 26, 151, 152, 154
- 22:21 — 126
- 22:22 — 126
- 22:24 — 126
- 24:7 — 126
- 27 — 150
- 27:26 — 26, 150, 153
- 28:58 — 150
- 30:12–14 — 253

Deuteronomy (cont.)		9:9 LXX	211
32:43	204	10:7	123
33:8–11	114	14:1–3	123
33:13–17	68	15	194
		16:1 LXX	212
2 Samuel		16:15 LXX	212
7:8	274	18:49	204
7:10–12	115	21:32 LXX	211
7:14	274	24	194
16:20–22	195	29	194
		29:7–8 LXX	148
1 Kings		30:2 LXX	211
1:10	62	32:1–2	19
1:12	62	33	194
2:13–25	195	34:24 LXX	211
2:6	195	34:28 LXX	211
2:9	195	35:7 LXX	211
3:1–2	195	35:11 LXX	211
3:5–6	195	36:1	123
3:9	195	39:10 LXX	211, 212
3:12	195	39:11 LXX	211, 212
3:16–28	195	39:14 LXX	212
4:29–34	195	39:17 LXX	212
5:7	195	39:18 LXX	212
5:12	195	44:5 LXX	211, 276
7:13–51	195	44:8 LXX	211
8–9	195	45	195
10:23–24	195	46	194
		47	194
Nehemiah		47:11 LXX	211
8:1–8	306	48	194
		49:6 LXX	211
Job		50	194
5:12–13	16	50:16 LXX	211, 212
35:7	16	65	53
		66a	194
Psalms		68	53
1:1	115	68:28 LXX	211
2	53, 195	70:2 LXX	211, 212
2:1–2	115	70:15 LXX	211, 212
5:9	123	70:16 LXX	211, 212
5:10 LXX	211	70:18 LXX	211, 212
7:18 LXX	211	70:24 LXX	211, 212
8	194, 204	71:1 LXX	211
8:6	204	71:1–4 LXX	212

INDEX OF ANCIENT SOURCES

71:2 LXX	211	102	53
71:3 LXX	211	102:17 LXX	211
71:7 LXX	211	110	53, 195, 203–205
72	53, 195	110:1	200, 204
72:13–15 LXX	148	110:3 LXX	211
75	194	111:3 LXX	211
76	194	111:9 LXX	211
78	81	114	194
81	194	115:1 LXX	146, 147
82	194	115:2 LXX	148
84	194	116:10	147, 148
84:8 LXX	212	117:1	204
84:11 LXX	211	117:14 LXX	212
84:11–14 LXX	212	117:19 LXX	211, 212
84:12 LXX	211	117:21 LXX	212
84:14 LXX	211	118	194
85:5 LXX	276	118:7 LXX	211
87	194	118:40 LXX	211
87:13 LXX	211	118:40–41 LXX	212
88:15 LXX	211	118:62 LXX	211
88:17 LXX	211	118:75 LXX	211
88:26–27 LXX	203	118:106 LXX	211
89	53, 195, 203	118:121–123 LXX	212
89:14	203	118:123 LXX	211
89:15 LXX	203	118:138 LXX	211
89:16	203	118:142 LXX	211
89:17 LXX	203	118:160 LXX	211
89:26–27	203	118:164 LXX	211
91:13	204	118:169–176 LXX	212
93	194	131:1 LXX	276
95:13 LXX	211	132	194
96–99	194	138	53
96:2 LXX	211	142:1 LXX	211
96:6 LXX	211	142:2 LXX	205
97:1b–2 LXX	212	142:11 LXX	211
97:2 LXX	211	143	205
97:2–3 LXX	189, 191	143:1	205
97:3 LXX	212	143:2	205
97:9 LXX	211, 212	143:3	206
98	190–94, 206, 207, 209	143:11	205
98:2	206, 207, 210	143:12	206
98:2–3	189–93, 207, 211	144:7 LXX	211
98:3	210	148	53
98:4 LXX	211	149	194
98:6	194		

Isaiah

Ref	Pages
1:9	123
2:2–3	85
2:10–17	278
10:22–23	123
11:10	204
14:2	85
25:5–7	85
28:16	123
29:14	275, 278
39:8	212
40	16
40:13	16
42:4	204
42:6	204
49:8	317
51:1–3	84
51:5	85
51:5–11	212
52	25
52:3–6	22
52:5	16, 22–24, 28, 39, 220
52:7	22, 24
52:11	274
53:1	84
53:1–3	84, 92
54:1	83, 84
54:3	85
55:4–5	85
56:1	191
59	212
59:7–8	123
59:14	212
59:17	212
60:17	212
60:18	212
61:8	212
61:11	212
62	212
62:1	212
62:2	212
63:1–6	212
63:7–64:11	212
63:8–9	212
65:1	232
65:2	67, 232

Jeremiah

Ref	Pages
6:4	270
7:9–11	16
9:22–23	276, 278, 284, 287
9:23–24	16
24:6	287
36	305
51:34	287

Ezekiel

Ref	Pages
2:8–3:3	305
20:34	274
20:41	274
36:16–27	16
37:27	274

Daniel

Ref	Pages
3:4	53
3:7	53
3:29	53
4:1	53
5:19	53
6:25	53
7	53
7:14	53

Hosea

Ref	Pages
2:3	123
2:3b	123
2:23	78
2:25	123

Amos

Ref	Pages
5:7	212
5:12	212
5:15	212
5:24	212
6:12	212

Micah

Ref	Pages
7	53

INDEX OF ANCIENT SOURCES

Habakkuk		Zechariah	
2:1–4	20	4:6	278
2:2	78	9	53
2:3a	151	9–14	115
2:4	20, 21, 26, 150, 151, 153, 189, 206, 207, 256		

Malachi	
1:2–3	122

New Testament

Matthew		6:25–29	308
9:20–21	69	6:47–49	62
10:16	204	8:17	276
12:41	62	20:25	64
13:54–58	178		
18:16	276	**Acts**	
		1:1	165
Mark		2:5	165
1:21	178	2:10	166
6:1–6	178	3:14	20
6:2–3	308	3:18	165
		5:33–39	310
Luke		7:43	64
1:3	165	7:52	20
1:68	275	8:1	165
2:29	69	9:1–2	174
4	178	9:11	99
4:15–17	178	9:15–17	241
4:16	102	9:30	99
4:16–21	83	11:25	99
4:16–22	178, 179	13	178
4:17–21	62, 63	13:13–15	83
4:20–22	178	13:14–15	178
4:28	178	13:15–16	178
5:17–24	309	13:42	178
7:36–50	309	13:42–47	166
8:41–42	69	14:1–6	166
9:54	62	15:1–2	182,
10:17–19	204	15:21	178
10:18–19	204	16	160
11:37–54	309	16:37	119
24:44	123	17:1–5	166
		17:28	105
John		18	162
5:39	254	18:2	162, 165, 168, 169

Acts (cont.)

18:4	166
18:6	308
19:1	162
19:8–9	166
21:39	99, 105
22–23	182
22:3	99, 100, 102, 310
22:14	20
22:25	119
23:1–10	310
24	162
25	162
25:11–12	119
26	162
26:14	105
26:32	119
28:17	176
28:21–22	162, 182
28:21–25	176

Romans

1–3	206
1:1–5	54
1:1b	202
1:1b–4	201
1:2	55, 255, 304
1:2–4	203, 205, 206
1:3	204
1:3–4	201
1:4	206
1:5	166, 214
1:5–6	202
1:7	169
1:13	166
1:16	171, 191
1:16–17	20, 21, 189–92, 209, 211
1:16b	192
1:17	15, 18, 151, 189–93, 206, 207
1:17b	206, 207
1:18–32	226, 232
1:28	275
1:29–31	283
2	16
2–3	221, 226–28, 232
2:1	227, 229
2:1–5	227
2:1–6	229
2:1–16	226
2:3–5	221
2:6–11	231
2:12–13	229
2:17	221
2:17–23	22, 24
2:17–24	222, 227–30
2:17–29	16
2:17–3:9	226, 227
2:21–23	24
2:24	23, 25, 39, 158, 220, 226, 229
2:25	229
2:25–29	249
2:29	255
3	205
3:1	221, 229–31
3:1–2	175
3:1–9	229–31
3:2	230, 258
3:3	229, 230
3:4	230
3:5	190, 229, 230
3:6	230
3:7	229, 230
3:8	39, 221, 229, 230
3:8c	230
3:9	56, 221, 229–31
3:9–19	56
3:9a	230
3:9b	230
3:10–12	123
3:10–18	25, 123
3:13	123
3:14	123
3:15–17	123
3:18	123
3:19	226, 227
3:19–20	254
3:20a	205
3:21	190, 205, 255
3:21–22	21, 191, 192, 210
3:21–26	192

3:22	190, 205	9–15	170
3:23–26	210	9–16	52
3:25	190, 205, 232	9:3	51
3:26	190, 205	9:3–5	167
4	19, 91	9:4	175
4–8	210	9:4–5	49, 56, 228
4:1–24	144	9:5	51, 52, 201, 203, 275
4:1–25	134, 135	9:6–13	135
4:2–3	33	9:7	122
4:3	33, 55	9:9	122
4:9–22	158	9:10–13	158
4:9–23	127	9:12	122
4:17	91	9:13	122
4:19	91	9:14	122
5:1–11	202	9:17	55, 122
5:2	202	9:25	78, 123
5:10–11	202	9:25–26	158
5:12–21	59, 135, 201	9:26	123
5:14	59, 60, 63, 65, 71, 80, 202	9:27	16
5:17	202	9:27–28	123
5:18–19	21	9:29	16, 123
5:21	202	9:33	123, 126
6–8	201	10	251
6:1–15	221	10:1–15	106
6:1–23	226	10:3	190
6:12	202	10:4	247
6:17	64	10:5	256
6:19–20	168	10:5–6a	257
7:1	168, 176	10:5–8	158
7:4	71	10:6–7	252
7:12	304	10:6–8	251, 253
7:12–16	175	10:6–10	251
8	203, 250	10:8	252–54
8:15	202, 203	10:9–13	202, 203
8:15–17	203	10:11	55
8:18–25	242	10:13	200
8:20–21	233	10:14–17	253
8:21	202	10:15	22
8:29–30	203	10:16	16
8:34	203	10:17	253
8:37	202	10:18	158
8:38–39	250	10:20	16, 232
9	122, 123	10:21	20, 232
9–10	123	11	23, 123
9–11	6, 15, 210, 232	11:1	232

Romans (cont.)		16:25–26	167
11:1–4	158		
11:1–5	168	**1 Corinthians**	
11:2	55	1–3	126
11:3–4	126	1–4	289
11:13–14	175	1:3	51
11:13–15	167	1:18–31	275
11:17–21	167, 183	1:19	275
11:17–24	39	1:23	243
11:22	56	1:28	288
11:24	167	1:30	190
11:26	18, 23	1:31	274, 276
11:26–27	126	2:1–5	243
11:28	167, 233	2:4	255
11:30–31	167	2:4–5	243
11:31–32	233	2:6	275
11:33	15	2:9–16	255
12:1–2	232	2:10	71
12:1–21	317	2:12	255
12:1–15:13	32	2:12–13	71
12:2	266	2:14	252
12:16	288	3:19	16
13	163	4:3	278
13:1–7	176, 217	4:8	202
13:4	176	4:9	281
13:13	283	4:14	245
14:1	175	4:18–21	245
14:1–15:13	163, 170	5–7	44, 54
15:3	51	5:3–5	245
15:4	20, 55, 176, 255, 312, 316, 319	5:5	280
15:7	51	5:9–11	283
15:8	210	5:13	126
15:8–13	167	6:9–10	283
15:12	201, 204	7:5	280
15:15–16	167	7:19	256
15:19	255	7:31	251
15:25	202	8:12–13	242
16	163, 168	9:9–10	71
16:3–15	168	9:10	105
16:3–16	169	10	81
16:7	168	10:1	80
16:11	168	10:1–2	135
16:19–20	204	10:1–4	60, 82
16:19b	204	10:1–11	60, 65, 70, 79, 89, 144
16:20	204, 280	10:1–13	82

INDEX OF ANCIENT SOURCES

10:1–22	81	2:14–6:10	147
10:4	51, 69–71, 81	2:14–7:4	275
10:6	59, 60, 63–65, 70, 74, 80	2:15–17	246
10:6–10	60, 81	2:16	253
10:7	89	3	87, 88, 240, 253, 256
10:11	60, 63, 69–72, 74, 79, 81	3–4	259
10:14–17	89	3:1–3	315–16
10:18–22	89	3:1–18	87
10:31	89	3:1–4:6	87
11:3–10	249	3:1–4:15	245
11:17–34	142	3:3	315
11:19–22	90	3:6	71, 245, 259
11:27	89	3:6–18	276
11:29	89	3:6ff.	245
11:31	89	3:7	253
12	243	3:7–11	247
12:4	243	3:7–18	135, 144
12:9	243	3:12–13	257
12:11	243	3:12–16	249
12:12	51	3:12–18	247, 254
12:13	243	3:13	247
13	243	3:14	254
13:10	243	3:14–15	255, 256
14:1–40	142	3:15–17	71
14:21	158	3:17–18	255
15	243, 244	3:18	253
15:3–4	55, 255	4	247
15:19	242	4:1	147, 257
15:25–27	204	4:1–2	257
15:28	243, 244	4:3–4	249
15:28b	204	4:4	241, 255
15:33	105	4:5–6	247
15:39–40	244	4:5–10	281
15:47–48	244	4:6	105, 274
		4:7–15	315, 316
2 Corinthians		4:8–11	147
1–3	284	4:8–12	148
1–9	278	4:11–12	148
1:1–2:13	275	4:13	146–49, 158, 274, 281, 282, 316
1:3	275		
1:5–11	315	4:13–15	147
1:8–9	281	4:14	147
1:22	255	4:15–5:10	244
2:3–4	275	5:5	255
2:11	280	5:16	252

2 Corinthians (cont.)

5:21	190	12:7	280
6:1–10	315, 317	12:9–10	281
6:2	251, 274, 317	12:11	275, 284
6:14–7:1	274, 275	12:19–20	287
6:16–18	274, 317	12:20–21	283
7:5–16	275	13	285–87
7:8	275	13:1	276, 278
8–9	275	13:1–10	287
8:15	274	13:10	287
9:9	274	13:4a	278
9:22b	283		
10	276–79	**Galatians**	
10–12	278	1	56
10–13	272–87, 289, 315	1:1	266
10:1	276	1:4	242
10:1–11:15	280	1:12	254
10:3	277	1:16	266
10:4	277	1:21	99
10:5	277	2	56
10:8	284, 287	2:10	288
10:9–11	245	3	27, 126, 267, 270
10:17	274, 276, 278, 284, 287, 317	3–4	90
11	276, 279–82	3:1	154
11:1–12:18	278	3:1–4:11	190, 219
11:3	276, 280	3:5	255
11:4	247	3:6	26, 126, 149, 152
11:5	275	3:6–8	135
11:12	285	3:6–9	144, 149, 152, 158
11:13	275	3:6–14	134, 146, 149–54
11:13–15	280	3:7	149
11:14	280	3:8	55, 149, 254
11:15	280	3:9	85, 149
11:16	284	3:10	150, 152–54, 158, 270
11:21–27	281	3:10–12	151, 153
11:22	276	3:10–13	152
11:23	281	3:10–14	26, 150
11:24	175, 281	3:10a	150
11:25	281	3:10b	153
11:25–28	281, 285	3:11	150, 151, 153
11:31	275	3:11–12	154, 256
11:32–33	281	3:11a	151
12	276, 281–85	3:11b	153
12:2	277	3:12	151, 256
12:6	284	3:12a	153
		3:12b	153

INDEX OF ANCIENT SOURCES

3:13	151, 152	2:8	21
3:16	78, 135	3:4–11	283
3:19–20	26	3:5	312
3:21	255	3:9	190
3:22	55, 56	3:17	59, 65
3:22–23	254	3:21	253
3:28	135, 282	4:4	105
4	126		
4:3	282	**Colossians**	
4:6	203	2:16–17	71
4:9	282		
4:21–30	85	**1 Thessalonians**	
4:21–31	60, 73, 83, 127, 134, 135, 158	1:5	240
4:21–5:1	267	1:7	59, 65
4:22	85, 91	2:2	281
4:22–23	33	2:13	240
4:24	33, 60, 61, 63, 71, 72, 78, 202	2:17–18	241
4:24–25	33	2:18	280
4:25	72, 83, 85	2:19	242
4:26	73	3:6	241
4:29	85	3:10	241
4:30	55, 91	3:13	241
5:1	202	4:9	242
5:14	242	4:15	241
5:22	105	4:17	241
6:11–17	249	5:2–3	270
6:11–18	122	5:3	220
6:15	242	5:10	241
		5:23	241
Ephesians			
1:3	275	**2 Thessalonians**	
1:20–22	204	2:9	280
2	198	3:9	59, 65
4:27	280		
5:14	105	**1 Timothy**	
5:19–20	142	1:20	280
6:11	280	3:6	280
6:12–18	277	3:7	280
		3:11	280
		4:11	59
Philippians		4:13	142
1:7	281	5:15	280
1:12–14	281	5:18	55
1:16	281		
2:5–11	289		
2:6–11	288		

2 Timothy
2:7	105
2:26	280
3:3	280
4:23	120

Titus
1:12	105
2:3	280
2:7	59

Philemon
1	281
9	281
13	281
19	121, 122

Hebrews
1–2	204
1:13	204
2:6–8a	204
2:7–4:11	71, 81
4:2	81
8:5	60, 64, 69–72, 74
8:5a	72
10:1	60, 71, 72, 74
10:25	183
13:24	183

1 Peter
1:3	275
3:18	20
3:21	62

1 John
1:26–27	242
2:1	20
4:1	256

Revelation
12:10–11	204

EARLY CHRISTIAN LITERATURE

Acts of Paul
22.4	68

Barnabas
7.3	68
7.7	68
7.10	68
7.11	68
8.1	68
12.2–3	66
12.3	67
12.6–7	66

Clement of Alexandria, *Paedagogus*
2.101.1–3	71

Clement of Alexandria, *Stromata*
1.11	114
6.89.2	114
33.6	114

Eusebius, *Praeparatio evangelica*
8.10.3–4	47
9.26.1	47
9.27.4–6	47
13.12.1–4	47
13.13.3–4	47

Irenaeus, *Adversus haereses*
1	68
1.8.4	69
2.23.1	69
3.22.3	71
4.14.3	69
7.1	68
7.2	68
8.2	69

John Chrysostom, *Commentarius in epistulam ad Galatas*
4.710	60

INDEX OF ANCIENT SOURCES

Justin, *Apologia i*
55	67
60.3–5	67

Justin, *Dialogus cum Tryphone*
40.1	68
40.1–3	67
41.1	68
41.4	68
90.2	66
91.2	67
91.3	66
91.4	67
111.1	66
111.2	66
112.2	66
114.1	63, 66
131.4	66
134.3	68

Origen, *Commentarii in evangelium Joannis*
10.110.55	70, 73
20.67	72
20.74	72

Origen, *Commentarium in evangelium Matthaei*
10.14.43	72
16.3.57	72
17.34.78	72

Origen, *Contra Celsum*
2.2.14	72
2.3.8	72
4.43–44	72
4.44.28	72
5.44.13	72

Origen, *De principiis*
4.2.6	72

Origen, *Homiliae in Exodum*
5.13	13

Origen, *Homiliae in Genesim*
6.1.25	72
7.2.19	72
10.2.42	72
10.5.22	72

Origen, *Homiliae in Jeremiam*
1.34.2	72
6.266.3	72
10.91.3	72

Origen, *Homiliae in Iosuam*
17.1	72

Origen, *Homiliae in Leviticum*
5.1.48	72
9.2	72
10.2.45	72
13.1.2	72

Origen, *Homiliae in Psalmos*
38.7	73

Origen, *Philocalia*
1.13	72

Orosius, *Historiae adversum paganos*
7.6.15–16	160

Ptolemy, *Epistula ad Floram*
5.2	70
5.8	70

Theodore of Mopsuestia, *Commentary on Galatians*
4.22–31	72

Apocrypha, Pseudepigrapha, and Dead Sea Scrolls

1 Enoch
- 38:2 — 20

1 Maccabees
- 1:56–57 — 304
- 3:48 — 178, 304
- 12:9 — 178, 303, 304

1QpHab
- 3 — 20
- 7 — 77
- 8 — 20

1QS
- VI, 6–8 — 138
- VII, 11–12 — 138

2 Maccabees
- 8:23 — 178

4Q164
- frag. 1 — 84

CD
- 2.14–3.3 — 80
- 20.20 — 191

Letter of Aristeas
- 176–177 — 178

Sirach
- 1:1 — 280
- 1:11 — 280

Testament of Levi
- 13:2 — 179, 180
- 18:12 — 204

Testament of Simeon
- 6:6 — 204

Testament of Zebulun
- 9:8 — 204

Other Jewish Literature

b. Kerithot
- 9a — 82

b. Yebamot
- 14a–b — 309

Josephus, *Antiquitates judaicae*
- 4.211 — 179
- 16.43 — 178
- 17.299–303 — 164
- 18.81–84 — 164, 166
- 20.115–117 — 178

Josephus, *Bellum judaicum*
- 2.229–231 — 178
- 2.280 — 164
- 2.291 — 178
- 2.292 — 178

Josephus, *Contra Apionem*
- 2.18 — 138
- 2.25 — 138
- 2.154–56 — 47
- 2.165–168 — 47
- 2.175 — 178
- 2.178 — 138
- 2.179–181 — 46
- 2.204 — 179
- 2.256–257 — 47
- 2.279–281 — 47
- 2.293–295 — 47

Josephus, *Vita*
- 134 — 110
- 219–223 — 118

… INDEX OF ANCIENT SOURCES

m. Pirqe 'Abot	
5:24	102

Philo, De opificio mundi	
128	178

Philo, De specialibus legibus	
2.62	178
4.61	47

Philo, De somniis	
2.127	178
2.92	217

Philo, De vita Mosis	
1.2–3	47

Philo, Hypothetica	
7.12	178
7.12–13	178, 179

Philo, Legatio ad Gaium	
1.2–3	47
132	173
155	173
155–156	178
155–157	172, 173

Philo, Quaestiones et solutiones in Genesin	
3.5	47
4.152	47

Philo, Quaestiones et solutiones in Exodum	
1.43	257

Philo, Quod omnis probus liber sit	
51–53	47
81–82	178

Greco-Roman Literature

Achilles Tatius, Leucippe et Clitophon	
1.6	118
5.24	118

Aeschylus, Eumenides	
1014–1015	105

Ambrose, Epistulae	
47	118

Andocides, De pace	
2	80
32	80

Aratus, Phaenomena	
5	105

Aristaenetus	
1.10.36ff.	118

Aristides, Orationes	
24.23	80

Aristophanes, Aves	
960ff.	118

Aristotle, De interpretatione	
16a.3–8	301

Aristotle, Politica	
3.8.2	105
3.14–18	194
5.10–11	194

Aristotle, Rhetorica	
1.9.40	80
1.15	17
2.20	80
2.21	17

Athenagoras	
1.8.5b	118

Athenagoras, Equites	
116–127	117

Athenagoras, *Nubes* 23	118	Euripides, *Iphigenia taurica* 763	118
Athenagoras, *Ranae* 51–52	118	Hermogenes, *Peri ideon* 2.10–12	111
Augustine, *Confessionum libri XIII* 8.12	118	Herodas 4.21–25	118
Augustine, *De civitate Dei* 6.10	225	Herodotus, *Historiae* 1.123–125	118
Cicero, *De oratore* 57	118	Homer, *Iliad* Σ–T	112
Cicero, *De republica* 3.15	222	Horace, *Epistulae* 1.19.34	118
Cicero, *Epistulae ad familiares* 9.20	118	Horace, *Satirae* 2.5.51ff.	118
Cicero, *Tusculanae disputationes* 5.116	118	Horace, *Sermones* 1.9	225
Cyril of Jerusalem, *Procatechesis* 14	118	Isocrates, *Ad Demonicum* 51	113
Dio Cassius, *Historia Romana* 60.6.6–7	161	Lucian, *Juppiter tragoedus* 1	118
Dio Chrysostom, *Orationes* 31.56	65	Lucian, *Piscator* 6	113
Euripides, *Bacchae* 794–795	105	Lucian, *Scytha* 10	111
Euripides, *Hippolytus* 856–874	117	Menander, *Epitrepontes* 211ff.	118
Euripides, *Ion* 8	105	Menander, *Thais* frag. 218	105
Euripides, *Iphigenia aulidensis* 34ff.	118	Ovid, *Metamorphoses* 9.569	118

INDEX OF ANCIENT SOURCES

Petronius, *Satyricon*	
129	118
Philostratus, *Vita Apollonii*	
4.17	118
8.1	118
8.31	118
Plato, *Leges*	
810e–812a	113
Plato, *Phaedrus*	
275D–276E	245
Plautus, *Bacchides*	
729–995	118
Pliny, *Epistulae*	
5.3.2	118
Plutarch, *Antonius*	
10	118
Plutarch, *Brutus*	
5	118
36.1–3	118
Plutarch, *Cato Minor*	
19	118
34	118
Plutarch, *De Alexandri magni fortuna aut virtute*	
340A	118
Plutarch, *De recta ratione audiendi*	
8.41E	113
Plutarch, *Tiberius et Caius Gracchus*	
21.2–3	217
Possidius, *Vita sancti Augustini*	
31	118

Pseudo-Heraclitus, *Allegoriae (Quaestiones homericae)*	
5.2	86
Pseudo-Longinus, *De sublimitate*	
13.4	18
14.1	18
Quintilian, *Institutio oratoria*	
1.1.5	111
1.1.33–34	118
1.3.1	111
1.8.12	17
2.7	18
10.1.76	111
10.3.25	118
Seneca, *De clementia*	
1.2.1–2	223, 225
1.4.2	223, 225
1.12.4	223, 225
2.2.2	223, 225
Seneca, *Epistulae morales*	
83	114
Strabo, *Geographica*	
4.5.181	99
6.2.8	105
14.5.13	99
14.5.14	99
Suetonius, *Claudius*	
25.4	160, 165
Suetonius, *Divus Augustus*	
39	118
Suetonius, *Nero*	
10	222
16.2	162
39	217
Suetonius, *Tiberius*	
36	164

Tacitus, *Annales*
  2.85   164
  12.12–13   222
  12.52   164
  13.4   222

Tryphon, *De tropis*
  1.1   86

Virgil, *Aeneid*
  6.851–853 222

Xenophon, *Symposium*
  4.27   118

INSCRIPTIONS AND PAPYRI

P.Freib.
  I 4   114

P.Hamb.
  II 136   112

P.Mich.
  inv. 4832 112

P.Oxy.
  III 622   114
  IV 671   114

P.Petr.
  II 49   114

P.Stras.
  inv. 2374 112

P.Tebt.
  3   114

P.Vindob.
  G 26740   112

Index of Modern Authors

Aageson, James W.	91, 263	Bernstein, Moshe J.	303, 307, 310
Abasciano, Brian	141, 147, 148	Berrin, Shani	78
Abrams, M. H.	30	Betz, Otto	61, 76, 77, 82
Achtemeier, Elizabeth	65	Bhabha, Homi K.	264, 277, 279, 283, 285, 290
Achtemeier, Paul J.	117		
Agamben, Giorgio	238	Binder, Donald D.	172
Alexander, Hanan A.	314	Bloom, Harold	43
Alexander, Loveday	108–10	Blumenfeld, Bruno	194
Allen, Amy	296–99	Boda, Mark J.	115
Allison, Dale C.	200	Boer, Roland	214, 262
Ando, Clifford	214	Böhl, Eduard	5
Archer, Gleason L., Jr.	4, 122	Bonner, Stanley F.	100
Arendt, Hannah	293, 295–99, 311, 312	Bonsirven, Joseph	5, 19, 76
Ascough, Richard S.	180	Booth, Alan D.	101
Ashton, John	237	Borg, Marcus	163
Atlas, Jay David	57	Botha, Pieter J. J.	138, 143
Aune, David E.	244	Bousset, Wilhelm	199, 206
Badiou, Alain	238	Bowman, Alan K.	116
Barclay, John M. G.	161, 164, 165, 173, 174	Boyarin, Daniel	41, 42, 239, 242, 244, 245, 255, 271, 289, 301
Bar-Ilan, Meir	138	Brändle, Rudolf	61, 164–66
Barns, Jonathan	113, 114	Braun, Willi	238
Barr, James	65	Brooke, George J.	77, 79, 82, 83, 114
Barrett, C. K.	64, 84, 231	Brown, Jeannine	34, 35
Bartchy, S. Scott	314, 318	Bruce, F. F.	76, 77, 161
Barton, Stephen C.	308	Brunt, Peter A.	213, 215
Bartsch, Hans-Werner	225	Bultmann, Rudolf	238, 239, 251, 252, 256
Bauckham, Richard	53, 194, 199, 308		
Baur, F. C.	239	Burtchaell, James T.	180, 181
Beale, Gregory K.	258	Byrne, Brendan	22
Beard, Mary	116, 137	Caird, G. B.	31
Beaugrande, Robert de	31, 32	Cameron, Averil	263, 266–68, 271, 277, 283
Beker, J. Christiaan	38, 252		
Belleville, Linda	87	Campbell, Douglas A.	11, 192, 197, 199, 202, 203, 206, 209–11
Benko, Stephen	161–63		

Campbell, John McLeod 208
Campbell, William S. 205, 316
Caputo, John D. 239
Caragounis, Chrys 159, 175
Carpzov, Johann 3
Carr, David M. 300
Carson, D. A. 4, 5, 258
Casson, Lionel 108
Castelli, Elizabeth 279
Champlin, Edward 216–20
Charlesworth, James H. 45, 47, 77–79, 200
Chau, Wai-Shing 256
Chirichigno, Gregory D. 4, 122
Ciampa, Roy E. 10, 56
Clark, Donald L. 100
Clayton, Jay 41, 42
Clemen, August 4
Cohen, Shaye J. D. 174, 223, 288
Cole, Susan Guettel 137
Collins, John J. 181
Cosgrove, Charles 85
Cothenet, Édouard 82
Cranfield, C. E. B. 52, 64, 189, 204
Cremer, Hermann 198
Crenshaw, James L. 300
Cribiore, Raffaella 101, 104, 109, 111, 137, 141
Crossan, John Dominic 270
Culler, Jonathan 238, 239
Dahl, Nils 231
Daly, Lloyd W. 99, 100
Daniélou, Jean 61
Danziger, Marlies K. 30
Das, Andrew 168, 169, 176, 177, 182
Davidson, Harriett 25
Davies, Philip 79, 81, 82, 86, 87
Davies, W. D. 19, 102
Derrida, Jacques 238–40, 245, 248–52
Dewey, Arthur J. 106
Dewey, Joanna 106, 107, 122, 142, 143, 219, 268, 300
Dimant, Devorah 47
DiMattei, Steven 10, 60, 83, 85, 86
Dochhorn, Jan 312

Donfried, Karl P. 159, 161, 163–65, 168, 172, 173, 224, 225
Döpke, Johann Christian Carl 5
Dover, Kenneth J. 108
Dressler, Wolfgang 31, 32
Drusius, Johannes 3
Duffy, Charles 31
Dungan, David L. 294, 302
Dunn, James D. G. 36, 50–52, 59, 65, 165, 166, 168, 174, 181, 183, 204, 208
Easterling, Pat E. 109, 110, 142
Eaton, J. H. 193
Eco, Umberto 190, 313
Ehrensperger, Kathy 12, 239, 273, 280, 293, 295, 298–300, 307, 308, 311, 313–15, 319
Elliott, Neil 11, 53, 215, 217, 224, 226–29, 231, 265, 281, 288, 297, 316
Ellis, E. Earle 4, 5, 20, 61, 64, 76
Engberg-Pedersen, Troels 245
Esler, Philip F. 162, 166, 171, 172, 183, 307
Fee, Gordon D. 242
Feldman, Louis H. 143, 301
Fernández Marcos, Natalio 121
Finlan, Stephen 48
Fiore, Benjamin 80
Fishbane, Michael 61, 83, 128, 139, 292, 316
Fisk, Bruce N. 11, 178, 180
Fitzmyer, Joseph A. 21, 77, 199
Forbes, Clarence A. 100
Ford, David F. 148, 274, 276, 278, 280, 281, 287
Foucault, Michel 265, 296
Frankfurter, David 271, 288
Friedman, Susan Stanford 42
Froehlich, Karl 65, 72
Furnish, Victor Paul 245
Gager, John G. 180, 181, 279
Gagnon, Robert A. J. 166, 176
Galinsky, Karl 222
Gamble, Harry Y. 23, 110, 137, 138, 141, 142, 179, 180, 269
Garnsey, Peter 214

INDEX OF MODERN AUTHORS

Gavrilov, A. K. 118
Gerhardsson, Birger 102, 107, 300, 308
Gibson, E. Leigh 271, 279
Gilliard, Frank D. 117, 118
Given, Mark D. 11, 241, 245, 255–58
Gombis, Timothy G. 198
Goodenough, Edwin R. 194, 217
Goodspeed, Edgar J. 168
Goppelt, Leonhard 59, 62–66, 76
Graham, William A. 306
Greene, Thomas M. 128, 129, 144, 145
Greenspoon, Leonard 121
Greer, Rowan 66
Grieb, A. Katherine 189
Guillet, Jean 63
Guinot, Jean-Noël 73
Haacker, Klaus 189, 191
Habermas, Jürgen 296, 298, 299
Haenchen, Ernst 162
Hafemann, Scott 88
Hanson, Anthony Tyrell 5, 20
Harris, Murray J. 257, 274, 278, 280
Harris, William V. 23, 116, 136–38, 141
Havelock, Eric 115
Hays, Richard B. 4, 6, 20–25, 27, 30, 36–39, 41, 42, 45, 60, 62, 66, 75, 87, 97, 98, 126–36, 143–46, 151, 158, 159, 166, 189, 190, 192, 193, 200, 204–208, 219, 220, 237, 254, 263, 291, 292
Hebel, Udo J. 41
Heil, John Paul 6
Hengel, Martin 177, 179, 199, 202
Hezser, Catherine 102, 103, 115, 138, 139
Hock, Ronald F. 100, 103
Hodgson, R. 114
Hogeterp, Albert L. A. 308–10, 312, 313
Hollander, John 36, 127–29, 144, 145
Holman, C. Hugh 31
Hooks, Bell 272
Hopkins, Keith 116
Horsley, Richard A. 213, 215, 217, 218, 220, 261, 265, 269, 273, 275, 297, 300, 316
Horst, Pieter W. van der 304

Howell, E. B. 105
Hübner, Hans 50, 52
Hughes, Philip E. 148
Huizenga, Leroy 190
Humphrey, J. H. 116, 137
Hurtado, Larry W. 199, 200
Hvalvik, Reidar 163, 165, 170, 174
Ingraffia, Brian D. 239
Iser, Wolfgang 36
Jaffee, Martin S. 301
Jameson, Fredric 214
Jeffers, James S. 164
Jennings, Theodore W., Jr. 240
Jewett, Robert 52, 189, 201, 220, 221, 224
Jobes, Karen H. 121
Johnson, Luke T. 159, 160, 166
Johnson, Mark 194
Johnson, W. Stacy 30
Judge, E. A. 166
Juel, Donald H. 89
Juhl, Peter D. 34, 35, 203
Junius, Franciscus 3
Kahl, Brigitte 282
Kaiser, Walter C. 5, 65
Käsemann, Ernst 52, 84, 204, 210
Kaster, Robert A. 101
Keesmaat, Sylvia 6, 43, 44, 75, 87
Kelber, Werner 106
Kennedy, George A. 103
Kenyon, Frederic G. 108, 109, 142
Kirk, J. R. Daniel 201
Kittredge, Cynthia Briggs 218, 287
Klauck, Hans-Josef 169, 241, 245
Knox, Bernard M. W. 109, 110, 118, 142
Koch, Dietrich-Alex 5, 191, 303
Kraabel, A. Thomas 172, 181
Kraemer, David 114
Kraus, Thomas J. 121, 122
Kristeva, Julia 41
Kugel, James L. 66, 302–4, 306, 307
Lakoff, George 194
Lambrecht, Jan 148
Lampe, G. W. H. 65
Lampe, Peter 165, 168, 174, 176, 182

Lane, William L.	165, 166	Moyise, Steve	10, 25, 27
Le Boulluec, Alain	74	Müller, Mogens	267
Légasse, Simon	65	Mullins, T. Y.	169
Leithart, Peter	207	Murphy-O'Connor, Jerome	171
Lenski, Gerhard E.	214	Najman, Hindy	304–6
Leon, Harry J.	166	Nanos, Mark D.	11, 83, 161–63, 165, 166, 170, 171, 175, 176, 181
Levinas, Emmanuel	319		
Levine, Lee I.	172–74, 177, 178, 308	Nicole, Roger	4
Lieu, Judith M.	180, 181	O'Neil, Edward N.	103
Lim, Timothy	76, 77	O'Neill, J. C.	231
Lodge, John G.	6	Olbrechts-Tyteca, Lucie	231
Longenecker, Richard N.	5, 51, 82	Olbricht, Thomas H.	117
Lüdemann, Gerd	161	Olsson, Birger	308
Lukes, Steven	293	Osborne, Grant R.	32
Luther, Martin	150, 238, 239, 256	Ostmeyer, Karl-Heinrich	59, 65
MacLennan, Robert S.	181	Overman, J. Andrew	181
Malherbe, Abraham, J.	104, 204, 242	Parenti, Michael	216
Manson, T. W.	168	Patte, Daniel	61
Marrou, H. I.	100, 104	Perelman, Chaim	42, 231
Marshall, I. Howard	4	Perkins, Pheme	281
Martin, Dale B.	238, 244	Perri, Carmela	42
Martin, Ralph P.	270, 278	Perrot, Charles	45, 83
Martyn, J. Louis	21, 162, 256, 282	Pettit, Henry	31
Mason, Steve	171	Pietersma, Albert	151
Mays, James Luther	193	Polaski, Sharon H.	266, 287
McCant, Jerry W.	278	Porter, Stanley E.	10, 11, 29, 33, 39, 54, 76, 97, 104, 105, 107, 110, 115, 117, 119, 120, 128, 129, 143, 181
McCutcheon, Russell T.	238		
McDonald, Lee Martin	104		
McLay, R. Timothy	120, 122	Price, S. R. F.	213, 218, 265, 273
Meeks, Wayne A.	81, 180, 242	Prigent, Pierre	68
Meggitt, Justin J.	216	Punt, Jeremy	11, 12, 264
Metzger, Bruce M.	108	Rad, Gerhard von	50
Michel, Otto	4, 6	Randolph, Thomas	4
Middleton, J. Richard	194	Reed, Jonathan L.	270
Millar, Fergus	265, 284	Rendtorff, Rolf	314
Millard, Alan	103, 110, 120, 137, 141, 178	Renner, Timothy	112
		Richardson, Peter	159, 161, 164, 165, 171–73, 224
Miller, Merrill	4		
Mitchell, Margaret M.	65, 79–81	Rieger, Jörg	274, 279, 281, 283, 286, 288
Moo, Douglas J.	32, 51, 52, 166	Riesner, Rainer	160, 165
Moore, Stephen D.	262, 264, 269, 277–79, 282, 284	Robbins, Vernon K.	106, 107
		Roberts, C. H.	141
Morgan, Robert	189, 192	Rochberg-Halton, Francesca	305
Morgan, Teresa	100, 104, 111–13	Roetzel, Calvin J.	217, 271, 272, 280
Morgan, Thaïs E.	41	Rorty, Richard	238

Rosner, Brian S.	44, 54		286, 289, 291–93, 300, 303, 312, 313, 315–17, 319
Roth, Cecil	77		
Rothstein, Eric	41, 42	Starr, Raymond J.	109, 110
Rowe, C. Kavin	189, 200, 202, 203	Ste. Croix, G. E. M. de	214, 216
Runesson, Anders	172	Stegemann, Ekkehard	161, 164, 166
Rutgers, Leonard	164, 171, 224	Stemberger, Günter	309
Rutherford, Ian	111	Stern, Menahem	142, 143
Ruthven, K. K.	33, 34	Sternberg, Meir	2, 26, 27, 289
Saller, Richard	214	Stockhausen, Carol K.	85, 90, 270
Sanders, E. P.	177, 178	Stone, Michael	307, 309
Sawyer, John F. A.	137	Stowers, Stanley K.	166, 227–31, 265
Schäfer, Peter	223, 301	Strange, James	177
Schiffman, Lawrence	83	Strenski, Ivan	238
Schneider, Bernardin	254	Stroumsa, Guy G.	268, 269
Schottroff, Luise	270	Stuckenbruck, Loren T.	308
Schreiner, Thomas R.	161, 168, 176	Stuhlmacher, Peter	44, 50–52, 204
Schürer, Emil	47	Sugirtharajah, R. S.	262, 272
Schüssler Fiorenza, Elisabeth	299, 306	Surenhusius, Guilielmus	5
Schwartz, Seth	304, 312	Talbot, Mary M.	29
Scott, James C.	47, 215–18, 270, 297	Theissen, Gerd	134
Scott, James M.	270	Thiselton, Anthony C.	204, 269, 288
Seesengood, Robert P.	283, 284	Tholuck, F. A. G.	4
Segal, Alan F.	244, 254, 273	Thomas, Rosalind	107, 300
Segovia, Fernando F.	261–64	Thomas, G. S. R.	163, 166
Seidman, Naomi	301	Thompson, Michael	32
Seifrid, Mark	189, 193	Thorsteinsson, R. M.	169
Sherwood, Yvonne	239	Thrall, Margaret	148
Shinan, Avigdor	177	Torrance, J. B.	208
Silva, Moisés	121, 269, 270	Tov, Emanuel	294, 303
Simonetti, Manlio	65	Toy, Crawford H.	4
Skeat, T. C.	109, 141	Turpie, David M.	4
Slemon, Stephen	281	Ulrich, Eugene	295
Slingerland, H. Dixon	160, 161, 163, 165, 224	Usher, Stephen	111
		Vermes, Geza	77, 269
Slusser, Michael	117	Vollmer, Hans	4, 6
Small, Jocelyn Penny	141, 142	Wagner, J. Ross	5, 25–28, 36, 77, 79, 85, 87, 93, 98, 140, 158, 159, 166, 171, 263, 291, 292
Smith, D. Moody	5		
Snyder, H. Gregory	307, 308		
Sommer, Benjamin D.	43	Walters, James C.	164, 170
Spivak, Gayatri C.	277, 279	Ward, Graham	239
Stamps, Dennis L.	119	Wartenberg, Thomas E.	293, 298, 299
Stanley, Christopher D.	4, 6, 11, 23, 24, 87, 89, 97, 98, 111, 112, 121, 126, 128, 134, 135, 137, 141, 146, 149–53, 155, 157–59, 207, 237, 266, 267, 274, 276,	Watson, Francis B.	5, 19–21, 26, 27, 75, 87, 88, 151, 163, 256
		Weber, Max	294, 295

Wedderburn, A. J. M. 159, 161–63, 166, 168, 182
Weinfeld, Moshe 208
West, Stephanie 111
Whiston, William 3
White, John L. 47, 169, 194
White, L. Michael 172
Wiefel, Wolfgang 159, 161, 162, 166, 169, 170, 173, 174, 224, 225
Wilamowitz-Moellendorff, Ulrich von 105
Wilcox, Max 46
Wilk, Florian 17
Wilson, Stephen G. 177, 181, 231
Wire, Antoinette Clark 219
Witherington, Ben, III 7, 51, 52, 161, 165
Wold, Benjamin 308
Woolf, Greg 223
Woollcombe, K. J. 65
Wright, Benjamin G. 151
Wright, N. T. 34, 53, 85, 91, 198, 200, 201, 204, 208, 220, 269, 274, 287
Young, Frances 148, 274, 278, 280, 281, 287
Youtie, Herbert C. 116
Zanker, Paul 213, 218
Zetterholm, Magnus 51, 308
Žižek, Slavoj 238

www.ingramcontent.com/pod-product-compliance
Lightning Source LLC
Chambersburg PA
CBHW021114300426
44113CB00006B/151